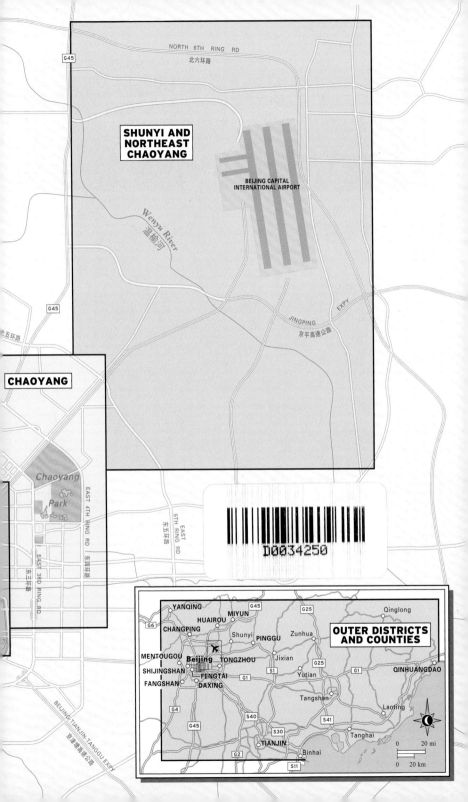

NORTH 6TH RING RD
北六环路

G45

**SHUNYI AND
NORTHEAST
CHAOYANG**

BEIJING CAPITAL
INTERNATIONAL AIRPORT

Wenyu River
温榆河

G45

JINGPING EXPY
京平高速公路

CHAOYANG

Chaoyang Park

EAST 4TH RING RD 东四环路

EAST 3RD RING RD 东三环路

五环路

EAST 5TH RING RD
东五环路

D0034250

BEIJING-TIANJIN-TANGGU EXPY
京津塘高速公路

**OUTER DISTRICTS
AND COUNTIES**

YANQING
HUAIROU   MIYUN   G45   G25   Qinglong
G6   CHANGPING   Shunyi   PINGGU   Zunhua
MENTOUGOU   Beijing   TONGZHOU   Jixian   G25   G1   QINHUANGDAO
SHIJINGSHAN   FENGTAI   G1   S1   Yutian
FANGSHAN   DAXING   Tangshan
G4   Laoting
G45   S40   S41   Tanghai
G2   TIANJIN   Binhai
S30
S11

0   20 mi
0   20 km

Contents

At Home in Beijing

Welcome to one of the most populous cities in the world. Beijing is an exhilarating mélange of the exotic and the international, of tradition and modernity. There's a constant energy here, a buzz of excitement and optimism about what's to come next. Stroll along the streets at night and you'll hear it bubbling out of restaurants, bars, and cafés—the cacophony of chatting, laughing, and shouting, what the Chinese proudly describe as *rènao.* You'll sense it as you cram onto local buses and subways with throngs of other commuters, and again after dark as entertainment quarters pump out music from sun up to sun down.

Yet despite this energy, Beijing has never developed the frenzied, chaotic feel of many other parts of Asia. Its orderly tree-lined streets are wide, dispersing the intensity, and its apartments generous. Outside of rush hour, it's easy to forget that there are millions of people going about life around you.

Language barriers, pollution, and traffic are fixtures of life, and everyone has the odd "China Day," a day of frustration that ignites longings for home. One moment you'll be pushed and shoved, lose your place in the queue, and have near misses with arrogant drivers who take the right of way over pedestrians. But in the next moment you will suddenly fall in love again after tasting the most incredible barbecued meat or succulent Peking duck.

Your life here will be what you make it or are willing to shoulder. The gains you'll make by immersing yourself in this fascinating culture are well worth the occasional hassles. The key to getting the most out of Beijing is to throw yourself in head first. You may find yourself staying here far longer than you initially intended.

▶ WHAT I LOVE ABOUT BEIJING

- The sense that if you're not currently doing something great then that opportunity is just around the corner.

- The feeling of freedom. Living in a modern communist country does not curtail your lifestyle one bit.

- How safe I feel walking home alone along a quiet, dark street at 3am.

- Perfectly flat terrain, wide bike lanes, and electric scooters that you can park anywhere you like.

- Beijing Duck (no one calls it Peking Duck here).

- The abundant but short-lived mass of blossoms in spring.

- The constant change. Things you want may not be here now, but wait a couple of months and they probably will be.

- Next-to-free public transport. An average trip in a taxi will be the equivalent of US$4.75 (RMB30); a subway ride US$0.32 (RMB2); and the average bus ride US$0.15 (RMB1).

- The exhilaration of going to one of the many fresh-food markets, which stock everything from freshly roasted sesame oil to hand-made noodles, to shockingly cheap avocados.

- The enthusiasm with which locals accept foreigners, whether they speak a word of Chinese or not.

- Extremely wide roads that seem to make the city far less intense and populated than it really is.

- The infinite and ever-expanding number of restaurants and bars.

- The fact that you can go out for a fine meal for about a quarter of the price that you'd pay in the States.

- Free home delivery–for almost anything.

- The constantly surprising diversity of Chinese people living here.

- Streets and markets that dedicate themselves to one thing, whether it's photographic equipment, musical instruments, or trophies.

- The fact that going for a massage doesn't have to be a luxury.

- Free Wi-Fi in virtually every café and bar.

- The endless social and networking opportunities for expats.

WELCOME TO BEIJING

© PENGYOU91/123RF.COM

INTRODUCTION

China is one of the most economically and politically influential countries in the world, and Beijing is the driving seat. A city of almost 20 million people, it is also one of the country's most populated cities, and you're moving here to be part of it all.

Beijing has been the capital of China off and on for hundreds of years, and its name has changed almost as many times as its title. It's been Khanbaliq, Yanjing, Zhongdu, Peiping, and, of course, at various periods of history, Beijing.

That's a lot of change, and possibly a very difficult grounding on which to form a strong identity. But this has always been the way and, in fact, seems to be just part of its nature. For thousands of years it has been an important place for trade, business, and politics, and so has attracted a diverse variety of residents. Today it continues to be regarded as the political, educational, and cultural heart of the entire country, and, as such, it also offers incoming expats an amazing and life-changing experience.

For university students, life has a culture of its own very different to that on the east side of the city. The western side of town is relatively new. Not too many years ago, villages stood here, but now they've all been torn down and replaced by soulless shopping malls and digital markets. It lacks the refinement of the east and can feel a little chaotic, but it's a fun and easygoing place to be if you're a student. Many come to study Mandarin (generally referred to here simply as Chinese), but an increasing

© RADIST/123RF.COM

number of internationally respected, non-language-related courses are also available (taught in English).

Entrepreneurs will also find a wealth of opportunities in Beijing. It might be the capital of the world's second biggest economy, but there are still many gaps in services and trade that a pair of foreign eyes might quickly spot and take advantage of. In recent years, the government has eased some of its regulations on foreign investment, so doing business here can be a little easier than in former years. There are still huge challenges for the foreign businessperson, however. You'll likely find that the work culture, business ethics, and bureaucracy vary radically from what you're accustomed to, and for some, this can be too difficult to endure.

The Beijing workplace is definitely still a Chinese-dominant environment, and if you've spent time in Hong Kong you might be shocked by the difference. If you don't speak Chinese, it can be hard to find a job in a field that doesn't relate explicitly to using English, be it an English teacher or writer for a local expat magazine, and rarely do these kinds of jobs promise to bring you wealth. Beijingers frequently work long hours, and you'll be expected to, too. If you work late one night you'll still be required to turn up at 8 or 9 the following morning. In smaller towns of China, a workday might begin at 10am, break at noon for a long lunch, and then conclude at around 4:30 or 5pm. But in Beijing, there's no such luck. A typical Beijing day starts at 9am, people clog the elevators at 12 sharp to get out for their half-hour lunch break, then are back to the office, where they stay until possibly 7pm.

Outside of work and study, Beijing holds an ever-changing array of attractions and things to fall in love with. Almost any night of the week you can meet your friends for a relaxed, cheap dinner close to home, and no one will think of the need to turn it into a big night. Any night of the week you can go out for a cocktail or two, and again, you don't have to spend an arm and a leg. Eating and drinking here is an extremely casual affair.

You can visit the 798 Art District, where former factories have been repurposed into an almost endless collection of progressive art galleries. You can bar-hop between rooftop bars that sit amid historic courtyard houses and overhanging trees. You can skate or ice-bicycle around the frozen Houhai lake in winter. And you can spend your time in one of the many beautiful parks doing tai chi or kung fu with the locals.

Admittedly, adjusting to Beijing life when you first arrive can be a little awkward, and everything seems like a hassle. Even after six months it can feel like living in a bunker, where nothing is available and nothing works. Just simply going to the bank or buying household goods can send your blood pressure skyrocketing. But, over time, as you work your way into the city, and discover its ways of doing things, you'll start to wonder how you'll readjust to life back home. You won't always find that life is cheap here, but when you master how to live it, you'll find it addictively convenient.

BEIJING OR PEKING?

Many people ask the question, "When did Peking change its name to Beijing?" But really, the question should actually be, "When did the spelling of Peking change to Beijing?" because for those living in Beijing and who spoke the standard Mandarin dialect (pǔtōnghuà), it has always been Beijing, or at least 北京. It wasn't until foreigners came in and tried to romanize the language (to make it intelligible for themselves) that it took on the form of Pékin and Peking.

Various theories account for the Pékin and Peking spellings, but invariably the point at which confusion occurs is regarding what's called "aspiration" and how that is coded on paper. Essentially, aspiration is the hissy air that comes out when you produce sounds like "t" and "p," compared, respectively, to the sounds "d" and "b." Some argue that early linguists to China used phonetic coding such as the old postal system to romanize what they heard. This system would have given the written form of "peking." Other theorists blame the mixup on the traveling Jesuit priests of the time, who typically came from countries speaking romance languages, such as French,

Spanish, Italian, or Portuguese. In these languages, sounds such a "p" and "t" are not aspirated, so, to the priests' ears, the unaspirated sound at the start of Beijing would have sounded just like a "p." They wrote it down, and the rest of us adopted it. (As to why many Westerners like to use a French-style "j" sound rather than a clear crisp "j" sound as the Chinese do is less clear.)

The Chinese government decreed in the 1970s that the capital's name should be spelled "Beijing," in line with what had become the official phonetic system, pīnyīn or Pinyin. It wasn't until the late 1980s, however, that it was really taken onboard. Today a few countries around the world continue to drag the chain, and even Beijing itself seems to have been remiss on few points of correction. One of the city's biggest universities, Běijīng Dàxué (or Běi Dà for short) is still referred to as Peking University when dealing with foreigners, and you're just as likely to hear Peking opera said as you are Beijing opera. But you can definitely leave your Peking duck at home—here it's Běijīngkǎoyā (Beijing roast duck), every time, without fail.

The Lay of the Land

While Italy is clearly a boot, China is lovingly thought by its people to resemble a chicken, and Beijing sits right in the middle of the chicken's neck. It's neither lapped by a sea nor threaded by any river worthy of note. Instead, it's a dry and increasingly dusty land-locked domain. So with no port or any major body of water to its name, how did it become the capital of this vast country?

Despite its portless existence, Beijing's development and history has in reality been greatly influenced by its geography. It covers a total area of 16,801 square kilometers (6,487 square miles), making its size somewhere between that of Connecticut and New Jersey. It sits at the northern point of the North China Plain, a far-reaching territory that, overall, also takes in much of Hebei, Henan, Anhui, Jiangsu, and Shandong provinces, as well as the city of Tianjin. The plain's southern border extends to the Huai River, still a good distance north of Shanghai. In the east it reaches out to the Yellow Sea and to the Bohai Sea in the northeast. The North China Plain is a large stretch of flat, fertile land, uninterrupted by mountains or rivers, and so, in ancient times, it made a perfect environment for communities to thrive and interact. The terrain made for quick and easy horseback movement, farming yielded bumper crops, and communication was relatively unimpeded. This also meant that languages within these areas remained relatively similar—unlike, for example, the Shanghainese or Cantonese dialects farther south in the country. Its relative flatness, however, made it vulnerable to intruders from the northern steppes, and so came the Great Wall.

Beijing's center sits at just 44 meters (146 feet) above sea level, and its northwestern corner is only 10 meters (33 feet) higher than its southeastern corner. The northern and western limits are, however, bounded by mountain ranges that rise to an average of 1,000-1,500 meters (3,281-4,921 feet) in height. Beijing's highest mountain, Ling Shan, reaches up to 2,303 meters (7,556 feet). On a clear day, the Western Mountains (part of the Taihang range, which extends into Beijing from Hebei) are surprisingly visible. Have a drink at the top of Park Hyatt or the Shangri-La's Summit Wing in Guomao and you'll enjoy a full view of them. University students up in Haidian have them as a constant backdrop.

Beijing is not part of a province but is a municipality directly governed by the national government. In China, there are three other such cities—Shanghai, Tianjin, and Chongqing. Beijing is completely surrounded by Hebei province, except for Tianjin, which sits at its southeastern corner. The actual urban area of Beijing, which covers approximately 1,000 square kilometers (about 386 square miles), is concentrated down in the southern central part of the municipality.

This urban area is largely circumscribed by a set of five ring roads, numbered two to six (the absent First Ring Road is a bygone of the 1920s). For the large part, life goes on inside the Fifth Ring Road, which runs for 98 kilometers (61 miles), sits at an average distance of about 10 kilometers (6 miles) from the city center, and encompasses just five of the districts. The remaining areas beyond this point are dramatically less populated and predominantly rural—although this is rapidly altering with farmlands seized for construction and flashy golf courses for the wealthy.

BEIJING'S DIVISIONS

To help with the administration of the city, Beijing is broken up into 14 districts and two counties. Until fairly recently, there were 16 districts, but in July 2010, the government merged the four innermost districts into two—Chongwen district was absorbed into its larger, more powerful northern neighbor, Dongcheng district, and, likewise, Xuanwu district became part of Xicheng. Together, these particular districts formed the old city, which was once surrounded by a city wall, of which remnants can be seen along the southeast section of the Line 2 subway route. The wall had nine gates in total, and today many neighborhoods sitting along this line still bear the word "men" (门, gate) at the end of their names, such as Dongzhimen and Qianmen.

For most expats, life exists in only a handful of districts. Chaoyang district is, by far, home to the greatest population of expats, and so has developed a strong international character. Other areas that are also typically worked in, lived in, studied in, or shopped in by foreigners include: Dongcheng, Haidian, Xicheng, and the suburban Shunyi.

The other suburban areas that surround the city's core include: Changping, Tongzhou, Daxing, Fangshan, and Mentougou districts; and to the north of these are the rural areas of Yanqing county, Huairou district, Miyun county, and Pinggu district.

WELCOME TO BEIJING

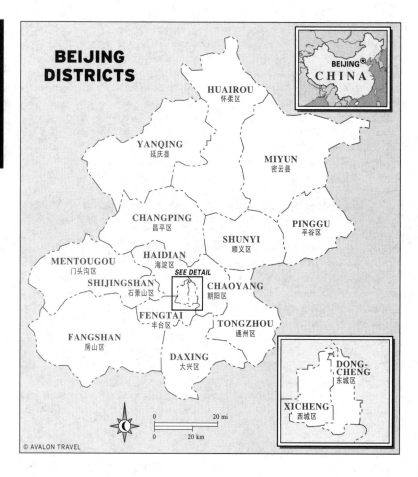

If you choose to live out here, you'll definitely impress the locals, not to mention fellow expats, who typically venture out this far for recreation only—a day of hiking, a walk on the Great Wall, or a spot of skiing in winter. Drives out here from the city center can take 1-3 hours. For example, a trip to the Nanshan Ski Resort in Miyun county takes about an hour (thanks to the fantastic highway out to the area); a visit to Simatai, a more remote, less refurbished section of the Great Wall close to the Hebei border, will require about 2.5 hours of driving.

WEATHER

Beijing has a continental monsoon climate, with moderate humidity. In summer, temperatures generally climb to an average of 26°C (79°F) in July, but days can definitely hover in the 30s and spike into the 40s. The humidity can indeed get a little sticky at this time, but the rest of the year generally feels very dry—unlike Shanghai, and completely incomparable to Hong Kong. A testament to this is the almost total absence of clothes dryers in homes. Hang your clothes up at night and they're dry in the morning.

In winter, temperatures plunge to an average of -4°C (25°F) in January. It's not unusual to have a week or two straight where days top out at -5°C (23°F) or less and get down to -15°C (5°F) at night. Add a nice Siberian wind to that and things get really chilly.

Despite these unpleasant temperatures, however, homes in Beijing are typically extremely well insulated against the outside elements. In winter, most homes around the city are centrally heated by the government. Around November 15, the city's thermal managers turn on the coal, radiator, and other heating systems. This date can be moved forward if temperatures fall below 5°C (41°F) for five consecutive days. On March 15, give or take a few days, they turn them off—an exercise that not only has environmental consequences but which is estimated to cost around RMB1.913 billion (US$300 million) every year. Fortunately the government is taking serious steps to improve this situation, and is initiating more environmentally friendly and cost-effective methods for heating the city.

Spring temperatures are perfect, and the city bursts to life with an explosion of blossoms. The downside of this season is the wind. This is definitely the windy season. A lot is made of the sand or dust storms that come in from the encroaching Gobi desert in the northwest. Prior to the year 2000, they were a serious problem, frequently coating the city in thick yellow dust and exacerbating health problems. After a particularly serious sandstorm on April 1, 2000, the government rallied to launch a massive reforestation project, referred to as the Beijing Tianjin Anti Dust Storm Project. The storms do still happen—perhaps two to four times in a given spring—but they're far less severe than they once were. Far from being like a scene from *The Mummy,* they're more like a yellowish version of a highly polluted day. A more intrusive problem you'll

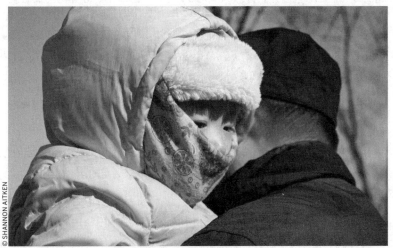

© SHANNON AITKEN

Icy Beijing winters require complete covering up.

face on a more frequent basis is the general dust and dirt that gets swept up on any windy day. Extensive construction work, littering, and dryness give gusts plenty to throw at you. Don't be afraid to don a face mask, which can be readily found at any convenience store. Another downside to spring is that some years it can seem to come and go in the blink of an eye. You'll feel like you're just starting to savor the outdoors again when you need to retreat back in to escape the heat.

Hands down, fall is the best season. Winds are minimal, temperatures feel luxurious, and the autumn colors that paint the city are stunning. At this time hordes of locals head out to Xiang Shan (Fragrant Hill) in the city's far northwest to see the red leaves on the mountains. A well-timed walk along Dongzhimenwai Dajie, close to Sanlitun, however, will leave you with photos of a street densely lined with brilliant golden leaves.

Beijing's average rainfall is 630 millimeters (25 inches), with most of this occurring in July and August. The downfalls are usually fairly short-lived and rarely interrupt your plans for the day, and other than the disappearing trick the rain seems to play on the taxis, it's usually a welcome way to freshen up the stuffy, polluted air. Winter is much drier, and there may be no more than two to four snowfalls, and seldom anything worth getting your skis out for.

FLORA AND FAUNA
Flora
If humanity had not stamped a big heavy footprint on Beijing, the city would today sit in the midst of a deciduous, broad-leafed forest. Unfortunately, the foliage—both type and quantity—that covers the land here today is very different from how it once was. Over the centuries, much of the native flora of the area has been taken over by introduced species, destroyed by wars or land clearing, or flattened by farmlands, orchards, villages, and other by-products of urbanization. Even in the more remote rural areas, a high proportion of the native species have been replaced by oak, aspen, and birch. By the time 1949 rolled around, Beijing had been stripped to just 3.2 percent of forest coverage.

For the last 60 years, however, the city has been trying to rectify the problem. Mao Zedong appreciated greenery, and in the 1950s he took it upon himself to initiate a campaign to promote tree and flower growing across the country. In 1981, the fourth session of the Fifth National People's Congress put in place a resolution that stipulated that every able-bodied citizen between the ages of 11 and 60 needed to "volunteer" to plant three to five trees every year. This doesn't necessarily mean the citizens are personally heading out with shovels and seeds to do a bit of gardening. Instead, they can pay a small amount to an approved tree service to plant trees on their behalf. Today, the Beijing Tianjin Anti Dust Storm Project continues the push. In truth, there are many sandstorm belts around China, but Beijing, being the capital, had the privilege of being chosen to be the guinea pig for this radical reforestation scheme. Consequently, over the last several decades, billions of trees have been planted; grasslands, watercourses, and ecological parks are being managed; and around 500,000 residents farming on eroded land have been relocated. Green cover has now reached more than 26 percent in the municipality. In addition to this, the government has also put in place regulations to protect urban trees—cut down a tree that's "larger than a building" or older

© SHANNON AITKEN

the flora of Jingshan Park

than 100 years of age without prior permission from your district planting bureau and you could cop a fine of around RMB500.

Today, Beijing's plant life can be extraordinarily beautiful, especially in spring and fall. If you're really keen to see the flora up close, it's best to head out to Mentougou, Huairou, Miyun, Fangshan, or Yanqing. Not so far out, Haidian also has a lot of stunning plants and trees in places such as the Summer Palace and the Old Summer Palace (Yuan Ming Yuan, Gardens of Perfect Brightness). Closer to the Central Business District, there is a multitude of parks filled with luscious cultivated plants, particularly all manner of cherry blossoms. In spring some of the best places to visit to see these include Longtan Park in southern Dongcheng (a must-see), Beihai Park in Xicheng district, and Zhongshan Park, just to west of the Forbidden City. But really, almost any park will put on a flashy show for you at this time of year.

Around town, typical tree species lining the streets include aspen, juniper, Japanese pagoda, and locust. The city also has many wonderful rare and historic trees, such as Chinese arborvitae, Chinese juniper, and Chinese pine, which are typically found in temples and parks. Thousands of them are more than 100 years old, and some are more than 1,000 years of age.

Fauna

It's hard to believe, especially when living in among the high-rises of Beijing, that the municipality is home to hundreds of species of wildlife. China has the greatest number of animal species in the world, and Beijing got its fair share of them. Birds alone account for more than 400 species.

Despite the massive ongoing development of the city, these numbers have actually been increasing in recent years. This is due not only to the general reforestation efforts but also to the focus these projects have had on native plants and landscapes. The Olympic Forest Park, for example, has been designed with a natural ecosystem in mind—it has marshlands, grasslands, woodlands, and a lake. This and other such eco-friendly parks have dramatically increased the potential habitats for wildlife.

Typical birds that can now be seen around the municipality—beside the dominant sparrows and magpies—include the beautiful nuthatches and azure-winged magpies, herons, swifts, swallows, mandarin ducks, and cranes. Mammals, such as hog badgers and macaque monkeys, are also increasing in number. Around your apartment in the city, you might also spot a weasel, particularly if you live around the *hútòng* (alleys) or Dongzhimen. If you do see one, locals will tell you it's good luck. For some serious wildlife watching, you can also head to Beijing Botanical Garden or farther afield to Chenjiapu valley (although, theoretically, here you would have crossed from Yanqing county over into Hebei).

Beijing's wildlife still faces many challenges, however, and not all species are increasing in number. Pollution is still an issue, as is the ever-expanding urban girth. Many of the eco-parks are not only isolated from each other but they're also manicured for human appreciation rather than animal—short grass, tidy foliage, walkways for the increasing numbers of tourists. Even the new sleek apartment complexes in the city lack the nesting potential of the eaved buildings of earlier years. Additionally, Beijing residents are still not particularly savvy about how to treat wildlife when they encounter it. There may be an increasing understanding of and love for pet dogs, but when it comes to wildlife many people don't understand the impact that touching or feeding has on the animals and their existence. All these factors have led to a recent decline in the numbers of many species. Grass-roots associations, such as the Beijing Birdwatching Society, are trying to tackle many of these issues through education and research.

On another aspect of the wildlife topic, if you have nightmares of seeing unusual species spiced up on Beijing menus, there's no need to worry. This is really a preference of southerners, and so, unless you're a guest at a designed-to-impress business dinner at a traditional imperial restaurant, the most "exotic" thing you might see is donkey or bullfrog. Beijingers are not partial to dog, and snakes, scorpions, and bugs on sticks tend to be limited to the "nobody goes there but tourists" Donghuamen Night Market by Wangfujing.

Social Climate

Beijing is a hard city to define. Whenever you think you've nailed your understanding of one aspect of life here, someone puts a chink in your theory. There are currently close to 20 million people, and more than 7 million of these are migrants who've come to the capital for work and to study. It's a huge mixing bowl of Chinese ethnicities, of people who have different interests, fashion and food tastes, values, and ethics.

CULTURE OF MATERIALSIM

There is a distinctive atmosphere of ambition. After centuries of hardship, wars, famine, and now fierce modernization where homes can be torn down one day and replaced with a shopping center the next, there is a general feeling of insecurity. The costs of living are skyrocketing, while competition for jobs only gets harder with every additional migrant entering the city. There is little room for dreams of a hippy existential existence. Many will tell you that Chinese are practical first, idealistic second. Before they can dream they need to acquire the hallmarks of stability—a secure job, a car, a home, marriage, and a child, and often in that order.

Ambition in Beijing means striving for one of two things—money or a position of power. Locals refer to such people as *quángui, quán* meaning to have power or rights, and *gui* referring to having money. Either can go a long way toward lubricating the path of life in Beijing. Officially, workers within the government don't earn much money, but when you're standing at the top of the ladder of power and your coffer is overflowing with *rénmài* (networks and contacts), you might well as be a millionaire.

Despite a history of socialism and religions such as Buddhism, Taoism, and Confucianism, the city is increasingly materialistic. And when you've got it, you flaunt it. The Chinese still have a deeply embedded concept of "face," and in many ways these days, face is coded by a monetary value. SUVs and luxury cars, designer goods, multiple apartments, multiple children, and oversized pedigree dogs are prized symbols of wealth. Even when they can't afford it, many feel obligated to spend lavish amounts of money on ostentatious gifts or dinners, just to "give face" to their boss or important connections.

Fortunately, not everyone is like this, but unfortunately the wealthy and their glittering goods can shine such a blinding light on the day-to-day life that you sometimes find yourself looking at the city through glasses that are anything but rose-colored. Rather than seeing the good, it becomes easy to see greed and arrogance. Step out to cross a road and a black Audi muscles its way past you; suddenly all your blissful thoughts burst like soap bubbles. Breathe deeply, and think back to your lovely Chinese teacher or your charming colleague.

An easy way to access the warm spirit of Beijing is to spend some time within the Second Ring Road, where *hútòng* life is still strong and the sense of community apparent. The majority of people here are Beijingers who have been in the city for generations. Folks sit around in large groups late into the summer nights and are extremely neighborly, sharing food they've cooked or brought back from the market, or jumping to help when a problem arises. They're extremely proud of their heritage, and will spend an hour telling you all about their culture and traditions if you give them an ear. Sadly, this flavor of life begins to disperse as you leave the limits of the Second Ring and is almost nonexistent between the Third and Fifth. In the older apartment communities, resident retirees will say hello as you come and go, and keep an eye on your bicycle for you. In the newer, flashier complexes, life is anonymous. Get in the elevator of your apartment complex on your way to work in the morning and your neighbors may be more likely to stand preening themselves in the mirror on the way down than to say hello.

CULTURAL ATTITUDES

The Chinese pride themselves on being hardworking, and in your time here you'll meet people who will validate this idea in every regard, and others who will blot it from your mind entirely; you'll encounter people who'll go to extraordinary, selfless efforts to help you, and others who won't lift a finger or simply raise a suggestion if your issue strays even slightly from their immediate area of concern. It's this constant stream of contradictions that keeps Beijing intriguing. There are those who are fiercely

© SHANNON AITKEN

Get to know your neighbors by joining in a game of Chinese checkers.

nationalistic and those who try feverishly to assimilate to Western ways; there are many who look down on physical risk-taking as an insult to their parents who gave them their body, while others play chicken with cars and buses while riding their scooters. Some value beauty above any other quality, and some dress for work like they had planned to spend the day at home on the couch. There are twenty-somethings who giggle with embarrassment when you ask them if they have a boyfriend and others who use abortion as a regular form of contraception. Some are extraordinarily thrifty and frugal with their money, and some throw it about like confetti in a ticker-tape parade. Beijing is mercurial and resistant to definition.

Many years ago, Beijingers were a pretty conservative lot, but this is quickly changing. Change is just a way of life these days, and many embrace it or, when it's unpleasant, quietly accept it without protest. Today, many once-taboo behaviors no longer turn heads. An increasing number of people live together before they get married; the lesbian and gay community has an ever-more-obvious presence (the transgender crowd is still a little bit too out there), and dramatic body piercings and tattoos are the trend du jour. A well-regarded expression used to be "the nail that stands out gets hammered down," but if you visit the university area of Haidian or simply ride the subway, you'll see this is an endangered notion.

EDUCATION AND EMPLOYMENT

One area that does have unwavering diligence, however, is education. In Beijing, education is the be-all and end-all of life as a teenager knows it. And the pinnacle of this the Gao Kao, the high school examination that opens or locks the gateway into university. From the time children begin primary school to the time they sit the Gao Kao, their lives are dominated by study, often from 7am to 11pm. Without a good result, they're unlikely to get into a good university; if they don't get into a good university, their chances of securing a good job are drastically reduced; without a good job they are set for a life of struggle that will affect their ability to support themselves and their aging parents and grandparents. Even if they do get into university, many youths have no choice about what major they do and end up spending a lifetime in a profession that they have no interest in. It's a dismal view and one that places extreme pressure on Beijing's young people.

According to the Beijing Municipal Bureau of Statistics, Beijing's registered urban unemployment rate in 2011 was 1.39 percent, a figure that is relatively low compared to many other cities (the national rate at the time was 4.1 percent, according to the National Bureau of Statistics of China). The figure is possibly a little overly inspiring, however. Of this 1.39 percent, approximately 38 percent are under the age of 35, and many people, in order to save face, actually refuse to register themselves as unemployed and so don't get factored into this figure. Additionally, many who do have jobs, such as waiters or street cleaners, earn as little as RMB800-1,500 per month, an amount that falls far below the average monthly rental price in the city. Even well-educated people can find themselves stuck in jobs earning less than RMB3,000 a month. Beijing life is far from the slums of India or the favelas of Brazil, but you'll often hear it referred to as *hěn kùnnan* (tough and full of hardship).

English is frequently seen as the panacea to this bleak situation. Private English schools are massive money spinners in Beijing, feeding into the belief that English will snag them a high-paying job. Students can spend RMB30,000-100,000 on courses that promise fluent spoken English. Every year, thousands of students flock abroad to obtain a foreign education in America, Australia, England, Canada, or New Zealand. Unfortunately, taking such steps doesn't always guarantee a more lucrative future. Even a *hǎiguī* (a student returning from abroad) may not get a look at anything over RMB5,000 a month.

FAMILY

Aside from education, one other aspect of life in Beijing that remains relatively unaltered is respect for the family. Those of the 1980s generation, and the kids of thereafter, are often described as being increasingly selfish and egocentric, thanks to the one-child policy and its decisive effect of focusing the attention and affection of both parents and two sets of grandparents on a single child. (Bear in mind, not every young person fits this modern-day emperor profile—there are a good many lovely, generous youths.) Yet despite this sharp change of culture and the growing devotion to materialism, the family still strongly influences an individual's life. Several generations continue to live contentedly together under one roof, and come vacation time, young people will join the exodus of people from Beijing back to their hometowns to share their few days of annual leave with their families. Even when their children are fully grown adults, parents can have a lot of input into their choices and lifestyle. It's a quick lesson many expats will learn if they embark on a relationship with a local.

BEIJING AND FOREIGNERS

Beijing's early history with foreigners wasn't particularly harmonious. Merchant brothers Nicolo and Matteo Polo visited the city in 1261, at which time the city was the place of Kublai Khan's Mongolian empire, and referred to as Khanbaliq. They actually did okay. It's thought that these were the first white people the khan had ever seen. A few years later they returned with Marco, Nicolo's son, and again it was a reportedly cheerful experience.

For the next 600 years or so, however, relationships between the East and West went downhill. Westerners didn't really find their way back to China until the time of the Ming dynasty in the 14th century, and at that time the Chinese weren't interested in relationships of any sort, including trade. When the West tried again in the 18th century, they met with a race that was firmly convinced of being the center of power. The arrogance and ignorance of both sides sparked new tension and conflict. Such was the distaste for foreigners that they weren't even allowed to live in the city until the 1860s, and this came only after a messy end to the second Opium War. At this time foreigners were given the right to set up legations, and a handful of diplomats from various countries lived a sheltered life inside their walled compound. Given that these foreigners were there to garner concessions rather than provide any real benefit for the Chinese, it left a bad taste in the locals' mouths, and by 1900, the locals had had enough and laid siege to Legation Quarter. In 1919 on May 4, thousands of students set about protesting the Treaty of Versailles and condemning the influence of the West on their country.

So much has changed since then. There is still the obvious puffing of international chests, but on a daily basis life is extremely cordial. In contrast to the turbulent past, there now possibly might not be another city in the world where foreigners are generally so easily accepted by the locals. As long as you tick all the boxes at the visa office, life here goes relatively smoothly. Sure, on the rare occasion you'll encounter an individual with a racist comment to make—but which country is without such people? It certainly isn't the general feeling that you'll have as you go about your day, and the doors that are open to the common person are generally open to foreigners, too. In fact, there are many instances where you'll feel you have comparably more liberties, such as the freedom to take your holiday when you choose rather than at the same time as the rest of the country or the lack of obligation to follow certain cultural mores.

One of the first things you'll notice when you move to Beijing is the curiosity of the locals for foreign faces. There might be certain sections of the city, such as Sanlitun, Lido, or Guomao, where people won't look twice at you. But if you live or work outside these areas then inevitably you're going to run into one of the millions of migrant workers who are new to the city and its strange inhabitants. Get on the subway or bus and it's unlikely that you won't be stared at by somebody. If you have blonde hair, or particularly children with blonde hair, then you'll cause an even greater stir. It can be a hard thing to adapt to when you come from a country where staring at a stranger is considered rude or even hazardous. It can also interfere with one's dating radar, as women, men, young, and old can all stare at you with the same prolonged blank expression. You'll soon get used to hearing the term *lǎowài* or *wàiguórén* (foreigner) said by children and even adults as you walk past.

In a dramatic reversal of the 1919 student uprising, many young people today have a strong attraction to the West and its influences. Steve Jobs gained iconic status, and an almost nationwide sense of mourning ensued when he died in 2011. KFC, which set up its first shop just near Tian'anmen Square in 1987, is not only often considered a flash place to take a date, but now competes with the hundreds of outlets of McDonald's, Starbucks, and Pizza Hut that have spread over the city. Unfortunately,

© SHANNON AITKEN

Many young locals think the KFC near Tian'anmen Square is the ideal place for a first date.

such places have come to define "Western food," and for those who love the intricacies of their own country's cuisine, it will be painful to constantly hear the locals say they "hate Western food."

Chinese people do like to generalize. If you're proud about your cultural heritage, for example if you're Canadian and hate to be mistaken for American, or a New Zealander and hate to be mistaken for an Australian, or have any such notion of personal identity, throw it in the trash now. If you have a white face, your nationality is "foreigner." Be ready to hurdle assumptions that you can't eat spicy food or won't nibble on any variety of offal; get ready to combat presuppositions that you can't understand a single word of Chinese, let alone read it; you might even want to tackle to presumptions that all foreigners shower in the morning or that all foreigners are lazy. On the upside, this pervasive homogenization of the West and its people does often give you the element of surprise, which can be highly entertaining. If you have an Asian face but are Western-born, then your experience will be very different. You might not get gawked at on a general basis, but should you suddenly start speaking perfect, unfaltering English on your cell phone while on the subway, then you'll find that all eyes are on you.

One previously held assumption that has done a bit of a backflip in recent years is the belief that all foreigners are wealthy. This attitude still seems to hold some value at tourist hot spots, such as the Silk Markets, but it appears to be losing ground as the Chinese gain confidence in their own financial position. Previously, foreigners were typically employed on padded salaries and substantial packages, which led to negative vibes and didn't do much for relationships with the poorly paid locals in the same office. Today, unless you're being brought in by an international company, the sun has all but set on those heydays.

It's not difficult to make friends here, and the Chinese are extremely friendly and welcoming. You'll be invited out to lunch or dinner, or KTV (the local term for karaoke). Their curiosity creates an avenue to chats or interaction, and in many cases language barriers can be overcome by food or copious drinking. (Letting yourself get drunk in front of them can earn big bonding points.) Expats do tend to gel together quite readily, and it's highly likely that your closest friends will be fellow expats, but it's rarely such a black and white "us" and "them" situation. Go out to the bars of Gulou, Houhai, Wudaokou, or Sanlitun and you'll see mixed groups everywhere, enjoying regular friendships as well as culture.

HISTORY, GOVERNMENT, AND ECONOMY

If you find it hard to pin Beijing down into a particular category of culture, don't accuse yourself of a lack of insight. The city has been in constant flux ever since people set foot in it. It's had countless name changes and has been ruled under almost as many different systems. While China's major ethnic group is Han, Beijing has for much of its history been ruled by other cultures, predominantly those from the north, such as the Mongols and Manchurians. It has experienced war and peace, has been both built up and razed, was held by the Japanese, and been attacked by Europeans. The last 50 years have perhaps been some of the most stable of its entire history, politically and economically.

Beijingers are a mixed bunch. Many are extraordinarily honest, friendly, and helpful; others will lie through their teeth to make a buck. To get your head around the diversity of the city and its people, it's important to know how it got here.

© SHANNON AITKEN

History

PRE-IMPERIAL BEIJING

Across hundreds of thousands of years, Beijing has been a suitable place to live and farm. Separated by millennia and, eventually, by layers of soil, various groups have made it their home.

The first group that appears to have lived here were our predecessors, a species of *Homo erectus* locally referred to as Peking Man. They lived in the southwest of modern Beijing in the area of Zhoukoudian, in Fangshan district. In the 1920s and '30s an international team of archaeologists started digging around in the caves of Zhoukoudian, after having heard reports of unusual bones being found in the area by local villagers. Often working in freezing conditions down 40-meter-deep crevasses, they uncovered more than 200 bone fragments, including skullcaps. The unearthed fossils indicated that at least 40 people had lived at the site around 200,000-750,000 years ago. Unfortunately, during the Sino-Japanese war (1937-1945), there was a bit of a slipup, and in an effort to safely keep the relics away from the occupying Japanese, someone actually lost them. Sadly, the pieces have never been found, and rumors as to their whereabouts are colorful and inconclusive—some say they are buried under a tree in Ritan Park (tree found—no relics); others say they sank with the MV *Awa Maru*, a Red Cross relief ship that was mistakenly torpedoed in 1945 by the American submarine USS *Queenfish* (the wreck was found after a five-year, multimillion-dollar search by China—no relics). Digging at Zhoukoudian resumed after the war, but the discoveries later made were far less impressive than those of the previous excavations. You can now visit the Zhoukoudian Peking Man Museum to try to get an insight into this people's existence. However, thanks to the signature pieces going walkabout, you might feel a little nonplussed about having made the hour-or-so journey to get there.

The next group of people found to have moved into the area couldn't have gotten much closer to where the center of the city now sits. In 1996, workers excavating the ground to build the Oriental Plaza on the corner of Chang'an Jie and Wangfujing Dajie (about 700 meters from the Forbidden City) uncovered a large collection of stone age tools and bones. These were somewhat younger than those of the Peking Man clan, being a mere 24,000-25,000 years old, but impressive nonetheless. Rather than flattening the site with the construction, however, the owners paused for about six months to examine the fossils carefully, then built around it. So now, below ground, wedged between one of Beijing's ritziest shopping malls and the Wangfujing subway station on Line 1 is the Beijing Wangfujing Paleolithic Museum, housing the remains of people who lived not by shopping but by hunting on what was then a place of verdant plains.

Other such discoveries around the municipality point to Beijing's continuous suitability for habitation. In Changping district in the north and Fangshan district in the southwest, for example, implements of other ancient settlements have been found, showing that farming was popular here even just 6,000-7,000 years ago.

THE BEGINNING OF THE DYNASTIES

Evidence of China's dynastic past begins around 4,000 years ago with the Xia dynasty reportedly kicking things off in about 2070 BC. This dynasty established itself farther

© SHANNON AITKEN

Gates of the former ancient city wall can still be found around the city and continue to provide important geographical landmarks.

south in the country, however, and Beijing doesn't really get a mention in history books until about 1046 BC, when the Zhou dynasty put paid to the Shang.

At this time, King Wu of the Zhou dynasty took it upon himself to dish out parcels of land to his friends and family. Two of these were in the Beijing area. The first was Ji, a walled city, which would have been situated in today's southwest area of Guang'anmen, in Xicheng district. Ji sat just north of Beijing's largest waterway, the Yongding River, and along an important trading route between the south and north. It also had the advantage of being close to the ready supply of water that came from Lotus Pond. The pond still exists today in Lianhuachi Park (Lotus Pond Park), just near Beijing West Railway Station, and gives a brilliant display of flowers for much of the year.

The other area was the state of Yan, farther south, which depended more on the ebb and flow of the Liuli River. It's thought that this is one of the major reasons that Yan, as it expanded, moved its capital to Ji. Consequently, Beijing has also been referred to as Yanjing (燕京, Yan Capital), and hence the name of one of the city's most widely consumed beers.

The Zhou dynasty continued to rule in various forms for roughly the next 800 years, being one of the longest-surviving dynasties of China's history, but in 221 BC it was outmatched by the mighty Qin empire, which had already expanded from its homeland in the west and had now conquered all other six states in China. This was the first time all of China had been united under a single empire and leader. He was Qin Shihuang, China's first emperor.

IMPERIAL CHINA

Qin Shihuang was partial to China's west, Xi'an in particular, so Beijing didn't immediately assume the position of capital. Instead it remained just a provincial city for

© SHANNON AITKEN

Ancient temples, such as Dongyue Temple on Chaoyangmenwai Dajie, can be found scattered throughout the city.

much of China's first 1,000 years of imperial rule. Time and time again over this period, the emperors reconfigured the country like pieces of a puzzle. At one point, Han emperor Wudi sliced up the country into 13 provinces, and the surrounding territory of Beijing became the province of You, or Youzhou (幽州), and Ji remained its capital. But then under the Western Jin dynasty (AD 265-316), Yan's capital moved to a city that was farther west and Ji was downgraded to a mere county seat.

After the Western Jin dynasty was overtaken by people from the northern steppes in around AD 304, things got a little messy for several years with a succession of short-lived kingdoms controlling various places at various times, and again splitting the country into north and south. Eventually, the Northern Wei regime took control of northern China and reasserted Ji as the capital city of Youzhou. There was another problem, however. Another prefecture had been created to the east, laying the foundation for what would one day be known as Tianjin. It was called Jizhou, and it soon took the name Ji for its county seat. The original city of Ji then simply took up the name of Youzhou.

Thankfully, a major identity crisis in Youzhou was averted and this name somehow stuck for roughly the next 500 years until almost the end of the Tang dynasty. The Tang dynasty did dabble with another name change, though. They had broken up the country into smaller pieces to help administer it more easily. Instead of prefectures, there were now 300 commandaries, so in 742 Youzhou became Fanyang commandary. This lasted for about 16 years before it reverted once again back to its former name of Youzhou.

While many of China's early dynasties favored the west over Youzhou for their capital, to the nomads from the north it was a valuable entry point into the fertile land south beyond the mountains, and worth squabbling over. The northern nomadic Liao dynasty (also known as the Khitan empire) took over northern China in around

936 and made Beijing a secondary capital. They called their new city Nanjing (南京, Southern Capital).

The Song dynasty, which was ruling China in the south, wasn't too happy about the northern competition, so they asked the Jin dynasty (or the Jurchen people), another group of nomads from the north, to help them oust the Liao dynasty. The Song didn't expect that these northern wanderers would be strong enough to pose any threat to them in this agreement. The Jin, however, were powerful. They convincingly annihilated the Liao, then took Nanjing for the Song and renamed it Yanjing. They were on a roll, however, and set themselves on a southward course to defeat the Song. A 10-year struggle ensued, and finally the Song were brought to their knees. In a desperate move to secure peace, they conceded all of northern China to the Jin. The Jin dynasty then decided to move its capital, which had been up in Huining Fu in northern Manchuria (south of today's Harbin), down to Beijing. So doing they gave the city yet another name, Zhongdu (中都, Central Capital). This was situated in the southwestern area of Beijing, around what is now Xuanwumen and Beijing West Railway Station. The Niu Jie Mosque, built by the Liao and situated on Niu Jie (牛街, Ox Street), is one of the relics from this period and is still worshipped in today.

The problem that seemed to face all these northern conquerors was that once they made it down into the plains of northern China, they settled in, they sinicized, they became Chinese. No longer needing to maintain the vigilance of a nomadic life but enjoying the southern lifestyle, they became sedentary and, like those before them,

© SHANNON AITKEN

Guo Shoujing (1231-1316) was a celebrated scientist and astronomer during the Yuan dynasty.

became vulnerable to new encroachers from the north.

From the early 1200s, a new wave of Mongols began to make its push for Beijing, and this time it was truly a force to be reckoned with. In 1214-1215 Genghis Khan led his Mongol forces into Zhongdu, sacking it first and finally, after a protracted and bitter battle, making it his province. He again restored the name of Yanjing and pushed the Jin to the south.

Following through almost 50 years later, his grandson, Kublai Khan, took his turn with the city. In 1271 he proclaimed the birth of the Yuan dynasty and claimed Yanjing as its capital. At first he had envisaged his new capital to be by the Luan River in Xanadu, in present-day Inner Mongolia, but in the end, like others, he thought Yanjing ideally situated between his northern homeland steppes and the sweeping North China Plain in the south. It was only natural that another name change was in order, and Yanjing now became Dadu (大都, Great Capital) in Chinese or Khanbaliq in Turkic. It seemed that this young khan had a penchant for town planning and began a lot of things that gave modern Beijing its current orientation. When he arrived in the city, much of it was still in ruin thanks to Granddad, so he set about making some improvements. He moved the center of the city northeast, and so established present-day Beijing's vertical axis. The Drum Tower (Gulou) was built in 1272, marking the city center; he also expanded the size of the city and erected a wall around it. Much of this was incorporated into the later city walls of the Ming and Qing dynasties. *Hútòng,* the narrow alleyways that seem to define "authentic Beijing," came out of the Yuan period, their crisscross pattern imprinting the city's core. The 12 parallel *hútòng*—Dongsiyitiao (1) to Dongsishi'ertiao (12), including the famous Dongsishitiao (10)—that still score inner Dongcheng district today are some lingering examples. Likewise, the six "seas" of Beijing, a connected series of lakes, were dominant features of Kublai Khan's capital. Starting just from Jishuitan (near the northwest corner of Line 2), Xihai (West Sea), Houhai (Back Sea), and Qianhai (Front Sea) collectively are known as Shichahai but, more often than not, simply get called Houhai. The string of lakes continues south with Beihai (North Sea) and Zhongnanhai (Middle and South Sea), which sit just to the west side of the Forbidden City. Though the lakes came from the Jin dynasty, they became a key point of commerce during the Yuan dynasty. Xihai was the starting point of the Grand Canal, a major trade route that joined Beijing to Hangzhou in southern Zhejiang province by a 1,776-kilometer-long (1,104-mile-long) series of natural and manmade waterways. The canal's entry point at Xihai meant that the area became a bustling place of business. (These days the Grand Canal is functional only between Hangzhou and Jining in the south of Shandong province.) The whole lake area is still a major hub of activity in the 21st century, but the form of trade is a little different. Today it's surrounded by cafés, restaurants, and terrible karaoke bars—perhaps not something Kublai Khan would have envisaged for his beautiful lakes.

Dadu's trade-route position as well as its increased water supply meant that the city quickly prospered and grew in size, population, and status. Despite the strong position that Kublai Khan established, however, the city was taken almost 100 years later in 1368 by the northward-bound Ming dynasty. Again, a name change felt needed, and Dadu now became Beiping (北平, Northern Peace). At the time, Nanjing in Jiangsu province (just above Shanghai) was serving as the Ming capital. Not known for being warm and fuzzy, the Ming set about making some dramatic changes. The first Ming emperor, Hongwu, was decidedly suspicious of anyone with an education, such as the courtiers, so he led with a strong authoritarian fist. He abolished many of the vital ministries and surrounded himself with a sort of secret service of eunuchs, who were apparently trustworthy because of the lack of a penis. Hongwu did, however, have the extreme generosity to give his then 10-year-old son, Zhu Di, a spectacular gift—the city of Beiping. Hongwu outlived his three oldest sons, so when he died in 1398 his title was passed not to Zhu Di, but to his grandson Zhu Yuwen, the son of the late crown prince. The new emperor was a little bitter over his uncle's power up in Beiping, so he sought to minimize it. Uncle Zhu Di, however, proved to be the mightier of the two, and after a four-year civil war he took Nanjing and boldly declared himself to be the Yongle (永乐, Eternal Happiness) Emperor.

Finally, in 1403, Beijing took on its modern-day name for the first time. It wasn't yet the capital, but it was raised to a position of power similar to that of Nanjing. The Yongle Emperor wanted to do a bit of renovating before he decreed it his capital. So over the next roughly 20 years he boosted the city with a massive reconstruction program. It's thanks to Yongle that Beijing took on much of its present-day structure. The inner city wall was completed, which, though torn down more than 500 years later in 1965, greatly determined how the city would develop to this very day.

During this time the Forbidden City was also constructed, as was the Imperial City, an extension of the Forbidden City. This took in the lakes and gardens immediately surrounding the Forbidden City and gave the royal set exclusive use of the best recreational areas to be had in all of Beijing. In 1420 Yongle also bequeathed the Temple of Heaven (Tiantan Park) to the city. Large sections of the Great Wall were also constructed during Yongle's time. Finally, in 1421, Yongle seemed content with his city and decreed it the capital of China.

Part of Yongle's reasoning behind moving the capital to Beijing was to better protect his dynasty against those marauding steppelanders. Not long after his death, however, incursions from the north began once again. So to further fortify the city, the city wall was extended in the south in 1553. This section protected the southern suburbs and the Temple of Heaven. Like the inner city wall, this was also torn down in the 1960s, to make way for the Second Ring Road.

While the Ming dynasty was definitely a time of growth and development, it was also a particular time of destruction. Winter has always been harsh in Beijing, and the residents at the time logged the surrounding forests for firewood until they were all but barren. When the trees ran out, people turned to coal. The impact on the environment would have severe long-lasting effects on the city.

The Ming dynasty was also hit with a host of epidemics, including various forms of the plague. The epidemics killed hundreds of thousands of people and left the city badly weakened. This, and a protracted period of disorder, banditry and rebellion, eventually left the regime open to defeat. The Manchu Qing dynasty seized on the opportunity, maneuvered its way into the city, and in 1644 commenced China's last dynastic reign.

While many thought the Qing dynasty to be a time of laziness and stagnation, it was also a time of great revival and opulence. Though the Qing were Manchus, holding dominion over a country of a predominantly different ethnicity, they managed to maintain power for almost 300 years. It's thought that some of this was through authoritarian weight throwing, but also by sinicizing. They took on Chinese characteristics, ensured the people were adequately fed, and fostered the arts. They became protectors of the Chinese culture. It was in this period that art forms such as Peking opera were born.

They did, however, do a lot to hold on to their own identity. In fact, their bias toward their own people greatly influenced the geographical distribution of Beijing's wealth. Many of the Han Chinese were moved to the south of the city, to the former districts of Xuanwu and Chongwen. Here the streets developed in a more laissez-faire fashion, their alignment in a not-so-heavenly north-south-east-west orientation. North of Chang'an Jie, however, the Manchu nobles and military groups enjoyed the more manicured environment. Palatial gardens were created up here, including the Summer Palace and Yuan Ming Yuan (the Old Summer Palace).

The Qing dynasty also had more influence from abroad than any other dynasty—both constructively and destructively. They fought a series of battles with British and French troops, and on most occasions were soundly beaten and required to concede territory. After the first Opium War (1839-1842), China was forced to cede Hong Kong to Britain; then during the second Opium War (1858-1860), the Anglo-French forces burned and looted Yuan Ming Yuan to take revenge for the treatment of Western troops. Other reparations included Beijing ceding territory just south of Tian'anmen Square to establish the Legation Quarter (now a fine-dining precinct), an area for foreign embassies. This later became the target of the Boxer Rebellion, in which a Chinese group referred to as Boxers, angered by foreign influence and concessions in China, took siege on the complex. Again, after foreign powers sent in troops to defend the Legation Quarter and its hundreds of occupants, China was forced to make reparations, this time in the form of silver. The costs of the reparations badly damaged the strength of the Qing regime and of the Chinese's confidence in it.

Foreign influences over the Qing period weren't all bad, though. Foreign input assisted developments in many areas of life, including policing, education, medical practices, banking, and rail. And, for better or for worse, this also had an influence on the city's architecture.

THE REPUBLICS OF CHINA

As the 19th century tipped into the 20th, things continued to unravel for the Qing dynasty, and China's 2,000-plus-year dynastic way of life rushed to a close. In 1911 it was faced with the Xinhai Revolution. This was a series of uprisings and rebellions from both visible and underground anti-Qing groups, such as Sun Yat-sen's Tongmenghui (Chinese United League). Sun Yat-sen had spent years gathering funds and anti-Qing supporters in order to topple the Qing regime. At the critical moment, however, to avoid civil war he handed the presidency of the new Republic of China to the rebellious Qing general Yuan Shikai, who had somehow managed to force the abdication of the emperor. Sun Yat-sen's Tongmenghui joined with several other parties to form the Chinese Nationalist Party (the Guomindang or the Kuomintang) and established a system for voting. When the first Chinese elections were held 1912-1913, the Nationalist Party won convincingly. Yuan, however, didn't like the idea of sharing his place in the sun, and took extreme measures to ensure that it didn't happen. It was fast becoming clear that the man had tendencies for megalomania.

Sun Yat-sen was aware of this and rebelled. He tried to spark a second revolution, but instead ended up fleeing into exile to save his skin. Yuan tightened his grip on the leadership by taking over the presidency of the National Assembly. Following this he ousted the Nationalists, dissolved the party and the constitution, and moved to found a new dynasty, naturally with himself as the new emperor. Of course, having just gotten rid of their last emperor, the locals weren't too happy with this, so within a year Yuan had been forced down from his heavenly position, and within months of that, in June 1916, he died. What ensued was more than a decade of confusion and fighting across China. The country tumbled into an unstable position where warlords squabbled for power, and a successive chain of presidents attempted to establish control.

The discontent was highlighted in 1919 during the May 4 Movement. Students, angered by terms of the Treaty of Versailles (areas of China that had previously been

© SHANNON AITKEN

reminders of the Communist Party's rise to power at Tian'anmen Square

conceded to Germany were, instead of being returned to their motherland, handed over to Japan), began an uprising. The protests included a demonstration at Tian'anmen Square, where more than 3,000 students gathered.

Amid the mess, in 1921 the Chinese Communist Party (CCP) found its feet. Its founding members included Mao Zedong and Zhou Enlai. The party's rise to supreme power, however, would be slow and painful, not truly taking the lead position for another 28 years. Before that, the country was still to be ruled first by the warlords of the Beiyang regime, and then by Sun Yat-sen's successor, Chiang Kai-shek, and his Nationalist party. When Kai-shek did seize power in 1928, he moved the capital back to Nanjing, and poor Beijing, yet again, took back the name of Beiping and was relegated to simply being the capital city of Hebei province. Consequently, it was suddenly deprived of the funds for development that it had enjoyed under the Beiyang leadership.

The CCP and the Nationalists had joined forces to successfully defeat the Beiyang warlords, but at this point, the Communists had a change of heart and decided to turn on the Nationalists. This was a bad move. Chiang Kai-shek and his forces viciously suppressed their opponents. Thousands were killed, including Mao's second wife, Yang Kaihui, and Chiang went into full-scale attack mode against the Communists.

The Communist Red Army at that time was predominantly stationed in Fujian and Jiangxi provinces in the south, and it was these latter troops that met with particular trouble. Chiang's soldiers' initial tactic was to corner and starve them. At first, the Communists put up a fight, but, after great losses, made a decision to flee. And so, in 1934, the Long March began. Setting off on a circular route to the north and west, crossing some of the harshest terrain and mountain ranges in China, they evaded their enemy. It's alleged that the Red Army walked 12,500 kilometers (8,000 miles) in just over a year and that thousands died along the way. Around 87,000 soldiers had set off from Jiangxi, but fewer than 10,000 made it to their final destination of Yan'an in Shaanxi province. But through all of this, Mao at last began to firm his position at the top of the Communist ladder.

The Long March demonstrated the hatred the two parties had for each other, and yet, at the end of it, they saw the Japanese as more repulsive than each other. Ever since the early 1930s, Japan had been encroaching on northern China (Manchuria). They had already taken the Great Wall and were threatening Beiping's security. After an exchange of fire between Japanese and Chinese soldiers down at Marco Polo Bridge (also known as Lugou Bridge, about 15 kilometers southwest of Tian'anmen Square), war was declared. So, once again, the two parties joined forces to wage the second Sino-Japanese war (1937-1945). Japan, however, quickly took control of Beiping. They proclaimed it the capital of northern China and revived the name Beijing, yet again.

The city remained under Japanese control for eight years. Compared to other Chinese cities, however, the Japanese handled it with a fairly soft hand. Historic structures were generally preserved, the economy grew, and many locals worked in Japanese companies. As part of the overall plan to humiliate and destroy the confidence of the Chinese people, however, Japan did decide to attack China's institutes of higher learning. Peking University, one of China's proudest places of learning, was shut down, and some of its buildings were even transformed into brothels and bars for the Japanese soldiers. Many of China's other cities, particularly the southern capital, weren't so "lucky." Nanjing was gruesomely attacked in what has become known as the Rape of Nanjing (often called the Rape of Nanking). An estimated 300,000-plus Chinese were killed, many savagely raped and tortured, and it has been argued that this was perhaps the single most atrocious act of genocide in the World War II period. It has left long-term scars on the entire country. Many Chinese today, even those born long after the carnage, openly despise the Japanese. Relationships are gradually improving, however. In Beijing today, there are many bustling Japanese restaurants, and you'll find the occasional young Chinese person who looks not to the West for cultural inspiration but to Japan.

By the end of the war in 1945, tensions flared again between the Nationalists and the CCP. Though together their efforts eventually led to Japan's surrender in 1945, it had not brought them any newfound unity. And where the Nationalists had by that time driven the country to near bankruptcy, the CCP had instead garnered a strong national following.

On October 1, 1949, Mao at last took center stage, and upon a podium at Tian'anmen Square he declared the People's Republic of China and Beijing its capital.

The first 5-7 years of Mao's leadership were some of his best. Land was redistributed and the economy showed signs of improvement. In 1956, however, people got a taste of what was to come. Mao launched the Hundred Flowers Campaign, in which people were asked to express their opinions about the government. Those who did raise an objection, however, were promptly incarcerated. People quickly learned their place, and Mao laid the foundation for a healthy respect for obedience.

The next challenge to fall on the people's shoulders was the Great Leap Forward of 1958-1960, part of Mao's second Five Year Plan, which aimed to modernize the country. It was at this time that China really began to set its sights on matching itself with the West (a goal that is still blatantly apparent today). Mao believed China was capable of surpassing the economy of the United Kingdom in 15 years and of the United States in 20-30 years. He believed grain and steel production would be the yardsticks with which to judge this by, so he set about redistributing land into large communes, and "encouraged" people everywhere to turn their backyards into furnaces. It's estimated there were about 60,000 such furnaces around the country. Being run by people who had absolutely no idea about steel production, however, meant that almost everything they produced was unusable. When Mao would make his tours of the country to inspect the progress, people would jump to impress him. Furnaces and transported crops were fashioned alongside his train route just ahead of him so that he could see the bountiful gains of his plans. The true result, however, was utter devastation. Many of the able-bodied people had been sent off to work on steel, so there was no one left to work the land, and even if there was, they often had no tools to work with, as these had been melted down or destroyed for steel production. Even many of the crops that were successfully harvested were sent to Russia rather than fed to the starving Chinese people who had produced them. China was billions of *rénmínbì* in debt to Russia, and Mao stubbornly wanted to prove the country's strength by paying it all back in an agreed period of time. In 1959 China was hit by severe drought, tipping the country into catastrophe. Crops failed and millions died from starvation. Those who opposed were punished, and often killed. Figures of those who died from famine or militant killings range from around 14 million to more than 40 million. Historians such as Yang Jishen (author of banned book *Tombstone*, one of the most respected accounts of the Great Chinese Famine) suggests 36 million individuals. Author and producer of *China History Podcast* Laszlo Montgomery compares that figure to the total population of the states of Alabama, Alaska, Arizona, Arkansas, Colorado, Massachusetts, and Washington, D.C.—every single person dead within three years, thanks to one man's bad policies, which were compounded by a year of inclement weather. It was the worst famine in the world's recorded history.

Following the disaster of the Great Leap Forward, the government lost confidence in Mao, and he was forced to resign from his position as Head of State (though he still got to keep his powerful position of Party Chairman). Moderates Liu Shaoqi, Zhou Enlai, and Deng Xiaoping then took over the running of the country, and, in late 1960, the Great Leap Forward was abandoned.

Like a cat with nine lives, however, Mao made a comeback in 1966, and this time it was with an attack on what he believed were growing capitalist elements within the party and country. It became known as the Great Proletarian Cultural Revolution, and it ran from 1966 to roughly the time of his death in 1976. The revolution's goal was to impose Maoist theory and socialism on society. So-called "revisionists" were to be removed, through violence if necessary. China's youths rallied to the cause and responded by forming the Red Guard. The Red Guard went around attacking anything or anyone that represented the West, capitalism, religion, or old traditions. Any rivals were purged from the political system, and the country's medical and educational systems were destroyed, along with its culture and many of its religious and historical relics. An intense and pervasive sense of distrust developed among the people. People were "outed" for alleged anti-socialist behaviors, and millions were abused, tortured, publicly humiliated, and displaced.

AFTER MAO

Stability within China didn't really begin to take shape until two years after Mao's death, when Deng Xiaoping took control in 1978. In 1980 he began a process of "reform and opening up." Though he never officially held office as the head of state, head of government, or the general secretary of the CCP, Deng was the country's paramount leader until 1992 and is greatly respected for the gains that he brought to the nation.

One smear on his glowing career, however, came in 1989, when the country was reminded that things were not yet completely open. For seven weeks, starting April 15, thousands of students gathered at Tian'anmen Square, calling for economic reform, freedom of the press, accountability of officials, and political liberalization. The government at first offered some concessions, but when students wouldn't budge the military was called in and on June 4 brutally suppressed the demonstration. No official figures were released, but reports of the numbers killed range from many hundreds to several thousand, and even more wounded. Today the topic is strictly taboo on the mainland, website content relating to the issue is blocked (except for official versions of the incident), and many young people have no knowledge of the event at all. People are acutely aware, however, of the risk of gathering in large groups. At the hint of any protest, the government cracks down on Internet activity, potential gathering sites, and on known activists and dissidents. And there is no city in China that is more closely monitored by the government than Beijing.

When Mao took power, he began a "generation" system of leadership. Together with Zhou Enlai, Liu Shaoqi, and Zhu De, he represented the first generation, from 1949 to 1976. Deng Xiaoping was of the second generation (1976-1992). It was under Deng Xiaoping that the one-child policy was introduced in 1979 to try to stem the unsustainable population growth. The third generation (1992-2003) was led by Jiang Zemin at its core. The fourth generation (2003-2013) had Hu Jintao at the helm, with the grand collection of titles of general secretary of the Communist Party of China, president of the People's Republic of China, and chairman of the Central Military Commission; Wen Jiabao served as prime minister. China's newly sworn-in group represents the fifth generation, with Xi Jinping as the general secretary of the Communist Party Central Committee, chairman of the Central Military Commission, president of the People's Republic of

© BRYAN MULLENNIX/123RF.COM

A larger-than-life portrait of Mao Zedong hangs over the gate of the Forbidden City.

China, and chairman of the Central Military Commission, followed by Li Keqiang as the premier of the State Council.

In general, since the time of the second generation, the city of Beijing has prospered and developed at a mind-boggling pace. In this time there have been many major events that have signaled its entry onto the world stage. The 2008 Olympics were a tremendous success and catapulted the city forward in its international status, and the opening of the T3 Beijing Capital Airport, designed by British architect Norman Foster, at last gave it a terminal worthy of global travel. It may have taken much longer to get to this position than Mao anticipated, and required slightly more humanistic approaches, but Beijing seems to now be nearing a relatively level playing field with the West.

Government

Beijing is one for four special kinds of cities in China. Like Shanghai, Tianjin, and Chongqing, it's a top-tier, freestanding municipality, autonomous in that it doesn't answer to its surrounding province (in Beijing's case Hebei) but directly to the national government. These cities have the same political, jurisdictional, and economic rights as a province.

To try to better manage Beijing and its millions of people, the government has broken the municipality up into 14 districts (Dongcheng, Xicheng, Chaoyang, Haidian, Fengtai, Shijingshan, Tongzhou, Shunyi, Changping, Daxing, Mentougou, Fangshan, Pinggu, and Huairou) and two counties (Miyun and Yanqing). Each of these districts and counties is led by its own local government and an elected mayor. Overseeing them all is the Beijing People's Congress, Beijing's top legislative body. Representing the People's Congress is the mayor of Beijing, the municipality's highest-ranking government official. Since 2012, that man has been Wang Anshun. As the Beijing mayor, Wang has the same level of power as the provincial governors, so when it comes to the city's taxes, budgets, and administration duties, Wang is the man.

The Chinese Communist Party (CCP), however, always remains the supreme body. Wang, therefore, is still outranked by the secretary of the Beijing committee of the CCP. That honor goes to Liu Qi, who, in that role, had the pride of being president of the Beijing Olympics Organizing Committee in 2008.

Being the capital, Beijing is home to most of China's top organs of power, including the National People's Congress (NPC), the State Council, the Central Military Commission (which is in charge of the People's Liberation Army, or PLA), and, most importantly, the headquarters of the CCP. Together with the grand structures that house these and other political bodies in the city, the government has a very clear and commanding presence in the city.

CHINA'S POLITICAL SYSTEM

China is divided into 22 provinces (it likes to call Taiwan its 23rd province; Taiwan likes to think differently); five autonomous regions (Guangxi, Inner Mongolia, Ningxia, Xinjiang, and Tibet); four municipalities; and two Special Administrative Regions (SARs), these being Hong Kong and Macau.

The political system that rules these divisions is made up of three main arms—the party, the army, and the state—and these do not have equal power. The party is the paramount body, and the army (i.e., the PLA) and the state answer to it.

The party, that being the Chinese Communist Party (CCP; or the Communist Party of China, CPC), is strictly controlled and very organized. Through a lengthy, highly selective approval process, people become members of the party. Once they become members, there are strict laws within the party that they must abide by. Despite the arduous vetting process, there are still around 80 million CCP members, making it the world's largest political party. Every five years the CCP holds a National Party Congress (not to be confused with the state-level National People's Congress). At the National Party Congress the two main objectives are to inform people of any important changes to the party's ideology and to elect new members. The last National Party Congress, the 18th, was held in October 2012, and it was there that Xi Jinping and Li Keqiang were officially "elected" as the new president and premier, respectively (in reality the decision had been made well ahead of this event).

Of course, not every party member can have a major position, so the 80 million get whittled down into a finely pointed cone of command. Of the general collection of members, around 2,000 attend the National Party Congress. From this, around 200 elite members form the Central Committee. These people are selected from far and wide—ministers, high-ranking military men, even CEOs from state-owned companies. The Central Committee is where the real power really starts to kick in. Around 25 men are then extracted from the Central Committee to form the Politburo (short for political bureau) and, from there, the elite of the elite, the nine-member Politburo Standing Committee, which makes all the heavyweight decisions. To sharpen the nib even further, these select men are numbered from one to nine—number one being the top of the Chinese Communist Party, the general secretary of the Central Committee; i.e., Xi Jinping.

The more practical matters for running the country happen at the level of the state. The state works around a People's Congress system, and it too is distinctly hierarchical, whereby the lower levels elect the higher levels. This means that the district- and county-level governments of each province or municipality elect the members of their respective People's Congress, and all the People's Congresses then elect the members of the National People's Congress (NPC). The governor or mayor of each region also gets a seat at the NPC. The NPC, being the highest organ of power, has the power to then elect or depose the top names in the Supreme People's Court and the Supreme People's Procuratorate (the country's top body for prosecution and investigation). Towering above all of this is the CCP.

Some compare the NPC to the U.S. Congress. The NPC's deputies, however, far outnumber the U.S. congressmen and -women, with a representation of close to 3,000 people, each elected for a five-year term. About two-thirds of these are also members of the Communist Party. The other third is made up largely of non-Communist representatives. Contrary to how it may seem, China does actually have a multi-party system. There are eight other legally recognized non-Communist parties, such as the China Democratic League and the Revolutionary Committee of the Guomindang. The election and approval process, however, barely makes it possible for members to rise above the lowest level of congress, and added to that, China has no provision for non-Communist parties to establish themselves as a company, so they have no legal way to build funds. Despite their presence at the NPC, however, the Communist Party has the final yea or nay on any decisions made. So, in practice, yes, the system is basically Communist.

There seems to be very little the NPC can't do. It can elect the head of state, namely the president; approve the appointment of the premier of the State Council; interpret the constitution and supervise how it's enforced; enact or alter laws relating to crimes, civil affairs, and state organizations; oversee the country's economic and social plans; supervise the performance of the State Council, the Supreme People's Court, and other such bodies; draw up state laws; manage treaties with other nations; and much more. It does all this just once a year in a two-week-long plenary session. In reality, many of the decisions have actually already been made over the year by the NPC Standing Committee and the Politburo, and the meeting on the whole simply serves to ratify those decisions.

The congress is held every March in the magnificent Great Hall of the People beside Tian'anmen Square, and it coincides with the Chinese People's Political Consultative Conference (CPPCC). Both the NPC and the CPPCC are often referred to as the Two Meetings. While neither meeting truly has much independent power, together they create a media frenzy. The Two Meetings provide forums where China's current concerns and plans can be put forth, as well as an opportunity with which to try to groom public opinion.

The NPC's leading man is the president (Xi Jinping), and though this position is more ceremonial than functional, he can appoint the head of the State Council (or the State Government). This is where all the ministers and ministries reside. The head of the State Council is the premier, and since March 2013 this has been Li Keqiang.

How do the premier and the State Council fit into the political structure? Well, while it's the party that issues the directives for how they want the country to be modified as per party ideals, it's the responsibility of the State Council to make sure these turn into a reality. It's the State Council that creates the actual working laws and administers and enforces them. It covers everything from the environment and housing to banking and finance. Of course, the State Council must answer to the party, but as the premier is also the number three man on the Politburo Standing Committee, it's potentially a fairly tight relationship.

For now China's political system is still highly controlled and socialist. Figures such as former president Wen Jiabao have pledged to allow more democracy and pluralism into the mechanisms of society, but with censorship and a highly government-controlled legal system, progress here as yet remains limited. Where Xi Jinping and Li Keqiang will take China in the next five years, we're just beginning to see.

Economy

CHINA'S ECONOMY

For the last 30 years, China has been one of the world's fastest growing economies, averaging at about 10 percent growth per year. Of course, this staggering figure can't be discussed without mentioning Deng Xiaoping, who, against great resistance, managed to transform the country out of near devastation to one that was highly productive, organized, and market-driven.

The time of Deng is referred to as the period of reform and opening up. He developed a whole new way of thinking for the Communists. Though a proponent of Leninism and Marxism, he devised "socialism with Chinese characteristics"—a mixture of state-owned enterprises with a market economy. Deng could see the errors of Mao; however, he took a diplomatic approach and refrained from trashing his former leader's name. Mao was "seven parts good, three parts bad," Deng said and advised that Mao's "accomplishments must be considered before his mistakes." So, respecting the people's lingering loyalty for Mao, Deng pushed forward with profound economic and social changes. He removed class barriers. Those of the old landlord class, who had suffered severely during Mao's regime, were again allowed to find work, and even capitalists could join the Communist Party. The massive ineffective farming communes were broken up and peasants were permitted to earn a profit. China's market was opened up to foreign trade, and companies such as Boeing and Coca-Cola soon began to develop relationships with China. Deng also improved relations with the United States, Japan, Singapore, and Britain, and successfully negotiated the return of both Macau and Hong Kong from Portugal and Britain, respectively.

In his time, Deng stipulated three bold financial goals, and he came close to achieving all three within his own lifetime. The first was to double the 1980 gross national product (GNP) so as to ensure the Chinese could actually clothe and feed themselves; he did this in 10 years. The second was to double this number again before the year 2000. He accomplished this five years ahead of schedule. The third, due for a completion check in 2050 and clearly well on its way, was to raise the GNP level per capita to a level equal to that of medium-developed countries.

Deng had a strong influence on the government long after he stepped down from any official roles, and even after his death in 1997, his policies have continued to help succeeding leaders drive the economy. In 2001 China entered the World Trade Organization, resulting in further economic liberalization and deregulation.

Figures from the World Bank highlight various impressive gains made by China over the last few decades. In 2004 those living below the poverty line in China accounted for 2.8 percent of the population—down from 6 percent in 1996—while gross national income (GNI) per capita was at US$4,930 in 2011, up from US$1,100 in 2002. At the end of Mao's reign the GDP was at about US$152 billion. Deng's reforms took a while to kick in, but by 1990 the GDP had risen to US$357 billion, and just eight years later it hit the trillion mark. In 2011 China's GDP was at US$7.298 trillion, about US$7.8 trillion behind the United States.

At the end of 2012, there were some signs of China's economy beginning to slow down. Some have argued that this was due to the government pushing excessive investment in earlier years. The Chinese government, however, argues that the GDP contraction was in line with its plans. The government is currently into its 12th Five Year Guideline, running 2011-2015. The Five Year Guidelines (previously called Five Year Plans, and still frequently referred to as such) are the economic and social goals outlined by the government for a given five-year period. The current guideline, if achieved, will radically change China's economy. Just some of its goals include: expanding domestic consumption while maintaining stable economic development; modernizing agriculture to create the new socialist rural villages; and promoting energy savings and environmental protection.

BEIJING AND ITS FORTUNES

While China's economic success seems impressive enough, Beijing's success is astounding. It's often been said that Shanghai is China's key hub for business, and that Hong Kong is the cutthroat domain of capitalism, yet from many perspectives they both seem to pale in comparison to Beijing. Perhaps one figure that highlights Beijing's economic domination is its number of Fortune Global 500 companies. In 2012, China had 73 of the *Fortune* Global 500 companies, second only to the United States with its stash of 132 *Fortune* 500s, and a smidgeon ahead of Japan's 68. After that, the closest countries are France and Germany, both with 32 companies each.

Beijing alone claims 44 of China's 73 *Fortune* Global 500 companies. This puts it ahead of not only France and Germany, but leagues ahead of any other Chinese city, including Hong Kong, which has only four, and Shanghai, which does mildly better with six. On top of this, list king *Forbes* also has China down for nine companies in the top 100 of its 2012 "The World's Biggest Companies" list, seven of which are situated in Beijing.

Where other parts of China seem to be contracting, Beijing is relatively robust. The city's GDP reached RMB1.6 trillion (US$253.3 billion) in 2011, up 8.1 percent from 2010, and according to the Beijing Municipal Bureau of Statistics, the capital's GDP again increased by 7.2 percent year-on-year in the first half of 2012.

The average salary in Beijing is likewise rising dramatically. Far above the average earnings of their fellow countrymen and women, Beijingers each enjoyed an average GDP of RMB80,394 (US$12,447) in 2011, which the Beijing Municipal Bureau of Statistics said was close to the levels of developed countries. Even adjusting for the slight difference in GNI, this figure still put Beijing into the World Bank's category of a "high income" economy.

Take away taxes and the like, however, and Beijingers have an average disposable income that's a little less comfortable, just RMB32,903 (US$5,170). This is about 40 percent of GDP per capita, which is still about 10 percent lower than many developed countries. In April of 2012 official figures put Beijing's inflation rate (CPI) at 3.5 percent (0.3 percent above the national average). When living a life in downtown Beijing, however, this might sometimes feel a little off. It's not unusual to hear stories of rent being jacked up by 20 percent between lease periods. Gasoline prices at the pump went up by around 50 percent between 2009 and 2012, and food seems to constantly be more expensive than the last time you bought it. Professor Patrick Chovanec of Tsinghua University's School of Economics and Management ran his own Beijing-based "KFC index" experiment to illustrate. Over a period of two years and eight months, between 2009 and 2012, his standard meal—large popcorn chicken, small fries, and a large Coke—went up by 53.5 percent, from RMB21.50 to RMB33.00. This was somewhat higher than official figures, which put food inflation at 5.6 percent in July 2012.

In 2011, the unemployment figure in Beijing was 1.39 percent, a relatively low number when compared to other Chinese cities. Those under the age of 35 accounted for 38 percent of the unemployed population. Additionally, the city is still in need of skilled staff for various industries, including IT, manufacturing, avionics, transportation, and agricultural development.

DEVELOPMENT OF THE SUBWAY AND INFRASTRUCTURE

Over the last several decades, the government has made massive investments to boost Beijing's development. The Olympics alone led to a major injection into infrastructure, yet the rapid expansion didn't end with the closing ceremony. Since 2008 alone, 11 subway lines have been added, with plans for a total of 19 by 2015. This will mean an estimated total investment of around RMB200 billion (US$29.2 billion). It has also encouraged new and increased concentrations of companies around transport-rich areas. It will also free up many of heavily congested roads in Beijing—theoretically. A second airport is also in the pipeline, this one to be located 46 kilometers (29 miles) from the city's center in southern Daxing district. Due for completion in 2017, this will connect Beijing even more strongly with port city Tianjin (already connected by high-speed train) and surrounding Hebei province.

Another key contribution to Beijing's economic rise is the development of major commercial hubs. Just some of the major financial development zones include the Beijing Central Business District (CBD), centered around Guomao in Chaoyang district; Wangfujing in Dongcheng district; Xidan and Financial Street (Jinbao Jie) in Xicheng district; Tianzhu Airport Industrial Zone in Shunyi district; Yongle Economic Development Area in Tongzhou district; and Zhongguancun Science Park in Haidian district. There are dozens more and most have highly concentrated mixtures of business, residential, and lifestyle facilities.

BEIJING'S INDUSTRY

While China's two dominant sectors are industry and agriculture, Beijing's major revenue spinner is the tertiary industry. In fact, in 2011, the service industry accounted for about 75 percent of GDP, with a contribution of RMB1.2 trillion to the total figure. Finance, information technology, and scientific research, such as the pharmaceutical industry, were the key contributors to that percentage.

The banking sector is almighty in Beijing, and typically generates more than RMB126 billion a year. In 2012 that added up to around 15 percent of Beijing's total GDP. While the Chinese can surprise you with their ability to pay massive amounts upfront in cash, lending is a significant part of the banks' business. In 2012 Beijing banks had accumulated RMB4.2 trillion in outstanding loans, RMB3.55 trillion of which was in local currency (a 12.4 percent increase on RMB loans from 2011), along with RMB650 billion in foreign currencies.

It seems that some of that might be from the real estate industry, which is another

AVERAGE MONTHLY SALARIES IN BEIJING

Accountant: RMB10,000-15,000+
Brand marketing manager: RMB20,000-28,000
CEO of an advertising agency: RMB70,000-100,000
English teacher*: RMB5,000-16,000
Executive secretary/personal assistant: RMB13,000-21,000
Finance director: RMB65,000+
HR manager: RMB20,000-35,000+
IT programmer: RMB5,000-9,000
Legal secretary: RMB6,000-5,000
Marketing executive: RMB6,000-12,000
Mechanical engineer: RMB10,000-16,000
News editor: RMB5,000-8,500
Office assistant: RMB7,000-10,000
Public relations manager: RMB20,000-30,000
Project manager: RMB24,000-40,000
Quality-control manager: RMB14,000-24,000
Regional sales manager: RMB26,000-36,000+
Senior architect: RMB25,000-45,000
Translator: RMB8,000-18,000+
Web editor: RMB6,000-19,000+

*Added by author.
Source: Survey of salaries in Beijing, Shanghai, Shenzhen and Guangzhou in 2012 Q1, by recruitment firm J.M. Gemini. Current surveys are available via www.imsinasia.com.

phenomenally successful sector in the municipality, and which after a cooling in 2011 was back on fire in 2012. The Beijing Municipal Bureau of Statistics reported that the total commercial housing sales in Beijing in August 2012 were 31.2 percent higher than they were the previous year, despite new policies being imposed in 2011 that set limits on the number of residential properties people could buy.

Beijing is currently placing emphasis on the development of high-tech industries and modern services, such as outsourcing, and cultural and creative industries. In 2010, the value-added output of the cultural and creative industry grew by 13.6 percent, resulting in a fat contribution of RMB169.2 billion to the city's GDP.

Other major industries in the city include tourism, telecommunications equipment, transportation equipment, chemicals, machinery, metallurgy, and food processing. Foreign trade also plays an important role in the economy, with major exports including mechanical and electronic products, vessels, and clothing. In agriculture, wheat and corn are the key crops.

Finally, the people in Beijing are big spenders. Beijing's consumption increase is thanks not only to the higher incomes of the residents but to the millions of tourists that flock to the city year on year. In particular, residents like to spend their money on housing, cars, and communication devices. Previously, Wangfujing and Xidan were the locally favored places to spend money, but these days major shopping districts are cropping up everywhere. Guomao, Sanlitun, Haidian, Chongwenmen, Chaoyangmen,

© NORA JANG

Tourists and the money they spend are an important part of Beijing's economy.

Dongzhimen, and Fuxingmen are just some of the places boasting impressive collections of shopping malls. Foreign-invested stores, such as Carrefour, Ito Yokado, Ikea, Muji, Apple, and many others, have also spurred on development in the local market.

Finally, while many of Beijing's companies are state-owned, the private sector has been rapidly developing. By the end of 2010, there were approximately 496,000 private enterprises, an increase of more than 200 percent in less than 10 years.

PEOPLE AND CULTURE

After a history of instability, turmoil, and famine, personal security is a major concern to Beijing families. This is exacerbated by the constant pressure of living in a heavily overpopulated city with intense employment and marital competition.

Beijing is a place of paradoxes, and you'll fail abysmally if you try to box people into a single definition. While many will squash themselves into a hot sweaty bus to save a single *yuán*, others will flaunt their new Maserati outside nightclubs. Some will quaff cocktails of traditional and Western medication to maintain optimal health while others chain-smoke chemically dubious cigarettes. Many passionately embrace traditions, while others are bewitched by anything shiny and new.

Given a long and not-too-distant history of famine and turmoil, people here prioritize personal security over spiritual things such as love. Marriage is paramount, and it's the men who have the pressure of having to provide a dowry of a car, apartment, and stable job.

For the most part, the people of Beijing are warm and open to change. They're forgiving of those who don't speak Chinese and often even embarrassed if they're unable to speak English themselves. Rather than racing to be adults, they're young at heart and playful well into their 30s. They love to laugh, to go hiking in spring, to sit around for hours eating communal meals, and, above all, to share their pride in their country.

© SHANNON AITKEN

Ethnicity and Nationality

By the end of 2012, Beijing's population had reached 20.69 million people, and every year, more and more people continue to squeeze into the capital. Fortunately, figures over recent years suggest that the rate at which the city is getting more crowded is finally beginning to slow.

China has 56 ethnic groups, and they are all represented in Beijing. The Hans are the largest group by far, accounting for more than 95 percent of all Chinese people. The next most populous ethnicities include the Hui, Manchus, and Mongolians. Expats make up around 120,000 of Beijing's population, just 0.006 percent.

What characterizes Beijing, however, isn't its ethnic groups, but the blend of Beijingers and non-Beijingers or, rather, the migrants coming in from other provinces and cities to work or study. Around 400,000 migrants arrive in Beijing every year, and currently they make up about 36 percent of the city's population. Approximately one in every three Chinese people you'll meet will have come from somewhere like Hebei, Hubei, Inner Mongolia, Sichuan, and so on. The migration has its benefits. You couldn't be in a much better city for authentic, ethnically diverse cuisine. Demographically it evens out the age distribution problem (making the ticking time bomb of the aging population look subtly better, at least on paper). It also evens out the gender imbalance. Beyond that, the migrants contribute greatly to Beijing's growth at both labor and management levels. Beijing's manufacturing industry relies heavily on migrants, with these non-locals making up around 40 percent of Beijing's manufacturing staff.

The mass migration also has obvious consequences and is putting serious strains on the city's infrastructure. This places the government in a difficult position. On one hand it needs to control Beijing's population, which some experts say is already beyond approved levels, while on the other hand it needs migrants to maintain the prosperity of the city. Its main tool for managing this is the *hùkǒu* system (residential status). In the capital, having a Beijing *hùkǒu* is like gold.

Communism and Class

Communism is something of a mixed bag in Beijing. There is perhaps no other city in China where its presence is so palpable. Imposing government buildings abut residential neighborhoods and tower over common thoroughfares. Bodies of troupes march the streets, and from time to time full-pomp military displays demonstrate the party's might and rouse the national spirit. Even uniforms of anything from a hairdresser to a security guard can be confusingly military looking. Red banners hung from walls or railings by party community groups impel people with Communist slogans of social unity, and Mao's portrait forever hangs imperiously over the entrance to the Forbidden City. Businesses will also readily feel the hand of the government at work. Bureaucracy is an art form here—you'll need to stand in more queues, sign more pieces of flimsy paper, and go to more separate government offices to have something approved than you've ever experienced elsewhere, and then at the government's whim, you may need to do it all again because of a change in policy. Locals can wake up one day to find a red 拆 (*chāi,* demolition) character painted on their door and, no matter how passionate their resistance, be relocated the next, all in the name of progress.

From a more day-to-day perspective, however, Communism, especially in its fundamental concepts of comradeship and equality of wealth and power, seems to be more of a veneer. In reality, Beijing is fiercely capitalistic and competitive. The government's "socialism with Chinese characteristics" ideology has allowed them to pursue capitalist ideals while maintaining socialist control, without loss of face. Money is both the worshipped idol and the all-powerful motivator of society, and there is a flagrant, increasing gap between the haves and have-nots. Where once the motto of life was "the nail that sticks out gets hammered down," ever more people fight tooth and nail to be the shiniest star on the stage. Luxury items become badges of status, and success in life is measured not by love or contribution to society, but by ticks on a socially mandated checklist: car, apartment, spouse, secure job with potential to climb—even fashionable furniture is starting to become mandatory. While the poor remain vulnerable, the rich are threateningly powerful. The luxury goods market in Beijing is flourishing, and the wealthy segregate themselves ever farther away from the stragglers, secluding themselves in private clubs, in VIP rooms at bars, or in simulacra of Western-style gated communities, such as the notorious Orange County development near the airport.

Not everyone is consumed by desire for money and possessions, but with the media devouring and regurgitating an image of opulence, and with stories of bribery and corruption arising in close succession, your collective image can get a little tainted.

According to the 2012 *Hurun Report,* Beijing is now home to most of China's wealthy, with 179,000 millionaires (defined as those with RMB10 million/US$1.6 million or more) and 10,500 super-rich (those with RMB100 million/US$16 million or more). Yet, breathing the same air are workers who get by on a few dollars a day, making a living by collecting used boxes, carting coal, or manufacturing the goods that have made the rich rich. Migrant workers, many with university degrees earned years ago, sleep in crammed dormitory-like accommodations, often on the outskirts of town, and work in dangerous conditions with minimal to no protection. Beijing may not have the slums of India or the favelas of Brazil, but it certainly is very conscious of its blue collars (蓝领, *lánlǐng*), white collars (白领, *báilǐng*), and gold collars (金领, *jīnlǐng*).

Customs and Social Values

Given Beijing's ethnic makeup and migrant population, the local culture is far from homogenous and is difficult to define. You'll see all kinds of behavior here—some that will endear the city to you, others that will downright repulse you. Yes, people spit, so get used to it. You'll see worse. Many in Beijing are well traveled and educated overseas, and have begun to blend Western social values with their own. Others have had essentially no real exposure to Western life, and live by a more distinct, traditional set of Chinese ideals.

Within a family, circle of friends, or work group people are considerate, generous, and wonderfully warm. Expect to be invited to frequent dinners or have people willing to help you at the instant a problem arises. There is, however, often little

© SHANNON AITKEN

A mother and son stroll in Ritan Park.

consideration for anything outside one's personal sphere. People cough and sneeze without covering their mouths, dump rubbish outside their front door, shout into cell phones in the subway, and jump the queue if there's the slightest hint of a gap. And in a country of more than 1.35 billion people, no matter where the person comes from, there is no strong concept of personal space. If you pay too much attention to the things that irk you, you'll give yourself ulcers. This is China, not the West, and values are different.

To live a more Zen-ful, less agitated life here, abandon your own Western notions of public courtesy. Do not expect anyone to hold a door open for you—in fact, expect them to let it slam in your face; do not expect people to let you out of the elevator or a vehicle before they scramble in; do not expect a car to give way to you even if you have a green light; and, if you're planning to drive, repress the idea that the thank you wave ever existed. Without any such expectations, you will cruise through life much more agreeably, and no doubt at times even be pleasantly surprised.

Trying to understand how culture and etiquette have evolved in Beijing can help you better appreciate why people have the values they do. Some of it has been influenced by religion and Communism, but much of it has also been forged by a relatively recent history of severe poverty, famine, and the unrelenting daily competition created by living in the most populated country in the world. Though the general standard of life has improved dramatically, there is still a survival-of-the-fittest mentality. In recent years a lot has been made in the media regarding lack of compassion of the Chinese, with stories of people walking past injured people on the street. Unfortunately, it's not that simple. Not only is knowledge of first aid all but nonexistent, but those who do help are often accused by the injured of being involved and forced by the police to pay out large sums of money. No proof required. People have become rightly scared to offer a helping hand. Getting involved in someone else's accident is something even you should think twice about doing when here.

There are other distinctive aspects relating to culture in Beijing. Two of the most important are *guānxi* (关系), or relationships, and *rénmài* (人脉), or contacts. These are deeply valued here and are a fundamental part of life, particularly when doing business. Having friends, family, or business relationships that can help you is much more important than in the West.

There is a strong sense of hierarchy in China, particularly in the workplace. Bosses are rarely addressed by their first name but by their position. Criticisms or disagreements are given indirectly in order to save face. This can make getting to the core of an issue or resolving a problem tedious and time consuming. On the other hand, some comments can be frightfully frank. "Wow, you've put on weight!" is not something people are shy about saying. In many cases, this is really just a way of showing their intimacy to you, showing that they know you well enough to notice small changes. If you pay attention, they'll probably be just as quick to tell you you've lost weight, too (*"Nǐ shòu le!"*). It's often said that Chinese people will openly ask you how much you earn, but from personal experience this really doesn't get asked that much these days. Instead, people definitely will very freely ask you how much something you bought cost. Again, to them, this isn't being rude. In part it's pure curiosity, as they like to be up to date with what's happening, but it can also be because they care about you and don't want you to have been ripped off. To avoid answering a question that you think is too personal, simply tell them *"Wǒ wàng le"* ("I forget").

If you're looking for Western examples of politeness, you might not see what you want to see. But there are in fact many niceties routinely practiced here, things that Westerners would probably be quite ambivalent about. For example, gifts are frequently given for no apparent reason, hosts regularly offer food or drinks to guests, and in business situations people often stand up when someone new enters a room. People may not say thank you quite as often as is almost habitual in Western culture, particularly between close friends or to service people such as shop attendants. Saying "thanks" to a close friend can even sometimes be felt to distance your relationship because the obligation to do things for each other is already inherent in the relationship. A person will also detect your respect or politeness by the way you address them—*shīfu* for a taxi driver, *āyí* for a woman who's older than you, *fúwùyuán* for a waiter, or *lǎobǎn* for a male in charge of a shop or stall. The list goes on, but it's helpful to have a few of the common ones in your repertoire.

DINING ETIQUETTE

For day-to-day dining, Chinese people are generally pretty easygoing when it comes to etiquette. There are no obvious rules about eating with your mouth closed or talking with your mouth full, about putting elbows on the table or slurping your soup. Dining etiquette is more about the mechanics of the meal than about the way that you eat.

Unless dining at a Western restaurant, you'll find eating is almost always family style, with dishes put in the center of a round table and everyone helping themselves. It can often appear that people order gluttonously, and that at the end of the meal there is an excess of leftovers. Some of this comes from the goal to ensure one's guests are well fed. Rather than an empty plate being seen as compliments to the chef, it can actually be interpreted as having under catered and leads to a loss of face for the host. Fortunately, there is a healthy habit of asking for a doggy bag and taking home any uneaten food.

In more formal circumstances, such as at business dinners or family gatherings, there are a few rules you should know about. The seat farthest from the entrance is reserved for the guest of honor, and then the level of hierarchy decreases as you go around the table, with the lowest on the ladder seated closest to the door. Ladies first doesn't apply here. The guest of honor is the first person to dig in, and this then gives everyone else the green light. You'll need to get used to the one menu per table custom. Traditionally

© SHANNON AITKEN

Chinese people love to eat out in large groups, and hotpot is one of the most popular ways to do that.

the person taking care of the bill also does all the ordering. It's best to leave it this way in formal situations and happily be surprised by the parade of dishes that then ensues. For casual dinners amongst friends, however, it is acceptable (especially in expat hubs) to prompt the waiter to bring you additional menus.

Paying for the bill is perhaps the most obvious point of difference. These days, in purely social situations, younger people occasionally like to go Dutch, which they call *AA-zhi* (*AA*制), but it's still not the norm. More often one person will take responsibility for both ordering the entire meal and paying the bill, and this is usually the person who initiated the dinner. If this hasn't been made clear from the start, an ostentatious display of determination to pay the bill can often take place at the end of the meal, occasionally with people yelling and semi-wrestling in front of the patiently waiting waiter. It can actually be seen as impolite not to offer to pay the bill, even if you're the invited guest. Those wishing to avoid the bill scene at the end of the meal can discreetly pay the bill by making a bogus bathroom dash. If you do end up being the recipient of the meal, it's quietly expected that you'll even things out with a counter invitation at a restaurant of similar or higher standing in the near future.

One final example of dramatically different etiquette is the way in which you get the waitstaff's attention. While in the West it's standard to raise a hand or simply make eye contact and nod, in China it's the norm to call out a loud and clear *"fúwùyuán!"* ("Waiter!") Waitstaff don't routinely patrol restaurants, but do instead listen out for a call. Once you get used to it, you'll find it extremely practical and efficient, and when you go home to your own country where you need to return to waiting quietly for a waitress to catch your eye, you're sure to feel quite debilitated.

LIQUID CULTURE

One cornerstone of culture in China, particularly in business situations, is drinking. The Chinese love to drink, in copious quantities, and though the beer doesn't have much of a kick in a single bottle, *báijiǔ,* the alcohol of choice in the north for business meetings, certainly does. Sharing a drink with your companions and even getting rolling drunk in front of them is a sign of both respect and trust, and is a key tool for cementing relationships or securing business deals.

In China you'll come to be very familiar the expression *"gānbēi,"* which can equate to "cheers," but more closely to "bottoms up," given that its direct translation is "dry glass."

Toasting is almost a ritual of dining, for both men and women. People not only do one big toast at the start of the meal, but individuals will randomly pipe up throughout the evening. The amount people drink each time varies, with some sipping and others literally drying their glass. A junior person is more likely to dry their glass when drinking with a senior person, while the latter may take only a sip. At company events, key managers and junior staff will work their way around to every table, toasting and drinking to each group. Getting tipsy is no cause for embarrassment. The guests of honor may not always schicker themselves into oblivion, but it is standard for them to dry their glasses with the host at least once during the meal.

Understanding how to clink your glass is something else to aware of. To show respect, especially to someone of seniority, you should dip your glass so that its rim is lower than his or hers when you clink. Sometimes people become so determined to get the lowest position that the drinks end up in the food.

Refusing to drink and let down your guard won't do much to improve relationships. If you do need to abstain, you should come up with a good excuse at the start of the meal and do your best to overcome the possible slight in other ways.

FACE

While to us, losing face might seem like another expression for simple embarrassment, in reality it runs much deeper in the Chinese psyche. It's a complex system of stature or shame. One can lose face, save face, or give face. Loss of face can cause acute anguish, and can also exacerbate an already bad situation. Losing one's temper in public, criticizing someone in front of others, or being shown up can all lead to loss of face. On the other hand, if you know how to give face—make someone feel important or valued—then it can deepen relationships and improve efficiency.

In general life, if you apply good Western manners, you'll get along fine in Chinese society. In business, however, understanding face is critical. Face will affect everything from how well you can manage your team to how smoothly a contract goes with a new business partner. Fear of losing face can result in employees sitting silently in a meeting and passively agreeing to an idea that they secretly know has major flaws. It can gag them from voicing their complaints about a problem to you, and it can divert a business partner from telling you that they can't make the next shipment that they promised you.

You'll quickly discover here that Chinese people almost never say "no" or "I don't know." It can result in a big loss of face, so these fatal words are usually avoided at all costs. Instead you might be met with a "Maybe," "Perhaps," "We'll think about it," "That sounds interesting," or even a blatant lie. Translation? They can all be ways to

MIND YOUR CHOPSTICKS

Here are some etiquette tips to ease you into the hearts of your Chinese friends:

- Never stand your chopsticks in a bowl of rice (it's reminiscent of a grave).
- Ensure the spout of a teapot never points directly at anyone on your table.
- Show respect to someone by adding food to their plate or topping up their glass whenever the tide runs low.
- Give face to someone by making a toast to them at any random moment during the meal.
- Always take a gift if you are invited to someone's home.
- Never serve guests cold water. It should be somewhere between warm and hot.
- Don't split the bill. If someone else pays, repay them by taking them out for dinner.
- Take food from the shared plates with the back end of your chopsticks (if others are doing this).
- Always leave a little on your plate to give the impression you're well fed.

actually say "no." It can be incredibly frustrating for a Westerner not accustomed to such ambiguous or evasive communication, and you need to become better at reading body language rather than just listening to words. If you feel the answers you're getting are strangely inadequate, try to word your questions in a way that may help the person save face if the answer does happen to be a negative one.

On a similar point, you too, should avoid a direct "no." Save the other person face with an indirect reply along the lines of, "I'll get back to you." Giving face can be done through simple etiquette practices, such as the customary habits at dinners, but it can also be given through thoughtful gift giving, and by knowing who to mention and when to mention them in speeches or at meetings. If you're coming to Beijing to work as a manager or to conduct business deals, it will be highly valuable for you to learn more about the culture of face.

GIFT GIVING

Gift giving is an important part of Chinese culture, and a major part of relationship building. It is one way to show politeness and respect, as well as to give face. On the less heartfelt end of the scale, it's also a major tool for bribery and wheel greasing.

If a friend or colleague gives you a gift, don't open it in front of them unless they insist. Not opening the gift in front of the person shows them that it's not the gift that's important but their friendship. You can simply send a text message later after you open it telling them how much you liked it. Additionally, you can show your appreciation by buying them a gift in return. If you do give a gift to a Chinese person you may find that they refuse several times before accepting it. Be patient and stick with your offer, but also try to detect a sincere rejection of the gift if possible.

Unlike in the West, chocolates, wine, and flowers (especially white ones, which are for funerals) are not traditional gifts to give. Instead, the Chinese prefer items that

© LAW ALAN/123RF.COM

Red envelopes are used for giving money on special occasions.

aren't available in China, such as something from your home country: specialty food items, such as seasonal delicacies; spirits, such as cognac, whiskey, or *báijiǔ* (the Maotai brand in particular); and cigarettes. Expensive, beautifully packaged cigarettes are available, almost exclusively for the sake of gift giving.

Finally, when giving gifts, consider the number of items that you're presenting someone with. Just one can be considered miserly, especially if the item itself isn't expensive; four is unlucky; and eight is thought to be very fortunate indeed.

Red Envelopes

Red envelopes (紅包, *hóngbāo*) are envelopes filled with money, which are traditionally given to children and relatives at Chinese New Year, as well as to couples at weddings and to employees for their year-end bonuses. Unfortunately, the amount of money can be extremely contentious, even among Chinese people. In some cases, it might be just enough for children to get themselves a gift such as a T-shirt or an Xbox game, but in many cases it might be as high as RMB1,000 or more if it's for someone who needs to be impressed. The closer you are to the person, the more money it should be. If you're the boss, it's also expected to be more generous than what might come in other envelopes. If you're unsure of the appropriate amount to put in the envelope, ask your Chinese friends for their advice, and if in doubt, err on the side of generosity. A well-padded red envelope can be good for relationship building. For best effect, go to the bank to get new, crisp notes, and ensure the amount contains the numbers 6, 8, or 9, and not 4, 7, or 250. When handing the envelope to the person, hand it over like a business card—using two hands and facing toward the person. If it's for a wedding and there isn't an assigned person at the door to collect the envelopes, wait until the couple speaks to you and hand it directly to them.

Gender Roles

Like most things in Beijing, gender roles fail to fall into a neat, all-inclusive definition. Some women argue that they have equal lives, sharing housework and responsibilities happily with their husbands. Others disagree, believing they have fewer opportunities and much less power than their male counterparts. You will see a few things that suggest an homogenous society—female bus and taxi drivers are extremely common; various Beijing enterprises, such as the ubiquitous SOHO complexes, are spearheaded by women; and women will often be seen roadside, working alongside men, paving and landscaping. And then there's the behavior that would send a more blokish Westerner running in the opposite direction, such as a Beijing man's willingness to carry his wife's or girlfriend's purses around for her like a personal bellhop. This not only is a public signifier that the two are in a romantic relationship, it also shows that the woman has at least some hand in the relationship.

Beijing women are definitely in a better position than their rural sisters. They are treated more equally and do have more rights in the workplace. Yet when you look closely at what's happening in the ranks, there are many holes in the system, particularly at the power-wielding apexes of society.

Historically, Chinese women have never really had much power in the public sphere. They were forced to live with cruel foot-binding practices, lived as concubines, and were sold or married off. Confucianism frowned on powerful women and made them subservient to their fathers, followed by their husbands, followed by their eldest sons, should they be widowed. Mao came along and did manage to advance the role of women to some degree. His policies pushed women and men together, and he proclaimed that women held up half the sky.

In reality, this adage has proved to be more rhetoric than reality. Never, from the moment the Communists took power in 1949 to the present, has a woman sat in the Standing Committee, the highest organ of government. In fact they hold up only one-fifth of the entire Communist party membership, a figure staggeringly disproportionate to the near 50 percent of the total population that they represent.

In business, the upper echelons of authority are also boys' clubs. Though women are becoming more aspirational and financially independent, they're often overlooked for promotions and are frequently selected for their beauty and rejected for their child-bearing age. Many men in Beijing society still also believe that the male should be the bigger breadwinner, and it can be regarded as a loss of face to have a wife with a larger income. While Shanghai men may have earned themselves the reputation of enjoying cooking and housework, Beijing men have not. Even some of the more pro-Western men say they'd like their wives to be housewives to take care of them. Consequently, it can be difficult for progressive women to find an accepting partner. This has engendered the social stigma of being a "leftover woman" (剩女, shèngnǚ), a single, urban, educated woman, aged somewhere around 27 to 30. They have been accused of not doing their part by not only by some groups within society but also by the government, which now needs to deal with the crisis of around 20 million more men under the age of 30 than women under 30—a result of the one-child policy and the persevering preference for boy babies. The marrying age for women in China averages around

27 years, but one problem for women who pass beyond this age is that Chinese men tend to marry down—regarding both age and education. So it gets harder and harder to marry the higher they climb and the older they get.

Older men, on the other hand, don't seem to have this problem, especially when they have money. Not only is it not uncommon to hear of a much older man snagging a beautiful young bride, but the ancient days of the concubine lifestyle have taken on a modern manifestation. *Èrnǎi* (二奶, second wives) are now a social phenomena. These are the modern concubines of the rich and powerful. In exchange for sports cars, luxury goods, even apartments, these young women (usually under the age of 30) decorate their lover's life and show off the man's wealth. The real wives rarely approve, but for many of them absence of monogamy is such a standard situation in Chinese life that they turn a blind eye. Chinese women argue that they are more practical than Western women. As long as they feel financially secure, then they are content. And despite their apparent lack of position in the family, they can actually often exert significant influence on their husbands.

GAY AND LESBIAN CULTURE

Beijing might not be San Francisco, but the gay and lesbian culture is certainly alive and blossoming. Looking back into China's past, homoeroticism has always had its place in society. While Confucianism made almost no comment on lesbian relationships, it accepted sexual romps between men. As long as one could fulfill his procreative responsibilities, it wasn't an issue. Homosexual acts were just that, behaviors, and they weren't seen as a definition of someone's personality nor as an exclusive form of sexuality. It wasn't until Western concepts started infusing into China that homosexuality came to be seen as identifying who someone was and as a (now discredited) psychological disorder.

Today in Beijing, the gay scene is visible but not particularly flamboyant. In some circles it's accepted but is generally hush-hush and not talked about openly, especially inside families. With the older generation's deeply held beliefs about being married and continuing the family lineage, a young homosexual person is likely to get peppered relentlessly with questions by anxious family members about when they're going to settle down. If you're of the school that believes social factors influence homosexuality, cities like Beijing will be worth watching. With the out-of-kilter male-to-female ratio, there will be ample research opportunities to look at how gender imbalances impact sexual orientation and society's attitudes. For more information about the LGBT community in Beijing, contact the Beijing LGBT Center, via www.bjlgbtcenter.org.

EXPAT PROFILE: LGBT COMMUNITY

Twenty-six-year-old Michael comes from Belgium and has been working in foreign affairs in Beijing for more than two years. Though his weekdays are almost swallowed up by his job, he still has plenty of time for all the other things in life, including spending time with his friends in Beijing's gay community.

HOW WOULD YOU DESCRIBE THE LGBT COMMUNITY IN BEIJING?

Considering that Beijing has more than 20 million inhabitants, I can only imagine how big the gay community must be. Generally speaking, the gay scene in Beijing is very open-minded and has a welcoming attitude toward newcomers.

The most distinctive factor of the community itself is that it actually consists of two scenes: one that's more visible and one that's very underground. The major reason for this is the discrepancy in the mindsets of the majority of the Chinese population (but definitely not all of them) and that of the temporary residents (foreigners or expats). As a result, the visible scene consists of a colorful mix of all nationalities, whereas the underground scene is mostly Chinese.

WHAT'S IT LIKE TO BE GAY IN BEIJING?

For a foreigner, I would say it is very easy to be gay in Beijing. Chinese society has a strong sense of avoiding any personal (negative) confrontation, so everyone more or less minds their own business. I've never witnessed any hatred or bias toward myself or other gays, nor have I been openly questioned about my sexual preference.

Next to the easiness of Beijing gay life, I think the Beijing gay scene itself has some very interesting characteristics. Being partly embedded in an expat society whose members stay mostly on a short-term basis (as in most major world cities), the gay-scene is also constantly changing, so you can meet new people everywhere you go. At the same time this society still has a very strong family feeling to it, which also reflects upon the gay scene.

WHAT'S THE GENERAL LEVEL OF UNDERSTANDING OR BELIEFS ABOUT HOMOSEXUALITY HERE?

Even though the Chinese government deleted homosexuality from its list of mental illnesses more than 10 years ago now, it is still frowned upon by many locals. It's

Religion

A common complaint in Beijing today is that China has become an ethical vacuum, a country without a religious or moral compass, guided instead by greed and financial targets. Stories of crime, corruption, and loss of humanity fill the newspaper pages and provide fuel for explosive cyber rants. It's rare to hear people in Beijing talk about religion at all, and the only time most locals visit temples is during national festivals or when traveling to tourist spots. There is next to no discussion about the afterlife, but rather of how to have a more affluent here and now.

Religion began its downward spiral in China in the early 1900s, and then when the Cultural Revolution rolled through 1966-1976, it was all but obliterated. Places of worship were demolished, ransacked, or sequestered for secular purposes, and Communism, an ideology essentially opposed to religion, became the philosophy by

estimated that 80 percent of all gays living in China are still in the closet. Most of them remain married and live some sort of double life. A major reason for this is that most Chinese see it as their duty to produce offspring in order to make their parents proud and to obtain full completion in life.

HOW DO LOCALS REACT WHEN YOU TELL THEM YOU'RE GAY—OR DO YOU KEEP IT TO YOURSELF IN PUBLIC?

Honestly, Chinese people very rarely inquire about things that are very personal or emotional. For example, I've often been asked if I have a girlfriend, followed by the question of if I'm interested in having a Chinese girlfriend. I usually answer that I'm not interested in Chinese girls, after which there are no further questions asked.

So, you could say that I keep it to myself by dancing around the topic. If someone did ask me straight up if I were gay, though, I wouldn't have any problem with telling the truth. But so far this hasn't happened to me (yet) outside of the gay scene.

On the other hand, everyone at my job—including my Chinese colleagues—knows that I'm gay, and so far I haven't had any negative remarks, nor have I noticed any change in their attitude toward me.

WHAT ARE THE BEST PLACES IN THE CITY TO MEET OTHER GAY PEOPLE AND HANG OUT?

Support group: The LGBT center (www. bjlgbtcenter.org) is a great, open-minded place to meet gay people. You can also contact them for gay-related issues or questions you might have. There will always be someone there to listen to you.

Bars and clubs: Mesh is a lounge bar located in the Opposite House hotel and has a weekly gay night (on Thursdays). It's a great place to have a drink with friends and meet new people. Destination is considered the 7/7 party temple for gays in Beijing. Its smaller counterpart, Alfa, has gay party nights only on Friday. Finally, Kai Bar is one of those dance bars that turned gay, just because lots of gays started to frequent it.

These few venues are the staples of Beijing gay life nowadays. Other bars come and go, so keep your eyes and ears open. Because of the two scenes in the gay community that I mentioned earlier, these are the only venues that have willingly put themselves on the expat radar, so currently the list seems rather short.

which to live. Since the country's opening up in the 1970s, the Communist Party has relaxed the laws surrounding religion in society. Article 36 of the constitution even goes so far as to state that "Citizens of the People's Republic of China enjoy freedom of religious belief." The article's entire wording, however, allows the government a bit of maneuverability, allowing it to define what it sees as permissible. There are only five officially recognized religions—Buddhism, Taoism, Islam, Catholicism, and Protestantism—and even these must go through state approval processes. So while you will be able to attend Catholic, Protestant, Islamic, and even Jewish services, they may not always conform word for word to the services back home.

In an effort to reignite humanity, there has been talk of reviving Confucianism in schools. This isn't a religion but a set of ethical and philosophical teachings, and Confucius is considered not a god but a philosopher. This has been extremely controversial, however. It might foster social harmony, but it also propounds clear social hierarchies. So for now, it's been stymied.

© SHANNON AITKEN

St. Joseph's in Wangfujing

It's difficult to get accurate numbers on religious groups in society in Beijing. Those Chinese people who do follow a faith may not always admit to it. Additionally, Chinese often blend their religions or philosophies, taking a little from Buddhism, a dash from Taoism, and a sprinkling of Daoism. Other than traditional Chinese religions, there is a substantial Islam community in Beijing. In fact, on the west of the city in Xicheng district, an entire street, Niu Jie (牛街), is dedicated to the Muslim community, and includes the oldest mosque in Beijing. For comprehensive information on Muslim services around town, including restaurants and mosques, visit www.qingzhen114.com. Unfortunately, the site doesn't have an English version, but it translates readably through Google Chrome.

Around town you'll also find many Protestant and Catholic churches or communities, including **Chongwenmen Christian Church** (2 Hougou Hutong, Dongcheng district, near Chongwenmen subway station, Lines 2 and 5, exit B, 东城区后沟胡同丁2号, tel. 10/6522-9984), which runs bilingual services; **BICF** (Beijing International Christian Fellowship), an international nondenominational church (www.bicf.org), which runs services in various locations in both Chaoyang and Haidian districts; and **Nantang Catholic Cathedral** (also known as Cathedral of the Immaculate Conception and St. Mary's, 141 Qianmen Xidajie, Xicheng district, near Xuanwumen subway station, Lines 2 and 4, exit F, 西城区前门西大街141号, tel. 10/6602-6538). This is Beijing's largest Catholic church, and it runs English services on Sunday at 10:30pm. **Our Lady of China Beijing** also holds various Catholic services around Chaoyang and Shunyi districts, including Saturday at 5pm in the Shunyi area (passports required), Sunday at 10am at the Canadian Embassy (passports required), and Sunday at 4pm at St. Joseph Church in Wangfujing. For full details contact olcbjparish@aol.com.

Jewish groups also have several places to worship and gather, including **Chabad House** near Lido (Fangyuan Xilu, Chaoyang district, next to the south gate of Si De Park, 朝阳区芳园西路, 四得公园南门旁, tel. 10/8470-8238, www.chabadbeijing.com) and at the Capital Club Athletic Center with **Kehillat Beijing** (3rd Floor Ballroom, Capital Mansion, 6 Xinyuan Nanlu, Chaoyang district, 朝阳区新源南路6号京城大厦旁边的京城俱乐部3层, tel. 10/8486-2225, www.sinogogue.org).

The Arts

ART

Art in Beijing is confined mostly to art districts, including the most famous of them all, the 798 Art District near Lido in Chaoyang district, as well as Caochangdi, a little farther east and closer to the airport. These districts are often repurposed factories, converted into mazes of galleries of varying scale—some good, some terrible—as well as artists' studios. It's not clear exactly how many working artists live in Beijing, but some wager there may be as many as 10,000. The city is considered one of China's major art locations, and most Chinese artists are drawn here at some point in their career for a period of residency. In the past, artists dreamed of heading to the West, but now they see Beijing as an abundant source of inspiration and potential.

Beijing's art scene is dominated by commercial galleries. Art can be big dollars, especially for Chinese artists who have been able to make a name for themselves, and fortunately for them, Beijing's wealthy have an insatiable appetite for contemporary art and conspicuous consumption. Not all Chinese art, however, is about creating corporate or home jewelry for the nouveau riche. Many artists have their own position and are doing their own thing, making social comments or experimenting with new directions. It's surprising to see just how far some artists in Beijing push the envelope or gamble with censorship. There's the notorious bad boy Ai Weiwei, internationally renowned and well connected locally. Though the law has tried to shackle him, he has the power, family connections, and international following to provide him with some protection.

Smaller, more independent local artists can and do make potentially inflammatory statements about the state, but, for their own safety, it needs to be done on a smaller scale. On the whole, art is well supported in Beijing, and artists enjoy a little more liberty than the media. Some would say there is even more tolerance for artistic rebellion in Beijing than in other cities.

"There's no animosity toward art," says resident Canadian artist Michael Eddy. "It won't bring down the government."

In reality, it is has become a tool of the state. "It's the propaganda of freedom," says Eddy. "Art represents a post-industrial period, it's the icing on the cake for a developed country."

© SHANNON AITKEN

a sculpture in the 798 Art District in Chaoyang

FILM

If you're a film buff then life in Beijing can be both a love and hate situation. Love, because there is an endless supply of cheap pirated DVDs, with movies running only a few weeks behind release dates in cinemas abroad. Hate because 90 percent of the films screened overseas never make it to the big screen here.

Fortunately for you, unfortunately for the film industry, pirated DVD shops can be found all around town, selling all the movies you'll never be able to watch in the cinema for much less than it costs to go to the movies—compare RMB10 for a DVD to RMB60-120 for a movie ticket. What's more, the shop vendors run such slick operations that you can occasionally order something in, and if you luck out with a bad copy you can usually return it. The DVDs are actually graded for quality. If the movie is hot off the press and possibly still on at the cinema, it may have no number, and is probably a *qiāngbǎn* version (枪版, the grainy handheld camera kind where someone walks in or out halfway through the film). Avoid these. Next there are the DVD5 and DVD9 versions. DVD5 can be a gamble. Quality is dubious, subtitles unintelligible, and the actors are likely to suddenly start speaking fluent Russian mid-movie. DVD9 is the best quality for new releases, and the safest gamble. Older films, those a year or more out of the cinema, won't have any coding, but the quality will be almost as good as a genuine copy.

Though they may look it by their solidness and visibility, these DVD shops are not legal, and from time to time the police will do a sweep and shut them down. Wait a week, and back they are, restocked with all the latest blockbusters and classic keepers. Most expats build up a sizable collection of fake DVDs while here, but remember that despite the unchecked availability of fake DVDs in the city, they are illegal. You cannot ship them home, and if you do try to take them home with you and get caught, you may find yourself in a serious legal tangle.

In the cinema, foreign films are very rarely dubbed into Chinese, but rather subtitled. Chinese films, however, are not typically subtitled with English unless they're big-budget films and have an international target. If a foreign film does make it to the Chinese cinema, it may not have completely escaped the censor's razor—sex scenes, nudity or language, or imagery that suggests a negative comment on China will have been sliced.

One thing to be aware of here is that movies start bang on the dot, with possibly just a handful of ads and zero trailers. So you'd better be on time. Additionally, while movies can be expensive, there are plenty of ways to get a better deal. Look out for memberships and discount days or times. Group buy websites (such as http://t.dianping.com/Beijing or http://bj.meituan.com) are also extremely popular ways to get cut-price tickets.

MUSIC

One thing you'll notice in Beijing is that there are no major music stores. Occasionally you may see a dusty rack of CDs in a department store, but for the most part, music is downloaded freely. While the local equivalents of Youtube—Youku and Tudou—occasionally remove Western movies and TV shows, sites like Baidu make it incredibly easy to download whatever song you want, Chinese or international.

EXPAT PROFILE: MUSICAL NOTES

Tom Mattessi came to Beijing in 2004 and soon after set up his own company, This Town Touring (www.thistowntouring. com). The company books, plans, and promotes tours for international musicians and bands within Beijing and across China, and has a particular focus on rock music. When you head out to Beijing's bars, cafés, universities, or music festivals, you may well be listening to a band brought in by This Town Touring.

HOW WOULD YOU DESCRIBE THE BEIJING MUSIC SCENE?

Beijing is the coolest rock music scene in China. Most rock musicians come here from other parts of China, and there are a lot of bars and opportunities to play, regardless of ability or experience. There are lots of rock fans here, and plenty of people booking shows and helping bands.

HOW DO YOU THINK BEIJING COMPARES TO OTHER CHINESE CITIES?

Beijing is the heart of the rock music scene. In fact, given that most kids or bands who really want to devote their youth to rock music move to Beijing, the other cities tend to suffer. So there aren't really many bands in other cities, and so it's harder for them to develop. Beijing is the place to develop as a musician.

WHAT ARE THE BEST VENUES FOR ROCK?

Mao Livehouse is a great venue for rock. It's really well designed so that people go there to really focus on the music. Yugong Yishan is cool, too, and Old What is a great tiny punk venue just meters from the Forbidden City. Everyone loves Old What, and it's such a cool place for young bands to play their first gigs.

WHAT ARE THE BEST THINGS ABOUT MUSIC IN BEIJING?

It's easy to get shows if you're a young band, and there are lots of bars to play in. Practice places are cheap and easy to find, and you don't need to take your gear. All the bars have backlines so you just come with your guitar and you can play. The fans are open-minded; any band can play with any other band and usually people don't mind.

If you do want a hard copy, there are pirated CDs available in the DVD stores, or, for the real thing, you can purchase genuine copies from online stores such as Amazon.

Chinese music itself is largely pop and highly commercial. Canto pop is a favorite on the musical menu, as is anything by Korean boy bands. Live music of both niche and mainstream varieties is, however, plentiful. You won't often see concerts on the scale of U2 or Madonna here, but on almost any night of the week you can drop by a bar or club for some jazz, rock, indie, electro, or folk music.

Community

One of the most important ways for you to ensure you have an enjoyable and fulfilling life in Beijing is to connect with other people, and in Beijing it is incredibly easy to build a solid circle of friends with very little effort at all. The expat community is geared to networking and socializing, and no matter what kind of lifestyle you enjoy, you'll be able to find like-minded people here. There are specialized professional networking groups, mothers' groups, events for party people, and even hiking groups. Whatever your interest, you'll be able to find something compatible. Moving to a city that seems as foreign as Beijing may feel a little daunting, but you'll soon discover there are many other people in exactly the same situation as you and many more who are willing to lend a hand or give you their personal pointers.

MEETING THE LOCALS

It's not hard to meet locals in Beijing. In most workplaces you'll find that the majority of employees are Chinese, not expats, and Chinese people love to do things in big groups. It's highly likely you'll find yourself invited out with the entire office to karaoke (KTV) or dinner on a regular basis. Saying no to these invitations can even be detrimental to your business relationships. Outside of the office, Chinese people are also extremely friendly. You may be shocked by how readily people that you still consider basically strangers will invite you out for dinner. Unlike Hong Kongers, or even Shanghaiers, who are jaded by their city's foreign occupants, many Beijingers are still extremely curious about the outside world and keen to expand their circle of foreign friends. Whether or not you ultimately develop deep and lasting friendships with the locals here is less certain. Language and cultural differences can keep friendships from becoming close.

© SHANNON AITKEN

Build community by being a good neighbor.

As far as relationships of the romantic kind go, men will have no difficulty whatsoever. Like it or not, Beijing can be a candy store for the Western guy who is keen to date. Western women, however, don't have a high ratio of matchups with the local men. There are various speculations about why this is so, but, to offer a general argument, single Chinese men can often be much more reserved and less direct with Western women than Chinese women are with Western men.

WHERE TO MEET PEOPLE
Sports Clubs

Sports competitions in Beijing are not particularly fierce. On the odd occasion you may encounter someone refusing a night out on the town to attend training, but in most cases, sport is tradition-free and generally comprises a group of friends getting together on a Saturday or Sunday for a friendly match, followed by beer and pizza. Commitment is a limited entity here, and sports groups live by a "drop in if you're free" code—soccer teams perhaps being the one exception.

If your kids are heading to the international schools then no doubt you'll find your weekends filled with attending sports games, and you'll be sure to meet other parents through the spectator channel. If they'll be attending a local school, however, then you'll need to seek out extracurricular sporting options. In Beijing, academics trump sport, so other than a few stretches on the quadrangle, there isn't much emphasis on physical activity.

If you do want to get involved in sport, there are endless possibilities out there around the city. Soccer (called football here) is perhaps the most organized sport. **ClubFootball** (www.clubfootball.com.cn) organizes teams for kids, men, and women. Informal training is usually held one night a week in the Chaoyang area, and experienced players and newbies are welcome. For the more serious crowd, there is the **International Friendship Football Club** (www.iffc1994.com), where you can try to find a team, or if you have enough buddies you can create your own team, and then compete in the Premier League or First Division. It can be hard to find a place to kick a ball around, so if you're interested in putting your own team together, there are places such as O'le (http://ole-sports.org) or 26 Degrees (www.26csportscenter.com), which both have multiple football fields that can be hired.

Baseball can be a difficult sport to come by, and fields are few. **Sports Beijing** (www.sportsbj.org), which offers baseball, basketball, and many other sports for kids, is a good place to start asking questions. Adults can join **Mashup Sport & Social** (www.mashupsports.com). With a primary interest in expanding social circles through sport, Mashup organizes basketball, flag football, NFL nights, beer pong events, and more. Those into ice hockey can contact Beijing International Ice Hockey (www.beijing-hockey.com), which runs scheduled competitions from August to April. Rock climbing is also gathering momentum, and you'll find reasonable climbing walls at **Ol'e** (http://ole-sports.org) in south Chaoyang district, as well as inside Ritan Park in the warmer months. Outdoor climbing in out-of-town areas such as Miyun can also make for good weekend escapes. For sport on wheels, cycling is just starting to emerge. On the odd Sunday morning you'll see Lycra-clad teams relaxing with a post-ride coffee in Central Park. Groups such as **Beijing Peleton** (http://beijing.mongoliaprocycling.com) or **TriBeijing** (www.tribeijing.org) lead rides farther afield. Thanks to China's progress in the tennis world in recent years, as well as the government's determination to turn the China Open into a Grand Slam event, tennis clubs and courts are relatively easy to locate. Try such places as **Potter's Wheel** (www.potters-wheel.cn) in Chaoyang, **Broadwell Tennis Club** (sports.broadwell.cn) beside Chaoyang Park, **Kerry Sports** (www.shangri-la.com/beijing/kerry) near the Central Business District, or one of the universities in Haidian. For something more amusing, try **Heyrobics** (www.heyrobics.com), Swedish-style workouts that are popular with guys, girls, the super fit, and the non-athletic alike. Classes are held in multiple sessions around the Chaoyang and Shunyi. **Beijing Sailing Center** (www.beijingsailing.com) will get adults or kids out of the city for some fun time on the water. Come for a one-day course, or commit yourself to something longer. Kids can also make friends at the camps. Outside of these, you'll also find gyms, yoga studios, swimming pools, basketball courts, hiking groups, ice hockey clubs, Frisbee clubs, and even dragon boating clubs. If all else fails, you can head to your local park at dawn and join the locals for tai chi.

Volunteering

A fantastic way to get out into the community and really come to understand what's happening in Beijing and China as a whole is to volunteer. The expat nooks of the city are sleek and sanitized, but not far from where you'll live or work are adults and children who missed the elevator ride to wealth. Millions in the city are deprived of health care, education, shelter, or support and need a helping hand. While it mightn't seem very PC to pick and choose a charity, like anything in life, you'll probably do a much better job at something you have a vested interest in. So it will be far more rewarding if you take time to find a charity that is compatible with your interests and values.

Don't worry if you don't speak Chinese. Many existing charities and NGOs are managed by international teams, so not speaking the local language isn't necessarily going to be an obstacle. In fact, speaking English can be an advantage. Many volunteer groups eagerly welcome people who can teach English or write and edit.

Most of the major international organizations are represented. You'll find the likes of **Rotary** (rotaryclub-beijing.org), **UNICEF** (www.unicef.org), **Greenpeace** (www.greenpeace.org/china) and many others all quartered here. However, if you'd prefer something more local or personal, these too can be found. Just some of them include **Magic Hospital** (www.magichospital.org), which aims to help neglected, hospitalized, or other needy children by providing them with short-term or long-term entertainment or care; **Half the Sky** (www.halfthesky.org), which strives to provide love and care for institutionalized children who may or may never be adopted; **Prevention Through Education** (www.pte-china.org), which is working to prevent the growing HIV/AIDs epidemic in China through education; and Jane Goodall's **Roots & Shoots** (www.jgichina.org), which is making a big effort to tackle environmental and social issues via education. **New Day** (www.newdaycreations.com) has a well-established volunteer program. They welcome you to come and help with such things as caring for orphans, teaching English, visiting the elderly, serving the poor, or providing medical care. **Roundabout** (www.roundaboutchina.com, tel. 137/1877-7761), one of the city's most popular charities, is both a charity-based store in Shunyi and a happy recipient of jettisoned goods from departing expats.

If animals are your interest, there are various groups making an effort to change attitudes toward our furry friends. These include the **WWF** (www.wwfchina.org), **International Fund for Animal Welfare** (www.ifaw.org/china), and the **Beijing Human and Animal Environmental Education Center** (www.animalschina.org).

For an extensive list of charitable organizations in Beijing, visit the Community listings at www.cityweekend.com.cn or visit the Directory of International NGOs website (www.chinadevelopmentbrief.com/dingo). Alternatively, if this all seems too overwhelming, condense your options with **Rotaract Beijing** (www.rotaractbeijing. org), which connects existing volunteer organizations with the community through fun events and networking.

Networking and Mixers

Going to networking events is almost a standard part of expat life in Beijing, and you should never feel nervous about going to one—be it solo or with a friend. Though of course there are networking events where romantic matchups might be an ulterior motive, most are genuinely aimed at linking you up with new friends or business contacts. Most include a membership fee, and then reduced-price or free entry for members to specific events.

First, fresh-off-the-plane residents should head to one of the regular **International Newcomers' Network** (INN, www.innbeijing.org) meetings. Held in various places in Chaoyang and Shunyi, these low-key, friendly meetings give you information about living in the city and help you make some friends over coffee and cake.

If professional networking is your goal, several groups have been developed to help you expand your Rolodex. Arm yourself with business cards and sign up for one of the events with **VIVA Professional Women's Network** (www.vivabeijing.org), the Beijing chapter of **85 Broads** (http://secure.85broads.com), or **FCGroup** (www.fcgroup.org). FCGroup is a long-standing well-respected networking group in the city offering industry-specific events, such as nights for finance or the media industry. The various chambers of commerce also organize regular professional networking events. These include **Amcham** (www.amchamchina.org), **Austcham** (www.austcham.org), **Britcham** (www.britishchamber.cn), and the **Canada China Business Council** (www.ccbc.com).

Not all networking groups require a tie or suit, however, and a wide range of groups use entertainment to catalyze friendships. Needlepoint fans, male or female, can join **Stitch 'n Bitch in Beijing** (http://groups.yahoo.com/group/stitchnbitch_beijing), which meets over coffee and sweets to chat over crafty creations. Any mode of craftwork permitted. **Beefsteak and Burgundy** (www.beefandburgundy.org) is one for the boys and somewhat more exclusive, requiring an invitation and approval process to join. Members meet at Beijing's upscale eateries and gel via gastronomic interests.

Last but not least, international networking group **InterNations** has a Beijing circle (www.internations.org/beijing-expats). As a full member, you'll be able to meet up with groups covering a wide range of specific interests, including music, dining, or even ten-pin bowling.

Culture, Education, and Hobbies

There's no need for your hobbies or interests to go on hiatus while in Beijing. From cooking to photography, there are one-off classes and term-length courses in English to keep you active and to broaden your horizons. Two of the major staples for hobbyists are the **China Culture Center** (CCC, www.chinaculturecenter.org) and **The Hutong** (http://thehutong.com). Both offer a range of activities, with the CCC delving into history as well as taking the adventure-bound out on Great Wall hikes, and The Hutong is an all-rounder with Chinese medicine courses, cooking classes, life drawing, and much more on its events list. More cooking classes can be enjoyed at **Black Sesame Kitchen** (www.blacksesamekitchen.com). Set in a restored *hútòng* house off Nanluogu Xiang, this tiny cooking school-cum-restaurant runs intimate cooking classes headed by Chinese chefs.

It's definitely worth getting yourself on the mailing list for Sanlitun's **Bookworm** café (http://beijingbookworm.com). This expat den is not only a laptop hub for itinerant workers, it also holds an extraordinary number of events, arranging talks by authors, performance poets, journalists, and anyone else with something interesting to say.

The artistically minded have several options for expression. **Beijing Playhouse** (www.beijingplayhouse.com), an amateur acting group for adults and kids, produces Broadway shows such as the *Wizard of Oz* and *Guys and Dolls*. While it can be extremely rewarding, this group isn't for everyone, given its hefty time commitments. For something much less time intensive, **Beijing Improv** (www.beijingimprov.org) runs free bilingual workshops once a week for anyone who's willing to get up say the first thing that pops into their head. If, however, you'd rather chew through a plate of Sichuan chilies than stand up in front of strangers and ad lib, then simply fill a seat at one of the shows by its Mainstage English Players. The company's premier comedy troupe, they put on monthly shows, which sell out without fail.

Finally, if you need to tweak your technical skills, the **Expat Learning Center** (www.beijing-classes.com) is more of your typical adult education center. One night a week you can come here to study fashion design, photography, German, Photoshop, or many other interests.

Baby and Toddler Groups

While you might expect it's the kids who have the most difficulty adjusting to life in a new and foreign city, often it's the parents who struggle to adapt, especially those who have come for their spouse's job rather than personal interest. In Beijing, there is no need to feel alone, and there are various ways to make sure you're connected to help or just a friendly ear.

One of the main groups out there is **Beijing Mamas** (http://groups.yahoo.com/group/Beijing_Mamas). This friendly email group makes an excellent starting point for solving any problem you might have relating to kids. Whether it's for party ideas or a recommendation for a pediatrician, ask and you shall be answered.

If you fall pregnant while in Beijing and decide to stay here for the birth, you may need a little extra support. While the international hospitals are similar to what you'd expect at home, local Chinese hospitals, even the private ones, don't really pile on the TLC. Even first-time mothers won't get much in the way of prenatal or breastfeeding education. This is where **La Leche** (for English, contact Serena via xiaohua68847@gmail.com, www.llli.org) can provide some friendly support. The group meets to discuss such topics as the benefits of breastfeeding, getting started and family adjustments, overcoming difficulties, nutrition, and weaning.

Once your baby's born and ready to meet the world, you and your spouse can clue yourselves in on early childhood development at **KindyROO** (tel. 10/8527-5305, www. kindyroo.com). A program developed in Australia, KindyROO now has several centers in Beijing and offers bilingual, research-based classes for kids up to five years old.

Parents with kids with special needs in Beijing have a unique challenge. Disabilities are poorly understood and supported here, so you'll need all the help you can get. Fortunately, **Special Child Beijing** (special_child_beijing-owner@yahoogroups.com, tel. 139/1030-6022) is there to help parents of special needs kids, by sharing resources and learning from one another.

PLANNING YOUR FACT-FINDING TRIP

Beijing is a hard place to get your head around in just a few days. It's a vast, often indistinct city, and no single place wholly defines what it's like to live and work in. Lacking a harbor or the like, it has no single major social center. Tian'anmen Square and the Forbidden City are literally the center of the city, but there is a dearth of entertainment around them, and once you're done being a tourist, for most there are few reasons to go near them.

Despite its unwieldy size, however, Beijing is perhaps one of the easiest cities in the world to orientate yourself to, and tuning your internal compass will be a valuable part of your fact-finding trip. The whole city adheres to a very clear north-south-east-west grid, with Chang'an Jie running from east to west slicing the city into horizontal halves; a line of heavenly temples that connects south to north; and a set of concentric ring roads that encircle the entire city, giving you a reassuring sense of position wherever you are.

Depending on your interests and family situation, there are areas that may be better suited to you than others, and none are particularly close to each other. Very broadly speaking, university students tend to head to the northwest, families with school-age

© SHANNON AITKEN

children to the northeast, fashionable singles and couples to the central east, and those seeking a deeper culture immersion to the inner neighborhoods within the Second Ring Road. Interests aside, you'd also be wise to consider transport issues. Traffic is a major problem in the capital, and rush hour seems to have no limits. If your work involves a regular office-hours commute, it may be advisable to investigate the accommodation options around the office. Otherwise, when you land, you may end up spending more time on the road than you do at home.

Preparing to Leave

WHAT TO BRING
Documents

It used to be that you absolutely needed a visa to get into China, and while in practical terms this is still the situation, the laws have been softened a little in recent years. There is now a visa-free 72-hour window for citizens from a range of countries, including the United States, Canada, the United Kingdom, Australia, and New Zealand. For most people, however, the regulations governing eligibility for this are possibly so limiting that it may be better to apply for a visa anyway.

If you do plan to stay for a few more days, you must have a visa for China and a passport with at least six months remaining on it. Everyone who is traveling with you will need the same, including infants and spouses. You will also be required to have the name and details of a contact in Beijing. Given that the whims of different immigration officers are highly variable, it would be wise to also carry your official itinerary for China on you as well as proof of tickets out of the country.

It's unlikely that you'll be stopped by the police while you're in Beijing; however, it is the law that you should always have your passport on you. If this makes you uneasy, at the very least, keep a photocopy of your passport and visa on you at all times.

Clothing

Before landing in Beijing, definitely be aware of what season you're heading into, and be prepared for either extreme. In winter, Beijing gets somewhat chilly. A good, thick down coat will be essential, and will also mean you don't need to lug around extraneous layers when you step into the warm buildings. Don't forget the accessories—woolen hat, thick gloves, scarf, thermal underwear, and thickly soled shoes. Being well-dressed for this time of year will make touring a lot more comfortable. If you're coming in summer, light clothing is all you need, with perhaps just a sweater or jacket as backup if the temperature does dip. Midsummer days can get hot and a little humid, but it's still relatively dry compared to the clothes-drenching humidity of Hong Kong or Shanghai. Autumn and spring are cool to comfortable. One essential is comfortable shoes. Beijing is a vast city, and exploring its streets can be surprisingly tiring. Fashion, on the other hand, is pretty much an anything-goes situation. If you want to walk around in your pajamas, feel free, but if you want to dress up for lunch like you're headed for a chic nightclub, that will also work. There are no religious codes here, so baring shoulders or legs is completely acceptable, and, in fact, in summer, mini shorts and heels seem to almost be the uniform. If you need to be dressed in a suit, there are hundreds of

THE 72-HOUR VISA-FREE STOPOVER

If you can work in a stopover in Beijing on your way to somewhere else, you can now visit for 72 hours without a visa.

HOW TO APPLY FOR THE VISA WAIVER

1. You must tell the airline in advance of your intention to take advantage of the visa waiver.
2. You need to complete the relevant documents at the customs gate.

WHAT CONDITIONS APPLY?

1. You must be from one of the 45 approved countries, such as the United States, the United Kingdom, Australia, Canada, or New Zealand.
2. You must have a valid passport.
3. The visa is valid for travelers coming into Beijing via Beijing Capital Airport only, not by train.
4. You must have proof of an onward flight to another destination within 72 hours. This document needs to state the exact departure date and seat number. You must have purchased the flight in advance and not after arriving in Beijing.

5. You must be eligible for entry into your next destination.
6. You must stay within the limits of Beijing.

OTHER THINGS TO KNOW

1. While you're in Beijing, you will need to carry valid ID on you at all times. If you're staying with a friend or relative rather than at a hotel or hostel, you'll also need to register with the local police within 24 hours of arrival.
2. Should something unexpected happen, such as flight cancellation or sudden illness, you will need to go to the Exit and Entry Administration of the Beijing Municipal Public Security Bureau immediately to apply for a valid visa.
3. If you have a pet with you, the pet will not be able to leave the airport (guide dogs with correct documentation excluded).

For more information, visit www.bjgaj.gov.cn/eng or speak to a China visa specialist.

tailors who can whip something up for you in just a few days. For the latest opinion on who's the best, check on www.thebeijinger.com or send out a message on Yahoo group Beijing Café (you will need another member to invite you into the group first).

Miscellaneous

If you're coming to job hunt or network, business cards are essential. Most of the printing stores around the streets can do cheap and basic cards for you; however, other options include Jingjin Printing (judyzhu@jingjinprinting.com) and Huamei Printing (www.hmprint.cn), which can both deliver to your hotel or office.

You may also want to come with a ready supply of particular personal items. Sunblock, for instance, is sold as if it were expensive face moisturizer—in tiny bottles—so if you're used to family packs and are coming in summer, bring your own. If you have a medical condition that needs ongoing medication, bring a full supply that will see you through your entire visit. Most major medications are available, but not all. EpiPens, for example, are not available, and many mental health medications, such as Ritalin, can be difficult to come by. Nicotine patches are also all but impossible to get your hands on.

You will find that you are forever getting asked for passport photos of yourself, especially once you really start to settle in and apply or register for things. Be proactive and get a good supply of ID photos made up and keep these handy. Twenty photos of yourself might seem excessive, but you'll be surprised how quickly you'll hand these out. In most cases, these should be 48- by 33-millimeter glossy, full-color photos with a plain white background.

Money

You'll need to have *rénmínbì* on you from the moment you step out of the airport. There is no other legal currency. As at any airport there are exchange counters for changing money; however, also as at any airport, these are not the places to get the best value for your money. If you have an international credit or debit card, you should be able to withdraw money directly from the ATMs. It is worth checking with your bank ahead of time which banks in China it cooperates with, as not all ATMs will accept your card. The banks most likely to do so include ICBC (Industrial and Commercial Bank of China), Bank of China, and China Merchants Bank. Most banks exchange foreign currency into *rénmínbì* and require only a passport to do so.

How much you need to budget for each day really depends on you. If you're sticking to public transport, small local hotels or hostels, and local restaurants, your visit can be done for possibly RMB300-500 (US$48-80) for a single person per day. At the other end of the scale, if you'll be staying in four- or five-star hotels, eating at quality restaurants, and taking a taxi from place to place, you should budget for possibly RMB2,000 (US$320) or more per day for a single person. This all excludes long-distance journeys or visits to tourist sites, which can be as much as RMB100 for entry fees. Hiring a car with an English-speaking driver from an official rental agent can be about RMB650 (US$104) or more per day.

WHEN TO GO

If you want to believe that Beijing is a place of eternal fresh, sunny weather, come in fall, particularly in September or October. This is generally agreed to be the best time of year. The weather is temperate and the surrounding greenery turns into all manner of spectacular autumnal colors. Spring likewise has pleasant temperatures, and stunning displays of blossoms decorate all the parks and streets. Come March and April, however, the city can get surprisingly windy. Pop into a convenience store for a face mask if you want to avoid a mouthful of dust and dirt.

Winter generally peaks in January, but in some years it seems to have no shame in taking an early dip in December. Days can hover at around -5°C (23°F) and nights at -10°C (14°F) or less. Fortunately, buildings are well heated in Beijing, so, if you're not outdoors, you should be perfectly comfortable. Touring time will be a little shorter, with the sun rising at about 7:30am and going down at around 5:30pm. There is no daylight saving time in Beijing.

You'll get the most opportunity for exploring at the end of June when the sun rises at about 4:45am and sets at about 7:45pm. The weather at this time is warm to baking, with temperatures in the inner city usually somewhere in the high 20s and 30s Celsius (roughly 70s and 80s Fahrenheit) and occasionally over 40°C (104°F). The climate is generally slightly cooler in the outer suburbs throughout the year. This means that if you plan to make a trip out to the Great Wall in the far north, it can be a bitter experience in winter but a pleasant relief in summer.

© SHANNON AITKEN

Chinese New Year at Chaoyang Park is festive, but very crowded.

Besides the extreme periods of midwinter and midsummer, the other times to consider avoiding for your visit include the two major annual holidays: the Spring Festival, or Chinese New Year, which usually happens around the end of January or early February, and the October National holiday, beginning October 1. The advantage of Spring Festival, however, is that a third of the city departs for individual hometowns around the country, and the chronic traffic issues miraculously disappear. The downside is that many venues are closed and traveling outside of Beijing is expensive and tickets are hard to book.

If you're planning to visit schools for your children, check ahead with each individual school to see when it is closed throughout the year. Major holidays occur in winter and summer, and they will also be affected by the Chinese national holidays, Easter, and various other cultural holidays.

If you're coming to Beijing specifically to search for work, the time you really want to avoid is between Christmas and the 15-day Spring Festival. The city all but goes into hibernation during this period, and many employers are either out of town or thinking about being out of town. Decisions are put on hold, and potential new jobs are shelved. It's also the time that many locals, after having received their end-of-year bonus at Chinese New Year, hand in their resignation. This means that immediately after this period can be one of the best times to visit for job seekers.

Arriving in Beijing

ARRIVAL AND IMMIGRATION

Beijing currently has one commercial airport, Beijing Capital International Airport, which has three terminals—Terminals 1 and 2, and the newer Terminal 3. If you're coming in via an international flight it's most likely you'll land at Terminal 3.

When you arrive you'll first pass through heat detectors, which will possibly detect any rise in body temperature due to illness. After this you'll file through immigration. Signage is bilingual throughout the airport, as are the information desk staff. Compared to many other countries, in Beijing the customs process seems to be almost nonexistent. Once you collect your baggage you simply walk out the door, with the declaration of any goods almost completely voluntary. On the rare occasion, people may be randomly selected for inspection.

TRANSPORTATION

The airport is serviced by shuttle buses, taxis, and the subway (the Airport Express). Buses are the cheapest option, costing just RMB16 per person. They run from around 6am to 11pm or midnight, with some 24-hour options. Times vary for the different routes, so it's worth checking ahead. For a map and detailed information on airport shuttle buses, see www.travelchinaguide.com.

The Airport Express begins its morning run from the airport at about 6:30am and runs every 12 minutes until the last train leaves Terminal 3 at 10:50pm. It's RMB25 per person, regardless of which stop you get off at. Unfortunately, a lot of flights still land after the Airport Express stops, and the queue for taxis can begin to wind a little long after 11pm, so taking a bus or trying to choose an earlier flight might help. Before you get on the Airport Express, you'll need to put your luggage through a security scanner, so items such as pocketknives or kitchen knives that you checked for flying might be confiscated for the subway.

The Airport Express takes about 20 minutes from the airport to the final stop, Dongzhimen. This is a major subway interchange station as well as a large terminal for local and long-distance buses. To continue on to other subway lines, you'll need to buy another ticket (RMB2). If you are planning to use public transport on your visit, however, this will be a convenient time to pick up a travel card, also known as an Yikatong card, which you can purchase for RMB20 from one of the tellers in the subway station, with no ID or form filling required. This will help you swipe your way on and off Beijing's public transport, including the Airport Express. It's recommended to add RMB50-100 of credit to the card, and any remaining balance can be refunded when you return it.

Leaving the airport by road is less predictable than the Airport Express. The airport is about 25 kilometers (15.5 miles) from the city center. On a good run you might get to Lido within 20 minutes, Guomao within 30 minutes, or Wangfujing within 45 minutes. Land at the wrong time of day and these times could triple. For these locations, expect to pay RMB80-120, including road tolls. More information for all transport options can be found at http://en.bcia.com.cn; click on Traffic.

As a final pointer, it will help to have your first destination written down in Chinese

RENT A BIKE

Why not rent a bicycle to make your visit a little more interesting? Whether you're here for a few days or a long-term stretch, you can rent one of the thousands of public bicycles around the city. Simply swipe your card at a bike station, ride wherever you want, and then return the bike to any other bike station in the city. The first hour is free, then it's just RMB1 for every hour thereafter up to a maximum of RMB10 per day. You can keep the same bike for a maximum of three days at any one time.

Before you begin, you'll first need to go to one of the registration points with your passport and a travel card (Yikatong). Long-term residents will also need to show their temporary residence permit. Short-termers then pay a RMB400 deposit, while long-termers pay a RMB200 deposit. You'll also need to sign a contract and have at least RMB30 credit on your card. After you've returned the bike your deposit will be returned. Riders must be aged 18-65 and at least 130 centimeters (4'3") tall.

REGISTRATION POINTS

- Tiantan Dongmen subway station (Line 5), exit A2

- Dongzhimen subway station (Lines 2 and 13), exit A

While you can use the bikes at any time, registration times are somewhat limited. You can register 9am-1pm and 1:30pm-4:30pm Monday-Friday, or 10am-11:30am and 1:30pm-4pm on weekends. Call 400/1577-157 for more information (Chinese only).

Alternatively, if you'd like more options for time and bicycle style, including bikes for kids, there are private companies, such as www.bikebeijing.com (English available). You can also pick up cheap secondhand bikes from around the city for about RMB100-300.

characters and ready to hand to the driver when you get in the car. Having it written in Pinyin probably won't be helpful, and English almost certainly won't be. It's also unnecessary to tip your driver as tipping is not a custom in Beijing, and some drivers may even refuse to accept it if you try.

REGISTER WITH THE POLICE

If you are going to be staying with friends or relatives while in Beijing, you will need to go to the police station to register for a temporary residence permit within 24 hours of setting foot in the city. You won't need to do this if you'll be staying in a hotel or other similar legal accommodation as they'll do it on your behalf. You should go to the designated police station (*pàichūsuǒ*) for the complex in which you are staying, taking your passport and a photocopy of its ID page and visa page (the police will not do the photocopying for you and will be much cheerier if you come with copies already prepared); a copy of the lease; a photocopy of the landlord's ID card; and a copy of the deed to the property. It's possible that they won't ask for the latter two, but they may, so it will save time to have them handy.

While this registering process seems extreme and possibly even pointless, police do occasionally come knocking on doors to check registrations, particularly in some areas of the city, and especially at times of political tension. If you do not have your temporary residence permit, you can be fined anything between RMB50 and RMB500 per day. Registering is nothing to feel stressed about, however. It's a quick, simple, and

No.

临 时 住 宿 登 记 表
REGISTRATION FORM OF TEMPORARY RESIDENCE

表 (三)

英文姓 Surname	英文名 First Name	性 别 Sex	女
中文姓名 Name in Chinese	国 籍 Nationality	出生日期 Date of Birth	
证件类别 Type of Certificate	证件号码 Certificate No.	签证类别 Type of Visa	
签证有效期 Valid Visa	抵达时间 Date of Arrival	离开时间 Date of Departure	
住房种类 Housing Status	住 址 Address		

派出所联系电话：

离京时请将此表交回派出所

© SHANNON AITKEN

sample temporary residence permit

fee-free exercise, and will introduce you to a standard process that you'll need to be very familiar with when you become a Beijing resident.

Sample Itineraries

The length of time you can spend on this trip obviously depends on your individual circumstances. If you're flying in for an interview and a cram session on Beijing, there is now the 72-hour visa-free option. Be aware that you'll have to comply to the T with the regulations stipulated for the pass, otherwise you may find yourself turned around at the airport. It's not exactly the best amount of time to see the city, and you really won't get much of a feel for it, but, then, you do what you can.

A week is much more ideal. This will give you time to get a better feel for the different areas of the city, which can be as disconnected in lifestyle and distance as separate cities. You'll get a brief insight into housing standards, the layout of the districts, and the general feel of nightlife and entertainment. If you throw yourself into it, you'll even get a taste of the squeeze of the rush-hour subway and road traffic.

Two weeks here will definitely allow you to burrow yourself in a little better, to get a feel for the pace of work and life. You'll be able to visit a market or two and experience how those who live here shop and eat—something distinctly different from habits of the tourists. You'll have time to take in a few tourist spots as well as develop an awareness of the local culture that you may soon integrate with.

If your purpose on this trip is to explore school options for your kids as well as work and a home, there are international schools in the inner city, but the majority of international schools, including the most impressive ones, are located up around the border between Shunyi and Chaoyang districts, roughly an hour away from the Central Business District (CBD).

© SHANNON AITKEN

The clash of ancient and modern is the stuff of Beijing's everyday scenery.

For those on their way here to job hunt, it's advisable to come for at least a month. It's easy enough to pick up an off-the-books English teaching job within a few hours, but not necessarily a job that will provide you with a legitimate visa and contract. Getting replies or feedback from companies and HR departments can be a protracted experience, so it won't help to be in a rush. It will also give them, not you, the upper hand if they know you are on a tight time schedule and in a rush to sign a contract before you fly out.

THE 72-HOUR STOPOVER

If you're just flying in for an interview, the new visa exemption law may allow you to do it with a little less fuss. Trying to understand the city in such a minute amount of time, however, is next to impossible, so this really will be just a taste.

For this visit, it may be best to concentrate your time in the northeast corner, between the Second and Third Ring Roads, perhaps somewhere around Dongzhimen or Liangmaqiao. Both spots will give you easy access to commercial and social hubs, as well as a smooth route to the airport.

Consider adding a stroll around the following areas to your itinerary: Gulou, Sanlitun, Guomao, Central Park, or Lido. If your kids' education is at the top of your mind, you may want to add Shunyi to the list, although bear in mind it can take 40 minutes to an hour to get there.

When speaking to the company that you'll be visiting, ask them ahead of time to give you a few names of apartment compounds in the neighborhood. In Beijing, there is no real segregation between commercial and residential areas, so there will usually be somewhere to live within easy distance of the office.

Scour the rental ads on www.thebeijinger.com or walk into one of the real estate agencies near a complex you're interested in. If you're sure you want to live in an international-level house or apartment, there are many agents specialized in helping expats do just that. They may even be able to expedite your house-hunting time while you're here by driving you around to each complex at a pre-arranged time.

If at the end of your whirlwind visit you're still feeling completely ignorant about the city, don't worry too much. Simply consider living out of a serviced apartment complex for the first month when you do return in order to give yourself more time to work out what you want before signing a lease.

© KATHI SCHAMARI

The Forbidden City sits at the very center of the city, a constant reminder of China's political power and history.

ONE WEEK
Day 1

The inner-city area of Beijing—that part embraced by the Sixth Ring Road—is relatively organized and generally easy to orient yourself to, and the best way to do this is to start at the city's nucleus, Tian'anmen Square and the Forbidden City, the source of much of the city's culture and pride. The two landmarks are bisected by Chang'an Jie, the street that divides the entire city into north and south regions, and are part of the central axis that divides the city into east and west. In this immediate area, there is more than a day's worth of things to see and explore, and a wander around its streets will give you an insight into the city's mangle of ancient and advanced. This will be a day of possibly more walking than you'll enjoy, so be sure to wear comfortable shoes.

Start the day off early and head to the south entrance of the Forbidden City (Tian'anmen East or Tian'anmen West subway station, Line 1). A tour through the Forbidden City can take hours if you're a wanderer, but those on a mission can complete a direct path through the nearly kilometer-long complex in around an hour.

When you emerge on the north side of the Forbidden City, continue on to Jingshan Park. Though many a weary visitor nixes this option after finally escaping the labyrinth behind them, it is worth pushing yourself on up into the park. In the center is Jingshan Hill, a 46-meter-high (150-foot-high) mound that was made from the earth dug out to make the moat ringing the Forbidden City and the nearby canals. On a beautiful day from the temple at its peak, you can see the buildings of the Olympic Park directly north, the skyscrapers of Guomao to the east, the mountains of Haidian and beyond to the west, and the Forbidden City directly at your feet to the south.

A sharp contrast to the Forbidden City is Wangfujing, just a short walk to the east. This is one of the primary shopping destinations of the city for tourists and residents alike. There are several major shopping malls, numerous flagship stores, multistory bookstores, a toy store, and perhaps the best-known Western-friendly Chinese pharmacy in town. Wangfujing, however, is not just a place just for tourism and shopping. The area is also a major business zone. Oriental Plaza, in particular, which extends all the way from Wangfujing subway station (Line 1) to Dongdan subway station (Lines 1 and 5), is home to many international offices.

Note: If this is a weekend day for you, try to reorder your itinerary so this is a weekday (to avoid the crowds).

Day 2

Today you're going to get to know the older side of Beijing, that part of Dongcheng district situated just inside the north Second Ring Road. Roughly delineated by the square formed by Lines 2, 5, 6, and 8, the area is broadly referred to as Gulou, or rather the Drum Tower.

This small quadrant of the city has a completely different vibe and style than cosmopolitan Sanlitun, chic Guomao, family-friendly Shunyi, or student neighborhood Wudaokou. This is "old" Beijing, albeit slightly hipster style. This is the area of the *hútòng* alleyways, once the homes of the Ming dynasty's elite, now the locale of tiny bars and cafés, and eclectic boutiques. This is where the young and creative Chinese are setting up shop, sometimes with good results, sometimes downright cheesy. It isn't without a few tourist traps, but it's also the place that hides many of the local hangouts that expats navigate to, and is a choice place to live for those who want a little immersion in old-school Beijing. If you have any mind to try out a bicycle, this is the day to do it.

Starting from Lama Temple (Lines 2 and 5) you can wander the nearby Wudaoying Hutong, Guozijian Jie, and Fangjia Hutong. These three quiet, narrow streets have

© SHANNON AITKEN

The Drum Tower, or Gulou, is the centerpoint for one of Beijing's most eclectic areas of nightlife and shopping.

© SHANNON AITKEN

Beijng's old *hútòng* are filled with quaint bars, cafes, and shops.

been on a rapid roll in the last few years, with budding fashion designers, restaurateurs, and bar owners settling in.

You can grab a bite to eat along Gulou Dongdajie, or, alternatively, pick up a guitar from one of the numerous guitar shops along the street. Beiluogu Xiang (the north section of Nanluogu Xiang) and Baochao Hutong are also worth a visit. These two *hútòng* string off the north side of Gulou Dongdajie and in recent years have likewise begun to cater to night goers. Nanluogu Xiang is almost unavoidable, and if you need souvenirs, this is definitely the place to shop. Try not to just get stuck along here, though, and instead explore the much more interesting, much more local *hútòng* that run off it.

Apartments in the Gulou area are generally local in style and less likely to have high-level security (if any). For this reason, you'll easily be able to walk in and wander around the grounds, but, on the other hand, it will be tough to find an official who'll show you around. Check on the Beijinger website for local apartments, and drop into the real estate agents along the streets. Most will have two or three apartments that they can show you at a moment's notice. If you're by yourself and willing, the agents will probably even run you from place to place on the back of their scooter—which makes a fantastic way to discover the neighborhood.

Day 3

It's back to business today and down to the CBD and the area often generally thought of as Guomao (Lines 1 and 10). This is the location of some of the city's most iconic modern structures, including the China World Trade Center, the Yintai Centre, and the new CCTV Headquarters. It's also the spot for haute couture and fine dining. For expats who spend most of their time up around Gulou, where the bar for fashion is set just a tad above pajama level, it can be a wakeup to come here and be reminded that there is a well-clad set that circles in Beijing.

Unfortunately, Guomao isn't the easiest locale to stroll around. There isn't much street-side shopping to be done, and most of the shops are hidden within the large, distant complexes. China World Mall and the Beijing Yintai Centre Mall, connected by the subway station (Line 1), house all the big-ticket names, including Cartier, Prada, Bvlgari, and more. On weekdays come noon they become frenetic warrens of activity, with office workers rushing to grab something for lunch or shop. On weekends they seem more like museums.

Highlights of Guomao include the high-altitude restaurants. Grill 79 in the Shangri-La at the top of the China World Summit Wing claims the highest dining destination title in Beijing; however, China Grill, across the road in the Park Hyatt at the top of the Yintai Centre, could argue it has better views, thanks to the 360-degree design and the unobstructed floor-to-ceiling windows. Either way, if you're in Beijing on a heavily polluted day, the view will be worth nothing.

If you have time for house hunting, some of the residential properties within walking distance of the CBD include Pingguo Shequ (Apple Community) and Fulicheng, both close to Shuangjing subway station (Line 10). Fulicheng is more upmarket than Pingguo, and even more so is the newer Xanadu property, located on the north side of the CCTV Headquarters. Real estate agents are situated close to all the compounds, so if you can't find a property management member to give you a tour, you should be able to find a local agent who can.

Day 4

Today we move to a distinctively expat-heavy area, Dongzhimen and Sanlitun. If you live or work around either of these areas you'll find life incredibly convenient. International supermarkets are in surplus, both high-brow and casual restaurants are at hand, and all forms of public transport are at your door, including the Airport Express. If you live in this neighborhood you'll find that friends and colleagues are always just a short bicycle ride away. It's highly residential, so isn't terribly scenic, but some streets to be aware of include Dongzhimennei Dajie, Dongzhimenwai Dajie, Xingfucun Zhonglu, Sanlitun Lu, and Gongti Beilu.

Muster yourself to add some housing investigation into the day, and make a point of looking at different price brackets and compound styles to get a feel for what you're going to get for your money as far as facilities and quality are concerned. There are compounds that have a more international flavor to them, such as Embassy House, Season's Park, the various Diplomatic Residence Compounds (DRC), and Sanlitun SOHO, and then there are the more local-style communities, such as Min'an Xiaoqu and Huayuan Star Compound.

There are endless lunch and dinner options in the area, again from fine dining to the kind that may hospitalize you thanks to rank produce and absent hygiene systems. In cooler months, the hot pot restaurants along Guijie (the western end of Dongzhimennei Dajie) are cheap and fun, and will certainly give you a glimpse of the cacophonous atmosphere that typically accompanies local restaurants. Alternatively, head into Sanlitun for an unlimited selection of restaurants and bars.

Day 5

Today is the day to explore one of the more modern quarters of the city, that around the northeast corner of the Third Ring Road. It encompasses the neighborhoods of

Liangmaqiao, Sanyuanqiao, and Chaoyang Park. The area is home to one of the city's densest concentrations of international offices and is the halfway point between the airport and the inner city. If your company is sending you to China to work in its Beijing office, there's a good chance you will be here somewhere, and if you're coming to work at the American embassy, this is certainly where you'll be.

With its weighty collection of global businesses, the area naturally caters to the expat crowd. Among its towering modern and commercial constructions, you'll find markets, quality shopping malls, and a large collection of five-star hotels.

Start with a morning visit to Sanyuanli Market on Shunyuan Jie in Chaoyang district to get a feel for grocery shopping Beijing-style. You can walk here from Liangmaqiao subway station (Line 10, exit A), though keep your map handy as it's not exactly obvious. This market is microscopic by contrast to other fresh-produce markets around the city, but it's one of the best as far as quality goes, and many of Beijing's international chefs come here for supplies. If you're hungry, you can fill up on Chinese pancakes and fresh fruit.

Next, wander along nearby Tianze Lu, past the American embassy and up to Ladies' Street and the Laitai Flower Market (identified by the large stone elephants at its front door). This is an excellent place to visit when you're setting up home. The market burrows far below ground, and when you find your way down here you'll discover clothing, electronics, and more. If you're in dire need of some food from home, City Shop (www.cityshop.com.cn) is just around the corner from the American embassy. It's one of the best-stocked but priciest international supermarkets in Beijing. Alternatively, head across Liangmaqiao Lu to Lucky Street, where you'll find the South German Bakery, and a little further down is shopping village Solana.

Solana sits at the northwest corner of Chaoyang Park, one of the largest and most vibrant parks in the city. Not only is Chaoyang Park a place for festivals and events, it's also a key destination for those with sport on their mind. Take your time wandering around the park and grab some dinner at one of the restaurants near the west gate of the park.

Day 6

Today we go farther in the direction of the airport to yet another expat enclave, Lido, and then to 798 Art District, a sprawling community of ex-factories repurposed as galleries.

Lido isn't a place you'd likely come to on a tourist visit to Beijing, as there's nothing historical or scenic about it, but it is packed with conveniences that will give you a comfortable Western-style life should you decide to live here, and is popular with families. The neighborhood has grown rapidly in the last couple of years. Once, Lido Hotel and the little collection of outlets at the intersection of Fangyuan Xilu and Jiangtai Lu were the primary social spots, but now things have extended to including Indigo shopping mall and East Hotel, just down the road on Jiuxianqiao Lu. Wander around the streets and make some appointments to look inside a few apartments.

Unlike Lido, the nearby 798 is a major tourist magnet. Busloads of baseball-capped, flag-bearing Chinese tourists and international tourists alike flood the place on weekends, coming to see the repurposed factories as much as the artwork they're filled with. Regardless, the area is still an important part of life in Beijing and provides ample evidence of the city's rapidly shifting culture. Without doubt you will find yourself at 798 more than once in the future for large-scale events or simply a nice day out. While here you can discover contemporary Chinese and international art in the myriad galleries, shop in the boutiques, and enjoy lunch or a coffee in the many cafés.

To truly immerse yourself in the area, switch to one of the many hotels in the vicinity and experiment with travel time by heading to other parts of the city for lunch or dinner.

Day 7

So, assuming time is a little tight today, make today a simple half-day exercise of visiting a local market—and this doesn't mean the tourist-packed complexes such as Silk Street at Yong'anli (Line 1), Yashow beside Taikuli at Sanlitun, or Panjiayuan (Line 10). These headache-inducing hives are run by well-trained vendors deft at swindling ignorant newcomers, add little value to your trip, and are definitely not places that will become a part of your daily life once you live here.

If you're anywhere near the southwest of the city, consider instead a trip to Jing Shen Seafood Market (京深海鲜市场) in Fengtai district. Even if you don't buy anything, it's worth a visit just to see the astounding array of fresh produce that's flipping or crawling around. If you can get a Chinese speaker to help you, it's possible to buy your fresh produce downstairs and eat it moments later upstairs in the food court, where purchases from the market are cooked to order. You'll find it just a short walk directly south from Shiliuzhuang subway station (Line 10) along Guangcai Lu.

Alternatively, spend the morning in the southeast at Dongjiao market, which lies on Xidawang Lu, about 500 meters (1,600 feet) directly south of Dawanglu subway station (Line 1). This is not a tourist market. It's where locals come to equip themselves for almost anything they need—kitchenware, fresh produce, stationery, bedding, and even mangy goldfish or turtles. It extends all the way to the East Fourth Ring Road, and if you had time to explore beyond there you'd find it progressed into a further stretch of hardware goods.

TWO WEEKS
Days 8-9

Continuing on from the first week, extend your exploration of the city with a few solid days to do some home hunting in the areas you specifically have an interest in. If you've done your homework and read the Prime Living Locations chapter, you might now be starting to get an idea of where you'd like to live. Those who are heading here for university or the IT industry will do well do concentrate on Haidian district, specifically Zhongguancun, Wudaokou, and Zhichunlu, as well as Xizhimen and Jishuitan in Xicheng district. Though the latter two are not exactly university or tech spots, they are extremely convenient locations from which to get up to Haidian, they have a stronger traditional culture than Haidian or the eastern side of the city, and yet they still pulse with energy.

Those with kids, on the other hand, should spend the day sizing up the area on the border of northeast Chaoyang and Shunyi, where the majority of international schools are to be found. Be warned, though; transport out this way isn't quite as abundant as in the rest of the city, so you'll do well to hire a car and driver for the day.

Try to fit in some commuting to and from these places to your future office, especially at rush hour. Get a feel for the road traffic or the subway squash that you're going to possibly need to deal with on a daily basis. While having a driver will overcome many transport issues, traffic can be hellish.

Day 10

Though you may feel that time is tight on your fact-finding trip, taking a day to get out of the city will remind you just how big the entire Beijing municipality is. It will also introduce you to the concept of getaways, which is also an important part of expat life here.

Of course, there are few better places to head to than the Great Wall. This might seem like an outright tourist thing to do, but even for residents the Great Wall is an important part of what makes Beijing what it is.

There are several sections of the wall to choose from. The most commercial, least recommendable, but easiest to access section is Badaling in Yanqing county. You can hire a driver to get here, but you can also take an S2 train from Beijing North Railway Station, located at Xizhimen subway station (Lines 2, 4, and 13). Trains leave several times throughout the day and take 90 minutes to get there. It's a bit more civilized than trying to take the 919快 bus from Deshengmen bus stop, which is a somewhat disorganized maze of bus stops to the east of Jishuitan subway station (Line 2). For more information on the S2 train, visit www.travelchinaguide.com/cityguides/beijing and click on North Railway Station under Transportation.

A slightly more interesting section is Mutianyu. Again this teeters on the brink of being overly commercial, but it does have a combination of restored and "wild" wall. There are also quality restaurants around the area that are worth taking a break in. In addition, it comes with the fun of a cable car and toboggan ride, if desired.

© KATHI SCHAMARI

Expect to make a few trips up to the north to walk on the Great Wall, for your own sightseeing, or to play tour guide for relatives or friends who visit.

Perhaps one of the one of the most interesting stretches of the Great Wall is between Simatai and Jinshanling. Not recommended for the middle of winter, it's magnificent at almost any other time of year. This section of the wall is a lot farther out, requiring a three-hour drive to get there, and has some steep, challenging climbs. Those with vertigo or physical limitations might want to think twice about taking the hike between these two sections. You can organize the day for yourself, but there are also tour groups around town that run hikes that are well worth the money. One of the best is managed by the Beijing Downtown Backpackers (www.backpackingchina.com). Book a few days in advance to secure your place. Other tours worth investigating include those run by Beijing Hikers (www.beijinghikers.com) and the China Culture Center (www.chinaculturecenter.org).

Day 11

For today we investigate the neighborhood surrounding Ritan Park, defined roughly by the square created by the intersection of Lines 1, 2, 6, and 10. You're really in the thick of it within this sector. There is an intense concentration of business, housing, and lifestyle venues to be found here. It's one of the major diplomatic areas, with some excellent shopping options and even an outdoor climbing wall in the picturesque Ritan Park.

Start the morning with breakfast at Central Park, a short walk west from Jintaixizhao subway station (Line 10, exit A). This residential community is packed with excellent cafés, restaurants, and shops, and even if you don't live here, you'll often find yourself coming here for a meal. On sunny weekend mornings the cafés overflow with families and groups of friends enjoying an outdoor brunch.

The neighborhood is well serviced by high-level accommodation options, most of which will need prior booking with an agent to be seen inside. If you're not up for house hunting, however, there are other things that will impress. On Central Park's west side is The Place, a mammoth shopping complex divided by a football-field-sized LED screen that lights up at night like a humongous screen saver. The Place has a range of cafés and restaurants and shops, as well as an international supermarket (basement level).

From the western side of The Place, meander through the tree-lined streets south of Ritan Park, gradually arriving at Yong'anli subway station (Line 1). Silk Street (a horrid tourist trap, but occasionally useful) is unmissable on the northwest corner. If you visited Yashow Market beside Taikuli in Sanlitun, you'll think you're having déjà vu. The markets are remarkably similar and you'd be forgiven for forgetting which one you are actually in. Pick up a handbag, sweater, or pair of shoes while you're here—just remember to bargain hard.

Continue along Jianguomenwai Dajie (Chang'an Jie) toward Jianguomen subway station, where you'll come across two separate DRC compounds—Qijiayuan DRC and Jianguomenwai DRC—which are quiet and spacious, and worth investigating if you're prepared to spend above RMB20,000 per month for a two-bedroom apartment. The DRC compounds house many of the diplomats from the nearby embassies, but they are open to other residents. Just be sure to book an inspection ahead of your visit to secure a good look (www.dhsc.com.cn/fw_sc/index_en.aspx).

If you're inclined to live a little more locally, make your way over to the Second Ring Road into the area on the northwest corner of Chaoyangmen subway station (Lines

2 and 6). There is a dense collection of compounds that house an interesting mix of locals and expats. Wander inside and around the compounds on Douban Hutong and Nanmencang Hutong and explore the surrounding streets for a taste. There's no shortage of street-side real estate agents who will be able to give you a close-up inspection without too much notice.

Finally, finish the day with a visit to Ritan Park at around sunset. Take a break at the Stone Boat Bar, a cement boat-shaped bar that sits at the edge of a lotus pond. On a balmy summer's evening, there's nothing that will trigger an epiphany of loving your life in Beijing more than sitting on the deck here at sunset with a beer, watching the locals walk around the park en masse for their evening exercise.

If you're keen for something a little less sedentary and more in the way of cocktails and loud music, head to the cheesy but entertaining club Chocolate opposite the northwest corner of Ritan Park. This is the Russian hood of Beijing, and when not buying furs from the neighboring fur markets, the Russians are here drinking and dancing. Alternatively, Centro, at the Kerry Hotel, is a little more sophisticated and has live jazz bands most nights.

Day 12

Take a break from home hunting today and explore some of the markets around town. Many of these are large and sprawling, and you'll find an entire day can be taken up with one market alone. Those interested in anything fabric related should head to the Muxiayuan Fabric Markets, the mother of fabric markets, located in southern Fengtai district. You can get out at Donghuamen subway station (Line 10) and walk north along Nanyuan Lu, over the river and up toward the Third Ring Road. The biggest building to look out for is Jingdu Textile City.

For another fabric encounter, but of the ready-to-wear variety, hunt around the Zoo Markets (Beijing Zoo subway station, exit C or D), an overwhelming snarl of complexes and street-side shops dedicated to selling all manner of attire at wholesale prices. This is definitely a whole-day activity, and you may return to your hotel with a throbbing headache, but it's a fascinating window into Beijing, its migrant workers, and its appreciation for the wholesale market.

If kitsch is your thing, and it happens to be Saturday or Sunday, go to Panjiayuan (Line 10). This is definitely a tourist destination, but you can pick up some questionably antique souvenirs as well as plot out a few furniture or decoration items that you'll return to buy for your future home.

Day 13

A lot of expats make the east side of the city their home, and go only as far as Gulou and its immediate surrounds. Houhai becomes the fence over which they don't cross. With the east being a cornucopia of entertainment, it's easy to imagine there's nothing of interest beyond there. It's true, there are almost no expat enclaves in Xicheng district, and finding international supermarkets requires much more determination. But then, if you want to give yourself a more removed, more foreign experience without surrendering too many conveniences, this is the place. So, today, this is the area we explore.

Start with a walk around Sihuan Zonghe Market (四环综合市场), one of the nicest food markets in town. Also known as Rùndélì càishìchǎng （润得立菜市场）, it's a bustling market with hundreds of vendors, selling everything from handmade noodles to sesame paste made from freshly roasted sesame seeds. Sihuan Zonghe Market is to the west of Houhai and is a 15-minute walk from either Xinjiekou (Line 4, exit B) or Jishuitan (Line 2, exit C). If you're taking a taxi, have the driver drop you off on Deshengmennei Dajie just south of Xinjiekou Dongjie.

When you're finished at the market, don't leave—stroll around the surrounding *hútòng* and enjoy an older section of Beijing that hasn't been hipsterfied, at least not yet.

If you'd like to discover how the imperial set spent their days and what today makes the backdrop for China's Communist party, spend some time in the ancient Beihai Park (www.beihaipark.com.cn). Formerly an exclusive playground for emperors, empresses, and their family, Beihai Park is one of China's largest gardens. It covers a massive 69 hectares (170 acres), more than half taken up by a large lake.

History isn't the only thing that Xicheng has going for it, however. It's also known for its shopping. So for this, head to Xidan (Lines 1 and 4). When young Chinese are asked where they think the best place to shop in Beijing is, their answer is rarely Wangfujing or Sanlitun. Nine times out of 10 it's Xidan. A relatively condensed, walkable area contains a multitude of shopping malls, and given that tourists or expats are not the target market here, prices are often lower.

By now the day should be getting on, so finish it off with an evening infusing yourself in local culture at Meilanfang Grand Theatre, beside Chegongzhuang subway station (Line 2, exit B). This beautiful theater is named after one of the most famous Peking opera performers in China's history, and on most nights its stage is dedicated to preserving the art form. You may not understand a word of it, and it might not even be to your taste, but it's definitely much more authentic than the diluted, dramatic highlights that are put on show for tourists elsewhere in the city. This is where the genuine Peking opera enthusiasts come for much more sophisticated performances. Alternatively, if you are in the mood for a show but just not Peking opera, look into what's happening at the National Centre for the Performing Arts (NCPA, www.chncpa.org), situated on the west side of Tian'anmen Square (Tian'anmen West Station, Line 1). For tickets for either venue, speak to your concierge or contact Theatre Beijing (www.theatrebeijing.com, English available), which can deliver tickets to your door.

Day 14

If you've no more personal business to finish off today, say a farewell to the city with a visit to one of its major parks, Tiantan Park (http://en.tiantanpark.com, Tiantandongmen subway station, Line 5). Also referred to as Temple of Heaven Park, this is the site where emperors came to worship the gods and pray for a bountiful harvest. Starting from roughly 7am, the entire park is alive with activity, with the older generations congregating in groups to sing, dance, play badminton, or do tai chi.

Finally, if you've any inclination, energy, or time left for shopping after this, you'll find Hongqiao Market (the Pearl Markets) across the road from the east gate of the park. This is yet another complex for bargaining on rip-off Prada and Gucci items. Hongqiao, however, has a much stronger focus on jewelry than Yashow or Silk Street.

Practicalities

Unlike Hong Kong or many other international cities of the world, Beijing still is an affordable destination to visit. There are high-rolling hotels and there are quality, very comfortable budget hotels for around RMB300 per night. In fact, the price difference between a single room in a hostel and a room in a good budget hotel is often indistinguishable.

If you do go local, you'll probably find that the beds are just as soft as the tiled floor beneath them. Amenities will be basic and service isn't going to be the kind that makes you feel special. It is, however, quite likely that you'll have unlimited free wireless Internet in your room at whatever level of accommodation you stay in.

ACCOMMODATIONS
Dongcheng

There is no shortage of hotels in Dongcheng, especially around Wangfujing, where China's rich love to stay. Book yourself into one of the big-name five-star chains, or for something with more of the Beijing spirit, try one of the many boutique options. Newcomer **Temple Hotel** (23 Shatan Beijie, Dongcheng district, 东城区沙滩北街23号, tel. 10/8402-1350, www.thetemplehotel.com, prices not available at time of writing) is a stunning option. Set in a restored 600-year-old wooden temple sitting at the end of a dusty urban *hútòng*, this luxury hotel gives you a stark juxtaposition of the upper and lower echelons of Beijing. You'll find it just a short walk west of the National Art Museum of China and Dongsi subway station (Lines 5 and 6).

Another boutique hotel, this time by Gulou, is the **Orchid** (65 Baochao Hutong, off Gulou Dongdajie, Dongcheng district, 东城区，鼓楼东大街宝钞胡同65号, tel. 10/8404-4818, www.theorchidbeijing.com, from RMB680). Just a stone's throw from expat favorites as well as tourist hangouts, it's in an amazing location for both convenience and entertainment. The rooms are stylish and comfortable, and in warm seasons you can enjoy a drink on its gorgeous rooftop before heading off for some food, drinks, or live music at the nearby bars and restaurants.

More business-like is the **Park Plaza** (97 Jinbao Jie, Dongcheng district, 丽亭酒店，东城区金宝街97号, tel. 10/8522-1999, www.parkplaza.com, from RMB700). This is a straightforward, elegant hotel, which in itself is not going to give you any heady flavor of Beijing, but it is in an excellent location for the city in general and makes a convenient well-equipped base for exploring.

Budget accommodations in the neighborhood can be found at the friendly **Peking Yard** (28 Wangzhima Hutong, near Zhangzizhonglu subway station, Line 5, exit D, 北平小院国际青年旅舍，汪芝麻胡同甲28号, tel. 10/8404-8787, www.yhachina.com, from RMB105). Peking Yard is in a quiet *hútòng* away from tourist sites and right among the real homes of true local Beijingers.

If you're not fussed about hotel style, but just want something clean and practical from which to explore the city, you will probably be satisfied with **Beijing Hutong Hotel** (sometimes still going by its former name, Green Tree Inn, located inside compound at 46 Fangjia Hutong, Dongcheng district, 北京胡同酒店，东城区方家胡同46号, tel. 10/6403-2288, from RMB162). Far from flashy, it is, however, in a stellar location, being just a short walk from the Lama Temple (Lines 2 and 5) as well as many boutique shops, bars, and cafés.

Chaoyang

Wham bam in the center of the Sanlitun action is the **Opposite Hotel** (Taikuli, Building 1, 11 Sanlitun Lu, Chaoyang district, 瑜舍酒店, 朝阳区三里屯太古里1号楼, tel. 10/6417-6688, www.theoppositehouse.com, from RMB2,125). This chic 99-room hotel may be the kind of place you stay at on leisure holidays, but it's also extremely practical. Not only is it in a convenient location for work and for many embassies, but given that it feels like an integrated entertainment complex of Taikuli rather than an exclusive guests-only destination, it has also become a venue that expats routinely come to for dining and drinking.

For something more in the style of what you'll experience as an actual resident, check in to **Season's Park Apartment Hotel** (B36 Dongzhimenwai Dajie, Dongcheng district, 北京海晟国际公寓, 东城区东直门外大街乙36号, tel. 10/5166-0060, www. seasonsparkaparthotel.com, from RMB418). The hotel is part of a major residential complex popular with expats, so gives a very real expat experience, and it's situated within walking distance to the Sanlitun embassy area, the Sanlitun shopping and dining precinct, and the Dongzhimen transport hub.

Five-star hotels can be found all the way down the East Third Ring Road, from Sanyuanqiao down to Guomao in the heart of the CBD, at which point there is an explosion of premium hotels, taking up iconic locations on the city's landscape. Less obvious, but more practical from a fact-finding perspective, are places like **East Apartments** (59 Fulicheng, East Third Ring Road, Chaoyang, 北京全方位服务酒店式服务公寓, 朝阳区东三环路富力城59号, tel. 10/5862-3125, www.eastapt.com), which are a little farther down the road at Fulicheng, beside Shungjing subway station (Line 10, exit A). Many expats working around Guomao choose to live in either the residential section of this property or the other high-quality housing complexes in the immediate surrounds. A stay here puts you right by a shopping mall, an international cinema complex, and Melody KTV, one of the best karaoke places in town for English songs.

To give yourself some breathing space away from the commercial hot spots, stay a bit farther out at Lido in the new **East** hotel (22 Jiuxianqiao Lu, Chaoyang district, 北京东隅, 朝阳区酒仙桥路22号, tel. 10/8426-0888, www.east-beijing.com, from RMB798). This hotel is specifically aimed at the business crowd, and offers high-tech modern conveniences in a casual contemporary setting. If you have meetings in Liangmaqiao or Sanyuanqiao, it's just a 10-minute drive (in good traffic) and not much more on a bicycle. It will also be a good test location for if you have kids who'll be heading out to the schools at Shunyi.

Finally, one more that will help to immerse you for the short term in an expat lifestyle is **Lanson Place** (Tower 23, Central Park, 6 Chaoyangmenwai Dajie, Chaoyang district, 北京逸兰, 新城国际, 服务式公寓, 朝阳区朝阳门外大街6号, 新城国际23号楼, tel. 10/8588-9588, http://beijing.lansonplace.com). Located inside Central Park, these home-style apartments are well equipped, and just above a village-like setting of cafés and restaurants. Most guests are long-term here, so vacancies for short-term visits can be limited and you usually need to book early to secure a room. Daily rates are calculated from the monthly rate of the available room.

Xicheng District

Over in Xicheng district, almost any five-star hotel you could want to stay at is located by Financial Street near Fuchengmen subway station (Line 2). It's pure business in this part of town, and other than what's in the hotels, entertainment options have been slow to develop. To give your visit a little more interest, consider **Shichahai Shadow Art Hotel** (24 Songshu Jie, Xicheng district, 什刹海皮影文化酒店, 西城区松树街 23号, tel. 10/8328-7846, www.shadowarthotel.com, from RMB1,200, discounts for advanced bookings). This beautiful boutique hotel is buried among the *hútòng* to the west side of Houhai. It's the perfect spot to wander among parts of old Beijing that haven't quite yet been freight trained by tourism. If you'd like to get a taste of what it's like to live in a *sìhéyuàn,* among the locals and within arm's reach of streetside vendors, look into staying at **Templeside Deluxe Hutong House** (exact address dependent on house chosen, Xicheng district, 广济.邻国际青年旅舍, tel. 10/6617-2571, www. templeside.com, from RMB100). Set in two traditional *sìhéyuàn,* this quaint family-style guesthouse has hostel dormitories through to a deluxe VIP family room. Though great for the warmer months, it's possibly not the most comfortable option for winter.

Haidian District

If your company is sending you to Beijing to investigate options up in Zhongguancun, then let's hope they kindly treat you to a stay at the **Crown Plaza Beijing Zhongguangcun** (106 Zhichun Lu, Haidian district, 北京中关村皇冠假日酒店, 海淀区知春路106号, tel. 10/5993-8888, www.crowneplaza.com, from RMB1,488). There isn't much entertainment in the immediate vicinity of the hotel, but being close to Haidianhuangzhuang subway station (Lines 4 and 10) gives you easy access to both the technology and university areas, as well as Olympic Park.

A budget option is YHA hostel **Beijing Heyuan International Youth Hostel** (1 Zhiqiangbeiyuan, off Wenhuiyuan Lu, Haidian district, 海淀区志强北园1号, 文慧 园路, tel. 10/6227-7138, www.yhachina.com, from RMB65). It's set in a beautiful traditional-style building and is walking distance from Jishuitan subway station, making it a great central location between the universities and the city center. If you do want to be closer to the universities, however, then you could try PekingUni International Youth Hostel (150 Chengfu Lu, Haidian, 海淀区成府路150号, tel. 10/6254-9667, www.booking.com, from RMB60). While it's not the most stylish place to stay, its facilities are clean and tidy. The major plus of this hostel is its excellent location near Wudaokou subway station and many of the universities.

Northeast Chaoyang and Shunyi

When searching for a hotel out around this area, try to stay somewhere in the vicinity of the New China International Exhibition Center or Tianzhu town, just west of the airport. This is where the majority of international schools and homes are in Shunyi. It's close to the expressway and subway, so getting into town will be much easier. You'll find luxury abodes to softly cushion your visit, such as **Langham Place** (1 Erjing Lu, Terminal 3, Capital International Airport, 北京首都机场朗豪酒店, 北京首都国际

机场三号航站楼二经路1号, tel. 10/6457-5555, http://beijingairport.langhamplace-hotels.com, RMB1,119), which has received various awards for its facilities and food.

To get right in the thick of Shunyi life, book a stay in **Beijing Yosemite Club** (4 Yuyang Lu, Houshayu town, Shunyi district, 优山美地俱乐部，顺义区后沙峪镇榆阳路4号, tel. 10/8041-7588, www.yosemiteclub.com, from RMB700 twin/night). Yosemite is one of the major gated communities in the area, filled not with apartment blocks but villas. A stay here will give you a very good feeling for what life will be like for the kids with school and neighborhood friends, as well as what the commute into the office in the city will be like for you.

Outer Districts

If a day trip turns into an overnight one, then the outer districts have a few impressive accommodation options. Sometimes this can just be a room in the house of an entrepreneurial local. It'll be cheap, authentic, and usually will include a home-cooked dinner. If Badaling in Yanqing county is your destination, budgeters can stay at the **Great Wall Courtyard Hostel** (26 Chadaogucheng, Badalingzhen, Yanqing district, 北京八达岭长城岔道古城, tel. 10/6912-1156, www.courtyard.cc, from RMB80), which is ideally placed by the Great Wall. A nice idea is to arrive the evening before and stay here, then rise early in the morning to enjoy the sunrise on the wall, well before the tourists roll in.

Nearby you can enjoy much more magnificent accommodations at the **Commune by the Great Wall** (Great Wall, Exit 53 at Shuiguan, G6 Jingzang Hwy., 长城脚下的公社，北京G6京藏高速公路53号，水关长城出口, tel. 10/8118-1888, www.communebythegreatwall.com, from RMB2,488). A collection of individually designed houses scattered among the mountains, and accompanied by a private section of the Wall, the Commune is a grand but rather exclusive option.

For those who choose Mutianyu, there is the **Brickyard Eco-Retreat** (Beigou village, Bohai town, Huairou district, 怀柔区渤海镇北沟村, tel. 10/6162-6506, www.brickyardatmutianyu.com, from RMB1,380), a luxurious and beautifully designed hotel set in a quiet village by the wall. Prices don't come cheaply here either, but it will definitely give you the feeling of a unique resort with views of the Great Wall from your bed.

FOOD

Haute cuisine is something of a nascent concept in Beijing. The *Michelin Guide* has yet to bestow a single star on any restaurant here, and even the *Miele Guide* has eschewed listing any of the city's restaurants in its top 20. But that doesn't mean people don't love their food. Restaurants are an integral part of life in Beijing, with many rarely eating a meal at or from home during the week. This means that the city has a surfeit of restaurants, many of which essentially play substitute for the family kitchen. It's not standard to take a sandwich to work for lunch here—it's standard to join the lunch rush and eat at the nearest *jiāchángcài fànguǎnr* (home-cooking restaurant) or noodle restaurant.

Steer clear of any restaurant boldly advertising "English menu" or "We serve Western food." In most cases it will be a bad approximation of a very ordinary cafeteria back home. Almost without fail, Chinese restaurants have fully photographed menus, so

English can be bypassed. Additionally, unlike in Hong Kong or China's south, there are relatively few odd ingredients to make you squeamish. It's unlikely you'll come across anything much stranger than stomach or intestines.

Hygiene standards can be ghastly, and it's not always the tiny mom and pop stores that fall to shame. For this reason, unless you've had a personal recommendation for an obscure place, avoid anywhere that appears mysteriously empty or grimy. Unlicensed street-side carts can be especially hazardous to one's digestive tract.

If it's breakfast you're after, this again isn't a particular specialty of the city. There are numerous dim sum restaurants around town, some exceptionally good, but that's Cantonese fare, a cuisine that's often considered fine dining in the north. Beijingers tend to start their day by wolfing down *yóutiáo* (油条), a fried bread stick dipped into soy milk; a cup of *zhōu* (粥), a rice porridge more commonly known in the West by its Cantonese name, congee; *bāozi* (包子), a steamed bun stuffed with meat or vegetables; or possibly even a *jiānbing* (煎饼), a scrumptious crispy crepe that's fried on a large griddle and typically topped with egg, a hoisin-based sauce, green onions, *báocuì* (a fried cracker), and cilantro or lettuce. It's a satisfying breakfast, but come 1am or 2am it's also the local equivalent of the drunkard's slab of pizza.

Dongcheng

No visit to Beijing is complete without trying its signature dish, Beijing roast duck, or perhaps what you might know it as, Peking duck. In this neighborhood there are numerous choices for devouring it, and one of the favorites is **DaDong Roast Duck Restaurant** (5/F, Jinbao Place, 88 Jinbao Jie, Dongcheng district, 东城区金宝街88号金宝汇购物中心五层, tel. 10/8522-1234, www.dadongdadong.com). The owner is known for growing his own ducks just for his restaurants. It's one of a large handful of restaurants at the top of the list when the inevitable "Who does the best duck?" question is asked. For something more rustic, seek out **Siji Minfu** (off Qianmen Jie, 四季民福, 廊坊二条烤鸭店, 位于宣武区大栅栏廊坊二条18号, tel. 10/6301-4493). There are several branches of this restaurant around the city, but don't assume that they'll serve up the quality that this one does. This tiny wood-decorated restaurant is much more personal and less touristy than its sister venues, and is tucked in an exhilaratingly interesting nook of the city.

There are several other Chinese restaurants of note in the general area. These include Yunnan restaurant **Lost Heaven** (Ch'ienmen 23, 23 Qianmen Dongdajie, Dongcheng district, 东城区前门东大街23号, tel. 10/8516-2698, www.lostheaven.com.cn), situated in Ch'ienmen 23 directly opposite the southeast corner of Tian'anmen Square. It's one of the few Chinese restaurants that serve vibrant, high-quality Chinese cuisine in an elegant fine-dining setting, but at a reasonable price.

If you're dinging around Gulou, there's almost no need to give any restaurant details—just walk 20 meters in any direction and you'll encounter a place to refuel. But just in case you're in doubt, one of local establishments to consider is **Mr. Shi's Dumplings** (74 Baochao Hutong, Dongcheng district, 老石饺子, 东城区宝钞胡同74号, tel. 10/8405-0399). Though packed on most nights with more foreigners than locals, this crammed humble abode pumps out some of the tastiest dumplings in town. Be sure to try both steamed and fried options.

If the weather is warm, enjoy some local craft beer at **Great Leap Brewing** (6

Doujiao Hutong, Dongcheng district, 城区豆角胡同6号, tel. 10/5717-1399, www.greatleapbrewing.com). The boutique brewery is set in a *sìhéyuàn* complete with its own garden, and though not so roomy in winter, it's an excellent retreat when the weather warms up. This is definitely one of the harder venues to locate in the city, so study the map on the website carefully before attempting to find it.

Chaoyang

Chaoyang is the district for dining and drinking, and in every expat hub there are great places at which to satisfy your appetite. Just head up to the roof-top levels of **Taikuli** at the intersection of Gongti Beilu and Sanlitun Lu; or into **Nali Patio,** just next to Taikuli; or into **1949-The Hidden City,** which is hidden behind Pacific Century Plaza near the corner of Gongti Beilu and the Third Ring Road. All three places are packed with an immense variety of bars and restaurants.

As a move to Beijing seems on the cards, however, it's worth trying the local cuisine, as opposed to Cantonese or Sichuan food, which you might be more familiar with. Normally, traditional Beijing cuisine is an offal-driven, drab, even pungent style of food, but **Hong Lu** (6 Nansanlitun Lu, Chaoyang district, 红炉, 朝阳区三里屯南路6号楼南侧, tel. 10/6595-9872) has rescued its reputation. Just a short walk south of Taikuli, Hong Lu produces fantastic food, served by friendly staff who are proud of their flavorful dishes.

Down by the east gate of Ritan Park, try out one of the best hot pot venues in the city, **Nan Men Hotpot** (9 Ritan Donglu, Chaoyang district, 朝阳区日坛东路9号, tel. 10/8562-8899, www.hongyuan.cc). If you're not keen on the usual communal hot pot broth, this may be more to your liking. Diners have individual pots in which to dunk the fresh supply of ingredients.

Over in the CBD there is no shortage of low-key local eateries, but the area is more strongly associated with fine dining, thanks to its concentration of five-star hotels. One that will simultaneously offer you a spectacular view and good cuisine is **China Grill**, set on the top floor of the Park Hyatt Beijing (66F, 2 Jianguomenwai Dajie, Chaoyang district, 北京柏悦酒店, 朝阳区建国门外大街2号66层, tel. 10/8567-1234, beijing.park.hyatt.com). On a fine day or night, there isn't a restaurant with a better combination of scenery and food. After dinner head one floor down to the sexy **China Bar**, or down to the third floor to Xiu bar for people watching, cocktails, and live music.

Those in the Lido area also have a few good options up their sleeves, including the restaurants around Indigo shopping mall and the various options inside 798. One worth mentioning is Najia Xiaoguan (2 Jiuxianqiao Bei Lu, 那家小馆, 朝阳区酒仙桥北路2号, tel. 10/5978-9333), situated on the north side of 798, just outside the area's 707 Street. Though it isn't particularly well known by the expat crowd, locals love Najia Xiaoguan for its mouthwatering Manchu-style cuisine.

Finally, if you're interested in checking out Beijing's gay scene, make a stop at **Destination** (7 Gongti Xilu, Chaoyang district, 朝阳区工人体育场西路7号, tel. 10/6552-8180, www.bjdestination.com), situated near the west gate of the Workers' Stadium. Beijing's gay community might be a long shot from that of San Francisco or Sydney, but it does have a growing presence, and this fun and lively establishment is an important part of that, bringing in a rainbow assortment of international DJs to play throughout the year.

Xicheng

Xicheng has somewhat polarized eating options. There are local restaurants and premium hotel restaurants, and very little in between, especially as far as Western cuisine is concerned.

The majority of fine dining in Xicheng is done at the five-star hotels near Financial Street (Jinrong Jie), near Fuxingmen (Lines 1 and 2). Italian restaurant **Cépe** and Cantonese restaurant **Qi,** both in the Ritz-Carlton Beijing, Financial Street (1 Jinchengfang Dong Jie, 北京金融街丽思卡顿酒店, 西城区金城坊东街1号, tel. 10/6601-6666, www.ritzcarlton.com), often take up posts in Beijing's fine dining annals, as does progressive French restaurant **S.T.A.Y. in Shangri-La Beijing** (29 Zizhuyuan Lu, Haidian district, 海淀区紫竹院路29号, tel. 8610/6841-2211, www.shangri-la.com/beijing/shangrila), which you'll find closer to the National Library (Line 4) and Huayuanqiao (Line 6) subway stations.

For something more of-the-people, there are endless options, and if you end up living in the area, there will be new eateries to discover every week. To get you started, try a visit to **Wufangyuan** (248 Chengfu Lu, Haidian district, 海淀区成府路248号, tel. 8610/6264-0677). You might know Sichuan food by its reputation for spiciness, but this will awaken you to Beijing's other spicy incarnation, Hunan food. Alternatively, try **Xiao Diao Li Tang** (66 Baofusi, Haidian district, 海淀区中关村保福寺66号, tel. 8610/6264-8616), a traditionally decorated but creative Chinese restaurant with all manner of fun and delicious dishes.

Those in the mind to try hotpot seek out **Happy Hot Pot** (20 Zhichun Lu, Haidian district, 高兴火锅, 海淀区知春路甲20号, tel. 8610/8235-6062). Hotpot restaurants blanket the city, but this one sets the bar higher than most.

The **Xinjiang Islam Restaurant** (Xinjiang Provincial Government Office, Building B1, 7 Sanlihe Lu, 三里河路7号新疆驻京办事处院内B1楼, tel. 10/6833-2266) is located by the official office location for Xinjiang representatives. This cheap and bustling restaurant is touted to offer the authentic flavors of this far north-west region of China. Try the succulent lamb skewers (羊肉串儿, *yángròu chuànr*).

Haidian

Food in Haidian tends to also be at either extreme, although this is changing. The student population in the area means that at one end there are a lot of café-level eateries, but the growing concentration of commercial hubs also means it feeds the white-collared set, too.

High-level dining can be enjoyed at **S.T.A.Y.** in Shangri-La Beijing (29 Zizhuyuan Lu, Haidian district, 海淀区紫竹院路29号, tel. 10/6841-2211, www.shangri-la.com/beijing/shangrila), which you'll find close to the National Library (Line 4) and Huayuanqiao (Line 6) subway stations.

For something more of-the-people, there are endless options, and if you end up living in the area, there will be new eateries to discover every week. To get you started, try a visit to **Wufangyuan** (248 Chengfu Lu, Haidian district, 海淀区成府路248号, tel. 10/6264-0677). You might know Sichuan food by its reputation for spiciness, but this will awaken you to China's other spicy incarnation, Hunan food. Alternatively, try **Xiao Diao Li Tang** (66 Baofusi, Haidian district, 海淀区中关村保福寺66号), tel. 10/6264-8616), a traditionally decorated but creative Chinese restaurant with all manner of fun and delicious dishes. Those in the mind to try hot pot should seek out **Happy Hot Pot** (20 Zhichun Lu, Haidian district, 高兴火锅，海淀区知春路甲20号, tel. 10/8235-6062). Hot pot restaurants blanket the city, but this one sets the bar higher than most.

Northeast Chaoyang and Shunyi

If you chose Shunyi for an in-depth visit, you won't run short of Western-style dining options. For breakfast, lunch, or dinner, you can hit **Mrs. Shanen's Bagels** (5 Kaifa Jie, Xibaixinzhuang (next to Capital Paradise), Shunyi district, 顺义区西白辛庄开发路5号, tel. 10/8046-4301), which has lots of family-friendly and organic options. **Fuel** at Langham Place (1 Erjing Lu, Terminal 3, Capital International Airport, 北京首都机场朗豪酒店, 北京首都国际机场三号航站楼二经路1号, tel. 10/6457-5555, http://beijingairport.langhamplacehotels.com) is the place to go for ribs. An elegant lunch or dinner can be had at the **Orchard** (Hegezhuang village, Cuigezhuang township, Shunyi district, 顺义区崔各庄乡何各庄村, tel. 10/6433-6270). This superb restaurant serves European cuisine in countryside surrounds and uses organically sourced produce. There is also a playroom for the kids, making it a very popular choice for weekend family brunches.

There are good local options in Shunyi, too, so life in this corner of the city doesn't have to be 100 percent removed from a Beijing experience. Beijing duck can be enjoyed at **Jinbaiwan**'s flagship restaurant (10 Fuqian Xi Jie, Shunyi district, 顺义区府前西街10号, tel. 10/5116-0000), or for something less usual, book yourself a table at the posh **Li's Imperial Cuisine** (L3/301, Europlaza, 99 Yuxiang Lu, Tianzhu town, 顺义区天竺镇裕翔路99号欧陆广场3层301，新国展对面，tel. 10/8046-1748, beijinglijiacai.oinsite.cn). Imperial cuisine is often raved about and pushed at tourists, but, in fact, you usually walk away pretty nonplussed by the meal you had. If you are keen to try this historic cuisine, Li's Imperial Cuisine does a more approachable variation.

Outer Districts

There are few restaurants of note in the outer districts, and generally if you're in the area it can be hit and miss with what you find. If in doubt, at Badaling in Yanqing county, there are always the American fast-food staples on hand. A short drive from here, the county also offers the Commune by the Great Wall (Great Wall, exit 53 at Shuiguan, G6 Jingzang Hwy.,长城脚下的公社，北京G6京藏高速公路53号，水关长城出口，tel. 10/8118-1888, www.communebythegreatwall.com). A hotel best known for its architecture, the Commune also serves up decent regional Chinese fare. The hotel is literally by the Great Wall—just don't expect to be able to walk on it if you're only popping in for lunch.

Those who choose to go to the Mutianyu section in Huairou will have some of the best options. A local favorite is Shuntong Hongzun Yu, or Shuntong Rainbow Trout (Tianxian village, Bohai town, Huairou district, 顺通虹鳟鱼，怀柔区渤海镇田仙峪村北慕田峪环岛直行, tel. 10/6162-6088), which is a short drive northwest of the Mutianyu section of the wall. You'll get to sample the fresh, locally caught trout, together with a wide array of other excellent dishes, all in a pretty, waterside setting. A little closer to the Great Wall is a place better known to the foreign crowd, the **Schoolhouse** (12 Mutianyu village, 怀柔区 慕田峪村 12号, tel. 10/6162-6506, http://

© SHANNON AITKEN

The Schoolhouse at Mutianyu is often on the itineraries of tourists headed to the nearby Great Wall, but its Western-style food and service make it worthwhile for residents as well.

theschoolhouseatmutianyu.com), which serves quality Western and Chinese cuisine in a repurposed former school.

VISITING UNIVERSITIES AND SCHOOLS

If you need to investigate educational options, you will most likely head to one of several destinations—up to the middle of Haidian district if you're interested in university, or over to Shunyi district and parts of Chaoyang if it's for international schools, including nurseries right through to high school.

Universities

Most universities attended by expats are located around Zhongguancun and Wudaokou in the city's northwest. If you already have a university in mind, by all means, start there. However, if you're just up for a browse, start with the top two. First up is Peking University (北大, *Běi Dà*). A good launching point is the East Gate of the university (Line 4). Stroll around the grounds, sneak a look at some lectures, and try to inspect some of the university's dormitories and apartments. Following Peking University, head for a similar visit at its neighbor, Tsinghua University (清华大学, *Qīnghuá Dàxué*), the other university in the constant battle for China's number-one ranking position. You can walk here, leaving the East Gate of Peking University and heading east along Chengfu Lu toward the main gate of Tsinghua University. Alternatively, take the 355 bus from outside the East Gate, getting off at the third stop, Qinghua Dong Lu Xikou (清华东路西口), and then backtracking slightly to the main entrance. Both universities have exceptional campuses, which might easily take you an entire day to tour if that's what you're interested in.

If you're quick on your feet, however, there are some other options to fill up the afternoon. For lunch, consider a relaxing picnic in the nearby Yuan Ming Yuan (圆明园). To get here take either the 438 or 628 bus from the bus stop across from where you got off for Tsinghua University. Alternatively, if you'd like to explore the gargantuan digital markets of Beijing, head to either Zhongguancun or Haidianhuangzhuang subway station (Line 4). Computer malls interconnect like a maze between these two stations and sell any possible electronic device you could need.

For a third option, head to Wudaokou, which has a much richer student feel about it. Enjoy lunch at Bridge Café or Sculpting in Time café, both mainstays of student life, and both on Caijing Donglu, which runs along the subway line on the southwest side (exit B).

Following lunch, consider heading to one of the major universities perhaps most heavily populated by expats, Beijing Language and Culture University (BLCU). This is a short walk from Wudaokou subway station on the northeast side (exit A) of the southwest gate. The university's website (wwwnew.blcu.edu.cn) has a good map of the campus, which points out such things as the Admissions Office for Foreign Students, the dining halls, the gymnasium, and the library.

Schools

Schools are scattered all around the north and east of the city, including Harrow International School up near Beitucheng subway station (Lines 8 and 10) and Beijing City International School down near Shuangjing subway station (Line 10). Though both are in Chaoyang district, they are about 19 kilometers (12 miles) apart. Many of the international schools, however, are on either side of the Wenyu River, which forms the border between Chaoyang and Shunyi districts.

It's recommended that you have a driver organized for the day, as it'll be much faster and more convenient than trying to traverse the distances on public transport. The Shunyi and outer Chaoyang regions are sprawling areas with large distances between complexes and not much in between. Until just a few years ago this was largely countryside, and though it has developed at the speed of lightning, much of it still has a rural feel about it, sans the cows and chickens. If you're coming by subway, allow for about an hour altogether to get here from the CBD. Take Line 15 and get off at the China International Exhibition Center stop, not Shunyi station, which is much farther along in central Shunyi. A taxi from the inner city should take 30-60 minutes and may cost close to RMB90.

Just some of the schools in the area include the British School of Beijing (BSB), Dulwich College Beijing, Eatonkids International School, and the International School of Beijing (ISB) on the Shunyi side of the river, and the toddler to year 2 campus of Dulwich College Beijing, the International Montessori School of Beijing, Ivy Bilingual School, and Western Academy Beijing (WAB) on the Chaoyang side. Remember to book in with each school ahead of time so that you're ready to roll with appointments, and ask the school to help you meet up with some other parents for a chat while you're there.

You may also want to try to see some homes in the area. Some of the estates popular with expats include Dragon Bay Villas, Yosemite, Capital Paradise, River Garden, and Legend Garden on the Shunyi side, and Beijing Riviera and Lane Bridge on the

Chaoyang side. Real estate agents can show you through homes, but a good place to start is at the club house of each compound.

For lunch or dinner, there is plenty on offer around Pinnacle Plaza and Europlaza. Nothing here is particularly Chinese, and, in fact, it's perhaps the most Western-style place in Beijing. Staying around the neighborhood to eat, however, will give you the perfect opportunity to chat with a nearby table of foreigners about their personal experiences. Expats in Beijing are almost uniformly friendly and will no doubt give you their opinion about schools and life in Shunyi.

DAILY LIFE

© SHANNON AITKEN

MAKING THE MOVE

China's rules and regulations for those moving to the country can feel complicated and are liable to change at a moment's notice. Not only can it be difficult to bring in and take out your own possessions, but managing your own residency can be tricky. Straightforward immigration is usually not an option for most people born outside of China, and living here entails a regular process of renewals or extensions. The easiest path into Beijing is to have a job already waiting for you. Many, however, arrive on simply a tourist visa, find work, then change their visa over to one with more permanent status.

If you're going to be working with a China-based company that is experienced with employing expats, you'll find that all the hoops you need to jump through to settle in will be cleared in no time. If you're doing it completely on your own, however, things can feel complicated and bewildering. It's important to rally your patience, and to cross your t's and dot your i's. If you can afford one, a good relocation service can help expedite the setup procedures and eliminate the headaches.

© SHANNON AITKEN

Immigration and Visas

By moving to China, you're moving to a country that not only loves rules and regulations, but which also loves to change them seemingly at a whim. If your move here is connected with a well-established company or school, then most likely they'll hold your hand through the entire visa process. But if you're doing it on your own or with a less-experienced organization, you'll need to stay on your toes about what's right and what's not.

China demands that every foreigner planning to reside in the country has a valid visa, and unless you're from Singapore, Brunei, or Japan (in which case you'd get a 15-day visa-free window), you'll need it before you leave home. There are no on-arrival visas in Beijing, period. You will also need at least six months remaining on your passport, even if you're only going to be coming for a month or two. While Beijing has introduced the 72-hour visa-free entry law, this is purely aimed at people transiting through the country. It is not meant for giving people time to apply for a visa, and proof of an onward journey to another country is needed to qualify.

There are different visas to suit nearly every possible scenario. Whether you're coming for short-term study, to participate in a trade event, to work, or for an extended holiday, there is a visa to suit. The price, application process, and rules vary for each, and may even vary slightly depending on which embassy or consulate you apply at. As a general guide, you'll need to start working on your application about two months before your departure, and not more than three.

In most cases, if you're coming because someone else in your family needs to, you'll have the right to apply for the same visa as they do. As of July 2013, dependents—including unmarried or same-sex partners—can apply for the dependent residence permit as long as you provide certain documents, such as a marriage certificate or cohabitation certificate issued by the embassy of your home country.

If your dream is to work in China but you haven't nailed down a job just yet, you won't be eligible for a work visa (Z) or work visa (M). But don't despair. Though it can sometimes be almost impossible to get a job from outside the country, once inside you'll find it decidedly easier. In this case you can apply for a tourist visa (L) to get into China and then apply to change it over once you've found work. As long as it's a legal company with the rights to employ you, they should be able to assist you in the process. Be warned, though, if you think your mother tongue will automatically land you an English-teaching job, you'll be mistaken. In order to protect its young'uns from persuasion by untrained expats, the government now stipulates that teachers must have a bachelor's degree and two years of teaching experience. You will of course find smaller schools or institutions willing to overlook these laws, but in this case you'll probably find yourself constantly running the visa gauntlet and without any form of protection should your school one day decide to eighty-six you on your pay. Companies that operate this way nearly always come with problems so are best avoided.

Before you start your visa process, you'll need to get regulation passport photos. Some places will specify white background, others blue, but usually as long as it's one of these you'll be fine. Be sure to get at least a dozen copies and keep them in your wallet—it's amazing how many places and processes require a passport photo as you set your life up in Beijing.

If you are to apply for any kind of work-related visa, you will also need to prepare a certificate showing that you have no criminal conviction, which should be issued by the public security or judicial authorities from your country or place of permanent residence. This will need to be translated into Chinese by an official translation company and then authenticated by a Chinese consulate. To add to your criminal surveillance, you'll also be required to give fingerprints at some point down the track.

Once in Beijing, your visa and residence issues will be taken care of at the Exit-Entry Administration of Beijing Municipal Public Security Bureau. This is located near Lama Temple and Dongzhimen subway stations, at the northeast corner of the Second Ring Road. Unfortunately, it can be hellishly busy. If possible, get there before the doors open at 8:30am. If you have questions, this is not always the most helpful place to reach out to, and its website and help line will probably frustrate more than alleviate. In cases where you have visa problems, you'll often find that visa services can do magic.

Children and Visas

Every person, babies included, needs a visa to get into and out of China. They also need a passport to get out of and back into the United States and Canada. If your child, for some reason, does not have a passport, then the mother or father can have a "+1" added to her or his visa. The documents required for the visa application are just as needed for adults.

When children travel with one parent, China does not require any permission letter from the other parent; however, when they travel alone, a permission letter from the parents will be needed. Ideally, the letter should include: the child's name and date of birth; the specific details of the trip, if the letter is only being used for one trip; an expiry date; the full name, address, and phone number of the parent; a notarized signature of the parent. It's recommended that you also have this letter translated into Mandarin (simplified Chinese) and notarized. If your child is traveling with a guardian or other adult, this person's name should also be included on the letter. Sample letters can be found at: www.samplewords.com/child-travel-consent-form-international or www.voyage.gc.ca/letter.

Children are not required to have any particular vaccinations before entering China.

CHINESE VISAS

For some special situations, people are issued a diplomatic visa, courtesy visa, or service visa, but in most cases you'll fall under the category of "ordinary visas," which are broken up into 12 types as listed below. For the particular paperwork and steps required for each visa, visit sites such as www.ebeijing.gov.cn/visa, www.travelchinaguide.com, or www.visaforchina.org. Visa laws in China are in a state of constant change, so take the following as a guideline and check with your local Chinese visa office for the most up-to-date information.

Tourist Visa-L (旅游, Lǚyóu)

So your goal isn't to travel but to live and work or study in Beijing? Well, you still might need to apply for a tourist visa to get yourself into the country. If you haven't

THE BEIJING *HÙKǑU*

The *hùkǒu* system is a "permanent residency permit," held by each Chinese family. It's like a national passport, which effectively classifies a family as citizens–or noncitizens–of a given municipality or province, and limits movements by curtailing benefits of trespassers and dishing out advantages to locals. The system has been around in some shape or form since the Xia dynasty of 21st-17th centuries BC, and has been strictly used in China since the coming of the Communist Party in 1949. Over time it has been used to control the movement of the population. In the time of the Great Leap Forward it was used to organize people into rural or urban groups of workers. Today it defines the Chinese as permanent residents of a given area of China, such as Beijing, and those who are drawn here for the higher salaries and greater work opportunities give up many of their entitlements.

The Beijing *hùkǒu* is the most coveted of any *hùkǒu* in China. With a Beijing *hùkǒu*, a person has better access to health care, welfare, employment, and house ownership within the capital. And that's just the start of a raft of benefits.

Expats don't get a *hùkǒu*, and, compared to many Chinese people, we can move around the country with relative ease. Those Chinese who do try to make a living in the capital with a non-Beijing *hùkǒu* can find life to be considerably tougher. Without a Beijing *hùkǒu* families can not send their children to junior or senior high school in the city, and so children are forced to live in their hometowns with grandparents while their parents work in the city. They are limited to buying a single property, and that is only after five consecutive years of tax payments, after which they can also buy a single car, and they have the daily inconveniences of having to return to their hometowns for such things as passports or ID replacements if lost. Out-of-town teenagers are also less likely to get into country's best universities (most of which are in Beijing), given that entrance marks are lowered for Beijing *hùkǒu* holders.

There are ways for non-Beijingers to get their hands on a local *hùkǒu*, but it's getting harder and harder. RMB500,000 (US$80,400) is no longer guaranteed to buy one on the black market, and with recent scandals of dual *hùkǒu* holders, there are expected crackdowns on this kind of corruption. The legal gambles include graduating in a university and getting a state job that has a *hùkǒu* quota, investing RMB30 million (US$4.8 million) in the city for two consecutive years, demonstrating high-level technical skills, studying abroad for more than a year and earning a post-graduate degree, marrying a Beijing resident, or possibly getting one through a company. All have their catches and none is a straightforward sure thing.

The government understands that the *hùkǒu* system creates disparity and limits the flow of skilled people into the cities. It's already beginning to implement ways that make it easier for talented people to establish themselves in the city. Yet, to completely remove the *hùkǒu* system would be to risk a stampede of people into an already overcrowded city, and possible destruction of many rural areas, so there are no real signs of it being truly abolished just yet.

been able to secure an official role within China just yet, then this is a good way to start, as it's the only visa that doesn't require some kind of business invitation or proof of relationship. Tourist visas can be valid for up to one year, with a maximum of 90 days' stay before you need to head out of the country to renew it. The amount of time you'll be able to get on a tourist visa will vary depending on your country's current relationship with China.

Hopefully, this should allow you more than enough time to secure a job or study option. Once you do find a company or school that is willing to take you on, you'll need to arrange for your new visa type before you start. The government is particularly watchful these days of those on tourist visas. It's illegal to work or study while on one, and if you get caught doing so, you'll face fines and/or deportation. If you need to change your L visa to another type, such as an M or Z visa, you may or may not be able to do this in Beijing. Laws regarding this issue constantly change, however, so if you have any problems when trying to do this, contact a knowledgeable visa services office.

If you plan to make trips out of China while on your tourist visa, remember to get a multiple-entry rather than a single-entry visa, otherwise you'll find yourself with an extended holiday when you try to get back in. And don't forget, Macau and Hong Kong are classified as international travel and will use up your number of entries.

Visitor Visa–F (访问, Fǎngwèn)

Previously the Business Visa, the F visa is now for those are coming for short-term non-business trips (less than six months). Reasons for this can include involvement in an educational program, a cultural exchange, or a sports event.

It's illegal to work while on this visa, and if you do, you'll also risk being fined and deported, never to return to China again.

Work Visa–Z1 and Z2 (工作, Gōngzuò)

The Work visa is primarily for those who come to China for employment, and also for their families. The Z1 visa is for foreign workers working here for more than 90 days, while the Z2 visa is issued to those here for 90 days or less). The Z visa is about the best kind of visa that most expats could hope for, but it's not always easy to get. In reality this visa's lifespan is very brief, lasting only 30 days. In this period you need to apply for your Residency Permit. Residency gives you the freedom to come and go from the country basically as often or as little as you please for the life of your permit.

If you're the primary person applying for the visa, you first need to meet several criteria: You must be at least 24 years of age and no older than 60; you must have a bachelor's degree; and you must have two years of post-graduation work experience.

With all the paperwork required and the constant law changes, many expats find procuring a Z visa and Residency Permit downright challenging. If you find yourself in this situation, be sure to speak to a visa service first. Somehow there are often ways to get around things.

Business Visa–M (贸易, màoyì)

This visa has replaced the old F visa, and is specifically for those coming to China for commercial and trade purposes, such as a trade show or short-term business project. You will need to have an official invitation letter from the company that you will be working for or with.

Study Visa–X1 and X2 (学习, xuéxí)

The X visas are issued to students coming to China for more than 180 days (X1) and those coming for up to 180 days (X2). X1 visas require you to do a health check upon arrival and apply for the Residency Permit within 30 days of arriving.

Journalist Visa–J1/J2 (记者, jìzhě)

If you plan to come to Beijing to work as a foreign correspondent you'll need the right visa. If it's just a short assignment it will be a J2 visa, but if it's for a permanent position, you'll need a J1 visa, which lasts for one year. Your family will also be eligible for this visa. If you apply for a J1 visa, like the Z visa, you'll also have to apply for a Residency Permit within 30 days of arrival and get the health check. Those who will work as other staff members of a news agency or the like should apply for a Z visa.

Journalists, unsurprisingly, come under a lot of scrutiny in mainland China, so rather than draw attention to themselves, many local magazines and newspapers hire people under the classification of "foreign expert" and arrange a Z visa instead. In most cases, this is fine and doesn't cause any problems. Doing legitimate foreign correspondent work without approval, however, is highly illegal.

It can sometimes be a pain to have a J visa stamped in your passport, particularly if you're out of Beijing, visiting smaller towns and checking into the hotels there. It's like waving a red flag. Ultimately, it does, however, provide you with more protection if you are legitimately approved to be in the country and writing about it. Even if you write negatively, you'll have a bit of leeway. Without the visa, you have no protection should you write anything that ruffles the government's feathers.

Other Visas

In addition to these, there are several other visas available, including:

Residence Visa (D—定居, dìngjū)—A rare visa, bestowed on someone who has spent more than 10 years in China, has contributed in some significant way to the country, and who wants to live here permanently. It's most typically given to people who have married a Chinese citizen.

Transit Visa (C—乘务, chéngwù)—Especially for crewmembers on international aviation, navigation and land transportation missions and their accompanying family members.

Transfer Visa (G—过境, guòjìng)—Given to people who need to transfer through Beijing but not qualifying for or needing more time than permitted with the 72-hour visa-free period.

Family Reunion Visa (Q1/Q2—探亲, tànqīn)—The Q1 visa is for family members of Chinese citizens or permanent residents, while the Q2 visa is for foreigners visiting Chinese citizens and permanent residents short-term. The Q visa allows up to 180 days of stay. Q1 holders must apply for residency within 30 days of arrival. When applying for a Q visa, you will need a letter of invitation as well as documents verifying your relationship.

Talent Visa (R1/R2—人才, réncái)—The R1 visa is for highly skilled foreign professionals or those whose skills are urgently needed by China, and those who will be residing in China for a long time. The R2 visa is for similar professionals who need to be here for only a short time. R1 visa holders must apply for residency within 30 days of arrival.

Personal Matters Visa (S—私人, sīrén)—Given to foreigners coming to China for private activities, such as marriage, inheritance, adoption, or medical services.

Residency Permit and Health Check

The Residency Permit needs to be applied for within 30 days for all people carrying a Z, X, or J visa, aged 16 and over. To get your hands on this prized document, you'll need to go through a fairly detailed process first. The paperwork required for each visa type is slightly different, but in all cases you'll need to take an official health check.

The health check can actually be done from your home country, but it's recommended that you do it in Beijing at the Beijing International Travel Healthcare Center in Haidian. It's an interesting but slightly baffling procedure. Within just about an hour you zip around to about 10 different examination rooms, having such things as a blood pressure test, an eye test, an ECG, a chest X-ray, and a blood test (testing for HIV and syphilis). Not every health condition will rule you out from the permit, but conditions such as HIV will.

Some simple tips for the day: 1) Fast for at least 12 hours before you go; 2) Do not try to go in an orderly manner from room 1 to 10; just look for an empty door without a queue and go in. All that matters is that all boxes are checked off; and 3) Keep the receipt (*fāpiào*) for both this and the cab fare, as your company should be able to reimburse you. The exam will cost around RMB650.

If you change jobs, your Residence Permit can be changed. To do this, you'll need a release letter from your former company to give to your new company. If you're leaving your old company on bad terms, however, and they refuse to give you the letter, you will most likely need to take a trip down to Hong Kong or back home to process the visa from scratch from outside of China.

VISA EXTENSIONS AND TRANSFERS

One thing you don't want to do in Beijing is overstay your visa. Doing so can result in not only a hefty fine of RMB500 per day (up to a maximum of RMB10,000) but also potential expulsion from the country. For this reason, always be mindful of when that expiry date is approaching. Plan ahead for renewals or extensions as the processing time can take anything from 7 to 15 working days, depending on the visa type. Rather than leaving it to the last moment, contact a visa agency, such as Beijing Expat Service Center (www.beijingesc.com) or Beijing LEEO (www.cn-visa.com) at least one month in advance and you should find you'll have more options for how to renew your visa from within Beijing.

In the past, L visas could be extended twice from within Beijing, but as of July 1, 2013, that changed to once only and for a maximum period of 30 days. So now, after your first extension, you need to take an international trip somewhere to renew your visa. One possible L visa that you may want to consider is a one-year, multi-entry L visa. This allows you to stay for periods of up to 90 days each time before needing to cross the border to renew it. This doesn't come cheaply, however. Expect to pay around RMB7,000 and ensure you still have 17 days left on your existing visa.

For those who do intend to hang around in China in a somewhat dubiously legal capacity, a border dash every two to three months becomes a part of Beijing life. Common places to do this include Mongolia, Vietnam, or Hong Kong. If it's only an exit stamp you need, an alternative is to take a trip down to the beachside city of Xiamen in Fujian, then take a ferry over to Jinmen Island, which is part of Taiwan.

Constant visa runs add up, however. A return flight to Hong Kong, for example, typically costs around RMB2,500-4,000.

Renewing other visa types can be much simpler if you have the support of your company or institution. In some cases, such as for students wanting to extend a one-year visa, a letter of explanation will be required. For many of these visas the extension can be done from within Beijing, but will at times call for an international trip.

Transfers from one visa type to another, such as from an M to a Z1, can sometimes be done in Beijing, but often you may need to leave the country. When you do find yourself in this situation, contact the China Travel Service (CTS) in Hong Kong, Beijing Expat Service Center, or another visa service for help.

If you're changing jobs in Beijing and maintain the same visa category, such as a Z1 to a Z1, you should be able to stay in Beijing to do it—as long as you can a get a release letter from the company that you're leaving. Legally the company is required to give you the release letter, but if you left on bad terms and for some reason the release letter isn't coming your way, then you may need to make time for a trip to Hong Kong or a holiday back home and apply for a new visa from scratch.

Be careful about quitting your job if you don't have another job to immediately go to. Legally your current company is required to cancel your work permit when you finish up, and if your paperwork isn't being transferred to another company and you're not transferring visas, you'll be required to leave the country within seven days.

REGISTER WHEN YOU ARRIVE

Everyone, unless staying in a hotel, hostel, or university dorm, must register for a Temporary Residence Permit at their local Public Security Bureau (PSB) (*pàichūsuǒ*) within 24 hours. This includes even family members who are just on holiday, staying with you for a week. Registering can be a fairly quick, painless process, but not always. The manner in which the police will deal with you varies from police station to police station and officer to officer. Stations in student-dense areas, such as Wudaokou, are notoriously battle scarred and harsher on transgressors. The first time you register in a new location it's best to take your landlord or at least a local friend with you. Make sure you have your passport and your lease. If you don't register, you can be fined RMB500 per day. You need to then re-register every time you change address, job, or visa; marry; or come back into the country after a holiday. Door knocks by police checking up on registrations are quite rare, but they do happen, particularly in known expat areas. Failure to register within 24 hours can result in a fine of up to RMB2,000.

Moving with Children

It might seem daunting taking your children out of their home environment and moving them to a city as foreign as Beijing, but in most cases the culture shock is felt more by you than the kids. Beijing is perhaps the safest city in China, and kids can roam freely within their housing communities playing with their multitude of friends. Children are extremely welcome in China and there are few places they can't go. As shocking as it sounds, they can usually even go down to your local shop and buy your beer for you. There are lots of public parks, but these are likely to be a little different from the ones back home. They're more manicured and there are fewer places to kick

EXPAT PROFILE: PARENTING IN ANOTHER CULTURE

Having lived in China for more than five years, Kathryn is a parenting consultant and co-author of the book *Slurping Soup and Other Confusions*. This unique resource (www.slurpingsoup.com) provides actual stories by children living internationally (also known as third-culture kids) as well as activities that help them cope with the challenges.

WHY DID YOU CREATE THE BOOK?

We recognized that there was no resource for children and the transitions that they experience living internationally, so we decided to put the book together. It can be used anywhere in the world. It's really about parents helping their children with the typical transitions, whether they're moving to a place or leaving a place or living in a foreign place—adapting to the new place, understanding who they are, where they belong, and cultural differences as well as friendship change.

WHAT ARE THE BIGGEST CHANGES THEY EXPERIENCE?

It's certainly the cultural and language changes, the food, and people wanting to touch them and stare at them. They're just very curious about Western kids, and not only the blonde-haired, blue-eyed ones. They want to have their photo taken with them. This is a big thing for

little children. They've also left their friends behind.

HOW CAN PARENTS HELP THEIR KIDS BEFORE THEY MOVE?

Definitely get a copy of *Slurping Soup*! This is targeted for 3- to 12-year-olds. It can be difficult for these kids to voice their anxiety. The book provides a catalyst for the crucial discussions you need to have, and can be a window for the parent into the child's thoughts. Apart from the book, it's really listening to children's concerns and listening to their excitement, too. It's also about problem solving any of those concerns together; for example, getting them to come up with ideas for what to do about missing their friends.

Explore information about Beijing together, and see the move as positive and as an adventure. However, one thing some parents do is to just try to keep their children feeling positive the whole time and fail to recognize that it's also okay also to be anxious. You need to give your children permission to talk about their concerns.

It's also important for parents to recognize that each of their children may respond differently to the transition—one might sail along easily but for the other it might be really challenging. They need

DAILY LIFE

a ball around or swing a baseball bat with complete freedom. Typical park equipment, such as slides, swings, and see-saws are also generally not to be found in public places. A growing number of shopping malls, however, are starting to include play gyms, and there are various amusement parks around town, including the best one, Happy Valley, by the East Fourth Ring Road; Shijingshan Amusement Park out on the western side of Line 1; and Chaoyang Park.

The toy industry here is patchy. There are lots of cheap, breakable toys. However, the range is improving and broadening. If you want international-style toys, however, you'll pay the same price or probably way more than you do at home. Lego has become a fashionable toy, puzzles are highly loved, and computer games can be bought (mostly pirated) all over the city. If your kids like board games, bring these from home. For

to, again, really listen, and make sure they get one-on-one time with each child.

WHAT ARE YOUR TIPS FOR WHEN FAMILIES ARRIVE IN THE COUNTRY?
Look at guidebooks together and get out there and explore the city together. There is such a rich diversity of historic cultural sites to see. That's a wonderful bonding activity for the family, and this is so important because the family needs to provide a safe haven in the midst of all the changes.

Parents should get to an Arrival Survival meeting with the International Newcomers' Network (INN)–that's a must. They'll get to meet different service agencies as well. Get on Beijing Café and Beijing Mamas email groups. And say yes to all playgroups and invites for at least the first few months till you establish a circle of friends, and that might include attending the PTA meetings at your child's school.

Continue to really listen, rather than just saying "It's going to get better." Acknowledge their concerns and anxieties, otherwise that reassurance really only says "You shouldn't feel that way." Come up with strategies with them.

WHAT'S IT LIKE TO ATTEND AN INTERNATIONAL SCHOOL?
I think the biggest difference is the cross-section of children from all over the world. This opens up their minds to cultural di-

versity. It's interesting, dynamic, stimulating. There are lots of opportunities for them to explore their interests–sports, arts, language.

WHAT ARE THE DIFFICULTIES KIDS FIND IN LOCAL SCHOOLS?
Usually it's that they're very different from the other children, so again, it's really important that parents are listening to their children because there can be times when the school does not recognize bullying. In the international schools they would, but sometimes, in local schools they don't. You can come up with stories together to create strategies for how to cope, for example: "What about this little boy, what should he do?"

WHAT SUPPORT SERVICES ARE THERE?
Help is mainly through schools, particularly the counselors at the international schools. When you're making a decision about the international school, it's really important that you find out if these services are available. The international medical centers, however, also have terrific services. *Beijing Kids* magazine (www.beijing-kids.com) is also a great resource. It has lots of interesting information targeted at parents with children of all ages, and has all the upcoming events. And both this magazine as well as *Time Out Beijing* (www.timeout.com/cn/en/beijing) do guides about schools.

sports-related equipment and toys, you can try Decathlon (www.decathlon.com.cn), of which there are several stores around the city. Baby needs are available, again, in a widening variety that matches Western tastes. Stores such as www.baby-international. com can usually cover what you need, and for cheaper prices you'll often be able to pick up no-longer needed goodies from mothers on email group Beijing Mamas (http:// groups.yahoo.com/group/Beijing_Mamas).

Kids will surely miss some of their old chums and comforts, but the rich experiences make it all worthwhile. Not only will they have the opportunity to learn one of the most widely spoken languages in the world, they'll be mixing with a truly multicultural crowd. There is little time for kids to be bored in Beijing. Beyond the school-related activities, there are also sports clubs, nearby mountains for weekend outings, and a plethora of activity groups.

Different areas of the city will provide your kids with different experiences. Up in Shunyi, where houses with gardens are standard and large international schools abound, they'll experience as Western a lifestyle as possible in the city. On the other hand, if they live closer to the CBD, they may not have a private backyard to play in, but they will enjoy a much more authentic experience.

SCHOOLING

When it comes to schooling, Beijing has the resources to offer your children, whatever age they are, a quality education. There are three main styles of education in the city—local Chinese schools, international schools, and homeschooling.

The Chinese school system still typically relies on the old rote-learning technique, and students study long and hard all day for the sake of the *gāokǎo,* the university entrance exam. It's rare for expats to send their kids to these schools, but it's not unheard of, especially in the first several years. As obvious outsiders, they may, however, occasionally experience bullying. These schools are typically run in Chinese, but the more progressive schools have a Western slant and may offer some classes in English at the primary levels.

International schools are usually the ideal option for most expats. Academic standards are high and facilities, particularly of the larger ones, are exceptional. School fees are, on the other hand, exorbitant. If you're not being brought over on a package by your company and are doing it on your own, you may find the potentially RMB200,000 or more annual school fees unmanageable. In this case, shop around and consider other options.

A third path is homeschooling. In addition to online support from your own country's services, Yahoo-based support network Beijing Homeschoolers (http://groups. yahoo.com/group/beijing_homeschoolers) and the Beijing Westside Homeschool Co-op (http://groups.yahoo.com/group/BJWestsidehomeschool) help bring together Beijing families who are educating from home.

SUPPORT

Despite the relative ease of life in Beijing for kids, bumps in the road do happen, so it's always good to make sure you're connected with supportive groups and people. Yahoo email group Beijing Mamas can link you with hundreds of expat parents who have been or who are going through the same experience as you. Members are extremely friendly and willing to answer any questions. You'll encounter everything from people asking where the local pediatric dentist is to mothers selling no-longer-needed maternity wares.

Several magazines in the city provide the latest news on everything going on in the city relating to kids. These include Beijing Kids (www.beijing-kids.com) and City Weekend Beijing Parents & Kids (www.cityweekend.com.cn).

For times when professional help is needed, English-language counseling services are available in the city, such as through the Beijing International SOS Clinic Family Counseling Center (www.internationalsos.com) and the Family Counseling Center at Beijing United Family Hospital and Clinics (http://beijing.ufh.com.cn).

Just remember; the expat community in Beijing is close and very supportive—you only have to ask and there will be people there to help you.

Moving with Pets

While humanity toward animals hasn't always contributed positively to China's reputation, things in the capital are a little different, and improving. Down in Guangzhou you might still see exotic species on the menu at a restaurant, but up here at least, turtles aside, they're rarely seen. Added to this, there is a growing love and respect for canine companions in Beijing. Dogs are a ubiquitous part of life here, and while the older crew still love their Pekinese, the younger, wealthier crowd like to flaunt their new, pedigree breeds.

Wherever you plan to live in the municipality, every dog is required by law to be registered. There are two different sets of regulations, however, depending on where you live. If you plan to live within Beijing's eight major districts, roughly inside the Fifth Ring Road, you'll face a few restrictions on the number and type of dogs you can own. In an effort to improve public health and safety, the government has introduced a one-dog policy—one home, one dog—and a height restriction on dogs living within these areas. Outside the Fifth Ring, almost anything goes.

BRINGING YOUR PET TO BEIJING

A genuine move to China might not be complete without bringing Fido or Fluffy along with you. Fortunately China is quite accommodating with dogs and cats. If you're hoping to bring in a bird, hamster, or other species, however, these will be classified as exotic animals and not pets, and getting them into the country requires a whole lot more trouble and expense.

The actual process for bringing your cat or dog to Beijing can be a little complicated, and involves both your own government's requirements to get your pet out of the country and then China's to get your pet in. Specialist pet-moving companies can help manage this process for you, particularly if you're tight with time. You can, however, do this yourself with a little bit of planning and scheduling. The key is to start preparing for your pet's move two to four months in advance.

The first step is to get your pet microchipped (ISO-approved chips are recommended) if you haven't already done so. Why is this so important? By moving to Beijing, you're moving your pet to a country where rabies is a serious problem. The disease exists in every province, and even in the capital city. Europe and a growing number of countries will not recognize any rabies vaccinations done prior to microchipping, so, even though China does not require a pet to be chipped, when it comes time to leave China, you may face a problem. By microchipping now before you leave home, you'll be giving your pet a unique number and starting a verifiable record of their health.

Regarding the paperwork, you will need to have your visa in order. Various information sources will specify that this needs to be a Z visa, but in many cases a pet can be brought in on any visa, so you will need to confirm your own eligibility. One point without variation, however, is the stipulation of one pet per passport (not to be confused with one dog per household for registration). You will also need to get the following three documents in order:

• Official certification of recent rabies vaccination
• An official certificate to export your pet from your current country
• A health certificate or letter prepared by your vet in your current country attesting to your pet's health

The exact process varies from country to country and can change at a moment's notice, so it's best to check with your local vet first and your own country's relevant export/import department, such as the USDA in the United States. Most vets will have the forms on hand and can advise you on the overall process. The forms can also be downloaded from the department websites. In the United States the form is called APHIS 7001.

Your pet will need to have the rabies shot at least 30 days prior to entry and not a day over one year. Once your pet has been vaccinated and your vet has signed off on the forms, you must send them off to your local state office (e.g., USDA). For a small fee, they will then give you the official export certificate and rabies vaccination certificate. Importantly, keep these documents handy on you at all times throughout your passage to Beijing, especially if you're coming in via Tianjin or transport hubs other than Beijing Capital International Airport. Some forms of transport require local registration documents, but they'll be more lenient if you have these at hand.

One thing to prepare ahead of time is your pet's travel crate. It not only needs to fit the legal requirements of the airline but your pet should also be comfortable with it. Make sure you give your pet a few weeks to become familiar with the crate so that it doesn't create yet another fear on top of this already scary experience.

Now contact your airline to arrange the actual flight of your pet. Sites like www. PetTravel.com and Globy Pet Relocation (www.globypetrelo.com) can provide you with advice on how to make sure your pet makes the trip as comfortably and safely as possible. This may seem like the simplest part, but there are catches to be aware of. A particular one includes knowing whether or not your pet will be checked in as excess luggage (relatively easy for you to handle yourself) or as cargo. The latter can be difficult to coordinate, as it may involve you and your pet arriving at different times. A pet relocation company can help manage transport of your pets as cargo.

When you land, your pet will need to be quarantined for a mandatory 7-30 days in Beijing, courtesy of the Entry/Exit Quarantine Inspection Bureau. The length of time is dependent on where you pet is entering from. Those entering China from the

United States or Canada are subject to 30 days of quarantine, while those entering from rabies-free or rabies-controlled nations, such as Australia, New Zealand, Hong Kong, Japan, Singapore, Taiwan, or United Kingdom, are subject to seven days quarantine. You can feel assured that while quarantine won't be the Ritz, your pet will be treated humanely and with necessary care. There are no exceptions, however, even if your pet is elderly or has a pre-existing health condition; quarantine is essential and you will not be allowed to visit bearing bouquets of beef jerky. Only in some extreme cases will you be able to take your pet home early.

While the quarantine center is well managed, it's recommended you also have your pet fully vaccinated for kennel cough (bordetella) at least two weeks before you depart. Also book them in for an appointment at such places as ICVS or Doctors Beck & Stone in Beijing to have a general checkup as soon as they're released.

REGISTERING YOUR DOG

Now that your pet is in Beijing, you'll need to procure two more documents: the Beijing Animal Health and Immunity Certificate (a red book recording vaccinations) and a registration license (cats are off the hook for registration). The ICVS can help you out with the former, and your neighborhood police station (*pàichūsuǒ*) will arrange the latter. Ask your property management office for the correct police station for your area.

If you're going to be living inside the Fifth Ring, as most expats do, you'll be limited to just one dog, which, when fully grown, can be no taller than 35 centimeters (13.8 inches) from ground to shoulder. If you plan to bring in an additional dog, you'll need to find a friend who is willing to have it registered under their address. And if the dog is large, the address will need to be outside the Fifth Ring. Ultimately, in some circumstances, it may be easier for you to simply make the choice to live out beyond the city center. Once your dog is registered in the appropriate area, however, you can take it into any region of the city.

If your dog isn't registered or is large and living inside the Fifth Ring, it will be classified as a stray and could be rounded up by the government. Size and registration enforcements tend to be stepped up before all major holidays, and this may not be done by a uniformed police officer but a local neighborhood watch representative. Registration period is officially May 1, every year; however you need to register your dog as soon as you arrive.

When you go to the police station to register, you may need to take the following:

- Your dog (although not all police stations require this)
- Two one-inch passport-size photos of your dog—head shots taken front on
- Your own original ID (passport, residency permit, foreign household registration document, etc.)
- Your lease
- Permission from your local neighborhood housing committee (*jūwěihuì*—there's one in every neighborhood)
- Cash—initial registration within the eight districts is RMB1,000 (if you can provide proof that your dog is neutered/spayed you may be able to get up to a 50 percent discount); annual renewal is RMB500

It will take about a month to get the license, so until then, be sure to keep the receipt (*fāpiào*) handy at all times.

If you plan to live in Shunyi, which sits astride the Fifth Ring Road, or in a residential compound technically outside the Fifth Ring, confirm with the local Public Security Bureau to see if you can definitely register your large or additional dogs there.

LIFESTYLES FOR PETS

Life for pets in Beijing is reasonably pleasant, but unless you're planning to locate to Shunyi where housing rather than apartments is the norm, they might feel a little hemmed in by city life. Dogs are not allowed in public parks, but there are several dog parks and random grassy areas around the city where dogs can romp and play. Just be sure to check the parks' cleanliness—some of them can be a little sketchy at times. One great way to get your pet—and you—familiar with Beijing is to sign them up for some training with Doggy Thoughts (http://chinadogtraining.com), a professional obedience training center, which offers training not only for your dog, but also for you.

Throughout your time here, the government requires that your pet has annual rabies vaccinations. When you do this it is essential that you go only to official vaccination facilities displaying the gold government vaccinations plaque. Black-market drugs, bought from pet shops and the like, are typically fake, out of date, or have been stored in conditions that render them useless. Despite it being the law, compliance with vaccinations is staggeringly low, with about only 1 in 10 dogs in the city vaccinated. If you plan to take your pet outside your front door, it is critical it is protected. Infected dogs do not typically foam at the mouth like Cujo, so it's unlikely you'll know which dogs to steer clear of.

Another factor is the weather. Temperatures can soar up to around 40°C (104°F) in the summer and down to -10°C (14°F) in winter. So if you plan to bring in a malamute or a sphinx, it might feel a little unhappy at either extreme.

BUYING AND ADOPTING PETS IN BEIJING

There is no shortage of pets that run, fly, swim, and slither for sale in Beijing, but you should definitely approach with caution. Breeding is an extremely immature industry here, and all it takes to call oneself a breeder is to put two pets together and produce offspring. There are no regulations, no animal-protection laws, and breeding is predominantly about making money, which in China means churning out animals as quickly as possible. The result of this is that females are forced to reproduce too frequently and litters are removed from their mothers too early—creating poor nutrition on all sides. The gene pool of "pure" breeds is also a little too pure, and the inbreeding leaves animals riddled with complications for the rest of their lives. If you purchase a new puppy, kitten, or guinea pig from one of the local breeders, pet shops, or open markets, you'll quite likely find that it has problems, becomes sick, and perhaps even dies within a week or two.

A more strongly recommended option is to adopt. There are various shelters and rescue groups, such as Beijing Human and Animal Environmental Education Center (www.animalschina.org), the Little Adoption Shop (http://lingyangxiaopu.com), and Beijing Cat (www.beijingcat.org), which adopt or foster out pets. Not only are the

© SHANNON AITKEN

DAILY LIFE

the favorite pets of Beijing's elderly residents

pets often already neutered and vaccinated, they're often free and almost always completely healthy.

Once you have a new dog, it's advised to educate both him or her and your family about behavior. And don't forget about your *āyí*. Unfortunately, awareness of dog behavior and humane training methods is almost nonexistent in China. So if your *āyí* is going to be spending any time at all with your beloved pooch, then it's worth involving her in the program as well. Doggy Thoughts runs group classes as well as private training in people's homes, in either Chinese or English, and considers *āyí* a crucial part of this process.

TAKING YOUR PET OUT OF CHINA

While it might feel like you have enough on your hands with just moving *to* China, when it comes to animals, you must also be aware up front of what it takes to get them out again. Microchipping is only one of the steps. Given China's rabies status, many countries are particularly strict when it comes to allowing in pets that have been in China for any amount of time. This may require a process of rabies vaccinations and testing that begins many months ahead of your exiting China, and then varying levels of quarantine when your pet does land in the next destination. If you're planning to go to Australia or New Zealand, then things get really difficult. Neither of these countries has rabies and they want to make sure things stay that way. Animals coming from China must first reside in an approved intermediary country or region, such as the United States, Hong Kong, Japan, Singapore, or Hawaii, for six months, and then once they do land in Australia or New Zealand, they're then required to stay in quarantine for 10-30 days. There are no exceptions, even for disability-assistance dogs.

Just remember that every country is different, and laws are liable to change at a moment's notice. At the time of writing, getting your dog or cat back into the continental United States or Canada was a breeze. Outside of the required rabies vaccination

GUIDELINES FOR EXPORTING YOUR PET OUT OF BEIJING

COUNTRY	DIFFICULTY	PROCESS TIME NEEDED PRE-EXIT	PROCESS TIME NEEDED UPON ARRIVAL
U.S. (excluding Hawaii), Canada	Easy	30 days	–

Requirements for export from Beijing:
- Rabies vaccination 30 days to 12 months before entry
- No quarantine
- No microchipping
- No rabies antibody titer testing

Hong Kong	Moderate	30 days	4 months

Requirements for export from Beijing:
- Microchipping
- No rabies antibody titer test
- 4 months quarantine in Hong Kong

European Union	Moderate	4 months	0-6 months

Requirements for export from Beijing:
- Rabies vaccination
- Rabies antibody titer test (done at least 30 days after rabies vaccination). The titer test must be done at least 3 months and no more than 6 months before leaving China.
- Microchipping and/or tattooing
- No quarantine if above points are completed and clear. The United Kingdom, however, requires pets from China to be quarantined for 6 months.

Australia, New Zealand, Taiwan	Difficult	4 months plus 6 months in intermediary country	10-180 days

Requirements for export from Beijing:
- Microchipping
- Rabies and other vaccinations
- Rabies antibody titer test (done at least 30 days after rabies vaccination). The titer test must be done at least 3 months and no more than 6 months before leaving China.
- Six months in an intermediary country. Animals coming from China must first reside in an approved intermediary country or region, such as the United States, Hong Kong, Japan, Singapore, or Hawaii, for six months.
- Up to 30 days quarantine in destination country

(at least 30 days before and up to 12 months before entry), no microchipping, rabies antibody titer testing, or quarantine was needed, if the other requirements had been met. But expect this to change.

In general, start contacting your vet six months before you leave China. The exit process is not that complicated, just time dependent. Four months out, a rabies vaccination; 30 days later, a rabies antibody titer test; and then, finally, one month out, arrange remaining exit documents. Unfortunately, not everyone has the luxury of six months notice. This is where services such as ICVS and pet relocation companies can really step in and help, taking care of the process even after you've left. If your pet does require the rabies antibody titer test, bear in mind that this blood sample needs to be sent to an approved laboratory—none of which are in China. So this requires immediate export after the test is done. But as this is a blood product, it's not that easy to do. Pet relocation companies, such as Globy Pet Relocation China or WorldCare Pet Transport, are experienced with handling this matter and can help.

For more information on your next country, contact the relevant export/import body, such as the USDA; the Australian Department of Agriculture, Fisheries, and Forestry; or Biosecurity New Zealand.

Documents

Rabies Vaccination Certificate: Thirty days to 12 months before your departure, go to a valid animal vaccination facility—such as ICVS, Doctors Beck & Stone, or Guan Shang Animal Hospital—and have your pet vaccinated against rabies. After this your pet will be issued with the official Beijing Animal Health and Immunity Certificate (a red book).

Health Examination and Health Inspection Certificate: Not more than seven days before your departure, take your pet for a checkup at the Entry/Exit Quarantine Inspection Bureau animal hospital (Guan Shang Animal Hospital). There are no appointments, so get there first thing in the morning. Take your pet's red book with valid vaccinations, your passport, and about RMB800. Following this, you'll be given a Beijing International Companion Animal Health Inspection Certificate. The certificate usually takes two business days to be issued and is valid for seven days. Try to get there early to avoid the lines, and take a Chinese speaker if possible. Office hours are weekdays 9am-11:30am and 1:30pm-4:30pm (closed on public and national holidays).

Animal Health Certificate for Exit: Once you have the health inspection certificate, take it up to the second floor of the hospital and exchange it for the exit permit, also called the Animal Health Certificate for Exit. This will take about two days to process and cost about RMB100.

What to Take

If you'd moved to Beijing 10 years ago, you might have packed a little heavier, but today there is little you can't get here. Sometimes it might take a bit of searching, or be much more expensive than what you'd pay back home, but it is here. Fortunately, once you do locate it, chances are you can have it delivered directly to your door, often for free.

If you are planning on shipping a household of goods to Beijing, be warned that this can be an expensive and complicated process. If you are not a diplomatic worker or do not have one-year residency and working permits, then your shipment will be dutiable. In addition to this, you also must be in China before your goods are shipped out of your home country, so you'll need to be able to live for at least one month without whatever is in the cargo. One option, to give you more time to get your bearings, is to move into one of the many serviced apartments around the city. They're definitely not the cheapest option, but they will give you a comfortable, well-appointed, often family-friendly place in which to find your feet.

CLOTHES

Straight up, one major issue for expats in Beijing is clothing size. If you're particularly tall or broad, you're going to have difficulties. Though the northern Chinese are taller than their southern siblings, and while the average modern Chinese girth is increasing rapidly, the fashion industry is yet to reflect this. Therefore, expats of larger proportions typically need to resort to tailor-made attire or hold out for shopping holidays at home.

It's next to impossible to provide a realistic conversion between Chinese and American clothing sizes. From label to label, sizing swings like a pendulum in a hurricane. It's no surprise to squeeze into a Chinese extra-extra-large and come to the conclusion that, in your mind, it's really a medium. Generally, you can assume that if you're in the extra-large or above group back home, then you will have limited choices here, so come prepared. Note that China uses centimeters, so if you're used to inches, you'll need to convert.

Definitely keep in mind winter wear, from top to toe. There is no shortage of affordable winter wear here for the average size, but again, if you're of a larger build, comfortable winter boots, long johns, and trousers can be hard to come by. Many a well-built expat, especially unsuspecting ones from warmer regions, will find themselves suddenly poorly clad in Beijing's icy winters.

A particular garment category you may want to bring with you is underwear. Going by what's on the shelves, fat-bottomed girls (and boys) seemingly don't exist in China. If you typically reach for a women's size 8 at home, then here you'll need an extra large, and even that might be a tad cutting. Up top, things are no better. The alphabet of Chinese bras doesn't exceed a D cup, so well-equipped ladies must bring a good supply of bras.

As far as style goes, it's hit and miss, but things are improving at an eye-watering pace. Just five years ago, you would have needed to be satisfied with poor-quality knock-offs, high-waisted jeans, and unruly embellishments. Today, however, the choice of international brands is constantly diversifying. Zara, Gap, H&M, Adidas, Puma, Marc Jacobs, and Miu Miu are all here. Unfortunately, smaller brands are still not strongly supported. Instead, big, well-established labels are king. So if your preference is for niche names, you may need to look at online options. As for price, cheap clothes come by the container load in Beijing, but the quality definitely equates with the price. If you want genuine Western clothing, then expect to pay for it, plus some.

SHOES

Shoes can also present a challenge—for quality, style, and size. While the clothing industry has come a long way, unfortunately Beijing's shoe industry is still just shuffling along. Some expats simply resort to restocking when they make trips back home. If your feet are wide or above a size 8.5/42, you'll find rocky love here. That's not to say it's impossible to find larger shoes. There are a few specialty stores around the city, such as along Zhangzizhong Lu in Dongcheng district, and in 3.3 shopping mall in Sanlitun. There are also cobblers, such as Lao Yu at Bespoke Leather Shoes on Gulou Dongdajie, who have become accustomed to Westerners' big feet. Lao Yu can whip you up a good pair of leather dress shoes in four to five weeks for around RMB1,200-1,800.

If you have children and you like them in well-fitted shoes, this is another item to put on the to-pack list. Quality children's shoes, such as school shoes, are next to impossible to find. If you know before you leave which school your child will be going to go to, it's worth checking in ahead of time about the school shoe requirements. Shoe-store attendants aren't particularly podiatry savvy, and they'll be more interested in selling you a popular shoe than one that supports your child's foot.

ELECTRONICS

Beijing is not Hong Kong. Electronic items are not particularly cheap, and if they are you have to question their quality, genuineness, and potential lifespan. Because of this many people do actually try to buy electronics outside the country and bring them in. The government has become hip to this tactic, however, and will try to impose a duty on them as you bring them in the gates. Particularly under their watchful eyes are items like iPhones and computers. A simple tip: When coming into and exiting from China, make sure everything is out of its packaging and has an "already used" feeling about it.

Electronics markets in Beijing abound. The camera market in Wukesong in the west is a photographer's paradise, and the digital labyrinths of Zhongguancun up in the city's northwest are a computer geek's dream. For something more mentally manageable, however, there is Buy Now Hui in Chaoyang. Both *zhēn de* (genuine) and *jiǎ de* (fake) items are to be found at all of these places, so be careful, shop around first, and bargain hard. Even better, hide your foreign face around a corner and get a local friend to purchase on your behalf.

One item to leave at home is your DVD player. Nearly all DVDs in Beijing are pirated, that's no secret, and while they are surprisingly good quality, they quite often just won't work on a high-performance foreign player. Pick up a cheap, local-brand DVD player at the supermarket when you do your first grocery shopping.

FURNITURE AND HOUSEHOLD ITEMS

Unless you're partial to your own furniture, there's no need to bring it with you. Rental apartments in Beijing come fully furnished. While not always to your taste, the furniture should be in reasonable condition, and, if not, you can usually ask your landlord to change it, or instead use it as a bargaining point to reduce your rent. For whatever you don't have, homeware stores, such as Ikea and Muji, are here. Alternatively, it's easy to pick up a good deal from expats selling off their wares before they leave. Email group Beijing Café and website The Beijinger are good places to look.

If you're a keen cook you may want to bring your specialty gadgets with you. Microwaves, toasters, blenders, juicers, and even espresso machines can all readily be bought from markets, supermarkets, and department stores, but particular items relating to Western-style cooking often cannot. Kitchen stores that focus on Western products are starting to make a showing, so Western knives, pots and pans, hand mixers, cake pans, and so on are available, but items such as slow cookers, sandwich makers, and health grills can be almost impossible to come by. If you do plan to transport items with complex mechanical components, such as stand mixers, verify first how to ship them correctly so as not to damage them.

SHIPPING OPTIONS

Your shipping options will vary greatly depending on if you are moving everything you own or just a few items, and then whether or not you need the complete services

THINGS TO BRING FROM HOME

While you can buy most lifestyle products in Beijing, sometimes it can be difficult to find specialty items that you're used to having back at home. Some of these are simply not available at all, or they are, but just inconvenient, highly overpriced, limited in range or variety, or the quality is below the par that you know. Surveying a diverse group of expats, I found the main complaints were large sizes, quality children's products, and specialty ingredients. If you live in Chaoyang or Dongcheng, you'll have fewer issues, but the farther you get from these two districts, the fewer Western comforts you'll be able to get your hands on. One tip: Get to know websites such as Amazon China (www.amazon.cn), http://tmall.com, www.jd.com, and, if you've really got it going on and are willing to risk fake items, Taobao (www.taobao.com). View them through web browser Google Chrome, which can translate the whole page, and your world in China will open up. They're much cheaper, and most deliver free of charge within a day or two.

CLOTHING

- Large bras
- Large or broad shoes, for adults or kids
- Large pantyhose
- Large socks
- Large thermal wear
- Large underpants (women's size 10 and above)
- Quality children's clothes
- Quality, fitted children's shoes; e.g., school shoes
- Swimwear, especially bikinis

PERSONAL ITEMS AND BEAUTY PRODUCTS

- Clinique makeup
- Children's soap (paraben free)
- Deodorant
- Eye makeup remover
- Hair-removal products, such as wax strips
- Hairspray
- Quality facial cream free of whitening products
- Quality shaving cream
- Self-tanning products
- Shampoo and conditioner for blonde hair
- Specialty toothpastes; e.g., children's toothpaste with fluoride

of a relocation company or just a moving company. A good relocation company should be able to make your move to Beijing as stress-free as possible. They can offer such things as storage and housing and school finding. Moving companies simply get your things from A to B.

Regardless of the kind of company you choose, be sure to get several quotes and check their reputations. If you are moving a household of goods, the relocation team will probably come to your house to calculate the quote. If the quantity of goods that you're moving is small, however, and you know the volume, you can easily get online quotations. For extra peace of mind, you should also check that they are members of international quality-assurance groups FIDI and FAIM.

For most of us, air freight is just too expensive for anything more than just a few bulky items, so shipping by sea is usually the transport method of choice. From here,

DAILY LIFE

- Tampons
- Tinted facial creams

HEALTH ITEMS

- Advil pain reliever
- Alka-Seltzer antacid
- Antihistamines
- Benadryl antihistamine
- Children's pain reliever
- Cold medicine
- Contact lenses and solutions
- Diaper rash medication
- Epaderm and other creams for skin conditions
- Gaviscon heartburn relief
- NyQuil cold medicine
- Pepto-Bismol nausea reliever and antidiarrheal
- Tylenol pain reliever
- Vitamins and supplements

FOOD

- Agave
- Baby formula
- Bouillon cubes

- Buttermilk powder
- Food coloring
- Gravy mix
- Gluten-free products
- Lactose-free products
- Maple syrup
- Pecans
- Pop-Tarts
- Specialty baking products and spices
- Sugar-free products
- Velveeta

OTHER

- Crayons
- Footballs
- Greetings cards
- Home-schooling materials
- Magazines
- Nintendo 3DS games
- Non-Disney kids' DVDs; e.g., *Blues Clues, Veggie Tales*
- Quality children's dictionary
- Quality stationery
- Toys

there are three primary ways to send your things, which you'll need to be familiar with: full container load (FCL), less than container load (LCL), and groupage (GPG). FCL is the most expensive as it involves you using an entire container all to yourself. In an LCL shipment, your possessions are loaded into a wooden crate and shipped simultaneously with other crates headed to the same destination. GPG is the most cost-efficient method. In this, your possessions will share a container with those of other people going to the same destination. Given that other people may not be moving at the same time as you, this may increase the total transit time of your goods. Times for sea shipping will vary greatly, but you should generally allow 5-8 weeks, including customs.

The company you choose will need to be China savvy. Rules and regulations change here like the wind in spring, so if your company isn't on top of things you may find your goods are gathering dust at a port at home or in China. Companies such as Links

Moving Beijing, Santa Fe, Allied Pickfords, and Asian Tigers provide reputable services and have Beijing offices, and so are up-to-date with China's laws and exactly what you need to do to clear customs quickly.

CUSTOMS

Customs screenings at Beijing Capital International Airport are seemingly almost nonexistent. When you pick up your suitcase from the baggage carousel, you typically walk straight from the terminal with absolutely no further interruption. While, strictly speaking, it's not allowed, many expats even sneak through a favorite cheese or a nice piece of cured meat in their luggage. Importing a shipment of personal effects, however, is another beast entirely. If your possessions are coming in as freight, then there is a considerable amount of paperwork to be completed so that they'll clear customs and not attract a duty. One requirement you will need to fulfill is that your residency and work permits have no less than one year of validity on them. This can take a bit of coordinating, so make sure your relocation or moving company communicates with your new HR manager in Beijing to ensure dates match up.

Even if you tick all the boxes, your imports may still be liable for duty. To avoid this, remove everything from its packaging, don't stock up too much on any particular item, and report that it's used and for personal use only. Duty rates will vary and change, but typical values range from 10 percent for furniture up to 50 percent for any kind of alcohol. Wine is a favorite target of the government, so it's advised to leave any cases of your favorite reds or whites at home.

Other items that are put under scrutiny include religious literature, anti-Communist literature, and banned publications. Pornography is also a big no-no, as are gambling items, such as poker chips. If customs officials suspect contraband content, they can confiscate the item for checking, and may or may not ever return it. Additionally, while piracy and counterfeiting is a blatant source of business within China's borders, taking it in or out of the country can result in confiscation and/or fines.

If you have professional equipment that you need to import, China encourages the use of an ATA Carnet, for temporary admission of the items. To arrange this, contact the ATA Carnet Headquarters in New York (www.uscib.org).

Finally, another goods category to bear in mind is antiques. If you plan to pick up a few historic Chinese items to take home as souvenirs, you may not get them past the gates. China is very protective of its historical artifacts. Items produced before 1795 are prohibited from being exported, and items produced between 1795 and 1949 can be exported but require approval by the Relics Control Committee. Anything produced after 1949 can be exported.

HOUSING CONSIDERATIONS

It's possible that you might be worried you'll be living in a shoebox when you move to Beijing. But not to fear, Beijing is not like Hong Kong or Tokyo. Despite the population, architects here are a long way from adopting micro-loft or capsule-style accommodations. Apartments are quite spacious, and if you're lucky enough to be moving into a house, then you'll feel even more comfortable.

Building standards, however, vary dramatically. Workmanship and craftsmanship are not words that often pop up when talking about buildings in Beijing, and property developers often like to cut corners to save money. Don't let the gloss of a shiny new coat of paint blind you—sometimes the newer buildings can be fraught with problems while the older ones can be sturdier and more comfortable, though a little dim and closed in. Admittedly, the newer apartments can be free of the cockroaches and bugs that sometimes plague the very old ones.

Actually finding a place that suits your needs isn't always easy, and the people you need to deal with can be crooked and cunning. I've personally dealt with three different landlords and every one of them has been wonderful and very honorable. But I have no shortage of friends who have outrageous experiences to share. Unfortunately,

© SHANNON AITKEN

to even get to the landlords you first have to get past the agents, and unfortunately many of them here have earned their profession a very bad reputation. Buying is another headache altogether. It is possible, but there are some hurdles you'll have to jump first. Generally, the key to finding a happy home in Beijing is to take your time, consult a few different companies, and create a meticulous paper trail of everything you do.

Housing Options

There are various housing styles to suit your taste or needs, and the price point will obviously swing dramatically. On average, university students in share accommodation situations can expect to spend around RMB1,500-3,000 per person per month; couples living in a two-bedroom apartment in the inner-city are likely to be spending RMB6,000-15,000 per month, while a family living in a three-bedroom house with a yard will face rent to the likes of RMB35,000-65,000 per month.

CHINESE-STYLE APARTMENTS

A typical Chinese-style apartment is compartmentalized, so the kitchen, bedrooms, bathroom, and sometimes even the living room are individual rooms. These apartments can be a little dark and gloomy, with small windows that are set back by built-in balconies. They almost never have ovens, and only two-burner stoves, but will most likely come with a microwave, rice cooker, and fridge.

Furniture doesn't always match Western tastes, and though the landlord might have just refurbished it, it may in your eyes look like something from the hands of a colorblind scrapbooker. The bed is likely to be rock hard, and don't be surprised if there are extra pieces of furniture or objects taking over your abode—landlords frequently see their apartments as personal storage space.

Many older apartments in the inner city have only six floors and no elevator. Buildings with seven floors or more will have an elevator, but you'll need to check if this is 24 hours or not. Take relief in the fact that you may not be as high up as you think you are. In Chinese, the number four (四, *si*) sounds like "death" (死, *si*), so people avoid it at all costs. Your building, therefore, will probably be short of a 4th, 14th, and 24th floor, and possibly even a 13th for good measure.

Stairwells and corridors are not only dark but often become the storage

© SHANNON AITKEN

typical local apartment community

facilities for leftover bed frames, wardrobes, and everything else people don't want to throw away (and people really don't like throwing things away here).

Most of these apartments have government-controlled central heating, which usually gets turned on around November 15 and off around March 15. Because of their solidness, however, these apartments are usually cool in summer and warm in winter.

One of the nice things about living in the older complexes is that the communities of people that live there tend to be friendlier and more personable. The more expensive and modern the complex you live in, the fewer interesting interactions you're likely to have with your neighbors.

Security tends to be almost nonexistent in these kinds of compounds, and while it's unlikely you'll have to worry about things inside your apartment, downstairs your bicycle, scooter, and the battery in your scooter are easy pickings.

LUXURY APARTMENT COMPLEXES

If you'd prefer to live with the comforts you're accustomed to—Western-style decorations, spacious and bright living areas, functioning appliances—then these apartments are available across the city. Many come with their own gym and possibly a swimming pool, have large and well-tended gardens, and have their own convenience shops or restaurants. Most of the inner city apartments are already furnished, so if you prefer to furnish them yourself it will possibly require some negotiation.

These complexes tend to be filled with expats, especially in Chaoyang district, and many are staffed with English-speaking workers, so life can be much easier if you don't speak any Chinese. Just a handful of the more popular ones include MOMA and Seasons Park in Dongzhimen, Central Park and Millennium Residences in the Central Business District, Embassy House near the Sanlitun embassy area, and Beijing Riviera apartments in Shunyi.

For those wanting top-notch security, DRCs (Diplomatic Residence Compounds) are a popular choice. The newer DRC properties, such as Liangmaqiao DRC near the American embassy, tend to be more luxurious and offer more facilities, but are also more expensive than the older properties.

SERVICED ACCOMMODATIONS

If your reason for considering this option is having your bed made and your dishes washed, then you might just consider hiring an *āyí* (housekeeper), which will cost you around RMB50-70 for a couple of hours of cleaning or around RMB3,000 per month for a full-time English-speaking nanny who will cook, clean, and baby-sit.

Serviced accommodations are a good option, however, if you're only after short-term accommodations (up to six months) and your company is footing the bill. And again there are plenty of options to consider, including the Ascot Raffles City in Dongzhimen, Fraser Suites CBD in Guomao, and Four Points by Sheraton up in Zhongguancun. Website www.bj-servicedapartments.com can give you a quick introduction to many of the serviced apartments in the city.

If your budget is tight, consider staying in one of the local Chinese hotels. The Green Tree Inn inside Fangjia 46 near Lama Temple, for example, is a simple choice in a very cool location.

HOUSES AND VILLAS

If you're going to be living in a house—what is often referred to here as a villa—then it's highly likely you'll be living up in the northeast of the city in Shunyi district. This is the destination of expat families brought to Beijing thanks to a company arrangement, and with children who will attend one of the many international schools in the area. These estates, such as Yosemite Villas and Beijing Riviera Villas, are basically gated communities. Homes are complete with such things as rumpus rooms, gardens, and driveways. If you're not coming under the wing of a company, however, then you may well find the rent in these modes of abode exorbitant and out of reach.

Unlike apartments in the inner city, around 40 percent of villas are unfurnished. This is intentional, as the landlords here know that many expats come with a household of personal goods.

While you and your children will enjoy life in a wonderfully international neighborhood, if you want an immersive Chinese experience these are not the places to do it.

SÌHÉYUÀN AND PÍNGFÁNG

These are the homes of old Beijing, and are almost exclusively inside the Second Ring Road. A *sìhéyuàn* is a traditional form of northern Chinese architecture. It basically comprises four buildings facing inwards around a courtyard or garden. The north building facing south was traditionally for the head of the household, the two side buildings for the children, and then the south building, called the "opposite house" (and the name of one of Beijing's most popular boutique hotels and bar locations), was for the servants or where the family would gather to relax. Traditionally, every section of the *sìhéyuàn* is separated, so you may need to cross the courtyard to get to the kitchen or bathroom.

Many *sìhéyuàn* are owned by well-to-do government officials, but they're also now extremely popular with expats. Landlords have cottoned on to this fact, and so rent for one in good condition is unlikely to fall below RMB15,000 per month.

A *píngfáng* is basically a *sìhéyuàn* that has been subdivided into "studios," although many of them are more higgledy-piggledy and don't conform to the same principles as the fêng shui-driven *sìhéyuàn*. These are great for singles who want to mix with the locals. If you like to keep to yourself, however, *píngfáng* are not for you. Your lovely neighbors will no doubt come knocking on your door at random hours with offerings of dumplings and fruit.

The quality of *píngfáng* varies greatly. Many have been renovated and are fully self-contained. A *píngfáng* of around 40 square meters will possibly rent for around RMB3,000-4,000 per month. If you don't mind squeezing into something smaller, though, and if using the local public toilets and bathhouses is within your comfort zone, then you might even find a place for around RMB500 per month.

Sìhéyuàn and *píngfáng* are what give Beijing's *hútòng* their characteristics—dark and quiet alleyways with groups of neighbors huddling around tables to play *májiàng* (Mandarin for mahjong) or Chinese checkers. The pluses for living in them include the local experience in vibrant, colorful neighborhoods, as well as a potentially impressive entertaining space in summer. Away from major roads they can be wonderful retreats from the bustling city just outside, but they do come with their own set of drawbacks. Free of general traffic noises, they do have their own collection of quaint pedestrian sounds. They can be freezing cold in winter (especially if your bathroom is not attached to the living area), and heating them can effectively push your utility costs up by around RMB1,000 per month. In summer they're more prone to mosquitos and spiders (small web ones), and, being right at street level, they're incredibly dusty. Further, if you don't speak any Chinese, you may find managing problems a little tedious.

HOMESTAYS

If you're truly dedicated to immersing yourself in Chinese language and culture, then you can easily find yourself a local family to live with. Expat websites, such as The Beijinger (www.thebeijinger.com), have dedicated listings for homestays, and universities and private language schools will often provide services to set you up with a family. Many Chinese families want to rent a room out to a foreigner in exchange for the foreigner speaking to their child in English. Don't expect that the rent is going to be cheaper, though. It's still business.

UNIVERSITY DORMS

Dormitories vary widely from university to university in both price and quality. There are more local-style dormitories and then there are international ones. While many students prefer the immersion and convenience of campus life, many opt for off-campus lifestyles, believing that prices can work out to be roughly the same. If you're unsure, it might be worth trying a semester in a dorm. It's much easier to change your dorm situation than move from an apartment that has your name on a lease, and it's a good way to get to know your classmates.

Renting a Home

If you're coming over with the help of your company, chances are everything will be packaged nicely and you'll be guided to a home of your choice with relative ease and transparency. In this case you'll probably be handled by a reputable agent who understands your needs and deals with your transition in an international manner. If you're doing it on your own, however, and dealing with Beijing's local real estate agents, beware. The waters are muddy and filled with sharks that have a taste for ignorant expats. While it's certainly not difficult to locate a home by yourself, it's worth clueing yourself up first. It's also probably not the best time for you to flex your Mandarin muscles, even if you feel relatively fluent. Get a local friend, classmate, or colleague if you can, and take him or her out for dinner in exchange for chaperoning you through the rental process.

QUESTIONS TO ASK YOURSELF BEFORE YOU CONTACT AN AGENT
Where Do I Want to Live?

First up, decide which part of the city you want to live in. To do this, put commute time at the top of the list of factors to consider. Beijing might look well covered by public transport and roads, but traffic is constantly heavy and the distances are vast.

If you have a car, scout out areas that are by the ring roads or expressways, and if

HOUSING TERMS

ENGLISH	CHINESE	PINYIN
Bank	银行	yínháng
Contract/lease	合同	hétong
Deposit	押金	yājīn
Electricity bill	电费	diàn fèi
Gas bill	煤气费	méiqì fèi
Heating bill	暖气费	nuǎnqì fèi
Landlord	房东	fángdōng
Passport	护照	hùzhào
Pay	交	jiāo
Photocopy	复印	fùyìn
Police station	派出所	pàichūsuǒ
Real estate agent	房屋中介	fángwū zhōngjiè
Real estate agent fee	中介费	zhōngjiè fèi
Register	登记	dēngjì
Rent	房租	fángzū
Sign your name	签字	qiānzì
Tenant	房客	fángkè
Visa	签证	qiānzhèng
Water bill	水费	shuǐ fèi

you're going to rely on public transport, look for locations around subway hubs, particularly those where multiple lines intersect. Try to get as close as possible to the subway station, because in winter that 20-minute walk every morning in -10°C (14°F) temperatures can become a real low point of your day.

The bus network is extraordinarily extensive and cheap, but unless you have an affinity for sardines, it's probably not best to make this your first transport option.

Many of the major international offices are located somewhere in the central area of Chaoyang district. Most of the international schools, however, are up in Shunyi in the north. To get from the Central Business District to Shunyi during rush hour can easily take an hour, whether you go by subway or drive. The subways are also always jampacked at this time, so you can also forget that quiet morning read on the way to work. To work out roughly how much time a subway commute will take you, calculate three minutes for every station and add 15 minutes for any interchange. For example, a journey from Wudaokou station (Line 13) to Salitun, which is by Tuanjiehu station

(Line 10), is going to take around 50 minutes and cost RMB2. The same journey in a taxi could potentially take much longer and will cost around RMB50-60.

Some families prefer to live up close to their children's school and have the adults do the commuting to the CBD. Others have found it easier to base themselves in the CBD and have the kids commute happily with their friends on the private buses supplied by the schools, which ferry them safely from door to door. This system usually works well during the week. If your kids are involved in extracurricular activities, which they probably will be if at these schools, this may not work out so well, particularly on weekends when the buses don't run. You should contact your child's school to find out which housing complexes in the city its buses service.

If you're coming to Beijing to study, it's likely you'll spend a lot of your time up around Haidian district, possibly near either Wudaokou subway station for universities such as Beijing Culture & Language University (BCLU) or Tsinghua University, or Jishuitan subway station if you're headed to Beijing Normal University. If you like to go out at night, there is a lot around Wudaokou, but nowhere near as much as what's down in Gulou, Sanlitun, or Guomao, and regular treks down here can be off-putting. As a compromise, you could consider Xizhimen. This is a major transport hub and puts you halfway between school and a fulfilling social life.

After you've pinned down the general area, it's time to do some surveillance work and zone in on a few actual communities or residential compounds. Visit the area, see what facilities are there, and walk into the compounds. Get a feel for which ones suit you.

How Much Can I Afford?

When you begin a lease in Beijing you need to consider not only the monthly rent, but how much you're going to have to fork out up front. Rent here is typically paid on a quarterly basis, sometimes half yearly, and on the odd occasion yearly. When you sign a lease, it's fairly standard to pay the equivalent of one or two months' rent as a deposit, plus three months' rent in advance. So, on a RMB6,000 per month lease, that's at least RMB24,000 you would need to have ready to go when you sign. In some cases, particularly for apartments under RMB5,000, you may also have to pay an additional finder's fee to the agent, which is also the equivalent of one month's rent.

What Exactly Do I Want?

Clarify ahead of time exactly what you want in your home, and write it all down. This will hopefully minimize wild goose chases with the real estate agent. Specify how many bedrooms you want (be explicit if you want a studio or a one-bedroom, as these are typically lumped together), if you want it furnished or unfurnished (unfurnished can be difficult to come by in inner-city apartments, though not impossible), whether you want it in a complex with a gym or a garden, and so forth.

Apartments in Beijing are generally described first by their overall area in square meters, so this may be something to consider as well. An average RMB6,000 per month apartment around Dongzhimen, for example, should be about 80 square meters (861 square feet). Apartments down in expat hub Fulicheng (just south of Guomao) are a little larger. Average two-bedroom apartments here are about 120 square meters (1,292 square feet) and cost around RMB7,500. Occasionally, agents will factor in the foyer area outside an apartment, making it seem larger than it actually is.

HOW TO FIND A HOME

There are various ways to try to find a home in Beijing. You can use one of the several international-level real estate agents and relocation specialists, such as Bel & Well Property International (www.bel-property.com.cn) and Super Estate (www.superestate. cn). These companies are staffed by multicultural teams, specialize in dealing with foreigners, and understand the importance of service. You can also use local real estate agents, but these are another thing altogether. They will typically tell you anything to get you to a place, will show you fake photos, and when you discover it's a different place than the one you've been promised tell you that that other one was already taken (even though the ad may have been posted only hours earlier). They will most likely be in a different ballpark entirely when it comes to understanding what you want. The fun thing, though, is that many of them will drive you on the back of their scooter from place to place.

Many foreigners use sites such as The Beijinger or eChinacities (www.echinacities. com) to find an apartment. But be warned; these sites are swarming with local agents, and even though they will tell you they're not agents, they probably are. While expat sites are extremely helpful, the prices of apartments on them are usually heavily inflated, and the range is largely limited to the city's expat hot spot area.

© SHANNON AITKEN

popular local real estate agent Wo Ai Wo Jia

If you really want to tap into the massive range of homes that are out there across the entire city, local sites such as Wuwoo (www.wuwoo.com), Home Link (http://beijing.homelink. com.cn), Wo Ai Wo Jia (www.5i5j. com), and Ganji (http://bj.ganji.com) will get you there. Apart from Wuwoo, they are in Chinese only, but you can get around this by looking at the webpages via web browser Google Chrome and translating. When it comes to connecting with them, however, you're still going to need to be able to communicate in Chinese. And again be warned; probably 80-90 percent of the photos you see are not going to be genuine.

Another option is to keep your eye on postings on Yahoo group Beijing Café, or even post your own request there. Postings here are word-of-mouth, so it's most likely it will be a happy tenant leaving a good experience and wanting to help their landlord find a replacement.

Finally, there are usually real estate agent offices located close to every housing community. If you've found an area and a compound that you like, chances are there is an office on the block that covers that property. English is unlikely to be a strength in these offices. If the complex has a property management office, you might also want to go in and ask directly if they know of anything going. If you're lucky you can bypass the agent altogether and deal directly with the landlord.

REAL ESTATE AGENTS

Now that you're armed with some clear requirements, it's time to meet the real estate agents or deal directly with a landlord. Again, if you're going to be working with an international company, then things should be straightforward. At times some people worry that their agent has a biased relationship toward certain properties, and absolutely, this can be true. Some housing companies may "encourage" realtors to push their properties, especially during low seasons. An agent having good *guānxi* (relationships) with certain complexes isn't always a bad thing, however, and at times it can work in your favor. Agents with the best *guānxi* are likely to be the first to hear about new properties on the market. If you believe your agent hasn't done a wide enough search for you, ask them to look farther afield, and if they resist and give excuses, then simply find another one.

You need to be a little more savvy with local agents, and it's wise to use several agents in the same area rather than just one, as they often cover the same properties but quote different prices. Make sure you give them your list of specifications up front, and make it clear you do not want to look at anything that doesn't fit that criteria. Agents have been known to take people to several terrible apartments first and then finally to one that by comparison looks amazing. If you're dealing with them over the Internet, be clear that they need to send you genuine photos only.

While local real estate agents will do almost anything to suck you in, it's worth remembering that they are on your side, in the end. They do need your business, so when it comes to negotiating with a stubborn landlord, they can in fact be your friend. The inflated prices don't always come from them but rather the hungry landlords.

Unless you're dealing directly with a landlord, it's also possible that a finder's fee may arise. In Beijing this is typically equal to one month's rent. Though not a rule, in practice for properties over RMB5,000 a month the finders fee will be paid for by the landlord, and for properties under RMB5,000 by the tenant. This varies greatly from landlord to landlord, and is something that can be discussed when bargaining. If you're only considering renting places for around RMB4,500-5,000, then it might be worth calculating what you'll really be spending on average with the extra finder's fee factored in, and then look at better, slightly more expensive apartments for which that won't be a cost.

BARGAINING

If possible try to arrange a time when the landlord is there at the same time as the real estate agent. Real estate agents will work at virtually any time you need, so evenings can be easiest to connect with the landlord if they're working. Having the landlord present will make the bargaining process easier and more transparent, and will also

RENTING CHECKLIST

When you go to inspect a house or apartment, make sure you check a few critical parts.

Air conditioners: Do these work? Are they in the rooms you'll be in most?

Hot water: Is it really hot enough? Is it gas or electric? How many minutes before it runs out? Can you shower comfortably in that time? Is the hot water at all the faucets? For example, it might not be available at the bathroom sink.

Kitchen: Do all the burners on the stove work? Most apartments will have appliances such as a fridge, a microwave, and maybe a rice cooker. Check if they work. (There is unlikely to be an oven, but countertop options are cheap and easy to buy.)

Drinking water: What do you use for drinking water? Some high-end apartments and houses will have drinkable filtered tap water; however, often you may need to have a water dispenser and to purchase bottled water. Bottled water usually costs RMB10-22 per 19-liter (5-gallon) bottle. Watsons Water has an English-language service and is generally well regarded. Unfortunately, bottled water has been known to be fake, so try to purchase from a reputable seller. As this is something that's hard to be sure of, website www.myhealthbeijing.com suggests that the best option is to buy a quality-brand water filter, such as Aquasana, to install in your kitchen.

Bathroom: Most places will have a Western toilet, but if you're moving into a very old building it could be a squat toilet, and if you're in a *sìhéyuàn* or *píngfáng*, you might not have your own toilet at all. How well does the toilet flush, and can it handle "comprehensive" toilet use? Many toilets in Beijing don't cope even with

toilet paper, especially those in *hútòng* residences, and rather than flush it, you'll need to put it in a garbage bin. What's the water pressure like in the shower, and are there any signs of leaks between your apartment and the one above or below?

Bedroom: Again, does it have an air conditioner? What is the bed like? (Places like Ikea make a killing on selling mattress toppers to expats.)

Entertainment: Does it have a TV and DVD player? If not, these can usually be worked into your contract without too much bargaining.

Flyscreens: For anything from the ground floor to about the sixth floor, mosquitos can be a problem. Check for absent or unusually holey screens.

Telephone and Internet: Are these connected? The landlord should be responsible for covering the costs of having the facilities, such as the sockets, but you will mostly likely bear the costs of having them switched on. Normally the landlord or agent can help you set up your services. You usually don't have a choice which company you use, as given companies are assigned to particular complexes, but you should be able to select the speed of your Internet connection.

Outstanding bills: Be clear about the credit or debt existing on the water, gas, and electricity meters before you move in. Record the amounts/numbers on each meter and note down any payments made or credits given. If there are 100 units of credit on your electricity when you move in, for example, your landlord should deduct the value of this from your final settlement when you move out.

Fuse boxes and utility meters: Find out where all of these are and how to read and use them. Occasionally there is more than one fuse box, one inside your abode and another hidden outside in some obscure location. When you run out of electricity you will need to know where these are to flip the main switch back on.

Storage: Landlords here are notorious for using their rental apartments as their personal storage facilities. If they won't let you get rid of some of the unwanted furniture, try to negotiate the rent down in accordance with the reduced space.

Stairs and corridors: Are these clear of clutter and does the lighting work? Stairwell lights are often sound activated, so stamp your foot or cough like a local to see if it turns on.

Security: This varies greatly depending on where you are and what kind of property you're in. It's very unusual to hear of homes being broken into, but you should check what security systems are in place and that your door locks properly. If you're on the ground floor you should ask for bars to be installed if they're not already. Modern complexes will usually have security guards at the gate and require electronic cards or keys to get in. Regardless, strangers still do get in. Bolt your doors properly at night when sleeping. (I used to just use the simple switch that locked the handle, without bolting the door, and one morning I awoke to find some cigarette ash on my living room floor. My neighbors later told me that people use credit cards to slide open doors that aren't locked properly.) Check if there is a secure location to store your bike, scooter, or car.

Property management office: Find out if there is one and where it is on the property. Make yourself aware of what they can do for you. If you're expecting a large package in the post it may end up here rather than in your mailbox, and you'll need to be proactive about finding out if it's arrived or not—they're not going to leave a note under your door. They can often help with general maintenance problems inside and outside your apartment, lost keys, and occasionally utility bills.

The compound in general: Is the whole apartment complex and its grounds well maintained? You might not see bugs on the day you visit, but if the compound has an unusual amount of trash lying around, these might become a problem when you move in.

Around the block: What kinds of supermarkets, convenience stores, or restaurants are there in your hood?

The landlord or landlady: Is he or she transparent and trustworthy? For some landlords and landladies, renting out a home is pure under-the-table business, and they will not hesitate to throw you under the bus or out of the apartment if they can swing a better deal. Try to protect yourself by running some security checks, such as: Are they willing to arrange *fāpiào* (receipts) for every rental payment if you need them? Will they come with you to register at the police station? Are they using a standard contract from a rental agency (rather than something they've doctored up)? Will they give you a photocopy of their ID card? Is rent to be paid via a bank transfer or cash only? You can get some owners that seem to bomb with each of these questions but who are still good people, but you should try to size up their trustworthiness regardless.

give you the opportunity to suss out what kind of person you're going to be dealing with long-term.

You can usually assume that the rent advertised will not be the final price, and there is almost always room for bargaining. Again, the amount you can talk it down will vary from place to place. For properties for around RMB3,000-10,000 per month, you might try to bargain them down by RMB100-500 per month, and more for more expensive properties. Things to soften the landlord with are that you're clean and quiet, and most importantly, that you always pay your rent on time. When a landlord refuses to come down in price, you can try to have other things altered or added to the apartment—new furniture, an air conditioner installed in the bedroom, and so on. Landlords are often more willing to add things to an apartment than feel the loss of hard cash every month. Point out things that are inadequate or bad quality. Factors such as the poor direction of the building can even be worth raising. This won't work if you're in the prized north building of a *sìhéyuàn,* but generally eastward- or westward-facing buildings aren't highly desired.

Some apartments can be highly popular, and you'll find several people turning up at the same time to inspect it. One technique to improve your likelihood of securing the place is to always carry a wad of cash on you to inspections. It can be hard for a landlord to resist instant cash on their investment.

If you feel you might be here for a long time, it might be worth bargaining on the lease term. Between leases, rent can easily jump by 10-40 percent. By bargaining for a two-year lease you'll probably not only get a lower rent rate, but you'll avoid the jump in price when the year end rolls around. I have one friend who found a fantastic apartment in Sanlitun and was able to secure an impressively low price fixed for five years, with the guarantee that he would personally renovate the kitchen.

UTILITIES AND OTHER FEES

With so many new and old properties in Beijing, the utility systems and how to pay for them vary from place to place, so this is something to make sure you're clear about with your landlord or agent right at the start.

In most cases the landlord is responsible for the maintenance fees, the heating, and possibly the club fees if relevant. The rest is up to you. Setting up broadband and phone lines will sometimes be covered by the landlord, and sometimes by the tenant. Again it's a case-by-case basis and another potential negotiating point. Occasionally other fees crop up, but these are generally quite small. Bear in mind, if you're planning to live in a house, a *píngfáng,* a *sìhéyuàn,* or a modern apartment without the government's central heating, your electricity bills will jump through the roof in winter.

Some bills are paid monthly at the bank, but most often electricity, water, and gas are pre-paid on smart cards, and it's up to you to monitor and recharge these.

LEASES

If you're going through an international realtor or an expat-focused Chinese company then you may get an English version of the lease. The Chinese lease, however, is the only legal version, so make sure that what it says on the English version is what it says on the Chinese one. Get a third party to help you look over it. Be sure to check what

an example of a Beijing water bill

you will need to pay for. Generally the landlord is responsible for the general wear and tear of the property and its goods, and the tenant for any breakages.

Most leases are fixed for one year, or for two years with corporate accounts. It's hard to get short-term leases, but not impossible. Again this is a point of negotiation. If you want a short-term lease, look on sites such as The Beijinger for people who want someone to take over their lease. Alternatively, serviced apartments can definitely support you for short stays.

The lease will specify the rent and deposit, as well as dates of payment. Be sure to check how much notice you need to give without penalty. For two-year contracts, it can often be established that the first year is fixed and the second year is flexible in that there is no penalty for moving out early. On this note, don't forget to check with your company (if they are bringing you over) if there are any penalties for leaving early.

Make sure you complete an inventory of the furniture and property's condition to avoid disputes when you move out. Technically you can take the landlord to the local People's Court to try to settle a dispute if needed, but this is often more trouble than it's worth.

Another thing to clear up before you sign the lease is whether or not the landlord can provide you with *fāpiào* (invoices) for your rent. If you're in a corporate agreement this will be essential. But even if you're employed locally, you can often use the *fāpiào* to offset your own tax. Landlords don't always like to do this as it increases the tax, so if they refuse, you can try to bargain down the rent by about 5 percent.

MOVING IN AND REGISTERING

First, you must register at your local *pàichūsuǒ* (police station or PSB) within 24 hours of moving into a new home. If you don't, you risk copping a significant fine and possibly more serious penalties. Landlords or agents should accompany you, and it will definitely make the process easier if they do. Again, they may resist doing this for tax reasons. The agent will need to sort this out with the landlord, but regardless, this is something you can't avoid. You'll need the registration slip from the *pàichūsuǒ* when it's time to renew your visa and when your company applies for your working permit. Police often do random door knocks (especially around student areas) asking for proof of registration.

When you register, you need to do it at an assigned *pàichūsuǒ*, and these aren't always the most obvious stations, so, if your landlord or agent isn't accompanying you, ask one of them to explain exactly which one it is. Registering is free and generally quick and easy. You'll need to take your lease, passport (with visa), and photocopies of the photo page of your passport, the page with the most recent entry stamp, and the current visa. Some police may also require a copy of your landlord's ID card or a copy of the deed for the first registration. In the future, you will also need to re-register within 24 hours of any changes to your visas, passport, or address, and technically any time you leave the country for a holiday or business trip. This is much easier. You can go alone, and you only need to take your lease, passport, and the photocopies. In some areas, the police are lenient and friendly. Expat-weary police officers in foreigner hot spots such as Wudaokou, however, are known for being less tolerant and forgiving, so be particularly sure to register on time in these areas. If you're even a day late with registering you may be forced to write a letter of apology stating how stupid you were for not knowing the law and that you promise to never do it again.

Finally, be warned: When you move in, your new home will probably be a mess, especially if a local family has been living there before you. The kitchen will be covered in oil and it's unlikely that any cleaning will have been done. This is standard. Book an *āyí* to get in a day ahead of you and give it a good once over.

Buying

Buying property in Beijing used to be all but impossible for foreigners, but laws have relaxed considerably, and now, other than the hassle of paperwork, there are no particular restrictions that apply to foreigners. If all the requirements are complied with, a purchase can be completed within as little as two weeks. That said, laws do change overnight, so it will be important for you to deal with a real estate agent who is highly experienced and on top of the game, even if your partner is Chinese.

First, you can forget about owning anything for the first year. Foreigners are required to have studied or worked in the country for at least one year, and to have paid taxes for that period of time. You can take holidays out of the country during this period, but that will be deducted (calculated by your entries and exits at customs) from your total time. As a foreigner you're actually in a better position than Chinese people from other regions of China, who need to wait for five years before buying property in Beijing.

Beijing is not exactly the place to make money through property. Like many Chinese, you are limited to one property per family, and it's to be used as your place to dwell only. This is one of the rules the government has introduced to quell inflation. If you already have a property in Beijing and marry someone who also has a property, there is no penalty and you won't be required to relinquish it. Some couples have been known to divorce in order to buy a second property, then remarry after the deal has gone through, but the government is also trying to crack down on such behavior.

Property prices in Beijing have been on the rise for years now, and there is little sign of things changing. Prices are typically quoted in *rénmínbì* (RMB) per square meter, and anything inside the expat areas is going to take a big fat bite out of your bank account. An apartment in the Chateau Regency building in Lido in the northeast, for example, averages at RMB32,000 per square meter. So a three-bedroom 285-square-meter (3,067-square-foot) apartment there will tie you down for about RMB9,120,000 (US$1,436,286); an older-style 50-square-meter (538-square-foot) apartment near Zhongguancun may cost you RMB48,113 per square meter or a total of RMB2,549,989 (US$401,605).

CHOOSING A HOME

When you buy a home in Beijing, you must choose between a secondhand property and a new one. In order to curb speculation and prevent people from simply buying homes and selling them off a year or two later for profit, the government imposes heavy taxes on the sale of homes less than five years old, excluding the initial purchase of a brand-new property. If the property is older than five years, the taxes ease up.

Besides the reduced taxes, there are other reasons why brand-new (first owner) homes are cheaper. These are typically completely undecorated. It's highly likely they'll just be cement boxes without even paint on the walls. You will need to completely outfit it yourself. Given the rate of construction and buying, it's also likely that your home-to-be won't be finished for another year or two, so you'll be taking a gamble as to what it will finally look like and what the quality of the property management will be.

If your budget is limited to local services and you're unsure as to which part of the city you want to buy in, say you're deciding between Sanyuanqiao in the northeast and Chongwenmen in the southeast, then you may need to use two different real estate agents, as they tend to localize. On the other hand, if you have the budget for multi-million *rénmínbì* properties, you'll be able to use more international-level companies that can provide a comprehensive city-wide service for you.

PAPERWORK

The Chinese love paperwork, and when it comes to property buying they revel. Over the course of a property purchase a forest worth of documents will pass through your hands. First up you'll need to have your passport translated into Chinese and notarized. You'll also need a certificate from the Public Security Bureau verifying that you've been in China for one year to work or study. From here you can get the approval to purchase a property, which your agent should be able to help you with. After this, it's time to pay the taxes, a process that involves taking a number and getting in line. The better agents will help you with this.

In addition to the paperwork you personally have to put together, the seller also needs to provide various documents. These include a state land use certificate, a construction land planning certificate, a construction project planning certificate, a construction project commencing certificate, and a sales certificate.

Make sure you check the authenticity of all paperwork and that the seller has the legal right to sell the property. It's recommended that you engage a reputable lawyer to do this.

When it comes time to get the deed changed to your name, this is another harrowing waiting game. Expect to sit in a cacophonous hall for hours upon end, waiting for your number to be called. If all the paperwork you've brought with you is in order, you'll need to come back in a few days to collect the deed, though the wait this time will be a little briefer.

LAND RIGHTS

After you have bought a property, you may have the deed for it, but the land is only on loan. For residential buildings the land has a term of 70 years, for office developments its 50 years, and for entertainment or retail properties it's 40 years. If you take over a property, the period of time is transferred to you, not renewed. So if the previous owner had it for 10 years, you now have it for 60.

This is not an issue that many people seem to be worried about, however. The law is too new to have had an impact yet, and many speculate that in most cases it will just be renewed when the time comes, probably with some kind of tax or fee attached.

DOWN PAYMENTS AND MORTGAGES

Deposits are typically around 25-50 percent of the purchase price, and commissions around 1-3 percent of the purchase price. To keep your agent on task to the very end, it's advisable to hold off on paying the entire commission until the deal is completely finalized.

You can use your own bank back home or a local bank to take out a mortgage. While local banks don't have the pre-approval process, their interest rates can be much higher than what you'll be able to get in your own country. If you do need to use a Chinese bank, however, Citibank and HSBC are often successful options for foreigners, and mortgages can usually be done in U.S. dollars, Hong Kong dollars, or RMB. Your employer or your real estate agent may also have an existing relationship with a given bank, which is also worth investigating.

MOVING IN

Once you have finalized the payments as agreed and have the deed in your hands, it's time to move in. Property management fees will need to be paid, and this usually works out at RMB2-5 per square meter. Finally, ensure all the utilities have also been changed over into your name. That's it! Enjoy making it your new home.

HIRING HELP

One of the luxuries of living in Beijing is that hiring a housekeeper or nanny, locally referred to as an *āyí*, is extremely affordable. Even expats on modest local salaries often splurge for a cleaner to come in to give their home a weekly once over. For busy families and business people, an *āyí* can be a lifeline, giving you some breathing space to be able to spend quality time with your family or socialize. Be warned, though—it can foster the belief that housework gets magically done by itself.

Standards vary between both extremes, and though there are many who are loving and trustworthy, you'll hear horror stories of encounters with unconventional *āyí*. We walked in on our *āyí* doing leg exercises on the couch, and a friend came home early to find his *āyí* and her entire family strewn over the couch watching TV. Concepts of clean also differ dramatically, and if you're not assertive you may discover that the cloth that has been wiping your bathroom for the last six months has also been wiping your dishes.

A good *āyí*, however, can help you out with a wealth of day-to-day issues, from cooking and cleaning to bill paying and child care. If she can speak English, all the better. Many *āyí* become loved family members whom the children hate to part with.

It's important to be aware of potential problems of hiring an *āyí*. The less respectable ones have been known to make up stories of sick family members. Their employers then give them leave with pay to go and see the person, but the *āyí* pockets the money and moves on to the next family. These kinds of problems typically occur around Chinese New Year, when people notoriously collect their annual bonus and then disappear.

Āyí often have no training at all and have essentially walked in off the street, and unscrupulous agencies will tell puff stories about the *āyí*'s training and experience. Hourly rates can vary RMB15-50. For a good full-time *āyí*, expect to pay around RMB3,000 per month, plus one month's salary as an annual bonus at Chinese New Year. Rates may be higher if she can speak English.

Entrusting your baby, let alone your home, to a stranger can be a stressful task, so take steps to feel as confident in their service as possible. The best way to find a reliable *āyí* is word of mouth. Speak to people you trust and ask for personal recommendations for *āyí* or agencies. Beijing Café or Beijing Mamas can be good places to start. When you do contact an agency or an *āyí*, always insist on getting a copy of the *āyí*'s *shēnfènzhèng* (ID) and ask to speak to her references. You should also arm yourself with a battery of probing questions.

Selecting an *āyí* needs to be treated just like any employment situation, so this means clarifying such things as holidays and national days, hours, insurance, sick leave, overtime and penalty rates, bonuses, meal times, health checks, vaccinations, and salary review period. Try to get a feel for her personality and whether or not the two of you will click.

Questions to Ask the *Āyí* Agency

- What are the fees and refund policies?
- What is the agency's process for changing *āyí* or dealing with problems? Is there a trial period?
- What training does the *āyí* have? (Look for agencies that provide regular first aid training as well as cleaning and child-care training)
- Why did she leave her last job?
- What are the salary expectations?
- How much experience does she have with other expat families, particularly those with children?
- Does she speak or read English? How well?
- How does she feel about animals?
- What days and hours is she available?

- Is she able to cook, and if so, what kinds of food can she cook?
- If you need a live-in *āyí,* find out what her personal needs are.

Training Your *Āyí*

Once you do get an *āyí,* take some time to train her to work for you in the way that you prefer. Remember, every family has different standards and ideas, so it will take her a while to adjust from her last family. If you're not happy, however, don't be afraid to speak to the agency and ask for a new *āyí.*

Be straightforward, clear, and precise with your *āyí,* but also try to be patient and compassionate. Many *āyí* come from rural areas where the culture is very different, particularly toward child rearing. You may find that they do too much for your children, picking them up without allowing them to explore for themselves, or trying to pacify them the second they make a sound. You may need to be quite firm to ensure they follow through with your own methods. If they are cooking for you, you may need to specify where you want the food bought and how you would like it cleaned and prepared. Many *āyí* shop at the local markets and may not wash fruit and vegetables as you feel they should be washed.

If your *āyí* makes a mistake, be clear about the error, but speak nicely and try save her from losing face. The odd gift here and there will also go a long way toward securing a good relationship.

Agencies

These agencies are not recommendations by the author but are those commonly used by expats in Beijing. It's strongly advised that you speak to other expats about their experience with the agencies and independently assess their qualifications and service before hiring anyone.

- **Beijing Ayi Housekeeping Service,** www.bjayi.com
- **Beijing Huijia Ayi Housekeeping Service Company,** www.beijingayiservice.com
- **Beijing Sunnyhome Information Consulting Co.,** www.bjayiservice.com
- **Ex-Pats Life Service,** www.expatslife.com
- **MerryHome,** www.merryhome.com.cn
- **Nanny Beijing,** www.nannybeijing.com

LANGUAGE AND EDUCATION

Of all cities in China, Beijing is the major hub of education. It's home to many of the country's leading schools and universities, and offers expats a banquet of programs in Chinese language as well as English-taught undergraduate and postgraduate programs. Whether you want an intensive university-based Chinese-language course or a doctorate in a specialized area, this is the city to do it.

When it comes to childhood education, the Chinese education system still favors rote-learning over independent or creative thought. Class sizes are huge and schooldays long. The various international schools, however, offer programs and methods more in line with those in the West. They also have impressive campuses and active social communities. On the downside, their fees can be prohibitive if you're not coming over on a family-friendly expat package care of your company.

© YANG JUN/123RF.COM

The Languages of Beijing

ENGLISH

English is gathering momentum in Beijing, and most young Chinese people have at least a basic ability to use it. Even after years of school-based English lessons, they continue to fork out tens of thousands of *yuán* on private English tuition. Beast-sized corporations vie with each other for clients who believe English will allow them to bypass the ladder and take the elevator to the top.

The reality, though, is that English is still not the dominant workplace language, and, unless you live in a tightly sealed bubble of expats, many people around you will not have a level of English that will allow you to deepen your friendship beyond anything other than shopping or ordering at a restaurant. Waiters, local realtors, and shop attendants will often have reasonable English, but bank tellers and police officers may not. That said, most banks, travel companies, and cell phone companies have English help lines and websites. Never assume there isn't one—always check. You'll often be surprised and find you've been wasting time waiting for a Chinese friend to help when you could have quickly solved the problem yourself over the phone or online.

If you want to work in a Chinese company, then your Chinese skills had better be in tip-top shape. Most official information comes in Chinese, and the legal version of contracts is almost always the Chinese version, not the English version. Even in international companies, you'll often find that Chinese is a prominent language in the office.

Many extremely useful websites don't have English versions, and for those that do, updating them or furnishing them with complete information rarely seems to be a top priority. Sites such as Danwei and the Marco Polo Project, which provide translations of Chinese news and other writings, can offer windows into the written Chinese world. To get around the Chinese-only sites, try tools such as web browser Google Chrome, which gives reasonable translations of entire pages, and Mandarin Spot's annotate function (http://mandarinspot.com), which gives instant word-by-word translations.

Around town, the government is trying to make improvements on signage, especially for roads and on public transport. On the subways, English is everywhere and easy to understand. Street signage, however, is a little chaotic. Chang'an Jie, for example, the main street that runs through the city center, goes by English names that include Chang'an Street, Chang'an Road, Chang'an Boulevard, Chang'an Avenue, and Long Peace Street. These attempts at translation may make you feel temporarily at ease, but that will quickly pass when you try to use them on a taxi driver or anyone else who has mediocre English abilities. It really is best to forgo English words and commit yourself to learning the Pinyin and pronunciation of street names and buildings.

Ultimately, if you have no inclination or time to learn Chinese, don't worry. Many expats successfully get by with no Chinese. If you have the means you can employ an English-speaking *āyí* (housekeeper), who'll be able to take care of a wealth of problems for you, from paying the rent to negotiating with repair workers. Beyond that, the expat community in Beijing is extremely diverse and very welcoming to new members, and there are endless opportunities to form relationships with English-speaking people.

CHINESE

Firstly, no one says "Mandarin" in Beijing. You may see the word in the names of language schools, but other than that, Mandarin is simply referred to as Chinese, or *pǔtōnghuà*. While Beijing is home to millions of migrants from all over China, from areas where the dialects differ dramatically, everyone speaks the standard dialect in the big smoke. Accents do vary, but generally it's one language. Cantonese is almost never heard, and even films coming out of Hong Kong are increasingly being made in the mainland tongue.

Though you might assume Beijing, being the capital, would be the home of pure, standard *pǔtōnghuà,* it's not exactly. The Beijing accent can be extremely strong, weighed down by an almost guttural rolling "r" sound. For example, Sanlitun would be pronounced as *sānlìtún* in standard Chinese; however, your Beijing taxi driver is more likely to drive you to a place that sounds more like "*sānlìtérr*." Some people will tell you that these "r" sounds are laden on the Beijing accent only and not part of pure Chinese—this isn't true, but Beijingers do enjoy extra lashings of them.

Chinese is a tonal language, meaning changes in pitch alone can produce differ-ent meanings. In standard Chinese there are essentially four tones plus a neutral one (much better than Cantonese, which has approximately nine tones). The first tone is a high flat tone, the second a rising tone, the third a dipping or rather a low squashed tone, and the fourth a falling tone. For example (using a pronunciation that rhymes with sung, not sang), the first-toned *tāng* (汤) means "soup"; the second-toned *táng* (糖) means "sugar"; the third-toned *tǎng* (躺) means "to lie on your back"; and the fourth-toned *tàng* (烫) means "boiling hot."

If you can discipline yourself to pay attention to and learn the tones, you'll do much better. Not only will other people understand you better and vice versa, but you may find words seem to stick more if you've put effort into learning their correct pronun-ciation. I've been to various schools, and have found that I have better recall for those words that were taught by teachers who placed emphasis on tone. It's not always easy, and you might need to come up with some creative memory techniques to help you remember the differences, but the effort is worth it if you're serious about communi-cating in Chinese.

Though learning this language can be a little difficult, it is really interesting, and gives you wonderful insight into the culture. It's not that you need a sky-high IQ to master it, you just need patience and the willingness to immerse yourself a little. Accents vary considerably, so the way words are pronounced by those around you var-ies greatly. The grammar doesn't always seem to be logical, especially when you're first starting out, and if you don't know the tones, many words can sound exactly the same. The language is also often filled with idioms, set phrases, and what are called *chéngyǔ*, four-word phrases that usually have an interesting story behind them but, without ex-planation, mean nothing. Basically, imagine a language where people, young and old, routinely spout sentences padded by expressions like "a bird in the hand is worth two in the bush" or "never look a gift horse in the mouth."

WRITTEN CHINESE

Many expats shy away from written Chinese, *hànzì* (汉字), understandably arguing that they first need to be able to speak before they tackle writing. A little bit of study in this area, however, can really go a long way, even just in helping you learn how to recognize characters on addresses or to copy them for your taxi driver.

There is a system to it—each character isn't just a unique hodgepodge of strokes. Rather, characters are made up by varying combinations of set components. Many are pictographic, so the meaning jumps out at you without too much mental exhaustion, and most are systematically arranged to suggest sound and meaning. Once you familiarize yourself with the rule system behind characters and become familiar with the components, they don't seem so scary.

Written Chinese comes in two forms—simplified (*jiǎntǐzì,* 简体字) and traditional (*fántǐzì,* 繁體字). Simplified Chinese came into practice in the 1950s and 1960s when Mao made efforts to improve the general levels of literacy in the country. In simplified Chinese, several strokes from the original traditional character were condensed into a single stroke. For example the traditional form of *niǎo* (bird) is written as 鳥, but simplified it is 鸟. And if you look carefully, it does actually look somewhat like a bird. Traditional characters are still used in Hong Kong, Macau, and Taiwan, as well as in many subtitled Chinese films, but simplified Chinese is what is used in mainland China, Singapore, and Malaysia.

Memorizing how to handwrite Chinese characters—simple or traditional—is a mission that takes years of dedication. For good or bad, however, the importance of this has been somewhat demoted by smartphones and computers, which have made the need to handwrite characters all but obsolete. Outside of a school environment, the only time you may need to physically write out characters is when you're suddenly required to fill in a form with your name or address. It's not that people are moving away from using characters but rather that modern devices make it easy to instantly generate characters. Just type in the Pinyin, choose the correct character from the options that pop up, then continue to the next word. Your learning needs to be only deep enough for recognition rather than generation. These days, many Chinese people, even your teachers, will often fumble on how to write a character, and for most expats, the immense amount of time required to memorize how to physically write characters just doesn't equate to the value they get out of it.

© SHANNON AITKEN

Working out which bus you need in Beijing can be difficult if you can't read Chinese.

Most cell phones have built-in functions that allow them to toggle back and forth between English and Chinese input modes. Some computers also already have the software, and it's just a matter of finding out how to activate it. If not, there are various programs and apps out there, such as the popular http://pinyin.sogou.com, which you can download onto your computer or phone for free.

So how many characters do you need to know to be able to read a newspaper or be considered proficient? This is debatable, and figures typically touch on 3,000-4,000. The wonderful thing about *hànzì*, however, is that once you have a few hundred characters under your belt, you'll often find that your reading starts to become more reliable than your listening. Because of the way words are formed, you can often take a reasonable stab at the word's meaning, even if you've never been taught it. Characters also don't require any knowledge of tones.

One drawback to written Chinese is that the divide between written and spoken language is huge. Just because you may be fluent in speaking doesn't mean that you will be able to read a newspaper. In many cases there are words that are exclusively for writing and those that are exclusively for speaking—and trying to keep your words in the right basket when you're learning can be a headache. This is where self-directed learning of Chinese can be hazardous. Dictionaries don't usually point out what is for writing (书面, *shūmiàn*) and what is for speaking (口语, *kǒuyǔ*), so an over-zealous, bookish student might come out sounding like a misplaced Henry James character while trying to relate the latest episode of *Gossip Girl*.

Pinyin

Pinyin is the official romanized format of Chinese. It came into being in the 1950s and replaced various other forms that had been developed to make Chinese more manageable for the foreigner. Jesuit priests had been the first to try to turn this strange language into something readable to the outside world. Later came the Wade-Giles system and Chinese Postal Map Romanization. Pinyin was the Chinese government's own version.

At first Pinyin may appear to offer a more efficient language option than characters, but, while it helps learners get their heads around pronunciation and aids texting and typing, it's often less efficient for general reading. Just take the word *shi,* for example. Without considering tones, *shi* alone has more than 100 different meanings. Narrow that down by adding a fourth tone to it (*shì*) and there are still around 50 possible meanings to consider. It's just too much variability. Imagine trying to read a whole page, let alone a book, when you're guessing at the possible meaning of every single word. Change *shì* to the actual character you want, however, and the meaning becomes clear—for example, 是 means "is," 事 means "matter or issue," and 试 means "to test or try."

Many schools will offer you the option to study just with Pinyin, but the higher you get, the more you'll discover that books rely on characters.

Learning Chinese

WHERE TO LEARN

Beijing is definitely the city to come to to learn Chinese, and there is a banquet of options for doing so. You can plunge yourself into a comprehensive full-time four-year university program, right through to just having the odd private tutoring session in your own home.

Peking University and Beijing Culture and Language University (BCLU) are just two of the many university options for studying Chinese. They have a long history of teaching Chinese to foreigners, and the textbook you'll use will probably have been published by one of these two institutions. Universities offer undergraduate degrees in Chinese as well as intensive short-term courses. In all cases, they typically require four to six hours of class time every day, with a couple of hours of homework every night.

Before you hand over a single *yuán* for any program, it's worth investigating how many students will be in each class in the given program and what the teacher talk-time is like. In many university programs, classes have around 50 students and emphasis is on the teacher talking and the students listening. If your primary reason for moving to Beijing is work rather than study, you will also need to check if it will be possible to do both at the same time. Technically it's illegal for those on a student visa to work, and vice versa. Sometimes universities say they can get around this with a letter of permission from your company, but if you're dealing with sticklers for rules then you might come up against a brick wall, and universities are unlikely to refund your deposit if you need to pull out.

If you are on a work visa, another way around this is to go to one of the many private language schools around the city. Quality and prices vary greatly, as does their level of flexibility. Nearly all will offer a free trial class, so try out a few before you commit. These schools will almost always work out to be much more expensive than universities, and they'll try their best not to negotiate on price, but it is possible, especially if you're willing to commit to long periods of study. Before you sign up, again make sure you find out the maximum number of students that will be in your class. You may think you're entering a four-person class but later find the number has mysteriously risen to eight. Find out how the school allows for holidays and days off. I've been to some schools that allowed me to have as many holidays as I wanted without penalty as long as each break was a week or more, and then I've been to other schools where getting any time off at all once you'd laid down your money was like asking them to donate a heart. Most schools charge by the hour, but in reality classes are only 50 minutes long. Additionally, if you introduce a friend to the school, there is usually some kind of reward, such as a free lesson or two. If you don't remind them of this, they'll quietly let it slip by when the time comes.

The next option is having a private teacher. These can usually be recommended by friends or found on expat websites. Typical rates are RMB70-150 per hour. Lessons usually take place in cafés or in your home. An alternative is to find a language partner. Expat websites overflow with personal ads for language partners, and on the whole most people are pretty genuine, but a good proportion of them do have a little more than language learning in mind, and a handful of them can't be trusted at all. Meet in a public place the first time and avoid giving out your phone number or personal details until you've met them at least once.

Finally, there are online options. Choose from dictionaries, such as MDBG and Nciku; live lesson formats, such as from eChineseLearning or Sinoland College; and podcast programs, such as Chinesepod, a comprehensive online service that often covers real-life topics that the traditional culture-driven textbooks don't dare stray into.

WHAT TO LEARN

Most private schools focus on teaching *kǒuyǔ* (spoken language) rather than more formal language, such as that used in writing or more formal discussions. *Kǒuyǔ* is the kind of language you'd use in general social situations—with friends or neighbors, at restaurants, when going shopping. When you learn *kǒuyǔ*, you'll learn the Pinyin and relevant characters. If you're not interested in learning the characters, however, it's not hard to avoid them in the private schools. Teachers aren't too strict. Characters are a substantial part of university programs, however, and impossible to avoid.

Kǒuyǔ is extraordinarily important and useful; however, if your goal is professional language or language that can get you into really meaty conversations, you may feel it's just scratching the surface. University programs are more likely to delve into more formal or more detailed language that will allow you one day to speak and write with greater precision and color. Alternatively, you may want to find a school that will prepare you for the *hànyǔ shuǐpíng kǎoshì* (汉语水平考试), more commonly simply referred to as the HSK exam. This is the only standardized proficiency test of Chinese for foreigners, and equates somewhat to the English TOEFL exam. It's highly structured and graded from levels one to six, and covers reading, writing, listening, and speaking. Certain companies or schools may require that you have achieved a certain HSK level before you can be accepted. Many expats shy away from the HSK, claiming much of the language isn't useful and that too much emphasis is put on writing and memorizing characters. Not everyone agrees, and under a good teacher, it can be quite a thorough way to learn.

Education

When you first start to consider a life in Beijing, educating your child or children might cause a bit of anxiety. Though its MBAs and Chinese programs are world-class, the city has yet to become a global destination for most other areas of academia. Fortunately, Beijing offers a broad spectrum of choices—from the very local, strictly Chinese environment to the high-achieving, fully independent international school, many of which will proudly tell you that they have past students who have been accepted into Ivy League universities. In reality, the major determiner of where your child goes will not be a lack of options, but your budget. Before you move your family over here, it's critical to decide what education style or standards you're happy with, and if you can afford the school that meets those requirements.

To begin your search, look at the schools' websites, where you can check out everything from the admission process to photos of the school's latest social event. But this really isn't enough. The glowing marketing language and imagery that promote

Parents wait to pick up their children after school.

these sites can be misleading. That isn't to say they're deceiving you, but it does tend to have a homogenizing effect. Only a personal visit will really reveal a school's individual character and culture, so it's essential to line up a barrage of visits as part of your fact-finding trip.

Before you enroll your child into any school—local or international—make at least two visits to the school to get a clear feeling of what it will be like. Ask to be given a tour of the entire school (not just the highlights) and observe a class each visit to note the consistencies or inconsistencies. Watch how the teacher and students interact with each other, and ask to be put in touch with another foreign parent for their personal input. The big international schools are familiar with this process. The local Chinese schools, however, might be more guarded. They don't typically have the same kind of interactive relationship with parents that Western schools have, and information can be a like a stream, trickling in one direction. They may not be too willing to let you sit in on classes or talk to people independently. If the school isn't cooperative with your requests you'll have a good indication of how things will be once your child is enrolled.

LOCAL SCHOOLS

The Chinese school system is often characterized as being inflexible and extremely stressful for children. From the time they wake up in the morning till the time they go to sleep at night, a Chinese-school child's day is filled with classes, exams, and preparation for exams. If your child plans to sit the *gāokǎo* (the local equivalent of the SAT or university entrance exam) the local school system is 100 percent geared to do this. It's not really a style, however, that marries well with a Western education system. Learning is more passive—the teachers talk, the students absorb. Students rarely ask questions, often out of a fear of losing face, and there is little spontaneous interaction. There is also extensive emphasis on rote learning methods, mathematics, science, Chinese culture, and history. Creativity and independent thought are not strong points.

Not all Chinese schools are the same, however, and some schools are trying to make changes and introduce more creativity into their programs. There is also a growing number of private schools, which promise more international approaches to education and slicker environments. As things stand, however, even the most modern Chinese schools still find themselves shackled by the need to prepare their students for the same rigid exam system, so there remains a limit to exactly how liberal they can be.

Chinese school hours can be long—from as early as 7am to 4pm—and often require students to attend compulsory classes on Saturdays as well. In addition to the homework that they're already assigned to do, kids also face pressure to attend after-school tutoring or *bǔxíbān* (補習班), roughly translated as "cram classes." Extracurricular activities, such as sport, music, and art, do exist, but the range is unlikely to match the diversity of what you might be accustomed to in your home country. In countries such as America or Australia, the real pressure at school may crank up in the final year or two before high school, but in China, the pressure to do well in the *gāokǎo* is tangible from kindergarten. Children as young as seven or eight will have weekly tests, and their results are often posted on a school intranet for all parents to see.

In Chinese schools, class sizes are relatively large with 30 to 50 students per class. Students are randomly assigned into classes when they first start and will often stay in these same groups throughout their schooling, regardless of ability. There is no segregating of children with higher or special learning needs.

Chinese schools are extremely strong in objective subjects like math and science, and the skills carry over into everyday life—just watch to see how quickly and easily a Chinese person can recall a cell phone number that they've just seen. If such subjects are your child's passion, then maybe a Chinese school will work for them. It might not be to their advantage, however, if individuality or creative expression is more their thing.

In theory most local schools can accept foreign students, but in practice, many won't. If your child is fluent in Chinese this will give them a better chance, and if they have a Chinese appearance, this may also be a bonus. But if none of these factors help, then you may need to call on your connections and quite possibly hand over a well-padded red envelope (*hóngbāo*). Applications for admission are also relatively late, opening from around May to June.

If you can get your child in, you will find that school fees are much cheaper than what you might pay at an international school, possibly just around RMB28,000 per year. One option that many expat parents happily consider is to enroll their children into Chinese nurseries or kindergartens to give them a solid foundation in the local language, but then move them to an international school for the more formal education years.

Some Chinese schools are more expat friendly than others and several are actually set up with international departments. Fangcaodi International School, Beijing Ritan High School, The High School Affiliated to Renmin University of China, and Beijing No. 55 Middle School, for example, all have long-standing international programs. These schools are all run by the Chinese government and classes are taught almost entirely in Chinese. If your child doesn't speak Chinese before starting, they'll need to attend intensive language courses for the first semester. The standards and cultural diversity of these schools may differ from that of the major independent international schools in Beijing, but they do offer a deeper Chinese experience and are a slightly cheaper alternative if your budget is limited. These "semi-international" schools are well suited to preparing your child for entry into the Chinese universities, but it's advisable to ascertain whether their curriculums will set your child up for university back home. Some offer an International Baccalaureate (IB) program for an additional fee.

INTERNATIONAL SCHOOLS

International schools are generally the first choice for expats in Beijing. From nursery to high school, they offer quality education and a diverse range of extracurricular activities. Each school varies greatly, not just in fees, but in culture, curriculum, and the blend of nationalities at the school. Most of the international schools are well equipped; have internationally qualified, native-English-speaking teachers; and have curriculums that are tailored for their often-transient student populations.

Admission processes vary from school to school, but it's generally relatively easy to get your child into an international school, and it can often be done very quickly. The basic requirements are a foreign passport and the correct visa (such as Z, W, or J). You will probably also have to supply copies of your child's student records and a completed health check form from a doctor (the school can provide you with the correct form to give your doctor). Such schools aren't usually zoned, so your address is unlikely to affect your child's enrollment. One problem that you may encounter, however, is a waiting list. Many schools have a rolling enrollment system and accept kids throughout the year, but given that the new school starts at around mid-August, if you are moving to Beijing much later than that, there's a chance that the school you want might not have an immediate vacancy.

The international schools provide children with varying depths of experience of the local Chinese culture. Some schools, such as Yew Chung International School (YCIS), create bilingual learning environments; government-run international schools, such as

© SHANNON AITKEN

ISB is just one of many impressive international schools in the area.

Beijing World Youth Academy (BWYA), enroll both local Chinese students and foreign students; most schools include Chinese language as a compulsory part of their curriculum; and some schools compete with local schools in interschool sports competitions.

Trying to find a school that's close to your office shouldn't be too much of an issue if your child is little. International playgroups, preschools, and kindergartens can be found in nearly all the expat hot spots around the city. Many are even located in or beside apartment compounds, such as Etonkids International Kindergarten and Ivy Academy. For the older kids, the options are more limited in the inner city. Beijing City International School (BCIS) near Shuangjing, the British School of Beijing's Sanliun campus (up to age 12), and the Canadian International School of Beijing (CISB) Liangmaqiao campus are all within easy reach of the CBD; there are also several around Lido, near the northeast corner of the Fourth Ring Road. Most of the major international schools, however, are farther northwest, outside the Fifth Ring Road in Shunyi district. For an in-depth directory of all the international schools in Beijing, contact expat magazine *Timeout* or *City Weekend* for a copy of one of their annual Beijing school guides.

OTHER OPTIONS

Homeschooling is also a popular option, although it's not for everyone. While this will give you the benefit of spending lots of fulfilling time with your child or children, it is time consuming, tiring, and takes long-term dedication. A full homeschool program should involve 20 to 30 hours a week of teaching. A range of programs can be found online, such as K12 (www.k12.com), a popular program for American curriculums, and EdAlive, highly awarded educational software, which has been used widely across Australia's remote areas and which comes in different versions for different countries. Armed with such resources, you may still feel a little isolated, but you don't have to do it alone. Beijing has a well-established network for homeschooling. For more help, contact the Beijing Homeschoolers group at http://groups.yahoo.com/group/beijing_homeschoolers. There are more than 200 members, and if you don't already have a friend within the group, you'll need to send the group's manager an email requesting to be invited.

Finally, a handful of embassies around town, such as the German embassy and the Pakistan embassy, have their own schools. Entry isn't necessarily determined by which passport your child has, but you will need to investigate the curriculum choice for its relevance to your child and the teaching language. The Pakistan Embassy College, for example, offers a British curriculum taught in English, and follows the Islamic faith. The United States, British, and Australian embassies do not have their own schools.

CHILDREN WITH DISABILITIES

Many of the international schools can accept children with mild to moderate physical or learning disabilities. If your child needs more support than what you're able to get from the mainstream schools, however, then you may need to think seriously about living in Beijing. Beijing previously had a dedicated school for expat children with disabilities, which ran out of the Care for Children organization, but this closed in 2012. Your main options now are homeschooling and support from centers such as Eliott's Corner (the Beijing branch of Shanghai's Olivia's Place), a pediatric center that

THINGS TO CONSIDER WHEN CHOOSING AN INTERNATIONAL SCHOOL

SCHOOL FEES

Tuition fees at international schools can be hefty, and if your company doesn't include your child's education in your salary package, then some of these schools may be out of your reach. Total annual fees can range from around RMB85,000 (US$13,500) up to RMB233,000 (US$37,000), plus initial application fees of possibly RMB2,000 (US$317). For many schools, this includes extracurricular activities such as weekend sports and domestic excursions. For some schools, such activities may be an additional expense.

EXTRA EXPENSES

Make sure you're very clear about what is included in school fees and what isn't. At times some schools' fees may seem cheaper than others', but then you may find that expenses throughout the year will cause money to drip from your wallet. Things to ask about include textbooks, laptops, excursions or field trips, overseas holidays, after-school and weekend sports or activities, uniforms, lunches, and weekday and weekend school bus services. Ask other parents about their experiences.

CURRICULUM

Find out where and how the school's curriculum was developed. Most reputable international school will use a curriculum that will prepare students for university and college wherever they may end up in the world. For example, many use IB World School (www.ibo.org) programs and others use national programs from a given country, which have been adapted for international students. You may need to ask which tests they can administer. ISB, for instance, has more of an Ameri-

can influence, and can administer the SAT and the American College Test (ACT), among others. Check that the school has the appropriate accreditations. For more information relating to this, contact bodies such as the Council of International Schools (www.cois.org) or the Accrediting Commission for Schools Western Association of Schools and Colleges (www.acswasc.org).

THE SCHOOL'S CULTURE

Every school has its own culture, which may or may not appeal to you. Western Academy Beijing, for example, strives for an individualistic environment, where students are free from uniforms and interact with teachers on a first-name basis; the British School of Beijing prefers a more traditional private-school culture, in which students wear a uniform and stand when an adult enters the room. ISB has strong sports and performing arts programs, and also has a well-organized PTA. Consider their value system. Does the school prioritize exam scores above all else or does it also build other values into the children's days, such as caring, respect, responsibility, sharing, and so forth?

CULTURAL COMPOSITION

Some schools are more international than others. While many schools may have a fairly even mix of nationalities, others may attract more students from a particular country. For example, where one school might have a high proportion of Korean students, another might enroll more German or American students. The school's name isn't always an indication of the composition of students.

SUBJECT OFFERINGS

Of course the major subjects are all going

to be there, but some schools have additional subjects that may be important for your child. Children interested in a career in law may need Latin, or perhaps they need to study a given language as a native speaker rather than as a second language.

AFTER-SCHOOL ACTIVITIES

There is a healthy amount of interschool competition amongst the international schools, and if your child has eyes on one day turning into a pro athlete, you'll need to ask about each school's specialty.

STRESS AND PRESSURE

Most kids will experience pressure in the final years of high school, but in many schools in Asia, that pressure is on from the get go. Find out if your school has an expectation that students will be burning the midnight oil from the time they're 8 years old, or if sport and other recreational activities are encouraged. The more local influence the school has, the more likely that your child will feel the pressure of extra testing and extra study.

SPECIAL NEEDS

Not many schools have extensive services for either high achievers or kids with special needs. If your child has mobility challenges, accessibility is definitely something you'll need to investigate, particularly with more local-style schools. Beijing is not a particularly easy city to live in for people with disabilities. Understanding of capabilities is shockingly low, and well-placed ramps are sorely lacking.

ARE LOCAL CHINESE STUDENTS ADMITTED?

Most international schools are open only to students holding foreign passports, and local Chinese students are not permitted to attend. Some international schools, however, do enroll local students. You may want to consider this because schools that are exclusive to foreign students have greater independence and next to no influence on their curriculum from the local government. If local Chinese students are permitted into the school then the government is likely to have greater involvement in what and how things are taught.

BUS SERVICES

Most of the larger international schools have extensive bus services and will deliver your child from the door of your compound to school and back again. Not all provide weekend services. Unless you live in some out-of-the-way location, the school may be able to adapt a route if it doesn't already go to the place where you'll be living.

WHERE TO LIVE

Unfortunately the majority of the international schools are about an hour away from the CBD, and juggling work, home, and school life can be especially difficult when you first move to Beijing. Some families choose to live close to work and have the kids commute to school on the school buses. Others find it easier to live close to the school, which means that the kids will have the fun of living just a few doors down from their schoolmates, and that extracurricular activities are easy for you to manage.

The executive principal of the British School of Beijing, Michael Embley, recommends that families don't rush into signing a lease but first move into a serviced apartment (available at almost all high-level housing compounds) until they get a feel for what works best. You'll give yourself time to not only find a home that suits your family's needs, but also to really understand what commute time is like in Beijing.

provides occupational, physical, and speech therapy for children from birth to adolescence; and Side by Side, which offers support for kids with special needs and learning difficulties. A more Chinese-style school, Stars and Rain, provides schooling for and help for children with autism. Unfortunately, being located out east beyond the Fifth Ring Road, it's a bit of a hike from the typical expat's home.

Universities

Currently, all of the world's top 10 universities—according to QS World University Rankings—are from either the United States or the United Kingdom. The Chinese government, however, is determined that China will soon join this elite group and has set itself on a fast-track course to do so. What schools like Cambridge and Harvard did gradually over a century or more, China wants to achieve within the space of a single generation. This means it now spends billions of *yuán* every year on pushing two of its star universities toward a golden slot in the global top 10, and both are in Beijing—Peking University and Tsinghua University. Right now they're ranked at 44 and 48, respectively, on the QS scale. According to the 2012 China University Ranking by China University Application Center, the two universities went neck and neck for the top spot, with Peking seizing the first prize with a score of 98.1 out of 100 and Tsinghua with 97.6—the year before it was exactly the same figures, but in reverse.

One of the six criteria that the QS system use to rank a university is the number of international students that that university has, and China's universities are likely to score more highly on this factor in the coming years. As part of the efforts to increase its universities' standings, the Chinese government is working on making them more attractive to foreign students. There is an ever-expanding array of courses that you can do without so much as a *nǐhǎo* (hello), and education comes packaged in everything from an intense two-week course right through to a doctorate or associate's degree. Many international schools also have satellite campuses in Beijing, such as Stanford

© SHANNON AITKEN

Students can enjoy the beautiful grounds at Peking University.

University (at Peking University), the University of Colorado (China Agricultural University), and Rutgers Business School (at the Central University of Finance & Economics). Beyond this, hundreds of universities around the world have partnerships with Chinese universities to facilitate student exchange programs.

Unfortunately, one of the factors that may hinder China's rise in the global university ranking system is the fact that the relationship between the government and the universities is extremely tight. Not only are academic appointments often influenced by connections rather than academic excellence, but funding is also often dependent the exam results of its students. This means that teachers are often pressured to pass students, even if they never turn up to class. So, not only can results be falsely inflated, but if you're serious about really immersing yourself in education, you might find that you're surrounded by and involved in group assignments with students who couldn't give a hoot about studying. The fanatical study habits that got them into university don't necessarily hang around after Orientation Day. Also, because of the university admission system and a culture that prioritizes monetary gain over personal passion or interest, a shockingly high proportion of students are enrolled in majors that they have no personal interest in.

Aside from majors that directly relate to Chinese language or culture, another problem with doing an undergraduate or postgraduate degree at a Chinese university is that it's not always certain if it will be recognized back in your own country. While a Chinese degree in medicine or law may prevent you from picking up a scalpel or gavel back home, one in science, finance, or international relations may garner you more kudos. In general, postgraduate courses fare a lot better than undergraduate courses, and Beijing is becoming a popular destination for students who want a master's or doctorate with a Chinese twist.

There are more than 60 universities and colleges across Beijing, and standards vary greatly from one to the next, so if you are planning to do a full undergraduate or postgraduate degree, it may work out better to limit yourself to the top-ranking ones, in part because companies or universities back home may have actually heard of them, and because they are more likely to be more internationally savvy. Even then, you should still investigate whether or not your chosen course is going to be worth your time and money in the long run. Organizations such as the American Association of Collegiate Registrars and Admissions Officers (www.aacrao.org) or the UK Council for International Student Affairs (UKCISA, www.ukcisa.org.uk) can help you determine how respected the courses are likely to be valued elsewhere.

PROGRAMS

Chinese universities use the same structure for degrees as the West. Most of their undergraduate bachelor programs are four full years, master's programs are two or three years, and doctorate degrees are three years and up. To search online for both degree and non-degree programs, including those taught in English, you can use China's University and College Admission System (CUCAS) website (www.cucas.edu.cn).

Naturally, the vast majority of degrees offered in Chinese universities are taught in Chinese, though the number of English-taught programs is on the rise. Just a handful of English-taught bachelor programs include International Marketing at Beijing Foreign Studies University, Chinese Medicine at Beijing University of Chinese Medicine, and

International Trade at University of International Business and Economics. The servings of English-taught master's and doctorate programs are even more generous, particularly those relating to international relations or business.

FEES

As an international student, you're immediately going to pay more than a local student, but even then the difference may be as little as RMB5,000, and in most cases it will still be cheaper than what you'd pay at a university back home. While the average fee for a year at MIT will cost around US$40,700, a year at even Tsinghua or Peking University will cost less than half of that. In 2013, for example, the annual fee for a Bachelor of International Marketing (taught in English) at Beijing Foreign Studies University was RMB30,000 (US$4,700), and a Bachelor of Archaeology (taught in Chinese) from Peking University was RMB26,000 (US$4,150). An International Master in Business Administration (IMBA) from Tsinghua University was RMB94,000 (US$15,000), and a master's program in public policy from Peking University was RMB40,000 (US$6,400)—both taught in English. Then, most English-taught doctorate degrees from Beihang University cost RMB42,000 (US$6,700).

In addition to the tuition fees, there is also usually a nonrefundable application fee of approximately RMB600 (US$96) and an annual insurance fee of about RMB600.

SCHOLARSHIPS

Adding to its efforts to attract more foreign students to its universities, the Chinese government offers a considerable number of scholarships each year. While most universities offer their own scholarships—such as full scholarships that cover tuition, accommodations, meals, and medical insurance, as well as partial scholarships that cover full tuition or partial tuition—the Ministry of Education's China Scholarship Council and the Chinese government have also created several other scholarship funds. These include the Chinese Government Scholarship (CGS), the Beijing Government Scholarship (BGS), and the HSK Winner Scholarship, which is awarded to the top HSK test-scorers in each country where the test is administered. This particular scholarship can be applied for through your country's Chinese diplomatic office or HSK testing service. Application dates for these scholarships typically run from November to April (though this changes for different locations).

For more information on scholarships, visit the individual university's website, CUCAS, or the China Scholarship Council (www.csc.edu.cn).

APPLICATIONS

Applying for a university in Beijing as a foreign student has quite a few steps, and the entire process takes several months. UKCISA recommends that you start investigating your options as much as 18 months in advance. For undergrads, application dates are open from around early January to early March. It will then take until May or June to receive your acceptance letter, and then, only after that, you can apply for the appropriate visa. Postgraduate application dates may start and end earlier.

Academic years are typically divided up into two semesters of 18 weeks each. The year kicks off with the autumn semester, running from September until the end of January, and finishes with the spring semester, from February to June. There is also a summer period of 11 weeks that is broken up into a six-week vacation and a five-week term for various types of training or summer school.

Applying for a Chinese university isn't particularly difficult, but if you do it by yourself directly with the university, you may find aspects of it frustrating and baffling, particularly if you've just landed in Beijing. If this seems a little daunting or unclear, you can use services such as CUCAS or the Chinese Service Center for Scholarly Exchange (CSCSE), which will take care of everything for you for a fee.

Unlike the ferocious competition and exams that locals endure to get into the top universities, for foreigners it's relatively easy, as long as you can pay the fee. Standard requirements are that you have a foreign passport and your high school graduation certificate and transcript. You will also need to pass a government health check and be within a given age limit (typically 18-30 years for undergraduate degrees, although this varies greatly between universities). If you plan to do a degree that is taught in Chinese, you'll also need to have passed a given level of the HSK or New HSK exam (usually level 5 or higher).

If you have already accumulated credit points with a university in your home country, don't let these go to waste. Check to see if your university is affiliated with a Chinese university and apply to transfer your points for advanced credit.

ACCOMMODATIONS

Another expense you'll have to consider is accommodations. Most universities have several on-campus dormitories, some that particularly cater to the local Chinese students and some that cater more to the tastes of international students. The latter are generally more comfortable and modern, as well as more expensive—RMB40-80 per bed per day, or around RMB1,200-2,500 per month. Rooms do get booked up pretty quickly, so book online through the university's site ASAP, otherwise you'll find yourself needing to make other arrangements.

Rooms get booked quickly at Peking University's dormitory.

© SHANNON AITKEN

EXPAT INTERVIEW: STUDENT LIVING

Robin Lin is a Taiwanese American studying at Beijing Normal University. She's currently enrolled in a master's program for teaching Chinese as a foreign language.

WHICH DO YOU PREFER— ON CAMPUS OR OFF?

Having studied in Beijing for the past four years, and having had the experience of living in both on-campus and off-campus situations, I can confidently choose the former. The idea of living in the dorms may not seem like such a good idea to people who've already gone through that rite of passage during their bachelor's back home—I certainly wouldn't do it again if I went back home—but in Beijing the advantages far outweigh the disadvantages.

WHAT ARE THE COSTS?

With the mounting cost of rent, university accommodations are very competitive in price. At Beijing Normal University, a two-person dorm with shared bathroom is RMB1,200 per month, a two-person room with private bathroom is about RMB2,500, and a one-person room with private bathroom is RMB2,700 (this includes electricity, gas, and water, but not Internet). There is no living room and the kitchen is shared, but there are common areas to hang out in, and the canteen is cheap and passable.

WHAT ARE THE OTHER ADVANTAGES?

You can't beat the commuting time and the cost of living on campus. The morning commute is not fun in Beijing, no matter if you cab, bus, drive, or subway it. On campus, you can roll out of bed 10 minutes before your 8 o'clock class and still have time to pick up some steamed buns and soy milk on the way. There are other campus amenities that you can take advantage of, too, such as the cheap gym, pool, tennis courts, and cheap eats.

WHAT'S DORM LIFE LIKE?

During my first semester I lived off campus in a really cool apartment in the *hútòng*. However, I was very isolated and I didn't get to bond with my classmates. During the second semester, I lived in the dorms on campus and made loads of friends there. The people in the dorms came from all over the world, which meant that I had to speak Chinese because not everyone spoke English. The dorms are also a good place for networking and finding out about job opportunities. If studying and getting good grades are your priority, though, you'll need to be able to reject a lot of impromptu partying and hanging out. When my willpower is low, I simply hide out at the library.

HEALTH

Going to a local Chinese hospital could be one of the biggest cultural shocks you encounter in Beijing. The health-care system here, compared to what we're used to in the West, is chaotic and impersonal. There's not only no real family doctor system that weeds out the minor ailments, but millions of out-of-towners also make pilgrimages to Beijing every year to access its relatively superior health care. That means that hospitals are heavily overcrowded and expediency outranks any notion of customer service. Fortunately, thanks to the extensive range of international hospitals and clinics you can easily maintain high levels of care in a manner that you're accustomed to.

Traditionally, the Chinese have a long history of health care. It is a deep part of their psyche and at times seems to be almost like a religion. Eat cucumber and it will cool the "fire" within your body, or snack on some lychees and they will warm the body and improve circulation. They're fanatical about the temperature of drinking water and almost never drink it below room temperature. Even trying to get a cold beer in summer can be a problem.

Unfortunately modern society has muddied the more natural Chinese approach to health. Treatment here is now a cocktail of Western medicine and traditional Chinese medicine (TCM), and in a system where doctors are pressured to increase revenue from prescriptions, overprescribing is a huge problem.

© SHANNON AITKEN

Lifestyles are also changing. Very few people cook for themselves and instead often breakfast, lunch, and dinner from vendors and restaurants. Where the older generation routinely headed to parks to stretch or do tai chi, young children through to the middle aged are more likely to spend their free time in front of a computer or smartphone. It's not surprising that obesity is a growing concern.

As the capital city of China, Beijing is relatively clean and hygienic, but, as an expat, you will still no doubt still see some eye-opening sights from time to time. Turn a blind eye and walk on. Pollution is a serious problem as are food-production and -handling practices. Water safety is such an issue that filters are a more trusted option than bottled water. Sometimes it feels that life in Beijing is a minefield of health hazards.

Dr. Richard Saint Cyr, practitioner at Beijing United Family Hospital (BJU) and author of website MyHealth Beijing, believes expats can manage it, however. "You can definitely have a very happy and fulfilling life here, but you do have to take more precautions," he says. "You have to live better. You can't let yourself go here in China. You do have to be more aware, and take care of your kids more. You do have to be self-conscious about where you're buying your food and things like that. But if you do that you can still have many years of totally fulfilling life here."

Hospitals and Clinics

CHINESE HOSPITALS

As a newcomer to Beijing, it's only natural that you're going to have more confidence in a hospital environment that feels familiar to you, so checking yourself in to one of the vast, typically chaotic local Chinese hospitals is probably going to raise your blood pressure rather than lower it.

Unfortunately, when it comes to local hospitals, there is no shortage of horror stories—avoidance of treating foreigners for fear of them dying on hospital grounds, leftover blood and body fluids, outrageous under-the-table payments to doctors just so that they will see the patient, overprescribing by doctors who supplement their meager official income with bonuses from drug companies. The list goes on, and, in truth, the Chinese medical system is in need of a major overhaul.

It's not all doom and gloom, however, and there are many outstanding facilities that you should feel as confident in as you would in a hospital back home. Beijing in particular has benefited from improvements, and generally standards are now a long shot from what they were 10 years ago. It's also home to some of the best hospitals in the country, staffed with extensively experienced medical teams and equipped with top-of-the-line medical equipment. Medical techniques are also largely in line with those in the West, and while Chinese medicine is still popular, Western medication is now standard.

The issue is trying to sort the bad hospitals from the good ones. One way to start is to understand how hospitals in China are organized. First there are government hospitals. These are graded from level one to three, with level one being small county hospitals that are really more like clinics and best avoided; level two being medium-sized district hospitals; and level three being city-, provincial- or national-level hospitals. These top-level hospitals are large and comprehensive. They have specialist care

© SHANNON AITKEN

Beijing Family United Clinic offers Shunyi residents easy access to international-quality medical care for day-to-day issues.

units as well as teaching and research facilities. Each of the three levels is then subdivided further with a grading of A, B, or C. Officially, the top two hospitals in China are Peking Union Medical College Hospital (Xiéhé Yīyuàn), near Wangfujing, and the Chinese PLA General Hospital (Jiěfàngjūn Zǒng Yīyuàn) near Wukesong subway station in Haidian. Other 3A-grade hospitals in Beijing include the China-Japan Friendship Hospital (Zhōngrì Yǒuhǎo Yīyuàn) and Beijing Anzhen Hospital (Běijīng Ānzhēn Yīyuàn). These hospitals all have VIP or international wards with staff that have moderate to fluent English, and in many cases who have also been trained overseas. The VIP or international section costs a lot more than the sections used by the general public (a consultation downstairs might cost you RMB5-10, whereas upstairs time with a doctor will cost around RMB100-300), but you're likely to have almost no wait, will be treated in a more personal manner and in a more hygienic setting, and you'll also have someone who will walk you through each step of the process. Wards here are also a lot pricier than in the general area. For example, at the time of writing, a night at the China-Japan Friendship Hospital started from RMB300 for a small standard ward and went up to RMB3,800 for a posh deluxe suite.

Aside from the public hospitals, the government is also making a huge push to privatize many of its facilities. Currently those used most by expats tend to be ob-gyn facilities for childbirth. Again, inconsistency lurks in the private hospital area, so you do need to investigate ahead of time which hospital is up to par. Some offer service and treatment that approximates what you get in the West, but reports also suggest that some of these facilities still have difficulty attracting the top-level doctors because of the lack of government support and job security.

If you're not covered for the fully international hospitals or are simply keen to entrust yourself to the local system, just make sure you put some time into investigating your

VISITING THE HOSPITAL

Know the consultation times. In many local hospitals, weekends are for emergencies only. If you need a consultation, it's likely you'll need to visit on a weekday between 7:30am and 4:30pm.

Prepare to give up your entire day. Unless you're heading to the VIP wing, expect to spend a half to full day lining up and waiting around the hospital. It's a complicated process that thousands of people are trying to do at the same time.

Take a friend. If your Chinese is fair to fabulous, it's still best to take a local person with you. Language isn't the only barrier here—Chinese hospital culture is a world apart, as are the seemingly endless number of steps you need to work your way through from start to finish.

Bring cash. Many hospitals won't offer treatment without upfront payment, and international insurance isn't typically accepted, even the big insurers. Also, while some of the larger facilities may accept Chinese bankcards or international credit cards, some of the smaller ones won't. Prices vary from hospital to hospital and according to the treatment you get. If your visit is for something along the lines of a general checkup or treatment for a simple ailment, then your total bill might not exceed RMB100. Regardless, it might be worth coming with at least RMB1,000, just to cover yourself for any surprises.

Be ready for an IV. Whether you agree with the practice or not, you're probably going to get an IV stuck in your arm. From treating a cold to a bout of diarrhea, locals here love to hook themselves up to a drip. Even better, you'll probably be sitting in a communal room with dozens of other people doing the same thing. You can refuse.

Carry your own hand sanitizer. Bathrooms in local hospitals can get pretty funky and soapless. Bring your own.

Cater for yourself. Meals aren't automatically included in the cost of your stay at a hospital. You can definitely order meals, but they come at an extra fee.

Hire a carer. Chinese nurses don't always take care of such things as showering and feeding, but carers can be hired from the hospital to do this. If the sick person has a serious condition where the carer needs to be particularly careful, you'll need to check the carer's level of understanding. Most carers have little to no training. Depending on the situation, carers can be hired by the month (around RMB3,000), by the day, or by the task.

Get it filled. Often prescriptions are valid only on the day of writing, although some may last up to three days. And though you may be aching to get out of the hospital by the time it comes to get your prescription filled, it's wise to get it done at the hospital because the street-level pharmacies don't carry all medications.

Double check. If you're unsure of test results, the prescribed medicines, or even their dosage, you can always ask for copies and send them to a trusted doctor in your home country.

Tally up. At the end of your hospital stay, make sure that your bill is itemized—the chance that a mysterious charge has slipped its way into the total is big enough to warrant checking.

options ahead of time while you're fit and healthy. This is not a decision you want to make under a stressful situation.

The Culture

Don't expect to be treated with any form of sympathy when you go to a Chinese hospital. The doctors here have seen thousands before you, and most likely many in worse condition than you. If your doctor does waver toward a moment of tenderness, it'll quickly be extinguished by the recall of the endless crowd of people waiting outside ready to stampede in as soon as you're done.

If you're a tad on the prudish side, get over it. Privacy doesn't exist in this customer-service vacuum. There is next to no privacy in a local hospital and you can forget any sense of personal space. If you're taken off for an X-ray or test, it's quite likely that the husband of the woman in the bed next to you will be chilling out on your bed when you return. In the rush to get through the day's ocean of patients, doctors also often sit side by side in the same room, with patients lining up next to each other waiting their turn. Your diagnosis of irritable bowel syndrome will be of intense interest to the family and relatives at the neighboring table, who are wondering what kind of illness might be plaguing this wide-eyed *wàiguórén* (foreigner).

Doctor-patient relationships are another point of difference. Chinese patients typically accept the diagnosis that their almighty doctor decrees to be their problem and obediently leave with their basket load of prescribed medications. Practitioners here are not accustomed to two-way conversations where a patient might question a prognosis, so don't expect them to be up for a good probing chat. If you do have questions, don't be afraid to ask—you just might need to be persistent in trying to extract each and every detail.

Unfortunately the local medical system has also become enmeshed with a culture of "gift-giving." To have a chance at getting a good doctor, or at least one that appears at your bedside within a reasonable time frame, or to be bumped to the front of a long list of people waiting for a given test, gifts have become a necessary evil for many locals. Head nurses, physicians, people in position to grease a wheel or two, all are potential recipients of handsome gifts. Cash is too direct and can be frowned up, but an RMB1,000 voucher for a supermarket or a day spa goes down a treat, and perfume, alcohol, or even expensive cigarettes can advance one's number in the system. Unfairly for the locals, foreigners aren't always expected to take part in this process, and they may get preferential treatment simply because they are foreigners and carry a greater risk of face loss for the hospital should something go awry. If you do, however, find things going a little slowly, it might be something to keep in mind—just don't do it in front of anybody else; no one likes to be seen accepting non-birthday presents.

The Process

The be-all and end-all of the Chinese medical system is the registration process, the *guàhào*. Unfortunately, given that Beijing has the country's best hospitals and that adequate medical care is sorely lacking in almost every other city or province, millions of people are drawn to Beijing simply for health reasons. So on top of the general systemic problems, Beijing hospitals are under enormous strain as thousands of people heave through their corridors on a daily basis. There is no appointment process, so you need to get to the hospital as early as possible to take a number, just like lining up at a deli. Most hospitals open for registration at around 7:30am and close at 4:30pm, but it's gotten to the point that people will start lining up as early as 5am or, in some extremes, camp overnight, just to get a ticket. People have even begun to scalp registration numbers to make a buck. Using the VIP or international section should allow you to bypass this nightmare.

You must take your passport when you go to the hospital and, if you have one, your Chinese social insurance card. It's also best to carry some cash. Most Chinese hospitals will not accept international medical insurance, but some, such as Peking Union Medical College Hospital and China-Japan Friendship Hospital, will accept some insurers. Check their websites or call ahead to find out which insurance companies are accepted.

Nothing happens at a Chinese hospital until you pay. This doesn't mean you have to try to calculate the entire expense the moment you walk in the door; you typically pay step-by-step as each requirement arises. The first thing you'll need to pay is your registration fee, which will range from RMB5 to possibly RMB300 or more if you're seeing a specialist in a VIP wing. After this, every time you need to be sent off for a certain test or treatment, you'll first need to go to the cashier, pay for it, then head to the treatment area with receipt in hand. If you've shopped in a Chinese department store where they send you over to a cashier before they bag and hand over the shirt you've just selected, it's just the same.

As an example, imagine you suspect you've fractured your foot. First thing is to go to the registration desk to *guàhào* and choose which kind of doctor you'll need to see. It's up to you to self-diagnose and determine whether you need oncology, gynecology, or orthopedics. If you don't know, take a guess, and if you're wrong the doctor that you do see should hopefully refer you to the right one. Your registration fee covers your initial consultation fee. So now you hobble off to the appropriate section of the hospital and show your ticket at the relevant registration desk. Finally, the doctor will call your number. If he or she then sends you off for an X-ray, you'll need to go to the cashier to pay, get your receipt, then head off to have your scan. When this is done, you return to the doctor, scan in hand, and given that you've already seen the doctor once, you take priority over the other people lining up to get in. The minute the door opens, make your charge. It's highly likely that other people will still be lingering in the office when the doctor pulls out your X-ray and holds it in the air to examine it. If you don't demand that the other people get out, they'll stay to hear the diagnosis. Finally, let's say there's no fracture but your doctor prescribes you some painkillers. Take the prescription to the cashier to pay for them, then take the receipt to the pharmacy. At this point be prepared to wait for possibly an hour to collect your goods.

From your registration slip to the final prescription, make sure you hold on to every piece of paper like your life depended on it. If you have a Chinese social security card some of your costs will be reduced, either immediately or by a refund that will later be returned to you via your company or bank. The amount of the reduction will depend on the grade of the hospital, your job, and on the treatment. To encourage people away from the major hospitals to the smaller ones, the social insurance card offers bigger discounts at the level one and two hospitals. In some cases the insurance might be cover the entire amount, or in others it will be a percentage. There are some treatments that are not covered at all; for example, a specialty bed may not be, but a general ward bed should be.

INTERNATIONAL HOSPITALS AND CLINICS

Beijing has a growing range of international options, both at clinic level, where you can maintain a relationship with a family doctor and be treated for minor illnesses, through to full-scale hospitals with areas of specialization. These facilities are largely in line with what you'd be used to back in your home country. They're orderly, hygienic, and are staffed largely by expat doctors fluent in English. You can make appointments, and your passage through treatment runs much as it would in a Western hospital, without queuing at cashiers or scrambling for a place in the doctor's office.

One of the biggest complaints about the international facilities is about the fees. These days, they are pretty much in line with American medical fees, and if you're not insured, you may literally be bankrupted by your bill. Whether it's for medication, an X-ray, or a consultation, the amount that comes out of your pocket will potentially be 100 times more than what you might spend within the general section of a local hospital, and three or four times more than that from the VIP section of a local hospital. Standard consultations can range from RMB500 to RMB1,300, but if you decide to add on a few annual checkup items, such as a pap smear or blood test, you could quite easily tarnish your day with a bill of RMB5,000-6,000. In part it's true that prices are jacked up because many of these private facilities are money-making businesses that revel in the awareness of their predominantly fully insured clientele. In their support, they are expensive operations to run, and staffing them with foreign or foreign-trained doctors and staff doesn't come cheap. When you come here you are definitely paying for a different kind of experience.

It really is worth shopping around even between international hospitals, however. SOS and Beijing United Family Hospital (BJU) once almost monopolized Beijing expat healthcare, but with more private facilities entering the market and with the downward trend for well-padded expat packages, there is more incentive to compete on prices.

Aside from prices, it's important to know that not all the international facilities are comprehensive hospitals equipped to handle major procedures. While able to take care of basic medical conditions, places such as International SOS Beijing Clinic and the Hong Kong International Medical Clinic, for example, are not suited to tackle critical procedures. They will either transfer you to another hospital in the city or arrange for

Oasis International Hospital, Beijing's newest international hospital

COURTESY OF OASIS INTERNATIONAL HOSPITAL

DAILY LIFE

a medical evacuation to your home country or perhaps down to Hong Kong. In fact, some people argue that they do the latter far more often than is necessary. A medical evacuation to Hong Kong can easily cost $50,000 in transport costs alone. This may include a doctor and nurse, an ambulance out to the airport and then another one out onto the tarmac, a private jet to Hong Kong, and then another ambulance to the hospital. If you find yourself in a critical situation, it's best to go directly to the full-scale hospitals, such as Beijing United Family Hospital or Oasis International Hospital.

MATERNITY AND GIVING BIRTH

Aside from returning home, there are three basic options if you do decide to bring your child into the world in China's capital. There are the international hospitals, the private Chinese ob-gyn hospitals, and the local hospitals, again in either the general ward area or VIP/international section. If you give birth in one of the major international hospitals, then you probably won't notice much difference between the procedures you'd expect at home and what you'll experience here.

Local hospitals, however, may offer an experience that falls far short of your notion of an idyllic birth. Like many areas in Beijing life, the notion of customer service or customer experience is either not a consideration or just in its nascent form. When it comes to maternity, there is no exception. The private facilities differ dramatically from the public options, but, compared to what you might expect of a Western service, they still lack a few bells and whistles. On the flip side, as you can guess, staff at Chinese facilities are extraordinarily experienced.

If you choose one of the private Chinese hospitals, such as Amcare Women's & Children's Hospital, Mary's Hospital, or Beijing Alice Gynecology Hospital, visit ahead of time and compare. Find out if the hospital has an ICU or NICU unit (not all do), and what the level of English is with staff. You may need to hire a translator for dealing with your doctor. At times this can be done through the hospital. For extra help or advice, an extremely handy place to contact is email group Beijing Mamas. Simply post your question and someone who has used that hospital is bound to reply.

The more local you go, the less memorable—or perhaps more memorable—the experience will be. In a local hospital, after checking in, the expectant mother will find herself sitting side by side with other puffing, uncomfortable women and their families, waiting in line to be the most urgent before being wheeled off to the delivery room. It is considerably cheaper, however. A complication-free natural birth in the local ward of the China-Japan Friendship Hospital may cost around RMB3,000-5,000, including delivery and three days of care.

You may hear of various Chinese traditions surrounding birth—such as women needing to stay at home and keep their feet up for 40 days after the birth, or the mother-in-law rather than the father being present in the delivery room—however, things are changing. Women often return to work soon after giving birth, and while most Chinese hospitals won't let the man into the delivery room, some do. One thing that is entrenching itself into the culture here at an alarming rate is the caesarian birth. The World Health Organization recommends that a country's national rate for C-sections be under 15 percent. Today, however, many developed countries average around 20-30 percent. China, nationally, is a little over this figure. Beijing, however, averages around 50 percent. It's estimated that a third of these are medically unnecessary. Research shows that the primary reasons for the concerningly high figures include fear of pain and women wanting their baby to be born on an auspicious day. Eight, for example, is considered an extremely lucky number, while four is considered extremely unlucky. Additionally, financially, C-sections bring in much more money. So while women in Beijing are not only more likely to request a C-section, but hospitals are also more likely to suggest it. If a local hospital suggests a C-section, consider it with skepticism and get a second opinion.

Knowing the Sex

Chinese culture favors males over females, in part because the male is seen to be the one who will continue the family line and increasingly because the male will also be a bigger breadwinner and take care of the parents as they age. With this mindset still firmly the norm in society, the one-child policy has created huge problems. Abortions are not only excessively used as a form of contraception, but they have also been a quick way to remove a baby if it's a girl. Consequently, there is now a disproportionate number of men to women. To try to stop this, it's now absolutely illegal for medical staff to tell you the sex of your baby, even for foreigners being treated by foreign doctors in international hospitals. Expats have had mixed experiences with how lenient or strict staff are in letting them know the gender of their child, but occasionally a wink or a nod in a quiet moment with your specialist will satisfy your curiosity.

Nationality, Passports, and Visas

If you have a baby in China, you may need to be aware of the differences in laws governing nationality between your home country and China. First, China does not recognize dual nationality. Second, China's Nationality Law states that any person born in China whose parents are both Chinese nationals or one of whose parents is a Chinese national will have Chinese nationality. This means that even if you are an American citizen but your partner is Chinese, your child will automatically have Chinese citizenship. This can then become tricky when you need to apply for an exit visa for your child, because the Chinese government may not recognize the baby's American citizenship (even though the United States does). To legally leave the country with your child you may need to apply at your local Public Security Bureau to relinquish your child's Chinese nationality—a process that can take up to three months.

If your child does qualify for your home country's citizenship, you'll need to apply for both a passport and Chinese visa for the baby. You can do this through your country's embassy. Depending on where you come from, there are various steps to registering the birth of your child and applying for such things as a social security number and passport. Contact your embassy in Beijing for detailed information.

PRESCRIPTIONS AND MEDICATIONS

If you have a typical medical condition requiring ongoing medication, you shouldn't find any difficulty getting the necessary medications once you arrive in Beijing. Most standard drugs are available. Some, however, be difficult to come by. These can include those for rare conditions, drugs that are new on the market, and drugs for mental health. "Ritalin, for example, can be difficult to get," says Dr. Saint Cyr. "It's often out of stock, and sometimes you can get only a couple of weeks supply. It can be

EXPAT PROFILES: GIVING BIRTH IN BEIJING

Two expats share their experiences giving birth in local Beijing hospitals.

OLGA

Swedish expat Olga is very familiar with the Chinese lifestyle. She has lived in Beijing for eight years and is married to a Chinese man, so she admits she's somewhat of a sinologist. When she had her second baby in 2010, she chose Beijing Amcare Women's & Children's Hospital.

I chose a Chinese hospital firstly because I'm not really affected by culture shock anymore, and secondly, I was not on an expat package, so BJU wasn't considered. I did, however, want something nicer than what public hospitals can usually offer.

I had my first baby in 2008 in Sweden and overall it was a very positive experience. The prenatal care, however, was done in Beijing at Amcare. It was my first baby and I followed their schedule until the 33rd week and then flew back to Sweden. The prenatal care at Amcare was generally okay, much better than any public hospital would be, although still not perfect. I had to do a lot of research for myself. It was crowded, although not as crowded as nowadays.

When I fell pregnant with my second baby in 2010 I decided to go to Amcare again for the prenatal care. They are professional and experienced. It's just the personal attention that is always lacking. This time around, now knowing everything about pregnancy and childbirth, I designed my own visits: I did fewer prenatal checks than you should, and fewer tests and ultrasounds. I went for checks only when I felt I wanted or needed one. I would just say I was out of the city (you're supposed to buy the birth package and book the delivery time). I didn't because I was still looking for options.

I would love to have a home birth but it is illegal (in China), and water births are not perfect here. If I ever needed to have a planned C-section, I would not go to these private hospitals where it also costs a fortune. The Chinese are great with C-sections and the process is more or less the same everywhere, so I'd just arrange for a private room and that would be it.

I didn't need a C-section, however, and was still searching for alternatives. It got to the point, however, that it was too late to book the labor anywhere, and the hospitals said that they they were full. So, in the end, I decided that I would call Amcare when I went into labor, and if they wouldn't accept me I would call American-Sino, if no again, then Mary's Hospital and the various others I knew of. If I still was not lucky, then I would just go to the local hospital near my home. I was lucky, however; when my water broke, we called Amcare and they said to come over. We arrived there after midnight and it took about one hour for all the necessary tests for admission. The biggest surprise was they said that since the water had already broken, I couldn't get up from the bed, and I had planned to do a lot of walking to speed up the process.

Finally after everyone left, I was able to sleep, but then the contractions started. One hour later they took me to the delivery room, which was the same but a floor higher, strapped me to the monitor and tried to give me IV, but I refused. They said that everyone needed oxytocin (Pitocin), that this was the protocol. I was firm and said that if anything went wrong I would give them whatever they needed, but at this point I was taking responsibility for this. They also offered me an epidural, which I also refused. So then for the remainder of the time it was just waiting. Their support ended with my refusal for medical intervention. The whole crowd of doctors and nurses were just waiting for the push stage. In Sweden, it is just two midwives who are with you, and they try to give a lot of emotional support, massage, simple things that make you relaxed and comfortable. None of that exists here. It is nice to have your husband next to you, otherwise this part would be difficult to survive.

In Sweden, when the baby is coming they heat the room and lower the lights, which altogether creates a nice smooth transition for the baby and the feeling of a miracle happening. Here, you never forget you are in hospital.

They have never pushed in any way for a C-section. The delivery was pretty fast and they guided it well. They handled the baby well, but just because there are so many people in the delivery room, they do everything really fast. So if you do or don't want something to be done to your baby, you have to tell them this in advance as they may not ask you because it's just such a routine for them.

They all knew it was my second baby, so after the birth, they quickly left us alone without pushing water, formula, or any unusual advice.

The facility is nice and the room is spacious, and you don't need to bring anything with you (such as baby clothes, diapers, wet napkins, soap, or sanitary napkins), as you need to do in the public hospitals. We wanted to go home after 24 hours of stay and they were okay with this, but they wouldn't agree to discharging me any earlier. We didn't buy the package, but instead just paid for all procedures done and materials used and since I didn't use any medication during labor and we stayed at hospital for only one day, it was about RMB8,000 cheaper than the package at that time (normally at least RMB34,000 for a natural birth with three-day stay).

SABRINA

French expat Sabrina has also been living in Beijing for more than eight years. When she decided to have her baby in China, she chose Beijing Wuzhou Women & Children's Hospital (GlobalCare).

There were a couple of reasons why I chose a Chinese hospital. Firstly, we had heard some really good things about the equipment in local hospitals and, in fact, the ultrasound machines in Wuzhou seemed really new. A Chinese friend of mine, who gave birth at Wuzhou Hospital and was quite satisfied with the service there, advised me to choose a hospital close to where I lived. So while I was still able, I could ride there on my bicycle in 10 minutes.

I also chose Wuzhou because of the stories that I'd heard about [another popular Chinese hospital]. While a friend of mine was delivering, her translator fainted, and doctors and nurses chatted around her throughout the process, saying, "Look how lazy she is. If she can't push harder she'll still be here tomorrow." Unfortunately she could understand them. Another friend was offered a C-section when she was five months pregnant, her translator wasn't very good with medical language, and all her tests had "pregnancy at risk" written in bold red characters on them, because she was 35.

So finally I visited Wuzhou Hospital and asked to see someone so that I could ask some questions, and it turned out that they seemed ready to listen to the wishes of their patients. They even proposed water delivery, saying they were promoting natural methods (even though they warned me that it would be very very painful when I asked if they would allow me to not have an epidural).

Additionally, when I asked about the prenatal classes, I loved the answer: "Yes, we do. We have a one-hour yoga class once a month, and one session about feeding, pampering, and massaging the baby." When I asked about classes for such things as delivery preparation and breathing techniques, they replied, "Oh, that's okay, the nurse will tell you when and how to breathe in and out." So, perhaps I might need to work on that myself. They also have a session about how to become a brave and courageous mother. (I think I'd really like to participate in this one!)

As for the price, it was RMB30,000 for the delivery and a standard room that included both a real bed for a visitor and a huge bathroom.

DAILY LIFE

really inconvenient." Narcotics, such as extended-release morphine for chronic pain, can also be difficult to access, and if you can get it the quantity prescribed might be highly controlled. If you can't access a particular drug you may need to find a way to get it into the country, such as going home yourself to get it.

Dosages may also be different in Beijing than in your home country, especially for antibiotics, which are highly overprescribed. Unfortunately there is also a financial "perverse incentive," says Dr. Saint Cyr. "The hospital makes a 15 percent cut off most prescriptions, and after the government dropped its financial support from most hospitals, the hospitals do rely on prescriptions and procedures, and so doctors are pressured to prescribe or to prescribe expensive things. They may also prescribe IVs—intravenous hydration or intravenous antibiotics—which almost no Western hospital would do. It's basically a revenue maker. It's certainly not evidence based."

Most international hospitals and clinics have their own pharmacy, and it's best, and sometimes necessary, to use this if you have seen a doctor at that facility. Streetside pharmacies may not have the medication you've been prescribed, the medication from the clinic will be labeled in English, and you can set up a refill schedule on the pharmacy computer, meaning you don't have to see the doctor every time you need your medication.

Before you leave your home country, be sure to arrange a three-month supply of any medication, just to allow for a new system of care to be established. Additionally, when carrying medication while traveling, always be sure to keep a copy of the prescription or a letter from your doctor on you. You should also bring your medical records, or at least a summary or hard copy of your medical history, especially if you are on a complicated regimen of medication. Finally, when time comes to leave Beijing, don't forget to obtain a copy of your medical records. This can take up to a month to process from the hospitals, including the international ones, and requires you to visit the hospital's medical records department in person.

Dentists

As little as five years ago, it was extraordinarily common to encounter local people with stained, damaged teeth and breath that would knock you flat, but within just a few years there seems to have been a huge shift in culture toward oral hygiene. Supermarkets are stocked with every imaginable variety of toothpaste and breath freshener, and services and standards at dental clinics have improved and now cover everything from standard cleanings to cosmetic dentistry.

For general services, such as cleanings and fillings, prices are relatively digestible, even if you don't have insurance, and sometimes there isn't a huge difference between the reputable local clinics and the international ones. Cleaning, for example, will cost around RMB300-500 in both styles of clinics, while a single filling will set you back by RMB250-750 at a local clinic and by RMB600-1,500 at an international one. If it's your first visit to a clinic, an initial checkup fee may also be charged, ranging RMB50-200. Some of the larger local clinics, such as SDM Dental, Arrail Dental Clinic, and Joinway, may not always have English-speaking dentists, but there is usually someone there in the clinic who can translate.

On a day-to-day basis, you won't really need to adjust your habits too much. Dental hygienist and educator Pat Christie at IDC Dental recommends keeping a regular schedule for checkups, just as you would in your home country. On top of this, she suggests brushing at least twice a day with a fluoride toothpaste. "Beijing's water isn't fluoridated, so you'll benefit from any additional fluoride, including mouth rinses with fluoride. Fluoride boosts your teeth's resistance to decay, which is very important if you want to limit your dental visits while living here."

Finally, given the city's dryness, you may be inclined to drink more than usual. You should, however, avoid quenching your thirst with sugary drinks, Pat says. "Bottled tea and fruit juice are heavily consumed by the local population, but your dental health will benefit if you can avoid them. Brush as soon as possible after any sugar exposure."

Insurance

Living in Beijing without any form of insurance really is taking a gamble. These days medical costs are basically on par with those in the United States, and should anything serious happen to you, you may find yourself struggling to recover from more than just the illness. Even if you plan to stick to the local hospitals, a single night in a VIP suite at Peking Union (Xiéhé) can cost around RMB3,000 per night.

Expense aside, in many cases you won't even be treated if you can't either pay upfront or guarantee payment through an insurer. Another incentive for covering yourself is that many health-care policies build checkups into their coverage. Regular checkups are one way of staying healthy and catching things early. With appointments costing at least RMB1,000 at some international clinics, if you are paying directly out of your own pocket, you may be more likely to skimp on your health care and visit a doctor only when something goes wrong, which might be too late.

You may already have insurance in your home country, or pay into programs such as Medicare or Medicaid. Don't assume any of these will cover you in China. It's quite likely that they won't. Be sure to consult your provider before you depart your home country, and if you are covered in Beijing, find out exactly which hospitals they accept and whether or not medical evacuation is included.

The difficulty with choosing health insurance is that you need to wade through a seemingly endless array of options. If your company is going to provide insurance for you, then that will likely cut out a lot of the mental exhaustion of the selection process. Often international companies will collaborate with one or two providers, so then it's just down to you find the plan that's right for your individual circumstance. Even if this is the case, however, you should still check to see how comprehensively your given options will cover you in a worst-case scenario and if you can use a provider of your own choosing if preferred.

FINDING AN INSURER

There are various ways to try to sort through insurance companies. You can do it yourself by going directly to an insurance company; using an agent, who will have connections to various insurers; or speaking to a broker, who typically deals with a wide

DAILY LIFE

array of insurers and who can give you a better comparison of policies to try to match you as closely as possible to what you need.

Most international insurance companies are not licensed in China, but this isn't as scary as it may sound. If you're going to restrict yourself to the international hospitals and clinics it won't be a problem. You will, however, need a China-certified insurer if you plan to use local hospitals and if you need a *fāpiào* (invoice) for your insurance. There are ways to get a *fāpiào* through uncertified insurers, but this can be troublesome process and possibly more expensive.

Some brokerages also make it easy for you to quickly choose and buy insurance online. The problem is that you're likely to be unaware of the tricks and trips that are inherent with life in Beijing. It really is advisable to find a reputable broker who is willing to meet you face to face and who will give you frank advice and find a suitable plan for your situation. Speak to various brokers if needed. Ensure they're familiar with the local market and suss out how long they plan to be here—those who are in China for the long term are more likely to care about customer service and your return business when your policy rolls over. "It's important to speak to a broker who is knowledgeable about the small print and who isn't just trying to take your money and run," says local insurance professional Nika Feshchenko. Beyond that, find out how long the insurance company has been dealing with China.

While getting your insurance, ask about property insurance. Few expats have it, but it's quite possible that if someone else's property is damaged as a result of your property—for example if your shower's plumbing leaks into the apartment below—you'll be liable, not your landlord.

Broker options include locally experienced professionals such as Feshchenko, Pacific Prime, BrokerFish, Globalsurance, and many more.

WHAT TO LOOK FOR IN A POLICY AND INSURER

First of all, decide whether or not you're open to or interested in using local hospitals. If this is important to you, you will immediately have eliminated several choices on your list of potential insurers. Many of the most reputable international insurers are not accepted in local Chinese hospitals, but a few are making efforts to be locally certified. Chinese insurers are more likely to be accepted at local facilities.

Find out which hospitals the insurer can do direct billing for outpatient care with and under what circumstances. International SOS, for instance, will not do direct billing with your insurer if you are not a member. Then, for inpatient care, ensure the insurer can provide guarantee of payment (GOP). This can usually be obtained within a few days or even within a few minutes via fax if an emergency arises.

Just a few of the strong contenders for Beijing include Now Health International, AXA PPP Healthcare, Bupa, Cigma, Aetna, and Allianz Worldwide Care, but there are many more. Chinese private health insurance is relatively new and still developing. Some of the better-known companies include Ping An Health Insurance, Huatai Insurance, and AXA-Minmetals. Opinions vary as to local insurers' performance when it comes to customer service and following through on payouts, and it would be wise to speak to an independent broker or consultant to ascertain a company's current record.

Find out if there is guaranteed renewability, and if so, at standard rates. Not all policies offer this, and if for some reason you become too expensive over the year, they may refuse to renew your insurance at the end of the year. Alternatively they may jack up the price as you're now deemed a risk. Additionally, many expats have found that though they were happy with the first year of a given company's insurance, their premiums jumped dramatically for the following year for no apparent reason.

Know the lifetime limit of your policy. Some policies offer lifetime limits rather than annual limits. If you have a major medical incident, $500,000 of your lifetime limit of $1,000,000 may be used up in a few months. This may be fine if you just plan to use the policy while you're living in China and intend to return to a different insurer in your home country in the near future. Just check that usage of your lifetime limit won't affect your ability to sign with a subsequent insurer.

Know the individual allowances for your policy and how they relate to costs in Beijing. A bed at Beijing United Family, for example, cost around RMB7,000 per night at the time of writing. Examples of payments in the past for Beijing expats include: RMB150,000 (US$24,000) for a broken ankle; RMB400,000 (US$64,200) for a back injury; and RMB2 million (US$321,000) for the evacuation and repatriation of a healthy man who simply fell down a set of escalators and sustained a severe traumatic injury.

Find out if the company operates with a moratorium or by underwriting. If it's a moratorium, the company may be unlikely to pay for a condition, such as cancer, that may be pre-existing but unknown at the time you purchase your policy. This moratorium will last for a given period. If the condition arises within that period they won't cover you. Underwriting, however, assesses you at the time of signing and agrees to cover you for what is known at that time.

Find out if your policy is for expatriates only. Some policies will not cover you once you leave China. This may or may not be fine by you, but you should also know how or if they will refund any prepaid amount of money.

As for what to get, that's very personal. "At the very minimum you should get inpatient care plus repatriation," says Feshchenko. This said, some insurers are more willing to repatriate than others, even if this is included in your policy. FrontierMEDEX, for example, can provide basic packages that include emergency medical evacuation. Given that you'll be in China, you might also want to check if traditional Chinese medicine (TCM) is covered.

ALTERNATIVES TO INSURANCE

If the cost of insurance does end up out of your reach, there are some options that might soften a medical blow. Keep an eye out for specials and memberships. Many international facilities have memberships that, for an annual fee, will give you significant reductions. Oasis International Hospital and MedicGo International Medical Center also offer promotions, such as a package deal for a checkup, test, and medication.

SOCIAL INSURANCE

If you're going to be working in Beijing on a work permit, then you, together with your employer, will be required to make contributions to the social insurance system. In return, you'll receive a card that you can use to claim benefits relating to retirement, unemployment, medical treatment, workplace injury, and maternity. Theoretically, if you're paying into the fund, you're entitled to receive the same benefits as a local

Chinese citizen. This means that when you go to a local hospital for treatment or buy medication, you can show your social insurance card to get a reduction or refund on the costs. Unfortunately, as this applies only to public government hospitals, not private or international hospitals, very few expats make use of the payments.

Not every city has the same rules or contribution quantities, and Beijing differs from Shanghai and Guangzhou. As things stand right now, foreign workers in Beijing are required to make payments that will cover all five aspects of the plan—despite both unemployment and retirement ending your eligibility to be in the country. You will be required to pay around 11 percent from your gross salary, and your employer around 37 percent, with a salary cap of RMB12,603.

Before you begin working in Beijing, you should find out if your country is exempt from contributions. China has bilateral agreements with some countries, including Germany and South Korea, and employees from these countries won't need to pay. You must provide a certificate of coverage to be exempt. Currently U.S., Canadian, British, and Australian citizens are exempt.

If you have international health insurance, it's highly unlikely you'll ever make use of this money that you're paying out. Fortunately, however, you can get your own unused contributions back (not your employer's) when you leave the country. The rules governing the social insurance policy for foreigners, however, are new and not particularly transparent. Trying to get clear information about this entire system and process is extremely difficult. Speak to your HR department, contact Dezan Shira & Associates (www.asiabriefingmedia.com), or contact your embassy.

Preventative Measures

IMMUNIZATIONS

Beijing is a relatively safe city if you're just passing through, and many tourists forgo vaccinations altogether. As you'll be living here for an extended period, however, you should see your doctor at least four to six weeks before you leave home to discuss the current recommendations. If you or your children are already on a schedule of vaccinations, you should be able to continue that here in Beijing. You should, however, check with your child's new school in Beijing to find out about any particular local requirements. Recommended vaccinations for Beijing typically include diphtheria, tetanus, MMR (measles, mumps, and rubella), varicella (chickenpox), influenza, typhoid, tuberculosis, pneumococcus, and Japanese encephalitis (JE). Whooping cough (pertussis) is making a comeback, so it's strongly recommended that both adults and children are vaccinated against this. You may have already been vaccinated against hepatitis B, but you should also be vaccinated against hepatitis A. Hepatitis A is usually spread by close personal contact or by eating food or drinking water contaminated by feces, and, unfortunately, hand washing is not always a high priority for some of those in the local hospitality trade. A malaria vaccination is not always recommended for Beijing, but it is something to keep in mind should you decide to take a holiday down south to Yunnan or Hainan.

Another vaccination that should be strongly considered is rabies. Unlike countries such as New Zealand, the United States, and Australia where rabies just isn't a daily threat, in China it is a present and serious problem. Country-wide around 3,000 people die of rabies every year, and though incidences in urban Beijing are comparatively few, they do exist. There have been cases where expats have died after contracting the disease. All it takes is a bite or lick on an open wound from an infected animal, and then if no medical action is taken before symptoms begin to show in the person, the disease is 100 percent fatal. If you or your child is bitten by an animal, it's vital that you seek immediate medical treatment. If you had already been vaccinated prior to the infection, the treatment would be relatively simple. If you hadn't been vaccinated but receive immediate treatment before symptoms appear there is also a relatively successful post-exposure prophylaxis treatment, involving an injection of rabies immune globulin and several injections of rabies vaccine given over a 28-day period. The problem is that not only is this treatment expensive, it may also not be in ready supply in Beijing, and you may need to be evacuated to a place that has a supply of the rabies immune globulin. Much cheaper and more reliable is the pre-exposure vaccination, which is a series of three injections of rabies vaccine given over a month (on days 0, 7, and 21 or 28).

As to the quality of Chinese vaccinations, there is no need to be concerned. In the past standards were admittedly questionable, but they have since greatly improved and the WHO has now recognized Chinese vaccinations as being safe enough to export. Regardless, doctors have little choice anyway, given that it is now illegal for them to prescribe imported medications.

CONTRACEPTION

Despite being in a position to be a world leader in contraception, inspired by its one-child policy, China seems instead to be in an appalling position. It's not a topic that is comfortably spoken about, so people are commonly uneducated about safe sex practices. Consequently, unwanted pregnancies and abortions are quite near to being the norm. It's certainly not unusual for a girl in her twenties to have had four, five, or even six abortions. Despite this, birth control pills are readily available in Beijing. It was once possible to buy these over the counter at international pharmacies, but this has recently changed and you now need to get a prescription from your doctor. Be prepared to pay big bucks, however, if you shop here. A month's supply will possibly cost RMB250-300. Chinese pharmacies, such as the Cachet chain, also supply contraceptive pills, often over the counter, and usually at half the price. They may not always go by the same names, however. Dr. Saint Cyr also recommends bringing a three-month supply from home with you to give yourself time to find an appropriate replacement.

INFECTIOUS DISEASES

When it comes to infectious diseases, Beijing has its pros and cons. The weather for at least half the year is too cold in Beijing to make malaria transmission likely (it requires an average daily temperature of 20°C/68°F), and compared to many other areas of the country outbreak occurrences are relatively low. SARS, a pneumonia-like disease that had an outbreak in Beijing in 2003, is also rarely heard of these days. On the downside, Japanese encephalitis, rabies, and whooping cough are entrenched enough to be a continuing concern.

TOP 10 TIPS FOR STAYING HEALTHY IN BEIJING

A long-term resident of Beijing, Dr. Richard Saint Cyr of Beijing United Family Hospital (BJU) and website MyHealth Beijing has shared his top 10 tips to help you stay healthy while living in the big smoke.

TIP 1: RESPECT THE AIR POLLUTION, BUT DON'T BE CONTROLLED BY IT

Beijing has some of the worst pollution in the world, and even healthy people may still have problems on really bad days. You need to acknowledge and to *respect* this issue. Wear a mask while cycling if the pollution index is over 200. But also, keep some perspective and try not to get too caught up in worrying about pollution.

TIP 2: TAKE CONTROL OF INDOOR AIR

Ninety percent of our time is spent indoors, and air quality indoors can often be just as bad or worse than outdoors. Protect that 90 percent of your Beijing time with well-made air purifiers, special air-scrubbing plants, and proper ventilation.

TIP 3: DON'T WORRY ABOUT THE CLINICS; THE CARE IS VERY GOOD

Beijing expats are really lucky in that there are excellent clinics that can easily take care of almost all medical needs.

TIP 4: BUY ORGANIC FOOD— OR GREENFOOD LABEL

Here in Beijing, food safety is a major concern, and organic food in general has (in theory) much more government oversight than a standard local farm. Alternatively, government-certified foods with the GreenFood label are made with fewer pesticides and chemicals than regular produce. They're not as good as organic but they're better than nothing, and the prices are a bit cheaper than organic.

TIP 5: BUY A BIKE

The exercise value of riding a bike is crucial, and biking in Beijing's pollution is still healthier than not exercising at all. As for helmets, though it's rare to see them worn, they're still a lifesaver, and your children should definitely wear them as much as possible.

TIP 6: TO EVERY THING, THERE IS A SEASON

Each Beijing season has a few particular oddities:

Winter health problems usually include colds and influenza, as well as winter depression. The secret to avoiding the winter blues? Pamper yourself! For example, buy a foot soak; keep your skin moist; visit a local hot springs; take a weekend break in a hotel; take vitamin D.

Spring can come with sandstorms and catkin pollen. It can be a health hazard, but have a little common-sense

Likewise, STDs are a growing problem in China, and Beijing is no exception. From syphilis and HIV to gonorrhea and chlamydia, they are all here. This isn't helped by an unwillingness to talk about condoms, and using or suggesting your partner use one may incur loss of face. MyHealth Beijing recommends that during your time in Beijing you avoid sex workers; practice safe and low-risk sex; always use a latex condom; and get regular checkups, even if there are no symptoms.

avoidance and you'll be fine. Many Beijingers do have allergic hay fever problems in the spring, but most expats have fewer hay fever problems in Beijing.

Summer health issues include a major increase in gastroenteritis as well as travel-related diseases from expats' vacations to exotic and malaria-filled southern locales. Do your homework beforehand by researching your destination's health status on the CDC travel website (wwwnc. cdc.gov/travel). Additionally, prepare early—vaccines can be in short supply at this time of year.

Autumn is fairly mellow, so enjoy this all-too-brief moment of perfect weather by exploring Beijing's mountains and tourist attractions.

TIP 7: HAVE AN ANTI-INFLAMMATORY LIFESTYLE

In Beijing we are bombarded every day with air particles and gases both indoors and outdoors, as well as from chemicals in our foods. These are pro-inflammatory, causing free radical damage to our healthy cells, as well as setting off cascades of unhealthy hormones and enzymes that can slowly lead to many illnesses, such as heart disease and cancers. To fight off this damage: don't smoke; watch your alcohol intake; eat anti-inflammatory foods (e.g., vegetables and fruit); and speak to your doctor about supplements such as fish oil.

TIP 8: EXERCISE

China's number one killer is the same as all over the world: heart disease. You still need to focus on the basics of good body weight, exercise, proper foods, and not smoking.

TIP 9: TAKE CARE OF YOUR BODY AND SOUL

I see a lot of overworked patients who rarely sleep well, are totally stressed, and are too busy for exercise—all of which lower people's immune systems and set them up for illness. It's crucial that we constantly check in with our heart and soul and ask ourselves, "Am I happy here in Beijing? Am I neglecting something or someone, including myself?" If you do feel that life is spinning out of control, many of Beijing's clinics have professional counseling services.

TIP 10: WATCH OUT FOR SEXUALLY TRANSMITTED DISEASES

It is frighteningly common here to get exposed to bugs such as chlamydia and gonorrhea. There is also an alarming resurgence of syphilis in China – plus the usual suspects, such as HIV, herpes, hepatitis, and others. Practice safe sex and be careful where you buy your condoms—there have been recent scares with poorly made counterfeits. Stick to the big chains, like Watsons.

Published with permission from www.my-healthbeijing.com

Traditional Chinese Medicine

Chinese medicine is still alive and strong in Beijing, and if you have any inclinations to try it, there are plenty of options. Traditional Chinese medicine (TCM) is based on the principles of balancing the yin and yang in your body, and generally uses herbal, heat, or pressure treatments rather than Western-style drugs. It is said to be effective in treating an almost endless array of conditions, including skin conditions such as eczema and psoriasis, liver diseases, stress, depression, pain, weight problems, and much more.

One of the typical treatments still widely used is acupuncture. This uses long, fine needles to stimulate particular points in your body, aiming to adjust the flow of energy through and the functioning of a given organ. In many clinics, to ensure sterile conditions, you can purchase your own sets of acupuncture needles for the practitioner to use on you. While acupuncture is said to be able to treat a wide range of conditions, it's most popular for chronic pain, and even weight loss.

Cupping is another popular choice. In this practice, the practitioner uses a glass cup on a part of your body, often in similar positions to those for acupuncture. Suction is created either by heat or a pump. This is said to help blood circulation, and it leaves distinctive deep purple round bruises on your skin for all to see.

Beyond these, other treatment forms include scraping (*guāshā,* 刮痧), acupressure, moxibustion (*jiǔ,* 灸), massage (*ànmó,* 按摩), and traditional herbal medicine.

Some of the more popular TCM clinics and hospitals include the very busy Beijing Hospital of Traditional Chinese Medicine, Beijing Tongrentang Traditional Chinese Medicine Hospital in Dongcheng district, Beijing Hong Yi Tang Yiyuan near Sanlitun in Chaoyang district, Beijing Massage Hospital in Xicheng district, and the slightly more stylish Meridian Traditional Chinese Medicine Clinic near Lido. For a more Western-friendly option, there is Straight Bamboo TCM Clinic, which operates out of The Hutong.

Environmental Factors

One aspect of Beijing life that expats struggle to deal with most is the environmental issues. Pollution is a serious problem in all areas—air, water, and, in many parts of the city, noise and visual pollution. Food hygiene and food safety are likewise an ongoing concern for the public.

There are ways to get around the pollution problems, or at least reduce your exposure to them, but this usually means increasing your expenses by buying imported goods or gadgets, and perhaps curtailing your outdoor activities from time to time. Ultimately the environmental issues will be something you will need to accept or add to your list of cons when deciding to leave or stay.

AIR QUALITY

Air quality is a serious issue in Beijing. While there are definitely more "blue sky days" than there were 10 years ago, pollution readings are often at levels that rate as "very unhealthy" to "hazardous" by U.S. standards. Spring used to be notorious for its dust storms, which would taint the sky with a toxic yellow color. These do still occur every year, but with decreased frequency and intensity. The Chinese government is trying to take action to reduce the problem—such as limiting traffic, moving factories away from the city, cloud seeding, and tree planting—but the problem sometimes seems unrelenting.

There are 27 official monitoring stations scattered around the municipality collecting readings to produce the Air Pollution Index (API), and if you watch these on a daily basis, you can see that pollution levels swing greatly from day to day and place to place. Generally, the areas of Beijing that fall into the more polluted end of the scale most often include Shijingshan district (central west), Daxing county (south), and Yanqing

© SHANNON AITKEN

Pollution is an ever-present problem in Beijing.

county (far northwest). Miyun district (far northeast, and the place of Beijing's water reservoir), on the other hand, is almost always the least polluted. The inner city and Shunyi district typically fall somewhere around the middle.

Over the last year or so pollution monitoring systems in China have become a contentious issue, largely provoked by the American embassies in Beijing, Shanghai, and Guangzhou, which set up their own equipment within their own grounds and measured the immediately surrounding pollution according to standards set by the U.S. Environmental Protection Agency (EPA). They began releasing these figures to the public via hourly Twitter feeds (BeijingAir). This caused a national stir, not only because the numbers often differed dramatically from the official Chinese figures, but also because it highlighted the fact that the Chinese government was releasing more flattering figures, which were based on larger particulate matter (PM 10), rather than the smaller particulates (PM 2.5) that the EPA deemed to be more harmful. Stirred by public pressure, the government also began releasing PM 2.5 figures. Many of the official aggregated figures, however, still use the PM 10 data, and when put side by side with the health warnings of the EPA system, you'd think they were measuring different cities. For example, the Chinese system grades the air quality from I to V, with I (0-50) indicating Excellent (*yōu jí,* 优级) and V (>300) indicating Serious (*zhòng jí,* 重级). On the day of writing this very paragraph, the readings from the Beijing U.S. Embassy wavered between categories Unhealthy and Very Unhealthy, while the figures for the nearby Chaoyang Nongzhanguan station had a warning level of II (*liáng,* 良), or Good.

The pollution will no doubt dampen your enthusiasm for an active outdoor lifestyle, but sometimes it's important to be mindful of potential indoor pollutants. Cigarette smoke is of course one of the major pollutants in restaurants and bars. However, VOCs (volatile organic compounds) such as benzene and formaldehyde are also possible problems here because of the quality standards of construction materials. A new, freshly painted apartment may not be as pollutant-free as you think. "The indoor air pollution is just as crucial here in Beijing as the outdoor pollution," says Dr. Saint Cyr.

What Are Your Options?

Purchase air filters for your home, including your kids' rooms, especially if you plan to be here for several years. Do the research in your own country, ensure they filter for VOCs, and consider bringing them and the replacement filters with you—you may find they're cheaper at home. Popular brands available in Beijing include Torana Clean Air (Blueair) and IQAir.

Wear a face mask when in crowded spaces, such as subway trains, and when doing outdoor exercise on polluted days. It needs to be an N95-rated mask and not just a cloth one. Convenience stores, such as 7-Eleven, stock a range of basic masks, while stores such as the World Health Store, Natooke cycle shop, and Torana Clean Air carry more specialized options.

Keep your eye on the indexes. You can do this by downloading the China Air Quality Index app onto your tablet computer or smartphone. This app compares both official government readings of Beijing's air and the U.S. Embassy's reading of the air in central Chaoyang district.

WATER QUALITY

It's almost impossible to know what's in the water in Beijing—bottled or tap. Over the last several years, bottled-water companies have come under scrutiny and been accused of using everything from tainted water to bottles made from toxic recycled plastics. When you think you might be doing the right thing by buying the large bottles (a.k.a. barrels) of water rather than drinking tap water, what you might actually be doing is something worse. People often ask which brand of water is safest, but it seems reports conflict wildly. It's also not always obvious that what you're getting is the real deal, especially if the company outsources its distribution. It has been estimated that around half of Beijing's bottled water might be fake, such as bottles being refilled with tap water or fake labels altogether. Some companies place identification numbers on the tops of their bottles, which are said to vouch for the quality of the water.

Regarding tap water, you again will read or hear arguments from both sides, some saying you can drink it straight from the tap without worry, others saying it's toxic. The problem is that in any single part of the city either viewpoint might be right or wrong. Water quality varies from area to area, from building to building, and from day to day. The reason is that even though the water that leaves the government's treatment areas is largely drinkable, the plumbing on the way from there to your home is somewhat dubious. Pipes are frequently old, cracked, or improperly sealed at joints, and even if you live in a luxury apartment complex, it's not unlikely that developers have cut costs by using low-grade materials in out-of-sight places. This of course then increases the likelihood that your water may be mixed with such things as general silt and rust, heavy metals, construction-site runoff, fertilizers, or pesticides.

The water in Beijing is disinfected with chloramines, and this is nothing unusual. Chloramines are also the choice water disinfectant in many places in the United States and, if carefully controlled, are generally thought to be safe for consumption. What's more hazardous and difficult to control, however, can be the byproducts of disinfection—the chemicals caused by the reaction between the chloramines and the substances that combine with them along the way.

Unfortunately it doesn't stop at the drinking water. Shower or bath water may also have possible side affects. First, if there are chemicals and VOCs present, they are more likely to become vaporized when heated in the water, and so breathed in. "These are invisible but are a serious problem," says Charlie Tomson, CEO of American water filter company Aquasana. Second, even leaving potential toxins or carcinogens aside, many expats have found the water in Beijing to be irritating, especially to sensitive or eczema-prone skin, and damaging to hair quality or color. Some have also noted increased hair loss when they move to Beijing. Tomson, however, says that there is no clear evidence that this is from Beijing's water, but may often instead be related to the stress of moving to any new country.

Personally, my skin had always been much dryer in Beijing, and originally I put it down to the dry climate. I did see and feel obvious improvement, however, when I switched to using a filter on my shower. On the other hand, my Chinese neighbors tell me they have been drinking and bathing in the Beijing water all their life, and I can vouch for the fact that they all appear to be very healthy.

What Are Your Options?

At the very least, boil your water before drinking it. It won't get rid of heavy metals, but will kill the bacteria. Brushing your teeth with tap water should be fine, but for anything more than that, take precautions.

Avoid the barrels of bottled water. Unless you can 100 percent guarantee that your water is from who and where you think it should be coming from, and that the plastics are toxin free, it's best to bypass this option.

Get a filter system. This is generally becoming the preferred option. Things to look for include the size of particles that are filtered, that high-quality carbon is used, and that the filter is certified. Bear in mind that becoming "certified" in China can sometimes be expedited by means other than quality, so if the product has been certified abroad, this should put you at ease. Ideally the filter will be fully imported; however, check to see if it has been adapted for the Beijing water issues. Aquasana's China kitchen filters, for example, differ slightly from the American ones in that they have a pre-filter to remove the higher levels of sediment found in water here. Avoid buying your filter from sites such as Taobao, as it's quite possible they're fake. Water filters can be purchased directly through companies such as Aquasana, one of the most popular choices for expats. This is an American-run company and has English-speaking staff who will install it for you and who can assess your needs. Alternatively you can purchase filters via large retailers such as the World Health Store, Carrefour, or Dazhong.

In the end, it comes down to personal choice and what makes you feel comfortable. If you'd like to investigate the matter further, www.myhealthbeijing.com is a great place to start. Additionally, for more information on chloramines, water treatment, and possible health consequences, visit the EPA site at http://water.epa.gov.

FOOD QUALITY

Things don't get better in the food arena, and again it's an aspect of life that many Beijing expats realize they just have to deal with. From fresh produce to supermarket

DAILY LIFE

products to restaurant dishes, scandals relating to risky standards are prevalent. You could limit yourself to imported-only food, but you'll not only be blowing out your daily spending, you'll also be missing out on the wonderfully diverse food that is available.

The positive thing about Chinese food is that dishes typically include a multitude of ingredients, meaning every meal is a mega multivitamin. On the flip side, a lot of food is highly processed, salty and/or oily, or produced with money-cutting methods. Training of kitchen staff is also an on-the-job process, so attention to hygiene and safe food handling practices often falls anywhere between ordinary and shocking. Essentially this means both bacterial as well as chemical issues are to be confronted. The occasional bout of food poisoning is almost a given here, and hepatitis A spreading from the unwashed hands of kitchen staff, a more serious issue, is something to keep in mind when getting your vaccinations. Additionally, allergies of the West are not generally well understood by many locals. Popular ingredients include peanut oil, chilies, dried shrimp, and nuts. Awareness is growing, however, and you can usually tell the wait staff that you have an allergy and to not add a certain ingredient. (From a religious angle, the Chinese love pork. Sometimes it will not even be mentioned as an ingredient, and if the dish simply says "meat," then you can assume it's pork.)

What You Can Do

- Wash fruit and vegetables thoroughly before cooking or eating, and peel if possible. See the EWG guide to pesticides on produce (www.ewg.org).
- Eat at busy restaurants where the food is turning over quickly, and refuse cold rice. Request that no MSG be added (*búfàng wèijīng,* 不放味精).
- Avoid undercooked fish and shellfish. If you are eating seafood, try to choose imported options.
- Breastfeed your baby rather than rely on local milk products.
- Take multivitamins and other health supplements.
- Carry a pair of your own metal chopsticks to use at restaurants. Avoid the wooden ones, which are often poorly washed.
- Avoid street vendors—it's sad to say this, but this crowd unfortunately strikes out big time when it comes to food-handling practices and trustworthy raw produce.

SMOKING

If you're trying to quit smoking or detest the plume of someone's cigarette wafting into your face as you eat, then Beijing will be sure to test you. Smoking is still a huge part of everyday life here, cigarettes are incredibly cheap, and cigarette stores are prolific. Expensive cigarettes and cigars are even highly favored as face-giving gifts. In addition to the general evils of smoking, Chinese cigarettes are also typically of low-grade quality, and the premium-grade "imported" cigarettes are often fake. Add a daily dose of pollution and you really are risking your long-term health. For those who do want to quit, nicotine patches and gum are available from some international pharmacies.

The government isn't ignorant of the problem. China has the highest number of smokers in the world, totaling more than 300 million, and the Ministry of Health estimates that approximately 1 million people die of smoking-related illnesses every year, together with 100,000 people from secondhand-smoke (SHS) related illnesses. According to the WHO in China, "almost two-thirds of reproductive-aged women in China are routinely exposed to secondhand tobacco smoke at home, and over half are routinely exposed in their workplaces." Unfortunately, with the China National Tobacco Corporation responsible for a significant proportion of the government's income, hopes for a radical change any time soon are low.

Metropolitan Beijing does fare somewhat better than regional Chinese areas, and if you're at a foreign-owned venue, such as a Starbucks or fine-dining restaurant in the CBD, then it is unlikely anyone will light up. On the other hand, if you're in a local establishment, it's unlikely staff members will ask anyone to put it out. The smoking laws in such places still often mean nothing, and there is next to zero enforcement of them. People will flagrantly smoke right next to a conspicuously displayed No Smoking sign, and seem to be oblivious to the possibility that their smoke that is enshrouding you might be offensive.

Disabled Access

Unfortunately, if you or someone in your family has any kind of mobility challenge, the day-to-day issues you experience in your home environment are going to be magnified in Beijing. Generally the culture here is that disabilities are embarrassing and something to be pitied and hidden away. Even post-injury rehabilitation is a new and limited service here. It's an extremely rare thing to see anyone getting around in a wheelchair unless they're elderly or are dressed in pajamas and being rolled around hospital grounds; seeing people with amputations or neuromuscular disorders within the community is even rarer. When you do see someone with a visible disability, it's almost always a beggar who is using their disfigurement as a promotional tool to boost donations.

If you do happen to have an obvious disability, be warned that people will stop and stare shamelessly at you. And if you do need assistance to get anywhere, such as into a restaurant or down onto a subway platform, it no doubt will turn into a public spectacle with several staff kindly but perhaps overenthusiastically offering complete orchestration of the situation, together with a large crowd of onlookers. Unfortunately, the Paralympics came and went in 2008 with few long-term improvements to society as far as disabled access is concerned. Lifts and ramps that were installed were soon removed. The occasional stairlift still exists, but don't feel that you can rely on them being there or that they will be functioning.

Subways do actually have assigned carriages for wheelchairs, but in many cases the cars are so jammed with people that you must convince a number of people to get off the train so that you can get on. If you are able to stand, then you most likely will have to because there won't be a seat. Generally, buses don't have wheelchair options, and it can be hard to identify where to wait for the ones that do. For taxis, it can be hard to get a driver to stop and pick you up if you have a visible walking aid, especially if your chair or frame is collapsible and can easily fit in the trunk. On the other hand, there are a few barrier-free taxis (again, diminishing leftovers of the Olympic Games). Sightings of these are rare, and it's essential to book them. To do so, have a Chinese-speaker call the Beijing taxi center (tel. 96106) between 8am and 10am at least one day in advance.

Ramps at gutters are reasonably ubiquitous, but not all buildings have ramps at their entrances, and it's quite possible that a car will be parked in front of them anyway. Additionally, even if you or your loved one is not restricted to a wheelchair, subway stations are often several flights of stairs below ground, and escalators are most commonly only for coming up, not going down. In some cases, subway staff have been seen physically carrying a person down the stairs. Elevators are almost nonexistent at places of public transport. Similarly, in many older apartment buildings there may be no elevators at all or perhaps ones that operate during the day only. When nature calls, you're likely to also run into some frustrations. Accessible toilets are not extremely common, and those that do exist are often locked and/or double as storage rooms. Additionally, managing Beijing's typically small cubicles and squat toilets may be tricky.

Deafness and blindness seem to be two of the few conditions that get any kind of public attention or degree of acceptance. The Chinese deaf are often seen around town, signing to each other on subways or along the streets, and if you can read Chinese you'll be happy to know that it's basically standard for everything on TV to be subtitled. For the blind, sidewalks are uniformly paved with tactiles, the knobby tiles that are meant to aid navigation by touch. Sadly, these also uniformly end at power poles, newspaper stands, large holes, parked cars, and any other obstacle you can think of. There are no guide dogs, but you will occasionally see people with canes. From a career perspective, even for the deaf or blind work opportunities are limited, and the most common place that you'll encounter a person with a visual impairment is in one of the many blind massage centers around town.

Despite this, it's not all bleak, and there are ongoing efforts to make improvements. Prior to 1980 people with disabilities were derogatorily referred to as *cánfèi,* meaning disabled and waste, but today that's no longer used and *cánjírén* (disabled person) is standard. The reality remains, however, that life in Beijing for a foreigner with a disability comes with weighty challenges that you'll need to be ready for, and if you're a parent or care giver, you will need to be a strong advocate for your loved one. It's highly advisable that you make a fact-finding trip here before you commit to a life in Beijing, making sure to talk personally to expats who have lived here and who are perhaps in a similar situation. For extra information, you can contact Disability China, Handicap International, or the China Disabled Persons' Federation. There are also two illustrative posts by wheelchair travelers Rosemary Ciotti and Madeleine Wilken found in the Travel Archives at www.globalaccessnews.com. The dates may seem a little old, but the experiences the writers describe are still valid today and transferrable from the tourist sites of Beijing to the places of everyday life.

Safety

CRIME

When it comes to crime, Beijing is, for the most part, a fairly safe city. There is a constant presence of police almost everywhere you go, which reminds all of the government's watchful eye. Violent crimes against foreigners are infrequent, but they do occur and, over recent years, with somewhat more regularity. Petty crimes, on the other hand, such as bicycle theft or pickpocketing, are common. Scams are also extremely prolific. These may include sorrowful emails asking for financial assistance; pedestrians faking being hit by a cyclist or car and immediately demanding a huge payout; gas station attendants underfilling tanks; and people tampering with parked cars only to then demand a "help" fee to fix it when you return. Counterfeit money is also sure to fall into your hands on the odd occasion, particularly the RMB100 notes.

When violent crimes against foreigners do happen, most occur around bar areas, such as Sanlitun. These are fueled, of course, by alcohol, but also by the waves of xenophobia that occasionally ripple through China. Among other crimes, reports of black-cab and rickshaw drivers turning violent when foreigners won't pay the extortionate price they're demanding are also of concern. Bouncers and security guards can also provoke violence, occasionally grabbing people unnecessarily and using excessive force.

If you are the victim of theft, report it at the nearest police station within 24 hours, and make sure you get a police report if you intend to make a claim for it on your insurance.

POLICE

Expats have mixed experiences with police. In some cases the response service will be better if the police are aware that a foreigner is involved, yet in other cases, they may act more harshly. The legal system in many aspects is unreliable, and often the police will take matters into their own hands, negotiating a deal between you and the other party for financial compensation. People can be jailed for up to 15 days without so much as a phone call to a lawyer or a charge.

If you are arrested, you'll be taken to the Public Security Bureau (PSB), where you'll be questioned and possibly fined, jailed, or even deported, never to return. The list of offenses of detained foreigners is wide, and includes prostitution and certain religious activities. Penalties for crimes are often much stricter in China than elsewhere in the world, and include long prison sentences without parole as well as the death penalty.

ROAD SAFETY

Foreigners involved in traffic accidents may in many cases be accused of being at fault, even if they're not. *Do not* get involved in an argument with the other party, but instead try to diffuse any anger and sort it out in a safe location.

One of the greatest road dangers in Beijing is pedestrians, both being one and those around you. It seems that roads and road rules have developed faster than many people can develop road awareness, and it's shocking to watch many pedestrians and cyclists blindly step out onto the road or enter an intersection without looking. As a pedestrian yourself, you may be tempted to cross with the crowd. At times this works, but for some motorists the little green man is more a symbol for them to lay on the gas than the brake. Try to retain your own self discipline and cross when it's truly safe to cross, and never expect cars to give way.

As far as actual driving is concerned, thanks to the clogging traffic in the inner city, speeds are relatively slow, so collisions are usually mild fender benders. Out on the highways, however, fatal accidents are a serious and growing problem, with tens of thousands killed every year. Take extra caution when driving on open roads, and always drive defensively.

CROWDS AND PROTESTS

The government is highly suspicious of gatherings, and police will often shut down events such as parties at a residence that seem to be drawing too big a crowd. Protests do occur from time to time, especially at times of international tension. For example, at the time of conflict over the Diaoyu Islands (Senkaku), Japanese expats, China-based Japanese companies, and even Chinese owners of Japanese-made cars became targets of violence. In 2011, when worldwide Jasmine Revolution protests against authoritarian governments threatened to flare up in China, the government quickly neutralized the situation by rounding up potential activists, deploying large numbers of police, and ramping up censorship. It's strongly advised that you avoid areas of protest. Not only may you be at risk from acts of violence from crowds, but the police will not treat you favorably just because you're a foreigner.

PRIVACY

You should be under no illusion that your life will be private when you are in China. It's a well-known fact that the government regularly surveys emails, text messages, cell phones—any form of communication. Video cameras are ubiquitous throughout the city, and whether you are in an office, hotel, residence, or restaurant, there is a chance that you may be monitored, particularly if you are doing something of interest to the government. Diplomats, journalists with a J visa, and various bloggers are notoriously kept under watchful eyes. If you're involved with sensitive information it's highly recommended to be mindful of where and when you discuss it.

WHAT TO DO

If you are involved in a serious accident or are the victim of a violent crime, call the police by dialing 110. Following this, you may need to contact your embassy to see if you need legal counsel. If you're an American citizen, you can also contact the American Citizen Services (ACS), which will be able to advise you on both medical and legal avenues. For extra protection, you should register your residence in Beijing at your embassy, or with your country's government travel service, such as the Smart Traveler Enrollment Program (https://step.state.gov/step). There are various opinions on whether or not you should carry your passport on you. If you prefer not to, at the very least you should keep a photocopy of your visa and passport in your wallet or bag at all times.

Finally, for more and ongoing information, keep an eye on http://travel.state.gov or the Overseas Security Advisory Council (www.osac.gov) website.

EMERGENCIES AND NATURAL DISASTERS

If you've lived in virtually any major city of the Western world, the sound of emergency-vehicle sirens is almost as common as ring tones. In Beijing, however, there is a strange absence of emergency vehicles. Police, fire engines, and ambulances alike rarely beat their way along the roads with lights flashing or sirens wailing. If anything, they may have their lights flashing, but they'll crawl along at the same pace as the rest of the traffic, with few road users making an effort to clear a passage for them.

Beijing is luckier than most of China. Ambulance crews are a little better trained than they were pre-2008 Olympics, but they're still a far shot from international standards, and many are simply workers rather than real paramedics. Many vehicles are crude, poorly equipped, and simply for transport, not treatment. You may need to pre-pay for your ambulance before they'll take you (approximately RMB300). Additionally, once in an ambulance, you can not request which hospital to be taken to. In most cases drivers will be required to take you to the nearest state hospital. Given these factors, it's generally wiser to opt for a taxi or the closest available car if possible, and to accept that you may need to assume the role of medic. Be sure to have a quality first aid kit at home. Ready-made kits can be purchased from such places as International SOS and Beijing United Family Hospital.

Though Beijing is considered an earthquake zone, fortunately they're extremely rare. The last major earthquake was in 1976, 150 kilometers (93 miles) east of Beijing in Tangshan, Hebei province. It measured 7.8 on the Richter scale and killed more than 255,000 people. So, despite the infrequency, disaster planning is a big deal here and every hospital has a protocol.

If you have a medical emergency, there are various facilities with English-speaking 24-hour emergency hotlines. These include Beijing United Family Hospital, Beijing International SOS Clinic, International Medical Center Beijing, and Oasis International Hospital.

DAILY LIFE

EMPLOYMENT

China is a booming economy, and the lust for consumer goods is at fever pitch. In addition, it has the largest potential consumer base in the world. Sell a single ring tone to every person and you'll be a billionaire.

Companies come and go overnight, and the once-thrifty impoverished population now shops via smartphones on the subway. Local services can't always keep up with the demand. This makes Beijing a fertile and exciting ground for employment and profit. It does come with pitfalls, however, which can swallow up foreigners whole.

For those expecting to walk into a candy land of opportunities, take care and be prepared to lower your expectations. The vast majority of business here is still done in Chinese, and sometimes it feels like the only available jobs are for English teaching. Not only are Chinese companies beginning to prioritize local hires over expensive demanding foreigners, but there are more than 100,000 other expats that you'll also be competing with.

Setting up a business in Beijing can be a bureaucratic nightmare, and stories of expats being taken for a spin by dodgy companies are plentiful. Salaries and the packages that go with them are also extremely inconsistent. You'll no doubt have one friend who has hit the jackpot with a salary of RMB30,000 or more a month, housing, and international health care, and then another who scrapes by each month on a salary of

© SHANNON AITKEN

RMB8,000 that is half eaten up by the RMB3,000 they pay for their share of the rent on a mediocre apartment, and who hopes they don't develop any serious medical issues.

Beijing is like a green, spirited horse. It's going to buck and jump and even try to throw you off, but if you can grip on tight enough long enough that you come to understand it, you'll have the ride of your life.

Relocating

CONTRACTS

If the reason you're coming to China is that your company has a place for you here, then the process will flow relatively smoothly. Regardless, it's still important to check the fine details of your contract. Particular issues include how you are paid and taxed in China as well as at home. Some companies can split your salary into different currencies, perhaps one-half in U.S. dollars into your home bank account, and the other half in *rénmínbì*, which will go into a local Chinese bank account. While having *rénmínbì* will make your life here easier, if you do accumulate a lot of it, then it may be difficult or at least troublesome to get out of China when you finally leave.

It's likely your company will be offering you a range of benefits, including medical insurance, housing, and educational fees for your children. Look carefully into the medical insurance offered, and speak to a Beijing-based broker about how well the selected policy will suit your needs. Some international providers cover Beijing hospitals better than others.

Sometimes Beijing just doesn't gel well with a given expat and after a short period of time, he or she wants to return to home shores. Everyone's experiences here are different, and it can be hard to predict whether or not this will be you or someone in your family. Clarify with your company what would happen should you wish to resign from your Beijing post and return home. What costs will be covered or incurred, and will you still have a job to return to?

SPOUSES

For those being brought over to Beijing by their companies, there are usually provisions for their spouses and children. This will include setting your husband or wife up with the required visa and residence permit, and possibly covering health and education costs. Unmarried or same-sex partners may apply for a dependent residence permit in Beijing with a package of supportive documentation, e.g., a cohabitation certificate or marriage certificate issued by the relevant home country authorities, and other application materials required by the local authorities. Bear in mind that rules governing anything visa related change frequently and, of late, are particularly tight. Illegal residents or people employed while on non-working visas run the risk of copping heavy fines and being deported. It's highly recommended that you check with your nearest Chinese embassy several months in advance of your departure, with the Beijing Municipality Public Security Bureau (www.bjgaj.gov.cn), or with a knowledgeable China visa service to see what your current best options are.

Spouses are not allowed to work on the dependent visa, and if they want to, they'll need to apply for their own Z visa once they've found a company that is willing to employ them. As for a social life, however, they have little to worry about when it comes to making friends and being busy. Expats in Beijing are extremely friendly and always welcoming to new members in their ever-changing circles. There are endless social groups, such as the International Newcomers Network (INN) and Stitch 'n Bitch, not to mention cooking, hiking, craft, volunteer, and educational groups. Admittedly, Beijing *tàitai* (wives) are a much more powerful, organized group than the *jiātíng fūnán* (house husbands), so there is a ready supply of day or evening groups with a bias toward women. Men, however, might find new soul mates via Beefsteak and Burgundy, the Hash House Harriers, or one of the many sports groups.

The Job Hunt

While it's true to say that almost anyone can find a job in China, the Chinese authorities are not interested in attracting the unskilled, and regulations are ever tightening to ensure that the incoming talent perform duties not possible by the locals. That means Beijing is not the place for a gap year where under-30s can pick up a casual job behind a bar or serving tables in a restaurant. Jobs are primarily full time, and only occasionally part time. Anything resembling casual work is typically cash in hand, and not something that will pave the way for a visa.

English-language schools aside, Chinese companies rarely employ foreigners who aren't fluent in Chinese or who have premium-level skills that warrant the employment of a personal interpreter. That might seem a little limiting, but given that there are more than 25,500 foreign-funded enterprises in Beijing, you will find that a wide variety of jobs do in fact exist. Beijing is the workplace for foreign doctors, lawyers, high-school teachers, investment managers, chefs, hotel managers, and more. Currently there is a particular push for talent in engineering, pharmaceuticals, IT and telecommunications, R&D, intellectual property law, international patent affairs, and finance.

Regardless of the need, you won't simply be able to fall into these jobs—you'll need to come bearing the appropriate qualification, which, in most cases, means a university degree and a given number of years of experience. Unlike in some other countries, however, the level of your China salary will be inconsequential to your visa. Nobody cares how little you get paid here, as long as it's above the minimum wage. Doctorate holders may find that their entry into China can be expedited by the government's recent drive to attract top-level experts, the Recruitment Program of Global Experts 1,000 Talent Plan (http://1000plan.safea.gov.cn). Those who qualify will receive a lump-sum subsidy of RMB1 million granted by the Central Budget; a research subsidy of RMB3-5 million and a salary, as well as other attractive benefits for you and your family.

Trying to get a job in Beijing from your home country can be next to impossible. Chinese people put greater emphasis on personal relationships than emails and CVs, so if they haven't met you face to face, your well-worded applications will no doubt quickly be clicked into the trash.

If you are determined to come to Beijing to work, failing to secure an employer before you leave home can put you into a spot of difficulty—without confirmed employment, you won't be able to get a Z visa. A common technique for overcoming this obstacle is to arrive on a tourist visa (L), scout the job market once you have landed, and then have your visa changed over once a company wants you. But beware; the days of the perpetually lingering tourist are over. It was once the case that a border run every few months made it possible for people on L visas to live and illegally work in China for seemingly infinite amounts of time, but the government has now stamped a heavy boot on this behavior. So unless you want to be heavily penalized, it's best to secure yourself a legitimate working arrangement as soon as possible. Visa law reform has also meant that you will probably need to leave the country to convert your L visa to a Z visa when you do get a job offer. Many companies will be willing to cover the cost of the actual visa; transport, however, most likely will be up to you.

WHAT EMPLOYERS WANT

Employer standards in Beijing are high and getting higher. Not only is the capital city a magnet for educated workers from all over the world, it's also the city to be in for millions of aspirational nationals. What's more, these nationals are not only willing to work longer hours for less money than their foreign counterparts, many of them are also *hǎiguī*, ethnically Chinese people who have studied abroad and now return home to make their fortunes. *Hǎiguī* are particularly attractive to local employers—they're well qualified, viewed as more likely to stick around, are bicultural, and have the distinct advantage of speaking the mother tongue. At the top of the applicant ladder is the bilingual executive who has extensive experience working in multinational corporations.

Chinese employers that do want expats are generally looking for one who has the right blend of technical skills, general workplace skills, and bilingualism. Not every company or position is going to require that you speak Chinese, but unless you're planning to be an English teacher or have extensive work experience or a specialized skill set, then the more command you have of the language, the more competitive you'll be. Chinese is still the language of the workplace in Chinese companies, and if you can speak, understand, text or email even rudimentary levels of it, it will make life a lot easier. If Chinese is your only skill, however, you should consider upgrading yourself by enrolling in a course or two, such as in marketing, PR, management, or sales.

Chinese employees also favor people who understand the intricacies of the local culture—of what it means to give face and to save face. They want someone who respects the hierarchical chain and who is willing to put the company above a personal life without tallying up overtime hours or days in lieu. Team spirit is also an important character. Chinese workers frequently socialize together, after work and on weekends. If you're not a joiner, then you'll be frowned upon by management and the rest of your workmates.

According to recruitment agency Hudson, international firms in China employ about 85 percent of the expat workforce, with about 40 percent of the jobs being in sales and marketing; 20 percent in engineering; 10 percent in management, including accounting and finance; and about 5 percent in IT. Hudson states that only a small percentage of expatriates work for Chinese companies. Those who do are primarily engineers or managers in high-tech manufacturing firms.

WHERE TO LOOK

Ideally, in most cases, it's best to find a Beijing job from outside of China. If you're hired from abroad then you'll be far more likely to get a higher salary and a much larger benefits package. In a study done by Aon Hewitt in 2010, it was found that salaries for senior managers hired outside of China were 19.3 percent higher than those for senior managers hired from directly within the country. Their benefits packages were also dramatically fatter.

Not everyone can snag these kinds of jobs, however, and so the next step is to come here and search. Fortunately, finding work in Beijing really isn't hard. The main difficulty is finding something that is genuinely career-building and that pays you what you are used to getting paid. Thanks to rising standards, as well as the *hǎiguī*, these kinds of positions are comparably rare and highly competitive. These days, it's not good enough simply to be a foreigner—you have to have some goods to go with that. Some even say that the only real way toward wealth here in China is to find a gap and start your own business filling it. But if that's not you, there are various ways to go about finding a job.

First, there are the expat-driven sites, such as www.echinacities.com and www.thebeijinger.com. These sites post a real mishmash of offerings. They're the place to get your modeling jobs, voice-over jobs, teaching jobs, and other odds-n-ends jobs. Many of the advertised jobs here are cash-in-hand, unreliable if not illegal, and will probably not offer you a visa or any form of insurance. They're also not the first place to look if you want a high salary or senior management position. Regardless, it is worth keeping an eye on them when job hunting, as quality employers occasionally throw in an ad just to cover all bases.

Next you have specific job-search sites, such as www.zhaopin.com.cn, www.51job.com, www.chinahr.com, and www.chinajob.com. The level of English varies from site to site, and, excluding www.chinajob.com, most jobs advertised are for those who can communicate to some degree in Chinese. If you can't read Chinese, you can usually still do a search using English keywords—if the employer is interested in a foreign worker, then the ad will probably be bilingual. Unfortunately, these sites are also not really the place to go gold digging. Salaries offered are on the whole very local—often just RMB3,000-5,000 per month, and maybe, if you're lucky, RMB10,000 per month.

A step up is to look at global sites, such as the international section of major employment websites in your own country, or perhaps www.monster.com.hk/destination_china.html, which has a strong emphasis on China, or China-based www.careerbuilder.com.cn. LinkedIn is also a good option, as, unlike Facebook, this is not blocked in China and a growing number of Chinese people are using it. If you can translate a few of the basic details on your homepage (such as your Chinese name and profession) into Chinese you'll be found by more China-based employers. Headhunters and professional recruiters are also good options in Beijing, and most major companies have offices here. Just a few in town include RMG Selection, Hudson, Kelly Services, and Michael Page.

What seems to work best in Beijing is networking and using your *guānxi* or *rénmài* (your relationships or connections). In China it really is a case of who you know, and if you've been here for a while, then you'll often find that jobs seem to land in your lap. If you're new in town, it will help to work at this, and thankfully there is a surplus

TIPS FOR GOOD BUSINESS RELATIONSHIPS

- Show respect for hierarchy and acknowledge the more senior people first. If having dinner together, make sure they're seated in the best seat, which is usually the one farthest from and directly opposite the door (historically the seat safest from potential attackers).

- Relationships between China and the West are often tense and trust can suffer. Try to overcome this by showing an interest in and respect for the culture.

- If something embarrassing happens, manage the situation so that your Chinese colleague doesn't lose face.

- Give someone face by doing such things as mentioning them first when expressing your thanks.

- If you invite people for dinner, you pay the bill—never go Dutch or split the bill. If they invite you, try to offer to pay.

- Don't overdo gift giving. Money isn't suitable, nor is something outlandishly expensive.

- Don't be too direct when it comes to talking about the bottom line. Slow things down by talking about family or social things first. No matter how good your deal is, a Chinese person is highly unlikely to do business with you if they still consider you a stranger.

- Be prepared to *gānbēi* (bottoms up, or empty your glass) at business meetings and events. Getting so drunk that you need to make a dash to the restroom will probably make you the butt of a joke but will also endear you to your Chinese associates.

- When clinking glasses, always be sure that the rim of your glass is lower than that of the person you need to give face to.

- Don't be offended by personal questions, but skirt around them if you really don't want to answer.

- Understand that Chinese people probably won't directly say "no" or that they can't do something. Similarly, don't directly say "no," but say that you'll need to think it over and get back to them.

- Email is not always the best mode of communication. Chinese people will often fail to respond to emails, especially if the answer is "no." For general communication, take up the favorite option—instant messaging, such as QQ or MSN. Face-to-face communication is preferred.

- There's no need to bow in China.

- If meeting a senior associate, wait for them to initiate the handshake. If you outshine them with politeness it can cause embarrassment. Whether or not Chinese women shake hands is uncertain, just as in the West, so judge by each situation.

- Ask a Chinese associate ahead of time how you should respectfully address the person you'll be meeting.

- Always have business cards at every first meeting, and ensure they have your details in Chinese as well as English.

- If you can't speak Chinese, bring your own interpreter to business meetings.
For many more very practical tips in understanding Chinese culture and business, visit http://beijing.ischam.org and click on Cultural Tips under Business in China.

DAILY LIFE

The Beijinger website is the place to find or offer employment.

of professional networking options. These include organizations such as FCGroup, which runs regular industry-specific networking events; Viva Beijing Professional Women's Network; and InterNations Beijing Professional Networking. The various chambers of commerce, such as the American Chamber of Commerce (AmCham) or the Australian Chamber of Commerce (AustCham), are also good organizations to hook up with and frequently run their own networking events. Never go to any of these events without a deck of business cards, and always keep a few on standby for unexpected introductions.

THE INTERVIEW

If you're serious about applying for a job, then there are things to be mindful of when going for an interview with a Chinese company. First, try to be about 10 minutes early. Punctuality is extremely important and shows your enthusiasm. Bring your business cards and be ready to exchange them—even if you already have each others' details from emails. When you hand the card to the other person present it with two hands and so that it faces the person in the right direction. Don't be shy about asking how to correctly pronounce the person's name, and remember that a Chinese person's surname actually comes first, so a Wang Wei would be Mr. Wang, or a He Yingya would be Miss He.

The interviewer will be quite likely to start off by asking you questions about your general experiences in China, such as places you've visited or food you've eaten. Even if it seems inconsequential to what you're actually there for, this is a great opportunity for you to give the interviewer some face by elaborating on your love of the country and its culture. Generally, the interview questions will be similar to those asked in Western countries, but be ready for some of them to stray into areas that you're not comfortable with. It's not considered rude or intrusive by many Chinese people to ask about your

Zhaopin.com is one of China's biggest job search sites.

personal life or about matters relating to money. Keen on formulating plans, they will probably also throw you the "What's your five-year plan?" question.

When answering questions, try to maintain a level of modesty. While the modern, younger generations of Chinese people are often quite forthcoming about their highlights and competencies, the older generations still favor modesty. Avoid asking about the salary during the first meeting if you can, and instead show your interest by asking about potential for opportunities and development in the company. After the interview, send an email thanking them for their time and again expressing your interest in the job.

CONTRACTS, SALARIES, AND BENEFITS
Contracts

Unlike in the U.S., which in many states has "at will" employment systems (meaning you can be fired for any reason), in China, to be employed full time you must have a contract. And if you have a contract, then you need to pay attention to it and know exactly what's in it and what isn't. In Beijing, the legal version of the contract is usually in Chinese. You should, however, request that the contract be translated into English just for your own understanding, and then, if possible, have a second pair of eyes look over it to check that it's true to the original. In the past, many people worked in China based on verbal agreements, but with the country's developing legal system, this is quickly becoming a thing of the past. Employment contracts must now be completed for full-time employees within 30 days of the start date.

In China, employers, if abiding by the law, have very limited rights to unilaterally fire someone. There must be explicit evidence or records proving in detail how company rules or the contract were breached. An employee, on the other hand, can terminate the contract without reason, as long as they give the employer written notice 30 days in advance.

Before you sign with a company, you need to confirm that they have an employment license authorizing them to hire foreign employees. You won't get any of your permits if they don't have theirs. Be sure to know the term of your employment and what will and should happen if you decide to end your contract prematurely. The term of employment will be of particular importance to managers. For instance, there are various conditions in which a contract becomes open ended, such as when a contract has already been renewed for two consecutive terms. So if the person you've recruited turns sour, it can be difficult to terminate them and perhaps impossible to wait out the end of their contract.

Understand the conditions of your probationary period. This period may last one month for a one-year contract, or up to six months for a three-year contract. During this period you can be dismissed for any reason. You also may receive only a percentage of the actual salary; however, this can not be less than 80 percent of what you'll receive when your actual employment kicks in.

Finally, make sure you know exactly when you'll be paid (usually by a given date each month) and in what currency. Any benefits—such as housing or flights home—should also be written into the contract, as should expenses and reimbursement systems. Be clear about any deductions, such as tax and social insurance, any bonuses, how overtime is managed, and if there is any penalization system, such as bonus deductions for being late.

Salary and Benefits

The salary you get is going to depend a lot on your own luck, industry, and connections. Those in the teaching profession may earn anything from about RMB4,000 per month up to RMB30,000 for the highly qualified doctorate holders. Other industries might see salaries of RMB13,000-55,000 per month, together with packages that pad their salary by up to an additional RMB65,000 per month in value. Sadly the golden expat days are over, and companies, even international ones, are increasingly localizing, offering employees standard local rather than comfy international packages. It's ever more likely that your lifestyle won't be cushioned with a living allowance, school fees for your kids, bulk-billing international medical insurance, or even a flight home.

At the very least, and probably against your wishes, you should be provided with social security insurance, which is paid in part by you and in part by contributions from your company. The insurance covers five mandatory areas—maternity, medical, unemployment, pension, and work-related injury—and possibly housing. This makes you 35-40 percent more expensive than your gross payable income, and penalties can be imposed if your company doesn't comply. Whether you plan to use the insurance (which, at the time of writing, was not possible in the international hospitals and clinics) is irrelevant; it's compulsory. On the positive side, it's a little like forced savings, and the unused portion of your contributions should be returned to you when you permanently leave China.

Salaries in China, at least those in Chinese companies, are usually calculated for 13 months, with the 13th month being paid as a bonus at Chinese New Year. Confirm that you're not excluded from the bonus when you examine your contract. Some companies try to argue that foreigners don't receive the annual bonus, but this doesn't mean that your salary should be effectively less because you receive only 12 payments. If you're the manager of the company and decide to work with a 12-month system, you'll need to make it apparently clear to local employees that the 13th month has been spread out over the year, otherwise problems can arise when they suddenly feel you've shortchanged them at New Year.

Despite the infinite unpaid extra hours that many companies seem to expect of their employees, legally they should be paying overtime. Cultural instincts are strong, however, and few employees resist the pressure to work 10-hour days, even six days a week. If you find yourself in this situation, you have the right to state your case and object. Unfortunately, it's just not going to win you respect or opportunities for promotion.

Annual Leave

You might be in for a rude surprise when your get to the clause about annual leave in your contract. For most Chinese, the majority of their vacation dates come as a total of 11 fixed public holidays, with the major breaks at Chinese New Year and the National Day holiday in the first week of October. What could be more unpleasant than millions of people having their annual leave at exactly the same time as you? Though it sounds unfair, the government argues that it's one way to make sure companies give their employees adequate leave.

On top of the public holiday days, workers also get a set number of personal annual leave days. The legal minimum annual leave allowances are: zero days for the first year of your contract, five days for the second to ninth years of work, 10 days for the 10th to 19th years, and 15 days if you're still there at 20 years.

Foreigners working in local companies are increasingly likely to be given the same number of days as the Chinese staff. International companies, however, typically offer more. When negotiating your contract, ensure that the number of personal annual leave days and public holidays is clearly defined. To draw you in, a company may pad your actual number of leave days with the 11 legal public holiday days.

Maternity and Paternity Leave

The maternity leave laws in China are quite extensive, and they reflect the value of family in the Chinese culture. A pregnant woman (in a state-owned enterprise) is entitled to 98 days (14 weeks) of maternity leave, potentially longer for C-sections, and all women are also entitled to the maternity component of the social insurance scheme. It's generally illegal for employers to decrease a female employee's wages or to unilaterally terminate her employment while she is pregnant, on maternity leave, or in the nursing period (considered to end on the newborn's first birthday).

Beijing's laws concerning maternity leave pay differ from Shanghai's, and in many cases, pregnant women in Beijing are better off. In Shanghai pay rates are based on a set company average, so for some women that effectively means a pay cut. In Beijing, however, payments are based on the employee's average monthly salary in the previous year. So if the social insurance payments fall short of that amount, the company must make up for the gap. Additionally, if the social insurance payments exceed the original salary, the company can not pocket the excess.

Unfortunately, these strict laws surrounding maternity leave can sometimes produce negative side effects in the workplace, at times causing discrimination against women who are of child-bearing-age and reducing their chances of getting a job, and at times burdening a company with the costs of women who, after securing a job, disclose that they are pregnant and set off on maternity leave.

Paternity leave isn't really mandated. In some cases, it's said that a woman can give up a month of her maternity leave for the husband's paternity leave, but if they work for different companies, this means the companies have to negotiate. If paternity leave is important to you, make sure to have it included in your contract.

Sick Leave

Sick leave in China ranges from three months to 24 months, depending on how long you've worked for the company. During this time, it's illegal for the company to fire you. Generally you will need to provide a doctor's certificate, even if it's for only one day. In Beijing, the minimum salary paid during sick leave must be at least 80 percent of the minimum salary (in 2013 it was RMB1,400/month). Most companies, however, will allow you 10 sick days per year paid at full salary.

Resigning or Changing Jobs

If it does come to the point where you've decided to move on to another job with another company, perhaps even in a different city, it can be easy, or it can be complicated—this will depend on whether you're leaving the existing company on amicable terms or that they at least do things by the book; on whether you're moving to a job that fits within the same field of expertise as the one you're leaving; and if the new job is in Beijing or another city. For visa purposes, it's always best to have another job waiting for you before resigning, and to be sure that that company is authorized to employ foreigners.

The first thing you'll need when leaving is the employment release letter, stamped with the company *chop* (stamp), from your current employer. Unless there has been a serious breach of contract, companies are obligated by the Beijing Municipal Bureau of Labor and Social Security to provide these, and you won't be able to get a new job without one. Your current company should also cancel your work permit (Alien Employment Permit) but not your residence permit, which is good for as long as its date of validity. On very rare occasions, companies can become spiteful and refuse to give you the release letter. If this happens to you, you can go to the police station or to the labor bureau to file a complaint.

If the companies you're moving between have competent HR departments, transferring should be a seamless process. If you do need to manage the process yourself, you will need:

- A release letter from your employer with the company *chop*
- To transfer or cancel your employment permit at the labor bureau
- Your original university certificate, which should show a bachelor's degree or higher
- A CV, translated into Chinese
- A letter from your any of your former employers certifying that you have more than two years work experience

- Your passport and four two-inch white background photos
- Your residence registration slip from the Public Security Bureau
- The business license of your future employer and two certified copies
- Application forms, which also need a *chop*.

Visa agents can help you with this process, for a fee. For further information, visit www.ebeijing.gov.cn and click on Working in Beijing.

If you are staying within Beijing but changing industries and, therefore, the classification of your expertise for your work permit, in most cases this can be done from within Beijing and will not require the cancellation of your residence permit. Some expats have had different experiences. If you are changing cities, your former employer will also need to give you the work permit cancellation certificate from the labor bureau and company release letter with *chop*.

It's also important to remember that if you make any changes to your passport, you'll need to immediately have your company update your work and residence permits with the new details.

English Teaching Jobs

English is seen as the golden ticket to an overseas education and as the key to unlocking the gate of fortune. Millions of locals, from toddlers to retirees, are enrolled in English-language programs every year across China, and especially in Beijing. This makes for a generous number of jobs for foreigners—nurseries, primary and middle schools, universities, and countless private institutions have ready-made positions waiting for the native English speaker.

It used to be that having a white face meant that you could pretty much walk into any Chinese classroom and teach English, but things are changing, and Beijing is certainly one city where the government is monitoring who teaches its future generation. The State Administration of Foreign Experts Affairs (SAFEA) now strictly requires that you be a native speaker with a bachelor's degree as well as two years of some form of teaching experience. You'll also be required to have a TEFL/TESOL qualification. These can range from quick and cheap online courses to more intense programs, such as the seven-day TEFL in China certificate (http://tefl.chinajob.com) or the highly regarded CELTA certificate and DELTA diploma (www.cambridgeesol.org). CELTA courses are held all over the world. They typically run as one-month intensive programs and cost around US$2,000-2,500. If you intend to do one, it can help to shop around. You may find taking the CELTA in Thailand or Vietnam, for example, is much cheaper than doing it at home or even in Beijing.

Of course, there are always exceptions when it comes to qualifications, and many schools will turn a blind eye to the regulations. This puts both them and you at risk of serious penalties, and, again, won't qualify you for a Z visa in Beijing. If you really don't want to jump through the official hoops, then it's best to look into options in smaller, provincial cities, which may have less stringent rules and be willing to overlook holes in your CV.

2014-2015 PUBLIC HOLIDAYS

Festival	Date	Legal Public Holidays	2014	2015
New Year's Day	Jan. 1	1 day	Jan. 1-3	Jan. 1-3
Spring Festival	Varies according to lunar calendar	3 days	Jan. 31 (Jan. 30-Feb. 5 off)	Feb. 19 (Feb. 18-24 off)
Qingming (Tomb Sweeping Festival)	Apr. 4 or 5	1 day	Apr. 5 (Apr. 4-6 off)	Apr. 5 (Apr. 4-6 off)
May Day	May 1	1 day	May 1-3	May 1-3
Dragon Boat Festival	5th day of the 5th lunar month	1 day	June 2 (May 31-June 2 off)	June 20 (June 20-22 off)
Mid-Autumn Day	Aug. 15 of lunar calendar	1 day	Sept. 8 (Sept. 6-8 off)	Sept. 27 (Sept. 26-28 off)
National Day	Oct. 1	3 days (Oct. 1-3)	Oct. 1-7	Oct. 1-7

When applying for an English teaching job, there are pitfalls to look out for. Make sure you know exactly what the employment hours mean. Many will advertise that you need to work only 20 hours a week, but that probably means face-to-face time and doesn't include the many hours of preparation. Many private schools have sketchy practices, so always try to investigate the company you're looking at working for in advance. Ask for the school's credentials and request to be put in touch with other teachers. If you're still unsure, post a question on sites such as www.thebeijinger.com asking for other people's experiences, and make sure the person who responds is a foreign teacher rather than an agent.

If the company is not offering you a Z visa, then steer clear. This should immediately set off alarm bells in your head about this employer and their credibility. At the same time, check that they are registering you for your work permit in the same city that you'll be working in. Some companies sidestep various business restrictions by registering staff in cities outside of Beijing. This is illegal. Other suspicion triggers should include disregard for SAFEA's requirements and an offer that just seems too good to be true. A reasonable contract and salary offer may include a contract of one to three years, a monthly salary of around RMB10,000-20,000 before tax (full-time), return airfare after one year of service, private health insurance (domestic or international), social insurance, paid holidays and sick leave, and possibly accommodations, especially for the first few weeks if they are bringing you to China.

Teaching conditions vary from school to school—some will provide you with strong support and extensive teaching materials, while others will leave you to your own devices, which will mean you can do whatever you like but also that preparation is completely up to you and in your own time. As far as the students go, Chinese students are generally well behaved and eager to learn. If they can see that you have a genuine interest in helping them, adults and children alike are highly respectful and easily coerced into singing, dancing, or role playing for the sake of improving their English.

Self-Employment

BUSINESS POSSIBILITIES

Beijing has almost endless possibilities for business. For starters, there are 20,180,000 potential customers at your doorstep. To identify business opportunities, all you need to do is look at the key targets of the government's Five Year Plans. It's an instant source of inspiration for investment opportunities. If the government plans to target an area, then you can be sure the barriers to entry into that market will be reduced and possibly new investment incentives offered. For example, in the current Five Year Plan (2011-2015), just a few of the goals are to achieve an increase in domestic consumption; to spend 2.2 percent of GDP on R&D relating to innovation; to reduce energy consumption and increase use of green energy; and to increase the service sector. If you have a product or service that relates to any of these areas, it could be the perfect time for you in Beijng.

There is particular emphasis right now on innovation. "In the West, businesses are looking for people who can further develop an idea," says Israel Merica-Jones of business advisors Dezan Shira & Associates, "but in China they're looking for people who are creating new ones. They want that new thing, even if it might not be as good. There's a strong need for indigenous innovation. If you can present ideas in a brand-new structure people will want to start that conversation and have another drink with you."

Having a new idea will give you a good head start, but launching into the Chinese market isn't a challenge that everyone is suited to. The government can be heavy handed and the cultural mores can be difficult to fully understand and mesh with. The www.doingbusiness.org website of the World Bank and International Financial Corporation doesn't place China too highly in its rankings for ease of doing business. In 2012, out of 185 countries, mainland China was ranked 91st for "ease of doing business," 151st for "ease of starting a business," 181st for "ease of dealing with construction permits," and even 114th for "ease of getting electricity." Its best ranking was 19th for "enforcing contracts." In the subnational report, which compared 30 of China's cities, Beijing ranked sixth for ease of "starting a business," ninth for "enforcing contracts," and 12th for ease of "registering a property." Hangzhou, Shanghai, and Guangzhou claimed first prize for these factors, respectively.

If your idea relates to manufacturing, then you should know that the days when China was the cheapest place to have things made are numbered. Worker salaries are on the rise. In 2009 the minimum wage was RMB800 per month, in 2013 it was RMB1,400 per month, and the current Five Year Plan is pushing for it to continue increasing by no less than 13 percent on average each year. On top of that, you must factor in costs for quality control to ward off what Paul Midler (in his book *Poorly Made in China*) terms as "quality fade," the phenomenon that at some point in time quality of China-made products is inevitably going to fade, no matter how good the first few shipments were. "Foreign buyers have to be constantly on guard," says Steve Dickinson on China Law Blog. "Active intervention is costly and mentally exhausting. Most foreign buyers eventually tire of the process. However, such active involvement is the price of purchasing from Chinese manufacturers. Buyers that do not want to incur the cost should avoid China."

If you are prepared to take on these challenges, then you're in for an adventure and there are still plenty of advantages to doing business here. Chinese businesspeople move quickly. What might take months in the West can often happen within a few weeks here. The country might still be Communist, but in the workplace the Chinese are capitalists and the entrepreneurial spirit is flourishing. There is a palpable energy and drive for innovation wherever you go. "Just don't check your brains at the gate," warns China Law Blog's Dan Harris. "This essentially means that you should not get too taken in by China and you should still examine each deal for its business merits, just as though you were in Peoria."

HOW TO START A BUSINESS

There are various ways to start a business in Beijing. Many go it alone, others use agencies, and others find a local business partner. There are four major structures available to you: representative offices, wholly foreign-owned enterprises (WFOE), joint ventures, and foreign-invested partnerships. These differ in the amount of capital you need to have, the business scope, and the number of foreign employees that you'll be allowed to hire. Representative offices are the easiest to set up and don't require any registered capital. Their business scope is extremely limited, however, and are mostly just for market research and liaison with the home country. WFOEs are the most common structure that foreigners set up in China, and they can deal with just about any kind of business. They're most commonly used for manufacturing, service provision, and trading. Joint ventures are typically for those kinds of companies that can't be set up without a local partner, and foreign-invested partnerships are often used as investment vehicles and also for services. Each has its own pros and cons, and it's recommended that you speak to a professional who is thoroughly clued up on doing business in China, not just in your home country.

Starting a business in Beijing is time consuming and complicated. First you'll need to apply for an F visa (business visa) to get into the country. This gives you six months of validity and can be used simply for investigating business opportunities or for setting something up. Establishing the business can take between three and six months to achieve and involves numerous government departments—including the Ministry of Commerce, the Administration of Industry and Commerce, the State Administration of Foreign Exchange, the State Administration of Taxation, the Customs Office, the Quality and Technical Supervision Bureau, and the Statistics Bureau. About the simplest step of the process is making a company seal and getting the company name approved. You also need to set up a business bank account. This can be an extraordinarily complicated and exhausting process—you will probably be at the bank for around five hours on several separate occasions. If you're not competent in both written and spoken Chinese, find a patient and trustworthy Chinese person to help you through it.

If you're unfamiliar with the Chinese business scene, a soft approach into the market is via partnerships, starting with "soft partnerships," such as website mentions or co-hosting events, and finally moving to stronger commitments. Your partnership should begin to develop before you even set down in Beijing. Partnerships with Chinese people can help you overcome a lot of the obstacles that you would otherwise face as an independent foreigner. They do, of course, come with risks.

When looking for a partner, Merica-Jones says you should look for someone who has an office specifically in Beijing—not just in China. Given that most business operates according to *guānxi* (relationships), the company is less likely to have good connections in Beijing if they don't have a consolidated presence there. This is particularly important for Beijing because it means they are also potentially connected to those in the country's governmental hub.

When you go into business in China, make sure you know the laws. Assume nothing. In many regards the laws are similar to those in the United States, and in many regards they are different. China Law Blog points out joint ventures as a particular example of how many Americans go wrong. In joint ventures in China, owning 51 percent does not give you control of the company. Instead, control usually rests with whoever has the right to appoint the joint venture's representative and managing directors. Chinese businesspeople know this, but many Americans take the bait of the 51 percent carrot. This is China—if you become complacent and rest on what you think you know, you'll get caught out.

BUSINESS CONTRACTS

Historically, business contracts in China have been more verbal, but forget this idea, especially in Beijing. When doing business you'll need to stipulate every detail in the contract—do not assume the courts will fill in the blanks for you down the track if you get into a dispute.

Some argue that having too tight a contract is bad for building warm relationships with Chinese companies, that crossing every t and dotting every i causes loss of face. Additionally, they argue that the Chinese court system is so ineffective, it's not worth going through all the effort of formulating and agreeing on a contract. China Law Blog's Dan Harris concedes that there are cases where these this might be correct. He argues, however, that China's courts are "fair often enough" to make it ill-advised to do business in China without a contract.

"Having a well-written contract does not mean you will always win your lawsuit if you are forced to sue on it. But it does mean you will have some leverage if things go wrong and it does mean you will at least have a chance," he says.

Finally, never agree to an official "contract signing" date, and never tell your prospective partners when you'll be flying out of town. When asked how long you'll be in China, simply answer, "I'm here for as long as I need to be for this." Chinese businesspeople do want to get business done, too, but if they sense that they can win a few more points by stalling on concessions or adjustments right up to the day of signing and so putting pressure on you to compromise, they will. It's all part of the game.

EXPAT PROFILE: STARTING A BUSINESS

Adlyn Teoh came to Beijing in December 2004, leaving behind a career in the United States in medical tech process reengineering. She soon discovered a love for the city and saw potential for her to make a go of something she'd always had a passion for. So in October 2007 she set up Hias Gourmet Beijing. Based in the center of the city, Hias Gourmet Beijing runs food walks, Chinese cooking classes, and events for expats, tourists, and businesses.

WHAT DOES HIAS GOURMET DO?

We run food and market tours, cooking classes, team building activities, and corporate events. Our business model is built around the foundation of using food as a tool to share culture, heritage, and understanding, and using our profits to support social projects.

WHO ARE YOUR CUSTOMERS?

We have two main client target segments: travelers from the United States, Europe, and Asia; and corporate clients who are China- or overseas-based. Our corporate clients have included companies like Microsoft, Nokia, GE, and Moet Hennessey, as well as nonprofits and educational institutions such as International Finance Corporation (part of the World Bank) and Stanford University.

WHAT WAS THE GENERAL PROCESS OF SETTING UP HIAS GOURMET IN BEIJING?

First I had to set up a limited liability company in Hong Kong. I then used the Hong Kong company as an investing company to set up my China wholly foreign-owned enterprise (WOFE).

WHAT MISTAKES HAVE YOU MADE THAT WERE BIG LESSONS FOR YOU ABOUT DOING BUSINESS HERE?

No deal is a deal until the dollars are paid. Contracts can't really protect you. Also, if you can understand that many folks are out for short-term gain instead of long-term partnerships, it will help with strategies for dealing with local partners, suppliers, or clients.

WHAT HAVE BEEN SOME OF THE PLEASANT THINGS OR ADVANTAGES YOU HAVE EXPERIENCED BY HAVING YOUR OWN BUSINESS IN BEIJING?

To do well, my business requires me to have city and food knowledge, which means constant exploring and research,

Labor Laws

In some Beijing workplaces it can feel like labor laws don't exist. Workers can be expected to slave away until 8pm or 9pm every night and come in on weekends without an ounce of compensation or time in lieu, freelancers do work that they never get paid for, and people lose their jobs overnight. Often, staff quietly accept it or quietly leave. I've never personally heard of someone suing their company for unfair dismissal. The truth is, however, that in many cases an employee could well win if they took their employer to court.

Dan Harris of the China Law Blog says, "Employers in China have to follow a whole host of rules. Just because they often violate those rules does not mean they are not required to follow them. It also does not mean they will get away with violating those

and which for me is the most enjoyable part. I don't have regular work hours, so that means I don't need to deal with Beijing traffic. Furthermore, Beijing is an energetic city, and the people are really curious and willing to try something new, so that makes doing business here exciting.

WHAT HAVE BEEN SOME OF THE CHALLENGES OR DISADVANTAGES?

There is a lot of red tape and paperwork involved, and you need to be able to work patiently and under lots of uncertain conditions and deadlines. That said, the opportunities are exciting for an entrepreneur.

WHAT IS GENERALLY THE BIGGEST HEADACHE ONCE YOUR BUSINESS IS UP AND RUNNING?

HR is the biggest, most constant challenge. It can be difficult in Beijing to find and keep talent. For many expats, Beijing is still considered a transitional city, so they come and go within a year or two. Locals tend job-hop. It's also hard to find people with the magic combination of being bilingual and having the skills we search for.

WHAT EXCITES YOU ABOUT DOING BUSINESS HERE?

It almost seems like there is no limit to what you can do here. Business ideas don't just stay as ideas, they turn into reality.

WHAT ADVICE WOULD YOU GIVE TO SOMEONE WANTING TO SET UP THEIR OWN BUSINESS HERE?

Talk to as many folks who have successfully started and exited their business in Beijing. Also, talk to folks who did not make it—the most valuable advice would come from them.

Understand that the nuances of doing business vary significantly based on provinces as well as your industry. Learn about the legal structure options for foreign-owned businesses. Make your exit strategy plan part of your business plan.

There is no single place where you can go to learn about setting up a business in China. What you learn today may not apply tomorrow. So, you always need to have backup plans, and backups for your backup plans.

Finally, know that flexibility, speed, and honesty are valued traits in this city.

rules if sued. I'm not telling anyone to sue, but I am saying that it is our experience that the employee in China who actually stands up for his or her rights in China (at least as against foreign companies, which is all that we ever represent) usually prevails."

The fundamental requirements of China's labor laws stipulate fair and equal treatment of employees regardless of race or sex, that children under the age of 16 can not be employed, and that workers have the right to organize. The laws and regulations also establish standards for working hours and conditions, leave, and minimum wages.

For foreigners in Beijing, there are also five basic rules: You must be 18 years or older and in good health; you must have the professional skills and job experience required for the work of your intended job; you must have a clear criminal record; you must have a clearly defined employer; and you must have a valid passport or other relevant international travel document.

Technically, when you are here to work for a given company, it's illegal for you to be doing work on the side. Cash-in-hand jobs are, however, exceedingly common. It's just not recommended that you start getting regular sizable donations into your bank account.

Many local people don't even know their own labor laws, and it's highly recommended that you clue yourself in on your rights. If your own company doesn't give you a copy of the labor laws, you can access free online information from the many law firms specializing in this area, such as Wang & Wang and Broad & Bright Law Firm, as well as sites such as www.chinalawandpractice.com (subscription fee), www.chinalawblog.com, and the official government site, www.ebeijing.gov.cn (click on Working in Beijing).

Workplace Culture

To the uninitiated foreigner, the Beijing office can be a place of bafflement and frustration. The culture and expectations are often extremely different, and unfortunately, there isn't always the highest level of trust between the insiders and the outsiders.

When you first arrive in a Chinese office or begin to do business with a Chinese company, you may be deceived into thinking that communication—language barriers aside—is roughly the same. There are some subtleties to communication styles here, however, that may catch you unsuspecting. First, a Chinese person using English, particularly via text or email, can often come across as abrupt and impolite. This isn't intentional, and in business Chinese people are generally very polite. It's just that the Chinese language uses different ways to express politeness. They don't translate well into English, and so just get left out. English classes don't always teach phrases like "would you mind" or "could you please," so try not to be offended when they directly tell you "I want you to…" even if they're in a junior position to you.

Next, Chinese people don't like confrontation in the workplace, and this includes saying "no" or "I don't know," or "I can't do that." If your question comes via email, it's extremely likely that it will just be ignored outright, and if it's face to face, then you'll possibly get a meandering or inconclusive response, possibly even a yes, but then with no follow-through. People may promise to meet a deadline that they have no hope on earth of making. Others will simply tell you that they don't have the thing you need, when the real point is that they don't know what it is you're talking about. It can be an extremely frustrating thing to deal with and something you'll need to adapt to. Trying to structure your questions or the situation in a way as to let them save face may be a way to get the information you need.

At times you might want to point out a flaw in a boss's reasoning, shout out a disagreement, or put forth an idea that no one else seems to have had the imagination to come up with. Stop right there before you utter a word and bite your tongue. One, you don't want to make your boss look bad by disagreeing or saying something that he or she should have thought of. Two, it's not good to point out another's faults in front of others.

This indirectness may also at times come because the considerate person is trying to stop you from losing face. If you're falling short of standards they may hint so subtly at your lapsed judgement that you really don't know what they're talking about or that you miss it altogether. If you suspect this is happening to you, simply ask them to speak directly to you, telling them you want to do the best work for them and that you will feel respected rather than offended if they point out an issue to you.

Generally, non-Asian foreigners are given a fair amount of liberty, and a cultural faux pas or two will usually slide. If you're of Chinese origins, however, any ignorance is less likely to be laughed away, even if you clearly don't speak a word of Chinese. Those who do speak the language will be at an advantage when trying to interpret the nuances of the culture, and for those that don't, the best you can do is to launch into business here with enthusiasm, an open mind, patience, and a willingness to socialize.

The key to successful business in China is understanding *rénmài, guānxi,* and face. *Rénmài* is your networks and connections—the friend who knows someone at the local PSB, the buddy of someone on an approval committee; *guānxi* is the relationships you have with people; and face usually relates to something that either attacks or bolsters pride. Doing or saying something that results in an associate's loss of face can be a sure way to damage business.

Guānxi takes time to build in China, and you won't succeed here without it. Consequently, business can often seem painfully slow at the start. Your associates will need to build trust with you, and this can mean doing everything but business at the outset. It's a little like dating—you go out, you get to know each other, and then you start committing a bit more. People in China want to know you and to see you, and to be able to eat and laugh with you, even go hiking together first thing on a Sunday morning.

Though you might think this is the same the world over, it's somewhat exaggerated in China. In countries like America people are more likely to understand that it's a business relationship, but here that line between business and personal friendship gets a little muddy. In the States you might say that you're "having dinner with a business partner," but in China it would be "having dinner with a friend." Business is more family oriented, more integrated into your social life, and more likely to dip into areas that you might consider personal. In the West, this tends to happen more at the executive level, in China it happens whether you're an assistant or a CEO.

Drinking culture is heavily integrated with business culture in China. Depending on the nature of your job, you may find yourself under constant pressure to go out drinking with your colleagues, get sickeningly drunk, and even follow through with a bonding night at karaoke (KTV). While nothing businesslike may seem to happen on nights like these, you'll probably find that within the following few days things will get rolling.

Hierarchy is an important part of office life here, and it's rare to be on a first-name basis with anyone senior to you, particularly in a very local company. Senior people are frequently referred to by their title, such as *Lì Jīnglǐ* (Manager Li) or *Zhāng Lǎoshī* (Teacher Zhang), or at the very least *Lì Xiǎojie* (Miss Li) or *Zhāng Xiānsheng* (Mr. Zhang). Short of bowing, extreme deference is often shown to the "elites" of society. I was once told a story of two Chinese colleagues who spent six hours debating the wording of a single text message that was to be sent to a government official.

Transparency of Chinese companies is a common issue faced by foreign businesses, and bribery and corruption are deeply imbedded in the local society. There are many international companies in Beijing that successfully take a firm stand and refuse to become part of it. On the ground, however, particularly for smaller enterprises, it can make day-to-day life difficult if you do insist on not "tipping" the right people. Approvals may be stalled if not rejected, and you might find there are constant knockings on your door to assess your standards. If you're setting up shop or business, it can be helpful to chat with other businesspeople in the same complex or industry about their experiences and advice.

If you are bringing new ideas, they will definitely be embraced, but perhaps with much more enthusiasm than you might actually want. While the government is making efforts to tighten laws on IP theft and trademarking, enforcement is limited and it's still extraordinarily common for budding entrepreneurs to steal ideas and run. Many locals agree it is a problem, but it's a widespread issue and something often done with apparent indifference. An American interior designer friend of mine designed a chic and very popular bar in Sanlitun. One night she was sitting at a new bar in town and noticed the striking similarity in design between the two venues. She commented on it to the barman-owner, who proudly agreed, saying he used to work at the Sanlitun bar. When she told him she was the designer of the bar he was so excited and asked if she could advise him on how to fix a problem that he'd had with the measurements in his own bar.

There seems to be no shortage of cases where employees have learned the ropes and only months later opened their own version of the business. This isn't just a Chinese-expat situation. Chinese entrepreneurs also fall victim to highly observant staff. David Chan of Dezan Shira & Associates advises people to learn how to protect their business, even from their own employees. "Be wary of sharing too much know-how and giving one person too much responsibility," he says. "Give people different responsibilities so that one person doesn't do everything."

FINANCE

The time when everything was cheap in China has passed, and if you intend to continue enjoying the same quality of products or lifestyle that you have had in your home country, then most likely you'll be paying similar prices here. While public transport and utilities are amazingly cheap, rent and Western-style items can take hefty chunks out of the bank account. In Beijing, it really is up to you. If you want to save money and are willing to make a few sacrifices by living more like a local, it's quite possible for an individual to get by on the equivalent of about US$600 per month. If you want a European lifestyle with a driver and live-in nanny, it's here. It will just be much easier if you're on a company package or in a senior management position.

This said, issues relating to finance in Beijing can trigger anxiety attacks, even outright tantrums and hours of ranting and railing. The key to reducing stress here is to understand how to manage your money. That doesn't just mean knowing how to save it, but also about how to spend it. Using banks in Beijing can be one of the most exasperating experiences in Beijing, the kind of thing that makes you want to pack up your bags and go home. But there are ladders, tunnels, and other paths by which to cross the many obstacles you may perceive as a foreigner; you just have to put in a little effort to knowing what they are and how to cross them.

© SHANNON AITKEN

Cost of Living

Beijing is a city of extremes when it comes to the cost of living. Some will find that they can enjoy a lifestyle here that was never possible back home—a large home with a live-in housekeeper, a personal driver, enough savings to pay off a mortgage back home, and a social life filled with dinners at Western restaurants and black-tie events at five-star hotels. Others will scrape by from month to month on a basic salary, eating out most nights but at local street-side restaurants, and leaving China richer but only with experiences.

Your expenditure will be largely up to you. Despite prices hiking at dramatic rates, Beijing really does have the capacity to allow both thrifty and expensive lifestyles. Living on a shoestring might require some compromising on quality and international brands, but it's possible.

Beijing is also still considerably cheaper on average than many other international cities. In a 2012 survey conducted by Zurich-based financial firm UBS, Beijing ranked as 46th out of 72 cities for price levels (with New York at number 6 and London at 10). Then, in Mercer's 2012 Worldwide Cost of Living Survey, which looked specifically at the kinds of costs incurred by expats—including transport, food, clothing, household goods, entertainment, and housing—Beijing ranked as the 17th most expensive city for expats (above London at 25 and New York at 33).

The official Beijing inflation rates are hard to judge. Overall they hover at around 3-5 percent, but food and housing are substantially more. For many expats, these figures don't always seem to match what happens in their own experience. Back in around 2007, when re-signing your lease you could expect that the landlord would increase the rent by perhaps RMB200-300. In 2012-2013 it was more like RMB500-1,500.

You can choose to expose yourself to more or less of this inflation, depending on what kind of lifestyle you want and where you shop. You can lead an amazingly shallow-pocketed life if you live outside the Fifth Ring Road (Shunyi excluded) and stick to the locally produced goods, fake products, public transport, and local-style supermarkets. Try to maintain the lifestyle you had back home, and you'll find Beijing can be a very expensive city in which to live. Anything imported, organic, or classified as "luxury" is going to cost about as much as it cost back home, if not more. Unlike Hong Kong, Beijing is not the city to get cheap electronics—particularly the genuine ones.

Many expats fall victim to the higher prices, and a lot of this has to do with the way they shop. They get their groceries from Westernized supermarkets, which hike the prices up on local goods as well as the imported ones; they dine at Western-run restaurants; and they buy directly from Western-friendly shopping malls. As part of UBS's research, they also took a basket of consumer goods typically used by European families and used these to measure the actual spending power in each of the cities; i.e., the ability of foreigners to live like they live at home, but on a local salary. Beijing came out clinging to the 63rd rung. If you're going to be paid in your home country's currency or at least given a generous package, then you may not be affected by this depressing situation. If not, you might want to seriously reconsider the viability of moving to Beijing or at least be prepared to adapt and manage your spending more like a local.

MONTHLY EXPENSES

There is a range of lifestyles in Beijing, and how much money each of them requires each month is extremely different. Some expat families of four, for example, suggest that you need to have an annual income that's equivalent to US$200,000 to live a comprehensive Western lifestyle in Beijing.

University students usually have the best access to cheaper living. Shared accommodations can be as low as RMB500 per month in some extreme ascetic cases, university food is subsidized, and shops in the vicinity of the university grounds usually cater to the non-working population. A total monthly budget of RMB4,000-6,000 (excluding university fees) should allow you to enjoy a university lifestyle that includes cafés and nightlife, interspersed with the occasional *fāngbiànmiàn* (instant noodles).

For the locally employed single living in the inner city, life can a little more expensive. If you live in a Chinese-style apartment, eat predominantly at home or in local Chinese restaurants, and only occasionally splurge with a fine-dining dinner or shopping spree, you could get by on a net income of RMB7,000-10,000. This won't allow you to save much money, and if you plan to save for an annual trip home you'll really need to count your *máo*. If your salary exceeds RMB13,000 per month you'll feel much more comfortable and you should start to have some money to spare.

If you're an executive in the inner city and enjoy a New York shade of lifestyle, then ensure you have a job that pays you RMB20,000 net and above. This figure will allow you to live in a modern apartment, shop without too much stress, have taxis as your primary mode of transportation, and frequent Beijing's chic suit and frock establishments.

For families, a real lifestyle change will be required if you're not coming in under the wing of your company. Many local one-child families get by on a combined monthly income of RMB20,000-30,000. This covers a local way of life and local government schools. For most international families of four living in one of the villas in Shunyi, a salary of that level is not even going to cover accommodations. With a three-bedroom villa, international school fees for two kids, an *āyí,* a driver, groceries, and utilities alone, you'll be looking at a budget of around RMB70,000 per month. In fact, total monthly expenses might easily work out to be RMB90,000-100,000.

HOUSING

If you're aware of Hong Kong housing prices, don't let them give you a false impression of Beijing. On the contrary, homes in the mainland capital are generally very spacious, rarely attract a "shoebox" description, and are still often much cheaper than equivalent apartments in other international cities. According to UBS's survey, for example, a furnished four-bedroom apartment suited to someone in middle management, in an area of the city favored by such a person, would cost US$14,100 per month in New York, US$6,940 in Chicago, US$14,490 in Hong Kong, but only US$2,500 (RMB15,600) in Beijing.

If your company has you covered for your accommodations, this will probably translate into a very comfortable, fully furnished apartment or house in a security complex that's situated in a key expat part of town, such as Sanlitun, Shuangjing, Central Park, Lido, or Shunyi. For the locally employed, however, these numbers will be of little value. It's generally accepted by budgeting advisors that housing costs can acceptably take about 30-35 percent of your net income, and for this second crowd, that guideline is frequently exceeded—again especially for those who let their comfort zone have its head.

Modern apartments with security inside the Fourth Ring Road can go for RMB7,000-12,000 for a large one-bedroom, RMB8,000-22,000 for a two-bedroom, and RMB15,000-30,000 for a three bedroom. If you're willing to go to a Chinese-style apartment, then costs will be much lower. One-bedrooms can go for around RMB4,000-8,000, two-bedrooms for RMB6,000-10,000, and three bedrooms for RMB8,000-15,000. Sharing can be an effective way to either reduce your costs or have a better quality place for the amount you're willing to spend. For a ballpark figure for Shunyi homes multiply RMB10,000 per number of bedrooms—RMB30,000 for a three-bedroom house, for example.

Most rental homes in Beijing are fully furnished before you move in, so unless you want to decorate the home yourself, you won't need to outlay much to make it livable. Landlords can be quite stubborn about removing furniture, as they're using the place as a storage room. If furniture is shabby or just not to your taste, you can try to use this to bargain on the price. About half the homes in Shunyi, however, are intentionally unfurnished, given the high number of expats who do come over with their own furniture.

Utilities

Utilities are extraordinarily cheap, but they do differ somewhat between old and new homes, as well as apartments and villas. Older apartments usually work out to be the cheapest.

Electricity is about RMB0.5/kilowatt, which for many apartments pans out to be about RMB50-100 per month. This can go up in summer if you're using the air conditioner, but possibly also in winter if you choose to live in a *hútòng* home or other such place where you independently manage the heating. Heating a *sìhéyuàn* or *píngfáng* in winter can make your bills jump by close to RMB1,000 per month. Most apartments inside the Fifth Ring Road, especially the older ones, have state-run central heating (Nov. 15- Mar. 15). As a general rule, this fee is covered by the landlord not the tenant. Different complexes have different off-peak and peak periods throughout the day and year. If you're in a regular apartment this might not make a huge difference, but if you're in a *sìhéyuàn* or *píngfáng,* knowing the off-peak times can really help you cut costs. Ask your landlord or agent about the specific times for your complex.

Water is RMB4 per cubic meter, which might work out to be about RMB50-100 per month for apartments. Families in villas, however, may find their water bills get up to RMB350 per month.

Natural gas is about RMB1.2 per cubic meter, which can work out at about RMB100-300 per year. *Píngfáng* and *sìhéyuàn* units often have gas bottles rather than connected gas, and you'll need to refill these yourself. These cost RMB40 if you have a gas ID card (your landlord should give you this) or RMB100 without it. A single person will probably go through one of these bottles every month.

GROCERIES AND EATING OUT

Mainland-produced food products, be they packaged or fresh, have earned themselves horrific reputations in the last several years. Scandal after scandal seems to taint every corner of the food pyramid—including pesticides that cover tea, fruit, and vegetables; excessive levels of hormones in pork; melamine in milk products; and more. Even Chinese people clamor to get imported milk powder for their babies. If you're willing to turn a blind eye to the potential health issues, you can eat extremely cheaply, and as an unfussy single you could very easily get by on RMB50-100 a day. More and more expats, and even locals, however, are reaching for organic and imported goods, which, of course, are much more expensive and likely to expand your budget generously. Local M&Ms, for example, cost RMB4-5, while the imported American ones cost RMB9-10. A 600-milliliter carton of local milk costs around RMB6, a carton of local organic milk costs RMB13-15, and imported fresh milk costs RMB30-45 per liter. A family of four could very easily spend RMB2,000-3,000 per week on groceries.

The cheapest places to buy your fresh produce are the fresh produce markets, sometimes called wet markets. These are exciting places to go, and food is often three or four times cheaper (and fresher) than what you'll get at the supermarket. For example, an avocado at a produce market costs around RMB10, while at a "high level" supermarket it could cost as much as RMB40-80. The USB survey also took a basket of 39 food items and compared prices across the various cities. The average overall price was US$424. New York came in at US$552, London at US$436, and Beijing at US$463. Tokyo topped the rankings at US$928.

Local dining doesn't need to be expensive and can cost as little as RMB20 for lunch and RMB50 for a very filling dinner. Eating at a modern Western establishment in a place like Sanlitun or Guomao, however, can range RMB50-120 for lunch, RMB100-500 for dinner. Drinking out usually averages at RMB40-55 for beers and cocktails in local places and RMB70-120 in swankier places. If the price is strangely cheap you can be sure the alcohol is fake and that you'll wake up with a shocking hangover on the following day.

MEDICAL EXPENSES

If your company is following the law, they should be deducting approximately 10 percent of your salary each month for social insurance. In 2012 this was capped at salaries of RMB12,600.

Medical expenses can really add up, and if your company is not covering you for international health insurance then you could be forking out a fortune if you have a serious medical incident. To avoid a potentially catastrophic medical bill, take out international medical insurance. Rates for individuals start at around US$40 per month and move up to more than US$300 per month for comprehensive coverage for a family of four. If your company includes medical in your package, that's potentially more than RMB2,100 that you will save each month, plus the deductible.

EDUCATION

This can be another budget breaker. Western schools are around RMB180,000 per year per child, and preschools are around RMB65,000 (for a half day) per year, give or take a few thousand. If your company doesn't cover your child's education fees in China, this may be the deal breaker. Chinese education is significantly cheaper, but you'll need to consider carefully whether or not this will suit what you want for your child's future.

HELP WITH YOUR UTILITIES

Paying utilities is easy, once you figure out how to do it. With the diversification of Beijing's property market, there seem to be ever more methods by which to pay for your bills. In almost all cases they are prepaid, not billed after use. This system works by placing meters in your home, which need to be charged. They show how many units of electricity, hot water, or gas you have left.

There are two main methods for charging them: a rechargeable smart card (IC), which you add money to and then insert into the meter to recharge it; or a code number, which allows you to directly recharge your meter by making a payment via an ATM-like machine at the bank or online. Some meters are "smart" meters and can accept either method of payment, while some need a physical trip to the bank.

When you sign your lease, make sure you ask your landlord exactly how and where you pay each for utility. There should be more than just one bank that works for each card, so if your landlord tells you only one bank, ask the teller what other banks can also be used. Write it all down (it's very helpful to put a label on each card to remind yourself where to recharge it). If you're living in a higher-quality complex it's quite likely that the property management office or club-house has a 24-hour machine that allows you to conveniently recharge all cards. If you're lucky enough to have a trustworthy *āyí*, then often this becomes one of their assigned duties. One machine to keep your eye out for is a JiaoFeiYi machine (www.jiaofeiyi.net). These can recharge both smart meters and smart cards and work for all UnionPay cards.

RECHARGING SMART CARDS (IC)

The basic way to recharge your smart card is to go to the bank, get a ticket and wait in line, and then finally hand the teller your smart card and some cash. This can be a major headache if you try to do it at big, busy banks, such as ICBC. Try to find a smaller bank, such as the Beijing Rural Commercial Bank or China Everbright Bank. You may even find that many of these banks have machines that allow you to bypass the teller and do it yourself. Ask a security guard or bank worker to help you use the machine.

RECHARGING A SMART METER

If your meter can be recharged via a code number rather just physically with a smart card, congratulations—life is going to be much easier. There are various electronic options. First there is Internet banking. Check with your individual bank for how to do this.

Next, several banks, such as Bank of Beijing (北京银行) and ICBC (工商银行) have dedicated bill-paying machines (often 24 hours) at which you can directly add credit to your meter. Simply choose the option you need, punch in the code number of your home, swipe your bank card, and that's it. Unfortunately these machines are usually in Chinese only. Some ATMs will also provide this service, but again, you need to choose the Chinese format to access these services. Fortunately the bank security guards (or other loitering staff) are usually extremely helpful and will happily show you. It might help to write down or use your phone to take a photo of each step.

Alternatively, Zhifubao (Alipay) has automated processes to make this even quicker. As long as there is money in your Zhifubao account, it takes about a minute to recharge, and just about 5-10 minutes more for it to work its way to your meter. Zhifubao or Lakala on your mobile phone can be an alternative if you're completely out of power.

Finally, if cash at the teller is your only option, try your best to avoid the big banks, such as ICBC or the Agricultural

Bank of China (中国农业银行), and head to the smaller banks, such as Bank of Beijing or Beijing Rural Commercial Bank (北京农商银行). It's amazing how empty these banks usually are by comparison and how quick and painless paying bills can be.

I'VE RECHARGED MY CARD, WHY WON'T IT WORK?

First, make sure you hold the card in the meter's slot for around 10 seconds until it fully accepts the credit. Next, if you had let your power run out completely and sat in the dark before you bothered to recharge your electricity card, chances are the switch in your fuse box has shut off automatically. Check all your fuse boxes, and if one of the switches is off, flip it back on. Hopefully this is the problem. Make a habit of regularly checking your meter, and always recharge before it gets to zero.

WHAT IF I RUN OUT OF ELECTRICITY IN THE MIDDLE OF THE NIGHT?

Being suddenly plunged into darkness at 8pm on a weeknight is a major irritation to most Beijing residents, so you'll need to develop a habit of looking at your meter when you come and go from your home. There are 24-hour recharge options, such as JiaoFeiYi machines, but they may not always feel convenient at the time that you need them. It's highly recommended that you ask a neighbor as soon as possible where the closest 24-hour machine is.

If you have a smart meter system, then you'll still have a range of options at your fingertips. Major ICBC banks often have their bill payment machines located inside their 24-hour ATM lobbies. Of course there is also online and mobile Zhifubao and Lakala, as well as Lakala point of sale machines at convenience stores and supermarkets.

The Beijing Electric Power Corporation has an emergency service for night owls without power. From 7pm to 6am you can call the 95598 hotline number and they'll deliver a pre-charged card to your home. Theoretically there is an English helpline, but sadly the English-speaking assistant seems to be permanently out to lunch.

WHAT'S THIS OTHER WATER BILL STUCK ON MY DOOR?

This mysterious bill is a white piece of perforated paper with blue writing, entitled 北京市自来水集团有限责任公司缴费通知单. It covers such things as tap water and plumbing. At most they'll be stuck on your door every month, but in many places much less regularly. Water costs RMB4 per cubic meter (m3), so these could add up to around RMB40-150 per month. They can be paid at almost any bank. Pop into one of the quieter banks, such as China Everbright Bank (光大银行) or Beijing Rural Commercial Bank, pay in cash, and you'll be out in a jiffy. Alternatively, if you have an account with banks such ICBC, Bank of Communications (交通银行), or China Merchants Bank (招商银行), or with Zhifubao you can pay online.

WHAT IF I LOSE MY CARD?

Besides possibly needing receipts for tax reasons, they will come in handy if you lose your IC card or forget your number. When you sign your lease, your landlord may also give you the original paperwork used when setting up the IC cards. Keep this in a secure place. If you lose your cards, you can take the most recent receipts, your lease, and the original paperwork if you have it to the relevant utility office, and they'll replace it within a few minutes.

WHERE CAN I GO FOR MORE INFORMATION?

The government's www.ebeijing.gov.cn/feature_2/GuideToHeatingElectricityWaterAndGas gives fairly comprehensive but a little outdated information. A Chinese neighbor will probably be able to give you the best advice.

TRAVEL AND TRANSPORTATION

Bus, subway, and bicycle transport is so cheap that it feels free. It's only RMB2 to go anywhere you like on the subway, and if you use an Yikatong card (metro card) you won't even pay RMB1 to ride most buses.

Taxis are much more expensive but will probably still feel relatively cheap compared to back home. The minimum you'll pay to get in a cab is RMB10. A typical fare within the inner city is RMB20-30, and to get from the inner city to the airport will cost around RMB70-100, including road tolls. There are plenty of black taxis around town, which will do their best to try to extort you. Expect them to push an RMB20 fare up to RMB60-80 when it's raining.

Driving costs add up and really depend on your usage. Gas is about RMB8 per liter, and annual fixed expenses, such as registration and compulsory insurance, are RMB8,000. An English-speaking driver is likely to cost RMB4,000-5,000, excluding gas and tolls. Parking is fairly cheap by the hour if you're just at a shopping mall or restaurant, and may only cost RMB10 after a few hours. Where it will build up is for long-term or residential parking.

If you plan to travel around the country, trains are a little cheaper than flying, but sometimes the discount doesn't seem enough to warrant the extra time it takes. A return trip to Xi'an from Beijing (about 11 hours each way), will cost about RMB850 in a soft sleeper, while a round-trip economy flight (2 hours) can cost RMB1,000-2,500.

Your annual round-trip flights home will likely be much more expensive and may cost in the vicinity of RMB6,000-11,000, the latter price especially at Christmastime. Shop around for prices. Individual airline sites are usually, but not always, the most expensive option. Local online travel agencies www.ctrip.com and www.elong.com are English-friendly and often offer heavily discounted prices that the airlines themselves can't match.

ENTERTAINMENT

Of course, this is going to vary greatly depending on your tastes and lifestyle. There are plenty of national parks on the outskirts of town, which cost next to nothing to go for a hike in, and then there are horrendously expensive gyms that cost more than four times a local teacher's monthly salary. The city is scattered with amusement parks, KTV venues, museums, ice skating rinks, gyms, and scenic spots, so there are plenty of options. Giving just a very rough stab at prices, you're looking at spending roughly RMB100 to get into any major venue these days. At the start of 2013, for example, Beijing's answer to Disneyland, Happy Valley, was RMB100 for kids and RMB160 for adults, and Beijing's most popular ski resort, Nanshan, started at RMB120, which covered skis, chairlifts, and two hours of skiing.

The key to cutting costs with entertainment is discovering the discount systems. Groupon-like group-buying sites are extremely popular and can offer huge discounts on entertainment, including fine dining, drinking, travel (and almost anything else you want to spend your money on). They're particularly popular for cinema tickets. Unfortunately, these are uniformly all in Chinese, so you may need to draw on the help of your *āyí* or Chinese friend. Also, beware that there are thousands of these companies in China, and many have been shut down for offering fake deals and/or rotten service. Some of the more reliable ones include http://t.dianping.com/beijing, http://bj.meituan.com, and http://bj.nuomi.com.

Alternatively, keep your eye out for memberships and prepay options. If you're prepared to commit to a membership fee or paying out a chunk of money in advance, you'll get significant discounts. I prepay RMB1,000 at my hairdresser. This gives me a 20 percent discount on all services, and I just top it up when it runs out. At Mega Box cinemas (at Sanlitun and Zhongguancun), the annual RMB20 membership fee will get you 50 percent off tickets on weekdays and 30 percent off on weekends and holidays. Even if you use it only once, you'll already have saved.

Shopping

In previous years, people would come to China hoping to pick up cheap electronics or clothes. It is true that there are many things that are cheaper, but it really depends what you want and what kind of quality you're willing to accept. China is not a tax haven, and many imported goods are heavily taxed—wine in particular. For instance, at the start of 2013, the 16GB iPad Mini started from $329 in the U.S., and from RMB2,498 (US$400) in China. If something is unusually cheap then it's probably fake and likely to disintegrate after only a couple of uses. Custom-made goods, on the other hand, can be much cheaper than you'd ever be able to get at home. Furniture, curtains, tailored clothing, and printing, for example, are highly negotiable, and well worth considering having made here rather than bringing over. Getting them made can also be extremely fast, perhaps needing only a few days or a week or two.

As far as diversity is concerned, this is something that is ever improving. Just five years ago you might have been holding out for a trip home to stock up on your favorite brands, but the need for this decreases every year. Ikea was once the one-stop shop for expat households, but now there are more options. Not only is there an increasing number of international supermarkets and retailers, but Chinese tastes are also changing, so there are ever more products that align with Western preferences.

If you can't get something in Beijing, global Internet shopping can be a lifesaver, and many companies offer free international shipping. Avoid getting any international package delivered to your personal residence, especially if you have chosen standard postal delivery—it's shocking how many things never arrive. Instead, always have things delivered to a workplace, and always choose a courier option. Couriers in Beijing are excellent and it's rare to have problems. A minor difficulty is that they typically speak no English, so if your Chinese is just as good, include the cell number of a Chinese person in the delivery instructions.

WHERE TO SHOP FOR WHAT

Wherever you work or live in Beijing, there is bound to be a shopping mall within walking distance. New malls are incessantly opening, and each new one seems to compete with the last one for size and collection of retailers. The major malls to shop in these days include Lane Crawford, Shin Kong Place, Joy City, Solana, The Place, The Malls at Oriental Plaza, APM, Indigo, Taikoo Li Sanlitun, and newcomer Galaxy SOHO.

The exciting, and possibly frustrating thing about Beijing, however, is that there is actually a world of less-obvious places to shop—small streets in a unfamiliar parts of town, online shops, markets that only the locals seem clued in about. It's something that makes this an unendingly fascinating city. Expect to routinely be told about a hidden gem that you can't believe you didn't already know about. Beijing is not only filled with bustling markets, it is also dotted with streets and areas that have gradually developed over the years into the *it* place for a given item. Gulou Dongdajie, for instance, is the place to go for guitars and many other musical instruments. Wusi Dajie is the place to go for art supplies and framing. The streets around Yongdingmen

THE COST OF LIVING IN BEIJING

HOME

Salary	RMB4,000-60,000/month
Rent	RMB2,000-60,000/month
Electricity bill (apartment)	RMB100-200/month
Āyí (housekeeper)	RMB25-50/hr or 3,000/month

FOOD AND DRINKS

Dinner at a Western restaurant	RMB150-500 pp
Dinner at a local restaurant	RMB40-80 pp
Glass of wine	RMB45-90
Bottle of wine from the supermarket	RMB80-350
Cocktail	RMB50-120
Lunch in a local Western-style café	RMB45
University cafeteria lunch	RMB10
Whole free-range chicken	RMB50/kg
Big Mac	RMB16.50
Lunch of 3 bāozi (buns)	RMB6
Cappuccino	RMB30
Coffee of the day at Starbucks	RMB17
Local beer (from corner shop)	RMB3
Imported or craft beer	RMB20-60
Bottle of Coke, 500 ml	RMB3
Pack of local cigarettes	RMB10

HEALTH

International doctor's appointment	RMB300-1,200
Contraceptive pill (local)	RMB30
Contraceptive pill (international)	RMB250

Waidajie are where to go for all manner of stationery. And Malian Dao, also known as Tea Street, is, well, you can guess.

Antiques

For antiques with questionable antiquity and kitsch Chinese curios, head down to the Panjiayuan flee market (Line 10) early on Saturday or Sunday morning. Quality Chinese-style furniture can also be found at Gaobeidian Furniture Street (高碑店家具 一条街), a little south of Sihui (Line 1), beside the East Fourth Ring Road. Along this quiet backstreet, you'll find shops such as Lily's Antiques Furniture, which sell classic decorations and pieces of furniture that you'll most likely want to take home with you.

Membership at Western-style gym	RMB4,000-21,000/year
Pilates class	RMB200
One-hour massage (in expat-friendly spa)	RMB280
TRANSPORTATION AND COMMUNICATIONS	
Subway	RMB2
Bus	RMB1
10-km/20-minute taxi fare	RMB30
Gasoline	RMB8.5/liter
Basic bicycle	RMB100-500
Economy round-trip flight to Hong Kong	RMB2,000-4,000 (including tax)
Newspaper	RMB1
Internet	RMB1,700/year
Cell phone bill	100-200/month
SERVICES	
Haircut at Toni & Guy	RMB300-1,500
Haircut at a local salon	RMB30-200
Small-group Chinese-language class	RMB80/hour
ENTERTAINMENT	
Cinema ticket	RMB70
Pirated DVD	RMB10
Tickets for a live music act	RMB50-300
CLOTHING	
Shirt dry-cleaned	RMB12
Quality fake Prada bag	RMB600
Tailored suit	RMB1,000
Levi's jeans	RMB500-1,200

Books and Magazines

English-language books and magazines are increasingly easy to get in Beijing. You may still need to rely on incoming visitors for copies of the latest *Vanity Fair* or *Real Life,* but a handful of titles are available in international supermarkets and bookshops such as The Bookworm in Sanlitun, Page One, and Trends Lounge in the north tower of The Place. These are also the places to go for English books. Be warned, however; prices in such places are international and will likely incorporate the expense of shipping. Beijing's major local bookshops all have collections of English books, sometimes surprisingly large, and are usually cheaper than the international bookstores. These mega complexes include the Wangfujing Bookstore and Foreign Language Bookstore at Wangfujing, and the Xidan Books Building beside Xidan subway station. A much cheaper and potentially more convenient option is to use online bookstores, including www.amazon.cn, www.dangdang.com, and www.beifabook.com. Not all will accept international credit cards, but these three allow for cash on delivery. Rather than automatically defaulting to international bookstores for unusual titles it can worth checking here first. You might find that the book price works out to be the same, but you'll avoid the shipping costs.

Bicycles and Scooters

Cheap bicycles and electric scooters can be found just about anywhere in the city, including supermarkets such as Carrefour and Walmart. There are clusters of bike shops around particular streets, including along Dongsi Beidajie and Dongzhimen Neidajie in Dongcheng district. Expats on their way home frequently also try to hock their old pedals on The Beijinger website and on Beijing Café, so it's well worth putting out a call on either site if you're after your own set of wheels.

Camera and Camera Equipment

Camera shops can be found everywhere around the city, especially in the electronics zones, but there is no place better to get your fix than the Wukesong Camera Market, just a 10-minute walk directly north from Wukesong subway station (Line 1) in Haidian. This amazing market is packed with vendors selling all brands of cameras and camera equipment, both amateur and professional. You'll find the latest Canon or Nikon body or lens, as well as secondhand collector items. A good deal of the products are genuine but may not come with international warranties. Bargaining margins are also limited. The Lomography Gallery store, just north of Taikoo Li Sanlitun, will satisfy those with a Lomo fetish. Film, on the other hand, isn't so ubiquitous, and neither are good developers, particularly if you'd rather your photos didn't come back in an odd shade of green or blue. A few places that professionals and photography lovers choose to use include 798 Photo Gallery (www.798photogallery.cn) in the 798 Art District; Green View Club (www.greenviewclub.com), also in 798; and Photo Chance (www.photochance.com), just west of Dongsi subway station (Lines 5 and 6) near the National Art Gallery.

Clothes

You don't need to look far for clothes in Beijing, but not every place will carry what you're after. The Zoo Markets, a seemingly endless collection of buildings (located in Haidian, just near Beijing Zoo subway station on Line 4), is the place to go for wholesale-priced, no-name clothes and accessories. It's best to take a friend who is familiar with the area, otherwise be prepared to wander aimlessly, perhaps fruitlessly, in a search for gems among the thousands of racks of semi-terrible garments. Silk Street, the market complex at Yong'anli subway station (Line 1), and the almost identical Yashow Market, beside Taikoo Li Sanlitun, are the places to get classic fake Gucci, Prada, and the like. Hongqiao Market (www.hongqiao-pearl-market.com), just meters from Tiantan Dongmen subway station (Line 5), is similar again but has a much stronger focus on pearls and jewelry. If you can stand an atmosphere that borders on harassment and the need to bargain like you're bankrupt, then these venues do have their place. These are major destinations for tourists, but they can also be great places to pick up winter sweaters, T-shirts, sweatpants, scarves, and even costumes for fancy dress parties. For clothing that doesn't conform to mainstream styles, weave your way through the boutiques in 3.3 and Nali Patio, both places wedged between the north and south sections of Taikoo Li Sanlitun. Some of the stores here sell shoes or garments created by local designers, and some sell pieces that have been personally imported by the store owners. The major malls, mentioned above, are the places to find brands such Gap, Zara, G-Star, H&M, and so on. Young people in particular like to shop at Joy City in Xidan (Line 1) and at Qingnian Lu (Line 6).

Cosmetics

If you have particular preferences for cosmetics, you might find your appearance starts to look a little shabby in Beijing. Major brands such as Clinique, Clarins, Estée Lauder, Mac, Bobby Brown, and Sephora are all here, but the color ranges can differ from what you can get at home, particularly for foundations. Meibocheng Beauty Supplies City (美博城美容美发用品商城), across from the south end of Qianmen Jie, is a maze of wholesale vendors selling everything from hair treatment products and shampoos to fake nails. Online store www.lefeng.com is popular with locals for major brands, but Strawberrynet.com is a good option for international brands and colors, and given that products ship free of charge from Hong Kong, they usually arrive in just a few days.

Electronics

For electronics, the major zone in Beijing is Zhongguancun, Beijing's own Silicon City. Enormous buildings sitting side by side become multistory burrows of digital wares. The main concentration of shops and markets is between Haidianhuangzhuang (Lines 4 and 10) and Zhongguancun (Line 4) subway stations. It can be extremely overwhelming and headache-inducing. For those who balk at the commute to Zhongguancun or simply prefer something more mentally manageable, an alternative is Buynow (百脑汇, *Bǎinǎohuì*), situated on Chaoyangmen Waidajie just north of Ritan Park. Beware that both places have their good share of fake products, and bargaining will be essential. Online stores www.amazon.cn and www.jd.com are great for everyday items.

Grocery Shopping

While you might not be able to get each and every item that usually fills your pantry, Beijing does have a lot of options for grocery shopping. "International" supermarkets are easily found all over the eastern side of town, and the major chains favored by

© SHANNON AITKEN

Walmart stocks an amazing range of products as well as ready-made food to go.

expats include Jenny Lou's, Jenny Wang's, April Gourmet, and City Shop. For ultra laziness, most of these shops home deliver. Relying on these kinds of shops is easy, but getting into the habit of shopping only here is not going to do your bank account any good. Many of the international products carried in such stores can also been found much more cheaply in the international aisles of Carrefour and Walmart. If you're after specialty baking items or ingredients, you might find what you're looking for on Taobao. Various online vendors here (such as Yipin Chuwei, http://ypcw.taobao. com; Beijing Global Gourmet Shop, http://hqms24.taobao.com; and Ziwei Hongbei, http://ziwei365.taobao.com) sell imported items that seem almost impossible to buy in mainstream shops, and many have a small physical store that you can visit if preferred.

Supermarkets stock meat, fruit, and vegetables, but the best way to shop for fresh food in Beijing is at the produce markets around the city. Perhaps the star venue for expats and Western chefs in the city is Sanyuanli Market on Shunyuan Jie, close to Liangmaqiao subway station (Line 10). Prices here might be a tad higher than at other local markets, but quality is good, and many of the vendors, including the butchers, have English on their signs. Just a few of the other major markets include Dongjiao Wholesale Market (south of Dawanglu subway station, Line 1); Sihuan Zonghe Market, a little west of Houhai; Yuegezhuang Wholesale Market, in Fengtai by the West Fourth Ring Road; and Nanhu Market, a Korean favorite, on Nanhu Nanlu in Wangjing. For a haul of fresh seafood, make your way to the enormous Jingshen Seafood Market on Shiliuzhuang Xijie in Fengtai district, just south of Songjiazhuang subway station (Line 5).

Given that the produce markets don't refrigerate the meat and fish, it's best that you get there early in the morning, especially in summer before the day heats up. If this isn't your style, two butchers that have more of a Western feel are Boucherie Michel in the expat hub of Xingfucun Lu, west of Sanlitun, and Chez Gerard, a tiny gem of Western goods on a narrow *hútòng* (alley) connecting Wudaoying Hutong and Guozijian Jie, near the Lama Temple. Another alternative is to shop online via Australian meat supplier Elders (www.elders.com.cn). They're based in Shanghai, but delivery to Beijing is free if you order over RMB1,000 worth of goods—something not hard to do if you order a couple of cuts of meat and a bottle or two of wine.

Contaminated food is a serious issue in China, thanks to shoddy standards at various links in the production chain. Organic products are consequently in increasing demand. They can be hard to get in local supermarkets, but international supermarkets have a better offering, and then there are shops that specialize in the greener goods. Lohao City (www.lohaocity.com) is perhaps the strongest contender and has various outlets around town. Smaller companies such as Wonder Milk, Green Yard (www.greenyard.cn), Little Donkey Farm (www.littledonkeyfarm.com), and Guoren Green Alliance (http://lvselianmeng.taobao.com) make a concerted effort to produce food that's closer to nature. Email group Beijing Organic Consumers Association (http://health.groups.yahoo.com/group/beijing_organic_consumers) can put you in touch with like-minded healthy shoppers, with whom you can share tips on where to buy what. Kosher groceries can be picked up at a lot of the international supermarkets, but for a more select range, visit www.chabadbeijing.com or www.kosherbeijing.com.

Homeware and Kitchenware

To deck out your abode with homeware and kitchenware, you can plunge yourself into Beijing's only Ikea outlet, beside the North Fourth East Ring Road in the Wangjing area. It can be chaos in here—husbands sleeping entirely under the covers of beds, children jumping up and down on sofas—but it is the place to get of staples that can be hard to come by elsewhere in the city, such as tea towels and fitted sheets. Alternatively, try Muji (www.muji.com.cn), which is an upscale Ikea with heavier price tags. Designs are minimalist and classy, and they also carry a cool range of stationery. If you don't mind the catering look, you can bargain for cheaper wares at Dongjiao markets, or head just a short walk west of Beijing South Railway Station (Line 4) to the Beijing Hotel Equipment Corp (HEC, 酒总酒店设备). This is particularly the place for those wanting to set up a restaurant or café, but home cooks will also find their hearts racing as they wind through the floors of kitchen equipment at far less than in conventional stores. If you're up in Haidian, you can establish your kitchen with a visit to Five Golden Star Market (金五星百货批发城), on Xueyuan Nan Lu (near Sidaokou).

Sporting Goods

Like anywhere in the world, if you want top-notch sporting goods, you may need to seek out the specialist retailers; however, places such as the Faya Sports Factory Stores (法雅体育工厂店) and the Decathlon outlets (www.decathlon.com.cn) around town will impress with their Olympic-sized range of sports goods. The goods in these stores are also predominantly genuine.

Toys

New China Children's Store on Wangfujing Jie was once the major place to shop for toys, but now there are many other choices. A mainstay is Tianle Toy Market, just behind Hongqiao market near Tiantan Dongmen (Line 5). This a good choice if you just want something cheap, or a lifetime supply of colorful stickers, but if you're

DAILY LIFE

© SHANNON AITKEN

HEC Hotel Equipment Depot is just one of the many different wholesalers that make setting up home exciting and affordable

worried about tiny pieces breaking off and getting into the mouth of your little one, then it might be wise to seek other toy vendors. You'll be impressed by the gargantuan Beijing International Toys City, which is the largest wholesale and retail toy store in northern China, and conveniently located just west of Liujiayao subway station (Line 5). ToysRus (www.toysrus.com.cn) also has a presence in Beijing, with one store smack bang next to Taiyanggong subway station (Line 10) in Capital Mall and the other in Chaoyang Joy City by Qingnian Lu subway station (Line 6).

Other

There really isn't much you can't get in Beijing, although it might seem contrary to this when you first touch down. There are flowers, candles, and exotic goldfish hidden in the Laitai Flower Market near Ladies' Street; unending reams of fabric at what has just collectively become known as the Muxiyuan Fabric Markets, spreading upward from the north side of Dahongmen subway station (Line 10) in Fengtai District; and floor after floor of spectacles at Beijing Glasses City just north of Panjiayuan subway station (Line 1). For free things, look to Beijing's branch of the Freecycle Network (http://groups.freecycle.org/FreecycleBeijing). Join the group's email network and you can give away or put your hand up for things without a price tag.

BARGAINING AND SHOPPING CULTURE

Shopping malls are much alike anywhere in the world, but there's definitely a par-ticular cultural trait that may drive you out of the store rather than into it. Shop at-tendants will shadow you around like the proverbial fly, often following intrusively close. Perhaps the most useful expression you could learn is *"suíbiàn kànkan"* (随便看看), meaning "I'm just looking." If this doesn't free you from your shepherd, go for something more direct: *"Búyòng gēnzhe wǒ"* (不用跟着我), "No need to follow me."

That usually does the trick. In department stores and local-style stores, they may use a cashier desk system, rather than a direct payment to the person you select the goods from. The salesperson will give you a receipt, which you take to the cashier. The cashier will take your money and stamp the receipt, which you take back to the salesperson to collect your things.

There is no bargaining in mainstream shopping, but it is a big part of the shopping culture here, and anyone who lives in Beijing will at some time encounter it. Bargaining is pretty much used in anything that isn't a mainstream commercial premise, such as fresh produce markets, tailors, wholesale markets, and so on, and your foreign face may cause instant inflation.

Many guidebooks advise you to start bargaining by cutting a vendor's original price down by about 70-90 percent, and that's definitely true in tourist hot spots. The most optimistic salespeople are to be found at the Silk Markets, Panjiayuan and Yashow, where more than half the trade is wide-eyed naïve tourists coming in by the busload. A "silk" tie that you should ultimately be able to get for RMB20-50 might start at RMB500. Cut them down to a low price, and only raise your offer fraction by fraction as they lower theirs. If they don't accept your final price, walk away, and if they come running after you, then you've got a deal. If they let you go, then you know you've really gone too low. There are usually plenty of other vendors selling the exact same thing, so now you have your baseline. Most vendors at these markets have enough English for bargaining and will understand "cheaper." If not, you can try your Chinese: *"Tài guì le,"* meaning "too expensive," and *"piányi,"* meaning "cheap."

Such heavy-handed bargaining might not go down well at places where the clientele is predominantly local and the profit margin is much smaller. The Zoo Markets, for example, may give you only RMB5-20 off the price of a piece of clothing.

Generally the rule is that the more you buy, the better you can bargain. If you can manage to make the vendor laugh, then your chances are even better. Chinese people enjoy a good round of bargaining, but if you insult them by insisting on a ridiculous offer then they'll be less likely to offer you their actual best price. If you are going to go for a rock-bottom price, say it with a friendly smile. Getting angry isn't going to get you a good deal.

Try to find out ahead of time from a Chinese friend what the item should cost. If you go in blind then you might be a sitting duck for being taken advantage of or, the opposite, trying to undercut them too much. Definitely decide how much you're willing to pay for something before you mention a price, and take your time.

It's good to develop a relationship with a vendor that you have success with. You can easily come back again and request the same price as last time, or even have your friends come and shop for the same price. Vendors love to know that they're going to get your return business, so it can help your bargaining to tell them that you'll use them again if they give you a good price.

Tipping

There is no expectation of tipping in Beijing, be it for restaurants, taxis, or bars. If you are determined to tip, be ready for a struggle. Some people will outright refuse to receive the tip, and you may even have people come running after you to return the cash you "forgot" on the table.

SHOPPING AND PAYING ONLINE

Beijing is a vast city, and the thought of running from district to district just to buy something can be enough to make you make do with the more expensive, more convenient alternatives. The online shopping world, however, is the key to transforming your concept of convenience in Beijing. Products are cheaper, there's almost nothing you can't buy, and delivery is fast and usually free. It just takes a little bit of effort to adapt to and to get yourself set up. So here are some tips to get started.

Make sure you have an up-to-date operating system on your computer, especially if you're not using a PC with Windows but are on a Mac. Many sites requiring any kind of financial transaction won't work on anything older than Snow Leopard. If you can't get things to work on your computer, explore the smartphone or iPad versions.

Be ready to experiment with different browsers, especially for Internet banking. Internet Explorer is most successful, while Opera, Safari, Firefox, and Chrome vary in their compatibility with different websites.

Most of the good sites are completely Chinese, so if you can't read characters, try viewing pages through Google Chrome. The translation function might result in obscure grammar for detailed documents, but it's usually perfectly adequate for making shopping selections and payment choices. Of course it can help to have a Chinese friend guide you through the process the first few times. Have them save your address and other details in Chinese so that you can copy and paste any time you need to enter them into a digital form. For other browsers, you can download the Annotate bookmarklet from mandarinspot.com and get word-by-word translations on any webpage. When searching for a product, try using the English word. You'll probably find that what you want comes up.

Not all shopping sites need you to have online banking set up. Many, such as Amazon and JD.com, will accept cash on delivery, so there's basically no risk. Beijing's couriers (*kuàidì*) are fantastic and will usually call before or when they arrive to check if you're in. If you're not, they can come back at a better time or day. The only problem is that it's highly unlikely they'll speak English, so if you don't speak Chinese, it's probably best to have your goods delivered to a workplace.

Online Shopping
Taobao

Taobao (www.taobao.com) is the hero online shopping site in China, something akin to eBay, but without the bidding. All manner of sellers, fantastic and terrible, are doing business here, and there's almost nothing you can't get. When you think you need to add a personal haul to the suitcase of an incoming friend, stop and look here first. Your mystery item could well be here. While the majority of Taobao sellers are good, there is a risk of buying fake goods or being scammed, so familiarize yourself with how to check a seller's reliability.

Taobao can seem a little overwhelming at first, but there is no shortage of English-language guides out there on the Internet for how to use it: http://taobaofieldguide.com and www.taobao.com/go/act/global/teach, for example, are great places to start. If you still feel a little unsure, however, you can use a Taobao agent, who will help you source what you want and even help you make the payment by using such methods as your home country's Paypal account. They add on a small commission for the service.

Perhaps the most standard method for making payments on Taobao is via Zhifubao, but you can also use Lakala or a JiaoFeiYi machine, or add money to your Taobao account at the post office.

AMAZON

Don't default to getting books sent from the States and paying the possibly US$50-plus shipping charge. Amazon China (www.amazon.cn) might just have the book here, which will be delivered to your door within one or two days, without any shipping costs for purchases over just RMB29. You can use online payment systems or pay cash or swipe your Chinese bank card on delivery.

JD.COM

This site (http://jd.com) works almost identically to Amazon but has a stronger focus on electronics. It accepts online payment systems, or pay cash or swipe your Chinese bank card on delivery.

DANGDANG

Dangdang (www.dangdang.com) works like Amazon and JD.com and has a strong focus on books. Some locals argue it's cheaper than other sites, but it pays to compare all three sites. Cash on delivery is also available.

LEFENG AND STRAWBERRYNET

Lefeng (www.lefeng.com) is the place for all things cosmetic. Locals love it, but some product ranges are still limited by what is better suited to the Asian complexion. Strawberrynet (www.strawberrynet.com) can be a savior and is also linked to Zhifubao. To pay with Zhifubao, however, you will need to use Strawberrynet via the Chinese-language option, not English.

HUIHUI

Most of the online shops cross over in what they sell, so it can be a nightmare trying to shop around for the best price. Download the Huihui add-on (http://zhushou. huihui.cn) and it will help you find the best prices for a product in a single search. It works for all major browsers—just click on the blue 其他浏览器 below the Explorer icon for other browser options.

FLIGHTS

The two major flight websites in China for domestic and international flights are www. ctrip.com and www.elong.com. They are both English friendly and have good customer service. Both accept international credit cards and international Paypal payments, as well as domestic cards and Zhifubao. Ctrip has the advantage of also accepting cash on delivery of tickets, as long as you'll be paying for them in the departure city.

Payment Systems
JIAOFEIYI MACHINES

This is perhaps your easiest option for all payments. Firstly, these incredibly handy machines are almost completely bilingual, so, unlike with virtually every other payment

© SHANNON AITKEN

Wu Mart (not to be confused with Walmart), one of Beijing's big local supermarkets

system in the city, you may feel confident using them without your usual Chinese hand holder. They accept any UnionPay card and can help you pay for almost anything—Zhifubao, electricity, Taobao, mobile or fixed line phone bills, road toll cards (ETC card), bank transfers, and more. You can find them in supermarkets, such as Carrefour, Wu Mart, BHG, Bonjour, and Walmart; the lobbies of banks; some shopping malls; and more. Just note that while bank transfers under RMB5,000 transfer immediately, amounts over this figure can take up to a day to be processed. To pinpoint your nearest machine, visit www.jiaofeiyi.net/map/map.php or download the app for iPhones and iPads.

ZHIFUBAO AND TENPAY

Zhifubao (www.zhifubao.com), also known as Alipay, and its direct competitor Tenpay (www.tenpay.com), are the local equivalents of Paypal. They might not let you shop in many of your favorite stores back home (yet) but they do have some additional automated functions that can make them worth setting up for an easier life in Beijing. Zhifubao, the more established of the two, is particularly popular. With just a few clicks, you can use it to quickly transfer money to a friend (who also has a Zhifubao account), add credit to your cell phone, and pay for electricity at any time of day or night (if you have a code system rather than an IC card). You can use it to pay for products on any of the online shops listed here as well as many more.

Setting up a Zhifubao account is extremely easy and quick, as long as you can read Chinese or have a Chinese friend to sit next to you at the computer. Connecting the account to your bank account, however, is where you will likely encounter a problem. To make the link, the system requires a *shēnfènzhèng* number to be entered. A *shēnfènzhèng* is the form of identification used by Chinese people and has about 15 numbers. As a foreigner you don't have one and your ID at the bank is your passport, which at the time of writing wasn't accepted by Zhifubao. It's best to speak to your bank to find out if and how your particular bank account can be linked to Zhifubao or Tenpay.

If you can't connect your bank to Zhifubao, there are other ways to get money into the account. You can give a Chinese friend some cash and have them transfer it to your account via theirs, or add money yourself via a payment at a Lakala machine. It works a bit like buying a recharge card for your cell phone.

HOW TO BUY SOMETHING ON TAOBAO USING LAKALA:

1) Choose the Lakala payment option on Taobao, then note the transaction number (交易号), which should also be sent to your mobile.
2) Go to a Lakala terminal.
3) Select option 3 (淘宝支付宝充值付款) to choose Taobao.
4) Next, select option 1 (为支付宝交易号付款) to input the transaction number.
5) On the next screen enter the transaction number then hit the red 确认 (Confirm) button.
6) On the next screen you will be asked to enter the amount you need to pay (请输入金额). Enter the amount and press 确认 (Confirm) again.
7) Now enter your phone number (请输入您的手机号码) and press 确认 (Confirm).
8) A summary of the information will appear on the next screen. Press 确认 (Confirm).
9) It will then show you the transaction amount, plus the processing fee (含手续费). Press 确认 (Confirm).
10) You will now be asked to swipe your bank card (请刷卡付款) and then enter your PIN (请输入密码). After you do this press 确认 (Confirm). A receipt will then be printed. Done!
To put money into your Zhifubao account, the steps are similar to those above. For point 3, however, you should instead select option 2 (购买支付宝充值号) to buy a recharge number. If you make any mistakes at any point, press 返回 to return.

LAKALA

Lakala is a relatively new but rapidly expanding payment system. It works in a similar way to Zhifubao, but rather than storing your money it really is more about transferring money from your bank to wherever it needs to be. You can use it to transfer money between different banks, pay off a Chinese credit card, recharge your cell phone, check the balance on your Chinese debit card, pay bills for cooperating stores, purchase goods on Taobao, add credit to Zhifubao or Tenpay, and more. Transactions incur a minimum fee of RMB2 and a maximum of RMB50.

In general, when using Lakala to pay when online shopping, you select the Lakala option when you reach the payment step. You will then be given an order number, which you take and enter into a Lakala terminal, website, or mobile device, after which you swipe your UnionPay bank card to make the payment.

There are various ways to access Lakala. The most straightforward way is at convenience stores such as Quik or 7-Eleven, or at supermarkets. They look like a point-of-sale (POS) machine and are usually set up just inside the door. The store person or a Chinese friend can help you make the transaction if you're unsure. Then there is a cell phone app, which can be downloaded for free, but which must be used in conjunction with a device that you plug into the headphone jack, which allows you to swipe your UnionPay bank card. There is also a home POS machine and a device that can be used with your computer—all of which are available for sale from the www.lakala. com or online stores such as Amazon and TMall.com.

PAYPAL CHINA

If you're going to be earning *rénmínbì* rather than dollars, you may want to think about opening a Chinese Paypal account, especially if you have continuing payments to make back home but don't want to use your savings there to do that. You may have already set up a Paypal account in your home country, but to have it working successfully with your Chinese bank account you need to create an account from scratch via Paypal China, which is all in English, so it's simple. You will need to set up online banking with your Chinese bank account and connect the two. This can be helpful when it's time to buy gifts for family or friends, or for paying off credit cards. Some people even use it as a method for returning money to their home country.

Banking

If you ever wonder where the trees have gone in China, it's probably to make the endless sheets of paper used by the banks. A simple transaction at the bank can yield four or five copies of receipts, each "chopped" with the all-mighty red *chop* (a stamp).

This is perhaps one part of life in Beijing that will make you cringe. Despite the focus on wealth, banks seem somehow out of step with the progress happening elsewhere in the country. People wait for often an hour just to make a simple deposit, and the elderly start queuing outside the bank in the morning so they don't have to sit inside and wait when it does open. A trip to the bank can be the most baffling, exasperating moment of your week.

While times differ, most banks operate 9am-5pm Monday to Saturday. Many, however, also open on Sunday.

It's hard to say which bank is the most expat friendly, as they all seem to have a deficiency in some regard, but the ones that have the most obvious affinity with foreigners include China Merchants, Bank of China (www.boc.cn), the Industrial and Commercial Bank of China (ICBC, www.icbc.com.cn), and China Construction Bank (www.ccb.com). There is definitely no shortage of banks, however. Other big players include the Bank of Communications (www.bankcomm.com) and the Agricultural Bank of China (www.95599.cn), although it's rare to hear of expats using that latter, which specializes in financing the rural and farming sector.

ICBC is the largest bank of them all in terms of staff and branches. Its branches are so prolific that they can quite often be found within a kilometer or two of each other. The Bank of China, which specializes in foreign-exchange transactions and trade finance, is a bank often used by those in international trade. Citibank and HSBC also have strong presences here. The Chinese branches of such banks, however, typically use different systems to their branches elsewhere in the world, so you will not be able to manage your money directly from China. China Merchants Bank can generally be relied on for having branch and phone staff that are more fluent in English.

China UnionPay is China's single card-processing company, similar to PLUS or Cirrus. It connects banks and businesses within China and abroad. You'll see its logo on your bank card, at ATMs, on online shops, and anywhere that it can be used. Many international Visa, MasterCard and other cards can also be used here. However, you may need to use particular banks or ATMs for your card to work, and in some cases international credit cards won't be accepted at all. If you encounter difficulty using your debit or bank card in Beijing, check with your bank to see which Chinese banks it cooperates with.

© SHANNON AITKEN

DAILY LIFE

ICBC, one of China's biggest banks

CURRENCY

The official currency used in Beijing is the *rénmínbì* (人民币). This is the legal tender for mainland China, but not Taiwan, Hong Kong, or Macau, although on some occasions it may be accepted. It shares the name of the bank by which it is issued, the Zhōngguó Rénmín Yínháng (中国人民银行), or rather, the People's Bank of China, the central bank. *Bì* (币) means "currency," so it can be said to mean "the people's currency." The currency code can be RMB or CNY, and the symbols used include ¥ and 元.

The basic unit of the *rénmínbì* is the *yuán* (元), often colloquially referred to as the *kuài* (块), which means "piece" and is the equivalent of saying "buck" or "quid." The *yuán* is then divided into 10 units called *jiǎo* （角）, colloquially called *máo* (毛); the *jiǎo* is also divided into 10 units, called *fēn* (分). *Fēn* are almost never used these days, except by banks, but nevertheless seem to accumulate in a jar in your home because of their uselessness. Even *máo* seem to be used only in convenience stores and supermarkets; everywhere else rounds up or down to *yuán*. When shopping, you will most likely hear the shopkeeper say something like *"shí kuài qián"* (十块钱), meaning "10 pieces of money."

Rénmínbì banknotes come in the form of 100, 50, 20, 10, 5, and 1 *yuán*, as well as 5 and 1 *jiǎo*. On the rare occasion you might run into a now out-of-print 2 *yuán* or a 2 *jiǎo*. As for coins, you will encounter the 1 *yuán*, the 5 and 1 *jiǎo*, and possibly the 5, 2, and 1 *fēn*. Depending on how you shop, it can be quite possible to get about without a single coin passing your hands.

Exchange Rates

In the past, the *rénmínbì* was fixed against the U.S. dollar. However, as China has moved toward a global market economy, it has been devalued to help make China's exports more competitive. Since 2005, the exchange rate of the *rénmínbì* has been allowed to float within a narrow margin and is pegged now not against the U.S. dollar but by a basket of international currencies. At the time of writing the general exchange rate hovered around US$1 to RMB6.2.

It was argued in the past that the *rénmínbì* was highly undervalued, but measures have been taken in recent years to appreciate it so that it is closer to its true value, and the Chinese government has said that it intends to increase the exchange rate's flexibility and eventually make it a reserve currency.

Prior to 2010, international trade needed to be done in U.S. dollars via the People's Bank of China, which acted as the exchange point between foreign and domestic companies. U.S. dollars would be sent to the central bank by foreign companies, and the bank would then pay the respective Chinese companies according to its controlled *rénmínbì* rate. Conversely, local companies trading internationally would pay the central bank *rénmínbì* and the bank would issue the U.S. dollars. Since 2010, the government has begun to liberalize trading and has allowed a growing number of countries to settle directly in *rénmínbì* rather than converting to U.S. dollars. Keen to increase international use of the *rénmínbì* over the U.S. dollar, the Chinese government is slowly allowing more countries hold *rénmínbì*. There are many countries now, for instance, in which you can now hold deposits of money in *rénmínbì*.

OPENING AN ACCOUNT

Opening a standard bank account is extremely easy and—queuing aside—relatively quick. In most cases all you need is your passport and visa, and occasionally your residence certificate. Most companies will help you set up a bank account when you start work, usually with the bank that they already have a relationship with. Doing it yourself, however, is simple. When you walk into the bank, say to the front desk: *"Wǒ xiǎng kāi ge zhànghù"* ("I want to open an account," 我想开个账户). If you need to open a business account this is a completely different ballgame, which takes hours, multiple trips, extensive documentation, and a whole lot of patience.

The major branches of the different banks usually have someone who speaks enough English to get you through this simple exercise. It will be helpful if you have your address and other personal details written down in Chinese so that they can write them on the forms for you. Be ready with your phone number, email address, local phone number, residential address, and a next of kin and their phone number. When you give your name it should match your passport exactly; however, be sure to note down precisely how they record your name—for example, if they put your family name first, use all capitals, or push your given name and middle names together to form a single word. This is exactly how you will need to use it in the future with any transactions, such as with online shopping. One letter or space out and it won't work.

Most basic *rénmínbì* accounts simply require a deposit of RMB1 to open. You will also be asked to select a six-digit PIN. The account will be processed immediately and you will walk away with the card in your hand. Major banks offer foreign currency accounts, time-deposit accounts, and checking accounts. All have different requirements, so check with the individual bank as to what will be needed.

It's recommended that you simultaneously have the bank open mobile phone, telephone, and Internet banking in order to avoid having to come back into the bank to do this at a later time. They all require paperwork and more *chop* stamps, so this can't be done independently or over the phone. Having a Chinese-speaking friend with you for this will be extraordinarily helpful as there will be lots of questions and instructions. Be aware that not all banks provide good online service for all computer types, especially Apples. So if using online banking is important for you, this should be a major factor to investigate when choosing your bank.

Online Banking

While Chinese people swear by online banking, for expats it can be a real headache—you know it's potentially a lifesaver, but it often seems just out of reach. The English versions of most banks' websites are downright rotten, in both design and functions offered. If you want the full range of functions, including online shopping and transfers, you will most likely need to use the Chinese-language version.

Most Chinese banks also use complicated security systems, such as plug-in USB keys, for their Internet banking. Apple users will have even more headaches. At the time of writing, only a handful of banks, including Bank of China, ICBC, and China Merchants, allowed Apple users to access online banking, but then of these only ICBC then gave Mac users the complete range of functions. China Merchants, for example, allowed Mac users to use the General Edition online banking, which allowed for viewing account details, but not the Professional Edition, which allows for shopping and transactions. For this you needed to have a PC.

You may need to upgrade your operating system—anything older than Snow Leopard won't work for any online payment service, even Zhifubao. Next, you will need to go into the bank with your passport to register for online banking. This may cost a small fee. They will help you set up your online banking account, but once you get home, you'll also need to download software from the bank's website onto your computer. Next, you may need to experiment with browsers. Windows Explorer generally works best with Chinese sites, while Opera, Safari, Firefox, and Chrome have varying levels of success.

Most banks have English-language hotlines, so before you jump into online banking, it's recommended to call them first to ask exactly what the requirements are for banking and what functions will be available to you with the computer system you have.

With fully fledged online banking, you'll be able to check balances, transfer payments to other banks, and pay for products at online stores, such as Taobao, JD.com, and so on. Even if your landlord has an account in a different bank, you'll be able to pay your rent without leaving home. You will, however, still need to familiarize yourself with the Chinese on the screen.

Phone Banking

Many banks now offer banking from your cell phone. Again, this isn't always easy for a foreigner as you'll probably find the software is in Chinese only and may require a *shēnfènzhèng* number for ID. If things don't work on your computer, this can be an avenue worth exploring. Despite the lack of support for Apple computers, iPhones and iPads are, together with Android devices, accepted by most banks' mobile software.

One service that's highly useful to have activated is a phone SMS alert system, which works on both standard and smart cell phones. For a minimal fee, you can receive a text message whenever any kind of transaction occurs into or out of your account. If you can't access Internet banking, it's a very simple and efficient way to track payments and withdrawals, and you can set this up over the phone in just a few minutes.

ATMS

ATMs are everywhere throughout the city, so you'll never be far from one. The Bank of China, ICBC, and China Merchants Bank are most likely to accept international cards. On the other hand, if you have a UnionPay card, you can withdraw from virtually any machine in the city, albeit with a RMB2 fee if the ATM is not from the same bank as your card. Additionally, all ATMs have English as an option, so they're easy to use.

ATMs in China still use the old system of spitting your money out before returning your card, so be careful to not walk off leaving your card behind. It's good to get into the habit of taking a receipt whenever you make a transaction. This will have the details of the terminal on it, so at least if you do forget your card, you will have the details of the machine that your card was lost in. If you didn't get the receipt, note down location or branch details of the ATM and report these when you call the bank's hotline number. The bank is likely to reissue you with a new card rather than return the old one, which can take up to about a week to do.

ATMs have a wide range of functions, such as deposits, account transfers, even bill payments. The specific services offered differ from machine to machine, some with comprehensive services, others withdrawals only. Unfortunately, many of the more "residential" style services, such as bill payments, become available only when you select the Chinese-language option. Bank staff can usually take you through the steps. ATM bank transfers, a function available in English mode, make doing things like paying rent to your landlord extremely quick and easy. You do, however, need to make the transaction at an ATM belonging to your bank, and your accounts must both be with the same bank. If not, you'll need to go into your landlord's bank and make a deposit at the counter or perhaps use a service such as Zhifubao or Lakala to transfer the money.

CREDIT CARDS

It can be extraordinarily tedious to get a Chinese credit card as a foreigner, and most foreigners simply give up altogether, opting for a standard debit card. Requirements differ slightly from bank to bank, but in general, to get a credit card, you will need to show your residence permit, passport, proof of salary, and work permit. Other supporting documents that are not essential but helpful include proof of local house or vehicle ownership, and a debit card with the same bank and three months of transactions. If approved, you should receive your card within 15-30 days. Given the complexity of applying for a credit card, it can smooth the process if you can get your company to assist you.

International credit cards are widely accepted in Beijing, although you shouldn't rely on smaller shops and restaurants or businesses being able to use them. When they are accepted, there is often an additional transaction fee of 3-4 percent, which would not be charged if you paid in cash or with a UnionPay card.

EXCHANGING MONEY AND GETTING IT OUT OF THE COUNTRY

There are various ways to get money out of the country. If you are legitimately working in the country and paying taxes, then there is no daily or annual limit, and it can be done without too much difficulty. If you are accumulating money earned on the side, however, and wish to take this out of the country, then you will encounter obstacles for large amounts. The country needs to control how much money leaves and enters the country, so it imposes strict rules on free-flowing cash.

Converting *rénmínbì* into dollars can be done at almost any bank. Each bank varies slightly in its rules for how it can be done, so it's best to call ahead to check what you need to do. Generally, if you don't have official work status here, you are limited to exchanging up to US$500 per day. All you need is your passport to do this. If you do have a work permit, however, you are limited only by the amount you have earned. You should take your passport, a tax statement showing income of at least the amount you want to change, and your work contract, and then you should be able to change any amount you like.

Exchange rates are generally fixed, so shopping around for the best price won't yield significant benefits. Many hotels can also exchange cash for you, but their commission is slightly higher than those at banks.

Wire transfers can be done at the bank, although it can be an arduous experience. Not high on the customer service priority list, this process can take an hour or two to achieve. If you don't have proof of valid income and tax, you'll be limited to US$500 per day. If you have a good Chinese friend, however, you could have them transfer up to US$2,000 per day to a foreign account on your behalf, but you will be chipping out of their annual ceiling of US$50,000. Make sure you call ahead to find out exactly which branch you need to go to, as not all branches offer this service. You don't want to be standing in a line for an hour just to be told you're at the wrong place.

Western Union (www.westernunion.cn) offices are found throughout the city, located in the Postal Savings Bank of China, Agricultural Bank of China, China Everbright Bank, Shanghai Pudong Development Bank (SPDB), and China Construction Bank. You'll need to take your passport, and the maximum daily transfer is US$500.

You can fly your cash out of the country, but make sure you know the limit. You can legally carry up to US$5,000 or the equivalent in another currency, or up to RMB20,000 out of Beijing without needing to declare it at customs. If it exceeds this amount it can be confiscated. Also be aware that *rénmínbì* isn't freely exchangeable outside of China, and it might be difficult to change back home. Hong Kong is the easiest place to change *rénmínbì*, but exchange rates outside of China are sure to be a downer.

Alternative methods include using a Paypal account. One method is to establish a new Paypal account in China connected to your Chinese bank account, and the other is to send a payment request to your (Chinese) self and then pay yourself with a Chinese credit card. There is also the option to simply withdraw money at an ATM in your home country using your Chinese UnionPay bank card. UnionPay (http://en.unionpay.com) has extensive relationships with banks around the world, such as the National Australia Bank, Bank of New Zealand, and Bank of Hawaii, as well as non-bank-specific ATM networks. You can simply go to these ATMs in your home country and withdraw money with your Chinese card. UnionPay debit and credit

DAILY LIFE

© SHANNON AITKEN

China Construction Bank, one of the preferred banks for many locals and an increasing number of expats

cards beginning with 62 and debit cards with 9 can all be used to withdraw money from ATMs in the United States. In fact, about 90 percent of all ATMs in the United States accept UnionPay cards. So, even if they don't carry the UnionPay logo, it's worth having a go. Withdrawals with UnionPay cards in the United States are based on the RMB exchange rate of the same day. Daily transactions are limited to the equivalent of RMB10,000 in whatever currency you are withdrawing; however, additional limitations may be imposed by the specific Chinese bank that your card belongs to. For exact details on this you will need to contact your Chinese bank. There will be an additional fee of around US$1.50-5 per transaction. The bank that you are using in your home country may have its own charges applied, so again you will need to check. ATMs at Citibank, Chase Manhattan Corp, Wells Fargo Bank, and United Commercial Bank in the United States, however, will not charge these fees. Being able to use your UnionPay card outside of China is something to keep in mind when simply holidaying as well. Before you leave China, check which banks in the country you're going to accept UnionPay cards because coverage is patchy rather than universal.

Taxes

CHINA TAXES

Tax in China can be baffling. Tax laws are constantly changing, many are not explicitly published, and those that are don't always mirror what happens in practice. Laws also differ significantly between cities. What happens in Beijing is not what happens in Shanghai or Guangzhou.

Individual Income Tax (IIT) in China is typically managed by your company, so for general employees, there is very little to do or worry about if your company is doing things by the book. Your tax will be taken each month from your salary and there is no "doing your taxes" at the end of the financial year. Just be sure to keep your pay slips. You are legally allowed to take home any or all of your net Chinese income, but you'll need these to prove that you've paid the same amount or more in tax to do it. Those liable for paying tax include those: 1) with an annual income of RMB120,000 or more; 2) receiving a salary and remuneration from two or more employers in China; 3) generating income abroad; 4) generating taxable income without a withholding agent; 5) who fit other requirements as specified by the State Council. Failure to pay tax can attract penalties.

Tax in China is calculated on a progressive scale, and the type of company you work for as well as your position will affect the rate at which you're taxed. Employees are taxed on the income remaining after social security payments, a fixed amount of RMB4,800, and other deductions have been taken out. In 2012 the tax rate ranged from 3 percent on monthly salaries of RMB1,500 or less up to 45 percent for monthly salaries of RMB80,000 or more. Most expats fall into rates of 20-30 percent. A few online websites have simple tax calculators to help you work out roughly what you'll be getting in your bank.

Tax rates are the same for both locals and foreigners. Foreigners do, however, need to be aware of two important distinctions—one being length of stay, and the other being position seniority. The longer you live in China, the more of your income becomes liable for taxation within China. Senior executives, such as CEOs, can be liable for taxation on all Chinese income starting day one, whereas more junior workers will have a grace period of 183 days (90 days for countries that haven't signed the treaty on avoidance of double taxation with China) before all Chinese income is up for taxation. After five consecutive full years of stay, you are liable for tax on income made within and outside China, regardless of your seniority.

The Five-Year Tax Rule

If you live in China for five unbroken full years you are required to file IIT on worldwide income from the sixth year onwards. However, if you are outside of China for 30 consecutive days or at least 90 days in total in one calendar year, it will not be counted as a full year, and the five-year tax rule will not apply. The five-year rule will be reset and recommence from your next full year in China. Be aware that your departure and arrival days in China are counted as days in China, so you may need to add on two days to your time away to cover these. This law may seem like a far-off and irrelevant idea to many people, but time has a way of speeding by in Beijing, and with holidays structured as they are it can be hard to get enough time off work to take the required leave. This should be something you negotiate with your company well ahead of time and perhaps plan to take your extended China break between contract periods. You should also consult a China tax law professional to confirm current requirements.

Reducing Your Tax

Many companies can help you reduce your tax by having you submit receipts of various expenses, such as restaurants, groceries, or airline tickets. To do this you will need to ask for a *fāpiào* when you pay. The waiter or salesperson should then ask if you want a personal *fāpiào* (*gèrén fāpiào*) or a company *fāpiào* (*gōngsī fāpiào*). In most cases you'll need to tell them it's a company *fāpiào,* and you can hand them a business card with your company's details on it for them to use on the *fāpiào.*

A larger expense that has the potential to reduce your tax substantially is your rent. If your company is willing to claim your rent as part of your income—even though you may be paying the rent yourself—then you can effectively reduce your taxable income. It's a little complicated to do this, but it can definitely work out to be worth the effort.

If your company is willing to make the necessary adjustments, you will also need to make sure your landlord is willing to help you get receipts for your rent (a lot of landlords would rather their rental business remain under the table). It's best to get this sorted right at the start when you're negotiating your lease. The *fāpiào* will incur a 5 percent tax fee. Some landlords increase the rent to cover this, some tenants take on the cost—it's up to your powers of negotiation. Best case scenario is that your nice landlord does this all for you and hands you the *fāpiào* after each payment of rent, and you hand this to your company. If it's up to you, there are several documents to prepare. You need your passport, a photocopy of your landlord's *shēnfènzhèng* (ID card), a copy of your lease, a copy of the deed (房权证), and a completed invoice application form (北京市地方税务局代开发票申请表). This can be downloaded from the Internet. With these in hand, together with a payment of 5 percent of the lease, head to your nearest Beijing Local Taxation Bureau office (www.tax861.gov.cn). At this point it's relatively straightforward. They'll give you the *fāpiào,* which you then give your company so they can prove you have a lower level of income.

If you are planning to be here as a foreign invested enterprise (FIE), you will then also need to be on top of the laws regarding corporate income tax, value-added tax, withholding tax, business tax, consumption tax, and individual income tax.

The financial tax year runs from January 1 to December 31, and as an FIE you are required to file your tax and make payments on a quarterly basis. Business tax, VAT, and individual income tax returns are also filed on a monthly basis. This must all be done in Chinese, the legal language, but English may accompany it.

To ensure you are compliant with tax laws, there are many companies specializing in Chinese tax laws and payroll, including GNS CHINA (www.gnschina.com), S.J. Grand (www.sjgrand.cn), Dezan Shira & Associates (www.dezshira.com), and China Briefing (www.china-briefing.com), among many others.

U.S. INCOME TAX

Unfortunately, living abroad doesn't necessarily exclude you from paying or at least claiming income made in China, especially in countries such as the United States. If you are a U.S. citizen or U.S. taxpayer, you have an obligation to report your worldwide income to the IRS, whether you actually owe any tax or not.

It's important to know what your obligations are, and you may in fact find you qualify for tax exemptions. Just some of the questions to ask include:

- Am I eligible for exemption? If so, how much of my income is exempt?
- Can I claim foreign tax credit? This is where the tax paid to the Chinese government on your Chinese income is used as a deduction on your U.S. taxes. You will also need to check whether or not this credit can be taken in conjunction with any exemptions you have.
- Do I need to file a return for my spouse? What about if he or she is Chinese?
- What is a Foreign Bank Account Report (FBAR) and does it apply to me?
- What are my requirements for reporting foreign assets and what is Form 8938 (Statement of Foreign Financial Assets)?

The U.S. embassy's Beijing website can be a good place to start getting information. The embassy will also occasionally hold information events to notify you of your rights and obligations. Taxpayer appointments can be made at the U.S. embassy in Beijing by calling 10/8531-3983.

For specific information relating to taxation in the U.S., simply visit the IRS website (www.irs.gov) and search for "U.S. Citizens and Resident Aliens Abroad." You'll find the full IRS guide for expats located under "Current Forms & Publications," Publication 54 (www.irs.gov/publications/p54/index.html).

Investing

If you have the luck of being in Beijing on a company package, then you may well discover you're able to put away a nice amount of money each month. Saving your money in a Chinese bank account as a way of investing, however, isn't generally the recommended tactic. Interest rates aren't particularly high, so your money won't be doing much work for you. A large number of international financial planning companies operate in Beijing, and generally they recommend offshore options. Major companies that you can speak to include Montpelier, Austen Morris, Zurich, and Friends Provident.

Playing the stock market, particularly in Beijing, can be difficult for foreigners. At the time of writing, neither of the mainland's stock exchanges—the Shanghai Stock Exchange (www.sse.com.cn) and the Shenzhen Stock Exchange (www.szse.cn)—were completely open to foreigners. Chinese stocks are classified into A and B categories, and foreigners were permitted to invest in class B stocks only, which are generally highly risky and not especially profitable. The government is working to open the market to foreign trade, so this situation is changing quickly and worth keeping your eye on. Currently the most typical way to invest in Chinese companies is via mutual funds,

ETFs (exchange-traded funds), and Chinese companies listed on major international stock markets, including Hong Kong Stock Exchange (SEHK), the NASDAQ, and the New York Stock Exchange.

Unfortunately, a difficulty that comes with investing in Chinese companies is that a lot of the time, they're not particularly transparent and getting accurate information about their performance can be tricky.

Other avenues for investment in China include investing through business ventures. The government is keen to attract foreign money and so frequently offers incentives for foreign companies. A good place to start your investigation into opportunities is Invest Beijing (www.bjinvest.gov.cn), the government's official investment website.

COMMUNICATIONS

When it comes to phones and Internet, Beijing has got it handled. Internet speed is relatively fast and technology moves at lightning speed. Free wireless access is virtually standard at all cafés, and land and mobile rates are satisfyingly low—especially when you can hook into the range of package deals available. Unlike in many other countries, there also isn't a lot of choice here when it comes to carriers, and in many cases, you may not have a choice at all. So at least you don't have the headache of shopping around.

Unfortunately China is still a stickler for blocking sites such as Facebook and YouTube, but this is more of a hassle than an unfixable problem. With a VPN or proxy program installed on your computer you'll be able to leap these hurdles and continue on with relatively uninterrupted, unrestricted Internet use.

Postal services and media, however, tend to have their own local standards. Despite the ubiquity of China Post, the likelihood of a package reaching your hands through standard post is low to zero. Couriers are almost always the better choice, particularly when the mail is coming in from abroad. English-language media is limited not only in scope but in credibility. It may intrigue you for the first week of your fact-finding trip, but you'll soon be reaching for international publishers and broadcasters to access more information on China than you can get from on the inside.

© SHANNON AITKEN

Phone Services

COMPANIES

There are three phone companies in Beijing, all state owned—China Mobile (中国移动, Zhōngguó Yídòng), China Unicom (中国联通, Zhōngguó Liántōng), and China Telecom (中国电信, Zhōngguó Diànxìn). Within Beijing, China Telecom also operates under its local name of Beijing Telecom, particularly for landlines.

China Mobile is by far the largest telecommunications company in the world, boasting more than 700 million subscribers. It currently, however, has the smallest share of 3G pie, having only recently added this to its raft of services.

As far as which one is better, that's debatable. They are all on obvious paths of development, and standards today are much better than what you would have had even five or ten years ago. For coverage and customer service within China they are all roughly on par. In addition to that, prices don't vary greatly between companies. For this reason, when choosing a carrier, there are other factors worth considering more than individual prices or coverage. These include knowing what company already services your housing complex for phone and Internet, and then what package you can get for your cell; and secondly, knowing what wireless network system that both your home country and existing cell phone use.

LANDLINES

Landlines and ADSL Internet are the exclusive turf of China Unicom and China Telecom (Beijing Telecom), and when it comes to choice, there isn't one. The decision of which phone company covers which property is made by property developers and the Internet companies, not individual tenants. One phone company usually has exclusive rights to an entire community or apartment complex, and you can't change phone companies if you don't like the one you're with. Given that, both companies are relatively similar in price and quality, and good and bad experiences have been reported by users of both. If you are planning to buy a mobile phone on a contract system where you bundle your costs with your Internet, then it may be important to you to know up front which company you're going to be using at home. The landlord or real estate agent should be able to tell you who that is; you can also tell by the first numbers of the landline phone number. If it starts with a 6 or an 8 it's China Unicom, if it starts with 57 or 58 then it's China Telecom.

While it is your landlord's responsibility to ensure a phone line is available, it's up to you to pay for its connection. Your landlord or agent will usually help you do this. If not, take your passport and lease to your nearest China Telecom or China Unicom office. You should also know the first four digits of the apartment's phone number. If you don't know this, you can ask your neighbor for the first four digits of their number. The phone company will want this to verify that you are dealing with the right people.

To connect a phone line without Internet, the initial setup fee is RMB200. The ongoing monthly line rental fee is then RMB21.60. For local calls, the first three minutes are charged RMB0.22, and it's RMB0.11 for every minute thereafter.

If you intend to make international or long-distance domestic calls from your landline, you will first need to have this function added to your phone account. You can

CHOOSING A PHONE NUMBER

Numbers are a big deal in China—some are considered auspicious, others ominous. Any phone number brimming with auspicious numbers will be hard to get, and may even come at a price. In fact, in 2003 at a special auction of phone numbers Sichuan Airlines bought the phone number 8888-8888 for RMB2.33 million (then US$280,000). Phone shops will usually show you a list of available numbers from which to choose. If you do get a number you like, you'll be shackled to that phone company for as long as you're unwilling to relinquish the number. There is no number transfer system here.

If you search, you'll find varying meanings for almost every number, but the following numbers to this day still strongly influence people's behavior, from the phone number they choose, to the floor they live on, to the amount of money a restaurant deems suitable for a dish.

6 (六, *liù*): Six is considered to be a very auspicious number because it sounds like the Chinese word for "flowing" or "smooth." Even what some Western-

ers might think of as the worst possible number, 666, the Chinese believe to be extremely lucky.

8 (八, *bā*): This is the luckiest of all numbers in Chinese, and the more of them the better. This number carries the meaning of "prosperity" or "fortune." It's the reason Beijing held its opening ceremony for the Olympic Games at 8pm on 8/8/2008. Any date with this number is also extremely popular for weddings.

9 (九, *jiǔ*): The number nine means longevity and eternality. So again, the more nines you have, the longer you'll live. It's the reason why the Forbidden City is said to have 9,999 rooms and why the romantically inclined send 99 roses to each other.

4 (四, *sì*): This is the unluckiest of numbers as the pronunciation is similar to that of the word for death (死, *sǐ*). Any number containing it, including 14, 24, and so on, is tarnished. It's highly likely, therefore, that if you live on the 30th floor of a building there will be a few floors missing. Any phone number with fours in it should be cheap, if not free.

request this upfront when you first apply for the phone line, but it can be added at any point. Adding this service is free. At this time you should ask the phone company about their IP function offers. This is a five digit number that you dial before you start dialing the phone number. They occasionally have different deals or promotions, so the numbers can vary. Adding these to the dialing process can cut call prices by around 50 percent.

Calls to the United States are about RMB8 per minute on top of the local call rate, which works out to be RMB81.43 for a 10-minute call to the United States. Halve that if you've added in an IP code. IP cards can also be bought from phone stores, but these are no cheaper than using the IP service directly through your provider.

As for telephones, these can easily be bought at Walmart and Carrefour, Buynow, Amazon, 360Buy, and so on.

CELLULAR PHONES

All three carriers provide mobile phone coverage. China Mobile is the largest by client numbers and uses a GSM system. The company launched its GSM 3G network (which is based on its own TD-SCDMA standard) in only 2010, and its share of the 3G market remains small. It has, however, been developing a 4G network, so this is something to keep your eye on. For now, the other two carriers dominate when it comes to 3G market. China Telecom uses CDMA2000, the same standard that is used widely throughout Southeast Asia and by many U.S. carriers, including Sprint and Verizon Wireless. China Unicom, on the other hand, uses W-CDMA (UMTS), the dominant 3G network throughout Europe, Australia, New Zealand, and much of Asia. It's also the network of choice for AT&T and T-Mobile in the United States.

Choosing a Provider (and Handset)

When it comes to the best value, the offerings are surprisingly similar, although China Telecom does tend to be cheaper on the whole. The trick to keeping your costs low is to find out what deals are available. Ask your Chinese friends and quiz the sales representative for what's currently on offer. People in China love the *tàocān* (套餐), which roughly translates as "set meal," and when activated, they can often save you more than RMB100 per month. Deals can include such things as spending RMB20 per month and getting free texts or calls to a given value in return. You don't need to be on a fixed plan to activate these—prepaid numbers have various money-saving options, too.

Before committing yourself to a mobile company or even a new handset, it can be useful to consider what kind of network you'll need to use most when outside of China, especially if you travel a lot. Like China, the United States uses both CDMA2000 and W-CDMA networks. Other countries, however, may use only one system. Your communication within the two countries will run a lot more smoothly if you're keeping to the same network type. If your home or primary business destination is Australia, for example, which uses W-CDMA, then a number with China Unicom and a handset that also supports W-CDMA will be the best combination. If you have a CDMA2000 SIM card from your home country that you would like to continue to use on your Chinese handset when back there, it may work out better for you to go with China Telecom here and a handset that uses CDMA2000. If you want or have an iPhone, you can strike China Mobile off your list. At the time of writing, negotiations between China Mobile and Apple regarding a China Mobile GSM version of the iPhone were still in a longstanding gridlock.

Another consideration, particularly for those who frequently fly back and forth between the mainland and Hong Kong, is a native number for both regions. These are offered by China Unicom only, and though more expensive than local numbers, they're cheaper than using the international roaming alternative.

Setting Up an Account

There are three options when it comes to paying for a phone or phone account in Beijing. The first is the prepaid option (预付费, *yùfùfèi*), by which you add money to the phone and then use it up. This is probably best if you make only a handful of calls each month, particularly as the valid period of your credit can last for many months. You can add credit by buying recharge cards (充值卡, *chōngzhíkǎ*) at newsstands and some convenience stores, or by transferring money via Zhifubao (Alipay), Lakala, or the JiaoFeiYi machines.

Next is a postpay method (后付费, *hòufùfèi*), by which you are billed monthly according to a plan (套餐, *tàocān*) and what you use. This is the option to choose if you already have a phone and expect to spend more than about RMB60 per month. To apply for this, go to the phone center with your passport and SIM card. You should be able to keep your existing phone number with the company, and in some cases you will also need to pay a deposit, though both of these points need to be confirmed when you visit the phone store. Bills can usually be viewed via the Internet or your cell phone.

Finally, if you need a new phone, you can sign yourself up for a phone contract (合约机, *héyuējī*), by which you commit yourself to one, two, or three years and minimum monthly payments in exchange for a new phone.

The third option is somewhat different to what you may be used to. In China, you do not gradually pay for the phone over the life of your contract, you pay for it upfront in full. Part of your upfront payment is then converted into a deposit that makes its way back to you in the form of phone credit over the life of the contract. The longer the time period and the more you're willing to commit yourself to spending each month, the more of your upfront payment is converted into a deposit. Let's take an iPhone5, for example, with China Telecom, which cost RMB5,288 at the time of writing. On day one when you walked into the store you needed to be ready to pay them the full RMB5,288. If you signed up for a two-year contract and chose the monthly payment of RMB49, they kept RMB4,788 as payment for the phone and placed a deposit of RMB500 in your account, which gradually returned to you each month as credit. Going to the other extreme, if you signed up for a 36-month period and agreed to spending RMB289 each month, the whole RMB5,288 was converted into a deposit, which would eventually all come back to you. There are other incentives bundled into the package, but these are the basics.

Once you sign your name to a given contract, it can not be changed, be it to upgrade or downgrade. So be sure you're making the right decision.

International Roaming

To set up international roaming, you need to physically go into a phone store to apply, taking your passport with you. You will need to pay a deposit somewhere in the range of RMB500-1,500, or more if you suspect you're going to be racking up a bill while abroad. The amount can vary depending on the carrier, your number, and where you're going. You can have this money added to your account simply as if it were prepay credit, or have it set aside exclusively as a deposit. Make sure you keep the invoice regardless.

If you are traveling to a country with the same network system as your Chinese carrier, then things are relatively easy. If you're going to an area covered by a different network, however, your phone company will probably provide you with an international SIM card to help facilitate the conversion. This card won't change your phone number. Whatever carrier you're with and wherever you're going, they should be able to provide you with international roaming; your handset, however, might not be so compliant.

If you have an iPhone5, you're in luck. This phone has an automatic function that allows it to switch between W-CDMA and CDMA2000 networks (although not between CDMA and GSM). So even if you're normally with China Telecom (CDMA2000) in Beijing, this will continue to work if you head to London or Singapore, which both use W-CDMA. Please note, you still need to go into a phone store to activate international roaming before you set off.

If you have another type of phone and you're going into an area where the network is different to that required by your handset, connection might be impaired. If you find that this is the case, the best solution may be to temporarily switch your card into a locally friendly handset.

To check your balance while out of China, you can either dial the phone company's hotline number or log in to your online account via the company's website. To add money while abroad, you may need to call on a friend on the mainland to help you. Alternatively, you can use online Chinese banking or Zhifubao.

You can leave the international roaming function activated as long as you like, no matter how many times you come and go from China. If your deposit was designated as a prepay, then your local calls will continue to eat into this amount when you're back in China, so you may need to top up your phone every time you go abroad, but you won't need to go into a branch to do this. When you finally decide to deactivate international roaming, go back to the branch with your passport and deposit invoice to cancel the function. It will take one month before you can return (again with passport) to collect the deposit.

Using Your Own Handset in China, or Your China Handset Abroad

So you have a much-loved or expensive phone from home and you want to use it in China. Chances are you can, but just don't assume that to be so. First, before you leave home, make sure the handset isn't locked to any provider from your home country.

Now the phone type. The main task is to select the right carrier in China for your phone—China Mobile if your handset requires GSM (but not if it's an iPhone), China Unicom if it's W-CDMS (UMTS), or China Telecom if it's CDMA2000.

Another thing to be aware of is that all carriers in China use SIM cards, so you need a phone with a SIM card slot. If you have an American CDMA2000 handset, such as those sold via Sprint and Verizon, you may not have one. This will be a problem. Unfortunately, your only solution then may be to buy a new phone or live on international roaming from the United States. If you have a GSM iPhone, this may also bring frustrations.

Internet

SETTING UP INTERNET ACCESS

Compared to many other countries, in China Internet access is extraordinarily cheap, and ADSL, at least, has no limit to the downloads you make each month. Like landlines, China Unicom and China Telecom (Beijing Telecom) are the only two providers, with China Telecom being somewhat cheaper. While some people may complain of the Internet here being slow in general, this is definitely not always the case and is sometimes the fault of your individual housing complex rather than the actual network provider. ADSL Internet is offered at speeds of 512 kb/s, 2 MB/s, 4MB/s, 8 MB/s, 12 MB/s and, in some rare cases, 20 MB/s, although, depending on where you live, you may not have access to every speed. Most people tend to use the 2 and 4 MB options.

If you're unsure of your length of time in Beijing you can pay by the month, which will cost around RMB120-170/month for a 2 MB plan. For this, however, you'll need to pay for or provide your own router, and if your stay is under three months, you will need to pay the installation fee, which is around RMB300.

You will get much better value if you pay upfront for a whole year of service. Not only will the provider usually throw in the installation fee and router for free but will also spice up the package with a few other freebies. A one-year 2 MB/s package with China Unicom, for example, costs RMB1,680 and includes a free home number and free cell phone number, plus 300 minutes of free talk time each month, which you can use up on either device.

Setting up the Internet at home is virtually identical to setting up a phone line. Again your landlord or real estate agent usually helps you. If doing it yourself, take your passport and lease to your closest retailer (call the phone company ahead to ask for locations), then, when you have done the required paperwork and paid the fees, technicians will come to your home and install the router. Unfortunately, very few technicians speak English, nor are they particularly familiar with Apple products, so getting through this stage of the process can be a little cumbersome.

PUBLIC INTERNET

One of the best things about life in Beijing is the almost unlimited free pubic wireless Internet. Cafés, bars, and even many restaurants become pseudo offices for freelancers and students. There are actual Internet cafés, but these are often grimy, dimly lit burrows with sour-smelling couches. On the odd occasion they may have their function, but it's almost always just as easy and twice as pleasant to go to a café. If you're simply after printing, photocopying, or scanning services, countless printers around town can handle these jobs for you. There is no expectation in Beijing that you should eat an entire menu as a way of paying "rent" for spending an entire day in a café. Many get by on a single coffee. The most anyone will do is possibly ask you to move to a smaller table during peak hours.

CENSORSHIP AND JUMPING
THE GREAT FIREWALL OF CHINA

China is, of course, well known for its censorship and blocking of various websites—Facebook, YouTube, and Twitter are just the beginning. You may also have trouble logging on to sites such as IMDB, Netflix, BBC, Dropbox, porn sites, and even occasionally Gmail. Thanks to a bitter past between China and Google, the company departed China and Google.com was blocked. So when searching for information on your computer or cell phone it won't work. If not using a proxy, you'll need to try such alternatives as www.google.com.hk (Hong Kong), www.google.com.au (Australia), www.ask.com, www.yahoo.com, and so on. You may even need to resort to local search engine options, such as Bing China (http://cn.bing.com) or (the big one) Baidu (http://cn.bing.com).

It's also well established that the government monitors user interactions. There is no privacy here and you should be aware that transmitting any sensitive comments or content carries serious risk. Even phone calls and message chats on Skype can be monitored. When particular national events arise, the government cracks down even harder.

You can avoid a lot of this by using a proxy server or VPN (Virtual Private Network), a server that you connect to that connects to another website on your behalf. It not

DAILY LIFE

© SHANNON AITKEN

Beijing isn't the place to come if you're worried about being watched.

only means that you can look at sites that are blocked but that it's harder for others to monitor what you're doing. It's contentious whether or not these are illegal, but there are endless private and government enterprises out there that also require proxies for the sheer secrecy of their own business, so a blanket ban on proxies or VPNs seems all but impossible.

Some proxies require you to download software, while others are accessed online via a given website. Prices vary, but you're generally looking at spending US$10/month or US$70/year. There are free ones, but these tend to get blocked extremely quickly by the Chinese government. The government is always improving its technology for tracking and blocking proxies, so it's possibly the case that only subscription services have the resources to stay ahead of the race.

Do your research before choosing your proxy or VPN. What's good right now may be blocked in six months. One place to start is Best VPN Service (www.bestvpnservice.com), which introduces you to most of major players. The websites of proxy or VPN providers may not always be accessible from within China, meaning you won't be able to get onto their homepage and download the software. To be on the safe side, it's advisable to set yourself up with a provider before coming to Beijing. Test out a company by emailing them a few questions and assessing their customer service. Even the best companies occasionally come under attack from the government and need to make adjustments to their software. You need a company that is enthusiastic about helping you modify your own settings as they modify theirs.

If you're curious about the latest news on what's blocked in China, you can visit http://GreatFire.org, although—no surprise—this site is blocked, too.

TABLET COMPUTERS

If you're just after an Internet package for your iPad or Android tablet, China Unicom and China Telecom offer various plans. Prices include packages such as RMB50 per month, or RMB600 for a one-year plan. Discounts can be found on their websites.

Postal Services

Going to the post office in Beijing isn't the most pleasant experience. There is next to no English available, particularly over the phone, and mailing a package always seems to require standing at numerous different counters to get the job done. Staff at the branches, however, are usually very friendly, and whether you speak English or not, in the end it all seems to work out.

China Post has branches all over Beijing, and most branches are open 9am-5pm Monday-Friday and on Saturday morning. The Jianguomen branch of the Beijing International Post and Telecommunication Office, beside the East Second Ring Road and just north of Jianguomen subway station (Lines 1 and 2), is perhaps the easiest branch for expats to manage their postal business at. They not only handle postal services but can also help you pay your bills, pay for tickets, make money transfers (Western Union), and even recharge your Taobao account. To do this simply go to the Postal Business Service counter and say *"Chōngzhí Táobǎo"* (充值淘宝). It always helps to have your passport on standby when you manage anything at the post office.

The average cost of sending letters around Beijing and China is RMB1. For international airmail, it's RMB6 for a small letter sent via airmail to the United States, Europe, Australia, or New Zealand, and about RMB475 for a medium package to the same areas. For an estimation of how much it will cost you to send a package overseas by post, log on to http://english.chinapost.com.cn. It's worth comparing prices with EMS, which may occasionally be even cheaper as well as faster.

Sending packages abroad by post is generally fairly successful and takes one to two weeks. Receiving anything from abroad via China Post, however, is almost invariably unreliable. At the very least you'll get that care pack of chocolate bars six months after it was sent. Never have packages sent to your home address if it's coming by post. Have

China Post offices are located all around the city.

DAILY LIFE

© SHANNON AITKEN

it sent to an office if possible. The address can be in English or Pinyin only, but it's highly recommended that you have it in Chinese too. An easy way to do this is to save the address in both English and Chinese and email it to family and friends for them to print out and simply stick on to the envelope or package.

If you are sending international packages, don't seal them up before you get to the post office. The post office staff double as customs officers so they'll rifle through your things looking for contraband. If you have any obviously off-limits things—such as a stack of pirated CDs or DVDs—they will not allow you to include them. Often anything over the value of RMB1,500 will also be refused.

There are various ways to contact China Post, including the 11185 hotline or via Beijing-specific sites such as www.bipto.com.cn (international) and www.bjpost.com. cn; however, you may find more luck by simply walking into a branch.

COURIERS

First, forget the word courier. In Beijing the word is *"kuàidì"* (快递), a term so often used that even expats relinquish the English alternative. *Kuàidì* are almost a standard way for individuals and businesses in the city to get all manner of things across the city and abroad. If you need to send a document or parcel to anyone within Beijing, it can be much more reliable to send it via EMS or SF Express than via China Post. On average this will cost just RMB10-20. If you'd rather go with a brand you know, all the major international courier companies are here in Beijing, including DHL, FedEx, TNT, and UPS. Offices and hotels occasionally have working relationships with a given courier company, so you may find it cheaper if you can do it through these.

Media

NEWSPAPERS, MAGAZINES, AND ONLINE MEDIA

English literature of any variety is somewhat controlled in Beijing, and any visit to Beijing Capital Airport might even give you the impression that it's all but banned outright. International English magazines are definitely hard to come by. International supermarkets occasionally stock a small range, most typically titles such as *The Economist* and *Time*. Page One bookstores also have a limited collection, but the biggest ranges are to be found in the Bookworm in Sanlitun and Trends Lounge in the Place. For international specialty magazines, look to Taobao, which can be a surprisingly good depository of current publications and subscriptions. Otherwise, you may need to arrange some kind of subscription and delivery system from your home country, wait for visitors, or look for digital options.

There are several locally published street and online magazines, including *Time Out, The Beijinger,* and *City Weekend,* as well as online-only magazines www.smartbeijing. com and www.echinacities.com. While these are indispensable for finding out what's going on around town, they do all tend to cover the same kind of thing. These are not magazines that will give you deep and edgy insights into issues of society. *The World of Chinese,* however, is a nicely designed English-language magazine that has a strong focus on modern Chinese culture.

If you're interested in contemporary Chinese writing, there are various journals

© SHANNON AITKEN

DAILY LIFE

Newsstands are the place to purchase the *China Daily* and *Global Times* as well as your mobile phone recharge cards.

dedicated to translation. These include *Asymptote* (www.asymptotejournal.com), *Chutzpah!* (www.chutzpahmagazine.com.cn), and *Pathlight* (http://paper-republic. org/pubs/pathlight). You may also want to try the Marco Polo Project (http://marco-poloproject.org), which translates modern Chinese writing.

English newspapers are even scantier than magazines, and it's no secret that the government has a heavy hand when it comes to pruning their content. There are two main English-language newspapers—*The China Daily* and *Global Times*—but being in English by no means saves them from the government's shears. They're both readily available from newsstands and convenience stores. Occasionally you might be able to get your hands on a copy of the *South China Morning Post*. This is an English-language newspaper from Hong Kong and can sometimes be picked up if you're visiting a hotel. Ultimately many expats simply turn to the websites of international newspapers for their news on the Middle Kingdom, as these can be much more penetrating than those based in Beijing. You may at times need a VPN/proxy to leap the Great Firewall to access them.

Both *Global Times* (www.globaltimes.cn) and the *China Daily* (www.chinadaily. com.cn) have online versions, as do two of China's largest news sources, the People's Daily (http://english.peopledaily.com.cn) and Xinhua (www.chinaview.cn). There are, however, other sites that allow you to gain insight into what's happening in the Chinese-language-only newspapers around the country. These include Danwei (www. danwei.com) and Baidu Beat (beat.baidu.com). These sites provide translations of stories run by China's newspapers. Other Beijing-based sources include the postings of respected foreign writers and correspondents, such as *The New Yorker*'s Beijing correspondent, Evan Osnos (www.newyorker.com/online/blogs/evanosnos). Professor Patrick Chovanec at Tsinghua University (http://chovanec.wordpress.com) is among the many others.

© SHANNON AITKEN

one of Beijing's most popular bookshops among expats

BOOKS

English-language books are much easier to come by. There are many large walk-in bookstores, such as Page One, the Bookworm in Sanlitun, the Foreign Languages Bookstore in Wangfujing, the Wangfujing Bookstore, the Beijing Books Building in Xidan, and the Zhongguancun Book Building in Haidian.

Other smaller bookshops to know about include Sanlian Shudian, near the National Art Gallery, and Timezone 8 in 798, which specialize in art books; and the Xinhua Travel Bookshop, on the northwest side of Chongwenmen subway station, which is one place to go to get maps of Beijing. If you'd rather browse than buy, there is the National Library of China (www.nlc.gov.cn), which is at its own subway station on Line 4.

If you know what you want, however, it's really worth shopping online. Amazon, TMall, 360buy, Dang Dang Wang, and Taobao are just some of the places that are threatening the cash registers at the real life bookstores. You can find a huge range of English-language books, plus delivery is most likely going to be free and quick.

Books printed in China are extraordinarily cheap. Novels might be only RMB20, and Chinese-language textbooks would be considered expensive if over RMB50. English books, on the other hand, are usually imported, so you'll find they sit on a different price scale altogether. Novels can easily range between RMB100 and RMB250. Alternatively, if you're not opposed to fake books, these go for around RMB20, give or take. They are, however, somewhat necessarily disposable. You'll probably find that pages fall out as you read, that the ink looks like the printing factory was squeezing every last drop out of their ink cartridges, or that sections of the story are missing altogether.

Occasionally titles are banned, so you won't find these in any mainstream sales place. International travel guides relating specifically to Beijing are also suspiciously absent, allowing for a monopoly on the genre by local publishers.

TELEVISION AND CABLE

The main television network in China is CCTV, and while it might share the acronym of a surveillance camera system, it actually stands for China Central Television. CCTV was founded in 1958. It has 22 channels, which cover such genres as documentary, comedy, entertainment, and drama. Turn on the channel and you are more than likely to see period dramas set in one dynastic era or another. The company was originally situated in the China Central Television Building in Haidian district, but now much of it has been relocated to the CCTV Headquarters in Chaoyang district near Guomao. This astounding complex was designed by architects Rem Koolhaas and Ole Scheeren and was finally completed in May 2012, eight years after it was first commenced. It is now one of the major iconic buildings of the city.

The only free-to-air English channel is CCTV NEWS (formerly CCTV-9), a channel that's about as stimulating as a hot cup of chamomile tea. Its key programs include News Update, News Hour, China 24, Asia Today, Biz Asia, Biz Talk, New Money, Culture Express, Sports Scene, Dialogue, and World Insight. Around these are other programs relating to Chinese culture and history.

CCTV-5 is occasionally worth turning on for sports coverage. Though it is entirely in Chinese and broadcasts of international events not particularly international, it may pass if you're keen.

In addition to CCTV's channels, there is also the local broadcaster, Beijing Television (BTV, www.btv.org), another government-owned network. There are 10 major stations on BTV, all in Chinese. Sports fans can also try BTV Sports Channel (BTV 体育).

As for "cable" TV, it is actually all satellite. There are Chinese satellite networks, and while extremely cheap, they just provide you with more Chinese-language stations from around the country rather than any new international options. Legal satellite needs to be applied for, and so, for individuals, isn't usually possible to get. If you're set to live in a luxury international housing complex, such as many of the estates around Shunyi, then it will quite likely be managed by your clubhouse or property management office and be included in your rent. Luxury hotels and sports bars are other places to visit if you have a dire need for some international viewing. There is a delay on the televising of international satellite programs, allowing the government to monitor and censor sensitive content. From time to time when controversial stories air, you may suddenly find yourself looking at a blank screen.

Locals have a way of getting around this, and there are numerous illegal operators out there who will install a dish and set you up for possibly just RMB1,000-3,000 per year. Reception for these can come and go as companies scramble their codes to try to throw off the pirates. Your satellite operator can usually crack the new codes and will, possibly for a little extra cash, supply you with the new ones.

RADIO

Like TV, radio in Beijing is state owned and so, much like television, is a vehicle for propaganda and news with a local perspective. If you can tolerate the phenomenal amount of advertising, there are many stations to choose from, although most are in Chinese. Those that are English-language or bilingual are run by China Radio International (CRI). While the broadcaster airs its messages throughout the world, in

Beijing its major stations include Hit FM (88.7 FM), Easy FM (91.5 FM), and China Radio International News (846 AM). CRI also airs such programs as China Drive, a bilingual news and lifestyle broadcast that airs seven days a week 5pm-7pm on Easy FM, and Chinese Studio, a five-minute language lesson that runs at the end of many programs, including China Drive. If you're fluent in Chinese, you may want to visit http://rbc.cn for a comprehensive list of Beijing stations.

TRAVEL AND TRANSPORTATION

Of all prices in the city, those of transport are the few that have *de*flated. With just RMB100 loaded onto your Yikatong travel card, you can easily jaunt around the city on the bus or subway for a month or three. Pedal power is no longer the main form of transport, having been squeezed out by cars, electric bikes, and scooters, but wide bike lanes remain on every street and cheap bicycles are easy to find, so it's still a good option.

For further distances or greater comfort, Beijing taxis are expensive by comparison but still cheap from an international perspective, and many expats travel in nothing else. Taxi drivers usually speak no English whatsoever, but, despite some misconceptions, they are literate, educated people. If you have your destination written down in Chinese for them, they'll usually have no problem finding it.

As for driving yourself, few expats ever get behind the wheel, but it is possible if you're game. An international license isn't accepted in Beijing, so you'll have to go through the local processes of getting a Chinese license. Buying a car will be more difficult. In an attempt to reduce congestion, the government has imposed a lottery

© NORA JANG

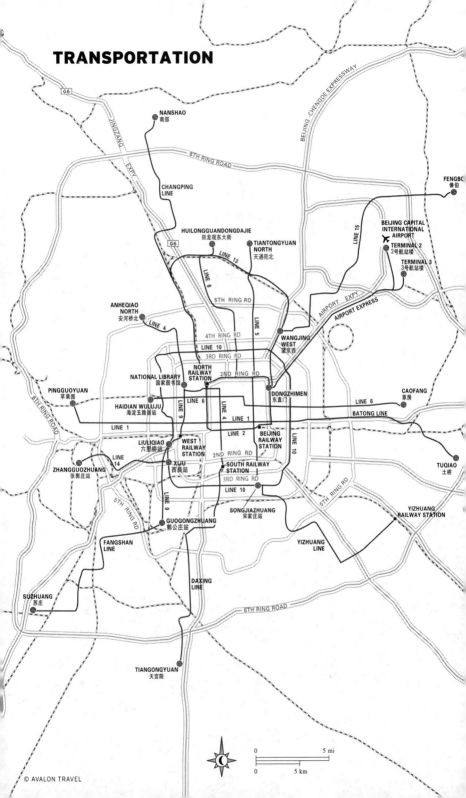

system on new registration plates to limit car purchases. To apply, you can log on to www.bjhjyd.gov.cn, although you may need a Chinese friend to help you do the rest.

By Air

According to the Airports Council International (ACI), Beijing Capital International Airport (or PEK on your ticket) is currently ranked as the second busiest airport in the world. It sits just behind Hartsfield-Jackson Atlanta International Airport in the United States, which holds the number one position. In 2011, 77,403,668 people went through Beijing's terminals, and this number has been climbing rapidly. Ten years ago it didn't even appear in the world's top 30 busiest airports. More than 70 airlines use its tarmacs on their way to more than 200 cities around the world.

The airport lies 32 kilometers (20 miles) northeast of the CBD. Though it's surrounded by Shunyi district, it's actually classified as being in a separated area of Chaoyang district.

A second airport for Beijing is said to be planned, rumored to be completed by 2017.

THE TERMINALS

Beijing Capital International Airport comprises three terminals—Terminal 1, which was completed in 1980; Terminal 2, which was completed in 1999; and Terminal 3, which was completed in 2008 just in time for the Beijing Olympics. Terminal 3 was designed by an international consortium of architects and is the world's second-largest terminal (second to Dubai). Its opening gave Beijing's capacity for international travel a major boost, and since this time Beijing has consistently ranked in the top 10 busiest airports.

Terminal 1 manages domestic flights, while Terminals 2 and 3 handle international flights and flights to Hong Kong, Macau, and Taiwan. A free shuttle bus runs between the terminals. For T1 it stops outside Gate 7, for T2 outside Gate 9, and for T3 outside Gate 5. Terminals 1 and 2 are actually located together, but most maps seem to not care about Terminal 1 and don't mention it. So if you discover you need to depart from T1, head to T2 and then follow the signs.

THE AIRLINES

Air China is China's national carrier, and to be frank, it's pretty horrible. Food, service, entertainment choices, even timeliness all fall way short of what you might expect from a national carrier. Its prices are rarely competitive. Few expats (possibly none) would rank it as their first choice. It is, however, one carrier that may offer you a direct flight if that's your priority. It has direct flights to Vancouver, Los Angeles, San Francisco, and New York, as well as to Sydney, Melbourne, London, and Paris. Other airlines that fly direct between Beijing and the United States include United, Delta, American Airlines, and Hainan Air. Hainan Air is one local airline worth keeping your eye on. It's one of the few Chinese airlines actually turning its attention to service quality. Its flights have an international feel and its ticket prices are competitive.

BUYING YOUR TICKETS

To book your China flights, you can go through the usual ticketing vendors, such as Travelocity, Expedia, or individual airline websites to buy your tickets, but within China there are also two very useful websites to investigate—eLong.com and www.Ctrip.com. Both offer competitive prices that are often way below those elsewhere, and both have good English services. These sites won't always allow you to directly earn points with your relevant points club, so either contact the club after you've purchased your tickets or present your club membership card first thing when you arrive at the check-in counter.

By Train

In Beijing, trains are used for long-distance journeys rather than everyday commuting, and when you make your first attempt at taking a train it can be a little intimidating. The stations are vast, crowded, dirty halls of people chewing on sunflower seeds or mandarins and spitting the remains on the floor. When boarding time for your train is announced your stomach dives at the horrible squeeze and chaos you're envisaging is about to happen. The constantly surprising thing, however, is that once you're through to the actual platform and boarding the train, it's all quite serene and organized. After they succeed in getting through the gate in the waiting hall, people behave in an orderly fashion, board their designated cars promptly, and settle in. Trains leave on time and get you to your destination in comfort.

You can get almost anywhere in China by rail, and at an ever increasing speed. In 2012 alone, the government added 6,366 kilometers of rail, 55 percent of which was for the high-speed rail (HSR) trains.

Trains in China are safe, even for women traveling alone, and while you should still keep an eye on your belongings, you never really hear of the kinds of problems that plague long-distance trains in other parts of the world. Another advantage to opting for a train journey is that while it's obviously longer than flying, you can almost always choose an overnight train. You arrive at the given station in Beijing an hour before the departure time in the evening and arrive hopefully refreshed the next morning with little interruption to your schedule.

One of the worst things about traveling by train is that it can sometimes

© SHANNON AITKEN

Train tickets can be purchased from train stations or from shops around town.

be incredibly hard to get a ticket. During any major holiday period (such as Spring Festival and the October holiday) people queue for hours outside ticket offices desperately trying to get any ticket they can to get back to their hometown. This is not the time to take an adventure on the trains.

Train guru Mark Smith and self-described "career railwayman" provides in-depth information about using China's trains on his website, www.seat61.com.

TRAIN STATIONS

Beijing has six passenger train stations, most connected to subway stations. These include: Beijing West Railway Station, Beijing Railway Station, Beijing South Railway Station, Beijing North Railway Station, Beijing East Railway Station, and the new Beijing Fengtai Railway Station. All but Beijing East Railway Station (mostly for freight) are connected to a subway station.

TRAIN TYPES

K trains are the slowest of the train categories, and though they're also the most basic, they're still reasonably comfortable. **T trains** are faster and are one up in quality from K. **Z trains** are considered the high-quality express sleeper trains; while **C, D,** and **G trains,** which include both high-speed daytime and sleeper categories, are the cream of the crop. These are the trains that are more likely to have the more expensive, more luxurious private first and second-class compartments. They're also more likely to have dining cars and snack bars, but in any case, it's highly recommended you go snack shopping before you board, just like the locals. A special **S train** category runs from Beijing North Railway Station directly to the Badaling section of the Great Wall. For more information about this, visit www.tour-beijing.com.

High-Speed Rail

Despite some hitches in its PR profile in recent years, China's high-speed rail (HSR) system is still on a ballistic course of development. Originally speeds ran close to 400 kilometers per hour, but today the trains are limited to 200-350 kilometers per hour (124-217 miles per hour), and rigorous testing systems have been put in place to avoid mishaps. As of the end of 2012, China's total HSR network stretched to more than 10,000 kilometers (6,214 miles), and the plan is to have more than 16,000 kilometers (9,942 miles) of track by 2020, with Beijing, of course, being a major hub for the HSR. Tickets for these trains are usually coded by the letter G.

TICKETS
Seat Classes and Pricing

On most Chinese trains there are basically four seat classes—soft seat, hard seat, hard sleeper, and soft sleeper. Not all are available on every train, and on the newer trains there are now often extra categories that foreigners would more typically equate to first class.

Putting these hard-to-buy posh options aside, the other classes are still relatively comfortable, though they do have open compartments and no curtains or doors. Sheets, blankets, and pillowcases are always spotlessly clean, and the bathrooms at

BEIJING'S TRAIN STATIONS AND DESTINATIONS

Station	Subway Line Location	Destinations
Beijing West Railway Station	Beijing West Railway Station, Line 9	Chengdu, Chongqing, Fuzhou, Guangzhou, Guilin, Hohhot, Kowloon (Hong Kong), Kunming, Lanzhou, Lhasa, Luoyang, Nanchang, Nanning, Qinhuangdao, Sanya, Shenzhen*, Taiyuan, Urumqi, Wuhan, Wuhan, Xiamen, Xi'an, and Zhengzhou. International destination includes Hanoi. *Planned to be moved to Fengtai Railway Station.
Beijing Railway Station	Beijing Railway Station, Line 2	Chengde, Dalian, Guangzhou East, Hangzhou, Harbin, Hefei, Qinhuangdao, Nanjing, Shanghai, and Shenyang; and international destinations of Moscow (Trans-Siberian Express), Pyongyang, Ulaanbaatar
Beijing South Railway Station	Beijing South Railway Station, Line 4	Nanjing South, Qingdao, Qinhuangdao, Shanghai, Shanghai Hongqiao (HSR), Tianjin (HSR)
Beijing North Railway Station	Xizhimen Station, Line 2, 4, 13	Chengde, Inner Mongolia (Hohhot, Yanqing (Badaling Great Wall)
Beijing East Railway Station	None (south of Dawanglu Station, Line 1)	Chengde, Qinhuangdao
Beijing Fengtai Railway Station*	Fengtai Railway Station, Line 10	HSR to Hong Kong

*Once operational, many services from Beijing West Station will move here.

least start off that way at the terminal (although make sure you come supplied with toilet paper).

What differentiates the experience is the comfort of the seat or bed. The cheapest and least comfortable option is the hard seat and then the soft seat. Next is the hard sleeper. The beds aren't particularly hard, but they are very narrow, so if you have a wider frame then you probably won't get a good night's sleep. In each compartment in this category, there are six bunks, three a side. The headroom is particularly limited, especially for the top bunk, and it's impossible to sit up straight. I've had both bad and good experiences in this category. At times people have been relatively quiet and

BEIJING'S HIGH-SPEED RAIL (HSR) LINES

Destination	Distance	HSR Time	Flight Time
Beijing-Tangshan	160 km (99 mi)	40 min (estimated)	N/A
Beijing-Tianjin	117 km (73 mi)	30 min	N/A
Beijing-Shenyang-Harbin*	1,700 km (1,056 mi)	2:30 hr, 5 hr	1:20 hr, 2 hr
Beijing-Guangzhou-Shenzhen	2,203 km (1,329 mi)	7:25 hr, 8 hr	3:15 hr, 3:10 hr
Beijing-Shanghai	1,318 km (819 mi)	4:50 hr	2 hr

*Due for completion by 2014.

respectful of others sleeping, and on other occasions I couldn't wait to get out and get away from my loud, smelly-footed co-travelers who sporadically spat from their top bunks down onto the carpet below.

The most comfortable option is the soft sleeper. The mattresses are slightly wider and softer. There are only four bunks per compartment, two a side, and the headroom is much loftier. The price is about two-thirds more than the hard sleeper.

When you select your ticket it's important to consider the position of the bunk. The higher the position the cheaper it is and the less comfortable it is because of space. The bottom bunk for both hard and soft sleepers is the most comfortable but the most expensive. You can sit with your feet on the floor when you're awake, and you have a small side table to put your things on. If you're traveling with a friend or two, it's definitely the most social way to travel, and if you're traveling anything more than 10 hours, you'll feel much less restricted.

As an example, an overnight train from Beijing to Xi'an in Shaanxi province can cost up to RMB159 for a seat; up to RMB274/283/293 for the top/middle/bottom beds in a hard sleeper compartment; and up to RMB426/445 for the top/bottom beds respectively in a soft sleeper compartment. A K train will take about 14 hours 52 minutes to get there, while a Z train will take 11 hours 11 minutes. Prices are the same for both trains. By comparison, a one-way flight from Beijing to Xi'an might cost RMB1,000 (including taxes) and takes around two hours.

How to Buy Your Tickets

The first thing to know about buying your train tickets is that it doesn't help to try to organize yourself too far in advance. Reservations don't open up until 10 days before departure for all trains, with new ticket rounds beginning at 9am each day. Reservation time can be shortened during peak periods. Thankfully Beijing is the terminal station for most destinations, as sometimes you can't buy the ticket more than two days

Beijing Railway Station is one of Beijing's busiest train stations.

in advance if the train is passing through. The Beijing to Hong Kong train can be booked 60 days in advance.

It's best to buy your tickets two to three days in advance, although you can check availability if you're concerned via www.chinahighlights.com/china-trains. During national festivals, however, primarily Spring Festival, May 1, and National Day on October 1, camp out at your nearest ticket office the night before tickets go on sale. To simply check for train times and prices, visit http://train.huochepiao.com and search by train number or station name.

To buy your tickets, you can visit any of Beijing's train stations, regardless of where you'll depart from. These often have 24-hour ticket windows, and Beijing Station and Beijing West Station also have English-language ticket windows. Only cash is accepted here.

Alternatively, there are around a hundred ticketing offices dotted around town, including in Terminal 2 at the airport. These are typically open 8am-9pm and charge a RMB5 booking fee.

There are also online options. Chinese-only site www.12306.cn (view through Google Chrome for a usable translation) is the official ticketing site and the most trusted. It is, however, in Chinese only and doesn't accept foreign bank or credit cards. You may find English sites www.tour-beijing.com, www.chinatrainguide.com, www. chinatripadvisor.com, or www.chinatraintickets.net more user-friendly. These kinds of agencies can also often work the system, allowing you to jump the queue and book far more in advance than you could yourself. Their prices do vary greatly, however, so be sure to compare.

If you're traveling with children, tell them to hunch—children under 120 centimeters (47 inches) travel free, and those 120-150 centimeters (47-59 inches) get a discount. Taller than this and they're considered big enough to pay full price.

Finally, don't forget; when you both book and travel (even to Tianjin), you and your companions will need your passports on you.

By Long-Distance Bus

Long-distance buses (长途汽车, *chángtúqìchē*) are an extremely affordable and convenient option for getting out into the countryside, as well as for taking yourself off on mini breaks to nearby cities and surrounding provinces, such as Datong or Pingyao in Shanxi province, Hebei or Liaoning province, Inner Mongolia, or Tianjin. While many will take you as far as Shanghai (RMB281-340) or Xi'an (RMB259), remember these are vast distances possibly requiring 10 or more hours on the road. A train or plane might be a better option.

There are two forms of long-distance bus travel—those that operate like public buses and run to a daily schedule, for which you turn up at the bus station, swipe your travel card or pay in cash when you get on, then get off at the stop you want; and then there are more coach-like services, which you can book through a travel site or office.

Local websites such as www.piaojia.cn/beijing/changtu.asp and www.e2go.com.cn can help you locate a local coach to almost anywhere in China, but again, these are in Chinese only. For services like these, you pay at the bus station, so it's good to look at the websites for schedules and then arrive early to secure a ticket.

Most long-distance buses to Beijing's rural areas are numbered in the 900s. For example, bus 936 from Dongzhimen will take you out to the Great Wall at Mutianyu for the bargain price of RMB16. Visit www.tour-beijing.com/public_bus for an extensive list of suggested long-distance buses for day trips.

A huge drawback to some of these buses or coaches, however, is the advertising that often screeches incessantly at you from TV screens. Roadside stops out in the countryside may also not be that appealing. Toilets can be a little scary (although no more than many in the CBD), and roadhouse snacks are likely to be things like instant noodles and packaged eggs, spam, or pickled vegetables.

The key long-distance bus stations to be aware of include Deshengmen, a short walk east of Jishuitan subway station (Line 2); Dongzhimen, right at the subway station (Lines 2 and 13); Pingguoyuan, out west at the very end of Line 1; Sihui, on the south side of Sihui subway station (Line 1); and Bawangfen, south of Dawanglu subway station and just south of Dongjiao markets. See sites www.travelchinaguide.com and www.beijingchina.net.cn for more information on exactly which bus station will get you where.

DAILY LIFE

Public Transportation

THE YIKATONG CARD

Lacking a memorable moniker like London's Oyster card or Hong Kong's Octopus card, Beijing's travel card gets called a few names by expats—IC card, smart card, Metro card, travel card—although I've never once heard anyone pull out an Yikatong, the official name, when talking about it.

It's also still a long way from being as useful as either London's or Hong Kong's card, and its major function is swiping to get on buses and subways. Theoretically, taxis are supposed to accept it, but taxi drivers hate it as the system is often faulty and frequently fails to transfer the money to them. If you do plan to use it, it's best to tell the driver immediately when you get in the cab.

The card's range of other services is ever expanding, and some of the places that it can be used include: bicycle rental stands around Dongcheng and Chaoyang districts; some parking stations; Sinopec gas stations; public telephones; some movie cinemas; some local fitness centers; many supermarkets, including Walmart, Wumart, Jinkelong, and Hualian; some convenience or fast food stores, such as Watsons, Quik, McDonald's, KFC, Cold Stone Creamery, and Holiland bakeries; and even Golden Elephant Pharmacies.

Yikatong cards can be bought and recharged at subway and train stations, as well as most post offices, some banks (especially CITIC), and some supermarkets. To buy them you must leave a deposit of RMB20, which you'll get back when you return it (if it's not damaged), plus at least RMB30 credit. You can load up to a maximum of RMB1,000 and make a maximum single payment of RMB500. There are designated places to return the card, which are mentioned on the official website, www.bjsuperpass.com (Chinese only).

If you would like to see your card-use history, visit the website and punch in the 17-digit number on the front of your card into the search box on the right of the homepage (where you see 卡查询).

TAXIS

Taxis are extremely easy to catch, except in the rain, and this is about the only form of legal transport you're going to get after 10pm or 11pm. If you don't speak Chinese then make sure you have the address of where you're going written down in Chinese characters for the driver. They will be able to read characters, but not necessarily Pinyin. Alternatively, have the phone number for where you're going so that you can call them and have them direct the driver.

Some people like to complain that Beijing's taxi drivers are rude or smelly, or both. But, while like in any city there is the occasional grump, most Beijing drivers are friendly and hardworking, and either just do their job emotionlessly or are extremely chatty and love it when they have a foreign passenger who can talk to them. If you don't speak any Chinese and clearly don't know where you're going, you're raising the risk that they will take you on a wild goose chase, but this is relatively rare, and there is no need to feel uneasy. If you do have a significant problem that is worth reporting, write down the driver's ID number, which is on the console, and remember to try to get a *fāpiào* (receipt) when you pay.

If you want a taxi for a whole day, you can occasionally bargain with the driver and agree on a fixed price. They'll keep the meter off and you can pay them at the end of the day.

Fares and *Fāpiào*

During the day, the taxi flag fall is RMB10 for the first three kilometers, and then RMB2 per kilometer for the rest of the ride. After 15 kilometers (9.32 miles), you'll notice the meter start going a little faster as the charge clicks over to RMB3 per kilometer.

From 11pm to 5am the flag fall is RMB11 for the first three kilometers, then RMB2.4 per kilometer, then RMB3.4 per kilometer after 15 kilometers. If you come to a standstill in traffic or ask a driver to sit with the meter on while you run into a building, you'll be charged the equivalent of 1 kilometer per 5 minutes.

If your journey exceeds 3 kilometers, you'll also have a RMB2 fuel surcharge added to the total price, which won't be shown on the meter or your receipt. There's no need to try to calculate the kilometers—if the meter still says 10.00 when you stop (or 11.00 late at night), then you won't pay extra. If it's more than this, add RMB2 when you hand over the money. If you do need a receipt for this extra RMB2, the driver can provide you with one. If you go through any tolls, such as from the airport into the city, toll fees will also be added to your total fare.

Further, if you want to avoid confrontation, be sure to have change (*língqián*). You'll make their day if you have the exact fare. You'll probably hear the driver say *"Yào piào ma?,"* meaning "Do you want a receipt?." If you do, say *"yào";* if you don't, say *"búyào."* It's good to get into the habit of taking your *piào*. These not only record the details of your driver and journey, which can be helpful if you lose something or have problems, but taxi receipts are a common form of collectible *fāpiào* to offset taxes.

Smoking is prohibited in taxis. You shouldn't smoke in them, and neither should your driver, but you'll definitely get the occasional driver who will. You have the right to have him or her put it out. If they won't, you can take their photo, note down their ID number, and report them by calling the hotline service on 10/6835-1150 or 10/6835-1570. Other possible times when you might have difficulty with taxi drivers is when you're only going short distances from particular places, such as the airport. If you only need to take the 10-minute drive from the airport to Shunyi, your driver may launch into a full-scale tantrum and try to refuse to take you. They've probably queued for 20 minutes or more outside the airport and don't like getting the dud fare. If you stay your ground they should take you—you'll just have to put up with them grumbling and complaining for the entire distance.

And a final tip: If you want to turn off the terrible advertising screen that is right in front of your face in the back seat, tap the volume button once to put it on silent and a second time to turn it off!

SUBWAY

This is the simplest, most reliable, and often the fastest mode of transport around town, but it's a relatively recent addition to the city. For two decades between 1981 and 2001 Beijing got by with just two lines, 1 and 2. Ever since 2002, however, the

© SHANNON AITKEN

The Beijing subway is a cheap and convenient way to get around most parts of the city center.

city's subway system has exploded. There are now 15 lines and 218 stations. By 2015 there will by 19 lines in service.

Subways cost a flat rate of RMB2, regardless of how many lines you need to use, and children under 1.2 meters (47 inches) ride for free if with an adult. The Airport Express costs RMB25, again regardless of which stop you get off at, Sanyuanqiao or Dongzhimen. By comparison, a taxi fare to Dongzhimen from the airport, including tolls, will cost RMB80-100.

It's best to buy an Yikatong travel card and simply swipe your way in and out of the gates; however, if you need to buy a one-off ticket, you can use the ticket machines. These all have English and are simple to use.

Subways generally run from 5am (the Airport Express starts at 6am) and finish at around 11pm. Rush hour is definitely a nightmare on many lines, particularly Lines 1, 2, and 5. At major stations, such as Guomao or Sihui, you may not even get onto the first several trains that pull in, let alone get down onto the platform. At these times, however, trains come every couple of minutes, while at low periods, they arrive about every 10 minutes.

Unfortunately, the subway doesn't always show the better sides of the locals. People will rush to get on before you get off, and some people will almost knock you over to get a seat if there is one. People cough and sneeze without covering their mouths, and bellow on their cells as if no one else were around. On the good side, no matter how crowded it is, people will make every effort to let you past so you can get off. To aid your passage, you can just say, *"xià chē"* ("getting off") or *"guò yī xià"* ("please let me past").

BUSES

Beijing's bus network is extraordinarily cheap, extensive, and convenient, but unlike the subway, it can be intimidating for an expat. There is virtually a total lack of English, and bus stop names are obscure. They're also not particularly designed for style or comfort.

Bus Routes

There are almost 900 bus route numbers in Beijing. Those numbered 1 to 100 operate within the Third Ring Road; those from 200-215 run only at night; the 300s are concentrated in the suburbs, such as Fengtai and Mentougou; the 400s ferry you back and forth from the inner city to the suburbs; 600s and 700s are common in most residential areas; and the 900s are what connect the inner city to Beijing's more rural districts, such as Changping, Yanqing, and Miyun.

There is no particular schedule for the buses. They come about every 10 minutes at most, and much more frequently during busy periods and on major routes. Most routes operate from around 5:30am to 11pm, but not always. Many finish by as early as 8pm. The 201-215 night routes run from 11pm to about 4:30am. To check, look up the bus on www.bjbus.com, www.baidu.com's map function, or www.mapbar.com, or look at the bus sign at your nearest bus stop.

Riding the Bus

You'll never blow your budget if you stick to the bus system. Standard inner-city buses cost RMB1 per journey when you buy a ticket onboard, and RMB0.4 if you use your travel card. This varies slightly for different routes and if the bus is air-conditioned or not. You can buy the travel card at most major subway stations and some major bus stops.

Buses have entry doors and exit doors. Get on at the door with the 上 (*shàng,* meaning "on") symbol—or where everyone else is getting on—and off at the door with the 下 (*xià,* meaning "off"). Swipe your travel card as you get on or pay the ticket seller on the bus. Sometimes you need to swipe when you get off the bus, but not always. Typically, buses numbered 1-599 need swiping when you get on only, and buses numbered 600 or higher require swiping when you get on and off. Basically, if there is a card reader at both the entry door and exit door then swipe at both; if the card reader is just at the entry door, then swipe once.

Finding Your Bus Route Online

Various websites can help you track down bus routes. These include Beijing Bus website (www.bjbus.com), Mapbar (www.mapbar.com), and the map function on Baidu (www.baidu.com), which works pretty much like the map function on Google. You can search by route number, destination, and by general location, and when a bus route is identified it will be highlighted on a map. Unfortunately all three sites are in Chinese. The good news is that they all work pretty well when viewed through Google Chrome and translated. It might take experimentation, but with a bit of trial and error, you might discover some handy information and open up more travel possibilities for yourself.

ILLEGAL OPTIONS

Various forms of private transport run around the city, many of dubious quality. These include black cabs, *bèngbèngchē* or *módī*, rickshaws, and *miànbāochē* (translated directly as "bread car," meaning "minivan"). All forms are illegal, and by riding in one, you risk being pulled over by police. It's rare, but not unheard of. If you experience any problems you'll also have no legal backup and zero sympathy from the authorities.

It's definitely not recommended you use these vehicles, but if you do, just take a few precautions, such as never getting into one unless you've agreed on a price first, never paying until you get to your final destination, and avoiding them if you're by yourself. If possible, try to use drivers that you are familiar with or that other people have recommended.

Black Cabs

Black cabs are everywhere in the city. They are unmarked and rarely actually black, but quite often have a sort of look about them that you get to know. They're typically older, cheaper cars, driven by a middle-aged driver who slowly cruises past you like a creepy stalker, leans over, and screams at you through his open window, *"Dǎchē?"* ("Need a ride?"). Others base themselves around specific apartment complexes, especially in the mornings. When it rains, many opportunistic car-owners will hit the streets and try to charge you extortionate prices.

Using a black cab always requires a bit of bargaining. You can usually get them down to about the same price as a taxi, and perhaps a fraction lower if your skills are good. In the rain, you've got no chance. They'll ask RMB60 for an RMB20 ride, and if you refuse they'll wave you on.

Despite their reputation, black-cab drivers are not all bad and can be extremely jovial. They don't have the stress of regular taxi drivers, and drive just when they want to. Many of them are happy with what they do and keep their cars spotlessly clean.

© SHANNON AITKEN

The *bèngbèng* (rear) and the electric bike are standard forms of private and often illegal public transport.

Bèngbèngchē

These are the little silver or green vehicles that seem to be half motorbike, half car. They zip around the city, driven by a chain-smoking retiree who seems to have dreams of taking pole position in the F1. Theoretically these vehicles are legal for people with physical disabilities, but you'll see many a suspiciously sprightly old chap with a disabled sticker slapped to his vehicle. The great thing about them is that they cut through traffic like a knife through butter, and get you where you're going in lightning speed for about RMB5. The reason is that they flirt with traffic rules, drive into oncoming traffic, and dart across flowing intersections with steely confidence. They are the cowboys of Beijing.

Rickshaws

Rickshaws were on the verge of extinction about five years ago, pedaled exclusively around tourist spots such as Houhai to give tourists an "authentic" experience. Since 2010, however, they've been making a bit of a revival in the inner city, especially around Sanlitun, Gulou, Ritan, and Houhai, as actual transport options. It can be damn hard to get a cab around these places at night, and the rickshaw drivers are taking up the slack.

Miànbāochē

These drivers don't tend to trawl the streets for passengers but rather get their business by word-of-mouth. They can be your best friend when you want to move house, and many will rent their van and driving services out for the day to take you and your guests out to the Great Wall or other such sites. For a whole day, they will probably ask for around RMB450-800, and again you'll need to bargain. When you need one, ask around. There's usually a friend or someone in the office who will have a contact number for a *miànbāochē* driver, and if not, ask for a recommendation on Yahoo group Beijing Café.

Getting Yourself Around

BICYCLES AND SCOOTERS

Beijing has fantastic bike lanes on every road, so bicycles and scooters are perhaps the most convenient way to get yourself from place to place, and you can park your bike virtually anywhere for free—although bicycle theft is a huge problem.

As far as safety goes, it's a little hazardous if you're a speed pedaler because pedestrians, other bike-lane users, and motorists are unpredictable—they'll stop, turn, veer, and cross your path without warning and without looking, often with a mobile phone in their hand. Ninety-nine percent of people don't wear helmets either. If you buck this trend, however, and ride with a good measure of defensiveness, it's relatively safe.

You can easily pick up a secondhand bicycle for around RMB100 if you're not fussy about style, or a new bike from large supermarkets, such as Walmart and Carrefour, for around RMB250-500. Such places even sell electric bikes.

Road bikes and fixed-gear bikes are now the trend, so you'll find an ever-greater variety of these bikes on sale around town, and while high-level European brands are yet to make a showing, brands such as Giant and Dahon are everywhere. Different frame sizes are difficult to find, so if you're particularly short or tall you may want to bring a bike from home, or opt for something from a store such as Decathlon, which reports to stock frames as large as 65 centimeters (26 inches). For a custom-made bikes, try Natooke (http://natooke.com) on Wudaoying Hutong near Lama Temple or Serk cycling (www.serk.cc) near Beixinqiao subway station (Line 5).

© SHANNON AITKEN

Public bike kiosks are found throughout the city, offering everyone a convenient and cheap way to get around.

Scooters are also prolific in the city and can start from around RMB1,500 for a gas-powered one, and RMB2,000 for an electric one, depending on the style you want. Electric bikes and scooters—or e-scooters—don't need a license. The downside of these bikes is that they tend to break down or have little problems from time to time; the upside is that these are usually cheap and quick to fix. Though some of these can zip along at 40-50 kilometers per hour (25-31 mph), they're ridden in the bike lanes, not on the main road. An infuriating given with an e-scooter is that at some point someone is going to steal your battery. Take it out of your bike whenever possible, and even leave your seat visibly unlocked so that potential thieves don't damage your lock trying to get in. For gasoline-powered scooters, see rules relating to motorcycles.

Bicycle Clubs

Cycling is increasingly seen as a form of leisure rather than just a mode of transport, and there are more and more cycling groups popping up around the city. Ask at any large bike shop for cycling groups, or try those run by Natooke, Serk, or Bike Beijing (www.bikebeijing.com). These kinds of groups are a great way to make new friends in the city.

Bike Sharing

As one of its efforts to curb pollution and traffic, in 2012 the Beijing government began a public bike-sharing system. It aims to have a fleet of 50,000 bicycles distributed at 1,000 service points across the city by 2015. Service points are at most subway stations and business areas, and bikes can be rented from one service point and returned to any other in the city.

At the time of writing, rates were free for the first hour and RMB1 for every following hour, with a maximum of RMB10 for the day. Bicycles can be hired for up to three consecutive days at a time, then, from day four it's an RMB20 fine until you return it.

To be able to use a bike, you need to register by presenting your passport, Yikatong card, and an RMB200 deposit, and signing a service contract. Then, simply swipe the docking stand for your bike of choice when you take it. Just make sure you check the brakes before pedaling away.

MOTORCYCLES

Straight up, riding a motorcycle in Beijing is not recommended. Thanks to the reckless and counterintuitive driving techniques of motorists here, it's extremely dangerous. On top of that, emergency responses by both bystanders and health services are not what you may be used to in your home country. If you are determined to ride a motorcycle in Beijing, be sure to buy quality safety gear and have international medical insurance.

Further, if you ride a gas-powered two- or three-wheeled vehicle, you need a genuine license, regardless of the bike's capacity. The government is cracking down on motorcycle infringements, and being a foreigner is not going to get you out of it. While many seem to dodge rules unscathed for years on end, there are also plenty of incidences where a foreigner has been caught on an unregistered motorcycle without a license, sent first to a Beijing prison for 14 days, then deported.

Buying a motorcycle is a little complicated, and there are many things to be aware of before launching into it. You can't just go out and buy any bike. There are approved sellers and approved processes.

For starters, there are two kinds of plates, a "Jing A" (京A) plate and a "Jing B" (京 B) plate. A Jing A plate can go almost anywhere in the city, except inside the Second Ring Road and on the Ring Roads, while a B plate is restricted to outside the Fourth Ring Road. So, if you live inside the Fourth Ring Road you'll need an A plate. But, to complicate this, you must also have an A plate if you're in one of the designated districts, including Chaoyang, regardless of the fact that your actual address hangs outside of the Fourth Ring Road. The capacity of your bike will also determine which bike has what plate and, thus, where it can go. Technically, anything larger than a 150cc is prohibited from inside the Fourth Ring Road.

The government stopped issuing new Jing A plates years ago, so when you're buying a new bike, the plate you'll get will be from an old bike that's been scrapped. This means they're extraordinarily expensive. Genuine Jing A plates can easily cost RMB25,000. The plummeting other downside to this is that in Beijing, if someone steals your plate, you can't replace it until it's been found. You could buy another plate, but you can't transfer the registration of your old plate from your bike for three years. One option: weld it to your bike.

It's best to buy a bike that already has a plate. But how do you know if the bike or the plate is genuine? Go through a large dealership and use an agent. While they'll add a hefty fee, agents will know how to get through the paperwork.

As far as licenses go, international licenses aren't recognized and this includes licenses from Hong Kong and Taiwan, so you'll need to go through Lao Shan training school (www.lsjx.cc), located out west in Shijingshan, to get your license. For more help and shopping ideas, visit motorcycle sites www.beijingriders.com, http://bj.58. com/danche, and www.cj750.net. You'll also find a lot of help and guidance from fellow motorcycle enthusiasts on www.mychinamoto.com.

Driving

© SHANNON AITKEN

One of the biggest complaints about Beijing is its unrelenting traffic problems.

There are already more than 4 million cars on Beijing's roads, and figures are on their way to blow past 5.5 million by 2015. As things are, it can already take an hour to pass a distance that you could pedal in under 10 minutes. If you choose to drive, you may get to have your own clean private space, and sing along to your own music, and know that even if it's raining you'll still get home, but will also be opening yourself up to a barn load of hassles.

The roads here are fraught with hazards, mercurial road rules, and punishing penalties. If you're caught drunk driving, you'll be toast, and if your car or motorbike is illegal you'll also be 100 percent at fault if you have an accident. Even if you so much as prod a wayward pedestrian, you'll be up for a creative sum of money. Somehow half the population here seems to have gotten their hands on the DIY Guide to Compensation and have no shame if there's even a whiff of a payout.

When you weigh up all the costs, including purchasing outlays, car insurance, health insurance, parking, fuel, fines, and so on, it's often much more economical to simply hire a driver with a car, and let them manage the stress and expenses. Additionally, before you decide to drive you should check with your work company and insurance company if you're permitted to drive. The insurance included in some expat packages doesn't always cover driving on Chinese roads.

DRIVER'S LICENSES

Getting your license is straightforward but it's not exactly effortless. An international license won't get you out of the carpark, but your existing license from your home country will at least put you at an advantage to getting a Chinese one in that you don't need to do a physical driving test, only a theory one. Never drive without a license here—it will put everything you have here at risk, including your work, your study program, and your assets. Deportation is only one of the possible penalties. Further, if you make any changes to your passport, always remember to update your driver's license accordingly.

To get your Chinese license, must be between 18 and 70 years of age. Some licenses will have height restrictions, and if you're diplomatic staff, you may not have to take the test. Most people, however, will need:

- A driver's license application form
- Your passport and a photocopy of it
- Your local residential registration slip from your local PSB
- A health certificate (This must be from a public hospital, not an international hospital. The Friendship Hospital and the China-Japan Friendship Hospital are acceptable.)
- Your original driver's license, a Chinese translation, and a photocopy of both
- Five one-inch passport photos (white background)

You can manage the process yourself or save a whole lot of *máfan* (hassle) by using the expat-friendly services, such as the Beijing Expat Service Center (www.beijingesc.com), FESCO (www.fescoservice.com), or Ex-Pats Life (www.expatslife.com). Companies such as these will usually take care of everything for around RMB650-1,000. If you do it yourself, it'll cost around RMB300 altogether, including the medical test, study book, license translation, license fee, and delivery of license.

If you do take care of things for yourself, you'll need to make several trips out to the Foreign Affairs Department of the Beijing Motor Vehicle Administration (BMVA) and manage your own health check at the local hospital. It won't matter which visa you have, as long as there is still three months remaining (if there is less than this you will only be able to apply for a temporary driver's license). Take all your paperwork to the MBVA and collect a test book while you're there. You'll need to return at the agreed time to do the computerized written test. This can be done in Chinese, English, Russian, German, French, Japanese, Korean, Arabic, or Spanish, and is 100 multiple-choice questions, of which you need to get at least 90 correct. If you do pass, your license will be ready within about five days, which you can pay to have delivered, and which is valid for six years. When it's time for renewal, you'll just need to redo the eye test, and you must apply 90 days before the license expires.

It's unlikely you'll be able to wing the test. The questions are randomly selected

TRAFFIC OFFENSES

Running a red light: 6 points, RMB200 fine.
Drunk driving: 12 points, license withheld for five years, fine, jail sentence.
Failure to wear a seatbelt: 2 points, RMB100 fine.
Failure to give way to a school bus: 6 points, RMB200 fine.
Talking on cell phone while driving: 2 points, RMB50 fine.
Concealing or using incorrect number plate: 12 points, RMB200 fine.
Exceeding speed limit by more than 50 percent: 12 points, licence may be revoked, RMB200-2,000 fine.

If you're caught driving at more than 50 percent over the speed limit, you'll lose your license. Beijing licenses have a 12-point penalty system, whereby you accumulate points (possibly in addition to being fined or sent to jail) for various offenses. Running a red light or speeding will earn you three points; driving without a seatbelt results in one or two points on your record; and drunk driving can lead to six or more points being added. If you accumulate 12 points within one year (starting from the time you get your license), you lose your license and have to re-sit for the test, potentially with some driver re-training thrown in. For more information on points, visit www.bjjtgl.gov.cn.

BEIJING ROAD RULES

Sometimes it might not seem that way, but Beijing does have hundreds of rules and regulations for the road. Here are some of the main ones you need to know.

Despite almost zero compliance, theoretically it is the law to wear a seatbelt both in the front and back of a moving vehicle. In a taxi, if you want to buckle up, best bet is to sit in the front passenger seat—although some drivers will try to talk you out of it by telling you it's broken or that their driving skills would impress Michael Schumacher. It seems the rule is a little up to interpretation. When I called the BMVA to check, they said "If seatbelts are there, you're required to wear them; if they're not, then you're not." Within the city proper where speed is slow due to congestion, crashes are fairly minor, but once you get out onto the open road your luck will often be determined by cavalier drivers for whom driving a new thing.

Vehicles (should) drive on the right-hand side of the road.

What you might understand as "right of way" probably isn't what applies here. In Western countries it typically implies whoever has the legally correct position goes first, such as at traffic lights. In China it's whoever gets there first. This means motorists will turn or merge straight into the path of others believing it's their responsibility to avoid a collision. In situations where it would normally come down to a mutual agreement, signaled by a nod or a wave, the Chinese will typically do the opposite—avoid eye contact and go ahead regardless. Few will use their indicators, as doing this can actually make it more difficult to turn or merge. Despite this apparent arrogance, however, there is relatively little road rage because pretty much everyone expects everyone else to do the wrong thing and is never shocked when they do.

Cars are prohibited from driving in bus or bicycle lanes.

Anything going slower than a maxi-

from 1,300 questions, many seemingly illogical, many outright bizarre, many confusingly translated. If you fail, though, you can sit it again for free. Fail a second time and you may have to start from scratch. The good thing is that the questions are worded just as they are in the study manual. There's even a fun smart phone and tablet app, China Drive (中国交规通), which you can download for free (some sites charge) to get all the questions. For more information, visit www.bjjtgl.gov.cn, or, for US$5, you can download the *Chinese Drivers License Guide* from www.themiddlekingdom.org.

If you don't already have a driver's license from your home country, you'll need to pass the medical check-up and traffic law exam first. After this you will have to go for driving lessons (a nightmare), then pass the physical driving test.

Temporary Licenses

Temporary licenses are available if you're staying for less than 90 days and have an L (tourist) visa, and can be used for rental cars only. Companies such as Hertz say they can do this in around an hour if done at their airport branch (Terminal 3), but in many cases it can take five days and will cost around RMB450. Find out exactly what you need well ahead of time. In most cases a temporary license still requires a visit to either the Foreign Affairs Department of the BMVA or the Vehicle Management Service Station at the airport (Terminal 3). You won't need to take any tests, but you

mum of 70 kilometers per hour (43 mph)—such as pedestrians, scooters, or bicycles)—is prohibited from using the expressways.

Cars must give way to pedestrians crossing at zebra crossings or traffic light crossings—but definitely assume they won't and look both ways before you put a foot on the road.

When an accident occurs, if possible, exchange license plate numbers, driver's license numbers, and insurance details. If anything is awry, such as no license plate, someone being injured, or the plate being not from Beijing, call 122 (traffic accidents) or 999 (private ambulance) and wait for the officer to arrive.

If you plan to drive to another city or province, especially Shanghai, but your car is registered in Beijing, check ahead for what restrictions might apply to you in that area.

As a motorist, if you hit a pedestrian or nonmotorized vehicle, you're automatically at fault—although if they were clearly violating some kind of law applicable to them your punishment may be reduced.

Car insurance is compulsory.

If you're caught driving at 50 percent higher than the speed limit, you'll lose your license.

If you're involved in an accident, the Beijing British Embassy's website recommends the following: Do stop the vehicle immediately—don't move it until requested to do so by the Public Security Bureau (PSB). If there are casualties, do call the PSB (122 or 110) and ambulance services (120 or 999). Do remain at the scene of the accident until the PSB arrives. Don't answer any questions put to you by the PSB about the accident, other than those confirming your identity, etc., other than in the presence of a legal representative. Don't speak to any casualties or bystanders about the circumstances of the accident.

will need your original driver's license from your home country, your temporary residence registration slip, an eye exam by an approved hospital, and four one-inch photos.

BUYING AND SELLING

Buying a car in Beijing has become a difficult process for those who go by the book. Again in an effort to reduce the hellish traffic conditions, the municipal government has created a lottery system for new car plates. In previous years, Beijing sold around 800,000 new cars a year, but since the lottery system has been in place, that has dropped to around 400,000. Chinese people not from Beijing, who don't have a Beijing *hùkǒu* (official local residency), can't apply unless they can prove they've lived and paid taxes in the city for five years. Foreigners are a little luckier—they only need to have been here for a year.

Before you can buy a car—new or old—you first need to have a number plate, and to get this you either need to offload some serious under-the-table cash (illegal) or put your name into a lottery for the chance to win the right to buy a number plate. This can be done via www.bjhjyd.gov.cn. Companies such as Car Solution (www.elsey-car.com) can help with this process as well as assist in buying or selling cars. To apply for the lottery, you'll need: a driver's license, a valid visa (any type) or permanent resident permit, a temporary registration slip issued from the local PSB (not one issued by your

© SHANNON AITKEN

Not sure what a road sign means? Visit the government's guide at www.bjjtgl. gov.cn/publish/portal1/

housing compound), a minimum of one year living in Beijing, and no other cars in your name in the city.

If you're moving into Beijing and someone from your company is moving out, they won't be able to automatically transfer the car over to you. They need to return their plate, and you need to go into the lottery for your own plate. Your chances of success are pretty slim. Hundreds of thousands may apply, but only 20,000 names are pulled out every month. Unsuccessful names roll over into the next barrel. If you do manage to win, you can then buy a car.

To buy a car, you should definitely go through a reputable dealer. If you later decide to sell the car in order to buy a new one, you can have the plate transferred to the new car without needing to go into the lottery again.

When you plan to leave the country you will need to officially deregister the car and sell it. Selling it could be difficult, though, as you may not know anyone who already has a number plate, and agents who can sniff the anxiety of an expat rushing to leave the country will offer criminally low prices. You won't be able to clear customs if the vehicle is still registered under your name. Basically, if you're planning to leave the country, plan your car's sale two or three months in advance and consider hiring a driver or using taxis for the remaining time.

Rental and Leasing

Renting a car in Beijing is definitely a way to overcome the buying problems. You can rent either short- or long-term, with or without a driver. Bear in mind that even if it's for a short trip, you won't be able to use an international license. You'll still need to apply for a temporary driver's license. Well-established car rental companies should help you with this. Rental for something like a Buick GL8 seven-seater will possibly cost around RMB10,000 per month, an additional RMB3,000 per month if you also want a driver, plus fuel costs. Deposits can be as much as RMB10,000, and an RMB1,000 deposit may be kept for one month (on your credit card) after you return the vehicle to cover any fines you may have chalked up. Some rental companies also require preregistration, so try to do this a few days in advance.

Companies such as China Auto Rental (CAR, www.zuche.com), Car Solution, or Beijing Auto Service Center are often used for longer-term rental, while Hertz (www. hertzchina.com) and CAR are experienced at providing short-term rental. Many companies, however, don't rent cars without drivers, even for periods of a year or more, so

DAILY LIFE

ask about this when investigating. If you are using a driver, you'll most likely need to have only cash or a credit card handy at when booking. Driving yourself requires more paperwork. You will need to show your passport and a Chinese driver's license, and may also need to provide a credit card, temporary residence registration slip from your local PSB, a guarantor letter from your company, and employment papers.

Renting cars is a new but rapidly growing industry in Beijing as locals are starting to see the value of taking off in cars for short trips rather than constantly owning a car. Car fleets often fall short of the demand, especially during national holidays, and often even on weekends.

DRIVERS

Rather than go through the risks and rigmarole of getting a car and driving yourself, an alternative option is to get a driver. This is a popular choice with families, especially those living out in Shunyi where public transport isn't as convenient.

You'll find lots of ads on expat websites, but it's recommended to go through official channels, such as car rental companies, as the drivers should have certain credentials and you'll have some backup if something goes wrong. Drivers typically cost RMB3,000-5,000 per month, not including fuel. Typical hours are 7am-6pm Monday-Saturday, although this is something you can negotiate. Of course, drivers are also available for one-off outings when you want to get out of town. These can be found through car hire companies or by word-of-mouth.

When you're hiring a driver, things to consider or ask about include whether or not they speak English; what their hours are and their ability to do overtime; what the driver's experience is with expats (service culture is very different here, so you might not want a first timer); what kind of vehicle he or she has and if it can accommodate your needs, such as a baby capsule or bicycle racks; if he or she is fully insured; and what their driving record is like. For full-time drivers, you should also discuss the end of year bonus. This is standard and is often equal to one month's salary paid at Chinese New Year before they return to their hometown for the holidays. If your company is hiring the driver for you then they will most likely cover this; however, you are often also expected to also give them your own *hóngbāo* (money in a red envelope), but the amount is at your discretion, and may be as little as RMB200-300. For any service person you entrust yourself to, you should always get a copy of their identity card (身份证, *shēnfènzhèng*).

Driving Days

You might assume driving on the weekends is easier than during the week, but not in Beijing. On the weekends, the road is open to anyone who has a car. But during the week, the government controls the number of vehicles by banning license plates ending with given numbers from driving within the Fifth Ring Road on particular days. For example, if your number plate ends with the number 1 or 6 you may not be able to use the car on Monday. The allocated days rotate every three months. Vehicles breaking these rules can be fined up to RMB300.

Additionally, cars registered in another province need to apply to come into Beijing, are banned from using roads inside the Fifth Ring during peak periods (7am-9am and 5pm-8pm), and must also follow the number plate system of restricted days.

To know which day you should be leaving the car at home, visit www.bjjtgl.gov. cn and click on the image of the number plate on the left of the screen. It's only in Chinese, but it's easy to understand. The main characters you need to identify include the days of the week: 星期一 for Monday, 星期二 for Tuesday, 星期三 for Wednesday, 星期四 for Thursday, 星期五 for Friday, and 公休日 for public holidays; 停驶 means "no driving," 尾号 means the plate number, and 和 means "and."

Filling Up

It can be hard to find a gas station in Beijing. However, www.aibang.com has a handy phone app, which can locate your nearest gas stations as well as a million other things. It is in Chinese, but this function isn't too complicated. When you open the application on your phone, go straight to the search box and type *jiayouzhan,* then select 加油站. Click on the top option that comes up, and then click on the blue marker symbol to bring up a map showing where you are in relation to the gas station.

Gas stations are not self-serve. An attendant will fill your car for you. Unfortunately, there have been many incidents of attendants underfilling by as much as RMB100, and charging the amount that was requested. Always get out of your car and check the meter. At the time of writing, gas prices at the pump were around RMB8 per liter (1L = 0.26 gallons). If you want to calculate your fuel consumption in Beijing, visit www.numbeo.com.

PRIME LIVING LOCATIONS

© SHANNON AITKEN

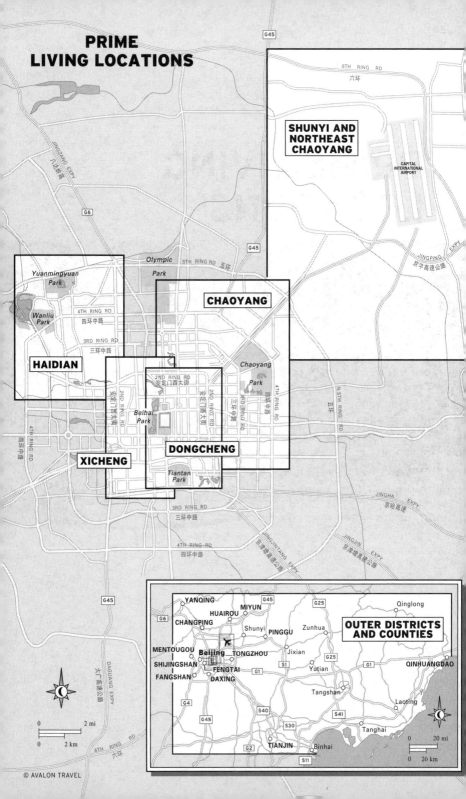

OVERVIEW

Beijing is an incomprehensibly large city. Stand at the top of any tower in its center and you'll look upon nothing but a sea of steel and concrete that engulfs every inch of land from that below your feet to the horizon in the distance. Fortunately—at least for sanity's sake—the expat population tends to organize itself into relatively specific locations, making it feel more manageable and sometimes even incredibly small, socially. The immensity of the city and the choking unrelenting traffic mean that people prefer to lay their hat close to work or school so as to avoid hours on the road or being jammed up in subway cars. This means there are various expat-friendly zones across the city, supplying foreign residents with home comforts and cushioning their daily experiences with moderate to high levels of English and international facilities.

The classic location choices for Beijing expats include Haidian district for students, Shunyi district for families with kids, Chaoyang district for city lovers, and Dongcheng or Xicheng for young singles or couples who want to experience traditional Beijing but can't quite tear themselves away from the convenience of city life. As Beijing is changing, however, the distribution of foreign residents is also changing. New subway lines are making previously bus-only neighborhoods more appealing, and the bloom of government-driven science parks is dispersing the population into new corners of the city.

This section covers the major districts that expats settle into, highlighting the

© SHANNON AITKEN

PRIME LIVING LOCATIONS

neighborhoods within them that are most popular, and alerting you to the places you may like to know about. The districts spoken about in detail include Chaoyang, Dongcheng, Xicheng, Haidian, and Shunyi, but information also touches on those that lie beyond the inner city and which have interesting options to help to make your Beijing life more complete.

DONGCHENG

Dongcheng is a wonderful part of the city that offers an intriguing mishmash of old and new. Like Xicheng to its west, Dongcheng still clings to the past with its *hútòng* and *sìhéyuàn*, but inside these structures the new is creeping in with eclectic boutiques, cafés, bars, microbreweries, and restaurants gradually repurposing the former spaces of Beijing's historical elite.

Dongcheng is more residential than commercial, so it's less likely you'll work here, but out-of-hours life is about meeting up with friends at a moment's notice at a local restaurant or bar and immersing yourself in the surrounding culture. Though threatened by modernization, Dongcheng is still a long way behind Chaoyang, so you won't find a huge supply of Western groceries or facilities immediately at hand. Fortunately transport is extremely convenient, and places like Sanlitun only a bike ride away.

On the other hand, it's not exactly an ideal choice for those with a family in tow. International schools are basically nonexistent, and there are few parks or rambling gardens in which kids can run freely. Spacious apartment complexes styled for Western comfort are also in the minority. The plus side to Dongcheng's more cramped conditions, however, is that life exists on the streets—people gather around on tiny stools to play poker or *májiàng* (mahjong), children play, and lovers argue out of the earshot of parents. A walk along the street can be like a walk through someone's living room.

© SHANNON AITKEN

the leafy *hútòng* of Dongcheng

XICHENG

Xicheng is a lot like Dongcheng—a shrine to Beijing's past with its ancient *hútòng* and architecture, and an ideal location for Beijing's super wealthy to buy out and transform former imperial homes into their own private palaces. Unlike Dongcheng, it is still markedly local. English-friendly facilities are relatively scarce and cafés that excel beyond a mediocre imitation of "Western food" are next to nonexistent. Expats do find their way out here, but their numbers thin dramatically a short distance west or south of Houhai. The lack of Western-centered services might be one explanation for this, but until a few years ago, Xicheng's reliance on bus transportation would have also stifled any appeal the district might have had for some. These days things are very different. Line 4 can shoot residents directly up into Haidian and its university and tech areas, while Line 6 can deliver them to bar hot spot Nanluogu Xiang or over to the CBD (Central Business District). Given this, Xicheng might be worth considering when you're house hunting. Its improved accessibility may now mean that you can enjoy the dual lifestyle of working or studying in a modern part of the city by day, and having an old Beijing experience by night.

CHAOYANG

Chaoyang is the most obvious choice for newcomers. It's not only the location of the CBD but also two of the three embassy areas. Consequently, over the years it has evolved into Beijing's most international district. It has the highest concentration of quality Western restaurants, bars, and brunch-loving cafés; English signage and service means you'll rarely have to break out a dictionary; apartments styled for Western taste are in ready supply; and there are more international supermarkets here than anywhere else in the city. When foreign brands foray into the Beijing market, it's usually here that they test the waters, and when an expat event is held the venue is almost always a Chaoyang one. Naturally, life in Chaoyang means minimal culture shock, and when you touch down you'll likely feel only the slightest of bumps as you adjust to your new life in the city.

The problem with Chaoyang, however, is that it is massive and encompasses places that are as disconnected in style as they are in distance. Simply living in the district will not automatically make everything that it holds convenient for you, and a good many parts of it are inconvenient and remain steadfastly local. The northeast corner of Chaoyang that neighbors Shunyi district, for example, is as remote to many inner-city residents as Shunyi itself, while for some parts of the far east and south of the district

© SHANNON AITKEN

pleasant and relaxing Ritan Park in Chaoyang

PRIME LIVING LOCATIONS

might just as well be Daxing or Tongzhou. For this reason it's not only necessary to thoroughly understand the location of neigborhood that you're interested in, but to also keep your eyes out for what you might be able to access more easily in the district next door rather than within Chaoyang.

HAIDIAN

The first thing that usually comes to mind when Haidian is mentioned is universities. This is the city's official academic district, and is home to the majority of Beijing's multitude of universities, including the country's two frontrunners, Tsinghua University and Peking University, as well as two other expat favorites, Beijing Language and Culture University (BLCU) and Beijing Foreign Studies University.

Given the intense concentration of campuses in the district, Haidian's character is decidedly student oriented. The population is youthful, and bars, eateries, and entertainment complexes cater to the crowd and its budget. Friends are never far away, and even if you don't live on campus, the atmosphere of university life is pervasive wherever you are.

Haidian is changing, however, and quickly. Though it's not going to lose the student population, it's now also making room and adjustments for its high-tech tenants. The government has chosen the district as its primary research and development base, and by providing attractive incentives to beckon start-ups and research units, it is diversifying the population into one that is also characterised by hip young entrepreneurs and scientists. Consequently, accommodations, recreation, and entertainment offerings are also expanding to suit the new wealthier, more adventurous clientele.

One major drawback to living in Haidian is that it's still a good distance from the CBD, regardless of the improved transport into the region. So while it might be an exciting and commercially inspiring place to live, the trade-off is that a night out in Sanlitun is a commitment most people don't want to make too often.

SHUNYI AND NORTHEAST CHAOYANG

While the internationalization of inner Chaoyang might make it a Chinese place with minimal culture shock, Shunyi and the neighboring northeast section of Chaoyang offer an almost total immersion into a Western lifestyle. This is the area of high-end, large-scale international schools and gated communities of multistory villas. Western medical facilities and supermarkets are all in the immediate vicinity, and though interesting shopping malls or stores are seriously lacking, daily needs are all at hand. Residents in the neighborhood are typically expats with families sent to Beijing on generous packages that come complete with a driver and car, a full-time nanny, and a private backyard for the kids to play in.

Life in Shunyi is a world away from that in such districts as Dongcheng, Xicheng, or Haidian, and given the considerable distance from these places, it can be easy to spend a number of years here and never get to know the real Beijing if you don't make a concerted effort to do so. If you don't have kids there is probably little reason to live out here, and if you do, there will be a surplus of opportunities to mix and make friends with those in your community.

To be clear, the Shunyi that expats generally speak of is just a microscopic part of the entire district, an area situated by the district's southwest border along the Wenyu

© SHANNON AITKEN

Pinnacle Plaza in Shunyi

River. Chaoyang district starts on the south side of the river, and its northeast corner by the river, identical in character to the Shunyi side, often gets grafted on to Shunyi to define a single residential concept. To any expat other than someone personally concerned that their mail is delivered to the correct address, these Siamese siblings are essentially the same neighbourhood.

OUTER DISTRICTS AND BEYOND

Beyond these key expat locations, there are 14 other districts and counties, all sparsely populated by foreign residents. These are the suburban and rural areas of the greater Beijing municipality, and they are home to working-class locals, apple orchards, mines, gargantuan wholesale markets, and the Great Wall. Transport to many of these areas is still highly limited, and the odd expat who does decide to sign a lease in one of them could well be an artist seeking estrangement from a city existence or a budding sinologist desiring complete and uninterrupted immersion into Chinese life.

Undoubtedly this isn't always going to be the case. Current developments in infrastructure and industry in Tongzhou, Yizhuang in Daxing, and Changping, for instance, already mean that foreigners will increasingly be needed outside the typical expat habitats. For now, however, these districts are primarily an expat's playground—offering places to hike, rock climb, ski, kayak, or enjoy a round of paintball.

DONGCHENG

As a whole, Dongcheng is possibly the most interesting district of Beijing. When historic sites were being dished out, it gobbled them up greedily, nabbing such places as the Forbidden City, Tian'anmen Square, the Lama Temple, and many, many more. For more than 700 years it has been home to emperors and modern-day politicians, so it's continually under the careful scrutiny. Today, there is a constant energy to both preserve it and modernize it.

From the time of the Yuan dynasty, in 1271, through the Ming dynasty and finally to the Qing dynasty, Dongcheng was a central part of Beijing life. Over that time, it made up the northeast quadrant of the city's core, with Chongwen District below it in the southeast, Xicheng in the northwest, and Xuanwumen in the southwest. In July 2010, Dongcheng absorbed Chongwen, garnering even more places of interest, including Tiantan Park and the beautiful Longtan Park. Chongwen, like its western stablemate, Xuanwumen, had historically been a district for the poor, and in the thriving modern Beijing it was still dragging behind. Both of these smaller districts merged with their wealthier northern neighbors in a plan to distribute government funds more equally and so foster their development. For this reason the various areas of southern Dongcheng rarely come up as suggestions for incoming expats, but should definitely

© SHANNON AITKEN

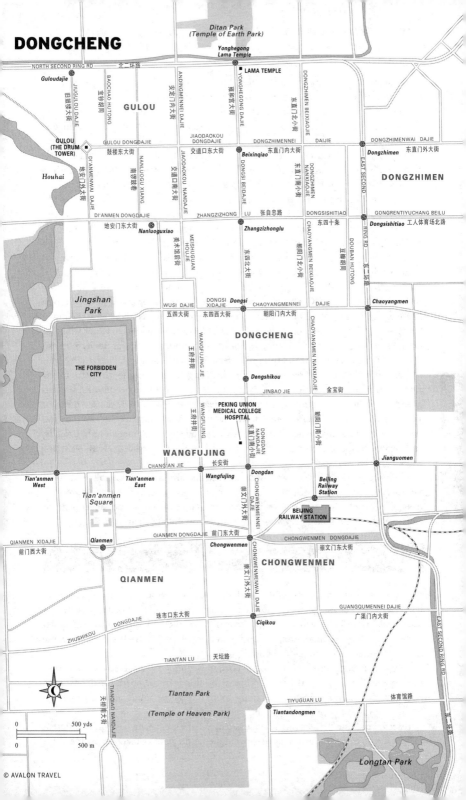

be considered as potential places to live. Rents there are still comparably lower, and infrastructure and shopping are improving at ballistic rates.

Despite Dongcheng's treasure chest of history, it's also a major center of modern business, retail, and politics. Perhaps nowhere else in the city has such a mélange of old and new, feisty high-rises flush against humble *hútòng* (alleyways) of traditional single-story houses. Come-as-you-are bars sit minutes from exclusive, members-only clubs, and while you won't see them walking the streets, many of China's celebrities also proudly lay their hats in some of the district's luxury apartment complexes.

One of the key features of this district is its convenience. Even if work is somewhere else in the city, Dongcheng is so central and the public transport so accessible that you can usually get to most places within the Third Ring Road within 30 to 40 minutes. While there are several preschools to choose from in the district, there isn't a high concentration of schools for older kids. Most kids will need to travel to Chaoyang or Shunyi, which can take as little as 15 minutes if they go to the Sanlitun campus of the British School of Beijing; 30 minutes if they head down or over to Beijing City International School (BCIS) in Shuangjing; or an hour if they travel up to Western Academy of Beijing (WAB) in Shunyi. Most of these schools generally have their own buses, so transport is unlikely to be a problem. University students may not find it as ideal, however, given that the commute from here to most of the major universities can take 45-60 minutes each way, typically in very crowded subways.

Generally the expats who do enjoy living in Dongcheng are those who want to feel a connection to and have interaction with the local culture and people, and yet also have modern facilities at their fingertips. It's ideal for those who love relaxed meals or a beer after work, live music, and eclectic shopping. You also can't, however, be too averse to the occasional (read: frequent) hawking and spitting, pungent public toilets, and general hustle and bustle. You're in the thick of it here, and it has it all—sophisticated and pedestrian.

There are relatively fewer family-style apartments, international schools, and facilities than in Chaoyang or Shunyi, but they are definitely here, and it is also a wonderfully safe part of town. If you have the means for one of the high-grade apartments or a private courtyard house *sìhéyuàn*), then your kids will have their own place to play.

Lay of the Land

Dongcheng covers an area of about 42 square kilometers. About 1 million people live here, and wherever you go, there's no real escaping that fact. On the plus side, a favorite feature of the area is its labyrinthine *hútòng* (narrow alleyways) and their traditional Beijing houses—low, single-story buildings. When you find yourself among these, life seems less intense and more neighborly.

Dongcheng basically covers the eastern half of Beijing's inner core, confined within the city's central axis and the East Second Ring Road. In the north it extends up to peek over the Third Ring Road, and in the south it hugs the South Second Ring Road but then spills out of this boundary below Tiantan Park.

Bisected by Line 5, the east and west partitions of Dongcheng have quite different feels. On the east, Dongzhimen, Chaoyangmen, and Jianguomen are businesslike.

Beijing's *hútòng* are full of tiny restaurants, bars, shops, hotels, and homes.

© SHANNON AITKEN

PRIME LIVING LOCATIONS

Two of Beijing's three embassy areas lie to the north and south of these areas, attracting a colorful array of expats and office workers to the surrounding apartments. In the northwest, from Lama Temple over to Gulou, ancient *hútòng* have been revitalized and are filled with an ever-increasing number of small Western-style boutiques, restaurants, bars, and Westerners seeking a taste of the *hútòng* life. South of here, from Dongsi down to Wangfujing, there are fewer foreign faces, but the diverse mix of Chinese here can be astounding. In some smaller, older apartments, young locals flatshare with two or three friends to a room, while down the road on Jinbao Jie, China's obscenely wealthy doll out their spare change on Lamborghinis, Bentleys, and Ferraris. Finally, crossing Chang'an Jie into the south, the character changes again. These days it's filled with Beijing's working class. Most of the old *hútòng* structures have been torn down and replaced by less-interesting high-density housing. There are fewer obvious expat enclaves, but the shopping is surprisingly good and there are two large parks to exercise and relax in.

EXPAT RESOURCES
Religious Services
There are several religious services in the area, covering various religions. For Islam, there is Dongsi Mosque. This ancient building was built in 1356 and rebuilt in 1447. It's just a couple of minutes' walk from Dongsi subway station, exit D.

Protestants can attend Chongwenmen Church, one of the biggest Protestant churches in the city, and an easy walking distance from exit B of Chongwenmen subway station. The services are in Chinese, but with English interpretation. Providing Chinese-only services, Zhushikou Church is located just near Qianmen, and Kuanjie Church is just near the south end of Nanluoguxiang on Jixiang Hutong. For English services, head to Haidian Christian Church.

Roman Catholics can visit St. Joseph's (also known as Wangfujing Church or East

Cathedral). An impressive building from the 1600s and renovated in 2000, it's not hard to miss as you walk up Wangfujing Dajie. Services are in Chinese and Latin, and in English on Sunday at 4pm. Alternatively, there's the beautiful St. Michael's Church (Dongjiao Minxiang), which is an easy walk west from exit A of Chongwenmen subway station. Services in Chinese, Latin, and Korean.

Those of the Jewish faith will need to travel over to Chaoyang to services at Capital Mansion.

Socializing and Networking

Happy hours are a great way to gel with your local community, and Dongcheng has quite a few that are sure to create strong bonds. Places to make your regulars include the Drum and Bell (across from the square between the Drum and Bell towers), which offers all-you-can-drink for ¥50 3pm-6pm on Sunday. Mao Mao Chong (on Banchang Hutong off the east side of Nanluogu Xiang) also frequently runs its own specials. Other bars prone to specials and worth warming a seat in include Great Leap Brewing, off Nanluogu Xiang (www.greatleapbrewing.com—you'll need to study the directions before trying to get here); Alba, on Gulou Dongdajie; Salud and 12sqm Bar, both on Nanluogu Xiang; and then Modernista, a stroll away on Baochao Hutong.

Fashion Exchange, held once a month, is a fun way to meet other people; groups meet to chat and swap items of clothing. Unwanted items left at the end of the gathering are donated to charity. The same group runs a local monthly support group called Life Changing. The group is a platform to address feelings of isolation, depression, anxiety, or other important issues in your life. Contact Stacey via lyflyshine@hotmail.com for either group.

While Dongdan Park, just south of Dandan subway station, is a noted gay meet-up point, those from the LGBT community who'd like to meet in a drinking environment can go to KTV spot Beijing Tenbar, set in Aihua Hotel northeast of Tiantan Park.

Salud, on Nanluogu Xiang, is often a good place to hear some lively music.

© SHANNON AITKEN

Naga Club is the place for lesbians on Friday and Saturday nights; and Seven Colors, up on Andingmenwai Dajie, is the place to sing, do a little disco, and be entertained.

Sports and Recreation
Sports (and drinking) enthusiasts will find support via Mashup Sport & Social (mashupasia.com). The group organizes a wide variety of league competitions, such as dodgeball, which runs at Dongsi Olympic Community Sports Culture Center near Chaoyangmen station, and coed and men's flag football, which is held at Ditan Sports Stadium, just north of the Andingmen subway station.

As for gyms, if you're willing to foot the typically RMB20,000-plus annual fee, most five-star hotels in the area will allow you access to their superb facilities and swimming pools, but other than that, there are many Western-style gyms around the city. Memberships range RMB2,000-8,000 per year. Some of the popular ones in Dongcheng include Powerhouse Gym, inside Ginza Mall at Dongzhimen; Amrita Fitness in the Swisshotel at Dongsishitiao subway station (exit C); Alexander Health Club in MOMA; and the very affordable East Gate Plaza Fitness Center, on Dongzhong Jie around the corner from Ginza Mall, which has its own basketball and squash courts. There are plenty of local Chinese gyms, too, and if you're happy with these, you'll be able to keep in shape for around RMB500, give or take, per year.

Where to Live

DONGZHIMEN TO JIANGUOMEN
Despite the Forbidden City being the official center of the city, to an expat living in this area, this feels like the city center. Almost everything is within an easy distance, and work and play can usually be juggled without spending too much time on the road.

Housing
Housing in this sector of Dongcheng is generally reliable and quite diverse, although it's also relatively expensive. Local communities, such as Min'an Xiaoqu and those around Douban Hutong and Nanmencang Hutong, range from around RMB4,500 for a one-bedroom up to RMB8,000 for a three-bedroom. Mid-tier apartments, such as East Lake, Season's Park, MOMA, and Beijing INN, are expat hot spots and are family friendly. Rents here average RMB6,000/month up to RMB28,000/month. For Western-style luxury accommodations, options include Embassy House, NAGA, and the newer Dangdai MOMA (complete with its own full-scale public cinema complex), which will easily set you back RMB38,000-plus a month. If you'd like to buy, properties go for around RMB30,000-50,000 per square meter. So that's about RMB1,500,000 (US$237,000) for a 50-square-meter (538-square-foot) studio up to RMB5,800,000 (US$917,400) for a 128-square-meter (1,378-square-foot), two-bedroom apartment. Apartments in the MOMA complexes average around RMB40,000 to RMB50,000 per square meter, with apartments ranging from around 80 square meters to about 350 square meters in size.

Education

Given its proximity to the diplomatic areas, it's no surprise that this area is scattered with several educational facilities. For youngsters, there's the Gymboree music and play center in Ginza Mall. MOMA Kids International Kindergarten takes kids up to six years old, whether you live in MOMA or not (although it's cheaper if you do). MOMA is also the place for kids, aged 8-12, to do Zumba classes, courtesy of ZumbAtomic. Ivy Academy has an English-language preschool and kindergarten campus in the East Lakes community. Then for older kids there is Beijing No. 55 Middle School and High School. More local than global, it does have an international department, and reports to bring students up to standards that will allow them to get into universities back in their own country. It's a popular choice for parents wanting their kids to have a more authentic Chinese education than what they would get in the fully international schools.

For adults, there is the Culture Yard as well as The Hutong. With both these educational gems in your hood, there's no excuse for not getting into your community and Beijing life. If you'd like to expand your knowledge of acupuncture, there's the China Beijing International Acupuncture Training Center. Mandarin schools in the area include That's Mandarin, Frontiers, and Rosefinch Mandarin.

Shopping and Dining

There's no shortage of department store shopping in this area of town. Dongzhimen alone has three major malls—Ginza, Guoson, and Raffles City—which all sit around the subway station. About two kilometers down the road is yet another major addition

looking from Dongzhimen subway station and bus station over to Raffles City

to the area, Galaxy SOHO, designed by architectural firm Zaha Hadid. At the time of writing, Galaxy was still a few months from completion, but given the SOHO empire's history in Beijing, and particularly with a name like Zaha Hadid attached to it, this one is bound to be occupied by a cosmopolitan collection of retail outlets, cafés, restaurants, and bars. If you're farther south, Cofco Plaza, a much older complex just past Chang'an Jie, can provide you with luxury homeware and clothing.

For grocery shopping, Ginza Mall and Raffles City both have well-stocked, though rudely overpriced, supermarkets. Ginza Mall also has Green dot dot, a supplier of organic nuts, snacks, and other ingredients. Just across the road at East Lake Villa, there is a Jenny Lou's international supermarket together with a Comptoirs de France Bakery, which sells good quality Western-style bread and all sorts of sinful indulgences. There is also a much bigger, much newer Jenny Lou's just down off Xinzhong Jie on the east side of Season's Park. If you're closer to Jiangguomen or Chaoyangmen, visit Chaonei Nanxiaojie Vegetable Market for fresh fruit, vegetables, and meat. It's on Chaonei Nanxiaojie, about halfway between Chaoyangmennei Daijie and Jinbao Jie.

Pharmacies selling Western medications are scarce in the immediate vicinity, but you are just a few minutes from the International SOS Beijing Clinic on Xinyuanli, which has its own pharmacy. Watsons stores exist in most shopping malls, but the most that these carry are vitamins, plasters, and personal care products. Alternatively, The Hutong offers a traditional Chinese medicine (TCM) clinic five days a week and runs frequent TCM classes.

Places of Interest
In itself, this section of town offers few particular destinations that will dramatically enhance your day. You can head to Nanxincang, the resurrected imperial granary of the Ming and Qing dynasties, to pick up a bottle of wine shop or dine at one of its quality Chinese restaurants, including one of the city's favorite duck restaurants, Da Dong Kao Ya.

The lesser known Tongjiao Temple and Nanguan Park can offer you a place of respite from the city. If you live in Min'an Xiaoqu, NAGA, or close to the Russian Embassy, the park makes a nice substitute backyard. You'll find it hidden away off Dongzhimen Beixiaojie, on Zhenxian Hutong. Alternatively, if you're farther south, closer to Jinbao Jie, you might find the untouristy Zhihua Temple a serene place to visit. It was built by a powerful and corrupt eunuch back in 1443 and today offers some of the most beautiful wooden architecture together with a view of the surrounding area.

Getting Around
In a district that is already highly convenient, this is the epicenter. Many places are within walking or cycling distance, and you're just a RMB10-15 cab ride away from the slick restaurants and bars of Sanlitun, or from the more bohemian nooks of Gulou. You're also right near the entry to Airport Expressway, so, in reasonable traffic, you can be at the airport in under 30 minutes, for around RMB80 in a taxi.

SUBWAY
The Dongzhimen to Jianguomen area is serviced by Lines 1, 2, 5, 6, 13, and the Airport Express. This makes it easy to travel within the Second Ring Road, but if you want to go farther afield, you'll probably need to change trains several times. This is also an intensely populated and busy part of town, so don't expect to get a seat on Lines 1, 2, and 5, even at 10 on a Sunday night. The Airport Express costs RMB25 and takes 20 minutes to get from Dongzhimen to Terminal 3, and it's far more reliable than going by road.

BUSES
The major buses worth getting to know in this area are:
• **1, 4:** If you need to get anywhere along Chang'an Jie, just jump on one of these buses.

EXPAT PROFILE: THE LOCAL FOOD SCENE

American-born Lillian Chou first visited the mainland's capital in 2008, and today, when the topic turns to food in Beijing, there are few people more qualified to lead the conversation. In her pre-Beijing life she worked as a cook, pastry chef, food show presenter, recipe developer, and food writer. Once installed in Beijing, she went on to explore the local food scene and reported her findings as food editor for *Time Out Beijing*. These days she continues to travel throughout China researching the cuisine, gives private food tours and cooking classes in Beijing, and is working on her first book.

WHAT FIRST BROUGHT YOU TO BEIJING?

I was working as a food editor for *Gourmet* magazine during the 2008 Beijing Olympics, and was working on recipes for food stories from provinces I knew little about. I'd traveled and lived in Asia for nearly eight years but had never been to mainland China. That's when I realized I needed to go, and a six-month sabbatical turned into a full-fledged move. I had no job and knew my Chinese wasn't very good and realized I needed to learn the language first. For me, Beijing offered the standard accent and was a part of China I knew very little about, so I went to study Chinese at university in Beijing.

WHAT WERE YOUR INITIAL THOUGHTS ABOUT THE FOOD SCENE WHEN YOU ARRIVED HERE, AND HOW DO YOU THINK IT HAS CHANGED SINCE?

I was so disappointed by what I saw. I thought Beijing would be a haven for excellent food and that tradition would have carried through. Instead I found the food horrible, oily, salty, and made without care. I felt Queens, New York, offered a similar range of provincial food but had nothing to compare it to. What traveling and my job as food editor for *Time Out Beijing* taught me was that my palate was very southern and very narrowed in its experience. The food of the north and imperial food overall are not written about in great detail in the West. And most of all I noticed the Chinese food in the U.S. was that of a certain genre in which good chefs were still allowed visas in the U.S., so the evolution of dishes seemed to stand still. This being Beijing, the roast duck was best reputed, but my first taste was dry and awful. Subsequent meals proved better but it took me years

24: Take a ride from Beijing Railway Station down near Chang'an Jie, directly north up to Dongzhimennei Dajie, and then over to the expat enclave in Xindong Lu.

106: A very handy bus, it can take you on a 13.1 kilometer journey from Dongzhimen station all the way down the path of Line 5 to shopping area Chongwenmen, over to Temple of Heaven Park, and finally to Beijing South Railway Station, where you can jump on an express train to Tianjin. It's a scenic route, but it can be slow, so if time is short, it can be quicker to take the subway to the train station.

107: Get yourself from Dongzhimen to Houhai via Nanluogu Xiang.

113 This useful bus passes Jiaodaokou (just to the east of Nanluogu Xiang), Dongsishitiao, the Workers' Stadium, Sanlitun, and then Guomao.

635: After passing Gulou, this bus heads past Nanluogu Xiang, Gui Jie, and Dongzhimen, over to Chunxiu Lu (embassy area), Tuanjiehu, Chaoyang Park (a major location for recreation and events), Ciyunsi (close to Yew Chung International School), and Kangjiagou (close to one of the city's favorite shopping malls, Joy City).

to learn to appreciate the subtleties of good roast duck.

WHAT DISHES DO YOU RECOMMEND PEOPLE TRY WHEN THEY FIRST GET HERE?

Beijing roast duck; noodles; Sichuan hot pot, which is unlike any hot pot I'd had before; hand-shaved noodles; Beijing's grilled foods, which are a very local specialty; the food from a selection of government provincial restaurants (not all are good, but some are excellent); imperial banquet food; *jiānbing* (a very filling bean crepe stuffed with egg and a crisp wafer), one of the more popular street foods; *lǘròubing* (a crisp bread filled with hand-sliced donkey), which is wonderful; dumplings, one of Beijing's specialties; and *mádòufu*, a hideous but delicious dish made of mung bean pulp that is unique to Beijing. Overall I would suggest experiencing a broad spectrum of foods, from humble dives to more upscale establishments.

HOW DOES FOOD IN BEIJING DIFFER FROM WHAT PEOPLE MIGHT BE USED TO OR WHAT THEY MIGHT EXPECT OF "CHINESE FOOD"?

Much of the Chinese food represented in America is like the food from the restaurant my family ran, and it was nothing like the food we eat at home. Saucy, sweet, heavily flavored dishes like egg rolls and chop suey don't exist here. The food in Beijing tends to have heavier flavors but in very different versions. For example, there is sweet and sour pork, but without the goopy bright sauce and pickled vegetables and pineapple that American versions offer. The dishes here are almost completely different from what's available in most parts of the United States and offer a very different taste of China.

WHAT ARE SOME OF YOUR FAVORITE RESTAURANTS AROUND TOWN?

I really can't answer that as things change constantly and many restaurants are inconsistent. It takes knowing what dishes are specialties. For duck, the choices are easier and well made at both Da Dong and Duck de Chine, but while other interesting establishments, such as Liqun, don't offer the best duck (in my opinion) they are in a *hútòng* (alley), thus a very special local environment. Bianyifang has a closed-oven method, producing a different type of duck, and there are many smaller local restaurants that do a good job.

915: This will get you from Dongzhimen to Shunyi, taking you via Sanyuanqiao, Lido Hotel, and 798 Art District.

LAMA TEMPLE TO GULOU

Life in the northwest of Dongcheng is about really enjoying Beijing life at its most colorful. Houses are houses, not apartments, shops are small, and there are plenty of rooftop bars and restaurants to make the most of the warmer months. That said, it's not for everyone and it does have its cons. It's dustier and dirtier; there are street noises that you'll find either endearing or repelling; and in winter, if you're in a house, you feel every day of it. Living in this neighborhood offers a quaint, romantic notion of Beijing, but you just might want to get to know it before you commit.

Housing

The overwhelming style of housing in this part of town is the *sìhéyuàn* and other varieties of single-story *hútòng* housing. There are apartments but these tend to be older-style accommodations—walk-ups some people call them. That means they have six floors, including the ground floor, and no elevator. If buildings are taller than this they usually do have elevators. The quality of the interiors in this area varies greatly. It's not uncommon to have a friend who's hit the jackpot—comparably lower rent, and furnishings by a landlord who's internationally savvy—while you look at place after place and find nothing but shabby, squatter-friendly abodes. So if you plan to move here, shop around and have patience.

The apartments north of the Second Ring Road are taller, slightly more modern. On this side expats are thin on the ground, and Western comforts less obvious. Cut off by a thick border composed of a road, a murky river, and a subway line, and stripped of its old *hútòng,* it feels very different on this side of the line than the other.

If you want to live in this part of town, you're looking at spending upwards of RMB3,000 for a one-bedroom apartment, RMB6,000-8,000 for a two-bedroom, and RMB10,000-plus for anything more. *Sìhéyuàn,* especially the restored ones, can easily go for RMB15,000 or more per month. It will be possible to find a cheaper place, but you'll probably need to be open-minded and easy going to accept the conditions and quirks.

There are not as many obvious complexes in this area, so finding an apartment typically involves days spent riding around on the back of a real estate agent's scooter as he or she takes you to an oddball array of homes.

If you are keen on moving into an established, secure community complex, there are a few to consider. Heping Xincheng (Heping New Town), just north of the Second Ring Road on Minwang Nan Hutong, has decent apartments for reasonable rents. A two-bedroom place will go for around RMB8,000 a month. There's also a veterinarian in the complex and nearby cafés and restaurants, and Lama Temple subway station is just two minutes' walk.

On the south side of the river, close to Lama Temple subway station, Yong He Villas can give a refined sense of *hútòng* life. The villas are modern and cosy, and come with a private outdoor area, which is great for kids. They are a little pricey, however (about RMB19,000 for a three-bedroom apartment), and don't have the facilities that similarly priced, large apartment complexes offer, such as a gym or pool.

One much-loved complex in the area is Noble Quadrangle (官书院, Guān Shū Yuàn). Despite its name, it's not a fancy serviced apartment block. It's actually very unpretentious but has good security and generally very solid apartments. The people who can manage to get an apartment here often say it's the best nook in town.

Purchase prices are similar here to the Dongzhimen region, but fewer properties dip below the RMB30,000 per square meter range. A 72-square-meter apartment, built in the 1980s, could set you back around RMB2,550,000 (US$403,000).

Education

Education options directly in this part of town are fairly limited. Beijing No. 1 Kindergarten Experimental Sister School, which offers a bilingual, modified version of the Chinese curriculum, can cater to kids aged three to six.

For adults, there is the Institute for Provocation, set in Heizhima Hutong, just off Nanluogu Xiang. It's a think tank and work space for visual and performing artists, architects, and designers. On the very same *hútòng,* cooking enthusiasts will find Black Sesame Kitchen, which runs a wide array of small, interactive Chinese cooking classes in a lovely traditional Beijing building.

Shopping and Dining

If you want big glitzy malls, this is not the place to be. The Global Trade Center (GTC) up near the North Third Ring Road is one of the major business hubs in the vicinity, encompassing a wide range of international brands as well as a movie cinema, gym, and spa. Most other shopping hot spots here are small, street-level, and forever mercurial. You'll be able to pick up clothes by nascent designers, quirky Chinese knickknacks, and musical instruments. Streets to spend your money in are Wudaoying Hutong, Fangjia Hutong, Gulou Dongdajie, and, of course, Nanluogu Xiang. These streets are forever growing and changing. A T-shirt store here today will be replaced by a waffle shop tomorrow, which will probably be replaced by a paper shop the day after. Nanluogu Xiang in particular can seem a little touristy, but at nighttime it's a true part of expat nightlife.

Supermarkets include locals Jingkelong (up in the north on Hepingli Beijie) and Tiankelong (on Jiaodaokou Dongdajie). A savior in the area is Chez Gérard Boucherie Francaise, a tiny provedore, located just off Guozijian Jie, which stocks everything from rib-eye and cheese to baguettes and wine. For a large range of fresh produce, try the Jiaodaokou Chaonei Vegetable Market.

Chinese pharmaceutical needs may be met at Tongrentang branch at number 6 on Hepingli Zhongjie, but for Western meds, your best bet is to head over to the International SOS Clinic in Chaoyang.

© SHANNON AITKEN

Boucherie Francaise stocks butchered meat and Western produce.

Places of Interest

There is such an eclectic mix of interesting places here that it's hard to imagine ever feeling bored. For music there are two of Beijing's hottest live music venues, Yugong Yishan and Mao Livehouse. Both places bring in quality international and local acts. There is a good scattering of bars, most within walking distance of each other, so barhopping is almost standard, and in the warmer months, most of them open up their rooftop decks.

This is not really the area for haute cuisine, but there are numerous cafés, such as long-time favorite Vineyard Café. Jiugulou Dajie, on the west side of the Drum Tower, is a great street to wander along and just choose a

© SHANNON AITKEN

Café Zarah is a favorite spot for many expats and their laptops.

restaurant at random. It's packed with a wide variety of fun eateries, with cuisines that include Yunnan, Vietnamese, Italian, and Malaysian. Alternatively, Café Zarah often exhibits art on its walls and is a popular place for to combine laptop work and coffee, as is Alba, a few doors down.

If getting outdoors is more what you're after, then this sector of the city has a variety of parks—particularly on the north side. The beautiful Liuyin and Qingnianhu Parks are here, as is Ditan Park (Temple of the Earth Park), one of the four historic sacrificial parks in the city (the others being Tiantan Park (Temple of Heaven Park) in the south, Ritan Park (Temple of the Sun Park) in the east, and Yuetan Park (Temple of the Moon Park) in the west. Ditan Park is a pretty place to wander and stretch, but it's also the site for many large-scale events.

If your inner tourist still thirsts for more historic sites, you'll also find yourself within easy distance from some classic structures. The Drum and Bell Towers (Gulou and Zhonglou), which sit side by side along the northern axis of the city, were originally places of ancient Chinese music and then became the timepieces of the Yuan, Ming, and Qing dynasties. Today they're very much tourist attractions, yet they have become such centerpieces of the immediate area that they define its character and feel.

East of the towers, on Guozijian Jie, is Confucius Temple. Initially built in 1302, it was once the imperial academy of ancient Beijing and the place in which intellectuals of the Yuan, Ming, and Qing dynasties offered their respects to Confucius. Today it's become a museum piece, and tourists come here by the busload. September is the best time to wander over, as it's the time they celebrate Confucius's birthday with music and dance.

And then, a block east, literally above Lama Temple subway station, is Lama Temple (Yonghegong) itself. The Lama Temple is also definitely a tourist attraction, but it remains a working Buddhist temple and monastery. In fact, it's one of the largest and most important Tibetan Buddhist monasteries in the world, and thousands of Chinese come here to pray. When your own family comes to visit, it's well worth taking them here. The architecture and artwork is magnificent and well maintained, and, unlike the Forbidden City, a visit here is extremely manageable and won't frazzle your guests with compressive crowds or hours of walking.

Living in the vicinity of the Lama Temple is sure to embed in your mind long-term memories of your Beijing home, which will come flooding back every time you smell incense. In the streets around the temple, vendors sell bundles of fragrant incense and the air is never without the scent of it.

Getting Around
This area is a great base from which to jump on the expressways, be it to get out to the Great Wall, the airport, or the 798 Art District. Though these places seem a good distance away, the roads out to them are good. You can be at Lido or 798 in 15 minutes, and the airport in 30. Unfortunately, it's getting to closer places, such as Sanlitun or the CBD, that can be a headache. Unlike the major roads on the periphery, the internal roads are narrow and seasoned heavily with traffic lights, so road traffic is constantly in a frustrating squeeze. During rush hour it can easily take an excruciating 45 minutes to make the 5-kilometer trip from Nanluogu Xiang to Sanlitun. So on a day-to-day basis, bicycles are a must—not only do they let you bypass the stalled road traffic, there's also nothing like pedaling through the *hútòng* or picking up some fresh produce from your local store and popping it in your basket. For social activities, everything is close enough that you can often forgo transport all together and just walk there, and at night, when everyone else is fighting for a cab, it's a relief to be able to stroll home.

SUBWAY
The Lama Temple to Gulou area is serviced by Lines 1, 2, 5, and 8, and few locations require anything longer than a 15-minute walk to get to a subway station. Thanks to the new Line 6, it's now much more straightforward to get to Haidian and its universities in the west, and much faster to get out to such locations as Chaoyang Park, Yew Chung International School, and Beijing Wuzi University in the east. The new Line 8 extension also transports you from the National Art Museum of China up to the Olympic area in the north and beyond.

BUSES
60: Take this bus to get back and forth between Gulou or Nanluogu Xiang and Wangfujing.

113: This super bus is worth keeping in mind. It will take you from the north along Andingmenwai Dajie, passing Liuyin and Qingnianhu Parks, down to Andingmen subway station, past music spot Yugong Yishan, over to the Workers' Stadium and Sanlitun, then all the way down the East Third Ring through the CBD to Guomao.

635: Take this bus to get from Gulou to Dongzhimen to Chaoyang Park.

701: If you need to visit Ikea, or are working or studying up in Wangjing, then this bus is for you. Get on at the south end of Nanluogu Xiang or Zhangzizhonglu, after which you'll pass the Workers' Stadium and Sanlitun before heading north to Beijing's only Ikea store (a little walk needed) and then Wangjing.

758: Starting from north beyond the Olympic area, this bus travels down

Andingmenwai Dajie to Ditan Park and Andingmen, then heads east at Zhangzizhonglu. From here it continues to the Workers' Stadium, Sanlitun, and Chaoyang Park.

DONGSI TO WANGFUJING

This is a culturally proud piece of Beijing. Not only is it home to the Forbidden City and Tian'anmen Square, it's also the burning hot spot for China's wealthy. Many expats can be found working here in the office buildings of Oriental Plaza at Wangfujing and browsing in its seemingly endless shopping malls. Socially, it feels a little disconnected or patchy. A night out here is usually bound to a single destination, so once dinner is over, for example, most expats jump in a taxi and head back to Sanlitun or Gulou for drinks.

Housing

Housing is almost polarized in this area—very local, or very modern and expensive. Around Dongsi prices are still similar to Dongzhimen and Gulou, but the closer you get to Wangfujing, the higher the prices rise. Expect to pay around RMB10,000 per month for a two-bedroom place, and RMB50,000 per month for a four-bedroom place. You should, however, also expect that you're getting high-quality apartments with modern facilities for these prices. Local apartments will almost definitely not have ovens, and will quite likely have Chinese-style fixtures, such as squat toilets. There aren't many long-term serviced apartments in the area; however, the Tower Apartments at Oriental Plaza are a good option. They're smack-dab in the heart of the area and are serviced by English-speaking staff. They do have facilities for kids, but as most guests staying here are businesspeople, your little ones might find themselves playing alone. For long-term accommodations, rates are approximately RMB18,000 for a one-bedroom apartment and RMB26,000 for a two-bedroom apartment.

Not the cheapest place to buy property, this area's housing requires an outlay of almost no less than RMB40,000 and beyond RMB70,000 per square meter. If you have dreams of owning a beautiful *sihéyuàn*, get ready to spend the equivalent of US$4 million or more.

Education

There's not much here for young English speakers, but adults will be able to access a few institutions. Cheung Kong Graduate School of Business (CKGSB), China's first private business school, is located at Wangfujing, and offers various MBA programs tailored to helping you understand the Chinese market. For more relaxed mind expansion, the Hutong Cuisine Cooking School, just off Dongsi Nandajie, will get you cooking dumplings and other traditional Chinese dishes. If you can speak Mandarin, then the Central Academy of Drama on Nanluogu Xiang is the place to ply your acting abilities.

Shopping and Dining

There are few places in the city with such a high concentration of major shopping venues, particularly down around Dongdan and Wangfujing. The star shopping spot right here is Oriental Plaza. It has a huge variety of international brands, both everyday and luxury. If that's not enough, just meters away you can try Beijing APM, home to

Beijing's flagship Gap store, and Intime Lotte. Two of Beijing's largest bookshops are also on this strip, the Foreign Languages Bookshop and the gargantuan Wangfujing Bookstore. Though the latter may seem a little intimidating and anti-foreigner, upstairs it has a generous selection of English-language novels and one of the most extensive ranges of textbooks for learning Mandarin. If this is their hood, expect your kids to nag you for regular trips to the New China Children's Store. It not only has strollers, cribs, bikes, and dolls galore, it also has a play area the kids will love.

On the east side of Wangfujing, Jinbao Jie is the place to spend big. "Elite" is the typical description of the clientele that haunt this manufactured street of wealth. Shopping mall Jinbao Place is filled with such names as Bottega Veneta and Gucci. Down the street, Aston Martin, Lamborghini, Bentley, Ferrari, Maserati, and Rolls Royce have all set up lucrative shops. It is a good street for Chinese fine dining, however. The Jinbao Place branch of Da Dong Kao Ya is a crowd pleaser, and the elegant Duck de Chine at 19492 is absolutely beautiful, and serves a great dim sum as well as delicious roast duck.

If bohemian is more your style, it's worth taking a stroll up Dongsi Beidajie, between Dongsi and Zhangzizhonglu subway stations. The clothing here is hit and miss, but there are eclectic shops and an ever-increasing range of new local designers setting up shop.

If you need art supplies, specialty shops are around the National Art Museum of China (Zhongguo Meishu Guan) on Wusi Dajie.

For supermarket shopping, those close to the Forbidden City can take advantage of local chain Tiankelong. If you're by Dongsi subway station, the three-story Wu Mart has everything from rice cookers to bread, but international products are few and organic products nonexistent. Oriental Plaza at Wangfujing has an Olé supermarket, which, though pricey, has a reasonably good supply of international and organic products. Specialty store Yipin Chuwei Baking Shop stocks Western baking favorites, including Madagascan vanilla pods (cheaper than at Jenny Lou's and April Gourmet), leaf gelatin, and Valrhona and Callebaut cooking chocolate. This is extremely hard to find as it's not really a shop but a tucked-away *píngfáng*, and the main source of business is via website Taobao. The owner isn't always there, so call ahead first. She doesn't speak English, so you might need to call on your translation friends for help. For cookware, pick up woks and other basic Chinese items from Xingsheng Yu Ri Yong Equipment on Dongsi Beidajie, just south of Beixinqiao subway station.

If pain strikes, there aren't many pharmacies in the area offering Western remedies. You do, however, have easy access to Wangfujing Drug Store, one of the bigger Chinese pharmacies, which stocks international prescription and over-the-counter medicines. A few doors down is another Western-medicine friendly chain, Golden Elephant Pharmacy. There are many branches of this store around the city—just look for the golden elephant logo.

Places of Interest

For a dose of pop culture and escapism, there are plenty of movie cinemas in this part of town. Beijing Changhong Cinema will suit those close to Dongsi, while those closer to Wangfujing can choose from the cinemas in Jinbao Palace, Beijing APM, and Oriental Plaza.

For a bit of outdoor meditation, your local parks are Zhongshan Park, to the left of the main entrance of the Forbidden City, and Changpuhe Park, a tiny but pretty strip of a park at the southeast side of the Forbidden City.

If your kids are learning Chinese—or, unlike you, are already having fluent conversations in it—then they might enjoy visits to the China Children's Art Theatre, just northwest of Dongdan subway station on Dong'anmen Dajie. While the plays and musicals presented are in Chinese, the stories are often Western classics, such as *Snow White and the Seven Dwarves,* and *A Journey with Hans Christian Andersen.* The Ma Lan Hua Art School, attached to the theater, offers acting and dance classes for children aged five to 12.

From a tourism perspective, your guests will think you live in the most convenient spot possible. Within easy walking distance, you have Jingshan Park, the Forbidden City, and Tian'anmen Square. There's also Wangfujing Paleolithic Museum, which is interesting, whether you are a tourist or not. When workers were digging up the site for Oriental Plaza, they uncovered the relics of several 25,000-year-old Chinese ancestors. You'll find the museum in the passageway from Wangfujing subway station up into the mall.

Getting Around

While everything is close at hand in this part of town, the downside is that there are no smooth-flowing arterial roads. You're really burying yourself in the heart of the city here. So unless you're willing to take the subway, you could be committing yourself to a lot of time personal time with your cab driver. In an ideal condition, let's say at 3am or during Spring Festival when the city virtually empties out, you're just a 10-minute drive from the CBD, 10 to 15 minutes from Sanlitun, and around 20 minutes from Beijing United Family Hospital, the major international hospital in the city. Put realistic traffic conditions into the picture, and those times double or even triple. The upside is that despite these times, if you do insist on cabbing it to work in the CBD, your 50-minute cab ride is still likely to cost you only about RMB30.

SUBWAY

Living here, you can take advantage of Lines 1, 2, 5, 6 and part of 8. The south section of Line 8, which will connect the National Art Museum of China to Daxing in the far south, is still under construction and won't be rolling until around 2015. Be warned that Line 1 is the most congested subway line in the entire city. During rush hour, keep luggage to a minimum, do not relax and unfold your newspaper, and do not expect anyone to stand aside. Just send a word of thanks to your deity of choice if you actually manage to get on and off.

BUSES

1, 4: These are the buses to get anywhere along Chang'an Jie.

110: Take this bus to travel past Dongdan, Jinbao Jie, Chaoyangmenwai, digital city Buy Now (Bai Nao Hui), the east gate of the Workers' Stadium, and Sanlitun.

120: A handy bus, this connects Qianmen, Tian'anmen, the Forbidden City, Wangfujing, Jianguomen, and Guomao before turning to head north, passing close to Ritan Park, the east gate of the Workers' Stadium, Sanlitun, and then up past the International SOS Clinic.

104: To get up to the parks in the north of Dongcheng, jump on this express bus. It travels from Beijing Railway Station to Dongdan, Wangfujing, Jinbao Jie, past the National Art Museum, close to Nanluogu Xiang, and then via Andingmen subway station to pass Ditan, Qingnianhu, and Liuyin Parks.

420: This bus takes you to a host of important locations, including (from south to north) Beijing Railway Station, Wangfujing, Chaoyangmen, the Lufthansa Center, the Kempinski Hotel, Ladies' Street, the American Embassy, Lido Hotel, 798 Art District (5- to 10-minute walk needed), and Wangjing.

QIANMEN, CHONGWENMEN, AND THE SOUTH

A lesser-known part of town, at least for expats, this area is increasingly convenient and practical. If your interests are all about bar-hopping and Western cuisine, you're putting yourself at a distance from the action in the north. But if you don't mind living among the locals, with local restaurants and the like at hand, then you might enjoy living here. Chongwenmen, in particular, is taking on a decidedly international color. It's also very accessible and quick to get to from the CBD. Qianmen has a few highlights that make it interesting, but on the whole it's very Chinese. There are few Western facilities, which, if you want total immersion, is a good thing.

Housing

Things are not much cheaper in this part of town, especially when it comes to places that have standards you might feel are comfortable. Well-appointed apartments can be found around both the New World and Glory Mall shopping complexes in Chongwenmen, but expect to pay anything from RMB4,500 and up for a one-bedroom place. You will be able to find places for around RMB2,500 a month, but expect terrible quality and kitchens you can't cook in.

Over toward Tiantan Park and Qianmen, rent is a little lower, with prices at around RMB4,000 for two-bedroom apartments. To find a place around here, however, you'll need to start looking at Chinese sites, such as http://58.com, rather than relying on the expat-friendly sites, such as www.thebeijinger.com, which don't really cover this region.

Apartment prices are a little lower here, particularly closer to the west. A wide variety of properties fall into the RMB22,000-30,000 range. A 90-square-meter, two-bedroom apartment, for example, may cost you around RMB2,020,000. Chongwenmen apartments are slightly higher and comparable to Dongzhimen.

Education

Educational options for expats are few and far between here in the south of Dongcheng. Youngsters aged 18 months to six years can attend Etonkids Bilingual Kindergarten, Midtown Campus. It's at Guangqumen, only a 10-minute drive from Jianguomen and Guomao. The campus features a bilingual Montessori curriculum, taught by bilingual teachers.

Golden International Dancing Academy offers classes on tango, salsa, rumba, belly dance, waltz, jazz dance, hip hop, waltz, and flamenco for both children and adults.

Shopping and Dining

This area might be lacking the elegance of its northern neighbors, but it definitely has a few shopping options. Glory Mall, just south of Chongwenmen subway station, has the usual brands that seem to clutter all shopping malls in Beijing, but it also has a few additional shops of interest, including Muji, H&M, and Calvin Klein. Other nearby malls include the large New World Shopping Centre, across the road, and Soshow to the south.

Hong Qiao Market (also known as the Pearl Market) sits at the east side of Tiantan Park. It sells the usual collection of clothing, shoes, and electronics found in other similar markets, but its big thing is jewelry—with pearls, coral, turquoise, amber, semiprecious stones, beads, and more. Bargain hard, especially if you're bulk buying, and feel free to have vendors custom-make a design for you. Above all, avoid the weekend if possible. Don't just rely on the main building here—there are lots of interesting shops in the immediate vicinity on the east side of the market (away from Tiantan Park). One such place is the Tian Le Toy Market. You won't find a great range of big-name toy brands that you'd get back home, but there is no shortage of cheap stuffed animals, dolls, remote-controlled cars, puzzles, kites, costumes, and art and craft supplies (upstairs).

A block farther east from here is Beijing's famous "sports street." Clustered between Tiyuguan Lu and Tiyuguan Xilu are shops selling all manner of sportswear and sports equipment. Don't be afraid to bargain.

Some tourist information sites might try to send you to the revitalized Qianmen Jie, which sits at the south end of Tian'anmen Square. Sure, go for a look, but don't go expecting sensational shopping. The buildings have been beautifully restored here to reflect the ancient pedestrian street of Beijing, but what fills them can be summarized as junk. Halfway down the street is an offshoot called Dashilan. This is also a tourist trap, but the farther in you go, the more interesting it gets, and it's a fun place to go to at night for street food and local cuisine. For a really special way to dine, try Capital M at the north end of Qianmen Jie. This will be the place you come to when you yearn for a weekend morning brunch, or for when you need a romantic night out.

For groceries, head to Carrefour on Guangqumennei Daijie, just east of Ciqikou subway station. Like all the Carrefour supermarkets, this monster has stress-inducing weekend crowds, reasonable prices, and a good range of imported goods—for far less than what you'll pay in one of the international supermarkets. There's also a big collection of Wu Marts close by, including by the subway at Tiantan Dongmen and just north of Longtan Park. If you're near Chongwenmen, you'll never go hungry, with major supermarkets in both Glory Mall and New World Department Store. The popular Chongwenmen Vegetable Market used to be in the area, but now it's nudged over into Chaoyang district, sitting at number 1 Guangqumenwai Daijie, but it's still worth a visit if you live close by.

Western-style pharmacies are farther from reach here. Wangfujing Drug Store is your closest bet, otherwise there are various local options, including a Tongrentang store just west of Ciqikou subway station on Zhushikou Dongdajie and a Golden Elephant Pharmacy in New World Department Store at Chongwenmen.

© SHANNON AITKEN

Dashilan is a popular place for tourists, but has a multitude of restaurants that attract locals, too.

PRIME LIVING LOCATIONS

Places of Interest

This neighborhood has a mixture of interesting features. Historic sites include Tiantan Park (Temple of Heaven Park) and Yongdingmen, the southern gate of the city's axis—although this latter structure is not the original (which was demolished in 1957), but a restoration constructed in 2004.

Inside Tiantan Park, various buildings draw in the tourists, religious structures used by the emperors of the Ming and Qing dynasties to pray to heaven for bumper crops. As a resident, however, you'll also find this park a satisfying place in which to wander and do modest exercise. It's pleasant for strolls and badminton.

To the east, Longtan Lake Park, being much more for the people, is more a place for genuine fitness. It's one of the few places in town to have a soft running track, and there are various public exercise machines. Kids will also have fun on the play equipment. There is a rock climbing wall, but this has sadly fallen into disuse.

Adults and kids can enjoy ice skating at New World Champion Skating Rink in Beijing New World Shopping Mall south of Chongwenmen station. This is one of the bigger skating rinks in the city and it's a family-friendly venue.

Other entertainment options include Show Max Multiplex Cinema, in Soshow shopping center, and Glory Mall Broadway Cinema just up the street. Both play Chinese and foreign films, and occasionally Chinese movies with English subtitles.

For more mentally engaging places, head to the Beijing Planning Exhibition Hall, just southeast of Tian'anmen Square. It's well worth making a trip here when you first move to Beijing to orientate yourself to the city. It features a highly detailed 302-square-meter model of the entire city and shows how the city looked in the past as well as how it might evolve into the year 2020. Legation Quarter (also known as Ch'ien Men 23), at one time the site of the American Legation, is a place for fine dining and occasional jazz events. Venues have come and gone from inside this handsome complex, but the

PRIME LIVING LOCATIONS

© SHANNON AITKEN

the restored Qianmen Jie, with Qianmen Gate in the background

highly awarded French restaurant Maison Boulud by Daniel Boulud and the Italian Ristaurante Sadler by chef Claudio Sadler have become Beijing classics, and provide you with impressive places to treat your guests. Complete the night with a show over at the Paul Andreu-designed National Centre for the Performing Arts (NCPA), which sits on the western side of Tian'anmen Square (although this is technically in Xicheng district). Red Gate Gallery, by the Dongbianmen Watchtower on Chongwenmen Dongdajie, is a leading local art gallery and well worth regular visits.

Getting Around

This is a densely populated part of town, so getting around can be a little tedious. Rapidly improving infrastructure is, however, making a difference. If you choose to cab it, expect to spend around RMB15 to get to Wangfujing, RMB20 to get to the CBD, and RMB30 to get to Sanlitun.

SUBWAY AND TRAINS

Currently the subway coverage here is patchy, but in one to two years, when Line 7 and the southern end of Line 8 are up and running, things will be noticeably better. As things stand now, you'll be limited to Lines 1, 2, and 5. These are, however, extremely useful and can have you at Wangfujing in a few minutes, to Guomao in 5-15 (depending on if you need to change lines or not), and to Sanlitun in around 30. Realistically you would need to allow 50-60 minutes to get to the airport, given the number of interchanges required.

Beijing Railway Station is also in the south Dongcheng region. Complete with its own subway station at the southeast corner of Line 2, it is typically the starting point for trains to Dongbei (including Harbin, Shenyang, and Dalian), Shandong (including Qingdao, Jinan), Shanghai, Nanjing, and Hangzhou, as well Inner and Outer Mongolia.

BUSES

A few of the key buses in the neighborhood include:

60: This bus passes Longtan Park and heads east to Tiantan Park and then up to Chongwenmen subway station, where you can transfer to Line 1 or Line 2 on the subway. Keep going and pass the Forbidden City, Nanluogu Xiang, Gulou, eat street Jiugulou Dajie, and finally Gulou subway station.

110: This route passes Tiantan Park, Chongwenmen subway station, Wangfujing, Chaoyang Hospital, the east gate of the Workers' Stadium, the Canadian Embassy, and the International SOS Clinic.

707: Another handy route, this bus can take you to Tiantan Park, over to Jinsong subway station on Line 10, and then all the way up the Third Ring Road, including Shuangjing and Guomao stations. It heads east at the Lufthansa Center and then past the U.S. Embassy to Lido and Wangjing.

XICHENG

Xicheng district, which makes up the western chamber of the city's heart, isn't always the obvious choice for newcomers to Beijing. It lacks many of the expat staples, such as supermarkets dedicated to stocking Western pantries, and bars and restaurants that cater specifically to foreign palates. But in that, it has its own charm. There is perhaps no other district in the city that has such a mixture of purposes and character.

In ancient times Xicheng's northern aspect (the area above Chang'an Jie) was home to the city's aristocrats, and the manmade lakes and parks around the Forbidden City were the exclusive playgrounds of the royals. Things are not entirely different today. Zhongnanhai (中南海), which you'll see on a map as the two lakes immediately west of the Forbidden City, is set off solely for the government. The lake's surrounding high-security buildings are the central headquarters of the Communist Party, and are what is sometimes referred to as China's Kremlin. The nearby *hútòng* (alleyways) and their *sìhéyuàn*—the Chinese equivalent of the American dream—are also once again becoming the homes of Beijing's moneyed. While the poor struggle to keep a grip on their inner-city homes, the rich are moving in, restoring and gentrifying the ancient buildings, and adding a few modern touches, such as private underground garages and luxury SUVs.

Zhongnanhai aside, Xicheng still boasts ample parks and waterways that the public

© SHANNON AITKEN

can access, including Beihai Park and Shichahai—the latter better known by its individual lake names of Qianhai (Front Sea), Houhai (Rear Sea), and Xihai (West Sea). Mind you, these are key tourist destinations, so they're not always the most tranquil.

Xicheng is also highly commercial. It has various business zones and some of the best shopping spots in the city. Whether you want to forage through wholesale clothing markets or shop for high-end couture, this is the district to come to.

Other advantages of setting yourself up in Xicheng include being able to immerse yourself in Chinese culture without really sacrificing too many comforts. Thanks to the new subway lines, the district has become extremely convenient. You'll be able to zip over to the east via Line 1, 2, or 6, and if you're anywhere along Line 4, getting to university in Haidian will be a breeze.

A final distinguishing feature of the district is its concentration of religious sites. Not only are Buddhist and Taoist temples to be found here, but it is also home to many of Beijing's most important churches and mosques.

LAY OF THE LAND

Xicheng is the second smallest district in Beijing (after Dongcheng), covering 51 square kilometers (20 square miles). This is almost twice the size it was prior to 2010, when it absorbed Xuanwumen district in the south. At the last census, taken later in the same year, the registered population in the area was 1.2 million people, making it the city's most densely populated district, with an average of 24,599 people per square kilometer. (Dongcheng came in second with 21,954 people per square kilometer.) It definitely can feel a little crowded in parts, especially at rush hour.

The district is roughly shaped by the western half of the Second Ring Road. The city's central axis through the Forbidden City and Tian'anmen Square forms its eastern border where it meets Dongcheng, and along its other borders it neighbors Fengtai, Haidian, and a smidgeon of Chaoyang.

Chang'an Jie cuts right through Xicheng's middle, giving it a belt that is heavily studded by stark and brutish government buildings. South of this, elements of the district's original character have long been flattened by bulldozers and replaced by stock standard local apartment compounds. There is little in this south half that will draw you to it on a regular basis. Muslim people may be the exception.

North of Chang'an Jie, the district morphs through more styles. Financial Street, Jinrong Jie (金融街), is perhaps the area's most glamorous strip. Located here are the head offices of many of China's Fortune 500 hundred companies, such as China Mobile and China Construction Bank. To meet the needs of its corporate tenants, a good handful of five-star hotels have set up shop. You'll also find one of the city's better storehouses of international fashion, Lane Crawford, nearby. A little east, between here and Tian'anmen, is Xidan, another important shopping neighborhood.

Farther north, the commercial sector gives way to the *hútòng* and old-world feel of Xicheng in its heyday. The streets that tuck in around Beihai Park, Jingshan Park, and Houhai are classic Beijing, and are filled with an eclectic range of eclectically stocked local shops. For the expats who do tend to settle in Xicheng, the northern side of Houhai, closer to Gulou, is where most can be found. Finally, at its northwestern most point, Xicheng ends at Xizhimen, a somewhat frantic, dusty commercial zone and major transport hub.

© SHANNON AITKEN

Xidan Beidajie is a popular shopping strip.

Where to Live

Xicheng really is what you want it to be, and as long as you park yourself next to one of the subway stations, nothing will be far from reach. There are several centers of activity in the district, and each has a very different feel. You can go for the business appeal of Financial Street, the old-world charm of Houhai and Deshengmen, or the chaotic city launching pad of Xizhimen. One problem is that this district doesn't get the same depth of coverage that eastern districts do from the expat websites and international relocation companies, so when you do a search on those sites, you may come up with nothing. Your best bet is to walk around the area and walk in to real estate agents. Homelink (www.homelink.com.cn) and Wo Ai Wo Jia (www.5i5j.com) are two of the biggest, and there may be someone in the office who speaks English. Alternatively, try Chinese house hunting site Ganji (http://bj.ganji.com/fang1). Be warned, though; this isn't really a Western zone, but it is the choice of Beijing's wealthy, so apartment prices are roughly on par with Dongcheng and Sanlitun, particularly for anywhere north of Chang'an Jie.

XIZHIMEN

You know you're in Xizhimen when you can see the iconic arching towers of CapitaLand Mall (凯德MALL), a bounteous shopping plaza that sits atop Xizhimen subway station (Lines 2, 4, and 13) and next to Beijing North Railway Station. Most activity in the area happens right here at this transport node. There are Western fast-food chains, a good supermarket, and several cinemas—Beijing Youth Palace Cinema (www.bjqng.com.cn) and China Film Cinema (www.cfc.com.cn), which, despite the name, shows more than just local films. In itself, Xizhimen is not especially picturesque or interesting—it's all about transport. From here you can jump on the subway to get to the university areas of Zhongguancun and Wudaokou, to head east to Gulou or Dongzhimen, or south to Beijing South Railway Station. If you're prepared to cycle, the bike lane along the North Second Ring Road and the adjacent river, from Xizhimen to Dongzhimen, is a particularly smooth and pleasant ride early in the morning.

Housing

Be clear about what you're after and the amount you're willing to spend. There are premium complexes and there are downright dumps. To keep in close to the area, include searches of surrounding neighborhoods, such as Jishuitan and Xinjiekou. Haidian district cuts in very close to Xizhimen, too, so when hunting, don't disregard a search just because it seems to be in a separate district. There are several reasonable apartment complexes northwest across the river in Haidian, walking distance from Xizhimen station, including Chang He Wan (长河湾) and Diamond Waterfront (钻河公馆).

Unlike other smaller subway stations, which have apartments virtually over the top of them, Xizhimen station is surrounded by heavy roads, so walks to the station can be a little tedious. A common practice is to find something more peaceful a little farther back and ride a bicycle to the station. Expect to pay around RMB5,000-6,500 for a Chinese-style two-bedroom apartment and RMB8,000-10,000 for a larger, semi-modern apartment.

HOUHAI, DESHENGMEN, AND GULOU

Laying your hat on the west side of Houhai can sometimes feel like you're cutting yourself off from places like Sanlitun or your friends in the east, but if you keep Line 6 or bus 118 in your mind when house hunting, you may not feel so stranded. A bicycle ride from here to Sanlitun may take as little as 20 minutes, depending on your pedal power. The neighborhood is overflowing with character, and many argue that this is truly the best place in Beijing to live.

Study the area on a map. There is west Gulou, the wedge that sits between the west side of Jiugulou Dajie and Houhai. Of all of Xicheng, this is probably where you'll find the greatest concentration of residential expats. There are some fabulous old *sìhéyuàn* complexes and older-but-solid local apartments here. Transport remains hyper-convenient, and you'll have copious bars, restaurants, and live music venues right at your doorstep. I would hesitate to say that there are many establishments of actual premium standards in the area, but beer is cheap and the karaoke plentiful. On top of that, Nanluogu Xiang and Baochao Hutong are just a short walk away.

Three of the major features of the area are obviously the Drum and Bell towers and Houhai, but another important structure is Deshengmen Bridge, which sits on the Second Ring Road just north of Houhai. This was once part of the northern city wall, which progress knocked down for the Second Ring Road and Line 2 subway track. The full tower is long gone, and its ancient archery tower and barbican are all that remain. Today it is the synapse for the Ring Road and the Badaling Expressway.

Moving southwest of Houhai, Western culture makes way for Chinese. The *hútòng* are lined with mom-and-pop stores selling everything from inner soles to specialty *báijiǔ* or soy sauce. Elderly people sit out by the street on small stools and crowd around tables to play cards or *májiàng* (mahjong).

Housing

Key names to look out for when doing your search include Ping'anli, Di'anmen, Xisi, Deshengmen, and Xishiku. Go to the area and wander around looking for a real estate agent rather than relying on expat resources. A two-bedroom *píngfáng* is likely to cost around RMB13,000 per month, while a small two-bedroom Chinese-style apartment may cost RMB5,000-7,000. If you're keen to share, you should be able to find a place where you're paying RMB2,500-4,000 per month for an apartment. A luxury *sìhéyuàn* can easily go for RMB25,000 or more per month. If this is your interest, there are companies such as Four Star Realty (www.shanghome.cn), which deal primarily in these kinds of properties.

FINANCIAL STREET

Financial Street—Jinrong Dajie (金融大街)—is just what you think it sounds like—a place for making money. The street kicks off with the People's Bank of China (the central bank) and continues with more bank head offices, towering office buildings, and five-star hotels built to accommodate the incoming businesspeople. Unlike Sanyuanqiao and Guomao, which are characterized by foreign or multinational companies, those located here are predominantly Chinese.

The culture here is money, so unless it's a custom designed to attract more fortune, you probably won't see too much by way of ancient practices. This is a working place. People come in, work, and then leave. Nightlife is next to zero. Shopping, on the other hand, isn't bad. You have Lane Crawford for the upper house, and Parkson department store for the everyday.

Housing

Serviced apartments abound here. These include The Apartments on Financial Street (www.jrjgy.com.cn), The Westin Beijing Financial Street Executive Residences (www.starwoodhotels.com/westin), and, a more affordable option, Beijing HWA Hotel (www.huaweihotel.com). The latter is a 15-minute walk toward the more cosmopolitan area of Xidan.

For something more permanent, there are also several quality apartment communities. These include Xipai International Apartments (西派国际公寓), which range from about RMB15,000 for a two-bedroom to RMB30,000 for a three-bedroom; Fenghui Yuan Xiaoqu (丰汇园小区), in which rent ranges from around RMB6,500 for a one-bedroom to RMB29,000 for a three-bedroom; or luxury community Zhonghai Kaixuan (丰汇园小区), which ranges from about RMB15,000 for a one-bedroom to RMB35,000 for a three-bedroom.

XIDAN

When you ask a local about where they like to go to shop, nine times out of 10 they'll tell you here. Situated at the corner of Xidan Beidajie and Xichang'an Jie, the area is a youthful and carefree interlude between the stern complexes of Tian'anmen and Financial Street. Cinemas, an ice-skating rink, restaurants, and cavernous malls populate the immediate area. Joy City (www.xidanjoycity.com), Grand Pacific (www.grandpacific-mall.com.cn), and Zhongyou Department Store (中友百货) are just three of the more popular ones for locals.

If you decide to locate to Xidan, things will be convenient, but it is unlikely you'll feel particularly at peace. On weekends the streets and malls can become overwhelmingly crammed with shoppers—even more so during sale periods—and in the morning, should you need to use Line 1, you'll be schooled on how crowded the city really is. The good thing is that you'll be just a short bicycle ride from Beihai, Jinshan, and Zhongshan Parks.

Housing

There are a lot of local apartments around Xidan, catering to the younger population. Expect to pay around RMB3,000-5,000 for a one-bedroom apartment and RMB7,000-12,000 for a two-bedroom apartment. For high-end luxury apartments, check out Cabinet Mansion (复地　西绒线26号), but be prepared to pay anything upward of RMB25,000 per month.

Expat Resources

RELIGIOUS SERVICES

Xicheng is home to some of the most important places of worship. Buddhism and Taoism are represented, but so are Islam, Catholicism, and Protestantism. In fact, the administrative offices of Buddhism, Taoism, and Catholicism are located here.

Catholics can attend services (Chinese) at **West Church,** also called Xizhimen Church (西直门天主堂, 130 Xizhimennei Dajie, 西直门内大街130号, Xinjiekou subway, Line 4, exit D, tel. 10/6653-7629, http://blog.sina.com.cn/westchurch). This is the newest of Beijing's four big Catholic churches (South, North, West, and East). **Xuanwumen Church,** also known as South Church or Nantang (宣武门天主堂, 141 Qianmen Xidajie, Xuanwumennei, 宣武门内大街前门西大街141号, tel. 10/6602-6538) is the oldest Catholic church in Beijing, and was established in the 16th century by Matteo Ricci, Jesuit missionary to China. It's a pretty building worth a visit, and has been listed for national protection. Services are in Chinese, Italian, and English (Sundays at 10:30am and 3pm).

The Church of Our Saviour, also known as Beitang, North Church, or Xishiku Tang (西什库天主教堂, 33 Xishiku Dajie, 西什库大街33号, tel. 10/6617-5198) is the largest Catholic church in Beijing and is known for its grand gothic architecture (Chinese-language services only).

Christians can attend **Gangwashi Church** (北京基督教会缸瓦市堂, 57 Xisi Nandajie, 西四南大街57号, tel. 10/6617-6181, www.gwshcc.org). The church was built in the 1860s by the London Missionary Society, but in 1900, it was burned down during the Boxer Rebellion. It was reconstructed in 1903 and remains an important center for Christianity today (services in Chinese and Korean only).

Muslims have pride of place in Xicheng, with not only a mosque dedicated to their religion, but an entire street of Muslim restaurants and shops that has blossomed around it. **Niu Jie Mosque** (牛街清真寺, 88 Guanganmen Nanjie, 牛街88号, tel. 10/6353-2564, Arabic services) is the oldest mosque in Beijing, being built in AD 996. Though the outside may look traditionally Chinese, inside it is influenced by Muslim culture. Additionally, there is **Dewai Mosque,** also known as Fayuan Mosque

Niu Jie Mosque, with its traditional Chinese architecture, is the oldest mosque in Beijing.

© MOHD FUAD SALLEH/123RF.COM

PRIME LIVING LOCATIONS

(北京德外清真寺, 200 Dewai Dajie, 德外大街200号, tel. 10/6201-6131, Arabic services), as well as **Jinshifang Street Mosque,** or Pushou Mosque (锦什坊街清真寺, 63 Jinshifang Jie, 锦什坊街63号, tel. 10/6603-6165, Arabic services). For more information on Islam in Beijing, visit www.islamichina.com.

Socializing and Networking

Much of the socializing in Xicheng is done in karaoke bars, and in the clubs and bars around Houhai. For more serious interactions, you can visit and involve yourself with the Dongjen Book Club, part of the Dongjen Center for Human Rights Education (18 Dashiqiao Hutong, Jiugulou Dajie, 旧鼓楼大街大石桥胡同18号, tel. 10/8403-4803, www.dongjen.org). This special *hútòng* café is a home for grassroots NGOs. Food and drink is cheap, and 100 percent of the profits go to the group's projects. Meet here to take part in its numerous activities or use it as a space for your own NGO meetings or rent some desk space for your office. If you're keen to do a bit of volunteer work, this is also a worthy place at which to put your hand up.

Sports and Recreation

Xidan might be crowded, but there's an interesting array of sports that you can try your hand at—in winter or summer—and a lot of it's thanks to the area's plentiful supply of water. In the warmer months, you can join the Beijing International Dragon Boat Team (http://beijingdragonboating.com). The club runs casual weeknight and weekend training sessions on Houhai, and also regularly travels to other cities in the country for competition. When temperatures drop and the lake freezes over, Houhai becomes an icy playground on which you can skate or ride ice bicycles or strangely converted "skate" chairs. The chairs might look mildly amusing, but pushing yourself around with metal sticks can lose its interest factor pretty quickly. If you'd like to keep up the skiing when the ice melts, head to Xiyue Ice Rink at the Xidan Cultural Center (喜 悦滑冰场, Level B3, 180 Xidan Beidajie, 西单北大街180号西单文化广场B3楼, tel. 10/6602-0050). It's underground below the large open square at Xidan subway station (Lines 2 and 4, exit A). If yoga is more your thing, there are yoga centers all over the district, but almost none are run in English. This is the challenge—or advantage— of living here. One approach is to search on Chinese listing site www.dianping.com, which can narrow down the options for you.

The Chinese, in general, don't believe in overt risk taking, so hard-core adventure sports aren't particularly abundant. It's a surprise, therefore, to find a free-diving base right here in Xicheng. If you're keen to take a deep dive without oxygen, con- tact Freediving China (www.freedivingchina.com). Based in Xizhimen, they often head out of the city for dives and training in better waters. For a hit at tennis, book a court at the The Xiannong Altar Xuanyuan Tennis Hall (先农坛体育场网球场, tel. 10/6301-0061). Set at the northeast corner of Xiannong Tan Park, it's easily acces- sible via Taoranting subway station (Line 4, exit C). Courts cost RMB230 per hour.

Education

Xicheng isn't known for its international schools, but a few prestigious local schools have international departments. **Beijing No. 4 High School** (www.bhsf.cn) is perhaps the best known. The school prides itself on its academic achievements and ability to get students into Beijing's top universities; then there is also **Beijing No. 8 Middle School Yihai International Campus** (www.no8ms.org or www.admissions.cn/yh8z), which offers nursery programs right through to senior middle school. The school has broad international relationships but has particular ties to Canada. **Beijing Yucai School** is set in beautiful grounds just west of Tiantan Park, beside Xiannongtan Park. Though strongly Chinese in character it has openings for international students and can pro- vide kids with intensive Chinese programs to bring them up to speed with the local language (www.bjyucai.com or www.admissions.cn/bjyucai). In general most of these schools require some level of Chinese language before kids start, and as a parent you may also find the culture between schools and caregivers hard to adjust to.

For adults in Xicheng, **Alliance Française de Pekin** (http://beijing.afchine.org) has a school at Deshengmen and offers a wide range of French courses, including business and intensive courses.

Health Care

Like anything in Xicheng, finding international services is more difficult, so you may need to make a trip to the eastern side of the city if you want the Western experience. May Flower Dental (www.mayflowerdental.com.cn) by Financial Street is very expat friendly and focuses not only on general dental treatment but cosmetic enhancements as well. High-level hospital care can be found at **Xuanwu Hospital Capital Medical University** (www.xwhosp.com.cn), just south of Changshun subway station (Line 2, exit D2) on Changchun Jie. This is a level 3, grade A hospital, meaning it's a top level hospital, and though it is a comprehensive hospital, it also specializes in neurol- ogy and gerontology. Not all, but some of its staff speak English. Peking University People's Hospital (http://english.pkuph.edu.cn) welcomes international patients and visitors, and is also one of the country's top-ranking hospitals. Almost 100 years old, this hospital strives to be one of the leading hospitals in the diagnosis and treatment of rare and complex disorders. It's on the southeast side of Xizhimen subway station (Lines 2, 4, and 13, exit D).

Those with heart conditions should be aware of **Fuwai Hospital** (www.fuwaihospital.org), situated close to Fuchengmen subway station (Line 2, exit A). This is the base for the National Center for Cardiovascular Diseases, and though it is a level 3 grade A hospital, it is exclusively for cardiac issues, so it shouldn't be your choice for flu or broken ankles. Another well-respected local hospital in the district is **Beijing Friendship Hospital** (www.bfh.com.cn, imd.cnkme.com/english/imc), a short distance west of Tiantan Park. This hospital offers a wide range of services, including a VIP/international wing. This hospital is a typical choice for patients from East Asia and is particularly well regarded for its kidney transplant operations.

Finally, one of China's leading pediatric hospitals is close at hand in Xicheng. **Beijing Children's Hospital** (www.bch.com.cn) is about half way between Fuxingmen and Fuchengmen subway stations (Line 2). Affiliated to Beijing Children's Hospital and located at its east gate is the **New Century International Hospital for Children** (NCICH, www.ncich.com.cn), a private hospital. In addition to all major areas of care it also specializes in pediatric eye care and pediatric dentistry. Some international health insurance providers, such as BUPA, Aetna International, and AXA, are accepted here.

SHOPPING AND DINING
Shopping

Aside from Xidan shopping street and the department stores near Financial Street, there are a few other places worth getting to know. Whether you live in Xicheng or not, at one point in your Beijing life you should definitely explore the Zoo Markets, named this because they sit across the road from the Beijing Zoo (which, if you're like many expats, you'll never explore for fear of having to look upon the woeful faces of the animals in their depressing enclosures). The Zoo Markets are a cluster of multistory markets along Xizhimenwai Dajie (Beijing Zoo subway station, Line 4), and if you don't want to have a headache by the time you've finished, beg a friend who is savvy with the labyrinth come with you. Winding your way from building to building, you'll find sunglasses, bags, shoes, jeans and clothing of every description, lingerie and more, all for rock-bottom prices. It's primarily for wholesale purchases, but single sales are accepted. Bargaining is required, but nothing like the Silk Markets or Yashow. Some of the most popular markets—if you can find them—include Jin Kailede (金凯利德), Dongding (东鼎), Tianle (世纪天乐), and Julong (聚龙) or Beijing Exhibition Center Plaza.

Xinjiekou Nandajie (Ping'anli subway station, Lines 4 and 6, exit A or B) is one of the other most-popular strips of Xicheng. Window shoppers and actual buyers will be well pleased by what they find. There are clothing stores, bicycle stores, restaurants, and more, but the feature item of this street is musical instruments. Come here for guitars, violins, flutes, pianos, or mouth organs. Many of the salespeople are musicians, so expect someone to suddenly break out with a performance.

Two other stores that you may be happy to know are in your neighborhood are the Beijing Books Building, unmissable at Xidan (exit C), and a large Sanfo (www.sanfo.com) outlet. The Xidan Books Building has an extensive selection of English

The Beijing Books Building at Xidan is a massive repository of all manner of books, including a large collection of English books.

© SHANNON AITKEN

PRIME LIVING LOCATIONS

books—possibly even better than the bookstores on Wangfujing—while Sanfo will re-ignite your passion for the outdoors with tents, sleeping bags, hiking gear, and the like.

Dining

The best restaurants are the ones you will happen upon by luck, or the ones that have been handed down by word of mouth from friend to friend and finally to you. But just to get you started, here are a few staples. Jiugulou Dajie, the street that runs along the west side of the Drum and Bell Towers, is lined wall to wall with restaurants and cafés. When you don't know what you want or where to go, this is a good fallback. There are delicious Yunnan restaurants here as well as Italian and Vietnamese. Added to your possibilities in the collection is Café Sambal (43 Doufuchi Hutong, 旧鼓楼大街豆腐池胡同43号, tel. 10/6400-4875), a Malaysian restaurant in a homey *hútòng* restaurant. Just off the east side of Jiugulou Dajie, it's technically in Dongcheng.

Join the queue of locals at Kong Yiji (2A Deshengmennei Dajie, 德胜门内大街后海南岸), at the northwest end of Houhai. Named after the hero of a famous Chinese story, this restaurant serves specialties from Zhejiang province, such as *dōngpōròu*, which is superbly soft braised pork in a caramelized sauce.

Yunnan cuisine is one of the more popular food styles of China—a little spicy like food from next-door neighbor Sichuan, fragrant and fresh like the food of the Southeast Asian countries across its southern border. For a good example of the cuisine, grab a table at South Silk Road (茶马古道, Unit 12-13, 19 Shichahai Qianhai Xiyan, 什刹海前海西沿甲19号12–13室, tel. 10/5971-6388), situated slightly west of Qianhai (southern part of Houhai) and a short walk from Beihai North subway station (exit B).

If you're on Financial Street, one particular highlight is Cépe. Located in the Ritz-Carlton Financial Street (1 Jinchengfang Dongjie, 金城坊东街1号丽思卡尔顿酒店, tel. 10/6601-6666), it crafts superb, delicate Italian food.

Don't forget Niu Jie down south. This Muslim neighborhood is food proud, and when people aren't here to pray at the mosque, they're here to eat in one of the many street-side restaurants. Look for the crowd and follow.

Places of Interest

Maliandao is Beijing's hot spot for tea. This ancient street has historic trade stories that have developed into what is today a street lined with small, large, and multistory tea purveyors. It is a bit of a tourist destination, but if you're in this neck of the woods it's a convenient but perhaps overwhelming place to get a simple cup of tea. To get here, take Line 9 to Beijing West Railway Station (exit B), then after exiting the south gate of the station, head east along Guang'an Lu. For other culinary adventures, wander the *hútòng* around Dashilan, just off Qianmen Jie. The section right next to Qianmen Jie is irksomely touristy and kitsch, but go deeper into the *hútòng* and explore the many too-narrow-for-cars alleyways. There are some interesting galleries and cafés tucked back here.

Xicheng district is also home to several important theaters. These include the stunning National Center for the Performing Arts (www.chncpa.org), on the west side of Tian'anmen Square; and the Meilanfang Grand Theatre, situated beside Chegongzhuang subway station (Line 2, exit C). The National Center for the Performing Arts is an iconic piece of architecture in the city, designed by French architect Paul Andreu, and nicknamed "The Egg" or "The Alien Egg." It hosts both local and international performances, such as ballet, orchestral music, and Western opera. Meilanfang Grand Theatre is the place to come for some authentic Beijing opera. You can find out more about each venue and buy tickets from http://theatrebeijing.com, which will deliver tickets to your door and accept cash upon delivery.

Then, for something of a more educational nature, visit the Capital Museum (www.capitalmuseum.org.cn) on occasion to see the elegant and contemporary displays of ancient artifacts. It's on the east side of Muxidi subway station (exit C). Beijing Zoo (www.beijingzoo.com) is also in the district, north of Xizhimen where Xicheng meets Haidian. The zoo is one of the biggest and most important zoos in China. It has one of the largest collections of rare and exotic species, and extensive traditional gardens and historic buildings. The pandas, China's most beloved animal, definitely get preferential treatment, but the enclosures of many other animals here put many people off ever setting foot in the zoo.

Across the road from the zoo on Xizhimenwai Dajie, you can expand your knowledge of the solar system at the Beijing Planetarium (www.bjp.org.cn). In addition to its exhibitions and displays it also has 3D and 4D theaters and two observatories.

PRIME LIVING LOCATIONS

Getting Around

SUBWAY

Xicheng is well connected to the rest of the city by subway. Currently five subway lines run through it—1, 2, 4, 6, and 13—and in 2014 yet another one—7—will be added to it south of Chang'an Jie, running east to west. This is ample to get you to most places in the city, albeit with a couple of changes to get you to such places as Sanlitun (Tuanjiehu, Line 10) or the airport. Interchanges between lines can add a good 10 minutes to your journey, particularly at Xizhimen between 13 and 2.

TRAINS

Beijing North Railway station, or Xizhimen Railway Station, was originally established in 1905. Though it was rebuilt in 2009 into a modern facility, coming here can still be a culture shock. As it's the city's most northern railway terminal, trains that depart here are primarily heading for Inner Mongolia and Liaoning Province. For just RMB6 you can also take one of the S2 trains, which depart roughly every half hour for the Badaling section of the Great Wall in Yanqing county. To confirm times, simply log on to www.travelchinaguide.com/china-trains and search for trains leaving from Beijing North and going to Badaling.

BUSES

The major buses worth getting to know in this area are:

44内/外: This bus is for those who don't like to be below ground, given that it essentially travels the exact same route as the Line 2 subway train, with the 内 going in a clockwise direction and 外 going anticlockwise.

90内/外: This loop route is shaped like an upside-down T. It can be handy if you live near Fuchengmen or Chegongzhuang and want to get up to Houhai, Gulou, or the Olympic area, or down along Chang'an Jie to Wangfujing. Again, 内 is clockwise and 外 is counterclockwise.

107: This handy bus travels from Chegongzhuang to Ping'anli and Houhai, then turns right onto Guloudong Dajie, where it continues east, passing Nanluogu Xiang, hot pot heaven Guijie, and Dongzhimennei Dajie, finishing at Dongzhimen station, or vice versa.

118: Possibly the simplest way to get to Sanlitun if you live in Xicheng, this bus starts west of Chegongzhuang West Station (Line 6) and travels directly along the one unbending series of roads—Ping'anli Xidajie, Di'anmen Xidajie, Di'anmen Dongdajie, Zhangzizhong Lu, Dongsishitiao, and Gongti Beilu—dropping you off in front of the Workers' Stadium (Gongti) before turning south on its way toward Hujialou (Line 10), right in the heart of the CBD.

Deshengmen Long-Distance Bus Station

When you plan to take a day trip out of town, chances are you may need to come here to get on your bus. Several buses, for example, head out to the Great Wall at Badaling (bus 877 is your best choice).

The terminus is extremely chaotic and unplanned. Buses do have allotted places to stop at, but working out just where they are can require a series of questions to people who look like they might know what's going on. Long-distance bus numbers can be a little tricky sometimes. Some numbers come with a character, such as a 快 or 内. Don't discount these characters when double checking your bus details; they can make a big difference to where you end up or how long it takes you to get there.

To see all the local and long-distance buses more clearly, go to www.bjbus.com, type in the route number in the fourth white search box (next to 线站查询), then when the map appears, click on the route number again to highlight the route. You may prefer to use www.mapbar.com/beijing. On the homepage, click on Transport Enquiry (公交查询), then Route Enquiry (路线查询), and finally type in the route number. Doing this through Google Chrome and translating can help.

PRIME LIVING LOCATIONS

CHAOYANG

Of all the districts in Beijing, Chaoyang is the one that expats are most likely to live in or at least spend a good portion of their time working or socializing in. It is the most international and most cosmopolitan of all the districts. Not only is it home to all three embassy areas, but it is also the district in which you'll find the CBD, nightspot Sanlitun, the 798 Art District, the Beijing Capital International Airport, the phenomenal CCTV Headquarters, and many other key places of business, leisure, and retail. There is nowhere else in the city that you will find such a ready supply of Western conveniences, including international supermarkets, international hospitals, and quality Western restaurants and bars. The area has been all but stripped of traditional China and replaced unapologetically with 21st century China.

The misleading thing about Chaoyang is that it's so vast that both living and working in Chaoyang isn't a guarantee that your life is going to be convenient. The district stretches for roughly 30 kilometers (19 miles) from north to south. That can easily convert into an hour's drive in Beijing traffic. For this reason, when deciding where to live here, it's better to think about the individual areas than the district as a whole.

© SHANNON AITKEN

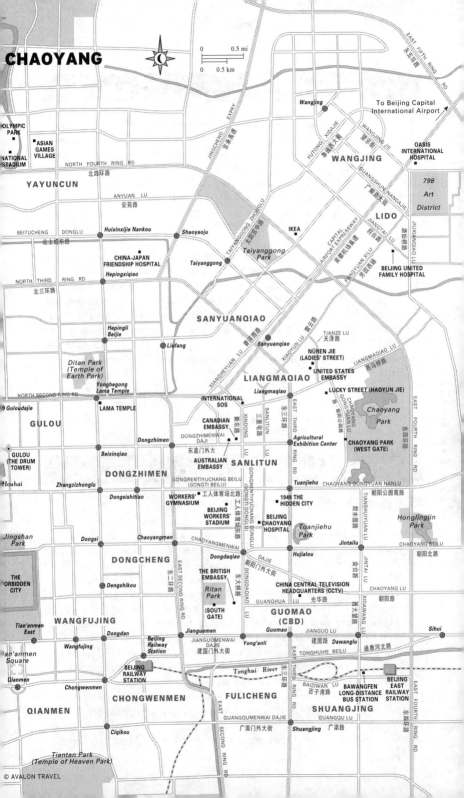

Lay of the Land

Chaoyang is the largest urban district in Beijing, sprawling over a massive 455 square kilometers (176 square miles). It spans the eastern side of the city from north to south, very roughly filling the area between the Second Ring Road and the Fifth Ring Road. Starting from the north and going clockwise, it shares borders with Shunyi, Tongzhou, Daxing, Fengtai, Dongcheng, Haidian, and Changping districts. While it's true to say that the farther east you go toward Shunyi or Tongzhou the less dense Chaoyang becomes, take a trip out on the Batong Line (an aboveground "subway" line extending east from Line 1) and you'll be shocked by how humanity's footprint seems to have no end.

While the populations in districts such as Dongcheng and Xicheng have grown relatively gradually in recent years, Chaoyang's population has been blooming. Between the last two censuses (2000 and 2010), it jumped by more than 1 million people, from 2,289,756 to 3,545,000. Granted, it does have more room than the other two for such expansion, and unlike the traditional *sìhéyuàn* complexes that enjoy some level of protection in Dongcheng and Xicheng, it has been open season on all such low-density structures out here. Any that did exist have for the most part been torn down and replaced by tightly grouped housing complexes or, the friendlier term, communities.

Being such a commercial and densely built up part of the city, Chaoyang can sometimes feel like an endless sea of concrete. Thankfully, it has several important parks that offer some respite from the rush and squeeze. These include Ritan Park, Chaoyang Park, and the Olympic Forest Park. If you have any of these within easy distance to home or work, life may feel a little more natural.

Where to Live

CENTRAL BUSINESS DISTRICT (CBD)

The CBD is usually pinpointed as the area immediately around Guomao, but we'll stretch the boundary just a little to take in the major areas that are all within a walkable distance from this point. Living right at Guomao would be an intense lifestyle indeed. Some people do it, living in such places as Jianwai SOHO or at the Park Hyatt Residences—basketballer Yao Ming is rumored to have an apartment here. Most expats, however, prefer to take a step back and live in one of the nearby communities.

A 15-minute walk or one stop south on Line 10 is the area of Shuangjing. It's an interesting place, and has a rich blend of both expats and white-collar Chinese. It lacks the warm friendliness of places like Dongzhimen, or really anywhere older Chinese apartments remain. Shuangjing is full of new money and *bālínghòu* (八零后), the term given to the generation of post-1980, after the one-child policy was introduced. Young people come and go to work each day with little time or interest to chat, while grandparents commune in the compound gardens below to look after grandchildren. Basic shopping is extremely easy in Shuangjing. A large Carrefour supermarket, a Lohao City, Viva Plaza (www.rfviva.com/home.php), a UME Cineplex, and the Today Art Museum are all in the neighborhood. Notions of DIY or the home handyman are

a typical traffic scene looking north up the East Third Ring Road from Shuangjing

© SHANNON AITKEN

PRIME LIVING LOCATIONS

not popular in Beijing—it's too cheap and easy to get someone else to do things for you—and consequently hardware stores are few and far between. Home Depot did try to make a go of it in Beijing but failed miserably. This being the case, Shuangjing expats prone to tinkering may find joy in the fact that a B&Q hardware store can also be found in Shuangjing, next door to Carrefour.

One stop east of Guomao is Xidawang Lu (or Dawang Lu on the subway line). Again, this is a major expat hub, and has been for many years. Luxury malls Shin Kong Place and China Central Place are here, but before they came there was already China Central Place (Huamao) and Blue Castle, apartment complexes that are a little older now but still favored by expats. An important resource in this area is the Dongjiao Markets, and whether you live in the neighborhood or not, you should come to this sprawling market for at least one visit. You'll find kitchenware, hardware, stationery, linen, fresh produce, almost anything. And all at bargain prices.

Now stretching out into the northwest quadrant of Guomao, life is very Western and city like. The area has a dense concentration of international lifestyle facilities, hotels, and apartment complexes, the main one being Central Park. Central Park is a collection of high-price-tag apartment buildings organized around a park-like setting. At the bases of the buildings, restaurants and cafés with outdoor seating, mini-supermarkets, and boutiques create a village feel, and even those who don't live here are drawn to the neighborhood on sunny days for brunch or lunch. In some ways Central Park is like an inner-city Shunyi. Rather than live out in the suburbs, many expat families choose instead to live here and either send their kids on the school buses out to school in Shunyi or northwest Chaoyang, or send them to the inner-city international schools. The surrounding streets complement the neighborhood with complexes such as The Place (Shìmào Tiānjiē, www.theplace.cn), a mega mall complete with a football-field-sized LCD screen; Parkview Green (www.parkviewgreen.com), an energy-friendly luxury

one of Ritan Park's various ponds, home to ducks and goldfish

shopping and office complex; and Ritan Park, a small but pretty park that creates a wonderful clash of old against modern surrounds.

Housing

Accommodations in this part of town don't come cheaply. Many of the communities are considered high-level or luxury. Of the well-known ones, Pingguo Shequ is probably the most affordable, starting at around RMB6,000 for a one-bedroom place. Pingguo is a modern Chinese complex. This means it has Western toilets and separate showers. However, apartments are unlikely to have built-in ovens or open kitchens. Fulicheng apartments have tighter security, are more family friendly, and have more options for style and size. Prices start around RMB6,500 and climb up to around RMB36,000 for a four-bedroom apartment. Apartments on the north side of Chang'an Jie are more expensive still. Prices are more likely to start from RMB7,500 for a one-bedroom and work their way up to RMB40,000 per month for a four-bedroom apartment in Blue Castle or Central Park. For premium-level luxury, investigate the options at Fortune Heights, where a nice three-bedroom apartment may cost you or your company RMB60,000 per month.

SANLITUN

Some expats love Sanlitun, enjoying its energy and its approximation of an international lifestyle, while some hate it, regarding it as akin to a manufactured tourist attraction without soul. Despite this, even those who detest the place find themselves brought here from time to time to dine, drink, or attend an event. And in a city where everything is so spread out, it is perhaps the one place in town where bar-hopping doesn't become an endurance sport.

There are several sections of Sanlitun worth familiarizing yourself with. The place that has become synonymous with Sanlitun itself is Taikoo Li Sanlitun (www.

taikoolisanlitun.com), a Swire property that is home to a multitude of shops and restaurants, a cinema, a supermarket, and Beijing's flagship Apple store. On the same block and just behind this you'll find Nali Patio, a building that is dedicated to both independent clothing boutiques and bars and restaurants; the 3.3 shopping mall, the former landmark of Sanlitun before Taikoo Li Sanlitun came along and stole the title; the Opposite House; and Taikoo Li Sanlitun North. Not to be forgotten is Sanlitun Houjie (Sanlitun Back Street), which runs immediately behind 3.3 and another complex called Tongli Studios. This street is a cacophonous clash of street vendors, drunken clubbers, hawkers, shoppers, and tourists. You'll find some of the best dives of backpacker bars here as well as pirate DVD shops selling everything that's still on the big screen, tattoo shops, and noodle bars. It is the human hot pot of Beijing.

Prior to the Beijing Olympics in 2008 none of the high-rises here existed. It was a dark, seedy-looking location that felt more like a red-light district. Today, vestiges of those days still cling to the back of Taikoo Li Sanlitun, but for the most part it's a bustling, youthful place, jam-packed with all levels of shopping, eating, and entertainment.

Diagonally across from Taikoo Li Sanlitun is a place that rarely gets given a clear name. On paper it's Courtyard 4, Nansanlitun Lu, but most people end up saying "near the Bookworm," referring to the café situated at the entrance to the whole area, or by whichever venue they find most identifying about the place. Enter from either Gongti Beilu or the top of Nansanlitun Lu, and you discover a warren of bars and restaurants, together with another restaurant complex, Hidden City 1949, which sits directly behind Pacific Century Plaza.

The Workers' Stadium (Gōngrén Tǐyùchǎng, or Gōngtǐ for short), just west of Taikoo Li Sanlitun, is also a crucial fixture in the area. Many of the surrounding streets take their name from it—Gongti Beilu (north) is the main road that runs east-west across Sanlitun, along with Gongti Donglu (east), Gongti Nanlu (south), and

© SHANNON AITKEN

Children play in the fountain at Taikoo Li Sanlitun.

PRIME LIVING LOCATIONS

PRIME LIVING LOCATIONS

© SHANNON AITKEN

Supermarket chain April Gourmet is the staple shopping venue for many expats.

Gongti Xilu (west), all potted with bars and restaurants of some description. Inside the gates of the stadium there are yet more restaurants, bars, clubs, and stores. One block farther west along Gongti Beilu is the Workers' Gymnasium, Gōngrén Tǐyùguǎn). The gymnasium has nothing to bring you to it on a regular day or night, but like the Workers' Stadium, on occasion it is the venue for Chinese or international music concerts as well as sports matches.

Finally, one other slice of Sanlitun is Xingfucun Zhonglu. You'll find this street at the end of the *hútòng* (alley) directly opposite the north gate of the Workers' Stadium. Xingfucun Zhonglu is home to international supermarket April Gourmet, French butcher Boucherie Michel, and a nice collective of restaurants and cafés.

What does this all mean for someone who lives here? Life can feel chaotic or lively, however you spin it; an imported carton of fresh milk or a wedge of French cheese is just a short amble away; and an impulsive beer or meal with a friend just an everyday behavior.

Housing

Housing options are somewhat mixed in Sanlitun. Though there are no real *hútòng* options, there are several older Chinese apartment buildings, such as those around Xingfucun Zhonglu. Rent will vary, but generally prices are likely to start at no less than RMB4,000 for a small and unimpressive one-bedroom apartment. Communities with a more modern or international design are many and include such places as Julong Garden, Sanlitun SOHO, Shimao International Center, and Sanlitun DRC. Rent for these kinds of apartments typically start at around RMB8,000-15,000 for a one-bedroom and climb to RMB30,000-70,000 for a three-bedroom apartment.

CHAOYANG PARK, LIANGMAQIAO, AND SANYUANQIAO

The area around Chaoyang Park (www.sun-park.com) is a wonderful place to live, particularly if you like outdoor sport. The park itself is great for carrying out your own personal training or joining up with group sports, and it has a wide range of facilities, including a tennis center, a badminton hall, basketball courts, football fields, and even its own amusement park. Chaoyang Gongyuan Lu (Chaoyang Park Road), which runs along the entire west side of the park, is a long-time favorite destination for expats. Starting at the north end near Liangmaqiao Lu, the road goes by the name of Lucky Street or Haoyun Jie. It's lined by restaurants and cafés, including the much-loved South German Bakery (www.germanbakery.com.cn) and organic store Lohao City. On the east side of the road here, you'll notice a very large dome. This is the Sino-Japanese Youth Center Pool (tel. 10/6468-3311, noon-10pm), and, as far as local swimming pools go, this is a serious pool with people who understand the etiquette of lap swimming. Clearly, though, an early morning swim before work is not the done thing in Beijing. Farther down the road, across the river, is shopping village Solana (www.solana.com.cn). It can be an interesting place to shop and is often the venue for events such as film premieres and the occasional fair. Continue down the road again, and it again transforms in style, this time into a youthful club and restaurant area.

Liangmaqiao and Sanyuanqiao, on the other hand, have a more corporate feel. This area is something of an extension of the CBD, and is populated by high-rise buildings and head offices of international Fortune 500 companies. It's also one of Beijing's other embassy zones, and includes the U.S. Embassy, among many others. Unsurprisingly, there is a big concentration of five-star hotels in the vicinity, including the Hilton, the Four Seasons, the Westin, and the Kempinski, all venues for important events and all with their own upscale wining and dining options.

Housing

Around the Chaoyang Park area, rental prices are similar to those in Sanlitun, particularly for smaller apartments. Studios can start from around RMB6,000-10,000, depending on the complex, and reach RMB25,000-30,000 for a two-bedroom place. If you need a larger apartment, however, such as a three- or four-bedroom place, you may find you can get more for your money out here.

Out by the East Fourth Ring Road, off the east side of Chaoyang Park, there are numerous high-density communities, such as Greenlake Place. If you don't have a car or a driver, you may start to feel that you're a little disconnected from the city. Getting to and from places like Sanlitun will feel like more of a hassle and you'll possibly feel more a part of Lido than the inner city.

Closer to Liangmaqiao or Sanyuanqiao, prices match the typical clientele. There are many serviced apartments and high-level luxury apartments with premium facilities. These include the Four Seasons residences, Capital Mansion, Beijing SOHO residences, and Liangmaqiao DRC, and typical rental fees at places like these range from around RMB20,000 per month to RMB60,000. It is definitely possible to find cheaper local-style apartments, but you'll never see these on the websites of international relocation services. For a broader awareness of what's out there, use Google Chrome to do a translated search of Home Link (http://beijing.homelink.com.cn/zufang) and see what the locals live in.

Lido's restaurant and shopping hub is near Hairun International Apartments, at the corner of Jiangtai Lu and Fangyuan Xilu.

LIDO AND 798

Lido and the 798 Art District sit between Sanyuanqiao and the airport. This location makes it a popular choice with families who need to juggle lives of kids in Shunyi or northwest Chaoyang with work in the city. Over the years expat homes and facilities have accumulated here, and in 2012 that took another big jump with the opening of Indigo shopping mall and business hotel East, both by Swire properties. One of the major advantages of living in the area is the proximity to the two major international hospitals, Beijing United Family Hospital (BJU) and Oasis International Hospital. Compared to many of the inner city areas, Lido has an almost village feel to it. Relative to the inner city, Lido is still heavily dependent on road transport, and come rush hour, the roads can become horrendously choked. But when the subway's north-south section (phase II) of Line 14 is completed in 2014, things will hopefully improve.

Housing

Compared to the inner city, there are some great-value apartments out this way. One-bedroom abodes may not seem much different, but you can easily find modern two- or three-bedroom apartments for RMB20,000-25,000 per month. Just a few worth looking at include Upper East Side (Sunny Shandong), Richmond Park, Chateau Regency, or, for something not quite as fancy but extraordinarily convenient, try Hairun International Apartments. These apartments are just above Jenny Wang's as well as Tom's, one of the best DVD shops in town, and are a short walk from Beijing United Family Hospital as well as Indigo Mall.

WANGJING

Wangjing is already close to becoming an uninterrupted extension of Sanyuanqiao. It also shares many similarities to Zhongguancun, Beijing's Silicon Valley, located in the west of the city in Haidian district. Various international high-tech companies are stationed here, including Siemens, Panasonic, Ericsson, Motorola, and Sony Ericsson. Gluing them all together is the Wangjing Science and Technology Park (also known as Wangjing Pioneer Park), which aggressively targets entrepreneurial *hǎiguī*, the overseas educated Chinese who now return to China. In 2014 Wangjing will be pushed even further in its status as a business center by claiming Beijing's next piece of world-attention-gaining architecture. Wangjing SOHO (http://wangjingsoho.sohochina.com/en), the second striking SOHO complex to be designed by the Zaha Hadid group, is due for completion at this time. In addition to it high-tech persona, Wangjing is also known for its South Korean population. The area has attracted so many Korean residents over the years that it's somewhat of a Korea Town. It's one of the best places to go to for authentic Korean cuisine, and if you like to buy Korean ingredients then the possibly overwhelming Nanhu market is an exciting place to visit.

Housing

There is a nice selection of housing options in Wangjing, and many are very reasonably priced by Beijing standards. If you require premium-level accommodations, then there are places such as Beijing Fairmont Residence, which are serviced apartments situated on Guangshun Beidajie, a very central point of the Wangjing area and right by Wangjing subway station. Olive and Do Hu Wan apartments are more affordable at around RMB4,000-17,000, and both have pleasant gardens to give you a sense of the outdoors. Somewhere in between are Central Palace, Fangheng International Center, and Baoxing Huating.

OLYMPIC AND YAYUNCUN AREA

A real luxury of living around the Olympic area and Yayuncun (meaning Asian Village, from the 1990 Asian Games) is your proximity to the Olympic facilities. The general area around the Bird's Nest (National Stadium) isn't especially beautiful, perhaps even bleak, but there are acres of cement for skateboarding and rollerblading. In winter you can come here to ice skate on the manmade rink. There is also the National Aquatics Center, better known as Water Cube (www.water-cube.com). It's one of the few Olympic venues open to the public. Visit for RMB30, swim for RMB50, or play in the water park for RMB200 (www.waterpark-watercube.com). There is also the National Tennis Center (www.chinatenniscenter.com). In addition to hosting the China Open, it has 17 outdoor and indoor courts that are open for public use from 7am to 11pm, at a price. North of the stadium, you have access to the Olympic Forest Park, a beautiful reforested area that has been developed with the goals of cleaning the city's air, regenerating native foliage, and attracting native birds. There are extensive running and walking tracks, which weave among manicured gardens and lakes.

On a map it may look inconvenient to live in this sector of the city, but for many people it can actually be extremely convenient. If your life exists anywhere between Zhongguancun in Haidian and Lido or Wangjing in the east you can get to and from each relatively swiftly from here. The roads are good and less congested than the inner-city roads. You can get to the airport in 25 minutes, and to either Zhongguancun or Wangjing in about 10 minutes. If you need to get into town, Line 5 and Line 8 are your rapid modes of transport. Universities such as BCLU or Tsinghua are just a short bus or bicycle ride away, and once the final section of Line 15 opens in 2014 they'll seem even closer. One drawback is that very few Western-style bars, cafés, or restaurants are immediately at your doorstep; however, public transport to get you to some is readily available.

Housing
Another advantage to living in this area is that affordable accommodations are plentiful and varied. At the upper end of the market there is Chateau Glory, with its ornate and opulent apartments that cost up to around RMB30,000 per month. If apartment living just isn't your cup of tea, something more humble and family friendly can be had at City House (倚林佳园), which comes about as close to a house and village experience as you can get in the inner city. It has the Olympic Forest Park at its door, and homes are low-density townhouse-style buildings. Rental prices range RMB15,000-22,000 for three- or four-bedroom apartments. For something a little lighter on the wallet, try Wanda Lake Palace (万达大湖公馆), which has large landscaped gardens and modern apartments ranging in price RMB11,000-25,000. There is, however, no need to spend even this much, and with the help of a local realtor you can easily find two-bedroom apartments for under RMB8,000 per month within the neighborhood.

Expat Resources

RELIGIOUS SERVICES
Unlike Dongcheng and Xicheng districts, which both have purpose-built churches, when it comes to Christian religions at least, Chaoyang has more of a makeshift arrangement. Christians and Catholics congregate in multi-use venues, and Christian groups, in particular, are typically interdenominational rather than representatives of a specific religious order. Beijing Chaoyang Church, a Christian church, is one of the few actual buildings dedicated to Christian worship in the district.

Many of the groups that do operate here are focused directly at the expat community, with the majority of sermons and other communication in English. Be aware that due to local laws you need to have your passport on you when you attend such services.

The two main Christian organizations in Chaoyang are the **Beijing International Christian Fellowship** (BICF, www.bicf.org) and the **Congregation of the Good Shepherd** (COGS, www.cogs-bj.org). BICF's Chaoyang meeting place is at the 21st Century Hotel Auditorium, located near the corner of Liangmaqiao Lu and Chaoyang Gongyuan Lu (Chaoyang Park Road), about 800 meters east of Liangmaqiao subway station (Line 10, exit C). COGS gatherings take place at the Capital Club Athletic Center at Capital Mansion, just a short walk west from Liangmaqiao subway station (Line 10, exit D), on Xinyuan Nanlu. Both organizations embrace denominational diversity and follow a Christ-centered belief.

If you'd like to enjoy worship inside a church, visit **Beijing Chaoyang Church** (60 Dongfeng Nanlu, Dongsihuan Beilu, 朝阳区东四环东风南路60号, tel. 10/6433-0511, http://chaoyangtang.org, English services on Sunday at 7:30am and 4pm). The church is across from the east gate of Chaoyang Park on Dongfeng Nanlu, just off the

East Fourth Ring North Road. There are no subway lines near here, but buses 973 and 988 stop right outside.

Catholics can attend Mass at the Canadian Embassy, located near Dongzhimen and Sanlitun on Dongzhimenwai Dajie. Held by Our Lady of China Beijing, Eucharist is held in English on Sunday at 10am. The parish also runs religion classes for adults and children, fellowship groups, and charity outreach activities. For full information email olcbjparish@aol.com.

Those of the Jewish faith can attend services at **Chabad Lubavitch of Beijing** (www. chabadbeijing.com), located at Fangyuan Xilu, beside the New Hope Oncology Center, next to the south gate of Si De Park. Alternatively, Jewish community **Kehillat Beijing** (www.sinogogue.org) organizes dinners and meetings with people who want to worship together. Join them at the Capital Club Athletic Center at Capital Mansion.

Islam is represented at **Beijing Changying Mosque** (北京常营清真寺, tel. 10/6548-4914, Arabic services). This ancient mosque was first built during the Ming dynasty (1368-1644). For overall space it is the largest mosque in suburban Beijing. The main hall holds 200 to 300 people for prayer. Women are also welcome to pray in the female hall. The new Line 6 subway has made it easy get here. You'll find it on Chaoyang Beilu halfway between Huangqu and Changying subway stations.

Alternatively, visit **Beijing Nanxiapo Mosque** (北京南下破清真寺, 129 Nanxiapo, Chaoyangmenwai, 朝阳区朝阳门外南下坡129号, tel. 10/8562-6316, Arabic services), which is much closer to the CBD, located near the northwest side of Ritan Park, off Chaowai Er Tiao.

SOCIALIZING AND NETWORKING

The very nature of living in Chaoyang is socializing and networking. Though the city is large, the expat world is small, and after an evening or two out on the town you'll start to recognize faces. People know people and six degrees of separation is an overly generous allowance for connections.

That said, when you first arrive in town, it will help to be a little proactive about building your social circles. The International Newcomers Network is an obvious place to start, but FC Group, VIVA Beijing Professional Women's Network, and InterNations also run regular events at interesting locations around Chaoyang.

There are also quirkier ways to buddy up. Wednesday trivia nights at Paddy O'Shea's (www.paddyosheas.com) are definitely more about beer and socializing than firing intellectual synapses. If that is more your thing, then head to the Bookworm's Pub Quizzes, which are a little more high-brow. Make sure you have yourself added to the Bookworm's email list. The team here does a phenomenal job of organizing social and informative events, hosting everything from wine tasting to international literary festivals. Beijing Hash House Harriers (www.hash.cn) frequently organizes runs in parts of Chaoyang, and though running is involved I'd hesitate to say the primary objective is sport.

SPORTS AND RECREATION

If you're in the right part of Chaoyang—by Chaoyang Park, the Olympic Forest Park, or even Si De Park in Lido—then maintaining an active lifestyle will come more naturally. For everyone else gyms or organized groups need to be sought out. Unless your

PRIME LIVING LOCATIONS

© SHANNON AITKEN

The south gate of Chaoyang Park is a place for sport, relaxation, and events.

sport is incredibly niche, you should be able to find it here, whether it's archery, kart racing, ice hockey, Thai boxing, or pole dancing.

Those around the Shuangjing and Xidawang Lu areas have a few good options to consider, both indoors and outdoors. International school BCIS, beside Pingguo Shequ, often shares its grounds on weekends or weeknights for sports group training activities. Beijing Ultimate Frisbee (www.beijingultimate.com) is one, as is Handball in China (www.handballinchina.org). For those who prefer to put movement to music, just a short stroll away is 22 International Art Plaza, home to Beijing Salsa (www.bjsalsa.com). Classes are available on a daily basis and include salsa as well as ballet, belly dancing, and many other dance styles. A little farther east along Baiziwan Lu, past the Fourth Ring Road, O'le sports center (http://ole-sports.org) has outdoor and indoor football fields, as well as climbing and bouldering walls. They organize other activities, including ski trips in winter and outdoor climbing in summer. Hokay Skating Rink (tel. 10/8576-8918) is also out in this direction, located inside Xinglong Park by Gaobeidian subway station (Batong Line, exit C). Come for a skate with the kids or join an ice hockey team.

If you're closer to Wangjing or northeast Chaoyang, 26 Degrees (26° 运动公社, 望京北侧崔各庄乡奶东村顺白路, tel. 10/8438-8177, www.26csportscenter.com) is a fantastic option. It has six full-sized football fields, as well as indoor facilities for five-aside games. It's about two kilometers (1.2 miles) north of Wangjing on Shunbai Lu on the west side of the Jingcheng Expressway. To get there take the Jingcheng Expressway and get off at exit 5B (not 5A). Take the first right after the exit, travel west for approximately 300 meters before turning left onto Shunbai Lu. It's about 500 meters down on the left. The website has directions in Chinese for taxi drivers.

Almost wherever you are in Chaoyang you can find yoga and Pilates, and there's perhaps no other district in the city in which it's easier to find bilingual or English-led classes. Most gyms offer yoga or Pilates classes, and there are also many dedicated studios. Just a few worth investigating around Chaoyang include Yogiyoga (www.yo-giyogacenter.com), the Yoga Yard (www.yogayard.com), Yihe 42° Yoga (www.yh42.com), Fine Yoga (www.fine-yoga.com), Alona Pilates (http://alonapilates.com), and Isofit Beijing (www.pilates.cn).

If it is a gym you're after, these too can be found all over the district. Many of the four- or five-star hotels have public memberships, but these don't always come cheaply. Kerry Sports at the Kerry Hotel in the CBD is perhaps the best known of the hotel gyms, and has some of the best facilities in town, with basketball and tennis courts as well as a stylish swimming pool and gym. Prices were being reviewed at the time of writing, but you can expect to pay in excess of RMB20,000 per year. Other interna-tional-quality gyms may cost somewhere between RMB5,000 and RMB15,000 per year. At the cheaper end of the scale Heyrobics (www.heyrobics.com) takes it outdoors, and for anything from free to RMB30 per class you can work up a sweat.

On a clear day, you may feel less inclined to exercise indoors and feel the need to take advantage of the blue sky and get out into nature. This is where clubs like Beijing Hikers or Beijing Climbing Club can be saviors. They arrange a diverse range of fun and social day outings to such places as Miyun or Shidu, and though their objectives are to explore the outer wilds of the Beijing municipality, their starting point is Chaoyang, and usually at the Starbucks by Metro Park Lido Hotel (simply known as Lido Hotel or Lídū Fàndiàn, www.hotellidobeijing.com). For prices averag-ing RMB400 per trip, you can have a refreshing day out in nature hiking or climbing, all expenses included and all transport taken care of.

EDUCATION

Inner Chaoyang might not have schools with the immense campuses like those out near and within Shunyi, but it isn't without quality options. In fact, many of the schools here are possibly more interesting culturally. Various local schools have long histories of accepting international students, such as Fangcaodi International School and Beijing Ritan High School, both near Ritan Park, as well as Beijing No. 80 High School, in Wangjing. Your children will learn and grow immersed in the local culture. Programs vary as to how much English is used, although by the higher grades usually all education is in Chinese.

As for universities, there are a few campuses in which expats can enroll. CAFA (China Central Academy of Fine Arts, www.cafa.edu.cn) in Wangjing is beginning to develop an international name for itself. Most courses are still run in Chinese, but it attracts many international Chinese-speaking students for its fashion design and ar-chitectural programs in particular. Even if you don't intend to study here, the CAFA Museum (www.cafamuseum.org), the college's gallery space, frequently holds events to show off the talents of its students to the public.

Beijing University of Chinese Medicine (www.bucm.edu.cn), is in the north near the China-Japan Friendship Hospital, close to Guangximen (Line 13, exit A) and Huixinjiebeikou (Lines 5 and 10, exit C) subway stations. This is a popular choice for international students wanting to learn authentic Chinese medicine in order to return to their home country to set up practice. There is no need to speak Chinese as many of the courses are run in English. There is a Chinese-language course offered, which in part is tailored to open doors for you to study TCM in its native language; however,

INTERNATIONAL SCHOOLS IN CHAOYANG

SCHOOL	AGE	WEBSITE
Preschool and Kindergarten		
Etonkids International Kindergarten	1-6 years	www.etonkids.com
The Family Learning House	1.5-6 years	www.thefamilylearning house.com
Ivy Bilingual School	2-6 years	www.ivyschools.cn
Ke Er International Kindergartens	18 months-6 years	www.keereducation.com
Combined Years		
3e International	2-9 years	www.3einternationalschool.org
Beanstalk International Bilingual Schools (BIBS)	2-18 years	www.bibs.com.cn
Beijing BISS International School	3-17 years	www.biss.com.cn
Beijing City International School (BCIS)	3-18 years	www.bcis.cn
Beijing World Youth Academy (BWYA)	9-18 years	www.ibwya.net
British School of Beijing, Sanlitun Campus (BSB)	1-10 years	www.britishschool.org.cn
Canadian International School of Beijing (CISB)	18 months-18 years	www.cisb.com.cn
International Academy of Beijing (IAB)	5-8 years	www.iabchina.net
Yew Chung International School of Beijing (YCIS Beijing)	2-18 years	www.ycis-bj.com
Universities		
China University of Chemical Technology		www.buct.edu.cn
Beijing International Studies University		www.bisu.edu.cn
Beijing University of Chinese Medicine		www.bucm.edu.cn
Beijing University of Technology		http://bjut.edu.cn
Capital University of Economics and Business		http://english.cueb.edu.cn
Communication University of China		www.cuc.edu.cn

some students argue that it's possibly not the best choice if your true and sole goal is to learn Chinese. There are better universities for that.

Another lesser-known university is Beijing University of Chemical Technology (wwwold.buct.edu.cn/english). While no one may have heard of it elsewhere in the world, it does have intensive long-term and short-term Chinese programs that, compared to the private downtown language schools, are relatively cheap. It's also less populated by expats than the big universities in Haidian, so you'll have a better chance of mixing with the locals. It's just across the road from Hepingxiqiao subway station (Line 5, exit B).

Not all of us, however, can fit a full-time Chinese course into our lives. Fortunately a plethora of private Chinese schools in Beijing target the less committed or less available. Just some of the better known (but not necessarily better) ones include Beijing Global Village School in Wangjing, New Concept Mandarin in Sanyuanqiao, Frontiers and That's Mandarin in Dongzhimen, Chinese Language Education (CLE) in the CBD, and The Bridge School, which is in numerous locations around Chaoyang. Satisfaction with each school varies according to individual goals and personalities. Your best bet is to ask around, and most importantly book yourself into several different free trial lessons before you commit to anything. As expats we're always coming and going, heading back home for a visit or off on business trips, so it's important to make sure you are fully aware of what happens to your payments when you can't attend class.

More leisurely courses can be found throughout Chaoyang, too. Atelier (www.atelier.cn.com), near Sanlitun, takes on artistic pursuits, such as creative writing, drawing, and photography, while the Expat Learning Center down in the CBD in Newtown SOHO (Dawanglu station, Line 1, exit C) can help you with the other notches you've been meaning to add to your belt, such as film making, web design, and Photoshop. Closer to Liangmaqiao and Chaoyang Park, the China Culture Center (www.chinaculturecenter.org) runs classes, talks, seminars, workshops, and discussion forums on topics surrounding Chinese culture. Make new friends while learning how to speak Chinese, cook Chinese food, do Chinese calligraphy, or practice reflexology.

HEALTH CARE

Of all districts in Beijing, Chaoyang has the most international clinics and hospitals, and your only real problem will be paying for them if you don't have international insurance.

In the CBD, head to Bayley & Jackson Medical Center if you're near the east side of Ritan Park, or go to Vista Medical Center if you're closer to the Kerry Centre on Guanghua Lu. Over at Xidawang Lu, GlobalCare Women & Children's Hospital, a private Chinese hospital, is steadily gaining more acceptance in the expat community for service that feels a bit more personal than perfunctory. One of the major clinics trusted by expats is the International SOS Beijing Clinic, located near Sanlitun, directly north of the Canadian Embassy. The clinic is an excellent resource for medical care, Western medications, and information; however, many mistakenly believe SOS to be a full-scale hospital. It does have a 24-hour emergency clinic, but the center isn't equipped to handle many medical conditions and will need to transfer some patients to other hospitals or will assist with repatriation if needed.

Eye problems can be treated at Beijing Aier Intech Eye Hospital (http://en.intecheye.com), just southwest of Panjiayuan subway station (Line 10). One problem in Beijing that many expats experience is that though there are thousands of spectacle shops, there are few fully trained optometrists, and usually the shop attendant will both test your eyes and sell you your frames. Beijing Aier Intech Eye Hospital is a multilingual facility, and specialist services include eye prescriptions, 24-hour emergency service, Lasik surgery, and treatment for eye disease. Direct billing is available for many international health providers.

In Liangmaqiao, nearby residents have access to the International Medical Medical Center (IMC), at the back of the Beijing Lufthansa Center and just a short walk from Liangmaqiao subway station (Line 10, exit C). Arrail Dental is just one block farther up Liangmaqiao Lu at the corner of Maizidian Jie.

In Lido we hit the jackpot. This is the hot spot of medical care. The Beijing United Family Hospital, with its various wings and clinics, is a prominent operation, but others include Oasis International Hospital, Amcare Women's & Children's Hospital, and Smart Health Medical and Dental Center.

The Olympic area has fewer purely Western services, though two of Beijing's leading local hospitals are close by if needed. Anzhen Hospital, a short walk south of Anzhenmen subway station (Line 10), is a highly regarded hospital and specializes in cardiology, while the China-Japan Friendship Hospital, near Huixinjie Nankou (Lines 5 and 10) and Shouyaoju (Lines 10 and 13) stations, is a top-level national hospital and has a VIP/international wing that expats should feel comfortable in.

Finally, animals are also well taken care of in Chaoyang. Doctors Beck & Stone have several clinics in Chaoyang, including one just west of Pingguo Shequ near Xidawang Lu, one at Chaowai SOHO in the CBD, and then their Chaoyang Park clinic, which is really more like Lido. The International Center for Veterinary Services (ICVS) is at Wangjing.

SHOPPING AND DINING
Shopping

There is no shortage of places to spend your money in Chaoyang, and wherever you go there is a hulking mall within walking distance. Usually it doesn't matter too much which one you go to—most are roughly the same, housing the same brands of clothes and eateries. A few stand out, however, such as Indigo in Lido, Nali Patio in Sanlitun, North Village in Sanlitun, China World Mall at Guomao, and possibly U-Town southeast of Chaoyangmen subway station (Lines 2 and 6), although the jury is still out on that one.

What can be more interesting is trawling your way through one of the many markets around the district. Some of them, such as Panjiayuan (Line 10), Yashow next to Taikoo Li Sanlitun and the Silk Markets at Yong'anli (Line 1), are dedicated tourist traps, with vendors like fully trained bloodhounds, capable of sniffing out naïve shoppers with loose pockets. Once you get to what the prices should be and how to get them, these places can be great for kids' dress ups, sports clothes, linen, and lots of other essentials. These markets are completely devoid of any genuine culture. For this, try Huasheng Tianqiao Market (a short walk south from Shilihe subway station, Line 10, exit D). It's a photographer's paradise. There are endless cultural items and trinkets, an ocean of aquarium fish, and hundreds of colorful crickets, which many

Chinese people still love to make a pet of, carrying them around inside their coats. If you wince at seeing cute pets in cages, however, you might want to skip it.

If you'd love to decorate your home with beautiful traditional Chinese furniture, acquaint yourself with Gaobeidian Furniture Street. The street is lined with shops, such as Lily's Antiques (www.lilysantiques.com) or Ju Yuan Zhai Classical Furniture Company, which go beyond what you'll find at Panjiayuan. Kit out your home with elegant oriental wardrobes, chairs and tables, or other decorations. If you can't find what you're looking for, there are craftspeople there who can build it for you. It's just east of Dawang Lu, a short walk south of Gaobeidian subway station (Batong Line, exit F).

Dining

Five years ago, you would have been impressed had you been able to find a premium steak somewhere. The bar was set by relaxed family eateries, such as Grandma's Kitchen and Annie's—both still around today and due respect for their consistency and service. But they're a long shot from fine dining. Today the dining scene in Beijing is astonishingly different. There are countless superb restaurants, and the majority can be found in Chaoyang district. The number-one place has to be the general Sanlitun area. Individual clusters of restaurants in the area make this the one-stop place for dining and drinking. Whatever cuisine you're craving, it's in the vicinity—Middle Eastern, Spanish, Malaysian, Thai, Italian, and of course every variety of Chinese. Surpassing even Gui Jie (Dongzhimennei Daijie) in Dongcheng, it's the most consolidated place of dining in the entire city.

Outside of Sanlitun, you can always find quality restaurants at the five-star hotels. Pop into any of the luxury hotels around Guomao, Dawang Lu, or Liangmaqiao and you'll enjoy a good meal, although for much more than street-level restaurants, plus 15 percent service charge. Weekend brunches are a huge thing in Beijing, and the hotels vie frantically with each other to our benefit. Each tries to create its own spin, but the real carrots are the brand of Champagne they pour and the size of their seafood counter. Families with young kids will probably love Bubbalicious Sunday Brunch at the Westin, while sophisticated pleasure seekers may be won over by the Grand Cru Sunday Brunch at the JW Marriott. Hotel brunches typically end up costing around RMB300-600 per person, so be sure to check the price so that your day isn't soured when your bill turns up.

Places of Interest

Chaoyang is packed with interesting places that can take up a position in your or your family's life to make it more interesting. Compared to the inner city, this part of town is relatively new, so places of interest tend more to be modern buildings than ancient treasures. There are architectural structures that will have you grabbing your camera, such as the CCTV Headquarters at Xintaixijiao (Line 10) near Guomao; the China World Tower, Beijing's tallest building, just a block away; and many of the Olympic buildings in the north.

Immerse yourself a little deeper with a visit to one place that has been protected, Dongyue Temple, an ancient Daoist temple from the Yuan period (1279-1368). It

© SHANNON AITKEN

The Workers' Stadium is a key landmark of Beijing, not only because of the events it holds but the surrounding streets that take their name from it.

covers 4.7 hectares (11.6 acres), which is always surprising considering the squeeze of modern commercial buildings around it. You'll find it on Chaoyangmenwai Daijie, halfway between Chaoyangmen subway station (Lines 2 and 6) and Dongdaqiao subway station (Line 6). More culture can be found at the Chinese Ethnic Culture Park (China Nationalities Museum, www.emuseum.org.cn/en), located near the Olympic Green (Olympic Sports Center subway station, Line 8, or Beitucheng subway station, Lines 8 and 10). This attraction was primarily built to appeal to tourists coming for the Olympics, but today it's still an enjoyable day out for the family and introduces you to China's 56 ethnic groups.

Kids will also enjoy the misleadingly named Blue Zoo Beijing (tel. 10/6591-3397, www.bluezoo.com.cn). This is a large saltwater aquarium jointly created by companies from both New Zealand and China, and it's situated at the south gate of the Workers' Stadium. Walk through the 120-meter-long tunnel and see thousands of tropical fish swimming around you. Entry for adults is RMB110, while kids under 12 cost RMB80. If the kids prefer to play, then check out FunDazzle, also by the south gate of the Workers' Stadium (tel. 10/6593-6193, www.bjgtfdl.com.cn). Adults can relax while kids play in the ball pit and on the climbing gym. If you're closer to Wangjing, a similar option is available at Family Box (www.familyboxes.com.cn).

In summer kids can splash around in Chaoyang's water parks. The city might be landlocked, but there are ample fake beaches and wave pools to keep the dream alive. In addition to the Water Cube's indoor water park, Tuanjiehu Pool (Hujiaou subway station, Line 10, exit B) near Sanlitun has a beach, pool with wave machine, and water slides. It's open June-August and can get very crowded on weekends, so go early to avoid the joy of adding yourself to a human hot pot. Chaoyang Park (www.sun-park.com) also has an impressive water park, again complete with beach, pool, and play equipment. Public hygiene is often a big concern in Beijing, and you're right to be a little edgy about what you might be dipping yourself into at some places. The Chaoyang water park, however, has the reputation of maintaining higher standards of cleanliness. Finally, if you're willing to go farther out, closer to Shunyi you'll find Crab Island and Merry Water World in northeast Chaoyang.

Adults can join in the fun at Happy Valley (http://bj.happyvalley.cn), at the corner of the East Fourth Ring South Road and the Jingha Expressway. This is Beijing's answer to Disneyland. There are a few other fun parks around Beijing, but this is the biggest and the one with the best rides. You may have heard horror stories about some fun parks in China, but there's no need to worry with Happy Valley. It's a well run and highly maintained park.

Essential locations in your GPS are art areas 798, near Lido, and Caochangdi, near the intersection of the Airport Expressway and the Fifth Ring Road. A trip to 798 can easily fill an entire day. In addition to the multitude of galleries, there are excellent cafés, tiny shops with quirky goods, and a constant stream of events. A good guide to Beijing's individual galleries and what's happening in Beijing's art world can be found at art site Artforum (http://artforum.com).

While you're out at Caochangdi, pop by the China National Film Museum (www.cnfm.org.cn). It's just inside the Huantie (railway circle) on Nanying Lu. A film buff's fantasy, this immense complex takes you through China's entire history of film, and may actually take up a good half of your day. Much of the content is in Chinese, but a lot of it is translated into English and is still extremely interesting.

Getting Around

SUBWAY

The subway in Chaoyang just keeps getting better and better. It now has 10 lines that pass through it, including Line 1 and the Batong Line, Line 5 and the Yizhuang Line, as well as Lines 6, 8, 10, 13, and 15 and the Airport Express. By 2014, Lines 7 and 14 will also contribute to it.

TRAIN

Currently the only major station in Chaoyang is Beijing East Railway Station, which is just south of Dawang Lu subway station (Line 1) on Baiziwan Lu by Dongjiao market. It is primarily a freight station, but you can take trains from here to Chengde as well as parts of Inner Mongolia and Shaanxi province. In the future, possibly around 2015, this station is set to be relocated to Tongzhou district.

BUSES

The major buses worth getting to know in this area are:

113: This useful bus connects the Olympic area to Guomao via Sanlitun. Get on at Guomao right in front of Jianwai SOHO (Dabeiyao Zhan, 大北窑站) and get off at Sanlitun Zhan (三里屯站) in front of Taikoo Li Sanlitun; the Workers' Stadium (Gongrentiyuchang Zhan, 工人体育场站); at Dongsishitiao Zhan (东四十条站) for the Poly Theatre; Jiaodaokou Nanzhan (交道口南站), which is a short walk through

© SHANNON AITKEN

Super mall Joy City is popular with locals here in Chaoyang.

the *hútòng* to Nanluogu Xiang; or at Beitucheng subway station (Beitucheng Xilu Dongkou Zhan (北土城西路东口站) for the Olympic area.

635: This bus is handy for socializing as well as exercising. Get on at Gulou Zhan (鼓楼站) or Baochao Hutong Zhan (宝钞胡同站) near Nanluogu Xiang, and ride it to Gui Jie (Dongnei Xiaojie Zhan, 东内小街站); Dongzhimen Zhan (东直门站); Chunxiu Lu Zhan (春秀路站), by April Gourmet; the Agricultural Exhibition Center (Nongye Zhanlanguan Zhan, 农业展览馆站) on the Third Ring Road; Tuanjiehu Zhan (团结湖站); Chaoyang Park (Tianshuiyuan Jie Beikou Zhan, 甜水园街北口站), by the southeast corner; and Ciyunsi Zhan (慈云寺站), by Yew Chung International School.

682: Those around Chaoyang Park may find this handy. Get on at Chengtie Beiyuan Zhan (城铁北苑站), near Beijing Yew Chung International School, then get off at Laitai Flower Market (Laitai Huahui Zhan, 莱太花卉站); Solana (Zaoying Lu Beikou Zhan, 枣营路北口站); Chaoyang Park West Gate (Chaoyang Gongyuan Ximen Zhan, 朝阳公园西门站); Honglingjin Park (Hongjinglin Gongyuan Zhan, 红领巾公园站); or one of the stops by Line 6, such as Balizhuang Nanli Zhan (八里庄南里站) or Qingnian Lukou Zhan (青年路口站) by Joy City.

404: Getting back and forth from Dongzhimen to Wangjing is extremely quick and easy with this bus. It travels right along Guangshun Beidajie and Guangshun Nandajie, before it turns on to Jingmi Lu to head directly to the Dongzhimen bus station.

915: The 915 is perhaps one of the most useful buses in the area, especially given the current lack of subway lines to the Lido area. Get on at Dongzhimen (Dongzhimenwai, 东直门外站) at the street on the west side of the bus terminal, then get off at Sanyuanqiao (三元桥站) at Lido Hotel (Jingshunlu Lido Fandian, 京顺路丽都饭店); Dashanqiao Dong (大山桥东站), which is a short walk to 798; Dongjiao Nongchang (东郊农场站), for Western Academy Beijing or Beijing Riviera villas; and then Shunyi Malian Zhan (顺义马连店站) for Pinnacle Plaza.

973: This bus connects Lido to Xiadawang Lu via the east side of Chaoyang Park. It starts from inside the Huantie (the rail circle) and passes through Caochangdi (草场地站), and heads south via 798 (Dashanzi Lukou Nanzhan, 大山子路口南站); Indigo mall (Jiuxianqiao Zhan, 酒仙桥站); past Chaoyang Church (Dongfeng Nanlu Zhan, 东风南路站); along the east and south sides of Chaoyang Park and then south to stop near Jintai Lu subway station (Jintai Lu Kou Nanzhan, 金台路口南站) on Line 6, and near Dawang Lu subway station (Bawangfen Beizhan, 八王坟北站) on Line 1.

HAIDIAN

Haidian district has a dual identity. On one hand it's known as the university district. Most of Beijing's universities are here, including China's top two, Peking University and Tsinghua University. If you live and work around Wudaokou or Zhongguancun in particular, you'll immediately perceive the university-town feel about it. At any time of day cafés are filled with students studying or gathered together. Boutiques sell clothes and goods that appeal to the student population, and bars and restaurants serve up passable budget-friendly meals.

Haidian's other persona is that of being China's own Silicon Valley. Twenty years ago it started as a bustling marketplace for electronics in Zhongguancun (*"cun"* meaning "village"). That's still here, but today, the area has also grown into what is now China's most important location for high-tech innovation, predominantly in the IT industry, but increasingly also in the aerospace, bioengineering, pharmaceutical, and financial industries. Haidian may have relatively fewer galleries and artists than in the city's east, but it is argued to be the most creative sector of the city.

This is something the government has intentionally been developing. In 1988, it officially launched the wordily titled Zhongguancun National Innovation Demonstration Zone, which fortunately has been cut back to Zhongguancun Science Park, or sometimes, just Z-Park (http://en.zgc.gov.cn). This is an official zone of the city that is

© SHANNON AITKEN

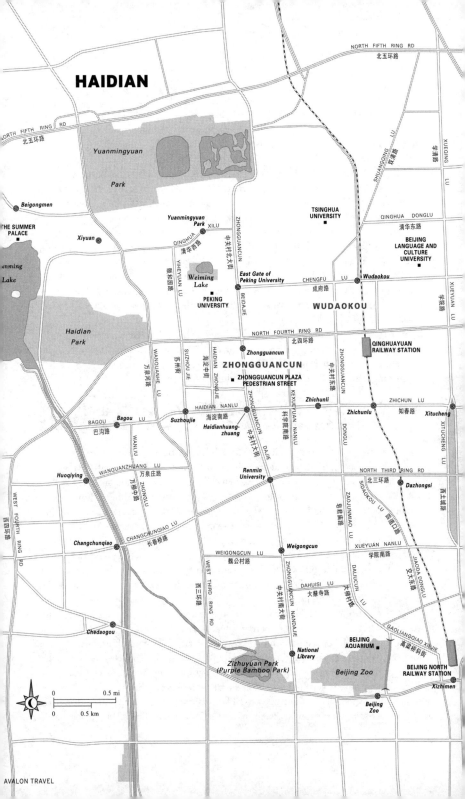

dedicated to attracting and incubating innovation in high-tech industries. Confusingly, the name doesn't just refer to Zhongguancun in Haidian, but to a collection of 10 sub-parks dotted around the entire city, such as Yizhuang Park in Daxing district and Electronics City near Wangjing. The Zhongguancun Haidian Science Park is the official name now given to the sub-park covering the actual Zhongguancun area, and this is the largest and most important sub-park of the entire Z-Park. It expands over a massive 217 square kilometers (84 square miles), nearly half of the entire Haidian district, and it's estimated that 20 percent of the entire nation's software industry revenue is generated in the Haidian Science Park alone. Enmeshed with residential and educational areas, it's one of the largest urban innovation zones in the world.

You'll find the head offices of many of China's biggest high-tech companies here, including Baidu, China's interpretation of Google; computer giant Lenovo; Sohu, a Goliath Internet company responsible for much of China's digital media; Youku, China's alternative to YouTube; and Microsoft's Asia Research and Development Headcounter. Even Google, which scaled back its China operations in 2010, still has an office in Haidian Science Park. In fact, more than 100 Fortune 500 companies have R&D offices in the region.

But Haidian isn't just all study and business. It also has some of Beijing's most important historical and scenic sites. When not working or hitting the books, you can enjoy visits to such places as the Summer Palace, Xiangshan (Fragrant Hills), Yuanmingyuan Park, and Recumbent Buddha Temple.

Lay of the Land

Haidian district sits in the northwest corner of urban Beijing, starting from the corner of the Second Ring Road and extending outwards far beyond the Fifth Ring. It is bordered by Changping, Chaoyang, Xicheng, Fengtai, Shijingshan, and Mentougou districts. It covers 431 square kilometers (166 square miles), making it just slightly smaller than Chaoyang district. At the last census in 2010 it had a registered population of 3,281,000 people—1 million more than in the previous census in 2000.

Inner Haidian is like the rest of urban Beijing—pancake flat. But you don't have to go far to get into the mountains that seem to suddenly rise out of the west and north. On a day when pollution isn't reducing your depth of field, they seem to be within walking distance. At the very least, a short bus or subway ride will get you out of the city and into the leafy hills.

To the rest of the city Haidian can seem like a world away, and it's a rare thing for east siders to make a trip out here to shop or dine. A trip up to Wudaokou from Dongzhimen will cost you around RMB50-60 in a taxi or about 45 minutes on the subway. Unsurprisingly, those who usually work or study out here, live out here. Transport to and from Haidian is increasingly convenient, and the only real problem you may have is getting home after about 11pm when public transport closes, at which point you'll need to rely on taxis. The airport is 25 kilometers (16 miles) from the center of the district, but access to the Third, Fourth, and Fifth Ring Roads makes the journey swift.

Where to Live

WUDAOKOU

Wudaokou is a youthful and vibrant place to be a part of. It's where most of Beijing's expat student population resides, and that includes people from China, the U.S., Europe, Japan, Korea, and many other parts of the world. Wherever you go you'll be immersed in a culturally rich environment. Though getting yourself down to Sanlitun or Gulou for a night out can feel like an arduous expedition, within Wudaokou everything is close at hand, giving it a real village feel. A friend and a coffee are just minutes away.

Given the number of startup companies around Zhongguancun and nearby Zhichun Lu, Wudaokou is also filled by go-getting entrepreneurs. People rise early in the morning and charge into the day, and there's a constant atmosphere of opportunity and willingness to make things happen. You might get a scent of this in the east, but here in Wudaokou it's palpable, and the person sitting at the table next to you in the café might be your next business partner.

Everything in Wudaokou is centered around Chengfu Lu and the subway station. There are shopping malls, cafés, bars, karaoke bars, street food vendors, and endless cell phone retailers on either side. Just a short walk west of the subway station is TusPark (http://en.tsinghua-vc.com), one of the area's most important science parks. TusPark is an initiative by Tsinghua University aimed at promoting technology innovation and entrepreneurship, and in addition to its internal business facilities, its tenants also include quality cafés and restaurants that appeal to Wudaokou's working crowd.

© SHANNON AITKEN

Wudaokou's cafes are important places for study, relaxation, and language exchanges.

PRIME LIVING LOCATIONS

Housing

Despite the number of students and universities in the area, housing is not cheap in Wudaokou. Sure, there are hovels, which you might be able to rent out for under RMB2,000 per month, but these are likely to be single rooms with boarding-house-style shared facilities. For one-bedroom places be prepared to spend RMB4,000-6,000 per month. Some of the better-known compounds in the area include Dongshengyuan (东升园) and Huaqing Jiayuan (华清家园), both on Caijing Donglu, which runs directly along the southwest side of Wudaokou subway station. Both are popular local housing communities with reasonable apartments that go for about this price range. Just outside their gates are Wudaokou's favorite establishments—the Bridge Café, Sculpting in Time Café, and bars Propaganda and Lush. On the northwest side of BLCU (Beijing Language and Culture University), Dongwangzhuang (东王庄) can be cheaper, though a little run down, while Furun Jiayuan (富润家园) on the east side of BLCU is a little pricier but much more modern. Setting yourself up with an apartment can take as little as a day or two if you're in a rush. Visit the real estate agents on Caijing Donglu and inside Huaqing Jiayuan, some of whom can speak English, and they'll take you around.

There are plenty of flatshare options, which you can find on the Beijinger website or on university notice boards, for example. Just be aware that most online ads are actually posted by agents, renting out rooms individually with no regard to how well you might get along. An alternative form of accommodation for students is to stay at their university. Most universities have separate dormitories or apartments for international students. The conditions are generally comfortable and spacious, and rent is typically about RMB2,500 per month.

Those here for business may prefer something a little more schmick. If that's the case, look into the Wenjin Hotel residences (www.wenjin.com.cn) right by TusPark, or at Longhu Tangning One, just south of Wudaokou station beside Zhongguancun No.2 Primary School. Prices in these properties start at around RMB7,000 for a one-bedroom apartment and at RMB12,000 for a two-bedroom.

One thing to remember in Wudaokou is that the police here are notoriously unforgiving and quick to fine or take action if expats don't respect the local registration laws. Make sure you register at the required *pàichūsuǒ* (police station) within 24 hours of moving into your apartment and then also immediately after you have any change to your visa or passport in the future. Take the originals and photocopies of your documents every time, even though you think they already have them.

ZHONGGUANCUN

Though only a five-minute drive from Wudaokou, Zhongguancun has a completely different feel. There is nothing village-like about it. It's a frenetic zone of high-rises, electronics, and shopping malls. When people talk about Zhongguancun, it's not about cute cafés or playing beer pong at bars—although there are several Starbucks cafés and a multitude of Western fast food chains in the area—it's about shopping or IT. The closest it comes to a community feeling is around Haidianhuangzhuang subway station (Lines 4 and 10, exit A2), where people set up stalls on blankets and in car trunks, selling anything from socks to cell phone covers, and where people stroll along the paved pedestrian street between EC Mall and supermarket Carrefour.

SHANNON AITKEN

Zhongguancun Plaza Pedestrian Street

PRIME LIVING LOCATIONS

Zhongguancun has a city feel about it, but with little glitz and zero glamor. The streets are lined with mall after mall, above ground and below. You can virtually walk the entire way underground from Haidianhuangzhuang subway station (Lines 4 and 10) to Zhongguancun subway (Line 4) and see nothing but shops, clothes, and electronic products lit by fluorescent lights. People come here to work in the various high-tech parks, and others are drawn from other districts to pick up their next hard drive, camera, or laptop.

Housing

Living within the center of Zhongguancun—anywhere between Zhongguancun Dajie, Haidian Nanlu, and the North Fourth Ring Road—can feel a little soulless. That said, everything is right at hand—several movie cinemas, a large post office, a Carrefour supermarket, and so on. Compared to elsewhere in the inner city, it can also be much easier to find affordable accommodations. You can start to find reasonable two-bedroom apartments from as little as RMB5,000. Quality can vary from shocking to fantastic within a single compound, but if you're lucky you might find one owned by a landlord who takes pride in the property.

Right in amongst everything is serviced apartment building Core Plaza (Lifang Ting, 立方庭) at 1 Shanyuan Jie. It's surrounded all the digital markets and malls. This is a relatively new complex with modern apartments and a large central garden. Prices start at around RMB5,000 for a studio. Nearby and also perfect for those working in Zhongguancun is Somerset Zhongguancun Beijing serviced apartments (www2. somerset.com). Prices range from around RMB19,000 per month for a one-bedroom apartment up to approximately RMB32,000 for a two-bedroom plus study.

These kinds of locations might be ideal for short-term stays, but if you're here for the long-term, you might want to reduce the constant intensity in your day. Toward the east or south of the center life can feel a little more tranquil. There are clusters of compounds on the east side of Zhongguancun subway station (Line 4), many of which have modern designs and nice communal gardens. Tianzuo International Center (天作国际中心), just south of Renmin University subway station (Line 4), has some impressive apartments, many with views of the surrounds, for surprisingly affordable prices. One-bedroom apartments might be found for RMB5,000 per month. You'll find it just off Zhongguancun Nandajie on Baiyi Lu, opposite the east gate of Beijing Institute of Technology (http://english.bit.edu.cn).

Expat Resources

RELIGIOUS SERVICES

Haidian isn't known for its places of holy worship, but with so much emphasis on science and business in the district, that isn't surprising.

Those that do subscribe to Christianity, however, may be impressed with the main church that is there—Beijing Haidian Church (海淀基督教堂, 39 Haidian Xidajie, 北京市海淀区彩和坊路9号, tel. 10/6257-2902, www.hdchurch.org), a short walk west of Zhongguancun subway station (Line 4, exit A). Though not in a traditionally expat heavy area, the church goes to great efforts to include its English-speaking community, more it seems than even many of the local churches in the east. Set in a lofty and bright modern building, the church holds English services every Sunday, English holy communion every second Sunday, and even has an English choir and English talk group.

Christian expat group Beijing International Christian Fellowship (BICF, www.bicf. org) also runs various weekly services and groups near Zhongguancun. Join meetings with the group at the Raycom Infotech Park (Tower C), located walking distance from either Zhongguancun subway station (Line 4, exit B) or Zhichunli subway station (Line 10, exit A).

Followers of Islam have a couple of choices. Madian Mosque (北京马甸清真寺, http://blog.sina.com.cn/u/1732042202) is set in an elegant traditional courtyard building on Madian Donglu on the southeast side of Madian Park, a short walk south of Jiandemen subway station (Line 10, exit D). It was built during the Qing dynasty and covers 3,800 square meters (40,903 square feet) and includes a prayer hall for women. Even older and larger is Haidian Mosque (tel. 10/6255-8296), a short walk north of Suzhoujie subway station (Line 10, exit A) at 19 Suzhou Jie.

SOCIALIZING AND NETWORKING

People in Haidian love to socialize, be it for work or pleasure. Universities will obviously generate a lot of activities through associations, sports, and groups, but there is more on offer elsewhere if you're up for it. Lush (www.lushbeijing.com), located on Chengfu Lu on the west side of Wudaokou subway station, is a regular host of events. Visit on Sunday evenings for open-mic nights, where you can get up and perform for a free beer, or test your knowledge on Wednesdays with their trivia nights.

More serious interactions can be had with the Zhongguancun Toastmasters Club (http://zhongguancuntm.blog.sohu.com), a branch of Toastmasters International. Events are held at the Haidian Art Culture Mansion, near Haidianhuangzuang subway

EXPAT PROFILE: LIVING IN OUTER HAIDIAN

Dirk is a freelance theater director, writer, and German teacher. He came to Beijing five years ago after traveling a lot in southern China, willing to learn and see a few things from a different perspective, and wanting to learn some Chinese. For the first few years he lived inside the Second Ring Road just near the Lama Temple, but then he decided to move out to Xiangshan in northwest Haidian district. Working part-time in Sanyuanqiao in Chaoyang, this means a commute of two hours each way by bus and subway several times a week.

WHY DID YOU DECIDE TO MOVE THERE?

I wanted to escape the air pollution in the city center and just occasionally get some fresher air. Unfortunately this is a wish that has been only partly fulfilled, as the dust cloud of Beijing frequently makes it out to Xiangshan—though I have to say the air quality still is definitely a bit better than in the city.

WHAT'S IT LIKE TO LIVE IN XIANGSHAN?

During the week (except in the touristy season) life around Xiangshan is more laid-back than in the city center. The locals meet in the morning at the marketplace, where fruits, vegetables, and clothes are being sold. There are loads of small noodle and dumpling places, as well as two Western-style cafés.

The highlight is Xiangshan Park, which has various tracks leading to the peak of Xiangshan (Fragrant Mountain) and Biyun Temple. The countryside is beautiful and has many hiking trails around the actual Xiangshan to discover. It's nice coming home from hectic Beijing in the night and seeing a light on the top of the mountain and sometimes even the stars in the sky.

WHAT ARE YOUR NEIGHBORS LIKE?

Most of them were originally farmers, but many of them now run different businesses in the tourism industry.

WHAT ARE SOME OF THE DRAWBACKS TO LIVING THERE?

In the "golden leaves season" and sometimes on the weekends, when loads of tourists flock to Xiangshan, it can get very noisy, and the streets and hiking trails become packed with people. It's also quite a long way to the city center, which is inconvenient, especially during rush hour. This is further exacerbated during the "golden leaves season," when it can take a long time to get in and out of the area in general.

WHAT'S YOUR APARTMENT LIKE AND WHAT ARE THE LIVING COSTS?

It's quite basic. I live in a simple room with basic furniture and a bathroom. It doesn't have central heating so it can get very cold in winter. It was built by a farmer, who added this extension onto the top of his own one-story house, and from my window I have a wonderful view.

WHAT KIND OF PEOPLE DO YOU THINK ARE SUITED TO LIVING IN XIANGSHAN?

Well, you're in the wrong place if you want to meet Westerners—there are only a handful living up here so far. I think this place suits people who don't have to work in the city center regularly, don't have to work at all, or may do a lot of work at home on the computer. It's for people who love the countryside around Beijing, wandering in the mountains, climbing hills, and enjoying a view of the big city from some distance. It's definitely a perfect place for all kinds of creative people, monks, and eremites who aren't yet ready completely to cut themselves off from the advantages of urban life.

Haidian Christian Church in Zhongguancun runs multidenominational services in both Chinese and English.

station (Lines 4 and 19, exit B). In a supportive and friendly environment, you can build your confidence and make friends through speech—using English.

Christian group BICF also runs get-togethers outside of its regular meeting place. One in particular is its Men's Monthly Breakfast at the Bridge Café. Join other gents and make new connections through your religious interests.

SPORTS AND RECREATION

Thanks to all the universities in Haidian, you'll have a surplus of sporting options at your disposal. Most of the universities make their facilities available to the public, so even if you're not a student, you'll be able to find a tennis court, basketball court, gym, or swimming pool—and for much less than what you would pay in a commercial venue. Renmin University and Beijing Sport University, for example, both have tennis courts that can be hired; Peking University and the China University of Geology have outdoor rock climbing and bouldering walls that are free to use, though dubiously maintained; while BLCU has a swimming center, athletics field, and gym. If you study at Beijing Sport University (BSU) you'll have international-class facilities available whenever you have a break.

In addition to the university options, Haidian has a wealth of other recreational possibilities. Relax or hike in one of the many parks around the district. Xiangshan (Fragrant Hills) is extremely popular with locals for hiking—maybe a little too popular for expats on weekends, especially during October when the leaves turn a vibrant red and hordes of tourists flock to see them. Get out here during the week and it feels entirely different. Fenghuang Mountain (www.bjfhl.com) farther out in Haidian's far northwest corner is a more tranquil option. To get here, take Line 4 on the subway to Beigongmen subway station. From exit A, walk about 200 meters around the corner to the 346 bus stop, and take the bus to the final stop.

You can also combine some hiking with yoga at Mountainyoga (www.mountain-yoga.org), out by Fragrant Hills. It offers yoga retreats, workshops, private tutoring, accommodations, and meals, and in between activities you can explore the surrounding trails.

For team sports, you can join clubs like Beijing Aardvarks (www.beijingaardvarks.org). Whatever your ability, age, nationality, or sex, they happily accept all new players. The team trains on Tuesdays at Beihang University (near Zhichunlu subway station) and at sports ground 26 Degrees on Thursdays—26 Degrees is actually out in Chaoyang northeast of Wangjing, but arranged busses leave from Pyro Pizza in Wudaokou and from outside the Jingkelong supermarket in Sanlitun (corner of Xindong Lu and Gongti Beilu) to take you there.

Alternatively, Frisbee training happens near Zhichunlu subway station (Line 10, exit G1), care of Beijing Ultimate (www.beijingultimate.com). The club holds weekly training and competes several times a year in such things as the China Nationals Ultimate Frisbee Tournament.

During winter when the lakes freeze over, you can break out your ice skates. Weiming Lake inside Peking University is free, although you'll need to pay to hire skates, and Zizhuyuan Park, on the west side of the National Library subway station (Line 4), has the largest ice course in Beijing. Skate it or have fun on the ice truck, ice ship, ice bicycles, or ice chairs. If you prefer to skate indoors, Champion Rink (www.championrink.com) is in Jinyuan New Yansha Mall. It has casual and club ice skating as well as an ice hockey club. Finding the rink, however, in this monster of a complex might cause you the most exertion of your day.

EDUCATION

It doesn't need to be said that Haidian is the place for further education. Students from all around the world come here to study not only Chinese, but many other majors and postgraduate courses. The most obvious choices are Peking University, Renmin University, Tsinghua University, Beijing Language and Culture University (BLCU), Beijing Normal University, and Beijing Foreign Studies University (BFSU), and if your main purpose is to study Chinese then these are good choices, but they may be out of your budget. If that's the case, some of the lesser-known universities may also be an option—and don't be dissuaded by a name that suggests that they teach anything but Chinese.

But what about for kids? There are definitely fewer expat-friendly educational choices in Haidian than in the east, and the choices that are here are not purely international, but rather local schools with an international department. The main exception to this is St. Paul American School, a private preparatory and boarding school on the west side of the Olympic Forest Park, about one kilometer north of Lincuiqiao subway station (Line 8).

In south Haidian, a short distance south of Yuquan subway station (Line 1), Beijing National Day School warmly welcomes international students, as do the schools attached to Renmin University and Tsinghua University farther north in the district. Tsinghua International School is perhaps the most international of the three. It requires students to hold a foreign passport and has a dynamic program directed carefully at preparing its students for university abroad. Admission fees are not cheap, but

SCHOOLS AND UNIVERSITIES IN HAIDIAN

SCHOOLS

School	Age	Website
Beijing National Day School	12-18 years	www.bjshiyi.org.cn
The High School Affiliated to Renmin University	12-17 years	www.rdfz.cn
Saint Paul American School (SPAS)	13-19 years	http://stpaulamerican.org
Tsinghua International School	6-12 years	www.this.edu.cn

UNIVERSITIES

University	Website
Beijing Film Academy	www.bfa.edu.cn
Beijing Foreign Studies University	www.bfsu.edu.cn
Beijing Institute of Technology	english.bit.edu.cn
Beijing Language and Culture University	www.blcu.edu.cn
Beijing Normal University	www.bnu.edu.cn
Beijing Sport University	http://en.bsu.edu.cn
Beijing University of Aeronautics and Astronautics (Beihang University)	http://ev.buaa.edu.cn
Central University of Finance and Economics	www.cufe.edu.cn
China University of Geosciences	www.cugb.edu.cn
China University of Political Science and Law	www.cupl.edu.cn
Minzu University of China	http://eng.muc.edu.cn
Peking University	www.pku.edu.cn
Renmin University of China	www.ruc.edu.cn
Tsinghua University	www.tsinghua.edu.cn
University of Science and Technology Beijing	http://en.ustb.edu.cn

they're much more approachable than many of the international schools in Shunyi or Chaoyang. Tsinghua International School, for example, starts from RMB89,000 for elementary school and RMB99,000 for high school. If you enroll your child for a second semester, the fee drops by 40 percent. Dormitory accommodation, if necessary, is RMB9,000 per semester for a two-person room.

In addition to direct schooling, little kids can also discover their nascent artistic talents at 3iArt (www.3iart.com.cn). The center is specialized in art education and offers art learning programs for children from preschool age to age 15. You'll find it located north of Xizhimen subway station on Xizhimennei Daijie, opposite Maples International shopping mall.

Finally, if you want to study Chinese but don't have the time or desire to do a university program, there are plenty of private Chinese schools in the vicinity. Just some of the better-known ones include Global Village (www.gvschinese.com) and Sinoland (www.sinolandchinese.com). Both are located in Wudaokou and relatively affordable. Sinoland places intense and ongoing emphasis on pronunciation, making sure you get each and every tone right so that people actually know that you want to "ask" *(wèn)* them something and not "kiss" *(wěn)* them.

HEALTH CARE

Haidian may have very few international health facilities, but it does have an abundance of health-care options. For starters, most of the universities have their own hospitals. These are typically basic level-one hospitals, which operate more like clinics for general ills and aches, but they're cheap and familiar with the international student population. Haidian then also has many of Beijing's top-level government hospitals.

One of the most important hospitals is the People's Liberation Army General Hospital (PLAGH), still sometimes going by its old name of the 301 Military Hospital (www.301hospital.com.cn). Being a general hospital it covers all areas of care for both the military and civilians. It is also one of the few hospitals in the district to have a VIP/international medical clinic (tel. 10/6829-5858), although English abilities are patchy. The hospital is conveniently located on Fuxing Lu (Chang'an Jie) at the southeast corner of Wukesong subway station (Line 1, exit C1).

Following on with the military theme, there is also the Air Force General Hospital (www.kj-hospital.com), located on Fucheng Lu on the east side of Xidiaoyutai subway station (Line 10, exit C); the Navy General Hospital (www.hjzyy.com.cn), also on Fucheng Lu, to the west of Baizhuizi subway station (Line 9, exit D); and the Armed Police General Hospital (www.wj-hospital.com), located on Yongding Lu about halfway between Wukesong and Yuquanlu subway stations (Line 1).

If going to a military hospital, however, makes you a little nervous, there is Peking University Third Hospital, also known as PKU Third Hospital (www.puh3.net.cn). This is also a top-level comprehensive hospital, but it's particularly respected for its work in gynecology and obstetrics, sports medicine, cardiovascular and orthopedic departments, in-vitro fertilization, and reconstructive surgery. It's closer to the universities on Xueyuan Lu near the North Fourth Ring Road, with its closest subway station being Xitucheng (Line 10, exit B).

Another non-military hospital to be aware of is the Beijing DCN Orthopaedic Hospital (www.dcn.org.cn/Eng). While this hospital isn't in the most convenient location, being out beyond the West Fourth Ring Road on Fushi Lu, it was the designated hospital for injured athletes during the Beijing Olympics and so can be worth the trip for the right injury.

Dental needs can be met out here by the same chains of clinics that service much of the inner city, including Arrail Dental (www.arrail-dental.com), Jiamei Dental (www.jiameidental.com), SDM Dental (www.sdmdental.com), and A&S Dental (www.

Haidian Hospital, located beside Haidianhuangzhuang subway station

© SHANNON AITKEN

PRIME LIVING LOCATIONS

aiyashi.com). An alternative to the private clinics is the Peking University School of Stomatology (http://ss.bjmu.edu.cn). Not just a facility for research and education, it also provides clinical care and emergency treatments.

SHOPPING AND DINING
Shopping

The most important shopping category in Haidian is electronics, and there are enough multistory digital malls here to completely bamboozle you. It's at once exciting and completely overwhelming. Navigating the various malls takes patience and a savvy Chinese friend. Get off at Zhongguancun subway station (Line 4, exit D) and you're immediately immersed in digital gadgets. Everything you could want is here—cameras, MP4 players, cell phones, endless cheap external hard drives, laptops, printers, computer hardware, software, DVDs—a lot genuine, a lot not. Bargaining is usually required. Some of the better-known malls to look for include Top Electronics City (鼎好电子商城, www.dinghao.cn), Hailong Electronics Market (海龙电子商城, www. hilon.com.cn), Kemao Electronics Mall (科贸电子城, www.zgccomo.com), secondhand mall Zhonghai Electronics Market (中海电子市场), and, the biggest of them all, Zhongguancun e-Plaza (中关村E世界数码广场, www.bjemall.cn).

Much farther south in Haidian, but definitely not to be forgotten, is the Wukesong Camera market (www.bjphoto.com.cn). This amazing market stocks everything the novice or professional photographer could need, including Holgas, Lomos, Rolleiflexes, antique secondhand cameras, sports-journalist-sized lenses, lighting equipment, books, specialty film, and bags. Modest bargaining can be done, but generally prices are fairly straightforward. You'll find it at 40 Wukesong Lu (Fourth Ring Road), a 10-minute walk north of Wukesong subway station (Line 1, exit B1).

Fortunately, Haidian is more than just fibers and motherboards. When you arrive, make a trip to Five Golden Star Market. This wholesale market is a cheap place

© SHANNON AITKEN

Zhongguancun is a head-spinning treasure chest of electronic gadgets and components.

to stock up on crockery, glassware, utensils, and cookware. And while there, you can acquaint yourself with the fresh food market next door. It's the place to get fresh meat and fresh fruit and veggies. Find it on Mingguang Lu, just south of Dazhongsi subway station (Line 13) on the east side of the railway line. Supermarkets are also big in Haidian. Three of the biggest include Carrefour (www.carrefour.com.cn), in Zhongguancun Plaza (Haidianhuangzhuang subway station, Lines 4 and 19, exit A2); Auchan (www.auchan.com) on the West Fourth Ring Road near Zizhuyuan Lu, and the Wal-Mart Supercenter (http://wal-martchina.com) by Zhichunlu subway station (Lines 10 and 13, exit B).

If you're interested in clothing yourself, there are also many places to find a bargain. One of the favorite spots for students is the Wudaokou Clothing Market. The market is geared toward the fashion-hungry student crowd, and these days it stocks a trendier, more upmarket range of clothing than many other markets. There are lots of Western and Korean brands, mostly fake, so be sure to bargain. It's located in Jinma Plaza at the corner of Xueqing Lu and Qinghua Donglu. If that's not enough, there is also Jinyuan New Yansha Shopping Mall (or Golden Resources Shopping Mall, 金源时代购物中心), on Yuanda Lu off the West Fourth Ring Road and beside Changchunqiao subway station (Line 10, exit A). The mall covers more than 550,000 square meters and was, for a fleeting time between 2004 and 2005, the world's largest mall. It's a collection of various mall brands and retailers, high-end and low, all located in the once gargantuan complex. Have a look at their promotional video on Youku (http://v.youku.com/v_show/id_XNTA3ODk3NzI0.html) to get a real feel for it. It's all in Chinese, but you'll get the gist.

Finally, on to books. Though the online book market in Beijing is big, cheap, and incredibly convenient, bookstores in Haidian are still going strong, for books in Chinese or foreign languages and textbooks. Plus, books in university libraries notoriously go missing or are just not put on the shelf so that they don't go missing—so it can be handy to know a good bookshop or two. Just a few of the stores you may find yourself in include Haidian Book City and the Zhongguancun Book Building, almost side by side at the intersection of the North Fourth Ring West Road and Suzhou Jie. There is also the Beijing Language and Culture University Press Store, located just inside the university's south gate on the left side. This is the supplier of almost half the Chinese-language textbooks on the market (Peking University Press monopolizes the other half), so it's one of the best places you could go to for Chinese textbooks.

Dining

Haidian isn't particularly known for its food, but it is the kind of place in which you'll discover a hidden gem or a tiny authentic place that only locals know about. Over the last decade, restaurants have catered largely to the student population, so you'll find endless cheap and cheerful eateries wherever you go. Korean and Japanese restaurants are both in plentiful supply, thanks to the number of these students coming to Beijing to study, and Western diner-style establishments are also popular. The food is hearty and portion sizes generous, though they may never quite match the standard of what you get at home.

The nature of dining in general in Haidian is on the verge of changing. Beijing's restaurateurs have cottoned on to the fact that not only are there many more adventurous, internationally minded businesspeople out here, but the student population is also wealthier than it once was. In the past high-end restaurant chains typically stuck to the east of the city—even Da Dong Roast Duck Restaurant, one of the most respected Beijing duck chains in Beijing, has yet to open a store on this side of town. But Wudaokou and Zhongguancun are beginning to look like culinary goldmines. Café Ricci, for example, situated in Tuspark, was one of the first high-end, Western-owned cafés to open first in Haidian and only later expand to other districts—normally it's the other way around, if at all.

When you first move to Haidian, there are some key places to know, especially if you're a student. These include Bridge Café, Sculpting in Time, and then bars Lush and Propaganda. These are all in the same location, 100 meters west of Wudaokou subway station, on Caijing Donglu. These venues are the staple eating, socializing, studying, and language-exchange venues of students, and you'll probably be introduced to them within days of arriving. Order a single coffee or a Coke and you can sit here all day without anyone asking you to leave.

Such kinds of places aren't expensive, and they usually have discount periods, but regardless, eating at them every day might not be within your means. For those who really need to tuck in the budget, there are the university cafeterias. The food is rarely said to be anything other than "okay" for quality, but without fail it's known to be cheap. Shop around the universities for variety. Tsinghua university is said to have some of the best dining halls out of all the universities and has nearly 20 halls to choose from in the entire campus.

Exploring the restaurant options in Haidian, however, is a must. So be sure to hound your local Chinese friends for their tips on where to go. One they may suggest is Wu Dai Yang Guan (五代羊倌, 29 Suzhou Jie, 苏州街29号, tel. 10/6265-8166). This home-style Shandong restaurant is set in a stylish traditional building and serves

some of Wudaokou's popular night spots, cafes, and shops

© SHANNON AITKEN

delicious authentic food for about RMB100 per person. Try the sliced lamb in family-style lamb soup (刀切羊肉和老家的羊汤), a tender, slow-cooked lamb dish in a wonderfully fragrant clear soup. Chinese people also love their Sichuan food, so you may also find yourself directed to Spice Spirit (麻辣诱惑, 15 Zhongguancun Dajie, 中关村大街15号, 中关村广场购物中心, tel. 10/5986-3088), at Zhongguancun Plaza. This is a chain that can be found all over the city, but it's extremely popular and affordable, has a fresh and modern environment, and incurs an average spend of about RMB75 per person.

At the upper end of the scale are the restaurant hotels, the most notable being S.T.A.Y. in the Shangri-La Beijing (Shangri-La Hotel Beijing, 29 Zizhuyuan Lu, 紫竹院路29号香格里拉饭店, tel. 10/6841-2211), situated west of Purple Bamboo Park, just across the West Third Ring Road. This is not only the place to enjoy immaculate and creative French cuisine, it's also a stylish place in which to have sophisticated business drinks in a manicured garden. Expect to spend around RMB1,000 per person for dinner.

Places of Interest

Haidian is packed with an abundant variety of places to visit and explore—both indoors and out, for kids and adults. This is largely thanks to the region of Beijing that its borders surround. While Chaoyang is almost entirely urban, Haidian is half urban, half suburban, giving it a collection of manmade as well as natural attractions. And because the imperial families pocketed it as their personal playground, there are ancient buildings galore and an abundance of beautiful lakes.

In the inner city, you can take advantage of a variety of facilities. The MasterCard Center (www.mastercardcenter.com.cn), beside Wukesong subway station (Line 1, exit B1), hosts international basketball matches as well as international concerts and other performances. Elton John has performed here, as have Westlife, Akon, and the Cranberries. More entertainment can be found at Haidian Theater (28 Zhongguancun Dajie, 中关村大街28号, Lines 4 and 10, exit B, www.bjshdjy.com), located beside Haidianhuangzhuang subway station. The theater not only screens the latest box office releases, but also presents concerts, opera, ballet, plays, and other performances.

Reading and immersing yourself in Chinese culture can be done at the National Library of China (National Library subway station, Line 4, exit A or D, tel. 10/8854-4114, http://nlc.gov.cn), the second largest library in the world (second to the Library of Congress in Washington, D.C.), and among its more than 26 million books it has a wide range of books in English. It's free to register for a reader's card, and this will give you full access to the public areas of the library. To do this you will need to show your passport when you apply. You can also borrow up to three books at any one time, for up to 31 days. English books can't be renewed, while Chinese books can be if not already reserved. The library is open weekdays from 9am to 9pm and on weekends from 9am to 5pm. The library is open to readers who are aged 16 and above, and the Children's Library is suitable for kids aged 6-15. Also along educational lines is the Beijing World Art Museum (www.worldartmuseum.cn/sjysg_en), on the south side of Yuyuantan Park, a short walk north from Military Museum station (Line 1, exit B). Rather than housing ancient Chinese relics, the museum pays homage to relics from elsewhere around the world, including ancient Egypt and Rome. It regularly curates fascinating exhibitions of different artists or periods of history from around the world. If it's the local culture that you want to delve into, however, there are several interesting Buddhist temples within the district, including Five Pagoda Temple (Wutasi), which is just east of the National Library subway station (exit C), and the Big Bell Temple (http://dazhongsi.org), which is a walkable distance from Dazhongsi subway station (Line 13, exit A), Zhichunlu subway station (Lines 10 and 13, exit B), or Renmin University subway station (Line 4, exit B).

For something more lively and just on the east side of the Five Pagoda Temple, there is the Beijing Aquarium. Unfortunately this is part of the Beijing Zoo (tel. 10/6217-6655, www.bj-sea.com); fortunately the two are nothing alike as a lot of money and care was put in to making this a special environment. You also don't even need to go through the zoo to get here as it's by the north gate of the zoo off the Gaoliangqiao Byway, just north east of Xizhimen subway station. There are feeding displays, sea lion and dolphin shows, and more than a thousand species of aquatic life to see.

One of the classic places to visit is the old CCTV Tower (tel. 10/6845-0715), at one time one of the more interesting buildings in the city before the new CCTV Headquarters, the Yintai Building, and the China World Tower came along and stole its thunder. Regardless, they're all in the east, and as far as things go in the west, this is still an excellent place to make a point of coming to. Located on the west side of Yuyuantan Park and the West Third Ring Middle Road, and standing at 405 meters (1,329 feet), antenna included, it is the tallest building in the area. There is an observation deck (RMB70 for entry) at 238 meters (781 feet), which gives you a 360-degree view of the city, and on a good day this means a bird's-eye view of the mountains extending into Hebei. The viewing tower is open until 10pm, giving you plenty of time to take in the city lights. Come a little earlier, however, as ticket sales stop at around

© SHANNON AITKEN

temple at Fenghuangling

9:30pm. There is also a rotating restaurant lower down, but it's generally agreed that the view is the highlight of the experience.

In addition to buildings, Haidian is also home to many beautiful parks, including Yuyuantan Park, loved for its profusion of cherry blossoms in spring and its frozen lake in winter; Yuanming Yuan (the Old Summer Palace); the Summer Palace, a stunning park of hills, historic buildings, and waterways; Haidian Park, often host to music festivals and other events; and Purple Bamboo Park (Zizhuyuan), a beautiful park set around a large lake and replete with traditional bridges, pagodas, and water lilies. Farther out there is the famed Xiangshan (Fragrant Hills), an expansive park of hills, historical relics, and lakes. Come to Xiangshan in mid-October to early November to see the brilliant display of red leaves—although be warned, any semblance of tranquility will be completely lost by the en masse visit of Chinese tourists who are there to do the same thing. On the north side of Xiangshan is Beijing Botanical Garden (www.beijingbg.com). This can seem a little far out for most expats, so relatively few ever come here, but it's worth making time for. Stretching over 401 hectares (990 acres), it is filled with historic buildings, conservatories, hot rooms and gardens, and more than 6,000 species of plants. It is also the location of Wofo Temple, Beijing's oldest temple, which was first built during the Tang dynasty more than 1,300 years ago. Inside the temple, there is a somewhat saucy looking Buddha, known as the reclining Sakyamuni statue.

Don't stop just at these venues, however; other places promise you a genuine escape from the crowds and the city. Take a day trip out into the mountains in northwest Haidian, hiking around such places as Yangtai Mountain, Dajue Temple in Jiufeng National Forest Park, or the peaceful Fenghuangling Mountain. They are far less touristy than the above-mentioned parks, and you may actually find yourself out here alone or with only the occasional passerby. Though seemingly a little out of reach, they can be surprisingly easy to get to with the right bus.

Getting Around

SUBWAY

The developing subway system in Haidian is making this part of town seem closer to the city center every year. It currently has five lines that pass through it, including Lines 4, 6, 9, 10, and 13, all of these making getting to university or work in the tech parks extremely convenient. By 2014 Haidian will also have the Western Suburban Line, which will provide direct access to the Summer Palace, the Botanical Garden, and Xiangshan, and by 2016 there will be Line 16, which will start in Fengtai district in the south, travel northwards inside Line 10, then up and out to the east side of Jiufeng National Forest Park and Yangtaishan Natural Scenic Area. There are also plans to connect Haidian directly to Tongzhou in the southeast of the city via rapid transport. As to when this will be completed, no one is yet sure.

TRAINS

There are no major train terminals in Haidian, but you can board trains at Qinghuayuan Railway Station, just north of Zhichunlu subway station (Lines 10 and 13), and Qinghe Railway Station, just north of Shangdi subway station (Line 13). The various S2 trains pass through both stations on their way to and from Badaling and Beijing North Station at Xizhimen, as do the 4471-4474 trains on their way to and from Chengde in Hebei province. Visit http://train.huochepiao.com and search by station name or train number to find out train times and fares.

The Fenghuangling area is easily reached by public transport and makes for a scenic day of hiking.

© SHANNON AITKEN

PRIME LIVING LOCATIONS

BUSES

The major buses worth getting to know in this area are:

331: Use this bus to get you down to Jishuitan by Line 2 or up to the Summer Palace, the Botanical Garden, or Xiangshan. Stops along the way include PKU Third Hospital (Beiyisanyuan Zhan, 北医三院站), BCLU (Beijing Yuyan Daxue Zhan, 北京语言大学站), Wudaokou (Wudaokou Zhan, 五道口站), Tsinghua University West Gate (Qinghua Daxue Ximen Zhan, 清华大学西门站), and Yuanming Yuan Park (Yuanmingyuan Nanmen Zhan, 圆明园南门站).

346: Take a break with a visit to the northwest of Haidian. Get on this bus right outside of Beigongmen subway station (Line 4, exit D), take it out past Bei'anhe (北安河站), which is about one kilometer from Dajue Temple and Yangtaishan, and get off at the very last stop, Fenghuangling, which is the starting point for hikes in the area.

466: This bus is for those who want to get over to the Olympic area in Chaoyang. Get on right outside of Zhongguancun subway station (Line 4, exit C2), near Wudaokou on Zhongguancun Donglu, just south of McDonald's (Dongshengyuan Zhan, 东升园站), in front of the Bank of China on Shuangqing Lu by the east side of Tsinghua University (Qinghua Donglu Xikou Zhan, 清华东路西口站), then get off at Lincuilu Zhan (林萃路站) for a short walk to the west gate of the Olympic Forest Park, or continue on through the center of the Olympic Park and up and around the east side of the forest park.

563: This bus connects many of Haidian's major attractions. Stops on the route include Xizhimen station (near exit D), Beijing Zoo (Dongwuyuan Zhan, 动物园站), the National Library (Guojia Tushuguan Zhan, 国家图书馆站), Beijing Institute of Technology and Beijing Foreign Studies University (Weigongcunlu Xikou Zhan, 魏公村路西口站), Renmin University (Wanquanzhuang Zhan, 万泉庄站), Haidian Park (Haidian Gongyuan Zhan, 海淀公园站), Yuanming Yuan (Poshangcun Zhan, 坡上村站), the Summer Palace (Ditie Beigongmen Zhan, 地铁北宫么站), and the very last stop, Xiangshan (Xiangshan Gongyuan Dongmen Zhan, 香山公园东门站).

656: This bus runs east to west, so it can be handy if you want to get to the Olympic area or even to Wangjing or 798 Art District. Some of the stops along the way include Beijing Sport University (Beijing Tiyu Daxue Zhan, 北京体育大学站), the east gate of Yuanming Yuan (Yuanmingyuan Dongmen Zhan, 圆明园东门站), the west gate of Tsinghua University (Qinghua Daxue Ximen Zhan, 清华大学西门站), Wudaokou (Wudaokou Zhan, 五道口站), BLCU (Beijing Yuyan Daxue Zhan, 北京语言大学站), China University of Geosciences and Beijing University of Science and Technology (Chengfulu Kounan Zhan, 成府路口南站), the Olympic Sports Center Stadium (Yayuncun Zhan, 亚运村站), within walking distance of Ikea (Wangjingqiao Xi Zhan, 望京桥西站), by Guangshun Nandajie in Wangjing (Futong Dongdajie Zhan, 阜通东大街站), 798 (Wanhong Xijie Zhan, 万红西街站), and even on to Indigo mall (Jiuxianqiao Zhan, 酒仙桥站).

SHUNYI AND NORTHEAST CHAOYANG

Shunyi district is an expat enclave as well as the residence of wealthy Chinese who dream the international dream of having a house, a white-picket fence, and a double garage in which to park their luxury vehicles—the first for its permitted days of driving, the second for the other days. Just six or so years ago, this was very much countryside with few amenities, while today it's Western suburbia transplanted into Beijing.

In almost all cases, the expats who live out here are families, those who have been sent by their companies on packages, and who have children attending the international schools. It can be a great place for those with school-age children—there are endless activities and sport options to keep the kids entertained, and the schools have a lot to do with that. It would be an unusual choice, however, for singles or couples without kids to move out here. There is next to no nightlife by city standards, bars and restaurants are also comparatively few, and to get to the city it takes 30 minutes to an hour or more, given good or bad traffic conditions. Plus, if you don't have a personal driver, you'll have the constant anxiety of not being able to get a taxi, let alone a driver who won't ask you to get out when you tell him or her where you want to go.

The character of Shunyi may actually be about to change dramatically over the next

© SHANNON AITKEN

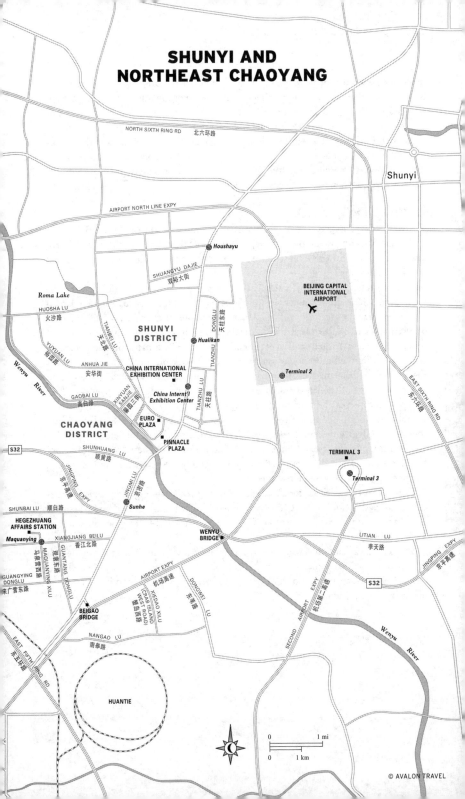

few years. New apartment complexes are being constructed at lightning speed out here by the government in an effort to alleviate the squash of the inner city. These are not luxury apartments, which until now, have been the signature abode of Shunyi. They are the apartments of the everyman. They are not being built out of sight in the far reaches of the district, but side by side with the gated villa compounds and the sweeping grounds of the impressively appointed international schools. At the last census in 2010 Shunyi had a population of 877,000 people—here's wondering what that figure will be in 2020 when the next census is due.

LAY OF THE LAND

Shunyi district is approximately 30 kilometers (19 miles) northeast of the CBD, straddling the Sixth Ring Road. Beijing Capital International Airport is encircled by Shunyi, but responsibility for this vital structure lies in the hands of a much more established district, Chaoyang.

Like the inner city, Shunyi's suburban area is also extremely flat. The entire district covers 1,020 square kilometers (394 square miles). Of this, expats tend to live in a minute portion of territory called Tianzhu town, one of the seven municipal areas of Shunyi. Tianzhu town is at the southwest corner of Shunyi and makes up just 13 square kilometers (8 square miles) of the entire district. The expat population occupies even less of this, with most homes and businesses located along both sides of the border that separates Chaoyang and Shunyi districts. The border here is etched by the Wenyu River, and most of the expat resources are on the Shunyi side of the river—such as shopping complexes and international medical clinics. However, many international schools and housing communities sit on the Chaoyang side of the river. Technically they are in Chaoyang, and if you do a specific Internet search for Shunyi facilities, you'll miss many of these, but in daily chit-chat, people living here or going to school here are still generally described as being "out in Shunyi." So for the simplicity of this chapter we'll maintain the status quo.

Shunyi isn't just all about the expat community. It is also an important zone for various industries, including Air China, which has its behemoth head office in Tianzhu town, and Hyundai, which set up its China head office and factory not far south of Shunyi subway station.

Shunyi subway station is where the real core of Shunyi is, the "village" from which the province took its name. Though this part of the district feels almost like a city itself, expats don't spend a lot of time here and generally prefer to head into the center of the city for shopping.

Where to Live

Housing

In the near future there may be cheaper options for apartments in Shunyi, something more local than the current selection, but for now, most accommodation styles and budgets align with those of expatriates who live comfortably on generous packages from their companies. There is a wide variety of home styles and decoration here, so do look around at several properties even within the one complex. The design tastes of landlords can swing from nonexistent to garish to elegant. Many homes have three or four levels, and generous backyards, some are semi-detached and others freestanding. If forking out for an entire villa isn't in your or your company's budget, some of the communities, such as Capital Paradise and Yosemite, have apartment complexes as well as villas. These are considerably cheaper than the villas and still reasonably spacious with three or four bedrooms. Don't forget to look into the facilities each compound provides for its residents as well. Gyms are just the start of what may be on offer. Spas, bike tracks, lakes, playground equipment, dog parks, and private or public swimming pools are just some of the built-in extras that some compounds have added to increase their attractiveness.

It's handy for you or your *āyí* (housekeeper) to be able to walk to your children's school to pick them up, especially as many schools require children to be picked up by a known or pre-arranged person in the afternoon. Nearly all international schools, however, have private bus services that can instead drop your child directly at home, wherever you live. So if you do happen to find a community that you like but which is not near your child's school, it shouldn't be a problem.

Some of the better-known estates on the Shunyi side of the river include:

© SHANNON AITKEN

Like most other housing communities in Shunyi and northeastern Chaoyang, Yosemite offers families multistory houses in safe and pleasant surrounds.

EuroVillage, Yosemite, River Garden (www.rivergarden-villa.com), Le Leman Lake, Capital Paradise, Gahood Villas, Dragon Bay Villas, and Rose & Ginkgo. On the south side of Wenyu river in Chaoyang there is Lane Bridge, Grand Hills, the traditional Chinese-style Cathay View (www.cathayview.cn), Quanfa Garden, Orchid Garden and Beijing Riviera (www.bjriviera.com). Prices vary greatly, obviously, depending on the specifications of the home, but in this area you're roughly looking at RMB17,000-26,000 (US$2,734-4,181) per month for apartments and RMB20,000-110,000 per month (US$3,216-17,690) for villas. Quanfa Garden, Capital Paradise, and Gahood Villas tend to sit at the cheaper end of this scale, while Yosemite, Beijing Riviera, and Grand Hills balance it at the other end.

Expat Resources

RELIGIOUS SERVICES

Continuing your religious practice will be relatively easy. The Capital Community Church (CCC, www.capitalcommunitychurch.net) represents the Protestant faith and meets at the Beijing Arts Exhibition Center on Sundays at 10am. You'll find it off Shunhuang Lu just behind the BD Flower Market, at the corner of Jingmi. For added convenience, the CCC has a shuttle bus that makes a run to many of the villa compounds before and after church. In addition to Sunday services, they have children's church and small groups throughout the week. Have scones, tea, or coffee after service at the English Tearoom right next door.

Catholic organization Our Lady of China Beijing offers religion classes for adults and children, fellowship groups, charity outreach services, and Mass in various places in the city, including in Shunyi at 5pm on Saturdays. All Masses are in English and take place in the same location as the CCC services. For full details, contact olcbjparish@aol.com.

Due to local laws, you are required to have your passport on you to attend services for either group.

SOCIALIZING AND NETWORKING

Unlike the CBD, Shunyi doesn't have many organized social groups, particularly those targeting networking of the business kind. A lot of socializing is done via school activities that naturally bring people together and through parent organizations associated with the schools.

Daystar Academy's kindergarten (www.daystarchina.cn) runs a toddler playgroup for parents with children three years old and under every Wednesday 9am-10:30am. It's a free program designed to bring parents of youngsters within the community together.

One very important group worth joining on at least several occasions is the International Newcomers' Network (INN, www.innbeijing.org). The group has firmly established itself as a resource for all newcomers. It can help you make friends, answer questions, and provide support if you're finding settling in challenging. INN meets in several places, and for Shunyi residents, that's for coffee on the third Thursday of every month, 10am-noon.

SPORTS AND RECREATION

The advantage of living out in Shunyi is that you have some great sports and recreation options at a relatively easy distance. A good many golf courses can be found out here if you're partial to a hit or two. Mind you, it doesn't come cheaply and is generally the signature sport of the local wealthy. The Beijing Riverside Resort Golf Club (tel. 10/8046-6566), for example, is at your doorstep just off Shunhuang Lu on the Chaoyang side of the river. It's an 18-hole, 72-par golf course, with total length of 6,428 meters (7,030 yards). The highlight of the course is the many water obstacles.

Water warriors can take advantage of post-Olympic sites by joining up with Ao Fan Sailing (http://aofansailing.com) at the Shunyi Olympic Rowing-Canoeing Park. The club not only runs summer camps, training, and competitions for sailing but also has kayaking and other water sports. For the frozen kinds of water sports, cross back across the Chaobai River and head a tad farther north to Qiabo Ice & Snow World (www.qbski.com/bj), the only indoor place where you can ski all year round in northern China, let alone Beijing.

Shunyi also offers residents equestrian clubs, hapkido, ballet and dancing schools, and swimming. Team sports are covered, too. The Beijing Devils make a serious commitment each season to playing hard, both on and off the rugby field. If you're not quite into full-contact rugby, however, the club also runs mixed touch rugby, offering you a less aggressive way to be social and keep fit. Most training and competitions take place in Dulwich College Legend Garden Campus. If you play cricket then join the very international Beijing Cricket Club (BCC, www.bjcricketclub.org). (The word for cricket in Chinese sounds very much like the word for baseball—compare *bǎnqiú* to *bàngqiú*—and some uninformed locals will try to correct what they think is your poor pronunciation of the latter.) The club holds Santa Fe League and Twenty20 League matches on weekends in Beijing, and participates in matches throughout the country. The BCC also holds its training at the Legend Garden campus of Dulwich College.

Of course, gyms aren't to be forgotten. When it's too polluted outside to run, you will likely be able to train indoors at your compound's clubhouse gym. If it doesn't have one, just some of the commercial gyms include Human in Motion (www.humaninmotion.com.cn) at Cathay View Garden. Alternatively, join a Heyrobics (www.heyrobics.com) class. What started as a quirky Swedish aerobics class has now developed into a diverse range of fun, energy-packed classes, which are held at various spots in the area.

EDUCATION

When people think of schools in Beijing—for expatriate kids—they think of Shunyi, so much so that you'd almost believe no international school existed in the inner city.

Shunyi's access to major roads, proximity to the airport, and its relatively undeveloped land has made it a magnet for well-funded private and international schools to build their ideal campuses on. Most of the international schools in Shunyi have been constructed in the last 10 years, with Keystone Academy and the new Harrow campus being two of the most recent newcomers.

Outside of the standard school facilities, however, there are several other educational support services. One of these includes the Learning Center (www.thelearningcenter.cn), which specializes in tutoring services for everything from kindergarten through to 12. They can coordinate with your child's school and also help them prepare for exams, such as the SATs.

Another important service in the neighborhood is Side by Side (www.sidebysidebeijing.com). This foreign-owned and -managed center helps those with special needs and learning difficulties, from preschoolers through to adults. They offer learning support, music therapy, behavior support, parenting sessions, family support, and workshops.

Education doesn't have to be all math and science, however. Mac Time Community Art Center (www.mactimeart.com), situated in Euro Plaza, can help bring out your or your kids' creative sides. There are kids and adults classes for pottery, film appreciation, calligraphy, oil painting, and more. In the same vein, if you dream of having your own romantic moment at a potter's wheel, then JOP (Joy of Pottery, www.joppottery.com) can set you up with the skills for this with bilingual pottery classes. In a relaxed countryside building, you can learn a variety of pottery techniques or simply come for tea. JOP is up in Shuipo village not far from the north end of Tianbei Lu.

For linguistic pursuits and to communicate better with your *āyí* or driver, Shunyi and northeast Chaoyang have schools to cater to expat families. You can easily find a private tutor, or for something more social, investigate options at schools such as Mandarin Express School (www.mandarinex.com), Live the Language Mandarin School (www.livethelanguage.cn), and the Bridge School (www.bridgeschoolchina.com).

Education options in the area can also extend to cooking—for you or your *āyí*. One of the frustrations that many expats find is that though their *āyí* are hard working and caring, their cooking skills are limited to family-style Chinese food, which is great, but you and your family might not want to eat it three times a day seven days a week. Christina's Catering Beijing (www.wix.com/tinasworkshop/tws) runs special classes dedicated to educating *āyí* to cook the kind of food Westerners like to eat, as well as classes for Westerners who want to cook the food their *āyí* like to eat.

Health Care

For day-to-day aches, illnesses, and dental problems, your main clinic in town is Beijing United Family Clinic (http://beijing.ufh.com.cn), prominently located in Pinnacle Plaza. Staffed by an international team and run like any good clinic in the West, it is a place that makes most expats feel at ease going to. Dental needs can also be taken care of at SDM Dental (www.sdmdental.com), in Euro Plaza. SDM Dental Clinics are internationally run practices and have English-speaking staff on hand.

There are no national-level or international hospitals in Shunyi. For this, your closest options are the main Beijing United Family Hospital (BJU) or Oasis International Hospital, both in Lido. Possibly not tremendously closer than a trip to Lido is Shunyi District Hospital (www.syhos.com), on the south side of Shunyi subway station. This is a second-tier hospital, meaning it's a district-level hospital rather than a national hospital. It has, however, been given a top grading for this level, and is a comprehensive hospital. For kids, Beijing New Century Harmony Pediatric Clinic (www.ncich.com.cn) is on Linyin Lu, not far from the Crown Plaza. This is a satellite clinic of the respected Beijing New Century International Children's Hospital. Though definitely more Chinese than the BJU clinic, it's staffed with experienced pediatricians

INTERNATIONAL SCHOOLS IN SHUNYI AND NORTHEAST CHAOYANG

PRESCHOOL AND KINDERGARTEN

School	Age	Website
Beijing Huijia Kindergarten	1.5-6 years	www.hjkids.com
Canadian International School of Beijing (CIS), Shunyi Campus	18 months-6 years	www.cisb.com.cn
Children's House International Montessori Kindergarten	0-6 years	www.montessoribeijing.com
Children's Community School Beijing	18 months-6 years	www.bjccs.org.cn
Children's International Bilingual Academy	18 months-6 years	www.clcbkids.com
Daystar Academy	0-2 years	www.daystarchina.cn
Eduwings Kindergarten	2-6 years	www.eduwingskids.com
Etonkids Bilingual Kindergarten	1-6 years	www.etonkids.com
House of Knowledge	10 months-6 years	www.house-of-knowledge.net
International Montessori School of Beijing	1-6 years	www.msb.edu.cn
Ivy Bilingual School	2-6 years	www.ivyschools.com
MSB Jiade International Bilingual Kindergarten of Beijing	2-6 years	www.eightbridge.com/msb1872/index.asp
Windsor Bilingual Kindergarten	18 months-6 years	http://legendgardens.windsorkindergarten.cn

COMBINED YEARS

School	Age	Website
International School of Beijing (ISB)	3-18 years	www.isb.bj.edu.cn
Beijing International Bilingual Academy (BIBA)	2.5-16 years	www.bibachina.org
British School of Beijing (BSB)	1-18 years	www.britishschool.org.cn
Dulwich College Beijing	1-18 years	www.dulwich-beijing.cn
Harrow International School Beijing	3-18 years	www.harrowbeijing.cn
Keystone Academy	6-18 years	www.keystoneacademy.cn
King's College Beijing	2-11 years	www.kingscollege.cn
Western Academy of Beijing (WAB)	3-18 years	www.wab.edu

and nurses from China and overseas, and has 24-hour multilingual services and consultations 9am-9pm.

SHOPPING AND DINING
Shopping

Shopping options in the Shunyi/northeast Chaoyang area constantly growing, and the nice thing about the options here is that there are a lot of artisans, people selling homegrown produce or artwork. You'll also find well-stocked international supermarkets catering to the local expat community.

Some of the most obvious places to shop include Euro Plaza on Tianbei Lu and Pinnacle Plaza around the corner on Xinyuan Yi Lu. Euro Plaza (www.bjeuroplaza.com) is your typical shopping mall, with fashion retailers, restaurants, and homeware. You'll find brands like Tupperware, Torana Clean Air, Costa Coffee, McDonald's, and KFC. Pinnacle Plaza has more of a village feel. Organic grocer Lohao City (www.lohaocity.com) is here, along with Starbucks, international supermarket Jenny Wang's (www.jennyshop.com.cn), and Beijing United Family's Shunyi dental and medical clinics. Just down the street at the gate of Capital Paradise, you can also shop for Western groceries at April Gourmet. If you'd rather get your groceries fresh from the farm, Beijing Farmers' Market is a regular activity in the area, typically held on the grounds of Daystar Academy. Across the river on Chaoyang side, De Run Wu Organic and Natural Store (tel. 10/8459-0809, jiyunliang@vip.163.com), run by a group of Buddhist farmers, sells food that they produce as organically as possible. They're on Shunhuang Lu near the BD Flower Market (look for the sign that says Danshui town) but also do scheduled home deliveries.

Walking distance directly north of Maquanying subway station is Beijing Scitech Premium Outlet Mall (www.scitechoutlet.com). You probably won't need to wait too long for somebody to suggest a visit here. Reminiscent of a Disneyland village sans the

© SHANNON AITKEN

Pinnacle Plaza

PRIME LIVING LOCATIONS

fun rides, it's a shopping haven dedicated to outlets of international brands, including Diesel, Calvin Klein, G-Star Raw, Lagerfeld, MaxMara, and many more.

Dining

The signature style of Shunyi establishments is family friendliness. Various cafés not only have kids' menus but also dedicated play areas. These include the English Tearoom (www.englishtearoombeijing.com); Fuel at Langham Place (http://beijingairport.langhamplacehotels.com), beside Terminal 3 at the airport; and Mrs Shanen's Bagels (tel. 10/8046-4301), next to Capital Paradise. Other cultures are also represented in the district. Those with an appetite for Indian can reserve a table at Taj Pavilion (http://thetajpavilion.com) in Euro Plaza; or if it's Japanese you're craving, Haru Teppanyaki and Sushi Bar (tel. 10/8046-5112) at Pinnacle Plaza is one of the town favorites. On the north side of Huosha Lu, Malacca Legend (www.malaccalegend.com) has become a popular establishment for those who enjoy Malaysian and Singaporean cuisine.

In northeast Chaoyang, familiarize yourself with the growing collection of cafés and shops at Cathay View Plaza on Xiangjiang Beilu (right by DD's Market). Brunch as well as healthy sandwiches and salads are the star items at Switch! Cafe (http://switchrestaurants.com), while Boulangerie Nanda (www.bnanda.com) produces delicious organic breads, cakes, fresh juices, and other treats. Not far away, Hegezhuang Village, the general area on the north side of Maquanying subway station, can be a surprising place to shop. It's home to the Orchard, a destination restaurant for city dwellers, and a staple of Shunyi residents. It grows much of its own produce and sells wares from local designers and artists. Five or so years ago you would have had a tough time finding it, but now, as other businesses have been drawn to it and the town has grown up around it, it's a well-marked central fixture.

Places of Interest

There isn't much in Shunyi by way of tourist sites, particularly of the historic variety. There is the Tunnel Warfare Site at Jiaozhuanghu Village (www.bjjzhdd.com), located in Longwantun town, at the northeast corner of Shunyi district closer to Pinggu district. This eerie museum is a reminder of the Chinese efforts against Japan and the Kuomintang in 1937-1945. The tunnels have been restored so the wartime atmosphere has been somewhat sanitized, but there are 800 meters of tunnels, as well as meeting rooms, command posts, individual shelters, and warehouses. Take the 934 bus to get here.

The most prominent place of interest in Shunyi is the New China International Exhibition Center (NCIEC, www.nciec.com.cn), across from Euro Plaza. In total, the entire site covers 156 hectares (384 acres) and includes 200,000 square meters of exhibiting space, comprising 16 separate, single-level, column-free exhibition halls of exhibition space. The center was explicitly designed for exhibitions, and so every hall in the center can be separated or merged to create smaller or larger exhibitions. It also includes office space, shopping, and fitness facilities. For upcoming conventions, visit www.chinaexhibition.com.

If you feel like you need a romantic escape, or even just a day of pampering, but don't

PRIME LIVING LOCATIONS

want to tire yourself out just getting there, make a getaway for the day to Chun Hui Yuan Resort (www.chunhuiyuan.cn/index.html). This is a superbly luxurious resort that has been built to take advantage of the natural hot springs beneath it. It focuses on all things relaxing and has specialty herbal baths, infrared light beds, massaging hot spring Jacuzzis, and a range of other baths.

More fun for the family can be found at Crab Island (www.xiedao.com) on the Chaoyang side of the river. Located just south off the Airport Expressway near Civil Aviation Museum (www.caacmuseum.cn), this amusement park cum convention center is fun for both adults and kids alike, with a fake beach, carnival rides, indoor archery, tennis, bowling, and much more. You can even cast a line in one of the indoor or outdoor fish ponds, depending on what kind of fish you want to catch. If you reel in one of the indoor sturgeons it will cost around RMB68 per kilo. Not far away, just a bit farther down Dongwei Lu, is yet another water park, Merry Water World, in Tulip Hot Spring Garden Resort (www.bjyujinxiang.com). While parents can soak in the hot spring tubs, kids can play in the large pool and on the water slides.

Getting Around

TAXIS

Most expats in this area have their own driver, so they may not have too many transport issues. On one day of the week at least, however, your driver's car will not be able to be on the road inside the Fifth Ring Road. This means you may need to resort to public transport. Your compound's clubhouse or property management office can usually help you order a taxi. During the day, you shouldn't have too many issues getting taxis from Shunyi into the city or back again, but late at night this can be more of a problem as taxi drivers don't always want to drive that far, knowing that it will be almost impossible to get a return fare. Many families also have a backup driver—a "black taxi" driver—who can help out when their official driver isn't available. While black taxis as a rule are not recommended, if you find a good one by reliable word of mouth then it can be worth saving their phone number.

SUBWAY

There isn't much to choose from here, just one subway line (Line 15), and the unpleasant thing about this line is that to get anywhere in the city you'll probably need to make two or three transfers, each adding possibly 10 minutes to your journey. The bus can actually be a lot more pleasant.

Those living on the Shunyi side of the river are closest to China International Exhibition Center subway station, but it's a considerable walk from most of the compounds. For Chaoyang siders, the stations of choice will possibly be Sunhe or Maquanying.

The Airport Express may be an alternative option for some. It's a direct route straight back and forth to the city with no intersecting lines except at Sanyuanqiao (Line 10). A ticket to ride this line is RMB25, regardless of where you get on or off.

TRAIN

Shunyi Railway Station, just south of Shimen subway station, has 10 trains that pass through it each day (see http://train.huochepiao.com for details). It's doubtful this will be a useful way for you to get into the city, given that the station is in the middle of Shunyi district. It may come in handy, though, if you want to do a weekend trip to Huairou or somewhere such as historic and beautiful Chengde in Hebei province, or Shijiazhuang, the capital city of Hebei province.

BUSES

The major buses worth getting to know in this area are:

850: This bus goes to two important destinations—west to the airport or south to Dongzhimen. Get on on Tianbei Lu directly across from the Crown Plaza hotel (Shunyi Maliandian Zhan, 顺义马连店站), or, for southsiders, near the BD Flower Market (Beidian Zhan, 北甸站) or near Grand Hills on the south side of the Jingping Expressway (Sunhe Zhan, 孙河站), and then head down to Lido, Sanyuanqiao, or Dongzhimen. Note: Sunhe Zhan here refers to the bus stop, not Sunhe Zhan the subway station.

855: This bus is best for those living in Rose & Ginkgo or Dragon Bay, as it runs along Huosha Lu. Take it to Wangjing, Ikea (get off at Futong Dongdajie Nankou Zhan, 阜通东大街南口站), Sanyuanqiao, or Dongzhimen.

915: This is basically the Jingmi Lu bus. It goes straight along this one road to deposit you directly into the city. There are several points you can get on or off at, including Shunyi Maliandian Daokou Zhan (顺义马连店道口站), opposite the Crown Plaza at Beidian Zhan, Sunhe Zhan, or near the Laiguangying Donglu intersection (Dongjiaonongchang Zhan, 东郊农场站), which is near Western Academy Beijing (WAB), and Beijing Riviera and Lane Bridge villas. From here you can continue on to Dashanqiao Dong (大山桥东) for 798; Jingshun Lu Lido Fandian (京顺路丽都饭店) for Lido; or continue on to Sanyuanqiao or Dongzhimen.

933: If business is calling you to subway Line 5, this is one way to get you there. Get on directly in front of Euro Plaza on Tianbei Lu. It will head out to Jingmi Lu before turning left and then left again onto Huosha Lu. It makes various stops along Huosha Lu before continuing west to the northernmost station on Line 5, Tiantongyuan North (天通苑北站).

934: This bus is your express into the city. Again it travels directly along Jingmi Lu. Get on at Jingmi Lu just near China International Exhibition Center subway station, at Beidian Zhan or Sunhe Zhan bus stop. It can take you to within walking distance of 798 (Dashanqiao Dongzhan, 大山桥东站), Lido, Sanyuanqiao, or Dongzhimen. You can also take this bus in the opposite direction to go to the Jiaozhuanghu Tunnel Warfare Site. Get off at Jiaozhuanghu (焦庄户), the very last stop.

942: This bus is just like 934, but has the added convenience of running along Yuyuan Lu, Anhua Lu, and Tianbei Lu before turning onto Jingmi Lu. This means it stops near Rose & Ginkgo, right outside of Dragon Bay Villas, at the north side of Yosemite, near Gahood, and then outside Le Leman Lake.

988: This bus is for those on the Chaoyang side of the river. It might be the slowest way to get you downtown with its numerous stops, but it is an option for you or the kids if you want to get to 798 Art District, Indigo shopping center in Lido, or Chaoyang Park. It passes Grand Hills, the Orchard, Quanfa Garden, Maquanying subway station, Cathay View, Lane Bridge, and WAB before getting onto Jingmi Lu and heading south.

OUTER DISTRICTS AND COUNTIES

It's rare for expats to settle into anywhere other than Chaoyang, Dongcheng, Shunyi, Xicheng, or Haidian, and the only kind of foot most of us step outside any of these is one clad in a heavy hiking boot. As far as land mass goes, however, this isn't even one quarter of the entire city. Beijing extends out in all directions for another 14,412 square kilometers (5,565 square miles), divided up into 11 more districts as well as counties.

Some of these, mostly those in the north, will become places you head to for fun, retreats, or tourism. They are populated by mountains and trails, guesthouses, hotels, recreational spots, winter ski fields, and, of course, the Great Wall.

Down in the south, things are a little different, and generally have a more industrial nature to them. In districts such as Fengtai, Fangshan, and Daxing you'll find monstrous sprawling markets, manufacturing, and agriculture. The government is pumping money into various locations in these regions to boost industry even further. Two particular examples of this are Yizhuang in Daxing and Liangxiang in Fangshang, both of which are being rapidly transformed into new economic zones, and Liangxiang additionally into Beijing's second university zone. New subway lines down into each area have sped up the progress, and come 2017-2018, when Beijing opens its second

© SHANNON AITKEN

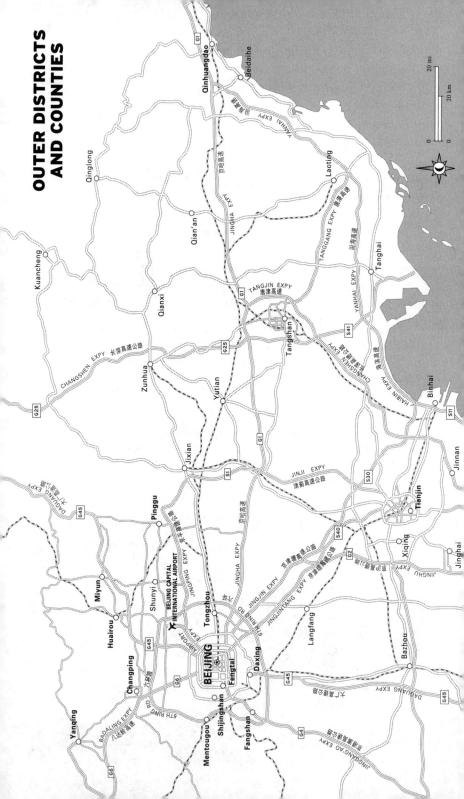

OUTER DISTRICTS
AND COUNTIES

international airport in southern Daxing, they will be rocketed into even higher levels of development.

Urban

FENGTAI DISTRICT

Fengtai covers the southwest corner of Beijing's urban area, stretching from along the South Second Ring Road down and out to the west beyond the Fifth Ring Road. One of the larger urban districts, it takes up 306 square kilometers (118 square miles) of land and is home to 2.1 million people.

The district is primarily industrial, but there are a few sites worth a visit, such as the kitsch but fun Beijing World Park (Guogongzhuang subway station, Line 9 and Fangshan Line, exit D, www.beijingworldpark.com.cn or www.kinabaloo.com/wp.html). The park has carefully copied miniatures of iconic buildings from around the world, including the Eiffel Tower, the Sydney Opera House, Angkor Wat, and Stonehenge. Other sites to visit in Fengtai include the historic Marco Polo Bridge (also Lugou Bridge, buses 309, 339, 624) and the Wanping Fortress, right at the start of the Marco Polo Bridge. Qinglonghu Park (www.bjqinglonghu.com) is also a nice spot to come for a weekend picnic or to lie on the beach beside the lake.

Not to be forgotten—nor confused with the often identically named park at the Olympic Water Cube—is the Happy Magic Watercube (欢乐水魔方水上乐园, 11 Xiaotun Lu, 小屯路11号, tel. 10/8860-9999). This is reported to be the world's biggest water park; not just for little kids, it has slides that would cause the most seasoned rollercoaster rider to hesitate. With a capacity to entertain around 30,000 people a day, perhaps the most challenging thing of the park, however, would be deciding whether or not to join the enormous mass of life-vest-wearing bathers bobbing in the wave pool. The park is open from around late May until the end of August (dates vary), and entry fees are RMB200 or RMB160 for kids under 1.5 meters (5 feet). To get here, take bus 338 or 507 from the Yuquanlu subway station (Line 1, exit D2) and get off at Meishikou (梅市口站).

There are some worthy shopping destinations to bring you south, including some of Beijing's most exciting markets. Get lost in the Muxiyuan Markets (Dahongmen subway station, Line 10, exit C2), where all things haberdashery can be found building after building and lane after lane. Stroll until your legs ache at Xinfadi Market, an immense collection of warehouses supplying much of the city with its produce. This is the epitome of wholesale, and is an astounding demonstration of how much food passes through this city. Entire warehouses are dedicated to a single produce item, such as mushrooms, eggs, or beef, and entire lines of trucks sell the exact same variety of fruit or vegetable from their open back doors. You'll find it on Nanyuan West Road (beside Xinfadi Bridge on the Jingkai Expressway, 新发地农产品批发市场, 丰台区新发地桥南苑西路).

Finally, buy all the kitchen equipment you could ever want at wholesale prices at the Hotel Equipment Corporation, or HEC (1 Kaiyangli Yijie, You'anmenwai, 酒总酒店设备, 北京, 丰台区右安门外开阳里一街1号, 东头条1号, tel. 10/8355-9988, www.hec.com.cn). Over four stories of culinary heaven, this market sells everything from baking goods to eight-burner stoves for restaurants. It's about a 10- to 15-minutes walk west from Beijing South Railway Station (subway Line 4).

If you do require a school in the area, Fengtai has Sino Bright School (www.schoolbj. com). Sino Bright offers an offshore school program from British Columbia, and specifically aims to help children prepare for university in Canada.

SHIJINGSHAN DISTRICT

Shijingshan is the third-smallest district in Beijing, after Dongcheng and Xicheng. It covers just 84 square kilometers (33 square miles) and sits out west at the tail end of subway Line 1. As recorded at the last census, 616,000 people call it home.

As far as expats are concerned, however, there is little here that brings it to their attention, and some may never even realize it's a district and not just the amusement park that it shares its name with. Shijingshan Amusement Park (Line 1, exit A1, www.bjs-jsyly.com) falls a little short of the thrilling standards set by Happy Valley in Chaoyang, but it makes a nice day out, queues are short to nonexistent, and those with young children will enjoy the kids' world, which is colorful and chock-full of rides and games.

There is more to the district, though, than rollercoasters and Ferris wheels. At its easternmost area, it's residential and gray, but as it extends out toward the Western Hills, city life gives way to nature. Badachu is a pleasant escape, and many come here not for the ancient temples and pagodas but to hike and explore the mountains. It's easy to get to, with several buses heading directly here from the city. These include the 347 from Xizhimenwai, the 958 from directly outside Gucheng subway station (Line 1, exit A), and the 972 from outside Pingguoyuan subway station (Line 1, exit C).

Other venues in Shijingshan include the Babaoshan Revolutionary Cemetery (www. bbsgmgm.com), the national cemetery of China. But this resting place isn't for the *lǎobǎixìng* (the common people)—this is a sacred place for those who worked for the revolution, great contributors to the country, and high-ranking military officials.

Shijingshan Amusement Park

© SHANNON AITKEN

You'll find it across the road from another point of interest, the Beijing International Sculpture Park, both a short distance from Babaoshan subway station (Line 1, exits B1 and C1 respectively).

Suburban

CHANGPING DISTRICT

Just north of Haidian, Changping in some ways feels like an annex of Haidian. Not only do many working or studying in Haidian choose to live here, but the government also has specific plans to rapidly develop it into a high-tech and university area. Infrastructure is being built and special policies are facilitating business development. There are already universities in the region as well as numerous high-tech hubs as part of the overall Zhongguancun Z-Park (www.zgc-cp.gov.cn). Two important ones are the Life Science Park (www.lifesciencepark.com.cn) and Changping Science Park.

The district itself spans a massive 1,344 square kilometers (519 square miles) and is home to 1,661,000 people. In the 10 years between the two national censuses this was a jump of more than 1 million people.

For now, rent is still relatively cheap up in Changping—you can quite easily find a large two-bedroom apartment for RMB2,000-4,500 per month. So if you're going to be up in Haidian for study or business then you may also want to keep Changping in mind. Making the trek down to places like Gulou, Sanlitun, or certainly Guomao is not going to be a nightly event, and your Western lifestyle choices are going to be slim, but once the soon-to-be completed north end of Line 8 is up and running, a trip to somewhere like Gulou or Nanluogu Xiang will take possibly 40-50 minutes.

When you're not working or studying, there are lots of things to do. The city's first museum to open to the public, the Chinese Aviation Museum (www.chn-am.com), is here. This is a muscly display of China's might. It has hundreds of planes on show as well as missiles and other weapons of destruction. Of course Changping also has the classic tourist sites, such as the Ming Tombs and the Jugongyuan Pass of the Great Wall, but there are less touristy places to get some respite in. These include the beautiful and peaceful Silver Mountain Pagoda Forest and Mount Mangshan National Forest. Head to either for fresh air and hiking away from the crowds. Mount Mangshan is particularly picturesque. It's the largest national park in Beijing and is situated on the east side of the Ming Tomb Reservoir, a short taxi ride north of Nanshao subway station (Changping Line). In winter you can return to the Ming Tomb area to ski in Beijing's largest ski field, Beijing Snow World Ski Park (Xue Shijie).

The adventurous can also look to Changping for shooting or winter skiing. There are two shooting options in the district, the North China International Shooting Range (www.bfshoot.com) and Aolin Shooting Gallery (Ao Lin She Ji, www.aolinshoot.com). The North China International Shooting Range is a more serious venue. You can choose your weapon, including anything from antique guns and sporting rifles to pistols and sniper rifles. You pay by the bullet, and with some bullets going for RMB30 each, you'll want to aim carefully. Aolin Shooting Gallery has a more recreational vibe, and in addition to shooting it also has paintball, barbecues, and, for better or for worse, is a wedding venue. Shotgun wedding anyone? Then, in winter, Jundushan Ski Resort (www.bjski.com.cn) becomes one of Beijing's favorite playgrounds. It's not only one of the closest ski fields to the inner city (about a 40-minute drive from downtown), it's also one of the biggest.

Finally, if kids will be in the picture in Changping, there are several education options. For younger kids there is Windsor Bilingual Kindergarten (http://vancouver. windsorkindergarten.cn), situated several kilometers directly north of the final stop on Line 5. Close by, Ivy Schools also has its Tiantong campus (www.ivyschools.com/ Schools-TT) and takes two- to five-year-olds. For older kids, Huijia Private School (www.huijia2000.com), a boarding and day school, uses an IB curriculum and offers grades from primary through to high school.

TONGZHOU DISTRICT

Tongzhou sits east of Chaoyang at the north end of the Grand Canal of China, and because of this it's an important agricultural region. Sadly much of this fertile plain is being developed, and a ride out this way on the aboveground Batong Line or on a bus feels like a dusty journey indeed. Tongzhou covers 906 square kilometers (350 square miles) and accommodates more than 1.2 million people, and like many of Beijing's regions earmarked for rapid-fire development, that number is likely to be entirely different come the next census in 2020.

As the inner city continues to blow out its belt notches, this is one of the areas in which the government has chosen to relieve the pressure. New housing developments and infrastructure are major items on the agenda. Not only will Tongzhou be eventually connected directly to Haidian by high-speed transport, but in the near future it will also be the location of the new Beijing East Railway Station, which will be a major hub connecting Beijing to the south, with high-speed train routes that include the Beijing-Tianjin Inter-city Railway and the Beijing-Qinhuangdao Inter-city Railway.

In the meantime, though, getting out past the East Fifth Ring Road is still quite convenient. It's serviced by both the Batong Line and Line 6, which run roughly every three to 10 minutes, depending on the time of day. Tongzhou Railway Station and Tongzhou West Railway Stations are in the district, which you can use to get to Huairou, Miyun, and into the city. The only problem is that, unlike on the subway, there are only a handful of trains every day and they are unlikely to be of use for a commute to work. On the upside, if you do choose to live out here, you'll get three to four times as much as what your friends in the city get for the same price, with new, modern three-bedroom apartments going for under RMB5,000 per month.

One of the main attractions out in Tongzhou is the Songzhuang artist village. But don't come here expecting to find another 798. This really is a village, and many struggling artists live privately in their studios, which are out of sight from the main street.

If local filmmakers wanted to shoot a Chinese Western, this would be an excellent location, with the main street of Songzhuang being the ideal backdrop for the final shootout. In summer, it's a hot and dusty location, and in winter it's unpleasantly frigid. Roadside shops peddle clichéd art and there is a modest number of good galleries. Many of these are open only when there is a given event on, so a spontaneous visit out here may leave you with the feeling that you've wasted your day. G-Dot Art Space (www.g-dotartspace.com), Artist Village Gallery (www.artistvillagegallery.com), Museum of Contemporary Art Beijing (MOCA, www.bjmoca.com), LDX Gallery

Hong Kong (www.ldxart.com), and Songzhuang Art Museum (www.artda.cn, songart-center@126.com) are some of the better-known galleries. To get out to the latter two, take the 938支9 bus from under Guomao Bridge and get off at Meishuguan (美术馆).

Schools out this way include the Ivy Tianshi campus (www.ivyschools.com/Schools-TS), for kids aged two to six; and the Beijing Shuren-Ribet Private School (www.shurenribet.org), Tongzhou's only K-12 independent coeducational bilingual boarding and day school, which is out by the Songzhuang artist village.

DAXING DISTRICT

Poor Daxing is so far down in Beijing that it often goes unnoticed, at least by the expat population. This is Beijing's southernmost district, and it spreads over 1,036 square kilometers (400 square miles) and is home to 1,365,000 people. Much of the district is a flat open plain, making it ideal for horse riding and farming. Until recent years its greenery and agriculture—particularly its grapes, pears, mulberries, and watermelons—were what fed its reputation. That all looks set to change now with the coming of Beijing's next airport, unsurprisingly touted to be the future world's-biggest airport.

Some attractions down here are worth knowing about; as a tourist you probably wouldn't go to them, but when here on a long-term basis you may find the time and interest to venture out to. Beijing Wildlife Park (tel. 10/9628-5360, www.bjwildlifepark.com), a safari experience, is available for those who want to see animals roaming freely. The park gets mixed reviews from animal lovers, with some arguing its conditions are better than the zoo in the city, others saying it's great for kids, and then those who still mourn the condition of the animals. It's a long way south, close to the Hebei border. To get here, drive directly south for about 44 kilometers (27 miles) along the Jingkai Expressway, which begins at the southwest corner of the Second Ring Road.

Something that will definitely impress skateboarders is Wooward Beijing skateboard park (www.woodwardbeijing.com). This state-of-the-art park boasts phenomenal indoor and outdoor skating zones, which you can skate, rollerblade, or freestyle on. The main drawback is the distance from the inner city. To get down here, take Line 4 down to Qingyuanlu on the Daxing section (exit A). About 200 meters (656 feet) north from here, take bus 841 to Xingminghu Resort (星明湖度假村).

FANGSHAN DISTRICT

Fangshan sits in Beijing's southwesternmost corner, and from the city center is a bit of a trek to get to. Depending on where you're headed, it could easily take around two hours to get there. It covers 1,990 square kilometers (768 square miles) of terrain, and within this there are plains, numerous rivers, and mountains. At the last census the population within the district was nearing 1 million people, living predominantly within several urban areas across the district, such as Liangxiang and Zhoukoudian.

The region has a colorful mix of industries. Its fertile plains mean that much of it is dedicated to agriculture, but coal stores, minerals, and building form other major sources of revenue. Though too far for the typical commuter, Fangshan has not avoided the government's gaze, and as favorable policies turn Liangxiang into a bustling economic zone, the diversity of Fangshan's resources is bound to broaden. Industries including everything from electricity and textiles to printing and the animal industry have been highlighted as potential areas for development.

Fangshan has numerous scenic and historic sites. Rock climbers frequently head to Shidu in the district's southwestern point to climb its craggy karst mountains. Many routes are already well established, and climbing groups, such as Beijing Climbing Club, make dedicated trips down here. In addition, Shidu is a leisure spot for local tourists who want to frolic in boats or throw themselves off a bungee jump gangplank—the star attraction of the location. There are various public buses to get down here and an infrequent train from Beijing West Railway Station. You can also book yourself on to one of the tour buses operated by the government, via the Beijing Hub of Tour Dispatch (tel. 10/8353-1111, www.bjlyjszx.com/english). These buses run only on weekends, so forget being able to avoid the crowd.

Other attractions to keep on the radar out this way include the World Heritage-listed Peking Man Site. This is the site upon which fossils of more than 40 hominids and thousand of artifacts were found, some of which were believed to have been around 750,000 years old. And though the majority of relics in the collection went AWOL around the time of the Japanese occupation, various items and molds still remain, which some still argue makes it an interesting day out. The limestone earth in the district is also responsible for various caves, some relatively preserved, others with multicolored light displays. Three of the largest in the area include Shihuadong (Stone Flower Cave), Yinhudong (Silver Fox Cave), and Xianqidong (Xianqi Cave). All three are quite spectacular, particularly Shihuadong, which has eight levels. Though only four of these are open to the public, the entire viewing route is still more than 2,500 meters (8,202 feet) long. To get to Shihuadong, take Tour Bus 7 (特7路) from outside Qianmen, Hepingmen, Xuanwumen, or Changchunjie subway station (Line 2); and to get to either Yinhudong or Xianqidong, take the regular bus 917 from Tianqiao long-distance bus station (east of Tiantan Park or from Liuliqiao East subway station, Line 9, exit E).

MENTOUGOU DISTRICT

Mentougou sits directly above Fangshan in Beijing's west. The district covers 1451 square kilometers (560 square miles), and, according to the 2010 census, just 290,000 live here, making it officially the least-populated district (or county) in all of Beijing. In fact, in the 10 years between the last two national censuses, it grew by only just over 20,000 people. Having no subway in the area doesn't really help things, but when the new Mentougou Line opens off the end of Line 1 in 2015 we might see a change.

The lack of population can also be explained by Mentougou's terrain. Approximately 93 percent of the district is mountainous, being part of the Western Hills. The hills are rich in natural resources, including coal, granite, and minerals, although, these days, many of the mines have begun to be depleted.

Within the area there are numerous sites that should be visited. These include the wonderful Cuandixia (爨底下), a tiny ancient village that sits in the nook of a ridge. Come here in spring when the mountains are full of color and stop in at one of the local homes to have lunch. It can take two or three hours to get here, so set off early. Take the 892 bus from Pingguoyuan subway station (Line 1) and then almost 2.5 hours and 55 stops later you can get off right at the village (Cuandicun Kouzhan, 爨底村口站). You'll probably be hassled by drivers outside Pingguoyuan subway station offering to drive you all the way there. Many will try to get RMB300 from you but in the end will usually accept RMB100. It's up to you, but be clear about the final price before you get in the car. There is an official ticket office into the village once you get there, and while no one is likely to even look at your tickets, it's better to buy them there than have the driver scam you for more money when they offer to purchase the tickets for you.

If you haven't yet fallen into the pit of complete temple apathy, then there are various temples in Mentougou to continue to satisfy your interest. Tianzhe Temple (or Pool and Mulberry Tree Temple) is not only one of Beijing's biggest Buddhist temples but is also one of the oldest, having been built during the Jin Dynasty (256-316). Alternatively, climb to the top of Miaofeng Shan, which stands at 1,291 meters (4,236 feet). From here you can see more temples, the Yongding River, and the city, and, if timing or luck is with you, you can enjoy the cultural festivities that are often held here as well as the rose fields at the mountain's base. Miaofeng Shan can be reached on the 929 or the M18 bus from Pingguoyuan subway station.

Rural

YANQING COUNTY

Yanqing county is located in Beijing's northwest corner and takes up 1,994 square kilometers (770 square miles). More than 317,000 people live among its mountains. Though few from the city come here to work, many come for recreation. The highways and transport up to Yanqing are good, so journeys up here can take anything from an hour to two hours, depending on where you're headed. One of the most well-known locations of the area is the Badaling section of the Great Wall. Although this is perhaps the least recommendable section of the Wall—thanks to the immense throngs of tourists, the nearby McDonald's, the complete restoration of the Wall and everything else that strips it of any original heritage—it is perhaps the quickest and easiest section of the Great Wall to get to. In addition to countless buses and tours that haul the people here, you can also simply jump on one of the S2 trains from Beijing West Railway Station (beside Xizhimen subway station) with usually no need to book the ticket in advance.

Yanqing isn't all about Badaling, however, and there are numerous other places to investigate. Longqing Gorge, which is farther north in the county, is a beautiful blend of cliffs and waterways. Admittedly, this is also a destination for local tourists seeking summer boating activities, horse riding, and even go-karting. So, if you can, avoid the weekend crush. To get here, take the 919 from Deshengmen bus station and, at the final stop, get a taxi for the remaining 15 minutes to the gate.

Out west in the Kangxi grasslands there's more horse riding to be done, in addition to barbecuing and free-spirited camping. This is not quite Inner Mongolia, but it's a good alternative if you need to stay near Beijing. The best time of year to come here is definitely between May and September before it becomes a barren wasteland over winter.

In winter Yanqing becomes the destination of skiers and snowboarders. Badaling Ski Resort is just three kilometers far from the Great Wall and has five main runs, the longest being 800 meters (2,625 feet) and a 2,300-meter (7,546-foot) road run. They might not be the most difficult of runs, but, regardless, reward yourself with a restorative dip in the nearby hot springs when you finish. Bus 919 from Deshengmen bus station will bring you directly here, or you can drive along Badaling Highway to Badaling Huaxuechang. Alternatively, Shijinglong Ski Slopes Resort, farther out in Zhongyangfang village in Zhangshanying town, has more runs on offer, including one run of more than 1,030 meters (3,379 feet). Difficulty levels are a little more challenging here, so snow enthusiasts may be more satisfied and, again, there are hot springs for post-ski recovery. To get here, take the 919 bus at Deshengmen and get off at Yanqing Dongguan (延庆东关), then walk 500 meters (1,640 feet) down Dongwai Dajie to take the 920 bus from Yanqing bus station (延庆汽车站), which will take you to Shijinglong Ski Resort (stop Xiaoluzhuang, 小路庄).

HUAIROU DISTRICT

Huairou district is between Yanqing and Miyun, and, as if squeezed in the middle by its two neighbors, it protrudes far into the north, claiming Beijing's northernmost point. It covers 2,123 square kilometers (820 square miles) and is home to 373,000 people. Per square kilometer, this makes Huairou the least densely populated region of Beijing with a piddling average of 175 people per square kilometer (compare that to Xicheng's 24,599 people per square kilometer). While 90 percent of this land is mountainous, and close to 70 percent is covered in forest, farmers are able to make a living in the district by growing chestnuts, walnuts, pears, apricots, and one of Beijing's favorite snacks, hawthorns. Importantly not only for them, but for all of Beijing, Huairou is rich in water. Its lakes and reservoir help supply the inner city with much-needed water.

Huairou isn't completely rural, however, and around the district are numerous townships. Make your way to any of these and you're likely to find a cinema, a theater, a shopping center or two, and low-level apartment buildings.

For the rest of us, Huairou is about getting out of the city and taking a break, be it for an event, a leisurely weekend, or a visiting family member who wants you to make their once-in-a-lifetime trip to the Great Wall your tenth. While there are the less-known, less-touristy sections, including Huanghuacheng and Jiankou, there is also Huairou's best-known section of the Great Wall, Mutianyu. Though undeniably tainted by tourism, it's still a far shot better than Badaling. Mutianyu is a nice blend of restored and wild wall, and still can be accessed easily from the city. People of any ability can explore the main section of the wall, and those who want a little more excitement need only to keep on walking beyond the general visiting area. Quaint restaurants and shops surround Mutianyu's base, and nearby several businesses, including the Brickyard (www.brickyardatmutianyu.com) and Red Capital Ranch (www.red-capitalclub.com.cn), have also established getaways that aim to complement the surrounds rather than destroy them. These kinds of places are not only good for a basic weekend away, they're a great option if you're looking for a venue in Beijing at which to hold an event or special celebration.

If you do want to put on a birthday bash, stag party, or the like out in Huairou, up the ante by camming up and firing off a few rounds of paintball at Senlimo (www.slmpaintball.com), west of Beitaishang Reservoir. Alternatively, if winter has set in, take the crowd to Huaibei International Ski Resort (www.hbski.com), in Huaibei town, north of the Beitaishang Reservoir. One of the bigger ski fields in Beijing, it has two advanced-level runs, an intermediate run, and four beginner runs, as well as the scenic advantage of being by the Great Wall.

To get out to Mutianyu Great Wall, take the 916 Express (916快) from inside the Dongzhimen long-distance bus station. At the final stop, Huairou Beidajie (怀柔北大街), change to local bus 936路支线 (Huairou-Dongtai, 怀柔至洞台) and continue for another 18.6 kilometers to Mutianyu.

MIYUN COUNTY

Miyun county is the largest of all Beijing's counties and districts, with a landmass of 2,229 square kilometers (861 square miles), and within that just 468,000 residents. It's one of Beijing's most picturesque areas, decorated by mountains, lakes, and farmland, not to mention air that is dramatically cleaner than in the inner city. Getting out here usually takes about a two-hour drive, or if by public transport it's a little longer and requires a bus to Miyun township and then a taxi.

Naturally then, the reasons people do make their way to Miyun from the city are not usually for work, but for recreation. It's to hike on wild or unrestored sections of the Great Wall—such as along the spectacular and often vertigo-inducing Simatai and Jinshanling passes—to visit the Miyun Reservoir (Beijing's main supply of water) or to hike around Black Dragon Pond.

Rock climbers also find love in Miyun. The rocks rising up around Bai He (or White River), on the west side of the Miyun Reservoir, are ideal for climbing climbing. Though still relatively undeveloped as far as climbing locations can be, there are already many established sport routes, as well as some traditional and aid climbs in the area. The rock is stable and there is enough variety to suit handlebar climbers as well as advanced multi-pitch enthusiasts. The main canyon can be hard to find the first time you come out here, so it's recommended to head out with a climbing group or friend who's familiar with the area for your first attempt.

Year round, people can also have fun at Nanshan Ski Resort (www.nanshanski.com). This is definitely Beijing's most popular, most high-tech, and best-maintained ski field. Many people are unaware that it's also a fantastic place to visit in the warmer months. Outside of the obvious winter sports, there is also water skiing, grass skiing, hiking, swimming, and, in fall, fruit-picking. Best of all, it's only about a 35-minute drive from the city along the Jingcheng Expressway. To get here by public transport, take the 980快 (express) from

© SHANNON AITKEN

Miyun county offers nice hikes for winter and a few manmade amusements.

Dongzhimenwai, get off at Miyun Xi Daqiao (密云西大桥), then take a RMB20 taxi ride the rest of the way.

PINGGU DISTRICT

Off to Beijing's far east, sheltered by Miyun in the north and Shunyi to its west, Pinggu district is 950 square kilometers (367 square miles) and is home to 416,000 people. One third of the land is a flat plain, and the remaining area is covered by mountains. Not much happens out in this neck of the woods, besides peach or watermelon growing. Freeways are sparse, the subway nonexistent, and there isn't a great deal on the government's agenda for its development.

For now at least it remains a quiet escape, most accessible for those on four wheels. In summer, Jinhai Lake, one of Beijing's biggest reservoirs, is a fun spot for water activities. Rent a motorboat, an inflatable boat, a row boat, or a jet ski. It's a long drive out of town, so to accommodate the visitors, a number of hotels have sprung up in the area together with locals offering home-cooked meals. Stay overnight and watch the sun set over the lake and the mass of fishing nets on the surface. The best time of year to come here is between April and October. To get here by public transport, take the 918支 from Dongzhimenwai and get off at Jinhaihu (金海湖), about 80 minutes later.

Finally, this wouldn't be a rural district if it didn't have a ski resort, and for Pinggu that is Yuyang International Ski Resort (www.yuyangski.com.cn). It has a 3,200-meter-long run for advanced skiers and even a ski school for novices.

Beyond Beijing

TIANJIN

Tianjin is almost like a sister city to Beijing. It's not only a neighbor sharing borders along sections of Daxing and Pinggu districts, but it also enjoys the same status as Beijing in that it's a freestanding municipality answering directly to the central government rather than a provincial government. The city has a long history of trade thanks to its geographical position and connections to water. Its eastern side runs along the Bohai Sea, and in its heyday, the Grand Canal cut right through the middle of the city on its way from Beijing to the south. So, for hundreds of years and still to this day, much of its commerce has been centered around port-related industries.

Today it's not really the most beautiful city you could visit. The constant trade and development over the years have worn away at it and turned it into an often-polluted industrial metropolis. As far back as the 15th century, the Ming emperors took a liking to it and made it into a walled garrison, and by the 1800s it had officially claimed its status as a trading port. By the 1930s it had become northeast China's most important economic center. Though Beijing has now trumped it on this account, that hasn't stopped Tianjin's progress, and the government has long-term plans to continue its transformation into a major international harbor as well as a key economic and ecological city.

This means the city has enormous potential for the international market. There are various areas zoned for high-tech development, and financial incentives are being dangled to try to attract foreign money and business. One of the most important zones is TEDA, or Tianjin Economic-Technological Development Area (http://en.investteda.org), which is right on the coastal area of the Bohai Gulf. The area is somewhat removed from the center of the city, but infrastructure and lifestyle facilities are in the works to make life here more comfortable.

In addition to business, however, Tianjin also has a wide range of attractions worth seeing. There are the former European and Japanese concession areas to explore, as well as the Huangyaguan section of the Great Wall, the Tianjin Water Park of China, Ancient Culture Street, and the Dabei Buddhist Monastery. Tianjin also has its own sightseeing Ferris wheel, the Tianjin Eye, which sits astride the Haihe river and gives you 120-meter-high (394-foot high) views of the entire city. Another very enjoyable way to see the city is to take a cruise along the river itself. In the 40-or-so-minute journey through the center of the city you'll wind past clusters of interesting architecture, such as the buildings of the Italian concession, and pass under an amazing array of bridges, each distinctly different, some trite copies of foreign designs, others interesting glimpses into Chinese architectural styles.

For most Beijing residents, though, Tianjin's attractions are only enough to bring them over for a day or two of sightseeing. Though transport between the two cities is cheap and convenient, and rent is much cheaper in Tianjin (good two-bedroom apartments can be found for around RMB2,500 per month), it's almost unheard of for someone to commute back and forth for anything other than the odd short-term project or meeting.

Getting Here

Getting to Tianjin from Beijing, or vice versa, is extremely simple. For those who have access to a car, there are several major expressways and highways connecting the two cities. Depending on your route, it's roughly 110 kilometers (68 miles) to Tianjin's city center, or 160 kilometers (99 miles) right over to Tianjin Port. On a good run, this can be made in about two hours, but the roads often become clogged with trucks. A better option is to take the high-speed train, which takes only 35 minutes. The trains are modern, clean, and efficient, and run every 15-20 minutes between about 6:30am and 11pm each day, in either direction. The only downside for many people is that they depart from Beijing South Railway Station (Line 4), which can take about as long to get to as the trip to Tianjin itself. Tickets cost RMB54.50, and sometimes less. The important thing to note is that some trains go to Tianjin Railway Station, which is the city's main station and centrally located, while others go to Tianjin South Railway Station, which is out of the way and not connected to the existing subway line. Regular-speed trains are also available from Beijing Station and Beijing West Railway Station. These are much cheaper, and take one hour fifty minutes and two hours, respectively.

Finally, there is currently no direct flight between Beijing Capital International Airport and Binhai International Airport in Tianjin. This may change, however, when Beijing's second airport opens in 2017. So, for now, if your entry to China is via Tianjin, you'll need to transfer to a car, coach or train.

QINHUANGDAO

Qinhuangdao is in Hebei province, about 300 kilometers east of Beijing on the coast of the Bohai Sea. Though the city itself has close to three million people, if you stick to

PRIME LIVING LOCATIONS

Take a short trip over to Qinhuangdao on the coast in northeastern Hebei province for some sailing or beach time.

the coastline, it can give you the feeling of being at a quiet seaside resort. As a Beijing resident, this is closest you can really get to a beachside getaway. There are three main areas worth visiting while you're here. These include Beidaihe, which is something of a seaside resort for the rich or powerful. It's also good for sailing and water activities. Beijing Sailing Center (www.beijingsailing.com) uses it as the base for their training and activities. Next, Haigang is the harbor area of the city and is home to Yanshan University, one of the top universities of Hebei province. Then finally, and perhaps most popular, is Shanhaiguan, the easternmost point of the Great Wall of China. Coming here to visit where the wall meets the sea somehow always feels like checking off an item on your bucket list.

Getting Here

One of the easiest ways to get to Qinhuangdao is to take a train from Beijing Railway Station or Beijing West Railway Station. Times vary depending on the kind of train you take. The faster D-category trains take about two hours and 15 minutes while other trains can take more than six hours. Tickets range RMB39-182 depending on both the train and seating or bed style. Alternatively, various tour groups, such as www.tour-beijing.com and the public buses with the Beijing Hub of Tour Dispatch (www.bjlyjszx.com), run short trips out here.

RESOURCES

© NORA JANG

Consulates and Embassies

IN THE UNITED STATES

CONSULATE-GENERAL OF THE PEOPLE'S REPUBLIC OF CHINA IN CHICAGO
100 W. Erie St.
Chicago, IL 60654
tel. 312/803-0095
www.chinaconsulatechicago.org

CONSULATE-GENERAL OF THE PEOPLE'S REPUBLIC OF CHINA IN HOUSTON
3417 Montrose Blvd.
Houston, TX 77006
tel. 713/520-1462
http://houston.china-consulate.org

CONSULATE-GENERAL OF THE PEOPLE'S REPUBLIC OF CHINA IN LOS ANGELES
443 Shatto Pl.
Los Angeles, CA 90020
tel. 213/807-8088
http://losangeles.china-consulate.org

CONSULATE-GENERAL OF THE PEOPLE'S REPUBLIC OF CHINA IN NEW YORK
520 12th Ave.
New York, NY 10036
tel. 212/244-9392
www.nyconsulate.prchina.org

CONSULATE-GENERAL OF THE PEOPLE'S REPUBLIC OF CHINA IN SAN FRANCISCO
1450 Laguna St.
San Francisco, CA 94115
tel. 415/674-2940
www.chinaconsulatesf.org

EMBASSY OF THE PEOPLE'S REPUBLIC OF CHINA IN THE UNITED STATES OF AMERICA
3505 International Pl., NW
Washington, D.C. 20008
tel. 202/495-2266
www.china-embassy.org

OUTSIDE OF THE UNITED STATES

EMBASSY OF THE PEOPLE'S REPUBLIC OF CHINA IN AUSTRALIA
15 Coronation Dr.
Yarralumla, ACT 2600
tel. 02/6273-4780
http://au.china-embassy.org

EMBASSY OF THE PEOPLE'S REPUBLIC OF CHINA IN CANADA
515 St. Patrick St.
Ottawa, ON K1N 5H3
tel. 613/789-3434
http://ca.china-embassy.org

EMBASSY OF THE PEOPLE'S REPUBLIC OF CHINA IN IRELAND
40 Ailesbury Rd.
Ballsbridge, Dublin 4
tel. 01/269-1707
http://ie.china-embassy.org

EMBASSY OF THE PEOPLE'S REPUBLIC OF CHINA IN NEW ZEALAND
Unit 2, 6 Glenmore St.
Kelburn 6011
tel. 04/472-1382
www.chinaembassy.org.nz

EMBASSY OF THE PEOPLE'S REPUBLIC OF CHINA IN THE UNITED KINGDOM OF GREAT BRITAIN AND NORTHERN IRELAND

31 Portland Pl.

London W1B 1QD

020/7299-4049

www.chinese-embassy.org.uk

IN BEIJING
EMBASSY OF THE UNITED STATES: BEIJING, CHINA

55 Anjialou Lu

Chaoyang District

美国驻华大使馆

朝阳区安家楼路55号

tel. 10/8531-3000

http://beijing.usembassy-china.org.cn

American Citizen Services

Emergency tel. 10/8531-4000

AUSTRALIAN EMBASSY, CHINA

21 Dongzhimenwai Dajie

Chaoyang District

澳大利亚大使馆

朝阳区，东直门外大街21号

tel. 10/5140-4111

www.china.embassy.gov.au

BRITISH EMBASSY BEIJING

11 Guanghua Lu

Jianguomenwai, Chaoyang District

英国驻华大使馆

朝阳区建国门外光华路11号

tel. 10/5192-4000

www.gov.uk/government/world/china

CANADIAN EMBASSY

19 Dongzhimenwai Dajie

Chaoyang District

加拿大大使馆

朝阳区东直门外大街19号

tel. 10/5139-4000

http://china.gc.ca

IRISH EMBASSY

3 Ritan Donglu

Chaoyang District

爱尔兰大使馆

朝阳区日坛东路3号

tel. 10/6532-2691

www.embassyofireland.cn

NEW ZEALAND EMBASSY: BEIJING, CHINA

3 Sanlitun Dongsan Jie

Chaoyang District

新西兰大使管

朝阳区三里屯东三街3号

tel. 10/8531-2700

www.nzembassy.com/china

RESOURCES

Making the Move

PLANNING YOUR FACT-FINDING TRIP

BEIJING INTERNATIONAL

www.ebeijing.gov.cn

This is the official information site about Beijing. Information covers all aspects of life in Beijing. However, it is often out of date and not particularly helpful.

TRAVEL CHINA GUIDE

www.travelchinaguide.com

An excellent resource about traveling in China by plane or train.

LIVING IN BEIJING
ANGLOINFO

http://beijing.angloinfo.com

Information on everything from housing to health care.

THE BEIJINGER

www.thebeijinger.com

This is one of the major sources of information for expats. Its search engine might not be the most powerful, but the information is usually in there somewhere once you work out the system. This is the go-to site for accommodations, jobs, classifieds, and language partners.

BEIJING KIDS

www.beijing-kids.com

This can be an invaluable resource for anyone moving to Beijing with children.

CITY WEEKEND

www.cityweekend.com.cn/beijing/

This is similar to the Beijinger. Its strength is its search engine for venues. Jobs and apartments are not its specialty.

MOBILE NATIVE

www.mobilenative.com

Extremely handy venue locater. Bookmark the cell phone version (www.mobnat.com) in your phone and you can show taxi drivers where you want to go using an English or Chinese map and address.

SMART BEIJING

www.smartbeijing.com

A recent addition to Beijing's collection of online street mags, giving you details on what's happening around town and where to go to buy what.

TIME OUT

www.timeoutbeijing.com

This is one of the more well-respected English-language magazines in Beijing. One of its many strengths is giving helpful information on markets and other shopping venues.

MOVING COMPANIES AND SHIPPING

AGS FOUR WINDS INTERNATIONAL MOVERS

www.agsmovers.com

Move your home or office by air, sea, or road.

ALLIED PICKFORDS

www.alliedpickfords.com

International mover with a Beijing office.

CROWN RELOCATIONS

www.crownrelo.com

International movers and relocation experts.

LINKS MOVING

www.linksmoving.asia

Links is one of the more affordable options in Beijing and is highly experienced with moving families in and out of China, as well as from place to place within Beijing.

SANTA FE

www.santaferelo.com

Santa Fe is one of the bigger relocation companies in Beijing and is widely used by companies needing to relocate staff internationally.

VISAS AND IMMIGRATION

BEIJING INTERNATIONAL TRAVEL HEALTH CARE CENTER HAIDIAN CENTER

10 Dezheng Lu, Haidian District
Hours: 8:30am-11am Monday to Friday
tel. 10/8240-3675
北京国际旅行卫生保健中心海淀分中心
北京市海淀区德正路10号

This is where you need to go for your official health check for your visa and residence permit. To get there, take the subway to Xi'erqi station on Line 13, then take a five-minute cab ride. Many taxi drivers won't know where it is, so keep the address and phone number handy.

EXIT-ENTRY ADMINISTRATION OF BEIJING MUNICIPAL PUBLIC SECURITY BUREAU

2 Andingmen Dongjie, Dongcheng District
tel. 10/8402-0101
www.bjgaj.gov.cn/
北京市公安局出入境管理处
东城区东城区安定门东大街2号

Theoretically this is the place to contact for all your visa questions and to manage your visa process. Neither the phone service nor the website is very user-friendly, though, so if you need help, here are a few other visa specialists that may be able to help.

ACCOLADE CORPORATE SERVICES LIMITED

http://accoladegroup.com.hk

BEIJING EXPAT SERVICE CENTER

www.beijingesc.com
Services include visas, driver's licenses, insurance, and police clearance.

CHINA VISA SERVICE CENTRE

www.mychinavisa.com

CHINESE VISA APPLICATION SERVICE CENTER

www.visaforchina.org

GET IN2 CHINA

www.getin2china.com

TRADERSLINK

www.traders-link.com
Visa and business consultancy services.

PET RELOCATION AND PET SERVICES

BEIJING CAT

www.beijingcat.org

Adopt a pre-loved or homeless cat.

BEIJING GUANSHANG ANIMAL HOSPITAL

www.chinapet.com.cn
In addition to being a general veterinarian hospital, it's also the place you'll need to bring your pets when they arrive in China.

BEIJING HUMAN AND ANIMAL ENVIRONMENTAL EDUCATION CENTER (BHAEEC)

www.animalschina.org
BHAEEC protects, rescues, and adopts out dogs and cats. Think about adopting a pet before supporting shoddy breeders at markets.

DOCTORS BECK & STONE

www.doctorsbeckandstone.com
International-standard veterinarian practice with many clinics around the city.

DOGGY THOUGHTS

http://chinadogtraining.com
American canine behavior specialist and professional dog trainer Dennis Schenk teaches basic obedience and runs puppy courses and behavior rehabilitation. Enroll you, your family, your *āyí,* and your dog in private or group classes.

GLOBY PET & ANIMAL RELOCATION

www.globypetrelo.com
Globy can help manage importing and exporting your pet in and out of China, particularly if you need to leave quickly.

INTERNATIONAL CENTER FOR VETERINARY SERVICES (ICVS)

www.icvsasia.com
The ICVS is a full-service, international-standard animal and pet health-care facility. It offers a comprehensive range of services, including vaccinations, boarding,

RESOURCES

and emergency care. The center is also an excellent source for up-to-date information on government regulations.

WORLDCARE PET TRANSPORT
www.worldcarepet.com
Assistance for getting your pet in and out of the country, whether you're here or not.

INTERNATIONAL SERVICES

AUSTRALIAN GOVERNMENT–DEPARTMENT OF AGRICULTURE, FISHERIES, AND FORESTRY
www.daff.gov.au
Information for taking animals into or out of Australia.

BIOSECURITY NEW ZEALAND
www.biosecurity.govt.nz
Information for taking animals into or out of New Zealand.

CANADIAN FOOD INSPECTION AGENCY
www.inspection.gc.ca
Information for taking animals into or out of Canada.

GOV.UK
www.gov.uk/take-pet-abroad
Information for taking animals into or out of the United Kingdom.

IRISH GOVERNMENT DEPARTMENT OF AGRICULTURE, FOOD & THE MARINE
www.agriculture.gov.ie/pets/
Information for taking animals into or out of Ireland.

IRS
www.irs.gov/Individuals/International-Taxpayers
Tax information for American citizens living abroad.

OVERSEAS SECURITY ADVISORY COUNCIL
www.osac.gov
Beijing Regional Security Office
tel. 10/8531-4111

TRAVEL.STATE.GOV
travel.state.gov
Consular services for United States citizens abroad, including travel warnings and advice.

UNITED STATES DEPARTMENT OF AGRICULTURE–ANIMAL AND PLANT HEALTH INSPECTION SERVICE
www.aphis.usda.gov
Information for taking animals into or out of the United States.

BEIJING SERVICES

BEIJING AMERICAN CENTER
Suite 2801, Jingguang Center, Hujialou, Chaoyang District
tel. 10/6597-3242
Center dedicated to cultural activities, educational resources, and offices that coordinate and support cultural and educational exchanges between China and the United States.

EXPATS LIFE
www.expatslife.com
Help finding *āyí*, drivers, and Chinese teachers.

RESOURCES

Language and Education

LANGUAGE SCHOOLS
BEIJING LANGUAGE AND CULTURAL CENTRE FOR DIPLOMATIC MISSIONS
www.chinesestudy-lcc.com
Various locations in Chaoyang district

BEIJING MANDARIN SCHOOL
www.beijingmandarinschool.com
Various locations in Chaoyang district

BERLITZ
www.berlitz.com.cn/beijing-language-center.html
Ritan Park, Chaoyang district

BRIDGE SCHOOL
www.bridgeschoolchina.com
Various locations in Chaoyang district and Shunyi district

CAPITAL MANDARIN
www.capitalmandarin.com
Various locations in Chaoyang district

CLE (CHINESE LANGUAGE EDUCATION)
www.chinaledu.com
Jianwai SOHO (Guomao), Chaoyang district

FRONTIERS
www.frontiers.com.cn
Dongzhimen, Dongcheng district

GLOBAL VILLAGE
www.gvschinese.com
Wangjing, Chaoyang district; Wudaokou, Haidian district

NEW CONCEPT MANDARIN
www.newconceptmandarin.com
Sanyuanqiao, Chaoyang district

SINOLAND EDUCATION
www.sinolandchinese.com
Wudaokou, Chaoyang district

TAILORMADE CHINESE CENTER
www.tailormadechinese.com
Guanghu Lu, Chaoyang district

THAT'S MANDARIN
www.thatsmandarin.com
Dongzhimen, Dongcheng district

ONLINE LANGUAGE TOOLS
ANKI
http://ankisrs.net
Free flashcard program to help you learn all your new words on your computer or cell phone.

CHINESEPOD
http://chinesepod.com/
Fantasitc podcast program with excellent hosts and real-life language rather than cultural propaganda.

CHINESE-FORUMS
www.chinese-forums.com
A long-running forum bringing Chinese learners together where any question about Chinese that could be asked is asked.

CHINESE HACKS
http://chinesehacks.com
Shortcuts, tips, and mini lessons.

FLUENTU
http://chinese.fluentu.com
Comprehensive language program, with lessons based on Chinese TV commercials and other commercial video content.

RESOURCES

HACKING CHINESE

www.hackingchinese.com

A site that focuses on how to learn Chinese rather than what to learn.

LANG-8

http://lang-8.com

An excellent free tool for those concerned about writing. Post an entry and native speakers will correct it.

MANDARINSPOT

http://mandarinspot.com/

Handy tool to bookmark on your computer to help you do word-by-word translations on any other website.

MDBG

www.mdbg.net

Easy-to-use online dictionary.

NCIKU

www.nciku.com

Fantastic dictionary with a multitude of useful example sentences and other learning tools.

PLECO SOFTWARE

www.pleco.com

Powerful downloadable dictionary for your cell phone.

SCRITTER

www.skritter.com

A fun program for your computer, iPad, or iPhone to help you learn how to handwrite Chinese characters.

TOSHUO

http://toshuo.com

Has a handy tool to help you type in Pinyin.

SCHOOLS—PRESCHOOL AND KINDERGARTEN

AMERICAN INTERNATIONAL ACADEMY OF BEIJING (AIAB)

www.aiab.com.cn

Chaoyang district

BEIJING HUIJIA KINDERGARTEN

www.hjkids.com

Various locations

CHILDREN'S COMMUNITY SCHOOL BEIJING

www.bjccs.org.cn

Northeast Chaoyang district

CHILDREN'S HOUSE INTERNATIONAL MONTESSORI KINDERGARTEN

www.montessoribeijing.com

Various locations

CHILDREN'S INTERNATIONAL BILINGUAL ACADEMY, THE

www.clcbkids.com

Shunyi district

DAYSTAR ACADEMY

www.daystarchina.cn

Northeast Chaoyang district

EDUWINGS KINDERGARTEN

www.eduwingskids.com

Shunyi district

ETONKIDS KINDERGARTENS

www.etonkids.com

Various locations

FAMILY LEARNING HOUSE

www.thefamilylearninghouse.com

Chaoyang district

HOUSE OF KNOWLEDGE
www.house-of-knowledge.net
Various locations

INTERNATIONAL MONTESSORI SCHOOL OF BEIJING
www.msb.edu.cn
Northeast Chaoyang district

IVY BILINGUAL SCHOOL
www.ivyschools.cn
Various locations

KE ER INTERNATIONAL KINDERGARTENS
www.keereducation.com
Chaoyang district

MSB JIADE INTERNATIONAL BILINGUAL KINDERGARTEN OF BEIJING
www.eightbridge.com/msb1872/index.asp
Chaoyang district

WINDSOR BILINGUAL KINDERGARTEN
http://legendgardens.windsorkindergarten.cn
Shunyi district

SCHOOLS— COMBINED AGES

BEANSTALK INTERNATIONAL BILINGUAL SCHOOLS (BIBS)
www.bibs.com.cn
Chaoyang district

BEIJING BISS INTERNATIONAL SCHOOL
www.biss.com.cn
Chaoyang district

BEIJING CITY INTERNATIONAL SCHOOL (BCIS)
www.bcis.cn
Chaoyang district

BEIJING INTERNATIONAL BILINGUAL ACADEMY (BIBA)
www.bibachina.org
Shunyi district

BEIJING NATIONAL DAY SCHOOL
www.bjshiyi.org.cn
Haidian district

BEIJING NO. 55 MIDDLE SCHOOL AND HIGH SCHOOL
www.bj55iss.cn
Dongcheng District

BEIJING RITAN HIGH SCHOOL
http://rtzx.bjchyedu.cn
Chaoyang district

BEIJING SHUREN-RIBET PRIVATE SCHOOL
www.shurenribet.org
Tongzhou district

BEIJING WORLD YOUTH ACADEMY (BWYA)
www.ibwya.net
Chaoyang district

BRITISH SCHOOL OF BEIJING (BSB)
www.britishschool.org.cn
Various locations

CANADIAN INTERNATIONAL SCHOOL OF BEIJING (CISB)
www.cisb.com.cn
Various locations

DULWICH COLLEGE BEIJING
www.dulwich-beijing.cn
Various locations in Shunyi and northeast Chaoyang districts

FAMILY LEARNING HOUSE
www.thefamilylearninghouse.com
Chaoyang district

RESOURCES

**HARROW INTERNATIONAL
SCHOOL BEIJING**
www.harrowbeijing.cn
Northeast Chaoyang district

**HIGH SCHOOL AFFILIATED
TO RENMIN UNIVERSITY**
www.rdfz.cn
Haidian district

HUIJIA PRIVATE SCHOOL
www.huijia2000.com
Changping district

**INTERNATIONAL ACADEMY
OF BEIJING (IAB)**
www.iabchina.net
Chaoyang district

**INTERNATIONAL SCHOOL
OF BEIJING (ISB)**
www.isb.bj.edu.cn
Shunyi district

KEYSTONE ACADEMY
www.keystoneacademy.cn
Shunyi district

KING'S COLLEGE BEIJING
www.kingscollege.cn
Northeast Chaoyang district

**SAINT PAUL AMERICAN
SCHOOL (SPAS)**
http://stpaulamerican.org
Haidian district

SINO BRIGHT SCHOOL
www.schoolbj.com
Fengtai district

SWEDISH SCHOOL OF BEIJING
www.ssbchina.se
Shunyi district

3E INTERNATIONAL
www.3einternationalschool.org
Chaoyang district

**TSINGHUA INTERNATIONAL
SCHOOL**
www.this.edu.cn
Haidian district

**WESTERN ACADEMY
OF BEIJING (WAB)**
www.wab.edu
Shunyi district

**YEW CHUNG INTERNATIONAL
SCHOOL OF BEIJING
(YCIS BEIJING)**
www.ycis-bj.com
Chaoyang district

UNIVERSITIES
BEIJING FILM ACADEMY
www.bfa.edu.cn
Haidian district

**BEIJING FOREIGN
STUDIES UNIVERSITY**
www.bfsu.edu.cn
Haidian district

**BEIJING INSTITUTE
OF TECHNOLOGY**
http://english.bit.edu.cn
Haidian district

**BEIJING INTERNATIONAL
STUDIES UNIVERSITY**
www.bisu.edu.cn
Chaoyang district

**BEIJING LANGUAGE AND
CULTURE UNIVERSITY**
www.blcu.edu.cn
Haidian district

BEIJING NORMAL UNIVERSITY

www.bnu.edu.cn
Haidian district

BEIJING SPORT UNIVERSITY

http://en.bsu.edu.cn
Haidian district

BEIJING UNIVERSITY OF AERONAUTICS AND ASTRONAUTICS (BEIHANG UNIVERSITY)

ev.buaa.edu.cn
Haidian district

BEIJING UNIVERSITY OF CHINESE MEDICINE

www.bucm.edu.cn
Chaoyang district

BEIJING UNIVERSITY OF TECHNOLOGY

http://bjut.edu.cn
Chaoyang district

CAPITAL UNIVERSITY OF ECONOMICS AND BUSINESS

http://english.cueb.edu.cn
Chaoyang district

CENTRAL UNIVERSITY OF FINANCE AND ECONOMICS

www.cufe.edu.cn
Haidian district

CHINA UNIVERSITY OF CHEMICAL TECHNOLOGY

www.buct.edu.cn
Chaoyang district

CHINA UNIVERSITY OF GEOSCIENCES

www.cugb.edu.cn
Haidian district

CHINA UNIVERSITY OF POLITICAL SCIENCE AND LAW

www.cupl.edu.cn
Haidian district

COMMUNICATION UNIVERSITY OF CHINA

www.cuc.edu.cn
Chaoyang district

MINZU UNIVERSITY OF CHINA

http://eng.muc.edu.cn
Haidian district

PEKING UNIVERSITY

www.pku.edu.cn
Haidian district

RENMIN UNIVERSITY OF CHINA

www.ruc.edu.cn
Haidian district

TSINGHUA UNIVERSITY

www.tsinghua.edu.cn
Haidian district

UNIVERSITY OF SCIENCE AND TECHNOLOGY BEIJING

http://en.ustb.edu.cn
Haidian district

SPECIAL SUPPORT SERVICES

BEIJING HOMESCHOOLERS

beijing_homeschoolers-owner@
yahoogroups.com
http://groups.yahoo.com/group/
beijing_homeschoolers
tel. 139/1030-6022
Support and networking for parents
homeschooling their kids.

BEIJING WESTSIDE HOMESCHOOL CO-OP

http://groups.yahoo.com/group/
BJWestsidehomeschool

CHINA DISABLED PERSONS' FEDERATION

www.cdpf.org.cn

Supporting the rights of and providing services for people with disabilities in China.

DISABILITY CHINA

www.disabilitychina.org

Supporting people with disabilities.

ELIOTT'S CORNER

www.oliviasplace.org

The Beijing branch of Olivia's Place in Shanghai, Eliott's Corner offers special-needs kids a range of supportive services and therapy. Based in Chaoyang district.

HANDICAP INTERNATIONAL

www.handicapinternational.be/en/china

Assistance for people with disabilities in developing countries.

SIDE BY SIDE

www.sidebysidebeijing.com

Support for children with special needs and learning difficulties, their families, and their networks through individualized special education, music therapy, behavior management, social skills training, and workshops. Based in Shunyi district.

STARS AND RAIN

www.guduzh.org.cn

A nongovernmental organization dedicated to helping kids with autism and their families. Based in Chaoyang district.

UNIVERSITY SUPPORT SERVICES

AMERICAN ASSOCIATION OF COLLEGIATE REGISTRARS AND ADMISSIONS OFFICERS (AACRAO) INTERNATIONAL EDUCATION SERVICES

http://ies.aacrao.org

A service that can help you assess the academic credentials of learning institutions in Beijing and anywhere else in the world.

CHINA UNIVERSITY APPLICATION CENTER

www.at0086.com/cuac/default.aspx

Assistance in finding and enrolling in the right course in China.

CHINESE SERVICE CENTER FOR SCHOLARLY EXCHANGE

www.cscse.edu.cn

Help with university enrollment and international exchanges.

Health

INTERNATIONAL HOSPITALS AND CLINICS

BAYLEY & JACKSON MEDICAL CENTER

www.bjhealthcare.com

BEIJING AIER-INTECH EYE HOSPITAL

http://en.intecheye.com

Eye hospital for everything from prescriptions to emergency care.

BEIJING PUHUA INTERNATIONAL CLINIC

www.puhuaclinic.com

Located near Shuangjing, this international clinic offers a wide range of medical care, including nutrition, dentistry, and ophthalmology.

BEIJING PUHUA INTERNATIONAL HOSPITAL

www.puhuachina.com

A high-quality, quiet hospital located near the south gate of Tiantan Park and near Beijing Tiantan Hospital. Many staff are fluent in English, especially during office hours when support staff are available. Many doctors have trained overseas, and so can also communicate with patients in English.

BEIJING 21ST CENTURY HOSPITAL

www.21-hospital.com
Suitable for minor procedures.

BEIJING UNITED FAMILY HOSPITAL AND CLINICS (BJU)

http://beijing.ufh.com.cn
This is the biggest international medical service in Beijing. It has general and specialty services, including oncology, rehabilitation, and counseling. In addition to its comprehensive hospital facility in Lido, BJU has various medical and dental clinics around Chaoyang and Shunyi districts.

HONG KONG INTERNATIONAL MEDICAL CLINIC, BEIJING

www.hkclinic.com
A health-care clinic for you and your family.

INTERNATIONAL MEDICAL CENTER (IMC)

www.imcclinics.com
A large-scale medical clinic with English-language service.

INTERNATIONAL SOS BEIJING CLINIC

www.internationalsos.com/clinicsinchina/en/Beijing.aspx
The go-to clinic for most of your family's medical needs and medication.

MEDICGO INTERNATIONAL MEDICAL CENTER

www.medicgo.net
Offers packages for simple checkups and treatments, as well as general practitioner services. Some staff speak English.

OASIS INTERNATIONAL HOSPITAL

www.oasishealth.cn
One of Beijing's newest comprehensive international hospitals—with some of the most stylish suites in town.

VISTA MEDICAL CENTER

www.vista-china.net
An international clinic to maintain your family's health.

CHINESE GOVERNMENT AND PRIVATE HOSPITALS

AMASIA INTERNATIONAL MEDICAL CENTER

www.asog-beijing.com
Formerly (and occasionally still) known as American-Sino, this hospital offers ob-gyn and pediatric services.

AMCARE WOMEN'S & CHILDREN'S HOSPITAL

www.amcare.com.cn
Though aimed at giving Chinese families international medical care, this is also frequently chosen by expat families willing to step away from the fully international facilities.

ARMED POLICE GENERAL HOSPITAL

www.wj-hospital.com
A large-scale comprehensive hospital.

BEIJING ALICE GYNECOLOGY HOSPITAL

www.fuke120.com

RESOURCES

BEIJING ANZHEN HOSPITAL

www.anzhen.org

Specializes in treatment of heart and lung diseases.

BEIJING CHILDREN'S HOSPITAL

www.bch.com.cn

Beijing's leading children's hospital.

BEIJING DONGWEN TCM CLINIC

www.dywjmed.com

An integrative traditional Chinese medicine (TCM) clinic aiming to make TCM accessible to the Western community.

BEIJING FRIENDSHIP HOSPITAL

www.bfh.com.cn

Chinese hospital with a VIP/international section.

BEIJING HONG YI TANG YIYUAN

www.guoyitang.com

Traditional Chinese medicine. No English is spoken, so take a Chinese speaker. Doctors are friendly and there is little waiting as this is a private clinic and a little more expensive than government facilities.

BEIJING HOSPITAL OF TRADITIONAL CHINESE MEDICINE

www.bjzhongyi.com

Registration fee varies from doctor to doctor.

BEIJING MASSAGE HOSPITAL

www.massage-hospital.com

Traditional treatments, which include massage as well as cupping and scraping.

BEIJING TONGREN HOSPITAL

www.trhos.com

One of Beijing's most important hospitals for ophthalmology and otorhinolaryngology.

BEIJING TONGRENTANG TRADITIONAL CHINESE MEDICINE HOSPITAL

www.tongrentangzyyy.com

Well-known chain of TCM hospitals and pharmacies.

CHINA-JAPAN FRIENDSHIP HOSPITAL

http://english.zryhyy.com.cn

A leading Beijing hospital well-known for its international, English-friendly section.

CHINESE PLA GENERAL HOSPITAL (301 MILITARY HOSPITAL)

www.plagh.com.cn

One of Beijing's leading hospitals.

FUWAI HOSPITAL

www.fuwaihospital.org

Specializes in cardiovascular diseases.

GLOBALCARE WOMEN & CHILDREN'S HOSPITAL (WUZHOU YIYUAN)

www.globalcarecn.com

Some English services are available. One of the many local hospitals that seem to equate "family planning" with abortions.

HARMONICARE

http://en.hmcare.net/index.html

International quality in obstetrics, gynecology, and pediatrics for both Chinese and Western families.

MARY'S HOSPITAL, WOMEN & INFANTS, BEIJING

www.mary.net.cn

Uses a Western model of health care and client service.

MERIDIAN TRADITIONAL CHINESE MEDICINE CLINIC

www.mingjingtang.com

Treatments range from massages to

acupuncture, moxibustion, and cupping, helping to treat such things as headaches, insomnia, menstrual pain, and more.

NEW CENTURY INTERNATIONAL CHILDREN'S HOSPITAL

www.ncich.com.cn
The English-speaking level of the staff is inconsistent.

PEKING UNION MEDICAL COLLEGE HOSPITAL (XIEHE YIYUAN)

www.pumch.cn/Category_1200/Index.aspx
One of Beijing's most highly respected hospitals. Skip the waiting by using the VIP/international wing.

PEKING UNIVERSITY PEOPLE'S HOSPITAL

http://english.pkuph.edu.cn
Important hospital for research and education. Welcoming to expat patients.

PEKING UNIVERSITY THIRD HOSPITAL

www.puh3.net.cn
One of Beijing's top hospitals, recognized for its gynecology and obstetrics, sports medicine, cardiovascular and orthopedic treatment, in-vitro fertilization, and reconstructive surgery.

STRAIGHT BAMBOO TCM CLINIC

http://thehutong.com/straightbamboo-clinic
An expat-friendly entry into traditional Chinese medicine, run out of expat center The Hutong in Dongcheng district.

XUANWU HOSPITAL CAPITAL MEDICAL UNIVERSITY

www.xwhosp.com.cn
Large comprehensive hospital specializing in neuroscience and gerontology.

DENTAL

ARRAIL DENTAL CLINIC

www.arrail-dental.com

BEIJING UNITED FAMILY DENTAL CLINICS

http://beijing.ufh.com.cn

BEIJING VISTA DENTAL CLINIC

www.vista-china.net

IDC DENTAL

www.idcdentalbj.com

IMC DENTAL CLINIC

www.imcclinics.com

JIAMEI DENTAL HOSPITAL

www.jiameidental.com

JOINWAY

www.dentalcn.com

OASIS DENTAL CLINIC

www.oasishealth.cn

SDM DENTAL

www.sdmdental.com

SMART HEALTH MEDICAL AND DENTAL CENTER

www.smarthealth.cn

SOS INTERNATIONAL DENTISTRY AND ORTHODONTISTRY

www.clinicsinchina.com

OTHER SUPPORT AND INFORMATION SERVICES

ALCOHOLICS ANONYMOUS (BEIJING AA FELLOWSHIP)

www.aabeijing.com

WORLD HEALTH ORGANIZATION (WHO)

www2.wpro.who.int/china/home.htm

Get up-to-date information on China-related health issues, such as disease outbreaks.

HEALTH PRODUCTS
AQUASANA
www.aquasana-china.com
An American-owned company providing filters for kitchen and bathroom water.

IQ AIR
www.iqair-china.com
Air filters for homes and offices.

PURELIVING—INDOOR ENVIRONMENTAL SOLUTIONS
www.purelivingchina.com
Have your home assessed for everything from the air and water quality to lead and mold.

TORANA CLEAN AIR CENTERS
www.toranacleanair.com
Air filters and humidifiers for your home as well as Totobobo masks for polluted days.

WORLD HEALTH STORE
www.worldhealthstore.com.cn
Buy everything from vitamins and face masks to water and air filters.

INSURANCE
ABACARE GROUP
www.abacaregroup.com
Meet face to face with agents knowledge-able about Beijing's specific issues to se-lect the right insurance plan for you and your family.

AIG
www.aig.com
International insurance services for individuals and companies.

BROKERFISH
www.brokerfish.com
An online broker that will give you a quick insight into what's available.

GLOBALSURANCE
www.globalsurance.com
Help selecting the right insurance package for you.

Employment

RESOURCES

JOB SEARCH
BESTALENT SEARCH
www.bestalent.com

FESCO
www.fesco.com.cn

HUDSON
http://hudson.cn

J.M. GEMINI RECRUITMENT SOLUTIONS
www.jmgemini.com

KELLY SERVICES
www.kellyservices.cn

MICHAEL PAGE
www.michaelpage.com.cn

RMG SELECTION
www.rmgselection.com

SETTING UP A BUSINESS, LEGAL HELP, AND INFORMATION
AMERICAN CHAMBER OF COMMERCE (AMCHAM CHINA)
www.amchamchina.org

ASIA BUSINESS
www.asiabs.com

**AUSTRALIAN CHAMBER OF
COMMERCE (AUSTCHAM BEIJING)**
www.austcham.org

**BEIJING MUNICIPAL BUREAU OF
LABOR AND SOCIAL SECURITY**
www.bjld.gov.cn

**BRITISH CHAMBER OF COMMERCE
IN CHINA (BRITCHAM)**
www.britishchamber.cn

BROAD & BRIGHT LAW FIRM
www.broadbright.com

**CANADA CHINA
BUSINESS COUNCIL**
www.ccbc.com

CHINA BRIEFING
www.china-briefing.com

CHINA LAW BLOG
www.chinalawblog.com

CHINA SCOPE FINANCIAL
www.chinascopefinancial.com
Up-to-date data, information, and analytics on China in English.

KING & WOOD MALLESONS (PRC)
www.kingandwood.com

LAW COMPANIES IN BEIJING
For an extensive list of U.S. law firms based in Beijing, look under U.S. Citizen Services/Legal Resources on the U.S. embassy's website: http://beijing.usembassy-china.org.cn.

LAWINFOCHINA
http://eng.chinalawinfo.com/index.asp

**NATIONAL BUREAU OF
STATISTICS OF CHINA**
www.stats.gov.cn

WANG & WANG
www.wangandwang.com

Finance

**BEIJING LOCAL TAXATION
BUREAU OFFICE**
www.tax861.gov.cn

JIAOFEIYI
www.jiaofeiyi.net
Pay all kinds of bills. For an interactive map of machines in Beijing, go to www.jiaofeiyi.net/map/map.php.

BANKS
AGRICULTURAL BANK OF CHINA
www.abchina.com

BANK OF BEIJING
www.bankofbeijing.com.cn

BANK OF CHINA
www.boc.cn

BANK OF COMMUNICATIONS
www.bankcomm.com

CHINA CITIC BANK
http://bank.ecitic.com

CHINA CONSTRUCTION BANK
www.ccb.com

CHINA DEVELOPMENT BANK
www.cdb.com.cn

CHINA MERCHANTS BANK
www.cmbchina.com

CHINA MINSHENG BANK
www.cmbc.com.cn

CITIBANK
www.citibank.com.cn

HSBC
www.hsbc.com.cn

INDUSTRIAL AND COMMERCIAL BANK OF CHINA (ICBC)
www.icbc.com.cn

PEOPLE'S BANK OF CHINA
www.pbc.gov.cn

STANDARD CHARTERED BANK
www.standardchartered.com.cn

Communications

NEWSPAPERS
BEIJING TODAY
www.beijingtoday.com.cn
Beijing city's only English-language newspaper. Government owned and run by the influential Chinese newspaper *Beijing Youth Daily*.

CHINA DAILY
www.chinadaily.com.cn
Government-owned national English-language newspaper. Available online, in convenience stores, and at newspaper stands.

GLOBAL TIMES
www.globaltimes.cn
One of the government's favorite national newspapers for distributing news to its English-reading population.

SOUTH CHINA MORNING POST
www.scmp.com
Produced in Hong Kong, this newspaper offers more independent views than the carefully guided papers produced in the capital. It can be hard to get, though. Find it in international hotels or subscribe online.

BOOK AND MAGAZINE SELLERS
AMAZON (CHINA)
www.amazon.cn
Shop via Google Chrome to translate, and have things delivered to your door, at which point you can pay in cash or by card.

THE BOOKWORM
http://beijingbookworm.com
Buy English-language novels, cookbooks, magazines, and even Moleskine journals.

PAGE ONE
www.pageonegroup.com
Somewhat new to Beijing, this English-books bookstore is quickly establishing itself in all the expat hot spots.

TRENDS LOUNGE
tel. 10/6587-1999
L214, Second Floor, The Place, 9 Guanghua Lu, Chaoyang district
朝阳区光华路9号世贸天阶北街时尚大厦2层L214
Come for a coffee or lunch and peruse what is perhaps Beijing's biggest offering of English-language magazines.

RESOURCES

TELEPHONE, CELL PHONE, AND INTERNET

CHINA MOBILE

tel. 10086

http://10086.cn/bj/

China's largest mobile carrier, despite its 3G service being relatively new.

CHINA TELECOM

tel. 10000

www.bjtelecom.net (For Beijing service)

www.chinatelecom.com.cn

Generally the cheaper option of the three. Coverage for fixed lines, cell phones, and Internet.

CHINA UNICOM

tel. 10010

www.chinaunicom.com

Currently China's strongest 3G network supplier. Coverage for fixed lines, cell phones, and Internet.

POST AND COURIERS

DHL

www.cn.dhl.com

EMS

www.ems.com.cn

FEDEX

www.fedex.com

SF EXPRESS

www.sf-express.com/cn/en

UPS

www.ups.com

Travel and Transportation

AIR

AIR ASIA (D7)

www.airasia.com

Budget Malaysian airline. Departs from Terminal 2.

AIR CHINA (CA)

www.airchina.com.cn

China's national carrier. Departs from Terminal 3.

CHINA AIRLINES (CI)

www.china-airlines.com

A Taiwanese airline. International flights from Beijing are via Taipei. Departs from Terminal 3.

CHINA EASTERN (MU)

http://easternmiles.ceair.com

Departs from Terminal 2.

CHINA SOUTHERN (CZ)

www.china-airlines.com

Domestic and international Chinese airline. Departs from Terminal 2.

DRAGONAIR (KA)

www.dragonair.com

A Hong Kong airline partnered with Cathay Pacific. Departs from Terminal 3.

HAINAN AIR (HU)

www.hnair.com

One of the nicer Chinese airlines, and one intent on offering international standards regarding service, food, and onboard entertainment. Departs from Terminal 2 for international and Terminal 1 for domestic.

HONG KONG AIRLINES (HX)

www.hongkongairlines.com

Flies primarily throughout Asia, but also London, U.K., and Moscow, Russia. Airline includes Hong Kong Express

RESOURCES

Airways (UO). Both depart from Terminal 2.

BUSES

BEIJING BUS

www.bjbus.com

Search for bus routes and bus numbers around Beijing (Chinese only).

BEIJING HUB OF TOUR DISPATCH

www.bjlyjszx.com

Government-run tours of the city, including a large range of cheap public tour buses that run direct from the inner city to outer-suburban destinations.

MAP BAR

www.mapbar.com/beijing

Search for bus routes and bus numbers around Beijing (Chinese only).

TRAIN

CHINA TRAIN

http://train.huochepiao.com

Search for trains coming into and departing from Beijing.

CHINA TRAIN GUIDE

www.chinatrainguide.com

A very useful search tool for trains around China.

SEAT 61

www.seat61.com

A handy guide to China's trains, including the Trans-Siberian Express.

TOUR-BEIJING.COM

www.tour-beijing.com

Search for and book train tickets.

TRAVEL CHINA GUIDE

www.travelchinaguide.com

Easy-to-use guide for China's trains.

GENERAL TRANSPORTATION

BEIJING SUBWAY

www.bjsubway.com

Information on Beijing's subway. Unfortunately, the English version of the site is downright lousy.

BEIJING TAXIS

tel. 96106

Book regular as well as barrier-free taxis. Call at least one day ahead 8am-10am. Chinese only.

BEIJING TRAFFIC MANAGEMENT BUREAU

www.bjjtgl.gov.cn

This is the official site for everything relating to driving licenses and road rules, including driver-training centers.

DRIVERS, CAR SERVICES, AND LICENSES

BEIJING AUTO SERVICE CENTER

www.ascbj.com

Buying, selling, rental, maintenance, and licenses.

BEIJING EXPAT SERVICE CENTER

www.beijingesc.com

Assistance for getting your Chinese driver's license.

BEIJING TOP RATED CAR RENTAL SERVICE

www.sxsdcar.com

Rent for day tours or ongoing use.

CAR SOLUTION

www.elsey-car.com

Buying, selling, rental, maintenance, and licenses.

CHINA AUTO RENTAL (CAR)

www.zuche.com

One of China's biggest rental car services.

RESOURCES

EXPATCAR
www.expatcar.com
Friendly service offering short-term rental for day trips through to year-long leasing.

EX-PATS LIFE
www.expatslife.com
Provides drivers, cleaners, car leasing, and driver's license assistance.

FESCO
www.fescoservice.com
In addition to employment and visa services, FESCO can help you zip through the driving license process.

FIRST CHOICE CAR RENTAL SERVICE
www.fccars.cn
Short- and long-term leasing.

HERTZ BEIJING
www.hertz.com.cn
Rent a car with or without a driver, for short-term or long-term periods.

ST AUTO CLUB
www.stautoclub.com.cn
Can help with car management and maintenance issues.

TRAVEL AGENCIES
CHINA CULTURE CENTER
www.chinaculturecenter.org
Cultural trips around Beijing and further afield.

CHINA HIGHLIGHTS
www.chinahighlights.com
Comprehensive travel service for Beijing and China.

CTRIP
http://english.ctrip.com
This is a China-based travel-booking service. It has some of the most competitive rates available and will become an important booking tool once you are living in Beijing. English information and phone service are both excellent. Ctrip has the advantage of offering cash on delivery for tickets purchased within China.

ELONG.COM
www.elong.net
ELong is a direct competitor to Ctrip and provides a similar range and level of service. It's worth comparing the two when purchasing flights, hotels, or tours.

QUNAR.COM
www.qunar.com
Popular and well-regarded travel booking site. Purchase plane and train tickets, and book hotels and holiday packages. Chinese only.

TRAVEL CHINA GUIDE
www.travelchinaguide.com
An excellent resource about traveling in China by plane or train.

Housing Considerations

REAL ESTATE AGENTS

BEL & WELL PROPERTY INTERNATIONAL
www.bel-property.com.cn

DRC (DIPLOMATIC RESIDENCE COMPOUND)
www.dhsc.com.cn/fw_sc/index_en.aspx
High-security, high-quality compounds, located near all the embassy areas.

FOUR STAR REALTY
www.shanghome.cn

GANJI
http://bj.ganji.com
Look where locals look. Reliability of photos and service highly varied and often dubious.

HOME LINK
http://beijing.homelink.com.cn

Real estate agent for properties Beijing-wide. Chinese only.

JOANNA REAL ESTATE
http://beijing.joannarealestate.com.cn
Help with locating high-end or family-friendly housing.

LIHONG
www.lihong.biz
Specialist in helping expats with an international budget find a home and settle in to Beijing.

SUPER ESTATE
www.superestate.cn
Help settling in as well as locating an office.

WO AI WO JIA
www.5i5j.com
One of the largest real estate agents in town. Chinese only.

Prime Living Locations

GENERAL

BEIJING REPORT
www.drben.net
This site might give you a headache to look at, and information is a little out of date, but it's still a great resource of information about Beijing, its history, its different regions, and its many attractions.

CHANGPING DISTRICT
www.bjchp.gov.cn
The official government portal on Changping.

CHAOYANG DISTRICT
http://bci.bjchy.gov.cn

The official government portal on Chaoyang.

DAXING DISTRICT
www.bjdx.gov.cn
The official government portal on Daxing.

DONGCHENG DISTRICT
http://en.bjdch.gov.cn
The official government portal on Dongcheng.

FANGSHAN DISTRICT
www.bjfsh.gov.cn

RESOURCES

The official government portal on Fangshan. (Chinese only)

FENGTAI DISTRICT
www.bjft.gov.cn
The official government portal on Fengtai.

HAIDIAN DISTRICT
www.bjhd.gov.cn
The official government portal on Haidian.

HUAIROU DISTRICT
www.bjhr.gov.cn
The official government portal on Huairou.

MENTOUGOU DISTRICT
www.bjmtg.gov.cn
The official government portal on Mentougou.

MIYUN COUNTY
www.bjmy.gov.cn
The official government portal on Miyun. (Chinese only)

PINGGU DISTRICT
www.bjpg.gov.cn
The official government portal on Pinggu. (Chinese only)

SHIJINGSHAN DISTRICT
www.bjsjs.gov.cn
The official government portal on Shujingshan. (Chinese only)

SHUNYI DISTRICT
www.bjshy.gov.cn
The official government portal on Shunyi.

TONGZHOU DISTRICT
www.bjtzh.gov.cn
The official government portal on Tongzhou.

XICHENG DISTRICT
www.bjxch.gov.cn
The official government portal on Xicheng.

YANQING COUNTY
www.bjyq.gov.cn
The official government portal on Yanqing.

Z-PARK
www.zgc.gov.cn
The official government site for the entire Zhongguancun Science Park, which is scattered right across the entire municipality.

Community

ORGANIZATIONS

AMCHAM
www.amchamchina.org

AUSTCHAM
www.austcham.org

BRITCHAM
www.britishchamber.cn

**CANADA CHINA
BUSINESS COUNCIL**
www.ccbc.com

DISABILITY CHINA
www.disabilitychina.org

GREENPEACE
www.greenpeace.org/china

**INTERNATIONAL FUND
FOR ANIMAL WELFARE**
www.ifaw.org/china

UNICEF
www.unicef.org

WWF
www.wwfchina.org

NETWORKING GROUPS

BEEFSTEAK AND BURGUNDY
www.beefandburgundy.org
Fine dining for the fellas. Invitation required from existing member.

BEIJING CAFÉ
http://groups.yahoo.com/group/Beijingcafe
A place to ask other residents any question you have at all about Beijing.

BEIJING HASH HOUSE HARRIERS
www.hash.cn

Drink, make friends, and occasionally run.

**BEIJING INTERNATIONAL
SOCIETY (BIS)**
www.beijinginternationalsociety.com
A nonprofit organization offering foreign passport holders an opportunity to hear about China from professionals and scholars on a wide range of subjects, including culture, history, arts, religion, economics, science, archaeology, the environment, and much more.

BEIJING LGBT CENTER
www.bjlgbtcenter.org
Equality, advocacy, and a whole lot of fun.

BEIJING MAMAS
http://groups.yahoo.com/group/
Beijing_Mamas
Share experiences with other moms in Beijing.

BEIJING ORGANIC CONSUMERS
http://health.groups.yahoo.com/group/
beijing_organic_consumers
Beijing residents interested in organic produce. The more than 950 members share resources, ideas, and information on how to live and shop healthfully and responsibly in the city.

85 BROADS
secure.85broads.com

FCGROUP
www.fcgroup.org
Connect with like-minded people over drinks at interesting venues.

INTERNATIONAL NEWCOMERS' NETWORK (INN)
www.innbeijing.org
Immerse yourself quickly into Beijing with this welcoming and informative group.

INTERNATIONS
www.internations.org/beijing-expats

STITCH 'N BITCH IN BEIJING
http://groups.yahoo.com/group/stitchnbitch_beijing
Art and conversation.

VIVA BEIJING PROFESSIONAL WOMEN'S NETWORK
www.vivabeijing.org
Nonprofit organization providing professional women with an opportunity to share knowledge, make meaningful connections, be inspired, and have fun.

PRIVATE CLUBS
BAYHOOD NO. 9 GOLF CLUB
www.bayhood9.com

BEIJING AMERICAN CLUB
www.americanclubbeijing.com

BEIJING HONG KONG JOCKEY CLUB
www.beijingclubhouse.com

CAPITAL CLUB
www.thecapitalclub.com

CHANG AN CLUB
www.changan-club.com

CHINA CLUB
www.thechinaclubbeijing.com

FOREIGN CORRESPONDENTS' CLUB OF CHINA
www.fccchina.org

SPORTS CLUBS
AO FAN SAILING
http://aofansailing.com

AUSTRALIAN RULES FOOTBALL CLUB
www.beijingbombers.com

BEIJING AARDVARKS RUGBY CLUB
www.beijingaardvarks.org

BEIJING CLIMBING CLUB
http://beijingclimbingclub.com

BEIJING CRICKET CLUB
www.bjcricketclub.org

BEIJING DEVILS RUGBY CLUB
www.beijingdevils.com

BEIJING INTERNATIONAL ICE HOCKEY
www.beijinghockey.com

BEIJING PELETON
http://beijing.mongoliaprocycling.com

BEIJING SAILING CENTER
www.beijingsailing.com

BEIJING ULTIMATE FRISBEE
www.beijingultimate.com

BROADWELL TENNIS CLUB
http://sports.broadwell.cn

CLUBFOOTBALL
www.clubfootball.com.cn

HANDBALL IN CHINA
www.handballinchina.org

HEYROBICS
www.heyrobics.com

RESOURCES

INTERNATIONAL FRIENDSHIP FOOTBALL CLUB
www.iffc1994.com

MASHUP SPORT & SOCIAL
www.mashupsports.com

O'LE
http://ole-sports.org

POTTER'S WHEEL
www.potters-wheel.cn

SPORTS BEIJING
www.sportsbj.org

TRIBEIJING
www.tribeijing.org

VOLUNTEERING
BEIJING HUMAN AND ANIMAL ENVIRONMENTAL EDUCATION CENTER
www.animalschina.org

HALF THE SKY
www.halfthesky.org

MAGIC HOSPITAL
www.magichospital.org

NEW DAY
http://newdaycreations.com

PREVENTION THROUGH EDUCATION
www.pte-china.org

ROOTS & SHOOTS
www.jgichina.org

ROTARACT BEIJING
www.rotaractbeijing.org

ROTARY
http://rotaryclub-beijing.org

ROUNDABOUT
www.roundaboutchina.com

RELIGIOUS
BICF (BEIJING INTERNATIONAL CHRISTIAN FELLOWSHIP)
www.bicf.org

CAPITAL CLUB ATHLETIC CENTER AT CAPITAL MANSION
www.thecapitalclub.com
Religious services are held here for both Kehillat Beijing and Congregation of the Good Shepherd.

CAPITAL COMMUNITY
www.capitalcommunitychurch.net

CHABAD HOUSE
www.chabadbeijing.com

CONGREGATION OF THE GOOD SHEPHERD
www.cogs-bj.org

ISLAM
www.islamichina.com

KEHILLAT BEIJING
www.sinogogue.org

OTHER GROUPS
BEIJING IMPROV
www.beijingimprov.org
Free bilingual workshops are run every Wednesday night in Dongcheng district, and the official team holds public performances roughly once a month.

BEIJING PLAYHOUSE
www.beijingplayhouse.com
Amateur acting group for adults and kids.

BOOKWORM CAFE
http://beijingbookworm.com
Get on the mailing list and enjoy events

such as author talks, wine tastings, and slam poetry.

CHINA CULTURE CENTER (CCC)
www.chinaculturecenter.org
Day trips, cultural activities, corporate events, and more.

COMEDY CLUB CHINA
www.comedyclubchina.com
Stand-up performances by local and international comedians.

HAIS GOURMET
www.hiasgourmet.com
Food tours and corporate events.

HUTONG, THE
http://thehutong.com
Join in cooking classes, cycling trips, photography classes, and many other interesting activities.

Emergency Numbers for Beijing

All emergencies: 110

Police: 110

Traffic accident: 122

Fire: 119

Ambulance: 120 or 999*

Beijing Emergency Red Cross Center: 999*

Local directory assistance: 114

*The 999 emergency number has an English-language service.

24-HOUR MEDICAL FACILITIES

Beijing International SOS Clinic: 10/6462-9112 (general) or 10/6462-9100 (24-hour emergency)

Beijing United Family Hospital: 10/5927-7000 (general) or 10/5927-7120 (emergency)

International Medical Center Beijing: 10/6465-1560, 10/6465-1561, 10/6465-1562, or 10/6465-1563

Oasis International Hospital: 400/UR-OASIS (400/876-2747)

EMBASSIES

Australia: 10/5140-4111

Brazil: 10/6532-2881

Canada: 10/5139-4000, 613/996-8885*, or 613/944-1310 (TTY)*

France: 10/8532-8080 or 137/0107-8733*

Germany: 10/8532-9000

Hong Kong Beijing Office: 10/6657-2880 or 852/1868

India: 10/8531-2500

Ireland: 10/6532-2691

Italy: 10/8532-7600 or 139/0103-2957*

Japan: 10/6532-2361

The Netherlands: 10/8532-0200 or 139/0112-4185*

New Zealand: 10/8531-2700

Singapore: 10/6532-1115

South Africa: 10/8532-0000 or 139/1171-1575*

Spain: 10/6532-3629

Sweden: 10/6532-9790

United Kingdom: 10/5192-4000 or 10/8529-6083*

United States: 10/8531-3000 or 10/8531-4000*

*After-hours emergency numbers for the given country's citizens only.

RESOURCES

Glossary

āyí domestic helper or nanny

Beijing duck sometimes known in the West as Peking duck; a classic dish of Beijing in which slivvers of roast duck are rolled into small pancakes with sauce and other condiments

Beijing opera a traditional form of Chinese opera in Beijing, sung in high-pitched voices and performed by actors dressed in ornate costumes

bèngbèng the name given to the small covered motorcycles that are often a form of (illegal) cheap transport to take people short distances

chop stamp or seal of a person, company, or organization; often required for official documents

dàjiē Chinese for avenue, but often also translated as street or boulevard

Dōngběi the northeast area of China, just above Beijing, comprising Heilongjiang, Jilin, and Liaoning, and formerly known as Manchuria

face the complicated concept of respect and status that governs relationships between individuals

fāpiào invoice

fǔlù side road, found running alongside the main road, typically used for turning corners, parking, and bicycle lanes

hǎiguī Chinese who have returned from being educated abroad

hóngbāo literally translated as red envelope, a packet in which money is given as a gift (sometimes simply refers to monetary gifts, with or without an envelope)

hot pot a popular form of eating suited to large groups, in which ingredients are purchased separately and cooked at will in a large pot of boiling soup

hùkǒu a Chinese person's registered residence; having a Beijing hùkǒu can be hard for Chinese people to get and is highly valued as it brings many advantages for life in Beijing; foreigners don't require these

hútòng traditional alleyways of Beijing, created by the walls of sìhéyuàn; these days largely confined to inside the Second Ring Road

jiānbing a standard street food in Beijing, in which a large pancake is rolled around egg, lettuce, sauce, and a cracker

jiē street

jīn 500 grams; a standard form of measurement when buying fresh produce

guǎngdōnghuà the Mandarin word for the Cantonese language

kuài spoken form for RMB1 or yuán

KTV karaoke

lǎowài a name meaning foreigner

lù road

májiàng popular noisy Chinese game played with small tiles, requiring four people sitting around a square table; often played on the street and in homes, and frequently involving gambling

pàichūsuǒ local police station

píngfáng a píngfáng is a one-story building (rather than an apartment block), which is typically found along the hútòng inside the Second Ring Road; one form of a píngfáng is the sìhéyuàn

pīnyīn phonetic system used to transcribe Chinese characters into romanized writing (Pinyin)

pǔtōnghuà the official spoken language of China, and the Chinese word for Mandarin

PRC People's Republic of China

PPT PowerPoint

shēnfènzhèng a Chinese person's form of identification, which they carry around with them at all times. It's required when doing such things as travelling domestically, shopping on some online stores, and registering addresses; foreigners do not have a shēnfènzhèng but instead must use their passports as ID

shèngnǚ a relatively new word, used to describe women over the age of about 27 who are still single, and which translates as "leftover woman"

sìhéyuàn a traditional Beijing house in which the entire house forms a square around a courtyard and faces inwards; the different buildings north, south, east, and west have different rankings

RESOURCES

of importance (often referred to as a courtyard house in English)

tàijíquán Mandarin tai chi, a martial-arts based exercise popular with the older generation

tàitai traditionally meaning "wife"; a word that is also applied to women who live a life of leisure, shopping, attending events, and enjoying the good life.

Taobao the most popular online shopping website

wàiguórén foreigner

xiàngsheng a traditional form of stand-up comedy, also known as crosstalk, in which two men banter back and forth. The humor stems largely from double meanings in words, and the art form is extremely popular in Beijing, especially with taxi drivers.

zhōu rice porridge often eaten at breakfast (what you might know by the name of congee)

Pronunciation

Mandarin Chinese is a tonal language, with four specific tones plus one neutral tone. This means that one word can have up to five different pronunciations, which are at times important to get right for your own preservation of face. Some people argue that a beginner shouldn't waste too much energy on learning tones, but in my own experience, if you put more effort into thinking how a word should be pronounced you will learn it more deeply. Plus, if you learn the correct pronunciation right from the start it sets a good foundation for your Chinese and prevents the need to go back later on and try to undo bad habits. It will also help your listeners understand you, as many locals do find it hard to make the jump in meaning if your tone has gone walkabout.

Tones are represented as accents above the vowels in Pinyin, the romanization of the Chinese characters. It's extremely important to learn how to correctly read Pinyin, the romanized form of the Chinese characters, so that your pronunciation is intelligible. Some letters, such as q or x, may not be pronounced as you think they should be, and if you try to say a word that uses them, you could end up flummoxing your listener. Some guidebooks use what may seem to be easier phonetic descriptions of words, but these are usually still way off target and in the long term unhelpful, as no Chinese character that you see in Beijing will be translated into anything other than standard Pinyin. Pinyin is easy to learn, and just a couple of lessons with a teacher will have you reading it correctly even if you don't know what you're saying.

PRONUNCIATION GUIDE

Tone	Description	Example	Chinese	Translation
1	A high, flat tone	tāng	汤	soup
2	A rising tone from low to high	táng	糖	sugar or candy
3	A dipping or squashed tone that falls and then rises again	tǎng	躺	to recline or lie on your back
4	A tone that falls sharply from high to low	tàng	烫	to scald or boiling hot
N	A neutral tone with no movement, most often in the second part of a two-"syllable" word	shī zi	狮子	lion

Some tones are easy to remember because perhaps emotionally they seem to match the meaning. For example, bù (不), meaning "no," has the downward stabbing fourth tone. But sometimes it can be helpful to use visuals or mnemonics to help you remember the tone. Dictionaries such as MDBG (www.mdbg.net) and Pleco (www.pleco.com) have color coding for tones, which can also aid memory. For example, to remember the different pronunciations of tang, you could think of the "flat" surface of a bowl of red soup, the "rise" of energy after eating a piece of yellow candy, lying on your back in a green field, and the "burning heat" from a bolt of blue lightning.

In addition to the tones, Chinese has a few other differences in pronunciation. Just some of these include:

q—Pronounced a bit like an English "ch" but made by concentrating the sound into a small point behind your front two teeth. The vowel that comes after it is usually produced in the same position.

ch—Again, like an English "ch" but flatter, wider, and farther back. It feels more relaxed then "q" and like your back teeth are helping to make the sound. Getting these two sounds right will make it clear whether you're saying qù (go, 去) or chū (out, 出).

x—This sound is produced by making an English "sh" sound but right at the front of your mouth where you'd normally produce a "s," and in a similar place to the Chinese "q." Vowels following "x" are produced at the front of the mouth.

sh—This is produced in a similar way to English "sh" but farther back like the Chinese "ch." Getting "x" and "sh" correct will make it obvious that you're saying either xiǎo (small, 小) or shǎo (少, lacking or few).

j—Again, rather than the English "j" sound that is produced with the sides of your tongue in about the middle of your mouth, the Chinese "j" is right at the front behind your two front teeth. The vowels that follow it are typically produced at the front of the mouth.

zh—This sound is much like the English "j" sound in "jump" or "g" in "George," only slightly farther back.

c—This is pronounced like a "ts." In English this sound occurs only in the middle or at the end of words, such as in kits or pats, but in Chinese it is found at the start of words, such as in "cù" (醋), meaning vinegar.

ü—This is produced much farther forward in the mouth than a usual "u" sound, almost in the same place that you would produce an "i" sound, as in "sit." It's sometimes written as a "v," which can also be used when typing or texting in Pinyin. Produced most often after an "n," as in nü (女), meaning woman, or after an "l," as in lüsè (绿色), meaning green.

This is how sounds work in Beijing at least. Go to Taiwan or to another province and things may be quite different. Beijing also has its own accent, which you'll easily pick up. The most distinctive sound is the "r" sound that gets added to the end of words. Sanlitun can be said just like that, but if you hear it from a taxi driver, it will most likely sound more like "Sanliturr."

Phrasebook

NUMBERS

ENGLISH	CHINESE	PINYIN
0	零	líng
1	一	yī
2	二	èr
3	三	sān
4	四	sì
5	五	wǔ
6	六	liù
7	七	qī
8	八	bā
9	九	jiǔ
10	十	shí
11	十一	shíyī
12	十二	shí'èr
13	十三	shísān
20	二十	èrshí
21	二十一	èrshíyī
22	二十二	èrshí'èr
23	二十三	èrshísān
50	五十	wǔshí
100	一百	yìbǎi
101	一百零一	yìbǎi líng yī
110	一百一十	yìbǎi yīshí
111	一百一十一	yìbǎi yīshíyī
200	两百	liǎng bǎi
1,000	一千	yìqiān
2,000	两千	liǎng qiān
10,000 (1,0000)	一万	yíwàn
100,000 (10,0000)	十万	shíwàn
1,000,000 (100,0000)	一百万	yìbǎi wàn
10,000,000 (1000,0000)	一千万	yìqiān wàn
100,000,000	一亿	yíyì
1,000,000,000 (10,0000,0000)	十亿	shíyì

DAYS AND MONTHS

ENGLISH	CHINESE	PINYIN
Monday	星期一	xīngqī yī
Tuesday	星期二	xīngqī èr
Wednesday	星期三	xīngqī sān
Thursday	星期四	xīngqī sì
Friday	星期五	xīngqī wǔ
Saturday	星期六	xīngqī liù
Sunday	星期天	xīngqī tiān
January	一月	yī yuè
February	二月	èr yuè
March	三月	sān yuè
April	四月	sì yuè
May	五月	wǔ yuè
June	六月	liù yuè
July	七月	qī yuè
August	八月	bā yuè
September	九月	jiǔ yuè
October	十月	shí yuè
November	十一月	shíyī yuè
December	十二月	shí'èr yuè

TIME

ENGLISH	CHINESE	PINYIN
today	今天	jīntiān
yesterday	昨天	zuótiān
day before yesterday	前天	qiántiān
tomorrow	明天	míngtiān
day after tomorrow	后天	hòutiān
weekdays	工作日	gōngzuò rì
weekend	周末	zhōumò
every day	每天	měitiān
last week	上(个)星期	shàng (ge) xīngqī
this week	这（个）星期	zhè (ge) xīngqī
next week	下(个)星期	xià (ge) xīngqī
last month	上个月	shàng ge yuè
this month	这个月	zhè ge yuè
next month	下个月	xià ge yuè

ENGLISH	CHINESE	PINYIN
last year	去年	qùnián
this year	今年	jīnnián
next year	明年	míngnián
spring	春天	chūntiān
summer	夏天	xiàtiān
fall	秋天	qiūtiān
winter	冬天	dōngtiān
early morning (approx. 6am-8am)	早上	zǎoshàng
morning (approx. 8am-noon)	上午	shàngwǔ
noon	中午	zhōngwǔ
afternoon	下午	xiàwǔ
evening	晚上	wǎnshàng
midnight	午夜	wǔyè
past	过去	guòqù
future	未来	wèilái
now	现在	xiànzài
early	早	zǎo
late	晚	wǎn
minute	分钟	fēnzhōng
hour	小时	xiǎo shí
half an hour	半(个)小时	bàn (ge) xiǎo shí
8am	早上八点	zǎoshàng bā diǎn
9:05am	上午九点零五分	shàngwǔ jiǔ diǎn líng wǔ fēn
10:15am	上午十点一刻	shàngwǔ shí diǎn yí kè
3:30pm	下午三点半	xiàwǔ sān diǎn bàn
9:45pm	晚上差一刻十点	wǎnshàng chà yí kè shí diǎn
10:55pm	晚上差五分十一点	wǎnshàng chà wǔ fēn shí yì diǎn
What time is it?	现在几点?	xiànzài jǐ diǎn?

GREETINGS AND USEFUL PHRASES

ENGLISH	CHINESE	PINYIN
hello	你好	nǐhǎo
good morning	早上好	zǎoshang hǎo
good night	晚安	Wǎn'ān
nice to meet you	认识你很高兴	rènshi nǐ hěn gāoxìng
wait a moment	等一下	děng yí xià

ENGLISH	CHINESE	PINYIN
fine/okay	好的	hǎode
good-bye	再见	zàijiàn
yes	对	duì
no	不	bù
thank you	谢谢	xièxie
you're welcome	不客气	búkèqì
I'm sorry	对不起	duìbùqǐ
please	请	qǐng
excuse me (to get attention)	打扰一下	dǎrǎo yíxià
excuse me (to get past)	过一下	guò yíxià
My name is____.	我叫	Wǒ jiào____.
Do you speak English?	你会说英文吗?	Nǐ huì shuō Yīngwén ma?
I don't speak Chinese.	我不会说中文。	Wǒ búhuì shuō Zhōngwén.
I don't understand.	听不懂。	Tīng bùdǒng.
I'll call a friend who speaks Chinese.	我要给一个会说中文的朋友打电话。	Wǒ yào gěi yí gè huì shuō Zhōngwén de péngyou dǎ diànhuà.
Where are you from?	你是哪国人?	Nǐ shì nǎ guórén?
I'm American.	我是美国人。	Wǒ shì Měiguórén.
Australian	澳大利亚人	Àodàlìyàrén
British	英国人	Yīngguórén
Canadian	加拿大人	Jiānádàrén
Irish	爱尔兰人	Ài'ěrlánrén
New Zealander	新西兰人	Xīnxīlánrén

GETTING AROUND

ENGLISH	CHINESE	PINYIN
airport	机场	jīchǎng
bicycle	自行车	zìxíngchē
bus	公共汽车	gōnggǒngqìchē
bus stop/station	公共汽车站	gōnggǒngqìchē zhàn
car	汽车	qìchē
expressway/highway	高速公路	gāosù gōnglù
passport	护照	hùzhào
plane	飞机	fēijī
subway	地铁	dìtiě
subway station	地铁站	dìtiě zhàn

ENGLISH	CHINESE	PINYIN
taxi	出租车	chūzūchē
Please switch on the meter.	请打表。	Qǐng dǎbiǎo.
train	火车	huǒchē
train station	火车站	huǒchē zhàn
visa	签证	qiānzhèng
We're here (stop here).	到了	dàole
one ticket	一张票	yì zhāng piào
two tickets	两张票	liǎng zhāng piào
How much does it cost?	多少钱?	Duōshao qián?
Where is____?	____在哪里?	____ zài nǎlǐ?
turn left	左拐	zuǒ guǎi
turn right	右拐	yòu guǎi
go north	往北走	wǎng běi zǒu
go south	往南走	wǎng nán zǒu
go east	往东走	wǎng dōng zǒu
go west	往西走	wǎng xī zǒu
go straight ahead	往前走	wǎng qián zǒu
far	远	yuǎn
close	近	jìn
near to ____	离-------很近	lí____hěn jìn
next to ____	在-------旁边	zài____pángbiān
opposite ____	在------对面	zài____duìmiàn
I'm lost.	我迷路了。	Wǒ mílù le.

ACCOMMODATIONS

ENGLISH	CHINESE	PINYIN
address	地址	dìzhǐ
apartment (high-end)	公寓	gōngyù
apartment (local)	民宅	mínzhái
bathroom	卫生间	wèishēngjiān
bed	床	chuáng
bedroom	卧室	wòshì
cable TV	有线电视	yǒuxiàn diànshì
deposit	押金	yājīn
electricity	电	diàn
heating	暖气	nuǎnqì
hostel	青年旅社	qīngniánlǚshè
hotel (cheap)	宾馆	bīnguǎn

RESOURCES

ENGLISH	CHINESE	PINYIN
hotel (premium)	饭店 or 酒店	fàndiàn or jiǔdiàn
hot water	热水	rèshuǐ
How many bedrooms?	有几个卧室?	Yǒu jǐ ge wòshì?
Internet	网络	wǎngluò
Is it furnished?	这个是带家具的吗?	Zhège shì dài jiājù de ma?
Is there an agent fee?	有中介费吗?	Yǒu zhōngjiè fèi ma?
kitchen	厨房	chúfáng
landlord/landlady	房东	fángdōng
lease	合同	hétong
real estate agent	中介	zhōngjiè
rent	房租	fángzū
sofa	沙发	shāfā
square meters	平(方)米	píng (fāng) mǐ
villa	别墅	biéshù

FOOD AND DRINKS

ENGLISH	CHINESE	PINYIN
apple juice	苹果汁	píngguǒzhī
bar	酒吧	jiǔbā
beef	牛肉	niúròu
beer	啤酒	píjiǔ
bottle	瓶子	píngzi
bowl	碗	wǎn
cash	现金	xiànjīn
cheers	干杯	gānbēi
chicken	鸡肉	jīròu
chopsticks	筷子	kuàizi
Coca-Cola	可口可乐	Kěkǒukělè
cold water	凉水	liáng shuǐ
congratulations	祝贺你	hùhè nǐ
credit card	信用卡	xìnyòngkǎ
drunk	喝醉了	hē zuìle
fish	鱼	yú
fruit	水果	shuǐguǒ
fruit juice	水果汁	shuǐguǒzhī
hot water	热水	rè shuǐ
meat	肉	ròu
menu	菜单	càidān

ENGLISH	CHINESE	PINYIN
milk	牛奶	niúnǎi
mineral water	矿泉水	kuàngquán shuǐ
napkin	餐厅纸	cāntīngzhǐ
noodles	面条	miàntiáo
orange juice	橙汁	chéngzhī
plate	盘子	pánzi
pork	猪肉	zhūròu
red wine	红葡萄酒	hóng pútaojiǔ
restaurant	餐厅	cāntīng
rice (cooked)	米饭	mǐfàn
seafood	海鲜	hǎixiān
soup	汤	tāng
soy milk	豆浆	dòujiāng
soy sauce	酱油	jiàngyóu
Sprite	雪碧	Xuěbì
table	桌子	zhuōzi
two bowls of rice	两碗米饭	liǎng wǎn mǐfàn
vegetables	蔬菜	shūcài
vegetarian	素食者	sùshízhě
vinegar	醋	cù
water	水	shuǐ
waitress/waiter	服务员	fúwùyuán
white wine	白葡萄酒	bái pútaojiǔ
wine	葡萄酒	pútaojiǔ
May I have the bill?	买单	Mǎi dān.
Do you have an English menu?	有英文菜单吗?	Yǒu Yīngwén càidān ma?
Do you have ice cubes?	有冰块儿吗?	Yǒu bīng kuài'er ma?
May I have a fork?	来一个叉子。	Lái yí ge chāzi.
May I have a knife?	来一个刀子。	Lái yí ge dāozi.
May I have a spoon?	来一个勺子。	Lái yí ge sháozi.
How many people?	几位?	Jǐ wèi?
two people	两位	liǎng wèi
three people	三位	sān wèi
I'm allergic to peanuts.	我对坚果过敏。	Wǒ duì jiānguǒ guòmǐn.
I'd like this.	我要这个。	Wǒ yào zhèi ge.
I don't want ice.	不要冰块儿。	Wǒ bú yào bīng kuàir.
Don't use MSG.	别放味精。	Bié fàng wèijīng.
Please give us another one.	再来一个。	Zài lái yí gè.

RESOURCES

ENGLISH	CHINESE	PINYIN
We have a reservation.	我们预定了。	Wǒmen yùdìngle.
Take away/ Put this in a doggy bag.	打包。	Dǎbāo.

SHOPPING

ENGLISH	CHINESE	PINYIN
Can I use a credit card/ bank card?	可以刷卡吗?	Kěyǐ shuākǎ ma?
cheap	便宜	piányi
Can you make it cheaper?	能再便宜点儿吗?	Néng zài piányi diǎn'er ma?
convenience store	便利店	biànlìdiàn
Do you have ____?	有___吗?	Yǒu____ma?
Do you have a PIN?	有没有密码?	Yǒu méiyǒu mìmǎ?
Do you need a bag?	需要袋子吗?	Xūyào dàizi ma?
May I have a bag?	给我一个袋子?	Gěi wǒ yí ge dàizi?
Do you have a member card?	有会员卡吗?	Yǒu huìyuánkǎ ma?
Forget it.	算了吧。	Suànle ba.
Enter your PIN.	输入密码。	Shūrù mìmǎ.
I'm just looking.	随便看看。	Suíbiàn kànkan.
How much is this?	多少钱?	Duōshao qián?
supermarket	超市	chāoshì
There's no need to accompany (follow) me, thanks.	不用跟着我, 谢谢。	Bú yòng gēnzhe wǒ, xièxie.
this one	这个	zhèige
Too expensive!	太贵了!	Tài guile!
vegetable (produce) market	菜市场	càishìchǎng
Where is ____?	____在哪儿?	____zài nǎ'er?

HEALTH

ENGLISH	CHINESE	PINYIN
acupuncture	针灸	zhēnjiǔ
allergy	过敏	guòmǐn
ambulance	救护车	jiùhùchē
antacid	抗酸剂	kàngsuānjì
antibiotics	抗生素	kàngshēngjì
antihistamine	(脱敏药) 抗组胺剂	(tuōmǐnyào) kàngzǔ'ànjì
antiseptic	消毒剂	xiāodújì
arm	胳膊	gēbo

ENGLISH	CHINESE	PINYIN
aspirin	阿司匹林	āsīpǐlín
asthma	哮喘	xiàochuǎn
back	后背	hòubèi
chest	胸	xiōng
a cold	感冒	gǎnmào
condoms	避孕套	bìyùntào
constipation	便秘	biànmì
contraceptive pills	避孕药	bìyùnyào
cough	咳嗽	késou
cough medicine	止咳药	zhǐkéyào
dentist	牙医	yáyī
diarrhea	拉肚子	lādùzi
dramamine	晕海宁/晕车药，这个说法我们最常用	yūnhǎiníng
doctor	医生/大夫	yīshēng/dàifu
ear	耳朵	ěrduo
eye	眼睛	yǎnjing
fever	发烧	fāshāo
flu	流感	liú gǎn
fire department	消防队	xiāofángduì
head	头	tóu
headache	头疼	tóuténg
hospital	医院	yīyuàn
ibuprofen	布洛芬	bùluòfēn
inhaler	吸入器	xīrùqì
itch	痒	yǎng
laxative	泻药	xièyào
leg	腿	tuǐ
lump	肿块	zhǒngkuài
nausea	恶心	ěxīn
neck	脖子	bózi
nose	鼻子	bízi
pain	疼	téng
painkillers	止疼药	zhǐténgpiàn
pharmacy	药店	yàodiàn
pill/tablet	药片	yàopiàn
plaster (Band-Aid)	创可贴	chuàngkětiē
police	警察	jǐngchá

RESOURCES

ENGLISH	CHINESE	PINYIN
sleeping pills	安眠药	ānmiányào
stomach	胃	wèi
swollen	肿了	zhǒngle
tampons	棉球	miánqiú
temperature (body)	体温	tǐwēn
tooth	牙齿	yáchǐ
vomit	呕吐	ǒutù
Call an ambulance!	叫救护车！	Jiào jiùhùchē!
Help me!	救命！	jiùmìng!
I need _____.	我需要_____。	Wǒ yào_____.
I'm diabetic.	我有糖尿病。	Wǒ yǒu tángniàobìng.
I'm ill.	我不舒服。	Wǒ bù shūfú.
I have asthma.	我有哮喘。	Wǒ yǒu xiàochuǎn.
It hurts right here.	就是这儿疼。	Jiù shì zhè'er téng.
My _____ hurts.	我_____疼。	Wǒ_____téng.
Take me to SOS.	送我到北京国际救援中心。	Sòng wǒ dào Běijīng Guójì Jiùyuán Zhōngxīn.
Take me to Beijing United Family Hospital.	送我到和睦家医院。	Sòng wǒ dào Hémùjiā Yīyuàn.

Suggested Reading

GENERAL

Chang, Jung. *Wild Swans: Three Daughters of China*. New York: Touchstone, 2003. Part memoir, part historical account, *Wild Swans* revisits the experiences of three generations of women in China. Chang weaves through the life of her grandmother, a warlord's concubine; her mother's experiences as a Communist during the Cultural Revolution; and her own foray into Communism and life beyond. It's a moving, deeply inspiring tale and has become something of an essential inclusion on the booklist of anyone visiting China.

Chang, Jung, and Jon Halliday. *Mao: The Untold Story,* New York: Anchor, 2006. This tome of a book takes the reader step by detailed step through Mao's life, from childhood to his rise to power in Beijing as Beijing's supreme leader, and through the Long March, the Great Leap Forward, and beyond. It's a condemning work that vilifies the leader, and some argue it should be read with moderate acceptance. Regardless, it is a provoking account of the man whose body still lies enshrined in the center of the city and whose portrait still hangs in glorious color at the entrance to the Forbidden City.

Ellis, Yi S., and Bryan D. Ellis. *101 Stories for Foreigners to Understand Chinese People*. Shenyang: Liaoning Education Press, 2007. If you want to know how to develop better relationships with your Chinese friends, start by bringing your Chinese etiquette up to scratch. This interesting and easy-to-read book takes you step by step through many cultural behaviors that are still relevant today, whether you are in Beijing, Shanghai, or Hong Kong.

FICTION

Chan, Koonchung. *The Fat Years: A Novel*. New York: Nan A. Talese, 2012. Banned in China, this futuristic and disturbing novel takes a hard look into a future China, and in doing so gives an honest perspective of the country today. Taking Beijing as its primary setting, this dystopian story is something of a Chinese *Brave New World* and looks at a country on the verge of world domination and which seems to have forgotten the lessons of its past.

Guo, Xiaolu. *Twenty Fragments of a Ravenous Youth*. New York: Nan A. Talese, 2008. This is an amusing story of a young Chinese woman's life as a film extra in Beijing. Like many others from around China, 21-year-old Wang Fenfang has left her impoverished peasant village and traveled to the capital in search of fame and fortune. She isn't ready for what awaits her in post-Cultural Revolution Beijing—a Communist city that is scrambling on shaky legs to modernize, nosy judgmental neighbors, corruption, and cockroaches.

Ha Jin. *The Crazed*. New York: Vintage, 2004. Student Jian Wan is given the task of looking after his professor, who has had a brain injury, and as the professor's outbursts reveal experiences from the Cultural Revolution, Wan sees parallels to his own life in 1980s China. Leaving love behind, Wan eventually heads to Beijing to join the student protests in Tian'anmen (consequently making this a controversial book in China).

RESOURCES

Min, Anchee. *The Last Empress: A Novel.* New York: First Mariner Books, 2008. This is a fictionalized account of one of the most notorious women in China's history, Empress Dowager Cixi. Not to be taken as fact, Min's novel leads the reader into the corrupt world of imperial China in Zhongnanhai, Beijing. Cixi is now a widow and mother of an emperor who has died from a venereal disease. She faces unrelenting deceit, power struggles, rebellion, incursions from foreigners, and, ultimately, the collapse of the Qing dynasty.

Wang Shuo. *Please Don't Call Me Human.* Boston: Cheng & Tsui, 2003. A satirical story about a Beijing taxi driver competing to find the nation most able to humiliate itself, which in the process makes a barely hidden slur at the Olympics.

NONFICTION

Boyd, Julia. *A Dance with the Dragon.* London: I. B. Tauris, 2012. Pulling together previously unpublished historical sources, this fascinating book opens a window into the world of Beijing's expats during the turbulent time between the Qing dynasty and the coming of Mao. Boyd illustrates vividly a world of diplomats, scientists, missionaries, and refugees, and the world that is in a hurricane of change around them.

Doctoroff, Tom. *What Chinese Want: Culture, Communism and the Modern Chinese Consumer.* New York: Palgrave Macmillan, 2012. This is an excellent insight into the modern Chinese consumer and a must-read for anyone hoping to succeed in business in Beijing. Doctoroff insightfully discusses what is driving the country as well as the psychology of its people.

Dodson, Bill. *China Inside Out: 10 Irreversible Trends Reshaping China and Its Relationship with the World.* Singapore: John Wiley & Sons, 2011. An insightful guide for anyone who wants to get to know today's China better. Exploring both business and society from a wide range of angles, it looks at the forces driving the Chinese population and where this superpower country is headed.

Halper, Stefan. *The Beijing Consensus: Legitimizing Authoritarianism in Our Time.* New York: Basic Books, 2012. This informative book looks at China's relationship with the United States, examining China's nonconfrontational strategies and soft power growth, gained through such avenues as extensive aid to struggling nations.

Han, Anna. *Doing Business in China: Cases and Materials (American Casebooks).* Eagen, MN: West Academics, 2012. This book might be a textbook, but it's well put together and makes a great general reference book for those operating businesses in China. The book covers key trade issues between China and the United States, such as intellectual property rights and trade deficits, recent political history, and many laws and regulations.

McGregor, Richard. *The Party: The Secret World of China's Communist Rulers.* New York: Harper Perennial, 2012. This is a spirited read about China's governmental power and how it has put its mark on everything in the country today. Fascinating for anyone wanting to know where China is headed and for anyone who is interested in how the regime has held and continues to hold its Communist grip on a modern Chinese society.

RESOURCES

Sandhaus, Derek. *Tales of Old Peking*. Hong Kong: China Economic Review Publishing Ltd., 2009. Sandhaus builds a picture of old Beijing, not through narrative but by pulling together an enormous array of articles, illustrations, photographs, and excerpts, and quotes from diplomats, emperors, sinologists, and visitors. It shows how life was then, and how very remote that is from what life and attitudes are like today in modern Beijing.

Scocca, Tom. *Beijing Welcomes You: Unveiling the Capital City of the Future*. New York: Riverhead Hardcover, 2011. One man's perspective on a diverse and rapidly changing city, set during the frenetic buildup to the Olympic Games in 2008. Keenly observing the city's many oddities and strengths, Scocca reports on interviews with architects, weather scientists, and many other experts assigned to ensure the Games' success. An interesting insight into how things can be managed in a modern Communist country.

Xinran. *The Good Women of China: Hidden Voices*. New York: Anchor, 2003. Former Beijing journalist Xinran began broadcasting an evening radio program in 1989, inviting people to share their personal stories and concerns by calling in or writing letters. At the time, such a show was unheard of and was naturally controversial as well as enthusiastically welcomed by women who had never before had a place in which to air their grievances or discuss personal issues. Xinran's book is inspiring, saddening, amusing, uplifting, shocking, and awakening.

ONLINE RESOURCES AND READING

Baidu Beat, http://beat.baidu.com. Baidu's English blog, Baidu Beat gives you an insight into what Chinese Internet users are looking for online.

Beijing Cream, http://beijingcream.com. News blog of what's happening in Beijing and around China.

Chovanec, Patrick. http://chovanec.wordpress.com. Patrick Chovanec is a professor at Tsinghua University's School of Economics and Management in Beijing, and he writes regularly about the nation's politics and economy.

Danwei, www.danwei.com. An informative website and research firm that tracks Chinese media and Internet, as well as providing translations of interesting news stories and posting media-related jobs. It's often blocked in China, so you may need a VPN/proxy service to access it.

Fallows, James, www.theatlantic.com/james-fallows. National correspondent for *The Atlantic* and formally its China correspondent, Fallows still keeps an occasional eye on what's happening in the People's Republic.

Osnos, Evan, www.newyorker.com/online/blogs/evanosnos. *New Yorker* correspondent in Beijing, Osnos writes regularly, succinctly, and with authority about politics and other newsworthy happenings in China. Worth adding to your RSS feeds.

The Peking Duck, www.pekingduck.org. A blend of personal journal, philosophy, news, and more from Richard Burger, the Beijing-based author of *Behind the Red Door: Sex in China*.

RESOURCES

Suggested Films

Beijing Bicycle. Directed by Wang Xiaoshuai. 113 minutes. Sony Pictures Classics, 2001. A quiet film that looks at the relationship that develops between two boys in Beijing when one buys the stolen bicycle of the other from a secondhand market.

Big Shot's Funeral. Directed by Feng Xiaogang. 100 minutes. Columbia Tristar, 2001. A comedy that has Donald Sutherland playing a hotshot film director who comes to Beijing to direct a historical epic. When he suddenly dies, communication problems surface and they decide to give him an imperial-style funeral.

Farewell My Concubine. Directed by Chen Kaige. 171 minutes. Miramax Films, 1993. The story of two male Peking opera stars—one who plays the male role in the onstage duo, and the other who plays the female role. Their relationship is damaged when the latter falls in love with the former in real life, offstage. This is a powerful film, depicting not only attitudes toward homosexuality in China in the 20th century, but also the changing culture of Peking opera—not to mention a photo album of Beijing itself.

Karate Kid. Directed by Harald Zwart. 140 minutes. Columbia Pictures, 2010. While this film can never compare to the original masterpiece, and though Jackie Chan teaches Will Smith's son, Jaden, kung fu, not karate, this latest version of *Karate Kid* is a stunning post-card introduction to Beijing, the Great Wall, and some of China's most beautiful locations. Once you've been in the country for some time, you'll also realize that the various locations are much more than a simple day's train trip away from Beijing.

The Last Emperor. Directed by Mark Peploe and Bernardo Bertolucci. 160 minutes. Columbia Pictures, 1987. A biographical film about the life of Puyi, the last emperor of China. Shot for the most part within the walls of the Forbidden City.

Lost in Beijing. Directed by Li Yu. 112 minutes. Films Distribution, 2007. Produced by a small, independent Beijing film company, *Lost in Beijing* touches on topics of prostitution, blackmail, and rape in modern Beijing, told through the story that unravels when a window washer sees his boss's wife raped by her husband. Unsurprisingly, this film was banned in China but was released internationally.

Love Is Not Blind. (失恋33天). Directed by Teng Huatao. 110 minutes. Perfect World Television Culture Co., Ltd., 2011. This low-budget Chinese comedy became a major success. In it, 27-year-old wedding planner Huang Xiaoxian discovers that her own boyfriend has been cheating on her with her best friend. While her workmate, Wang Xiaojian, helps her out she discovers who will really be by her side. Lots of Beijing location-spotting opportunities.

Summer Palace. Directed by Lou Ye. 158 minutes. Palm Pictures, 2006. A Chinese-French collaboration, the film follows the passionate relationship of two universities set against the backdrop of the 1989 Tian'anmen Square massacre. The film caused a lot of controversy and was eventually banned from China.

Together. Directed by Chen Kaige. 119 minutes. MGM, 2002. Thirteen-year-old violin prodigy Liu Xiaochun moves with his father to Beijing to chase their dreams of him becoming a world-class violinist. It's a touching movie of relationships and life's lessons.

You and Me. Directed by Ma Liwen. 83 minutes. China Film Group/Delphis Films, 2005. The story of a young girl who moves into a courtyard apartment in Beijing managed by an unpleasant old lady. Though it takes time and a few mishaps along the way, their relationship grows into true friendship and respect.

Index

www.moon.com

DESTINATIONS | ACTIVITIES | BLOGS | MAPS | BOOKS

MOON.COM is ready to help plan your next trip! Filled with fresh trip ideas and strategies, author interviews, informative travel blogs, a detailed map library, and descriptions of all the Moon guidebooks, Moon.com is all you need to get out and explore the world—or even places in your own backyard. While at Moon.com, sign up for our monthly e-newsletter for updates on new releases, travel tips, and expert advice from our on-the-go Moon authors. As always, when you travel with Moon, expect an experience that is uncommon and truly unique.

**KEEP UP WITH MOON ON FACEBOOK AND TWITTER
JOIN THE MOON PHOTO GROUP ON FLICKR**

MAP SYMBOLS

Expressway	○ City/Town	✈ Airfield	▲ Archaeological Site
Primary Road	⊙ State Capital	✈ Airport	🍾 Church
Secondary Road			⛽ Gas Station
Unpaved Road	⊛ National Capital	▲ Mountain	🌿 Mangrove
Ferry	★ Point of Interest	♣♣ Park	Reef
Railroad	▪ Other Location	⛷ Skiing Area	Swamp

CONVERSION TABLES

°C = (°F − 32) / 1.8
°F = (°C x 1.8) + 32
1 inch = 2.54 centimeters (cm)
1 foot = 0.304 meters (m)
1 yard = 0.914 meters
1 mile = 1.6093 kilometers (km)
1 km = 0.6214 miles
1 fathom = 1.8288 m
1 chain = 20.1168 m
1 furlong = 201.168 m
1 acre = 0.4047 hectares
1 sq km = 100 hectares
1 sq mile = 2.59 square km
1 ounce = 28.35 grams
1 pound = 0.4536 kilograms
1 short ton = 0.90718 metric ton
1 short ton = 2,000 pounds
1 long ton = 1.016 metric tons
1 long ton = 2,240 pounds
1 metric ton = 1,000 kilograms
1 quart = 0.94635 liters
1 US gallon = 3.7854 liters
1 Imperial gallon = 4.5459 liters
1 nautical mile = 1.852 km

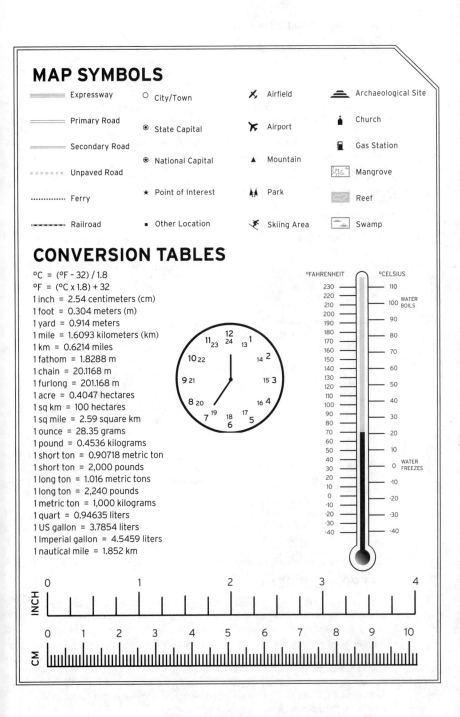

MOON LIVING ABROAD IN BEIJING

Avalon Travel
a member of the Perseus Books Group
1700 Fourth Street
Berkeley, CA 94710, USA
www.moon.com

Editors: Elizabeth Hansen, Nikki Ioakimedes
Series Manager: Elizabeth Hansen
Copy Editor: Deana Shields
Graphics Coordinator: Elizabeth Jang
Production Coordinator: Elizabeth Jang
Cover Designer: Elizabeth Jang
Map Editor: Kat Bennett
Cartographers: Kat Bennett, Lohnes + Wright,
  Chris Henrick
Indexer: Greg Jewett

ISBN-13: 978-1-61238-539-6
ISSN: 2331-6098

Printing History
1st Edition – January 2014
5 4 3 2 1

Text © 2013 by Shannon Aitken.
Maps © 2013 by Avalon Travel.
All rights reserved.

Some photos and illustrations are used by permission and are the property of the original copyright owners.

Front cover photo: red lanterns on Wangfujing Snack Street, Dongcheng District © Walter Bibikow/eStockPhoto.com

Title Page photo: lion statue and historical architecture in Forbidden City © Songquan Deng/123rf.com

Interior color photos: p. 4 red lanterns © Shannon Aitken; p. 5 flowers in Jingshan Park © Shannon Aitken; p. 6 (inset) Forbidden City © Kathi Schamari, (bottom) Beijing restaurant © Shannon Aitken; p. 7 (top left) the Great Wall © Kathi Schamari, (top right) lions at Beijing's Ancient Observatory © Shannon Aitken, (center) Beijing's Central Business District © 06photo/123rf.com, (bottom left) old doorway off Nanluogu Xiang © Shannon Aitken, (bottom right) local resident © Shannon Aitken; p. 8 (top left) unusual sight on a Beijing sidewalk © Shannon Aitken, (top right) arhats at the Temple of Azure Clouds © Shannon Aitken, (bottom) wish ribbons at the Temple of Azure Clouds © Shannon Aitken

Back cover photo: © Shannon Aitken

Printed in Canada by Friesens

Moon Handbooks and the Moon logo are the property of Avalon Travel. All other marks and logos depicted are the property of the original owners. All rights reserved. No part of this book may be translated or reproduced in any form, except brief extracts by a reviewer for the purpose of a review, without written permission of the copyright owner.

All recommendations, including those for sights, activities, hotels, restaurants, and shops, are based on each author's individual judgment. We do not accept payment for inclusion in our travel guides, and our authors don't accept free goods or services in exchange for positive coverage.

Although every effort was made to ensure that the information was correct at the time of going to press, the author and publisher do not assume and hereby disclaim any liability to any party for any loss or damage caused by errors, omissions, or any potential travel disruption due to labor or financial difficulty, whether such errors or omissions result from negligence, accident, or any other cause.

KEEPING CURRENT

Although we strive to produce the most up-to-date guidebook that we possibly can, change is unavoidable. Between the time this book goes to print and the time you read it, the cost of goods and services may have increased, and a handful of the businesses noted in these pages will undoubtedly move, alter their prices, or close their doors forever. Exchange rates fluctuate—sometimes dramatically—on a daily basis. Federal and local legal requirements and restrictions are also subject to change, so be sure to check with the appropriate authorities before making the move. If you see anything in this book that needs updating, clarification, or correction, please drop us a line. Send your comments via email to feedback@moon.com, or use the address above.